Lecture Notes in Computer Science 11058

Commenced Publication in 1973
Founding and Former Series Editors:
Gerhard Goos, Juris Hartmanis, and Jan van Leeuwen

More information about this series at http://www.springer.com/series/7410

Man Ho Au · Siu Ming Yiu
Jin Li · Xiapu Luo
Cong Wang · Aniello Castiglione
Kamil Kluczniak (Eds.)

Network and System Security

12th International Conference, NSS 2018
Hong Kong, China, August 27–29, 2018
Proceedings

 Springer

Editors
Man Ho Au (ID)
The Hong Kong Polytechnic University
Hong Kong, China

Siu Ming Yiu
The University of Hong Kong
Hong Kong, China

Jin Li
Guangzhou University
Guangzhou, China

Xiapu Luo
The Hong Kong Polytechnic University
Hong Kong, China

Cong Wang
City University of Hong Kong
Hong Kong, China

Aniello Castiglione
University of Salerno
and University of Naples Federico II
Fisciano, Italy

Kamil Kluczniak
CISPA Helmholtz Center i.G. GmbH
Saarbrücken, Germany

ISSN 0302-9743   ISSN 1611-3349 (electronic)
Lecture Notes in Computer Science
ISBN 978-3-030-02743-8   ISBN 978-3-030-02744-5 (eBook)
https://doi.org/10.1007/978-3-030-02744-5

Library of Congress Control Number: 2018962354

LNCS Sublibrary: SL4 – Security and Cryptology

This Springer imprint is published by the registered company Springer Nature Switzerland AG
The registered company address is: Gewerbestrasse 11, 6330 Cham, Switzerland

Preface

The 12th International Conference on Network and System Security (NSS 2018) was held in Hong Kong, China, during August 27–29, 2018. It was organized by the Department of Computing, the Hong Kong Polytechnic University, and co-organized by the Hong Kong Applied Science and Technology Research Institute (ASTRI).

The NSS conference series is an established forum that brings together researchers and practitioners to provide a confluence of network and system security technologies, including all theoretical and practical aspects. In previous years, NSS took place in Helsinki, Finland (2017), Taipei (2016), New York City, USA (2015), Xi'an, China (2014), Madrid, Spain (2013), Wu Yi Shan, China (2012), Milan, Italy (2011), Melbourne, Australia (2010), Gold Coast, Australia (2009), Shanghai, China (2008), and Dalian, China (2007).

The conference program included four keynote speeches, a workshop, and 35 contributed papers. We would like to express our heartfelt thanks to the keynote speakers (listed in alphabetical order by surname), Prof. Sihan Qing from the Chinese Academy of Sciences, Prof. Kui Ren from the University at Buffalo, Prof. Willy Susilo from the University of Wollongong, and Prof. Jaideep Vaidya from Rutgers University. The program this year also featured the ASTRI/NSS Cybersecurity Workshop, which included two sessions, namely, "Cybersecurity Technology Advancement" and "Security Issues Related to Blockchain."

This year, we received 88 submissions. Each submission was reviewed by two to four Program Committee (PC) members. The committee decided to accept 26 long papers and nine short papers. The accepted papers cover a wide range of topics in the field, including blockchain, mobile security, applied cryptography, authentication, biometrics, IoT, privacy and education.

NSS 2018 was made possible by the joint effort of numerous people and organizations worldwide. There is a long list of people who volunteered their time and energy to put together the conference and who deserve special thanks. First and foremost, we are deeply grateful to all the PC members for their great efforts in reading, commenting on, debating, and finally selecting the papers. We also thank all the external reviewers for assisting the technical PC in their particular areas of expertise. Last but not least, we are thankful to the authors of all submitted papers.

We thank the honorary chair, Prof. Jiannong Cao, The Hong Kong Polytechnic University, China, for his kind support of the conference organization. We are grateful to Dr. Lucas Hui, the workshop chair and representative of our co-organizer ASTRI. We would like to express our gratitude to the general chairs, Dr. Man Ho Au, Dr. Siu Ming Yiu, and Prof. Jin Li, for their excellent organization of the conference. We deeply appreciate the guidance from the Steering Committee, Prof. Elisa Bertino, Prof. Robert H. Deng, Prof. Dieter Gollmann, Prof. Xinyi Huang, Prof. Kui Ren, Prof. Ravi Sandhu, Prof. Yang Xiang, and Prof. Wanlei Zhou. Special thanks to the publicity chairs, Dr. Weizhi Meng, Prof. Tatsuya Mori, Dr. Kaitai Liang, the publication chair,

Dr. Kamil Kluczniak, the treasurer, Dr. Dennis Liu, local arrangements chairs, Ms. Carmen Au, Dr. Peng Jiang, and Ms. Catherine Chan, and the Web chairs, Mr. Jiachi Chen and Mr. Franky Lau.

We are grateful for the support of the K. C. Wong Education Foundation, Hong Kong. We would also like to express our gratitude toward our sponsors, the State Key Laboratory of Integrated Services Networks (ISN) and the National 111 Project for Mobile Internet Security. Finally, we would like to thank Springer again for its continuous support of the conference series, and the staff at Springer for their help with the production of these proceedings. We are indebted to the developers and maintainers of the EasyChair software, which helps tremendously with the handling of the submission and review process.

July 2018   Xiapu Luo
                                                               Cong Wang
                                                       Aniello Castiglione

Organization

Program Committee

Cristina Alcaraz	University of Malaga, Spain
Man Ho Au	The Hong Kong Polytechnic University, SAR China
Joonsang Baek	University of Wollongong, Australia
Silvio Barra	University of Cagliari, Italy
Alex Biryukov	University of Luxembourg, Luxembourg
Pino Caballero-Gil	University of La Laguna, Spain
Aniello Castiglione	University of Salerno, Italy
Arcangelo Castiglione	University of Salerno, Italy
Luca Caviglione	National Research Council of Italy, Italy
David Chadwick	University of Kent, UK
Chia-Mei Chen	National Sun Yat-sen University, Taiwan
Songqing Chen	George Mason University, USA
Ting Chen	University of Electronic Science and Technology of China, China
Wei Chen	Nanjing University of Posts and Telecommunications, China
Kim-Kwang Choo	The University of Texas at San Antonio, USA
Mauro Conti	University of Padua, Italy
He Debiao	Wuhan University, China
Wenxiu Ding	Xidian University, China
Jesús Díaz-Verdejo	University of Granada, Spain
Christian Esposito	University of Salerno, Italy
José M. Fernandez	École Polytechnique de Montréal, Canada
Yanick Fratantonio	EUROCOM, Graduate School and Research Center in Digital Science, France
Alban Gabillon	University of Polynésie Française, France
Ren Junn Huang	Tamkang University, Taiwan
Xinyi Huang	Fujian Normal University, China
Zoe L. Jiang	Harbin Institute of Technology, China
James Joshi	University of Pittsburgh, USA
Jörg Keller	FernUniversity in Hagen, Germany
Shinsaku Kiyomoto	KDDI R&D Laboratories Inc., Japan
Maciej Korczyński	Delft University of Technology, The Netherlands
Ram Krishnan	University of Texas at San Antonio, USA
Chin-Laung Lei	National Taiwan University, Taiwan
Jin Li	Guangzhou University, China
Kaitai Liang	University of Surrey, UK
Joseph Liu	Monash University, Australia

Zhe Liu	University of Waterloo, Canada
Giovanni Livraga	University of Milan, Italy
Xiapu Luo	The Hong Kong Polytechnic University, SAR China
Xiaobo Ma	Xi'an Jiaotong University, China
Weizhi Meng	Technical University of Denmark, Denmark
Chris Mitchell	Royal Holloway University of London, UK
Jose Morales	Carnegie Mellon University, USA
Tatsuya Mori	Waseda University, Japan
Kazumasa Omote	University of Tsukuba, Japan
Günther Pernul	Universität Regensburg, Germany
Carmela Piccolo	University of Naples Federico II, Italy
Florin Pop	University Politehnica of Bucharest, Romania
Chester Rebeiro	Indian Institute of Technology Madras, India
Stefano Ricciardi	University of Molise, Italy
Ruben Rios	University of Málaga, Spain
Na Ruan	Shanghai Jiao Tong University, China
Kouichi Sakurai	Kyushu University, Japan
Yang Shi	Tongji University, China
Masakazu Soshi	Hiroshima City University, Japan
Anna Squicciarini	The Pennsylvania State University, USA
Hung-Min Sun	National Tsing Hua University, Taiwan
Shamik Sural	Indian Institute of Technology, India
Kuo-Yu Tsai	Chinese Culture University, Taiwan
Yuh-Min Tseng	National Changhua University of Education, Taiwan
Chenxu Wang	Xi'an Jiaotong University, China
Chih Hung Wang	National Chiayi University, Taiwan
Cong Wang	City University of Hong Kong, SAR China
Steffen Wendzel	Hochschule Worms, Germany
Shouhuai Xu	University of Texas at San Antonio, USA
Lei Xue	The Hong Kong Polytechnic University, SAR China
Toshihiro Yamauchi	Okayama University, Japan
Wun-She Yap	Universiti Tunku Abdul Rahman, Malaysia
Kuo-Hui Yeh	National Dong Hwa University, Taiwan
Siu Ming Yiu	The University of Hong Kong, SAR China
Xingliang Yuan	Monash University, Australia
Haibo Zhang	University of Otago, New Zealand
Leo Yu Zhang	Deakin University, Australia
Tao Zhang	Harbin Engineering University, China
Zhenfei Zhang	OnBoard Security, Inc., USA
Zonghua Zhang	Institut Mines-Télécom, France
Yongjun Zhao	The Chinese University of Hong Kong, SAR China
Yajin Zhou	Zhejiang University, China

Contents

Secure Scheme Against Compromised Hash in Proof-of-Work Blockchain

Fengjun Chen, Zhiqiang Liu$^{(\boxtimes)}$, Yu Long$^{(\boxtimes)}$, Zhen Liu$^{(\boxtimes)}$, and Ning Ding$^{(\boxtimes)}$

The Department of Computer Science and Engineering, Shanghai Jiao Tong University, Shanghai, China
{chenfengjun,ilu_zq,longyu,liuzhen,dingning}@sjtu.edu.cn

Abstract. Blockchain is built on the basis of peer-to-peer network, cryptography and consensus mechanism over a distributed environment. The underlying cryptography in blockchain, such as hash algorithm and digital signature scheme, is used to guarantee the security of blockchain. However, past experience showed that cryptographic primitives do not last forever along with increasing computational power and advanced cryptanalysis. Therefore, it is crucial to investigate the issue that the underlying cryptography in blockchain is compromised.

This paper aims at the challenge that the underlying hash algorithm is compromised in blockchain. In 2017, M. Sato et al. firstly addressed the issue by proposing a framework of transition approach from the compromised hash algorithm to a secure one. Nevertheless, this approach is actually a hardfork if it is applied to proof-of-work blockchain, which is much likely to cause disagreement of the blockchain community and should be avoided accordingly. To fill this gap, we propose a softfork transition scheme to deal with the challenge that compromised hash brings into proof-of-work blockchain. Our scheme provides a secure transition in the case of compromised hash, keeping the validity of past data in the blockchain as well. We also show that a proof-of-work blockchain with our scheme is much more secure than the original one (i.e. without our scheme).

Keywords: Blockchain · Compromised hash
Softfork transition scheme · Proof of work

1 Introduction

Blockchain technology has attracted great interest of researchers and developers since Bitcoin [1] was proposed by Nakamoto in 2008. As the first remarkably successful and secure implementation of blockchain, Bitcoin took groundbreaking use of proof-of-work mechanism, to solve double-spending problem in cryptocurrency and maintain consistency of data in a decentralized environment. In proof-of-work blockchain, block is constructed with collected transactions and hash of previous block header by nodes called *miners*. Miners contribute computational power to competition in solving a hard cryptographic puzzle. In return for the

© Springer Nature Switzerland AG 2018
M. H. Au et al. (Eds.): NSS 2018, LNCS 11058, pp. 1–15, 2018.
https://doi.org/10.1007/978-3-030-02744-5_1

computational work, the miner who first solves out the puzzle will receive mining reward (i.e. newly generated coins) and transactions fee, and the block generated by him could have the chance to be accepted by the network and appended to the chain. To maximize the profit, rational miners will always follow the longest chain to do computation. Split from main chain may appear when two miners get solutions almost at the same time, but it will be eliminated soon when length of one branch outweighs the others. If an adversary maliciously intends to overturn transactions in a block followed by k block, the only way is to re-do computation to create another chain from this block overtaking the currently longest chain. However it is hard to succeed when k and the whole computational power in network are large enough. In Bitcoin, a block with 6 following blocks is usually considered safe since the success probability of generation of a branch from it overwhelming main chain, for an adversary with 10% computational power of the entire network, is less than 0.1% [1].

The underlying hash algorithm in proof-of-work blockchain is one of the key factors for security of the blockchain. More specifically, in proof-of-work blockchain, hash is used in computing reference of block (i.e. hash of previous block in each block) and proof-of-work puzzle, constructing Merkle Tree and hashing the transactions to be signed. Thus the hash algorithm adopted in blockchain should have sufficient security margin against known attacks. An eligible cryptographic hash algorithm ought to be computationally secure against pre-image, second pre-image and collision attacks. But history of cryptography showed that all hash algorithms can not stay computationally secure forever. Evolution in mathematical cryptanalysis and quantum computing are two main reasons to bring possible compromise to hash algorithm. The blockchain protocol will face severe security risk or even fail to work if the hash algorithms used are compromised.

To deal with the challenge, the most intuitive measure is to replace compromised hash algorithm with a more secure one, which is also a response to 0-day failure of SHA256 in Bitcoin contingency plans [2]. It is a kind of hardfork solution, i.e. an upgrade strategy adopting new form of blocks or transactions that are incompatible with original blockchain protocol [3]. However, hardfork is much likely to result in disagreement in the blockchain community. The success of hardfork depends on switch of the entire computational power from original blockchain protocol to new blockchain protocol. In the decentralized environment, such an agreement outside consensus protocol is hard to achieve in blockchain community. Danger of split of original blockchain will come even if only a small fraction of computational power staying at non-upgraded chain. Until now, Bitcoin has never implemented any hardfork successfully and safely without split [3]. Besides the intuitive hardfork, M. Sato et al. have proposed a transition approach to protect transactions in the case of compromised hash [4]. Their scheme utilizes proof of existence (PoE) model and archives transactions using a more secure hash algorithm. Nevertheless, this approach is also actually a hardfork if it is applied to proof-of-work blockchain.

This paper aims to tackle the challenge that the underlying hash algorithm is compromised in proof-of-work blockchain, as well as to avoid hardfork which is difficult to deploy without split of the original blockchain.

Contribution. With the proof of existence model given in [4], we introduce two-layer proof-of-work framework and then establish a novel transition scheme from the compromised hash to a secure one. As far as we know, this is the first softfork scheme against compromised hash in proof-of-work blockchain, which is more feasible, practical and easier-to-deploy than hardfork solutions since it is backward-compatible such that nodes that still run original blockchain protocol can admit blocks of new version, and softfork mechanism can completely avoid split of blockchain system when the majority computational power of the system fulfills upgrading blockchain protocol. Our scheme provides secure transition for a proof-of-work blockchain in the case of compromised hash, keeping the validity of past data in the blockchain as well. We also analyze the security of our newly-proposed scheme and show that a proof-of-work blockchain with our scheme is much more secure than the original one (i.e. without our scheme).

Paper Organization. The remainder of the paper is organized as follows. Section 2 introduces proof-of-work consensus, compromised hash and its impact briefly. In Sect. 3, we describe the existing solution to compromised hash in blockchain. Section 4 presents a novel secure approach against compromised hash. Finally, Sect. 5 concludes this paper.

2 Preliminaries

2.1 Proof of Work

In proof-of-work blockchain, miners compete in brute-force search to successfully solve a hard cryptographic puzzle and win reward for block generation. Practically the puzzle is to construct a block whose hash is less than a certain value, which also known as *difficulty of mining*. Only block that follows the latest block and has a hash value less than difficulty of mining will be accepted by network. In the view of long term, the received reward for mining is proportional to rate of computational power nodes contribute in network.

Within block structure, a *target* field indicates the difficulty of mining. For a blockchain where value domain of hash algorithm used by consensus is D, the probability of successfully finding an eligible block is as follows:

$$Pr[H \leq T] = \frac{T}{D}$$

Where H is the hash value of generated block and T is the value of target.

Target is not a constant value but will be adjusted periodically, to make block generation time stable when the network's overall computational power is changed. In Bitcoin, for example, *target* will be re-calculated every 2016 blocks to keep average block generation time at 10 min:

$$T' = \frac{t_{sum}}{14 * 24 * 60 * 60s} * T$$

where T is old target, T' is the new target after adjustment and t_{sum} is the accumulated time to produce latest 2015 blocks [5,6], which is calculated based on timestamp written by miners within block.

Beyond that, a *nonce* field is afforded in block to provide a enough space to find proof-of-work solution. Before computing to mine a block, miners should at first collect transactions and then construct a complete block structure. After that they fill *nonce* with a random value until hash value of the block meets target requirement.

2.2   Compromise of Hash

The basic security of an ideal cryptographic hash algorithm $h(x)$ can be defined by the following properties.

1. *Pre-image resistance.* Given a hash value y it is difficult to find a value x such that $h(x) = y$.
2. *Second pre-image resistance.* Given a value x_1 it is difficult to find a different value x_2 such that $h(x_1) = h(x_2)$.
3. *Collision resistance.* It is difficult to find two distinct values x_1 and x_2 such that $h(x_1) = h(x_2)$. Pair (x_1, x_2) is called a collision.

Collision resistance implies second pre-image resistance, while reduction from pre-image resistance to collision resistance is proved impossible [7]. In practice, collision always exists because of the fixed and limited output size of hash. Since the meaning of "difficult" here is infeasibility of breaking these properties in polynomial time, the three resistances indicate that there is no method for an adversary to modify a value without change of its hash value in a computational way.

Practically, security of a practical cryptographic hash algorithm can be estimated with its output size as a security parameter. A hash algorithm can be considered computationally secure when the possibility of successful attack in polynomial time is negligible. For a hash algorithm with k-bits output size, the computational complexity of brute force attacks to find a collision is $O(2^{k/2})$. Computational safety could be satisfied when k is large enough.

However in the history of cryptography, most hash algorithms suffer potential attacks, and breakages of them within certain amount of time are possible. Security of a hash algorithm does not fall abruptly, but will happen in a comparatively smooth process. In general, collision resistance is the relatively weakest part to be broken, followed by pre-image and second pre-image resistance. For example, widely-used hash algorithms MD5 and SHA-1 have turned out to be vulnerable to collision attacks – In 2005 Wang et al. firstly proposed efficient attacks to find collision for full version of MD5 within 2^{32} operations [8], and SHA-1 within 2^{69} operations [9] rather than 2^{80} for brute-force attack. The complexity of collision attack for SHA-1 is reduced to 2^{63} in later research. Until the first collision for full SHA-1 has been found under a practical attack by Google in 2017 [10], SHA-1 survives for over 12 years from proposal of the first attack in theory. Besides cryptanalysis on particular algorithm, quantum computing like Grover's fast quantum mechanical algorithm for pre-image attack [11], will accelerate the process of hash compromise as well.

2.3 Impact of Compromised Hash

Giechaskiel et al. have discussed potential impact of compromised hash algorithms used by Bitcoin [12]. In Bitcoin protocol, compromised hash algorithms results in steal of coins, double-spend and complete failure of the blockchain. Here we apply and extend their research into general proof-of-work blockchain protocol. We summary the impact in the aspect of mining, Merkle Tree and signature as follows.

Mining. Since the pre-image for a given hash value can be found through pre-image attack, miners can easily mine a block whose hash value less than target of proof of work. Thus split from main chain will be easier to happen. Moreover, an malicious adversary can use second pre-image attack or collision attack to mine two blocks with the same hash value. If the adversary has a sufficient control of network, he can transmit these two blocks into different network respectively. Since nodes always accept the first one they received and reject the latter, partition of the entire network consequently occurs and reverse of transactions become possible. In such case, blockchain protocol will fail to work.

Merkle Tree. Merkle Tree is constructed from transactions, and root of it will be put into block header for simplified verification. Generally, when computing a Merkle Tree with transactions, miners can include their own transactions with arbitrary data filled in some certain fields, e.g. input of *coinbase* transaction for Bitcoin [5,13] and *data* field in transactions for Ethereum [14]. With the help of these field, there may be enough bytes space for an adversary to launch second pre-image attack, to construct a distinct Merkle Tree with the same root value as an existing one. Therefore even a confirmed block is possible to be altered. The adversary can transmit the altered block to newly joined nodes and lead to failure of them to reach agreement with the network. Finally failure of the blockchain happens as well. Similar attack strategy can be applied to other specific fields within block structure, like the stored hash value of previous block.

Signature. Signature is computed based on hash of transaction in blockchain. If the used hash algorithm is compromised, two transactions as the hashed messages are possible to be found for a single hash value. The adversary can create a transaction with the same hash value as a on-chain transaction, such that these two transactions can both be acknowledged by network. For cryptocurrency like Bitcoin, as a result coins will possibly be stolen. Ownership of other data secured by signatures can also be broken.

3   Existing Solution to Compromised Hash in Blockchain

In this section we give an introduction and analysis of M. Sato et al.'s method [4] that applies proof of existence model with a decentralized manner into blockchain to resolve the problem of compromised hash.

3.1   Model of Proof of Existence

Sato et al. are the first to give the definition of proof of existence to describe validity of transactions in blockchain [4].

Definition 1 (Proof of Existence). *Supposing d is the data needed to be verified, we have the following definitions for d:*

- *poe_d: the proof of existence for d, which is calculated from d.*
- *$vpoe_d$: the data required for verification of poe_d.*
- *v: the verification algorithm outputing **true** only when input d and $vpoe_d$ are both valid, otherwise outputing **false**.*
- *A time-wise order can be obtained when poe_d is produced from d.*

Under centralized system poe_d is the signature produced by public key certificate from a trustful authority, while in decentralized scenario poe_d is determined by consensus of the whole network.

Proof of Existence for Blockchain. Under the model of proof of existence, we give a description of validity of transactions in blockchain. At first we define the following terms for blockchain:

- b_i: i-th block.
- tx_{ij}: j-th transaction in b_i ($1 \leq j \leq N_i$ where N_i is the number of transactions in b_i).
- hb_i: The reference of previous block b_i stored in b_{i+1}, i.e. hash value of b_i.
- $txid_{ij}$: The transaction ID of tx_{ij}, i.e. hash value of tx_{ij}.
- H_1: hash algorithm in use.

b_i is constructed as follows:

$$b_i = [hb_{i-1}, mkroot_i, [tx_{i1}, \ldots, tx_{iN_i}]]$$

where $mkroot_i$ is root of Merkle Tree calculated from $txid_{i1}, \ldots, txid_{iN_i}$.

Here transaction $tx_{ij}(1 \leq j \leq N_i)$ is the data d needed to be verified, hb_i is the proof of existence poe_d for d and b_{i-1} serves as $vpoe_d$ for poe_d. The verification algorithm v to check if tx_{ij} is existent is as follows:

1. Check d: calculate Merkle Root from $txid_{i1}, \ldots, txid_{iN_i}$ and check if it is equal to $mkroot_i$.
2. Check $vpoe_d$: calculate $H_1(b_{i-1})$ from $b_{i-1}(=vpoe_d)$ and check if it is equal to hb_{i-1} in b_i.
3. Calculate $H_1(b_i)$ and check if it is equal to hb_i in b_{i+1}.

3.2 Transition Scheme on Blockchain

Long-term signature scheme is a secure transition method originally designed for PKI (Public Key Infrastructure) model [15, 16]. It extends validity of digital signature and keeps a time-wise order of data relying on valid timestamps signed by a centralized trustful authority from PKI. Long-term signature scheme aligns model of proof of existence.

Sato et al. apply similar concept to secure transactions in the case of compromised hash in blockchain [4]. Their method can keep a block-wise order of transactions without participation of a trusted third party. Here we give a brief description of the method.

In proof-of-work blockchain once H_1 is compromised, poe_d will become an invalid PoE (proof of existence) for d because the mathematic relationship between them is broken. To deal with this problem, the transition scheme creates new PoE with a more secure hash algorithm H_2, to make verification of transactions available again. There are two ways to implement this method - basic transition procedure and support chain transition procedure.

Assuming that transition scheme starts from b_{M+1}, then we divide historical blocks $b_i (1 \leq i \leq M)$ into r groups of s blocks. Let b'_{M+k} be the new block constructed with H_2. Generation of new PoE poe'_d in basic transition procedure is as follow.

1. Calculate archive hash

$$archiveHash_k = H_2(b_{(k-1)s+1}, b_{(k-1)s+2}, \ldots, b_{(k-1)s+s})$$

2. Calculate new transaction ID $txid'_{(M+k)j}$ from $tx_{(M+k)j}$ with H_2

$$txid'_{(M+k)j} = H_2(tx_{(M+k)j})$$

3. Build Merkle Tree from $txid'_{(M+k)j} (1 \leq j \leq N_{M+k})$ with H_2 and set $mkroot'_{M+k}$ as the Merkle Root
4. Calculate hb'_{M+k-1} as follows:

$$hb'_{M+k-1} = H_2(b'_{M+k-1})$$

when $k = 1$, $hb'_{M+k-1} = H_2(b_M)$
5. Construct b'_{M+k}

$$b'_{M+k} = [archiveHash_k, hb'_{M+k-1}, mkroot'_{M+k},$$
$$[tx_{(M+k)1}, \ldots, tx_{(M+k)N_{M+k}}]]$$

6. Calculate new PoE

$$poe'_d = H_2(b'_{M+k})$$

where d is the collection of all transactions from $b_{(k-1)s+1}, \ldots, b_{(k-1)s+s}$ and b'_{M+k}.

After generation of b'_{M+k} for $1 \leq k \leq r$, each transaction in b_i for $1 \leq i \leq M$ will have corresponding new PoE protected by H_2, and the further blocks store newly collected transactions only, but not archive hash.

As mentioned in Subsect. 4.4.2 of [4], the above basic transition procedure is actually a hardfork since it inserts archive hash for past blocks into future blocks (that is, introducing new block structure into original blockchain protocol). Hardfork requires all nodes to follow new blockchain protocol to contribute computation but it always brings disagreement to blockchain community. The possible split can not be eliminated completely even if the computational power that still supports the original blockchain is very small. As a result, it will be divided into two blockchains. In example of Ethereum, after the DAO attack [17,18], a hardfork was processed from original chain to reverse state at the approval of majority of community members, but at the support of a minority of computational power the original chain still survived known as Ethereum Classic.

For the support chain transition procedure given in [4], new PoE poe'_d is stored in block from a second chain called support chain, which is maintained by the same or a part of miners of original chain, while block structure of original chain stays the same as before. As mentioned in Subsect. 4.4.3 of [4], proof-of-work competition is applied to one of these two chains, and both chains store the same transactions after completion of all archive hashes. Transactions verification is only conducted in original chain for most of time, but when dispute arises support chain will serve for final verification. This is a way of external protection. However, if proof of work is only applied to support chain, then proof-of-work mechanism in original chain should be removed. This is equal to introduction of hardfork into original chain, which results in the same issue as basic transition procedure. On the other hand, if proof of work is only applied to original chain, then block generation in support chain is not a computationally hard problem any more. Consequently, blocks in support chain will have no protection of accumulated computation. Even at some point where support chain has been maintained to be a very long chain, it is still possible for an adversary to take attacks on the compromised hash to replace blocks in original chain and then generate new corresponding support chain.

4 A Secure Approach Against Compromised Hash in Blockchain

In this section, based on the above proof of existence model, we introduce two-layer proof-of-work framework and then propose a softfork transition approach rather than a hardfork way, to provide a more feasible, practical and easier-to-deploy solution to the challenge of compromised hash algorithm in proof-of-work blockchain. Our scheme conforms to the model proposed by Garay et al. for secure blockchain backbone protocol [19].

4.1 A Novel Transition Scheme

To keep a proof-of-work blockchain secure, a transition from the compromised hash algorithm H_1 to a more secure one H_2 should be processed together with generation of new PoE. We define the following terms about proof of work with H_1 for block b_i:

1. $target_i$: current target for mining b_i.
2. $nonce_i$: the field that can be filled with random value to meet target requirement for b_i.
3. tsp_i: timestamp stored in b_i

When considering proof of work, b_i is constructed as follows:

$$b_i = [hb_{i-1}, mkroot_i, [target_i, nonce_i, tsp_i], [tx_{i1}, \ldots, tx_{iN_i}]]$$

In the following part, we let $target'_i, nonce'_i$ and tsp'_i represent corresponding parameters for proof of work with H_2. Adjustment rule of $target'_i$ can be set to the same algorithm as original blockchain protocol.

We assume that our scheme starts from b_{M+1}. Past M blocks will be divided into r groups of s blocks each, and we let $b_{M+k}(k \geq 1)$ be the block of new version. The new PoE is generated as follows:

1. Solve out H_1 puzzle: collect transactions and mine a complete block b_{M+k} that satisfies target of proof of work with H_1, i.e. using H_1 construct

$$b_{M+k} = [hb_{M+k-1}, mkroot_{M+k},$$
$$[target_{M+k}, nonce_{M+k}, tsp_{M+k}],$$
$$[tx_{(M+k)1}, \ldots, tx_{(M+k)N_{M+k}}]]$$

to subject to

$$H_1(b_{M+k}) \leq target_{M+k}$$

2. Calculate archive hash

$$archiveHash_k = H_2(b_{(k-1)s+1}, b_{(k-1)s+2}, \ldots, b_{(k-1)s+s})$$

3. Calculate transaction ID $txid'_{(M+k)j}$ from $tx_{(M+k)j}$ using H_2

$$txid'_{(M+k)j} = H_2(tx_{(M+k)j})$$

4. Calculate Merkle Root $mkroot'_{M+k}$ from $txid'_{(M+k)j}(1 \leq j \leq N_{M+k})$ using H_2
5. Calculate hb'_{M+k-1} as follows:

$$hb'_{M+k-1} = H_2(b'_{M+k-1})$$

where $hb'_{M+k-1} = H_2(b_M)$ for $k = 1$.

6. Construct outer block ob_{M+k}.

$$ob_{M+k} = [hb'_{M+k-1}, mkroot'_{M+k},$$
$$[target'_{M+k}, nonce'_{M+k}, tsp'_{M+k}]]$$

7. Construct the new block by

$$b'_{M+k} = [b_{M+k}, ob_{M+k}, archiveHash_k]$$

8. Solve out H_2 puzzle: mine b'_{M+k} to make it meet H_2 target requirement, i.e. fill $nonce'_{M+k}$ with random data such that to

$$H_2(b'_{M+k}) \leq target'_{M+k}$$

9. New PoE is generated as

$$poe'_d = hb'_{M+k} = H_2(b'_{M+k})$$

where d are transactions from $b_{(k-1)s+1}, \ldots, b_{(k-1)s+s}$ and b'_{M+k}.

Construction of outer block ob_{M+k} and new PoE hb'_{M+k} are respectively shown in Figs. 1 and 2.

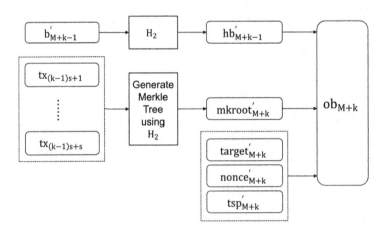

Fig. 1. Construction of outer block ob_{M+k}

Protection under H_2 of all historical transactions from $b_1, \ldots, b_M$ will be completed when b'_{M+r+1} is mined. For block $b'_{M+k}(k > r)$, new PoE is processed at the same way except to set $archiveHash_k$ empty. Chain structure of our solution is shown in Fig. 3. Since two kinds of proof of work for the hash algorithms H_1 and H_2 respectively both need to be solved out, we call the construction of the chain structure a *two-layer proof-of-work framework*.

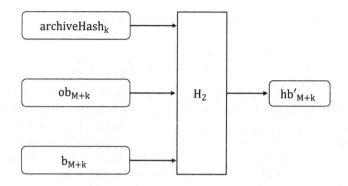

Fig. 2. Construction of new PoE hb'_{M+k}

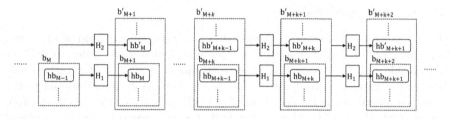

Fig. 3. Chain structure in our scheme

4.2   Verification Procedure in Blockchain

All participants in network can verify the validity of transactions when our scheme is implemented successfully. For nodes who run our upgraded blockchain protocol, as poe'_d is the new proof of existence for transactions, the algorithm v to verify $hb'_{M+k}(= poe'_d)$ is shown below.

1. Check transactions ($=d$)
   (a) if $1 \leq k \leq s$, then calculate $archiveHash_k$ from historical blocks $b_{(k-1)s+1}, \ldots, b_{(k-1)s+s}$

   $$archiveHash_k = H_2(b_{(k-1)s+1}, b_{(k-1)s+2}, \ldots, b_{(k-1)s+s})$$

   otherwise set $archiveHash_k$ empty. And check if this $archiveHash_k$ is equal to the stored $archiveHash_k$ in b'_{M+k}
   (b) Calculate $txid'_{(M+k)j}$ from $tx_{(M+k)j}(1 \leq j \leq N_{M+k})$

   $$txid'_{(M+k)j} = H_2(tx_{(M+k)j})$$

   (c) Calculate root of Merkle Tree from $txid'_{(M+k)j}, \ldots, txid'_{(M+k)N_{M+k}}$ and check if it is equal to $mkroot'_{M+k}$ in b'_{M+k}
2. Check proof of work and $b'_{M+k-1}(=vpoe_d)$:
   (a) Calculate $H_1(b_{M+k})$ and check if it meets the proof-of-work target for H_1 specified by $target_{M+k}$

(b) Calculate $H_2(b'_{M+k})$ and check if it meets the proof-of-work target for H_2 specified by $target'_{M+k}$
(c) Check if $H_2(b'_{M+k-1})$ is equal to hb'_{M+k-1} in b'_{M+k}
3. Check if value of $H_2(b'_{M+k})$ is the same as hb'_{M+k} in b'_{M+k+1}.

These upgraded nodes consider that a complete block is formed with b_{M+k}, ob_{M+k} and $archiveHash_k$. But in the view of old nodes that still run original blockchain protocol, they see b_{M+k} as a valid block, and ob_{M+k} and $archiveHash_k$ are transparent data to them. Therefore our scheme is a softfork strategy backward-compatible with original blockchain protocol. When verifying transactions, old nodes run the same verification algorithm as before, and do not check proof of work and Merkle Tree calculated with H_2.

4.3   Security Analysis

The key point to process our scheme safely is the implementation of upgraded blockchain protocol with majority computational power. In order to prevent the possible split, our transition scheme should be activated at a certain safe threshold of supported hast rate - that is, the dominant computational power should be migrated from original proof of work with H_1 to the two-layer proof of work with H_1 and H_2. Miners that still stay at original blockchain protocol recognize b_{M+k} within block of new version as a valid block, but upgraded nodes do not acknowledge the block generated by non-upgraded miners (i.e. b_{M+k}) as a complete block and will not follow it to mine further blocks. Therefore, according to the longest chain rule, branch generated only by non-upgraded miners will be given up by majority computational power switching to upgraded blockchain protocol. As for non-miners or light nodes, they do not contribute computational power and thus can still run original blockchain protocol.

Next, we consider the scenario where the adversary maliciously tries to mine an alternative chain with block of new version, to overtake the honest chain. Under hypothesis of rational man, miners always chase and extend the longest chain in order to maximize the benefits. Once the malicious branch outweighs the honest chain, rational miners will follow the malicious branch as the longest chain and abandon honest chain. As a result, blocks mined by honest miners will be overthrown and the adversary can benefit from it, e.g. taking back coins from transactions in honest chain. The probability of success for such an attack is related to the proportion of computational power that the adversary controls in whole network. To calculate out the probability, we first define the following terms.

- p_1 and q_1 are probabilities that honest miners and the adversary solve out H_1 puzzle respectively.
- p_2 and q_2 are probabilities that honest miners and the adversary solve out H_2 puzzle respectively.
- q_z is probability that the adversary overtakes honest chain from z blocks behind.

Then we can know that the relative probability for honest miners to find next block is $p = \frac{p_1 p_2}{q_1 q_2 + p_1 p_2}$ and for the adversary is $q = \frac{q_1 q_2}{q_1 q_2 + p_1 p_2}$. According to calculations in [1], we can compute probability P that the adversary overtakes the honest chain by the following formula:

$$P = 1 - \sum_{k=0}^{z} \frac{\lambda^k e^{-\lambda}}{k!} \left(1 - \left(\frac{q}{p}\right)^{(z-k)}\right)$$

Table 1. Solution to P less than 0.1% for different proof-of-work consensus, where q_1 and q_2 are probabilities that an adversary solves out H_1 and H_2 puzzle respectively, and z is the minimum number of blocks behind where an adversary can not generate an alternative chain overtaking the honest chain with probability more than 0.1%.

q_1	q_2	z	q_1	q_2	z
	0.10	2		0.10	4
	0.20	3		0.20	5
0.10	0.30	4	0.30	0.30	8
	0.40	4		0.40	12
	0.50	5		0.50	24
	0.10	3		0.10	4
	0.20	3		0.20	6
0.15	0.30	4	0.35	0.30	10
	0.40	6		0.40	17
	0.50	8		0.50	41
	0.10	3		0.10	4
	0.20	4		0.20	7
0.20	0.30	5	0.40	0.30	12
	0.40	7		0.40	26
	0.50	11		0.50	89
	0.10	3		0.10	5
	0.20	5		0.20	9
0.25	0.30	6	0.45	0.30	17
	0.40	9		0.40	43
	0.50	15		0.50	340

(a) Our Two-layer Proof of Work

q_1	z
0.10	5
0.15	8
0.20	11
0.25	15
0.30	24
0.35	41
0.40	89
0.45	340

(b) Original Proof of Work with H_1

The result of solving out P less than 0.1% for our scheme is shown in Table 1a. Compared with that for original proof of work with H_1 presented in Table 1b, we can see that two-layer proof-of-work framework in our scheme provides higher security since fewer blocks can reach the same security level of preventing chain from being reversed on the occasion that H_1 is risky to be compromised but still computationally secure.

Moreover, when complete break of second pre-image resistance or collision resistance for H_1 happens, transactions and blocks can not be modified under protection of H_2. In the case that pre-image resistance for H_1 is totally broken, i.e. x can be found in polynomial time for a given $h(x)$, solving out H_1 puzzle is not any more a hard job, but proof of work with H_2 and the majority computational power switching to the upgraded blockchain protocol can serve as the main guarantee to prevent malicious split and reverse of transactions.

5 Conclusion

This paper aimed to propose a secure solution against compromised hash in proof-of-work blockchain. Firstly, we analyzed the known approach given by M. Sato et al. which presented two transition procedures, i.e. the basic transition procedure and the support chain transition procedure. For the basic transition procedure, it is actually a hardfork which is difficult to be implemented since it always brings disagreement into blockchain community, while in the different case of support chain transition procedure, we observed that hardfork would also be introduced or support chain is risky to be tampered.

Then, we proposed the first softfork scheme against compromised hash in proof-of-work blockchain - a novel transition scheme with two-layer proof-of-work framework from the compromised hash to a secure one. Unlink hardfork solution, our scheme is backward-compatible such that potential splits from original chain can be avoided when the majority of computational power of the blockchain network migrates to our scheme. Furthermore, in our analysis we presented that a proof-of-work blockchain with our scheme can provide much more security than the original protocol in the aspect of resistance of malicious split attack.

Acknowledgement. We would like to thank the anonymous reviewers for their helpful feedback. The authors are supported by the National Natural Science Foundation of China (Grant No. 61672347, 61572318, 61672339).

References

1. Nakamoto, S.: Bitcoin: a peer-to-peer electronic cash system. In: Consulted (2008)
2. Bitcoin Wiki: Contingency plans - SHA-256 is broken (2015). https://en.bitcoin.it/wiki/Contingency_plans#SHA-256_is_broken
3. Bitcoin Wiki: Hardfork (2017). https://en.bitcoin.it/wiki/Hardfork
4. Sato, M., Matsuo, S.: Long-term public blockchain: resilience against compromise of underlying cryptography. In: IEEE European Symposium on Security and Privacy Workshops, pp. 1–8 (2017)
5. Okupski, K.: Bitcoin Developer Reference Working Paper, 30 June 2016. http://enetium.com/resources/Bitcoin.pdf
6. Bitcoin Developer Guide. https://bitcoin.org/en/developer-guide#proof-of-work
7. Stevens, M., et al.: Short chosen-prefix collisions for MD5 and the creation of a rogue CA certificate. In: Halevi, S. (ed.) CRYPTO 2009. LNCS, vol. 5677, pp. 55–69. Springer, Heidelberg (2009). https://doi.org/10.1007/978-3-642-03356-8_4
8. Wang, X., Yu, H.: How to break MD5 and other hash functions. In: Cramer, R. (ed.) EUROCRYPT 2005. LNCS, vol. 3494, pp. 19–35. Springer, Heidelberg (2005). https://doi.org/10.1007/11426639_2

9. Wang, X., Yin, Y.L., Yu, H.: Finding collisions in the full SHA-1. In: Shoup, V. (ed.) CRYPTO 2005. LNCS, vol. 3621, pp. 17–36. Springer, Heidelberg (2005). https://doi.org/10.1007/11535218_2
10. Stevens, M., Bursztein, E., Karpman, P., Albertini, A., Markov, Y.: The first collision for full SHA-1. In: Katz, J., Shacham, H. (eds.) CRYPTO 2017. LNCS, vol. 10401, pp. 570–596. Springer, Cham (2017). https://doi.org/10.1007/978-3-319-63688-7_19
11. Grover, L.K.: A fast quantum mechanical algorithm for database search. In: Proceedings of ACM Symposium on the Theory of Computing, pp. 212–219 (1996)
12. Giechaskiel, I., Cremers, C., Rasmussen, K.B.: On bitcoin security in the presence of broken cryptographic primitives. In: Askoxylakis, I., Ioannidis, S., Katsikas, S., Meadows, C. (eds.) ESORICS 2016. LNCS, vol. 9879, pp. 201–222. Springer, Cham (2016). https://doi.org/10.1007/978-3-319-45741-3_11
13. Bitcoin Wiki: Coinbase (2018). https://en.bitcoin.it/wiki/Coinbase
14. Wood, G.: Ethereum: a secure decentralized generalised transaction ledger. https://ethereum.github.io/yellowpaper/paper.pdf
15. European Telecommunications Standards Institute (ETSI): Electronic Signatures and Infrastructures (ESI); CAdES digital signatures; Part 1: Building blocks and CAdES baseline signatures. EN 319 122-1 V1.1.1 (2016)
16. International Organization for Standardization (ISO): Processes, data elements and documents in commerce, industry and administration - Long term signature profiles - Part 1: Long term signature profiles for CMS Advanced Electronic Signatures (CAdES). ISO 14533-1:2014 (2014)
17. The DAO, The Hack, The Soft Fork and The Hard Fork. https://www.cryptocompare.com/coins/guides/the-dao-the-hack-the-soft-fork-and-the-hard-fork/
18. Buterin, V.: Critical update re: DAO vulnerability, 17 June 2016. https://blog.ethereum.org/2016/06/17/critical-update-re-dao-vulnerability/
19. Garay, J., Kiayias, A., Leonardos, N.: The bitcoin backbone protocol: analysis and applications. In: Oswald, E., Fischlin, M. (eds.) EUROCRYPT 2015. LNCS, vol. 9057, pp. 281–310. Springer, Heidelberg (2015). https://doi.org/10.1007/978-3-662-46803-6_10

Analysis on the Block Reward of Fork After Withholding (FAW)

Junming Ke[1], Han Jiang[1,2(✉)], Xiangfu Song[1], Shengnan Zhao[1], Hao Wang[3], and Qiuliang Xu[1,2]

[1] School of Computer Science and Technology, Shandong University, Jinan 250000, China
junmingke1994@gmail.com
[2] School of Software, Shandong University, Jinan 250000, China
{jianghan,xql}@sdu.edu.cn
[3] School of Information Science and Engineering, Shandong Normal University, Jinan 250000, China
wanghao@sdnu.edu.cn

Abstract. The irreversible trend in clustering of mining power raises severe concerns on stability and security of PoW based on cryptocurrency. It has been shown that, in some case, reward of a mining pool can be significantly increased by deviating honest mining strategy. As a result, many attacking strategies are proposed to maximize pools' reward. Very recently, Kwon et. al. proposed Fork After Withholding (FAW) attack by combining selfish mining and Block Withholding (BWH) attack, which, as they stated, has a better reward than BWH. However, it is not always the case after our further investigation. In this paper, we firstly give a detailed comparison between the BWH and FAW attack, and show the implications behind them. We also consider honest mining to make the analysis of the block reward more clear. We demonstrate the imperfection of FAW in relative reward, reward after the fork and the fork state. Our main finding for FAW attack includes that the reward of victim pool increases faster compared to BWH attack, and for some cases, the attack should adopt honest mining strategy to maximize its reward, therefore, we present an improved FAW strategy, and propose a protocol for the pool's manager to resist FAW's attacker. Finally, we discuss the underlying flaws of FAW attack as well as countermeasures to alleviate it.

Keywords: Fork After Withholding · Analysis · Countermeasure

1 Introduction

Bitcoin is a popular cryptocurrency, first proposed by Nakamoto [13] in 2008. The Bitcoin system is peer-to-peer, and transactions take place between users directly, without an intermediary. Bitcion uses a proof of work scheme to limit the number of votes per entity, and thus renders decentralization practical, which

© Springer Nature Switzerland AG 2018
M. H. Au et al. (Eds.): NSS 2018, LNCS 11058, pp. 16–31, 2018.
https://doi.org/10.1007/978-3-030-02744-5_2

let the "miners" has the right to write the transactions. Bitcoin miners collect transactions in a block and vary a nonce until one of them finds the solution to a given puzzle [5,9].

In Bitcoin network, multiple miners join hands in order to form a mining pool to sum up their computing power with the aim of yielding a massive computing powerhouse. In such a mining pool every miner needs to regularly submit a proof of work to the pool manager to demonstrate their work towards solving the proof of work associated with a Bitcoin block [12]. Mining pool shares their processing power over a network, to split the reward equally, according to the amount of work they contributed to the probability of finding a block. Finding a valid solution leading to a new block depends on nothing but computation power, and consequently the pool manager distributes sub-puzzles to each miners. A miner engages in the sub-puzzle to generate partial proof of work (PPoWs) and submits corresponding solutions to the sub-puzzle. These PPoWs provide a relatively efficient way to find full proof of work (FPoWs). The difficulty of sub-puzzles is lower than the block puzzle. Therefore, the more PPoWs miners submit, the higher possibility FPoWs yields with. Once again, only FPoWs could obtain block reward.

Background. There has been increasing attention to the issue of stability and security of Bitcoin scheme (proof of work). In order to win the reward, the mining pool can adopt some unfair strategy to maximum the reward, and make the victim party (a pool or a solo miner) suffer losses.

There are many attacks on bitcoin scheme (proof of work), This paper focuses on the following four aspects:

Selfish mining is an attack on the integrity of the Bitcoin network [4,8]. This refers to such a scenario where one miner, or mining pool, does not publish and distribute a valid solution to the rest of the network. The selfish miner/pool then continues to mine the next block and so on maintaining its lead. When the rest of the network is about to catch up with the selfish miner, he, or they, then release their portion of solved blocks into the network. The result is that their chain and proof of work is longer, so the rest of the network accepts their block solutions and they claim the block rewards [3]. The selfish mining attack is a method for mining pools to increase their returns by not playing fair [11].

The BWH attack was introduced by Eyal [7]. An attacker joins a target pool and then submits only PPoWs, but not FPoWs, unlike honest pool miners [10]. Because the attacker pretends to contribute to the target pool and gets paid, the pool suffers a loss. Courtois et al. [14] generalized the concept of the BWH attack, considering an attacker who mines both solo and in pools.

From the above attacks, we could obtain a novel attack: Fork After Withholding (FAW) attack [15]. The core idea is that an attacker can split his computing power into two groups: innocent mining and infiltration mining, so as to attack a target pool (as with the BWH attack). However, in a BWH attack, when the attacker finds an FPoW as an infiltration miner, the attacker drops the FPoW; in an FAW attack, she does not immediately propagate it to the pool manager, waiting instead for an external honest miner to publish theirs, at which point she propagates the FPoW to the manager hoping to cause a fork (similar to selfish mining). Because the fork after withholding attack aims at causing fork, so the network delay will influence the attack's success rate. Of course, if the attacker combine the FAW and double spending, more rewards will be obtained than adopting only one of two attacks. However, the double spending could not be quantified in this scenario, so we are not going to discuss too much on this topic.

Motivation. Fork After Withholding is a new attack that combines selfish mining and a block withholding attack [15]. However, we would like to find where the fork after withholding attack is in Bitcoin or not exist. Unilaterally speaking, the fork after withholding attack would cause fork, which is an unusual case in Bitcoin network, we suspect there may not exist fork after withholding attack in the Bitcoin network. Besides, when fork after withholding first be proposed, the attacker's rewards have only risen 1% to 7% than honest mining. From a numerical point of view, the attacker's reward are indeed rising. However, if the attack cost too much, the attacker may not adopt these strategy in reality. On the one hand, this kind of attack is not as great as imagined, on the other hand, this attack may cost too much where we are easy to ignore. This paper gives an contrastive analysis on the attack, and intend to find some verifying points or some other interesting points.

Contribution. To our best knowledge, there is no research analyse the disadvantage on fork after withholding attack. This paper gives a detailed comparison between the block withholding attack and the fork after withholding attack. In this part, we find that in FAW, relative to the BWH, the victim pool's reward is increasing faster than the attacker's reward, and also, both in the withholding attack and the fork after withholding attack, the third party's reward (i.e. the honest miners) will increase all the time. Eventually, we find that the fork after withholding attack isn't as good as imagined. And this paper also use the results of the analysis to propose a simple system named Reputation System, which can help the pool's manager find the fork after withholding attack, if the pools manager finds the attackers and surely kick off the attackers. Meanwhile, this system will also take effort in the fork-permitted cryptocurrencies such as Ethereum.

2   Related Work

2.1   Withholding Attack Model

As mentioned in Sect. 1, the attacker can unfairly earn a greater reward through a BWH attack and a FAW attack, we demonstrate the whole attack model in Fig. 1. Not only the FAW attack against one target pool but also a generalized FAW attack against multiple pools simultaneously. FAW and BWH attacks can occur against Bitcoin and other cryptocurrency, which is based on proof of work scheme, such as Ethereum [6] and Litecoin [2].

2.2 Preliminaries

We refer the definition from [15].

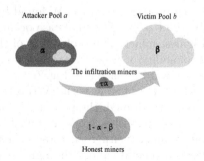

Fig. 1. Withholding attack model

There exit an attacker pool a, the victim pool b.

α: Computational power of the attacker,

β: Computational power of the victim pool,

τ: the infiltration mining power as a proportion of the attacker α,

c: Probability that an attacker's FPoW through infiltration mining will be selected as the main chain,

So the following proportion are derived from the above proportion naturally:

$\tau\alpha$: The infiltration mining power in the whole mining power,

$\alpha - \tau\alpha$: The attacker innocent mining power,

$\beta + \tau\alpha$: The whole victim pool computational power include the Infiltration mining power (Note that in withholding attack, $\tau\alpha$ computational power doesn't make any effects, but the situation is different in Fork After Withholding (FAW) attack).

$1 - \alpha - \beta$: The honest mining power.

We describe the attacker reward of the BWH attacker and the FAW attacker in Fig. 2.

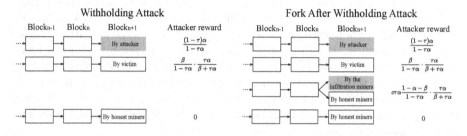

Fig. 2. The reward of withholding attack and the reward of fork after withholding attack

We can divide the BWH attack results in each round into three cases as shown in Fig. 2. In the first case, the attacker earns a reward through innocent mining. Because she as an innocent miner should compete with others who have total computational power $1 - \tau\alpha$, the probability of the first case is $\frac{(1-\tau)\alpha}{1-\tau\alpha}$. In the second case, the pool propagates an FPoW found by an honest miner in the pool, with a probability of $\frac{\beta}{1-\tau\alpha}$. The final case occurs when a valid block is found by an external honest miner. The probability of this case is $1 - \alpha - \beta$. As expected, the total probability of these three cases sums to 1. Then, we can derive the BWH attackers reward as shown in Fig. 2.

The FAW attack is just a little different with BWH attack in the fourth case, the attacker can generate a fork through the pool if she found and withheld an FPoW before the honest miner publish a block. Detailed, when a valid block is found by an external honest miner (neither the attacker nor someone within the victim pool), the attacker can generate a fork through the pool if she found and withheld an FPoW in advance. The probability is $\tau\alpha\frac{1-\alpha-\beta}{1-\tau\alpha}$. We can derive the BWH attackers reward as shown in Fig. 2.

2.3   Attacker Reward

The Attacker reward is given in [15]:

An FAW attacker with computational power α can earn

$$R_a(\tau) = \frac{(1-\tau)\alpha}{1-\tau\alpha} + \left(\frac{\beta}{1-\tau\alpha} + c\tau\alpha\frac{1-\alpha-\beta}{1-\tau\alpha}\right)\frac{\tau\alpha}{\beta+\tau\alpha} \tag{1}$$

The reward is maximized when the optimal τ value:

$$\bar{\tau} = \frac{(1-\alpha)(1-c)\beta + \beta^2 c - \beta\sqrt{h}}{\alpha(1-\alpha-\beta)(c(1-\beta)-1)} \tag{2}$$

Where: $h = (1-\alpha-\beta)^2 c^2 + ((1-\alpha-\beta)(\alpha\beta+\alpha-2))c - \alpha(1+\beta) + 1$.

At first, we state that FAW attack is equal to withholding attack when $c = 0$. When the infiltration miner mined a block, they would hide the block. In case of any honest miner mined a block, the infiltration miner would like to publish block to attain fork. $c = 0$ means the fork would never be controversial, everyone in the network will choose the honest miner's block to be the main chain. That is, There is no difference between the infiltration miner publish block or not, so there is no difference between the FAW attack and the withholding attack. More specifically, cause R_a is an increasing function of c, the reward from the FAW attack has a lower bound defined by the reward from the withholding attack.

According to the above description, in the case of the same mining power, the reward from the FAW attacker R_{FAW}, the reward from the withholding attacker $R_{withholding}$ and the reward from the honest miner R_{honest} should satisfy the following inequality (when $\tau \leq \frac{\beta}{1-\alpha}$):

$$R_{FAW} \geq R_{withholding} \geq R_{honest} \tag{3}$$

$\tau \leq \frac{\beta}{1-\alpha}$ means the infiltration mining power as a proportion of the attacker α should be greater than the victim pool mining power as a proportion the whole mining power besides the attacker's mining power.

3 Analysis

This section gives a detailed comparison of the block reward between the block withholding attack and the fork after withholding attack, respectively.

3.1 The Relative Reward

Case I. If all are the honest miner, than the reward of each party should follow the following expressions:

A miner a with α computational power: $R_a^I(\tau) = \alpha$.

A miner b with β computational power: $R_b^I(\tau) = \beta$.

The remaining computational power: $R_{remain}^I(\tau) = 1 - \alpha - \beta$.

Case II. For a block withholding attacker, the reward of each party can be represent as follows:

An attacker a with α computational power: $R_a^{II}(\tau) = \frac{(1-\tau)\alpha}{1-\tau\alpha} + (\frac{\beta}{1-\tau\alpha})\frac{\tau\alpha}{\beta+\tau\alpha}$.

A victim pool b with β computational power: $R_b^{II}(\tau) = (\frac{\beta}{1-\tau\alpha})\frac{\beta}{\beta+\tau\alpha}$.

The remaining computational power: $R_{remain}^{II}(\tau) = \frac{1-\alpha-\beta}{1-\tau\alpha}$.

Case III. For a fork after withholding attacker, the reward of each party can be represent as follows:

An attacker a with α computational power: $R_a^{III}(\tau) = \frac{(1-\tau)\alpha}{1-\tau\alpha} + (\frac{\beta}{1-\tau\alpha} + c\tau\alpha\frac{1-\alpha-\beta}{1-\tau\alpha})\frac{\tau\alpha}{\beta+\tau\alpha}$.

A victim pool b with β computational power: $R_b^{III}(\tau) = \frac{\beta}{1-\tau\alpha}\frac{\beta}{\beta+\tau\alpha} + c\tau\alpha\frac{1-\alpha-\beta}{1-\tau\alpha}\frac{\beta}{\beta+\tau\alpha}$.

The remaining computational power: $R_{remain}^{III}(\tau) = \frac{1-\alpha-\beta}{1-\tau\alpha} - c\tau\alpha\frac{1-\alpha-\beta}{1-\tau\alpha}$.

For the attacker, the attacker's reward is increasing:

$$R_a^{III}(\tau) \geq R_a^{II}(\tau) \geq R_a^I(\tau) \tag{4}$$

Meanwhile, the victim's reward isn't decreasing all the time, from the above:

$$R_b^{II}(\tau) \geq R_b^{III}(\tau) \tag{5}$$

For the case II, it is the same as that the attacker steals a portion of the reward from the victim pool. But for the case III, it is the same as that the attacker steals a portion of the reward from both the victim and the honest pool. Contemporary, when the attacker steals the reward from the honest pool, the attacker divided a portion of the reward and give it to the victim pool. Hence, the reward of the victim pool is increasing. Note that, in the withholding attack, due to $\frac{1-\alpha-\beta}{1-\tau\alpha} \geq 1 - \alpha - \beta$, the honest miners's reward is increasing. This is because the infiltration miner doesn't make any effects in the whole mining power, the whole mining power decreases, the ratio of the honest mining power increases, correspondingly, the reward of the honest miner increases.

Now we take a close look to the victim pool's reward. Due to $\tau \leq \frac{\beta}{1-\alpha}$ and $\alpha \leq 0.5 \leq 1 - \alpha$. We can get the follow inequality: $\beta \geq \tau\alpha$.

That is:

$$\frac{\beta}{\beta + \tau\alpha} \geq \frac{\tau\alpha}{\beta + \tau\alpha} \tag{6}$$

In case III, relative to the case II, we deemed that the victim pool's reward is increasing faster than the attacker's reward. Under some circumstances, however, it is not the optimal strategy for the attacker.

For example, for a victim pool with the higher computation power, like $\beta = 0.4$, the attacker pool's computation power is $\alpha = 0.2$, the remaining computation power is the honest pool: $1 - \alpha - \beta = 0.4$. The attacker pool hope to attack the victim pool, and make the reward of the attacker as close to the reward of the victim as possible. By this time, the attacker can adopt some strategies to increase his computation power. For instance, the attacker put forward this additional reward of the attacker pool to buy the computation power equipment, in order to achieve 51% computation power. Meanwhile, the attacker wish that the victim pool make as less reward as possible to buy the computation power equipment. As a result, the attacker won't adopt case III' strategy, especially the victim pool's reward is increasing faster than the attacker pool's reward.

3.2   The Reward After the Fork

Analysis. For a rational attacker, when the infiltration mining power find a block, and the honest mining power find a block, the attacker and the victim pool would follow the infiltration mining power's block. Then we will analyse the reward of the attacker and the victim pool after the infiltration mining power find a block. If the attacker still adopt fork after withholding strategy, then the reward will represent as follow in each step: $R_a(\tau) = \frac{(1-\tau)\alpha}{1-\tau\alpha} + (\frac{\beta}{1-\tau\alpha} + c\tau\alpha\frac{1-\alpha-\beta}{1-\tau\alpha})\frac{\tau\alpha}{\beta+\tau\alpha}$.

But if the attacker adopt honest mining with the infiltration mining power after the infiltration mining power publish a block (that means, after the infiltration mining power find a block, the honest mining power find a block.), we use $R'_a(1)$ to represent the reward of the first step and $R'_a(2)$ to represent the reward of the next step, then in the first step, the reward will represent as follows: $R'_a(1) = \frac{(1-\tau)\alpha}{1-\tau\alpha} + (\frac{\beta}{1-\tau\alpha} + (\alpha + \beta + g)\tau\alpha\frac{1-\alpha-\beta}{1-\tau\alpha})\frac{\tau\alpha}{\beta+\tau\alpha}$.

Where, g represent the fraction of the honest miner power will follow the infiltration mining pool's block. Due to the honest mining, then it will ended in the next step: $R'_a(2) = \alpha$. So the whole mining reward R'_a can represent as follows: $R'_a = R'_a(1) + \frac{\tau\alpha(1-\alpha-\beta)}{1-\tau\alpha}R'_a(2) + (1 - \frac{\tau\alpha(1-\alpha-\beta)}{1-\tau\alpha})R_a(\tau)$.

For convenience, we use the two steps reward represent FAW attacker's reward: $R_a = 2R_a(\tau)$.

From Eq. (3):

$$R_a(\tau) \geq R'_a(2) \tag{7}$$

We use $\underline{R_a(\tau)}$ to represent the lower bound of $R_a(\tau)$, because the lower bound of c is $(\alpha + \beta - \tau\alpha)$, that no honest miner follow the infiltration mining's block, and the infiltration miners are still adopt FAW strategy: $\underline{R_a(\tau)} = \frac{(1-\tau)\alpha}{1-\tau\alpha} + (\frac{\beta}{1-\tau\alpha} + (\alpha + \beta - \tau\alpha)\tau\alpha\frac{1-\alpha-\beta}{1-\tau\alpha})\frac{\tau\alpha}{\beta+\tau\alpha}$.

If the FAW attacker adopt honest mining after the fork, the lower bound of $R'_a(1)$ is represent by: $\underline{R'_a(1)} = \frac{(1-\tau)\alpha}{1-\tau\alpha} + (\frac{\beta}{1-\tau\alpha} + (\alpha + \beta)\tau\alpha\frac{1-\alpha-\beta}{1-\tau\alpha})\frac{\tau\alpha}{\beta+\tau\alpha}$.

Similarly, the situation is no honest miner computation power follow the infiltration mining's block. And we know:

$$\underline{R_a(\tau)} \leq \underline{R'_a(1)} \tag{8}$$

From (7) and (8), we will derived following inequations in some conditions:

$$R'_a \geq R_a \tag{9}$$

Which means, if we want maximum the attacker's reward, sometimes the attacker should adopt honest mining strategy when we use FAW attack!

The Improved FAW Strategy. For example, when $\alpha = 0.1$, $\beta = 0.15$ and $\tau = 0.2$, no honest miner computation power follow the infiltration mining's block, $g = 0$. We could calculate that when $c \leq 0.2492$, the attacker should be honest miner after the fork to maximize its reward.

At some points, when $R'_a \geq R_a$ is established, we specify the new FAW strategy based on FAW attack model as describe below.

An attacker can split his computing power between innocent mining and infiltration mining, aiming at a target pool (as with a BWH attack). When the attacker finds an FPoW as an infiltration miner, she does not immediately propagate it to the pool manager, waiting instead for an external honest miner to publish theirs, at which point she propagates the FPoW to the manager hoping to cause a fork, if the attacker innocent miner or the target pool publish a block, the infiltration miner would follow their block and don't propagate the FPoW. However, if the infiltration miner's block cause a fork, she will transform the strategy, from FAW strategy to honest mining strategy, that is, when the infiltration miner finds an FPoW, she will propagate the FPoW to the manager immediately. Until one party publish a block, the infiltration miner transform the strategy, from honest mining strategy to FAW strategy.

However, as discussed in [15], c is hard to confirm and changes frequently. And it's hard to determine how many honest mining power will follow the infiltration miner's block. Therefore, the new FAW strategy is hard to realize.

The Improved FAW Strategy's Game. In the Bitcoin network, pools can execute FAW attacks against each other as well. Let's consider briefly about game between two players, $Pool_1$ and $Pool_2$, Parameters for the analysis of the Improved FAW attack game are defined as below for $i = 1, 2$.

α_i: Computational power of Pool$_i$

f_i: Infiltration Computational power of Pool$_i$, i.e., $f_i = \tau_i \alpha_i$

In the FAW attack game between two pools, the lower bound rewards R_1 of Pool$_1$ and R_2 of Pool$_2$ are:

$$R_1 = \frac{\frac{\alpha_1 - f_1}{1 - f_1 - f_2} + (\alpha_1 + \alpha_2) f_2 \frac{1 - \alpha_1 - \alpha_2}{1 - f_2} + \alpha_1 f_1 f_2 \left(\frac{1}{1 - f_1} + \frac{1}{1 - f_2}\right) \frac{1 - \alpha_1 - \alpha_2}{1 - f_1 - f_2}}{2}$$

$$+ \frac{R_2 \frac{f_1}{\alpha_2 + f_1}}{2} + \frac{\alpha_1}{2}$$

$$R_2 = \frac{\frac{\alpha_2 - f_2}{1 - f_1 - f_2} + (\alpha_1 + \alpha_2) f_1 \frac{1 - \alpha_1 - \alpha_2}{1 - f_2} + \alpha_2 f_1 f_2 \left(\frac{1}{1 - f_1} + \frac{1}{1 - f_2}\right) \frac{1 - \alpha_1 - \alpha_2}{1 - f_1 - f_2}}{2}$$

$$+ \frac{R_1 \frac{f_2}{\alpha_1 + f_2}}{2} + \frac{\alpha_2}{2}$$

The above rewards is same like two-pool FAW attack game's rewards, there is a Nash equilibrium in the game, and the improved FAW strategy's game is the same scenario, there also exists a condition in which the larger pool always earns the extra reward, and the miner's dilemma may not hold.

3.3   Fork State

The infiltration mining power's action is similar to the selfish mining, but a little different. First of all, selfish mining is a pool's computation power selfish mining against the rest of the mining computation power. But the infiltration miner is selfish mining against the honest mining computation power, which is equal to $1 - \alpha - \beta$. When the honest mining computation power publish a block, if the infiltration miner has found the FPOW, he will submit his FPOW, and turn to the initial state. Then, if the attacker or the victim mining computation power ($\alpha - \tau\alpha$ and β) publish a block, even though the infiltration miner hides a block, he will not submit his FPOW, conversely, turn to the initial state. On the contrary, selfish miners can hide as many blocks as they can, with regard to the infiltration miner. When the infiltration miner find a block, he can't select transactions to form the next block, because he is not the administrator. Therefore, the filtration miner can't find the next block's hash value after he find the current block's hash value.

We have rebuild the state machine with transition frequencies of the fork after withholding attack (Fig. 3). State s = 0 means the initial state, State s = 1 means the infiltration miners hold a block, State s = 0' means the infiltration miners submit a FPOW (that means the honest miner also publish a block.). When the infiltration miner find a block with probability $\tau\alpha$, that means the infiltration miners hold a block, the state s = 0 transfer to the state s = 1. Similarly, the state s = 0 transfer to the state s = 0 with probability $1 - \tau\alpha$. After the infiltration miners hold a block, if the honest miners find a block with probability $\frac{1 - \alpha - \beta}{1 - \tau\alpha}$, the state s = 1 transfer to the state s = 0'. Also, the state s = 1 transfer to the state s = 0 with probability $\frac{\alpha+\beta-\tau\alpha}{1-\tau\alpha}$, including the attacker remaining mining power find a block scenario and the victim pool find a block scenario. The state s = 0' transfer to the state s = 0 with probability c, means the infiltration miner's block become the main chain's block, and the state s = 0' transfer to the state s = 0 with probability $1 - c$, means the honest miner's block become the main chain's block.

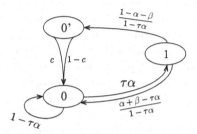

Fig. 3. State machine with transition frequencies of the fork after withholding attack

Is there still exist any other attack methods can be described as this type of state machine? or any "fork" attack can be formalized as this type of state machine? Limited by our research, we leave the analysis on the state machine with transition frequencies as an open problem.

In other words, the infiltration miner adopts a special selfish mining strategy, the infiltration miner can hide only one block, and this block will cause fork after the infiltration miner submit this to the administrator. For a rational manager, she will submit her FPoW as soon as she received the block from the pool's miners, since it would always be beneficial for him to submit a local FPoW. Even though there exist a block to be validated in the Bitcoin network. From the [15]'s opinion, considering the network delay, the infiltration miner's block can be the final valid block with probability c. However, in the Bitcoin network, for a normal mining process, we believe that fork is the small probability event, because two miners find a block together is the small probability event. The pool's administrator will realize that the infiltration miner computation power was hidden block after he received the infiltration miner's submission. In a short time period, this may be rational behavior for a pool's administrator publish the submission, like we discussed before, the reward of the victim would be greater than the reward of the infiltration miner if this submission become the final valid block. But in the long run, the long-term reward should be smaller than the pool deserved, because the infiltration miner will divided the victim pool's reward but make no effects most of the time. So, we have reached a consensus, from the perspective of profit, a pool manager should resist any BWH attacker if the pool manager knows, nevertheless, the pool manager will publish the submission at first.

4   Simulation

Honestly, we believe that the attacker's reward is very small compared to the honest mining. Consequently, we use $\frac{R-R_{honest}}{R_{honest}}$ represent the growth of reward R. Also, as we can see in Bitcoin network, the distribution of the mining pool are as Table 1 [1].

In order to approximate the actual situation, we assume that the attacker's computation power α and the victim pool's computation power β is not larger than 0.3. Figure 4(a)–(c) show the $\frac{R-R_{honest}}{R_{honest}}$ of the attacker, the victim pool and the honest miners, respectively, given terms attacker computation power α, when the victim pool's computation power is $\beta = 0.3$, the infiltration miner's computation power is $\tau\alpha = 0.2\alpha$, probability $c = 0.55$.

First of all, with the increase of the attacker computation power, the victim pool's reward decreases and the attacker's reward increases, however, the honest miner's reward is also increases, that means, when an attacker attacks a victim pool, the honest miner will profit from the attacking process. This is not a good news for an attacker's long term benefits, the attacker don't want "Two dogs strive for a bone, and a third runs away with it", if the victim pool counterattack the attacker's pool with block withholding attack.

Table 1. Computation power ratio

Pool name	Computation power ratio
Antpool	0.17
BTC.com	0.1332
BTC.TOP	0.1332
ViaBTC	0.1193
SlushPool	0.0846
BTCC	0.0572
BitFury	0.038
Others	0.2645

After that, in reality, the attacker's computation power α and the victim pool's computation power β is not larger than 0.3. The attacker's reward isn't increased very big as we imaged, $\frac{R-R_{honest}}{R_{honest}}$ only increases 0.5%–3%.

Figure 4(d) shows the lower bound reward after the fork, as we discussed in Sect. 3.2, we know the lower bound reward in next step, but we can't identify specific value in next step. Moreover, as discussed in [15], it is difficult to identify specific value c.

However, we know that the value c is lower bounded by $\alpha + \beta - \tau\alpha$, if the attacker adopt honest mining in next step, the probability of the attacker's chain be selected as the main chain is lower bounded by $\alpha + \beta$. From the Fig. 4(d), we can see that the reward of adopting honest mining will be greater than the

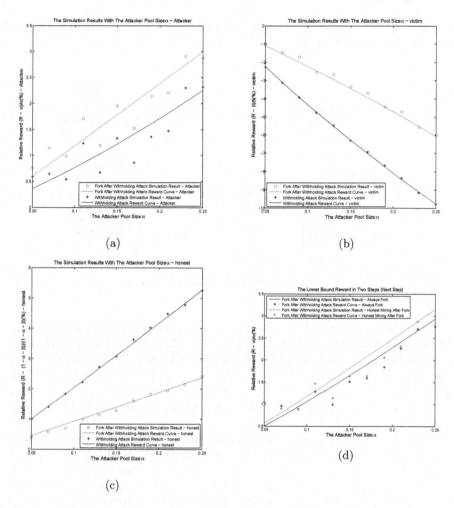

Fig. 4. Simulation results

reward of adopting fork after withholding in next step, however, the lower bound value isn't vary that much, only just 0.5%.

5   Countermeasure

For a rational manager, she will submits her FPoW as soon as she received the block from the pool's miners, since it would always be beneficial for him to submit a local FPoW. This may be rational for a short time period, but in the long run, the long-term reward should be smaller than the pool deserved. So, we have reached a consensus, from the perspective of profit, a pool manager should resist any block withholding attacker or fork after withholding attacker if the pool manager knows.

We proposed a reputation system for the pool manager, to help them find the fork after withholding attacker.

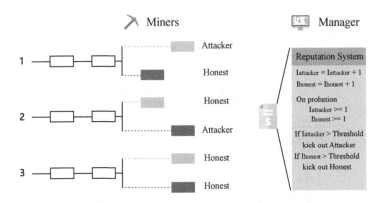

Fig. 5. Reputation system demonstration

From the perspective of the manager, when an attacker execute FAW attack, the manager will receive attacker's FPoW, after that, due to the network delay assumption, the manager will receive other's valid block. If the manager's network environment is good enough, the manager will receive other's valid block before she receive attacker's FPoW. This is possible because a pool's manager should be good enough for her mining task. This is demonstrate as Fig. 5 ①, ② and ③.

Also, in ①, ② and ③ may exist honest miner's fork, that means, a honest miner have find a valid block, and a honest miner in the pool have also submit FPoW, this is a small probability event. However, we take this event into our consideration, and define a value named *Threshold*. When the manager have cause a fork after he publish an FPoW, she will first thought this fork to be an accident, and calculate the coefficient of the identity equals to the old coefficient of the identity plus 1, this means the identity is found once. Then we observe any identity whose coefficient is greater than 1, if the coefficient is greater than the *Threshold*, the manager will kick out this identity, even this identity is the honest miner in reality. The meaning of the "kick out" is the manager throw this part of computation power out, and keep the remaining computation power mining in the pool.

We could consider if there exist an infiltration miner, he will submit his FPoW when he receive an unconfirmed block from the bitcoin network, and the manager first receive the infiltration miner's FPoW and she publish the FPoW as an unconfirmed block, but soon she will find there exist an unconfirmed block from the bitcoin network, but in the bitcoin, the true fork is small probability event. So the manager will realize that the miner who submit the FPoW is the infiltration miner. We should realized if the attacker never submit any FPoW and will never cause a fork in the Bitcoin network. In this case, the FAW attacker will degenerate into BWH attack, we could use other methods to find the BWH attacker [14], in this paper, we mainly focus on the FAW attacker.

There is an another reason why we define a value named *Threshold*, for some alter coins used POW scheme, fork is not a small probability event, so there exist a certain probability for a honest miner submit the FPoW and cause fork in the network, such as Ethereum, we define *Threshold* because we know that the FAW attacker will cause more fork rate, that is, $\frac{Threshold}{SubmitCount}$ than the honest miner, *SubmitCount* is the number of FPoW of this identity submitted. So if some identity's fork time more than the *Threshold*, the manager should kick out this part of computation power.

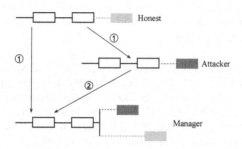

Fig. 6. Reputation system attack

However, the attacker can adopt another strategy in our system, show as Fig. 6. When a honest miner submit his FPoW to manager, the manager will publish an unconfirmed block, and the attacker in the network, or in the pool, will follow the previous block and find an unconfirmed block, when the manager received the attacker's unconfirmed block, he will calculate the coefficient of the honest miner, it will increase the honest miner's coefficient. Our suggestion is we could introduce time stamp scheme, when the pool manager publish a block, she could record the time in the system, and after that, in the certain time period, if there is another unconfirmed block in the Bitcoin network, the reputation system is online, beyond that time period, the reputation system is offline.

6   Conclusion

To summarize, this paper gives a detailed comparison between the block withholding attack and the fork after withholding attack. Eventually, we simulate the reward of the attacker, the victim pool and the honest pool in the block withholding attack and the fork after withholding attack. There are four mainly fundings:

At first, relative to the block withholding attack, in the fork after withholding attacks scenario, the victim pools reward will be greater than the victims pools reward in the block withholding attacks scenario. Then, both in the withholding attack and the fork after withholding attack, the third partys reward (i.e. the honest miners) will increased, which isn't a good news for the attacker, because in the miner dilemmas scenario, it is like Two dogs strive for a bone, and a third runs away with it. Third, when the attacker adopt fork after withholding attack, it is just like the infiltration miners publish a block and lead a fork, to make the infiltration miners block be the main chains block, in the next step, all the infiltration miners should adopt honest mining strategy to make the probability of being main chain increases. Finally, because the infiltration miners publish a block and lead a fork, compared to the block withholding attack, it is easy for the pools manager to find the fork after withholding attacks attacker. This paper proposed a simple system named Reputation System, used to find the fork after withholding attack, if the pools manager find the attacker and kick off the attacker. Meanwhile, this system will also take effort in the fork-permitted cryptocurrencies such as Ethereum.

Acknowledgments. This work is supported by the National Natural Science Foundation of China under grant No. 61572294, No. 61602287, Key Program of National Natural Science of China under grant No. 61632020, Natural Science Foundation of Shandong Province under grant No. ZR2017MF021, the Primary Research & Development Plan of Shandong Province (No. 2018GGX101037), and the Fundamental Research Funds of Shandong University under grant No. 2017JC019.

References

1. Block explorer. http://qukuai.com. Accessed 21 Dec 2017
2. Litecoin: The cryptocurrency for payments based on blockchain technology. https://litecoin.org/. Accessed 13 Dec 2017
3. Gervais, A., Karame, G.O., Wüst, K., Glykantzis, V., Ritzdorf, H., Capkun, S.: On the security and performance of proof of work blockchains. In: ACM SIGSAC Conference on Computer and Communications Security, pp. 3–16. ACM (2016)
4. Sapirshtein, A., Sompolinsky, Y., Zohar, A.: Optimal selfish mining strategies in bitcoin. In: Grossklags, J., Preneel, B. (eds.) FC 2016. LNCS, vol. 9603, pp. 515–532. Springer, Heidelberg (2017). https://doi.org/10.1007/978-3-662-54970-4_30
5. Tschorsch, F., Scheuermann, B.: Bitcoin and beyond: a technical survey on decentralized digital currencies. IEEE Commun. Surv. Tutor. **18**(3), 2084–2123 (2016). https://doi.org/10.1109/COMST.2016.2535718
6. Gavin, W.: Ethereum: a secure decentralised generalised transaction ledger. Ethereum Project Yellow Paper **151**, 1–32 (2014)
7. Eyal, I.: The miner's dilemma. In: IEEE Symposium on Security and Privacy, pp. 89–103. IEEE (2015)
8. Eyal, I., Sirer, E.G.: Majority is not enough: bitcoin mining is vulnerable. Commun. ACM **61**(7), 95–102 (2018). https://doi.org/10.1145/3212998
9. Bonneau, J., Miller, A., Clark, J., Narayanan, A., Kroll, J.A., Felten, E.W.: SoK: research perspectives and challenges for bitcoin and cryptocurrencies. In: IEEE Symposium on Security and Privacy, pp. 104–121. IEEE (2015)
10. Luu, L., Saha, R., Parameshwaran, I., Saxena, P., Hobor, A.: On power splitting games in distributed computation: the case of bitcoin pooled mining. In: IEEE Computer Security Foundations Symposium, pp. 397–411. IEEE (2015)

11. Madeira, A.: What is bitcoin selfish mining? https://www.cryptocompare.com/coins/guides/what-is-bitcoin-selfish-mining/. Accessed 12 Jan 2018
12. Bag, S., Ruj, S., Sakurai, K.: Bitcoin block withholding attack: analysis and mitigation. IEEE Trans. Inf. Forensics Secur. **12**, 1967–1978 (2017). https://doi.org/10.1109/TIFS.2016.2623588
13. Nakamoto, S.: Bitcoin: a peer-to-peer electronic cash system (2008)
14. Courtois, N.T., Bahack, L.: On subversive miner strategies and block withholding attack in bitcoin digital currency. arXiv preprint arXiv:1402.1718 (2014)
15. Kwon, Y., Kim, D., Son, Y., Vasserman, E., Kim, Y.: Be selfish and avoid dilemmas: Fork After Withholding (FAW) attacks on bitcoin. In: ACMSIGSAC Conference on Computer and Communications Security, pp. 195–209. ACM (2017)

Adding Confidential Transactions to Cryptocurrency IOTA with Bulletproofs

Peter Ince[1]($\boxtimes$), Joseph K. Liu[1]($\boxtimes$), and Peng Zhang[2]($\boxtimes$)

[1] Faculty of Information Technology, Monash University, Clayton, Australia
pinc0001@student.monash.edu, joseph.liu@monash.edu
[2] College of Information Engineering, Shenzhen University, Shenzhen, China
zhangp@szu.edu.cn

Abstract. IOTA, one of the largest cryptocurrencies in the world, is a platform that links together Internet of Things (IoT) devices and is specifically built for fee-free machine-to-machine micropayments and messaging. One of IOTA's core features is the Tangle - which is a new distributed ledger concept that tracks all payments and interactions. Despite its new features, there are some potential privacy issues associated when users combine the ubiquity and integration of the IoT and machine-to-machine transactions in our foreseeable future. In this paper, we describe an implementation that Bulletproof technique [9] with the IOTA platform to allow the hiding of transaction values and user balances.

Keywords: IOTA · Bulletproofs · Blockchain

1 Introduction

As technology becomes more and more integrated into our lives, many of the transactional relationships we have with technology or people will likely eventually be replaced by machine-to-machine transactions and payments.

One of the rising companies that is aiming to take this on is IOTA [20]; a "blockchain" (although IOTA is colloquially referred to as a blockchain, it's model is actual that made up of a Directed-Ac cyclic Graph, so it would be more accurate to refer to it as a DAGChain) built with the intention of enabling machine to machine payments and becoming the backbone of the Internet of Things.

IOTA aims to be more suitable for the Internet of Things through a few key measures;

– Unlike Proof of Work based cryptocurrencies like Bitcoin [15] and Ethereum [10] that require ever more powerful technology to secure the network and sign new transactions, IOTA requires only a minimal amount of processing power (similar to that required in Hashcash [3] as a counter measure to attacks on the network

© Springer Nature Switzerland AG 2018
M. H. Au et al. (Eds.): NSS 2018, LNCS 11058, pp. 32–45, 2018.
https://doi.org/10.1007/978-3-030-02744-5_3

- As there is no mining in IOTA, there are no transaction fees - making it more suitable for the micro-transactions of the future - as a payment of a cent quickly becomes infeasible when even the smallest of transaction fee is added
- As the network is modelled on a Directed-Acylcic Graph, and each transactions sent requires that two other transactions are processed, IOTA claim that the network will become more reliable as it scales to a larger level of adoption, unlike block based chains that typically have a set number of transactions that can be included in a block[1].

As with Bitcoin and many other cryptocurrencies; IOTA offers pseudo-anonymity based on hash based addressing that is not tied to an individual in any way. In the original paper for Bitcoin [15], Satoshi Nakamoto pointed out the weakness with this form of anonymisation; that the transaction is only not linked to other transactions if it has the exact amount of currency required associated with it. This creates a web of transaction inputs and outputs that can be linked and traced back to the original address. Researchers have been able to link not only transactions, but also linking the transactions to other information that could be used to identify individuals [1,5,11,21,22].

For example, in the study "Private memoirs of a smart meter" [13] Molina-Markham et al. showed that by analysing the usage data of three homes over two months, they were able to identify a range of details including number of people occupying the house; what were the hours people slept; and their eating routines [13]. If instead of just seeing usage of a single device; a bad actor was able to view the value, frequency and timing of all addresses; they would be able to infer much more than only our daily routines from the information.

Our Contributions. In this paper, we add Private Transactions to IOTA using the Vector Pedersen Commitments and RangeProofs technique (called *Bulletproofs*) outlined in the paper "Bulletproofs: Efficient Range Proofs for Confidential Transactions" [9]. This allows the value of each transaction to be known only to the sender and receiver, while also allowing the node and other users to validate that the transaction does not create new coins. Consequently, each addresses balance is also private to only the owner.

We first describe the changes made to the IOTA platform to support usage of Bulletproofs[2].

Finally, we suggest some future research and improvements that can be made to the modified platform to reduce space and improve performance.

Related Work. The work in this paper relies heavily on the work in "Bulletproofs: Efficient Range Proofs for Confidential Transactions" [9] to add private transactions to the IOTA platform.

---

[1] It is yet to be seen whether this claim is true in the long run, but there is evidence that it is not true is all cases, which will be covered in the background section.

[2] As we were working in Go, we have modified a Go implementation of the Bulletproofs paper - there are a few slight differences to the generator than in the reference implementation- https://github.com/wrv/bp-go.

In "Improving the Anonymity of the IOTA Cryptocurrency" [24] and a related blog post [25], Tennant described their research on adding private transactions to IOTA - focusing on Coin-mixing as a solution that meets the current requirements of the IOTA network.

In [25], Tennant also outlines the challenges with implementing Zero Knowledge Protocols within IOTA - as they are typically based on Elliptic Curve cryptography; making them incompatible with the Curl-P cryptographic algorithm IOTA uses, and also incompatible with IOTA's goal of quantum resistance.

2   Background

Before going through our contributions, we will give a brief background on IOTA, Bulletproofs and their supporting technology.

2.1   Internet of Things

Internet of Things (IoT) is a term that describes connected everyday devices such as cars, toasters, TV's, as well as RFID chips and various sensors and actuators that give the machine world a way to interact with our world without requiring direct input from us [2].

The earliest reference of the term was as the title of a presentation Kevin Ashton made in 1999 while working for Proctor & Gamble [2], and has continued to grow toward ubiquity.

2.2   Blockchain

Another technology that has seen a relatively recent explosion is blockchain technology. Bitcoin was the first known instance of Blockchain technology and was first described by Satoshi Nakamoto in the paper "Bitcoin - A peer to peer electronic cash system" [15] as a digital peer to peer currency that uses a chain of digital signatures to define a coin. By combining this coin definition with a distributed ledger - a distributed database that exists on all Bitcoin nodes - Satoshi could solve the double spend and verification problems that had previously been associated with digital currencies without requiring a central authority.

Since Satoshi Nakamoto's proposal and development of Bitcoin, we have seen an multitude of new technologies that built on their work.

Blockchains (also sometimes referred to as Distributed Ledgers) can be both public (a public blockchain is referred to as a cryptocurrency, and has a token or coin value attached), or private.

The idea of an immutable currency that is resistant to double spending is something that is becoming more and more important for the IoT as we move into this future of machine-to-machine payments. However, Bitcoin (and other blockchain based distributed ledgers) are unsuitable for this as they have significant space and power requirements for each node connected to the network.

2.3 IOTA

IOTA, one of the largest cryptocurrencies nowadays (with market capitalization more than US$5 billion), was created to solve some of the issues that made Bitcoin (and other blockchains) unsuitable for the IoT and to be used as a global payment method. Specifically, the ability to make micro-payments given the presence of transaction fees. For example; if a payment is in cents, a transaction fee a magnitude higher to guarantee delivery is not tenable [20].

Instead of using a blockchain to verify and secure the information stored in the Tangle, IOTA's distributed ledger, IOTA uses a Directed Acyclic Graph that requires that each node validate two transactions for each transaction that it wants to process. This validation scheme has the added benefit of reducing the typical energy expenditure associated with verifying (or mining) blocks on a blockchain.

As the Tangle grows and the small Proof of Work that is performed to create a transaction increases in difficulty, it is possible that the distributed energy expenditure may come closer to the energy expenditure of a block based network, although at this stage it is difficult to estimate if the network will grow to the size of Bitcoin, or experience the same longevity.

IOTA claim that the system becomes more efficient at processing transactions as the system scales (due to each new transaction processing two existing transactions) [20], not less like blockchain-based distributed ledger technology. However, this scaling requires that people run full nodes and not rely on public nodes, and there was an example in December 2017 of a spam attack using public nodes to disrupt the network [8][3].

IOTA's Tangle distributes the processing of transactions among many smaller nodes, whereas a blockchain (such as Bitcoin) packs all of the transactions into set 'blocks' that are processed at a particular interval, often determined by a Poisson distribution (Fig. 1).

Fig. 1. Visual display of the different between a DAG (the Tangle) and a blockchain - image reprinted from [14]

To ensure that the Tangle remains viable for smaller IoT devices, there is a process of 'snapshotting' (similar to the process of pruning in Bitcoin), which removes older transactions from the Tangle. However, in the future there will be

---

[3] It is worth noting that anything negative about IOTA on the web quickly attacks many critics; so the veracity of the claims in the article are also open to discussion.

Permanodes that store all of this Tangle data, ensuring the entire ledger is still available.

The functions of IOTA extend beyond just value transactions and includes support for zero value transactions that include a message to communicate between addresses.

Trinary/Ternary. One technical decision that the IOTA team have made that I have not seen in another blockchain project is the decision to use a ternary base system instead of a binary base system. David Sønstebø, one of the IOTA founders, has explained their choice in various places on the internet[4]. The IOTA project grew out of a project to create a ternary processor for the IoT, and David believes that Ternary will be used in the processors of the future; as it better represents how the mind works, and is used in other technologies such as spintronics and photonics/optical computing (Tables 1 and 2).

Table 1. Comparison between ternary and binary

Base	States		
Binary	0 1	Bit	Byte
Ternary	–1 0 1	Trit	Tryte

Table 2. The text "hello world" represented in trinary and binary

Base	Representation
Binary	hello world
Ternary	WCTC9D9DCDEAKDCDFD9DSC

Current State of Privacy in IOTA. In IOTA, a similar system of added privacy is used as to Bitcoin [15].

When a transaction is sent, the address the transaction was sent from is not used again and is replaced with a new deterministic address (deterministic indicating that all addresses can be determined from the private key, and are unique to that key).

However, because the address sending the value rarely has only the amount to be sent in it, in the transaction details (referred to as UTXO in Bitcoin and Bundle in IOTA), we can see the new values being sent to their new address, as

---

[4] David Sønstebø explaining the choice to use Ternary - https://www.reddit.com/r/CryptoCurrency/comments/6jgbvb/iota_isnt_it_the_perfect_cryptocurrency/dje8os2/?st=jgkpv09k&sh=05179241.

well as the transaction that is going to the receiver. This allows for analysis of the network to link pools of addresses and transactions together (Fig. 2).

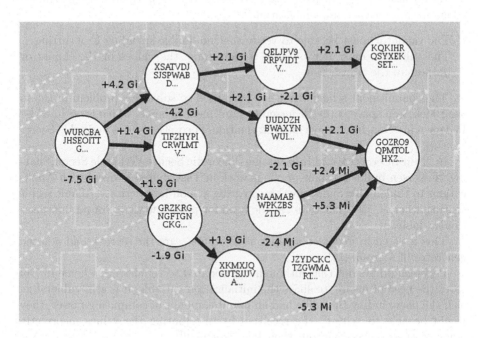

Fig. 2. Visual display of a series of transactions from a single address that show how a transaction is split - image reprinted from [25]

IOTA currently provides an encrypted messaging system, "Masked Authentication Messaging" [5],[6].

"Masked Authentication Messaging" allows a publish/subscribe messaging model that is secured by synchronous encryption. In this Contribution we are only focusing of the value transaction properties of IOTA.

2.4 Zero Knowledge Protocol

Pedersen Commitment Scheme. A commitment scheme in cryptography describes a method of secret sharing where the sender is able to hide (encrypt) the value/secret so that it cannot be read by anyone, and then to show (decrypt) the value/secret at a later point. It is also important that commitment schemes are binding; that the values cannot be changed after being hidden.

The original secret sharing schemes, which have become the basis for many such schemes we use today, were originally proposed independently by Shamir

---

[5] https://github.com/iotaledger/MAM.
[6] https://github.com/iotaledger/mam.client.js.

and Adi in "How to share a secret" [23] and by Blakely in "Safeguarding cryptographic keys" [7].

As we are dealing with privacy in blockchains, we have additional requirements for any privacy implementation;

- The validator must be able to verify that no double spending is occurring
- The validator must not be able to determine the values of the inputs or outputs of the transaction

The commitment scheme that has been used to solve this problem in the in the Blockchain space is the Pedersen Commitment Scheme, which is outlined by Pedersen in "Non-Interactive and Information-Theoretic Secure Verifiable Secret Sharing" [17].

In "Non-Interactive and Information-Theoretic Secure Verifiable Secret Sharing "Pedersen builds on their previous work in "Distributed Provers with Applications to Undeniable Signatures" by creating a "non-interactive verifiable secret sharing scheme" [16] that removes the need for prior knowledge of an initialisation variable.

This is listed in Pedersen's paper as g^s where s are the secrets, and g is the generator of a group [16].

Pedersen points out that although the updated secret sharing scheme in [16] saves the need of having to share the initialisation variable, it is still vulnerable; as if the party hiding the value had an infinite amount of computing power, they would be able to "cheat" the receivers by distributing the values incorrectly amongst the receivers without their knowledge [16][7].

Pedersen solves this in a new commitment scheme by

combining Shamir's scheme (see [23]) with a commitment scheme, which is unconditionally secure for the committer and furthermore allows commitment to many bits simultaneously.

The commitment scheme proposed in "Non-Interactive and Information-Theoretic Secure Verifiable Secret Sharing" is known as a "Pedersen Commitment Scheme", and allows the sender to hide the value of the transactions while still allowing the validator to confirm that no double spending in occurring, thus meeting the additional requirements for a commitment scheme in Blockchains we stated earlier in Sect. 2.4 on the facing page.

2.5   zero-knowledge Succinct Non-interactive ARguments of Knowledge (zk-SNARKs)

"zero-knowledge Succinct Non-interactive ARguments of Knowledge" were first introduced in Ben-Sasson et al.'s paper "SNARKs for C: Verifying program executions succinctly and in zero knowledge" [4].

There are several components that go into "zk-SNARKS" [4];

---

[7] In the cryptocurrency space that we are examining, this would allow the party hiding the value to double-spend their coins, thus creating new coins that should not exist.

- "preprocessing Succinct non-interactive arguments" [6] (SNARGs).
- "a SNARG of knowledge" [6] (SNARK).
- a "zero knowledge property" [4] - this adds the zk.

SNARGs. A SNARG is made up of a series of three algorithms that have characteristics that satisfy three conditions[8]

1. Completeness.
2. Soundness.
3. Efficiency.

There are two phases within the boolean circuit of a SNARG

- **The offline phase** - this is the key generator and is only executed once. The outputs are a proving key and a verification key [4]
- **The online phase** - this can be executed as many times as required. It uses the proving key to hide the input value into the proof, and then the proof can be verified using the verification key with the input [4].

SNARK. A SNARK is a SNARG that has a stronger requirement for Proof of knowledge [4][9].

zero knowledge. For a SNARK to become a zk-SNARK, the validator must be able to prove that the proof is true without being able to determine any information about the input that was put into the online portion of the boolean circuit listed in Sect. 2.5[10].

2.6 Bulletproofs

One of the challenges with zk-SNARKs is that they require a trusted setup that everyone can agree is setup correctly; and that if the parties involved in the trusted setup (or a portion of the parties) colluded to share the information generated instead of destroy it, could potentially create new coins within the network without anyones knowledge.

In the paper "Bulletproofs: Efficient Range Proofs for Confidential Transactions" [9], Bunz, Bootle et al. propose a new zero knowledge proof system that requires shorter proofs than prior work [12,19]; the shorter proof length making it more viable for use within a cryptocurrency (see Table 3).

---

[8] For a complete breakdown of the algorithms used to determine these criteria, see Sect. A.1 in [4].
[9] To see a detailed example of the formula for the Proof of knowledge, see Sect. A.2 in [4].
[10] For the zero knowledge formula, see Sect. A.3 in [4].

3   Implementation

3.1   Addressing and Transactions in IOTA

Addresses in IOTA function differently to cryptocurrencies such as Ethereum
[10] and Bitcoin [15] that each rely heavily on Elliptic Curve cryptography.
Instead their addresses are around Winternitz One Time Signatures (a variant of
Lamport One-Time signatures), and are created using their hashing algorithm
Curl-P.

Each user starts with a seed; a random string of 81 Trytes. This becomes the
user private key.

IOTA Wallets have no file that stores addresses or transactions, this seed is
all you need to access, spend and receive IOTA.

As reusing a One Time Signature can lead to the private key being revealed,
a new private key and public key is generated for each transaction.

Table 3. Comparison of proof sizes in bytes proving that m commit values are in
$[0, 2^{64} - 1]$ [9]

	$m = 1$	$m = 2$	$m = 16$
Confidential assets [18]	4 KB	8 KB	61 KB
Bulletproofs	672 Bytes	736 Bytes	928 Bytes

An example flow for a transaction is as follows;

1. Pre-generated seed is input (either by the user or the wallet)
2. The receiver address and the amount are entered by the user and the transaction is initiated
3. The wallet generates a set number of addresses (the default in the implementation we used started at index 0 and went to 100)
4. These addresses are sent to the API and transaction balances associated
   with that address are returned
5. The wallet checks that there is enough balance, and if so moves to create
   the outputs
6. The transaction output to the receiver is created
7. The spent outputs are created, if there is a remainder from the inputs used,
   a new transaction is generated with a new address belonging to the sender
8. The balance of all inputs and outputs is calculated, and if it doesn't equal
   to zero the transaction fails
9. A hash is generated of the collection of transactions (referred to as a Bundle in IOTA) and that hash is signed and the signature added to outgoing
   transactions (transactions with a positive value)
10. The wallet then continues the process of adding the transactions to the
    Tangle.

In order to use Bulletproofs, we need to use Elliptic Curves (specifically on the secp256k1 curve) with the addressing system - which typically has a different process[11]. However, we wanted to keep the flow for a transaction the same (or as similar as we could), so our address creation works as follows;

1. Pre-generated seed is input
2. Seed is converted to Trits and then to Bytes
3. The seed bytes are then used to create a Master Key (a Hierarchical Deterministic Key)
4. A new child key is created based on the address index provided (the key index starts from one, so one is added to the entered index)
5. This generates a new Keypair
6. To create an Address, we take the Public Key from the Keypair and compress it (compression takes the X value from the Elliptic Curve point and an indicator of whether the Y value is positive or negative, as the Y axis on the Elliptic Curve only has two values for each X value that mirror each other - one positive and one negative)
7. This gives us 33 bytes of data, which we pad into a byte array with a length corresponding to an IOTA address (48 bytes) which is then converted from Bytes→ Trits→Trytes.

This process gives us the address that can then be used for transactions.

So that we can incorporate Bulletproofs and hide values, we need to make a few changes to mechanism of building a transaction.

Receiving Values. Balances are still received in the same method as the original flow; but they are now encrypted with the public key of the address they belong to using AES. Unfortunately, we could not use the shared secret we generate with the Diffie-Hellman Key exchange in later steps, as transaction balances begin in the Snapshot (where the original balances are stored) and do not have a sender, so a public key is not always available.

Once the value of a transaction is decrypted, the total value of the inputs is calculated as normal and we move to creating the transaction outputs.

Outputs. To generate the outputs, the private key is derived for the first input address and generates a shared secret using a Diffie Hellman key exchange with the public key derived from the receivers address. This shared secret is used as a blinding factor in all of the Pedersen Commitments that represent the input and output values. This allows for the receiver to create the transaction for validation. The Pedersen Commitment for the values is then converted to a public key, compressed, converted to base58 and then Trytes to be added to the transaction.

---

[11] The different ways to create a Bitcoin wallet can be found on their official documentation - https://bitcoin.org/en/developer-guide#wallets.

The value is encrypted using the public key derived from the receiving address (which is either the receiver address for the main output transaction, or the newly generated address used to return the remaining value to the sender), and the resulting cipher text is converted to base58, then to Trytes to attach to the transaction.

Bulletproofs. For output values that are positive, we use the bulletproofs implementation to generate a proof to validate that the value is in the range of $[0, 2^{64} - 1]$. This proof is then serialized to bytes, encoded as Base58 and the resulting string is then converted to Trytes and attached to the Transaction. In this step we encode to Base58 instead of to Trits then Trytes (as we did with the addresses) as the Bytes→Trytes converter is only designed for Byte Arrays with a length of 48.

Finalizing the Bundle. Before signing the Bundle, we add up all of the Commitment Elliptic Curve points to ensure they equal the Zero point on the Curve.

The Bundle is then Hashed using Curl, and that hash is hashed using SHA256 and signed using the private key of the first input address.

Validation. As transaction values are hidden, the process of a third party (whether the IOTA Node or an individual user) being able to verify the transaction, and ensure that the total value of the Bundle is zero is extremely important.

Validation of a bundle has several steps;

1. Convert all of the Commitment values from Trytes back to Elliptic Curve points and add them together - ensuring that the final product equals the zero point on the Secp256k1 Curve.
2. For any transactions that don't have a blank range proof (in IOTA transactions this is represented by a long string of 9's), convert the Trytes back to bytes and rebuild the proof.
3. Send the rebuilt proof and the Commitment value for that transaction to the verifier and ensure it returns true.
4. Get the Hash of the Bundle, and Hash it with SHA256.
5. Convert the first input address back to a public key and use that and the hash of the bundle hash to verify the signature.

3.2   Other Changes to IOTA

Beyond changes made to enable the hiding and validating of values in Bundles themselves, we also had to make changes to the Milestone and Snapshotting process (these process essentially track and store changes to the balances stored in the ledger) to support the usage of a text value instead of a numeric value for the addresses. These changes do not cover all edge cases and were intended to support the examples and testing.

4 Future Work and Improvements

4.1 Multi-range Proofs

In this paper, we have only used the single range proof version of Bulletproofs [9]. However, Bunz, Bootle et al. also proposed a multi-range proof that would allow us to validate all of the positive output values in a single proof without too much additional overhead.

In order to implement this in IOTA, we would remove the range proof from the transaction itself and add it to the overall bundle. This would require changes to the way IOTA Libraries currently work, as they assemble the bundle in the API calls and not at the time of building the transaction when the private keys/seeds are available.

4.2 Adding Sender Addresses to Snapshots

As mentioned in Sect. 3.1, we must encrypt all values to the public key as a sender address is not always available. By adding a sender address to all balance storage, would could use the shared secret generated in the Diffie-Hellman Key Exchange, which produces a much smaller cipher text than the current method.

5 Conclusion

In this paper, we provide an implementation for IOTA that integrates Bulletproofs into the system. With this integration, transaction amount can be hidden from the public and thus privacy can be enhanced. Our implementation is compatible to the existing IOTA platform and can be regarded as a further enhancement for the next update.

Acknowledgment. This work was supported by the National Natural Science Foundation of China (61702342), the Science and Technology Innovation Projects of Shenzhen (GJHZ 20160226202520268, JCYJ 20170302151321095, JCYJ 20170302145623566) and Tencent "Rhinoceros Birds" - Scientific Research Foundation for Young Teachers of Shenzhen University.

References

1. Androulaki, E., Karame, G.O., Roeschlin, M., Scherer, T., Capkun, S.: Evaluating user privacy in bitcoin. In: Sadeghi, A.-R. (ed.) FC 2013. LNCS, vol. 7859, pp. 34–51. Springer, Heidelberg (2013). https://doi.org/10.1007/978-3-642-39884-1_4
2. Ashton, K.: That 'Internet of Things' Thing - 2009-06-22 - Page 1 - RFID Journal (2009). http://www.rfidjournal.com/articles/view?4986
3. Back, A.: Hashcash - a denial of service counter-measure, pp. 1–10, August 2002. http://www.Hashcash.Org/Papers/Hashcash.Pdf

4. Ben-Sasson, E., Chiesa, A., Genkin, D., Tromer, E., Virza, M.: SNARKs for C: verifying program executions succinctly and in zero knowledge. In: Canetti, R., Garay, J.A. (eds.) CRYPTO 2013. LNCS, vol. 8043, pp. 90–108. Springer, Heidelberg (2013). https://doi.org/10.1007/978-3-642-40084-1_6

5. Biryukov, A., Khovratovich, D., Pustogarov, I.: Deanonymisation of clients in Bitcoin P2P network (2014). http://arxiv.org/abs/1405.7418

6. Bitansky, N., Chiesa, A., Ishai, Y., Paneth, O., Ostrovsky, R.: Succinct non-interactive arguments via linear interactive proofs. In: Sahai, A. (ed.) TCC 2013. LNCS, vol. 7785, pp. 315–333. Springer, Heidelberg (2013). https://doi.org/10.1007/978-3-642-36594-2_18

7. Blakley, G.: Safeguarding cryptographic keys. In: AFIPS, p. 313 (1979)

8. Buntix, J.: IOTA Network Struggles Due to Lack of Full Nodes - The Merkle (2017). https://themerkle.com/iota-network-struggles-due-to-lack-of-full-nodes/

9. Bünz, B., Bootle, J., Boneh, D., Poelstra, A., Wuille, P., Maxwell, G.:Bulletproofs: Efficient Range Proofs for Confidential Transactions. Cryptology ePrint Archive (2017). http://web.stanford.edu/~buenz/pubs/bulletproofs.pdf, https://eprint.iacr.org/2017/1066.pdf

10. Buterin, V.: Ethereum Whitepaper (2015). https://github.com/ethereum/wiki/wiki/White-Paper

11. Koshy, P., Koshy, D., McDaniel, P.: An analysis of anonymity in bitcoin using P2P network traffic. In: Christin, N., Safavi-Naini, R. (eds.) FC 2014. LNCS, vol. 8437, pp. 469–485. Springer, Heidelberg (2014). https://doi.org/10.1007/978-3-662-45472-5_30

12. Maxwell, G.: Confidential Transactions, Content Privacy for Bitcoin Transactions (2015). https://bitcointalk.org/index.php?topic=1085273.0

13. Molina-Markham, A., Shenoy, P., Fu, K., Cecchet, E., Irwin, D.: Private memoirs of a smart meter. In: Proceedings of the 2nd ACM Workshop on Embedded Sensing Systems for Energy-Efficiency in Building, pp. 61–66. ACM (2010)

14. Najera, J.: Cryptos In 3 Mins – IOTA – SetOcean – Medium (2017). https://medium.com/setocean/cryptos-in-3-mins-iota-6dc02f4b8e27

15. Nakamoto, S.: Bitcoin: A Peer-to-Peer Electronic Cash System (2008). https://bitcoin.org/bitcoin.pdf

16. Pedersen, T.P.: Distributed provers with applications to undeniable signatures. In: Davies, D.W. (ed.) EUROCRYPT 1991. LNCS, vol. 547, pp. 221–242. Springer, Heidelberg (1991). https://doi.org/10.1007/3-540-46416-6_20

17. Pedersen, T.P.: Non-interactive and information-theoretic secure verifiable secret sharing. In: Feigenbaum, J. (ed.) CRYPTO 1991. LNCS, vol. 576, pp. 129–140. Springer, Heidelberg (1992). https://doi.org/10.1007/3-540-46766-1_9

18. Poelstra, A.: Mimblewimble, 1–19 June 2016. https://download.wpsoftware.net/bitcoin/wizardry/mimblewimble.pdf

19. Poelstra, A., Back, A., Friedenbach, M., Maxwell, G., Blockstream, P.W.: Confidential Assets. https://pdfs.semanticscholar.org/f498/297792fa142cefbe9afb7e61e11b3364851e.pdf

20. Popov, S.: The Tangle (2016). http://iota.org/IOTA_Whitepaper.pdf

21. Reid, F., Harrigan, M.: An analysis of anonymity in the bitcoin system BT - security and privacy in social networks. In: Altshuler, Y., Elovici, Y., Cremers, A., Aharony, N., Pentland, A. (eds.) Security and Privacy in Social Networks, pp. 197–223. Springer, New York (2013). https://doi.org/10.1007/978-1-4614-4139-7_10. http://www.google.com/search?client=safari&rls=10_7_4&q=An+analysis+of+anonymity+in+the+bitcoin+system&ie=UTF-8&oe=UTF-8%5Cnpapers2://publication/uuid/F5976E14-72A2-47A6-BB9F-4B3662F7E7BD

22. Ron, D., Shamir, A.: Quantitative analysis of the full bitcoin transaction graph. In: Sadeghi, A.-R. (ed.) FC 2013. LNCS, vol. 7859, pp. 6–24. Springer, Heidelberg (2013). https://doi.org/10.1007/978-3-642-39884-1_2
23. Shamir, A., Shamir, A.: How to share a secret. Commun. ACM (CACM) **22**(1), 612–613 (1979)
24. Tennant, L.: Improving the Anonymity of the IOTA Cryptocurrency (2017). https://laurencetennant.com/papers/anonymity-iota.pdf
25. Tennant, L.: Privacy in IOTA – IOTA @ UCL– Medium - 05/08/2017 (2017). https://medium.com/iota-ucl/privacy-in-iota-17112ac17a06

Burn After Reading: Expunging Execution Footprints of Android Apps

Junliang Shu[✉], Juanru Li, Yuanyuan Zhang, and Dawu Gu

Lab of Cryptology and Computer Security, Shanghai Jiao Tong University,
Shanghai, China
s.junliang@gmail.com

Abstract. Mobile apps nowadays are consuming and producing a mass of sensitive data. In response, a wide variety of privacy protection techniques and tools have been proposed since mobile users have the escalating privacy concerns. However, only a few privacy protection schemes consider how to thoroughly erase the runtime information of an app after its execution. Various traceable vestiges, called execution footprints, are kept by the device which could be used to steal and speculate user's privacy. We argue that a mobile operating system should not only establish sound isolation between different apps but also need to provide a fine-grained execution footprint expunging mechanism to ensure using an app confidentially. To achieve this target, MIST, a modified Android OS, to generate fine-grained data expunging policies, is designed and implemented. MIST is a lightweight ephemeral container, which does not require the support of specialized hardware or operation mode and it will be disposed of securely when in use apps. In this container, MIST persistently tracks every message generated by the app and then it deletes them during and after the execution. Experiments based on 200 apps show that execution footprints still have been neglected by the Android OS even after the app removal. By utilizing the expunging mechanism MIST provided, those footprints are erased to guarantee a private and confidential execution.

1 Introduction

The contradiction between forensics requirements and privacy protection has brought to the public since the FBI-Apple encryption dispute has burst out. Although robust cryptography schemes have been deployed to the mainstream mobile operating systems (Android and iOS), the unceasing attempts keep being made by investigators or attackers who try to break the protection. In particular situation, merely exposing the truth that some specific apps (such as healthcare

We would like to thank the anonymous reviewers for their valuable comments and helpful suggestions. This paper is partially supported by the Key Program of National Natural Science Foundation of China (Grant No. U1636217), the National Key Research and Development Program of China (Grant No. 2016YFB0801200), and a research grant from the Ant Financial Services Group.

M. H. Au et al. (Eds.): NSS 2018, LNCS 11058, pp. 46–63, 2018.
https://doi.org/10.1007/978-3-030-02744-5_4

app, life-style apps, and apps strongly relevant to user's privacy) have been execution can lead to a grave infringement on the privacy of the device owner. To refer individual behavior of the user, the primary sources of information exposure are **execution footprints**, which are modifications of system status due to an app's execution. The execution of an app always changes the system status and leaves an abundance of information on the device temporarily or permanently. These modifications may reveal various kinds of information (e.g., the name of the app) and can be used as digital evidence (e.g., whether a particular app has executed on the device).

Unfortunately, mobile operating systems often fail to erase such footprints to hide execution traces and protect user privacy. As a result, an experienced analyst can indicate not only the identity of the app but also the related operations. Take Android, the most widely used mobile OS, as an example. We reveal that except regular footprints such as files, many kinds of information, although unobtrusive, still indicate the execution of real app. With a study of 100 favorite Android apps mainly focusing on those related to Inter-Process Communication (IPC) or interactions with the OS, we investigated how apps generate footprints, and found When an app relies on intensive system services, some information will unintentionally leak to the system without being noticed. Even if under specific privacy protection enhancements, the surveillance state could still obtain data through conducting brute-force decryption, and also deduce relevant information from some encrypted but featured data. Also, we observe that Android does not provide a cautious data expunging policy and execution footprints remain for most apps even after the uninstallation.

To address this issue of data footprints, the critical steps include determining the sources where the execution footprints generate, and expunging remained footprints thoroughly after the execution/uninstallation. In particular, to execute an app on Android without being perceived by malicious observations as offline forensic analysis or online side-channel eavesdropping, a *private mode*, or say a private execution of the apps, is demanded to conceal the performance of the app and eliminate all those *footprints* left in the system. Private mode is firstly implemented as a *private browsing mode*, a standard security feature provided to prevent information leakage on modern web browsers such as Firefox and Chrome. It ensures that personal information (e.g., browsing histories, cookies, and cache information) are cleared once by the browsing session ends. However, to anonymize the execution of an app on mobile device is much more sophisticated. It involves a myriad of interactions with the OS such as file I/O operation and API invoking with sensitive permission requirements. A systematical solution for this problem is expected to conceal the execution information of specific apps.

To port such private execution function to Android, we design and implement MIST, a modified Android OS that enables an ephemeral execution for universal apps. With MIST, users can launch an app and execute it without being perceived by a later forensic analysis, despite the skillful analyst that could fully control the system and gain every aspect of the system information. During the ephemeral execution, the input and output of the app execution are managed delicately by fine-grained monitoring policies of MIST. For instance, MIST adopts a temporal partition encryption scheme to re-direct every file operation to a secure and ephemeral container. MIST also determines how to control the inter-process communication (IPC) during the app's execution: when the app generated data flow to the external environment, it either blocks the data flow or labels the system service as a tainted process. After the execution, MIST immediately sanitizes any possible leaked information. In this way, MIST proves that no footprints remain after the execution and thus protects the privacy of the user.

Compared with current privacy schemes on Android, MIST has the following advantages: (1) MIST conducts a fine-grained footprint monitoring based on an investigation of real-world Android devices and apps; (2) MIST implements a lightweight ephemeral execution to expunge footprint comprehensively, and it does not require the support of specialized hardware or operation mode (e.g., Trusted Execution Environment). To validate the reliability and usability of MIST, we conduct experimental evaluation with 200 popular Android apps. The evaluation first reveals many remaining data (according to the monitoring) as footprints and then it utilizes a set of forensic analysis tools to check whether typical footprints can be detected if the app executes in MIST. The results demonstrate that MIST expunges those footprints thoroughly against existing forensic analyses. The evaluation also shows that the performance overhead of MIST is acceptable for most application scenarios.

2   Footprint Expunging

The installation, execution, and uninstallation of an app modify the status of the device temporarily or permanently. Such modifications are defined as execution footprints if they can be used as digital evidences to refer specific behavior of the user (e.g., whether a particular app has been executed on the device). Mobile operating systems are expected to erase such footprints to hide execution traces and protect user privacy. However, modern mobile OS such as Android fail to achieve this target. In this section we first discuss the deficiency of Android system on expunging execution footprint and then present our enhanced strategy of practical footprint expunging.

2.1   Footprints of Android Apps

The Android OS provides a series of access control strategies to prove that each app only executes in an isolated environment. Ideally, the OS should guarantee that the status of the system keeps consistent whether an app has been installed or not. Apparently, this is infeasible since many apps must register themselves to the system to handle specific requests (e.g., write files to the disk and register themselves to some system services). Thus, a practical solution is to execute an uninstallation process and erase every vestige of the app. Nevertheless, current app uninstallation mechanism of Android does not guarantee such requirement. As shown in Table 1, recent studies related to execution footprints indicated that at least 11 items must be sanitized. Otherwise, each of them represents a class of footprint that may help track specific user behavior.

Table 1. Representative footprints of Android

Item	Footprint pattern
Memory [15, 18, 21–24, 28]	Kept in memory after the execution
Files [18–20, 27, 28]	Written to flash memory in plaintext
IPC [8, 32]	Transferred through IPC
Process status [31, 33]	Identified by other processes
Battery usage	App name kept after the execution
Network usage	App name kept after the execution
Screen [14]	Screenshot buffer captured by other apps or the system
Microphone [11]	Sound captured by other apps or the system
Sensor [13, 16]	Sensor data captured by other apps or the system
Keyboard input [6]	App identity referred by a third-party input method
System log	App identity recorded in system log files

However, only by enumerating such items we cannot understand the footprint issue comprehensively. From the viewpoint of footprint origins, we classify all execution fingerprints into four types and study them in a systematic way:

Footprint in Memory: Memory pages of an app process contain plenty of sensitive information that may reveal the identity of their creator or even the exact behavior of it [15, 21, 22, 24]. For instance, distinguishable strings, code segments, images, GUI layouts can be used to deduce certain user behavior.

Whereas, few app takes the initiative to actively erase used memory pages, making most sensitive data left in memory even if the running process is terminated. Android system does not consider this as an issue either, leaving a feasible attack window for the advanced cold-boot attack [10].

Footprint on eMMC: Most Android devices store files in the flash memory of embedded MultiMedia Card (eMMC). Files created by apps usually carry a lot of relevant information: both the content and the metadata (e.g., file name, directory structure) can be used as the evidence of app's execution [19, 27]. Once an attacker obtains the device, he can directly visit this information through dumping the partition image with forensic techniques (even if the partition is encrypted, it is possible to recover the image through guessing the password [1]). Unfortunately, Android lacks a secure data wiping mechanism and data written to flash memory is difficult to be wiped securely [4, 26]. Therefore, sensitive files often remain on the eMMC for a long time (even after a factory reset [25]).

Footprint in IPC: An Android app interacts with other apps or system processes frequently through IPC (mainly through Android's binder). Sensitive information may be leaked to other processes or remains in memory/flash [32] depending on the specific kind of IPC. In either case, footprints left on the device after the execution of their creators.

Side-channel Footprint: Except the memory pages and files directly and actively generated by an app, there are some unobtrusive footprints produced by the Android OS unintentionally. An adversary can also collect these footprints and use them to infer the behaviors of individual apps. In general, these footprints are divided into two major types: **runtime side-channel footprints** that can only be obtained while an app is running, and **legacy side-channel footprints** kept in memory or flash storage after the execution.

- *Runtime side-channel footprints.* A runtime side-channel footprint is a kind of information that can be gather by a (malicious) app with normal privileges [11,31]. Under the protection of Android's sandbox, typical runtime side-channel footprints include process name and UID of running apps. In Android, the system uses the package name as the process name of the app. By gathering process name through shell command **ps**, a malicious app easily obtains footprint of all the running apps. The sensors and microphone are also sources of data leakage. Previous researches have demonstrated the feasibility of inferring identity from such side-channel footprint [5,9,16,17,31].
- *Legacy side-channel footprints.* A legacy side-channel footprint is a kind of information related to the identity of the host app and is often kept by the Android system. Most kinds of these footprints are package names and UIDs logged by specific system monitors, which record system events such as the usage of system resources. some Android system components keep the sensitive runtime footprint of apps unintentionally. Although the threat model in this paper assumes that the OS and the device are both trustful, these footprints are somehow accessible without permission requests, leading an attacker to infer the behaviors of the device owner.

2.2 Footprint Expunging Strategy

The essential requirement for a robust footprint expunging strategy is that after the execution (i.e., the app process is terminated), even the user herself, knowing the execution details, could not able to recover any usable evidence of activities conducted on the device. Hence, the expunging strategy requires that any secret would not persist explicitly.

To achieve such goal, we consider four design principles summarized from real-world threats when sanitizing different footprints. These principles are based on either previous best practices or our observations. If a footprint sanitization scheme violates any of these principles, information may not be cleaned and thus can be identified as a footprint.

1. *Sensitive data in non-persistent memory should have a lifetime as short as possible.* Consider that an attacker could later acquire administration privilege to spy upon the entire memory space, the runtime execution data in memory must be wiped out to counter such attack. Hence, at the end of its lifetime, the data should be appropriately erased.
2. *Sensitive data should be encrypted before being stored in the persistent storage medium.* It believed that the secure deletion of disk data is not able to be fulfilled on the state-of-the-art storage medium of mobile devices. Therefore, any data written to the flash memory must be encrypted beforehand. The encryption key should be ephemeral and must only be kept in non-persistent memory. Thus this kind of data can be cryptographically erased when the execution is over by wiping the temporary key.
3. *The interaction of app and the OS should be censored so that sensitive data leakage can be filtered.* Confidential information sent from the app to the system processes is hard to clean thoroughly (the cleaning may crash the system). Therefore, a filter applied on IPC can block the leakage beforehand.
4. *The execution itself should be side-channel resistant.* In other words, its runtime information should not be gathered by a concurrently executed malicious program.

3   MIST

In this section, we present our solution to erase the app footprint on Android. We design and implement MIST, a system based on Android OS to offer a robust and comprehensive footprint expunging. MIST provides Android user the ability to run apps within an ephemeral container, leaving no recognizable footprint after being executed.

The design of MIST follows the four principles mentioned in Sect. 2.2. MIST achieves footprint expunging through providing the following features: (1) MIST offers in-time memory elimination right after the termination of the protected app to wipe the footprints left in memory. (2) MIST encrypts files to secure the footprints left in the persistent storage medium. (3) MIST monitors the interaction between the protected app and system services with fine-grained access control policy to restrict sensitive information leakage. (4) MIST obfuscates the identity of the protected app and control the access to specific system resources to avoid side-channel information eavesdropping and gathering.

3.1   Footprint Discovering

MIST conducts a comprehensive system monitoring strategy to record every possible behaviors related to footprint generating. As marked in Fig. 1, MIST implements an ephemeral container to keep monitoring sensitive information within this restricted environment. Several system components of Android are modified to achieve the design goals of footprint discovering and expunging, and the original app execution model has been re-implemented with additional or alternative steps.

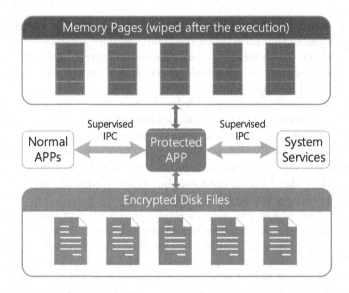

Fig. 1. The ephemeral container of MIST

Memory Monitoring. MIST records all used memory pages as footprints. Since MIST modifies the original Android OS and has the full control of the device, and thus it has the privilege to monitor every memory page used by the protected app directly.

File System Monitoring. MIST monitors an app's file I/O operations through checking all possible directories the app could write. Due to the restriction of Android sandbox, an app can only write files to several directories including its own private directory in the *userdata* partition, the SDcard, and a few temporary directories (e.g., `/data/local/tmp`). Hence the monitoring of an app's file I/O operations is implemented through checking these directories, and all data files modified by the monitored app are considered directly as footprints.

IPC Monitoring. In Android, there are many different ways to achieve data exchange between processes such as using `Intent` and `AIDL`, which based on Android's *Binder*. We monitor all IPC communication channels to investigate which system services a common Android app may use and what data these IPCs may transfer. We first modified the userspace library *libbinder.so*, which is loaded by most apps to implement IPC supervision. We also add monitoring code to the `IPCThreadState::talkWithDriver` function in `IPCThreadState.cpp` so that IPCs through a kernel driver can be supervised.

Side-Channel Footprint Monitoring. As discussed above, the side-channel footprints produced by the Android system may be stored in different system files. To discover such side-channel footprints, we use *Inotify* to monitor the entire file system during the execution of an app. All files that have been modified during the execution will be analyzed manually, and those contain recognizable data such as packages names and UIDs are considered as footprints.

3.2   Footprint Expunging

MIST executes an app in an ephemeral container and footprints are monitored and cleaned during the entire lifetime of the app. As shown in Fig. 2, to run an app, MIST first assigns to it an encrypted partition and installs the app with obfuscated identities (package name and UID). Then the execution is monitored to block sensitive information leakage through IPC or system logging. Finally, MIST eliminates memory pages of processes of both the executed app and some tainted services at the end of the execution, and removes the app through disposing runtime residue in system logs and erasing encrypted key. In this way, MIST sanitizes the execution footprints of the app thoroughly.

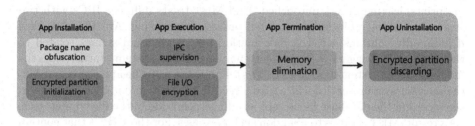

Fig. 2. App execution within the ephemeral container of MIST

Memory Page Elimination. Smart devices use volatile RAM to store in-memory data, hence by rebooting the device could the OS erase the remained data in memory thoroughly. Modern smartphones, however, are usually designed to work without a reboot for a long period. Once the attacker obtains the device, he can use memory dump tools such as *fmem* [12] and *crash* [2] to extract all physical memory pages (with root privilege), or physically access the memory (without root privilege). Most users would not reboot their devices for days, which makes the memory footprint issue even more severe.

MIST rewrites the corresponding memory space with null byte when a process terminates to deallocate the in-memory data generated securely. A kernel module is implemented to fulfill this task: it monitors the memory deallocation function in Android kernel, and whenever a monitored app exits or is killed, the kernel module reads the layout of virtual memory from /proc/<pid>/maps and calculates the address range to be eliminated. Then it passes the address of virtual memory should be eliminated and the PID of target process to a memory sanitization stub to erase all contents on those addresses.

File-System Encryption. MIST sets up an exclusive encrypted partition with an ephemeral key for each protected app. After that, all file operations of the protected app are redirected to this partition. MIST modified the `PackageInstaller` to change the default private directory to an exclusive encrypted partition which is set up before the installation. Then it uses `dm-crypt` to create this partition with AES-256-CBC and initialize an ephemeral key, which is then kept only in memory and will be wiped immediately after the uninstallation. During the execution, MIST hooks all file related operations in `libc` to redirect them to the encrypted partition, making sure that every recognizable footprints are only stored in this secure zone. When the app is uninstalled, or the system reboots, the ephemeral key for this encrypted partition is discarded and thus the sensitive data is cryptographically erased, leaving no recognizable footprints in flash memory.

IPC Supervision. MIST uses a configurable access control policy to supervise the IPC between the protected app and system services. The control policy only focuses on those IPCs initiated by the protected app and contain recognizable footprints, leaving others untouched. And MIST treats different IPCs with two strategies: message blocking or tainted process terminating. An IPC is blocked if it broadly contains sensitive information (e.g., individual strings related to the app), or it triggers a permanent changing of the system status (e.g., the modification of system databases or logs). For instance, if the app sends an SMS, the relevant system service will writes a record into system databases. However, the record in the database file is kept as a fingerprint due to the file wiping issue. As a result, MIST chooses to abandon such messages. For those IPCs that contain no sensitive information and only affect the status of the system temporarily (e.g., messages only kept in system memory), MIST monitors and restarts those tainted processes after the execution of the protected app, triggering the memory elimination of those processes accordingly.

Side-Channel Footprint Sanitization. Generally, MIST adopts an identity obfuscation strategy to protect sensitive information leakage against side-channel analysis. In detail, a protected app installed in MIST is assigned an obfuscated package name and a corresponding UID. We modified the `PackageInstaller` system service to assign a randomly generated package name during the installation. By doing so, the installed app runs like a new identity so that the information gathered by both malicious apps and system services would not leak the original identity. In addition, MIST utilizes relevant system functionalities to clean those side-channel footprints left in the memory of system services. For instance, the outputs of both `logcat` and `dmesg` produce sensitive information, and we can use shell commands provided by the system to clean them (`logcat -c` and `dmesg -c`).

For those side-channel footprints based on specific system resources such as sensor, microphone and input method, we disable these interfaces for other processes when an protected app is running. Besides, memory pages in the cache containing verifiable information will be removed if they are no longer needed. We can manually clean them through using a shell command `echo 3 >/proc/sys/vm/drop_caches`.

4 Evaluation

This section presents the evaluation results of MIST to show that it provides a comprehensive, usable, and efficient execution mode to expunge footprints of apps. In particular, we measure MIST from three aspects: (**1**) how comprehensively can MIST discover execution footprints of popular apps; (**2**) whether the footprint expunging policy works effectively, and would it affect the normal execution of both the app and the system; (**3**) what is the performance overhead of MIST.

4.1 Discovered Footprints of Popular Apps

Traces of executions are various and some of them are very stealthy on Android device, some execution footprints are often out of regular execution scope of an app. To discovering as many as footprints (especially those recorded unintentionally by the system or reside in system buffers) we conduct comprehensive experiments to help study how common app behaviors generate footprints. We collect the top 100 apps (covering 27 different types and each of them has been downloaded for at least one million times) from Google Play market for our experiments and execute them automatically with the `monkey tool` on two commodity Android devices (Nexus 5X and Nexus 6P) with MIST. Apparently, we found memory pages and files in app's sandbox and on the SDcard as footprints. Interestingly, we also have observed many stealthy footprints in IPC and system files.

Footprints in IPC: After tracing all the IPC interfaces during the execution of these apps, we pick up representative IPC interfaces and analyze them manually to find whether these IPCs leak recognizable runtime data of a individual app or not. Table 2 shows part of the analysis of those most frequently invoked IPC interfaces due to the limitation of this paper. Among these IPC interfaces, we found only a part of them leak sensitive information to the system databases. In response, we can define corresponding access control policy for those interfaces (as the **Policy** column in Table 2 illustrated). According to the analysis, not all IPC interfaces are forbidden for a protected app. Only those IPC interfaces that leak information to flash storage should be blocked (otherwise the corresponding system services for flash I/O should be modified).

Side-channel Footprints: Previous experiments [5,9,14,16,17,31] have shown that the screenshot, keyboard input, sensor data and microphone data can all make running apps distinguishable from other apps. Our experimental results demonstrate that many system logging services also leave legacy information on the device. After analyzing the result of whole file system monitoring, we then

Table 2. The (partial) analysis of most frequently invoked IPC interfaces

IPC interface	Leaked footprint	Access control policy
IContentProvider.insert	in flash storage	Forbidden
IActivityManager.startActivityAsCaller	in memory	Restart[a]
IPackageManager.getPackageInfo	in memory	Restart[a]
IActivityManager.broadcastIntent	in memory	Restart[a]
IGraphicBufferProducer.DEQUEUE_BUFFER	-	Allowed
DisplayEventConnection.REQUEST_NEXT_VSYNC	-	Allowed
IGraphicBufferProducer.DETACH_BUFFER	-	Allowed
IActivityManager.activityResumed	-	Allowed
IContentProvider.query	-	Allowed

[a]Restart the corresponding system service of IPCs.

manually analyse the modified files and find there are three kinds of data related to the identity of apps which have been executed:

- The *Batterystatus* file /data/system/batterystatus.bin is used to record the battery usage of each app since last full charge. Device owner can check it through *Setting menu* or shell command dumpsys batterystats for more detailed information. All these information discloses the behaviors of specific apps.
- The *netstats* file (/data/system/netstats/) is used to record the network-data usage of each app. We can also infer which apps have been executed through these files.
- The *task* file (/acct/uid/<uid>/tasks) contains the ever used PID of a specific UID (an individual app), and the change of this file can be used to confirm the execution of apps.

Besides the footprints left on the disk, there are also some system services keep recognizable footprints in their log outputs. For instance, Android inherits the logging system from Linux, providing a various way for viewing system log. We can use shell command dmesg to read kernel logs messages. Another logging system is the logcat system of Android system debug output, which gives an abundance of information about happened activities on the device Such kind of log messages are generated by the system services and cannot be cleaned by the user. A less noticed place is the Linux page cache, which also holds the data that may expose the execution of apps. The role of the Linux page cache is to speed up access to files on the drive. In other words, the Linux page cache always keeps the data related to files opened by running app.

4.2   Usability Evaluation

Expunging. After we proved that many footprints exist in current Android app execution model, we evaluate the usability of MIST (i.e., whether MIST expunges typical footprints) with real-world apps collected from Google Play. We utilizes five forensic analysis tools to detect footprint: Oxygen mobile forensic Suite is a mobile forensic software for logical analysis of smartphones and PDAs developed by Oxygen Software. Andriller is software utility with a collection of forensic tools for smartphones. Andriller can extract and analyse data stored in the userdata partition if the device is rooted. UFS Explorer is a data recovery software for data loss cases of different complexity. Here we use it to analysis the disk dump to recover deleted data related to executed apps. LiME is a widely used Linux kernel module to dump RAM contents of the device. In most cases, LiME is used to perform live memory analysis. In addition, we developed Side-channel FP Collector, an Android forensics tool based on our study of side-channel footprints of Android. It extracts the side-channel data and restores the behaviors of executed apps. We use these tools to analyze the following data as suspicious information leakage sources:

- memory dump of the Android system;
- dump of the *userdata* and the *SDcard* partitions;
- system database files;
- battery usage log;
- network usage log;
- files in /acct/uid;
- output of logcat.

We executed the tested apps in a device with MIST and in a native Android device, respectively. Then we used forensic tools to analyze both devices and compared the analyzing results. The results are shown in Table 3. For the native Android device, forensic tools detected many footprints listed in the Table. On the contrary, MIST expunged those footprints thoroughly and none of the forensics tools could discover useful footprint.

Compatibility. To test the compatibility of MIST, we expand our samples mentioned in Sect. 4.1 to the top 200 apps from Google Play. Each of them is executed on a Nexus 5X with MIST for 10 min with the monkey tool. We find some remarkable failures in this experiment and here we provide our analysis to these failures and our improvement to MIST.

In the beginning, we found that 80 out of 200 selected apps crashed. We analyze the crash log and find that most of them are caused by the inconsistent between origin package name and the obfuscated one. Some apps use system API getPackageName to get its own package name during runtime, and sometimes such package name is used to interact with components of the app. For example, the dynamically generated string "getPackageName() +'.a.b.c'" represents to a specific class within the app, app can use this string to visit this class through reflection mechanism. But in MIST, the return value of getPackageName has been changed to the obfuscated package name, which is inconsistent with the original one. Because we do not modify the class name synchronously, the app will throw the ClassNotFound exception when visiting the class through

Table 3. Footprint expunging using MIST

Forensics tools	Data source	Native android	MIST
Oxygen Forensics Suite	Disk files	photos taken by executed apps;	-
	System databases	SMS records and account records related to executed apps;	-
	Call logs	logs that contain package and activity names;	-
Andriller	Disk files	files that contain package names, recognizable strings and icons related to executed apps;	-
UFS Explorer	Deleted files	xml files, icons and pictures related to executed apps;	-
LiME	Memory dump	package names and recognizable strings left in memory;	-
Side-channel FP Collector	Battery usage	records that contain package names, icon and run time of executed apps;	-
	Network usage	records that contain package names and icons of executed apps;	-
	ACCT files	UIDs and PIDs of executed apps;	-

getPackageName. This problem also happens when the app visits resources defined in the *xml* files. Another problem is that some apps may conduct an Activity invoking through an Intent with hard-coded Activity name, which also involves the package name inconsistency.

To address this issue, we further modified the implementation of MIST: we modified the findClass function in the BaseDexClassLoader class to change the obfuscated package name to the original one and modified the function startActivityMayWait in package com.android.server.am to change the hard coded package name to our obfuscated one. Note that these package name patching only happen in the memory of the protected app and will not conflict with the installation process, and thus solves the inconsistency problem. After solving these inconsistent problems, All the 200 selected apps work correctly with MIST.

Since MIST provides a series of extra security features, it also brings some inconveniences to the users of protected apps. Users should reinstall the protected apps before the execution and some system services are disabled due to the IPC supervision. But considering MIST is designed for the users who have additional security demands, such compromises are acceptable while chasing the goal of leaving none footprint in the device.

4.3 Performance Overhead

The specific execution of an app under MIST inevitably introduces performance overhead. To evaluate the overhead of MIST precisely, we run the top 200 apps from Google Play automatically on both normal Nexus 6p and Nexus 5x with

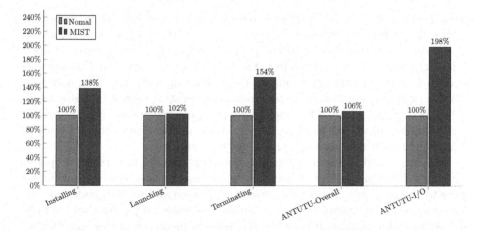

Fig. 3. Performance overhead of MIST

MIST using `Monkey`, and record the time each app spends on the installation, launching, and terminating stage, respectively. We also use the `AnTuTu` Benchmark (a state-of-the-art Benchmark suite in Google Play) to evaluate the running overhead of MIST.

The results of performance overhead are shown in Fig. 3. Among the three typical stages of app lifetime: *installing*, *launching*, and *terminating* we can see that the mostly influenced stage is the installation. The introduced encrypted partition operation in this stage brings a 38% (6.23 s) overhead on average to set up an encrypted partition. However, since the setup of the encrypted partition has been done before the execution, it will not affect the normal execution of the app. Moreover, after the execution, the memory elimination brings a 54% (0.06 s) overhead on average. Considering that these operations are only executed once for an execution, we believe that MIST does not produce a significant impact on user experience.

Except those operations happened before and after the execution, From Fig. 3 we can see that the use of MIST only slightly affect the normal execution: performance overhead for both the launching and the overall execution of an app are less than 6%. Note that although the overhead for the file I/O operation is 98% (due to the file encryption) according to the AnTuTu I/O testing, this is the maximum overhead since seldom app continuously reads or writes file during its execution as the Benchmark testing. Therefore, we argue that the overhead of file I/O is acceptable for most application scenarios.

5 Related Work

Private execution is first introduced to web browsers as private browsing mode. This mode guarantees that an attacker who takes control of the machine after the user exits private browsing can learn nothing about the user's actions while in private browsing. Although private browsing mode has already been supported by four major browsers (Internet Explorer/Edge, Firefox, Chrome, and Safari), recent study by Aggarwal *et al.* [3] points out that private browsing is used differently from how it is marketed. Xu *et al.* further shows that Chrome and Firefox do not correctly clear some of their browsing footprints [29], and they propose Ucognito, a prototype system to enhance existing private browsing mode of browsers. Similar to MIST, Ucognito adopts a filesystem overlaying approach with a sandbox filesystem to assure no persistent modification is stored. However, it only focuses on web browsing and is not universal.

To Generalize private execution on commodity systems, researchers proposed a myriad of design schemes. Lacuna [8] is a comprehensive system that allows users to run programs in *private sessions* of desktop and server Linux systems. It uses a special *ephemeral channel* to isolate the protected program and peripheral devices while making it possible to delete the memories of this communication from the host. However, it relies on a modified QEMU-KVM hypervisor to achieve this functionality and is quite heavyweight, and thus is demanding to be ported to Android devices. PrivExec [18] is an operating system service for private execution. It allows any application to execute in a private execution mode where storage writes will not be recoverable by others during or after execution. PrivExec only requires the modification of the operating system and is promising to be ported to Android platform. However, it does not consider the forensic deniability issue. TpriVexeC [7] improve the performance of private execution via keeping both I/O and runtime data of private applications in memory only. But it does not consider that the secure deallocation and sensitive runtime data may be leaked if memory forensic analysis is employed.

For Android system, CleanOS [28] is a representative system that fulfills memory encryption based protection. It identifies and tracks sensitive data in RAM and on stable storage and encrypts it. CleanOS leverages a trusted, cloud-based service to manage encryption keys, and evicts a key to the cloud when the data is not in active use on the device. Because it mainly focuses on in-memory objects encryption and does not consider the comprehensive behaviors of an app thoroughly, CleanOS may either leak sensitive information via system services interaction (file I/O, IPC, system API invoking) or be incompatible with many standard functionalities provided by the OS. AppShell [30] is a practical Android app private execution solution that supports both in-memory and on-disk data protection by transparently encrypting the data, which requires neither framework modification, nor the root privilege. However, it is possible that sensitive data may reside in places that cannot be touched by AppShell.

Compared with them, MIST provides a more comprehensive footprint expunging mechanism on Android. We demonstrated it in a comparison between MIST and previous solutions related to footprint expunging in Table 4: except MIST, other solutions all fail to achieve footprint expunging on Android for violating at least five items.

Table 4. Comparison to other footprint expunging solutions

	MIST	PrivateDroid	CleanOS	Lacuna	Privexec	Ucognito
Memory	Y	N	Y	Y	Y	Y
File	Y	N	Y	Y	Y	N
IPC	Y	N	N	Y	Y	N
Process status	Y	N	N	Y	N	N
Battery usage	Y	N	N	-	-	-
Network usage	Y	N	N	-	-	-
Screen	Y	N	N	Y	N	N
Microphone	Y	N	N	-	-	-
Sensor	Y	N	N	-	-	-
Keyboard input	Y	N	N	-	-	-
System log	Y	N	N	Y	N	N

[1] "-" indicates that the tested solution works on Linux, which contains no such footprint.

Some researchers use sandboxing techniques to protect Android app against the attack from malwares. Android app sandboxing provides each app a separated execution environment so that third-party apps can't detect and tamper the execution of protected apps. According to our threat model, we assume the attacker has physical access to the device, which means the attacker can analyze the disk and memory data directly. That's why MIST provides features that not considered by sandboxing techniques such as filesystem encryption and memory page elimination.

6 Conclusion

In this paper, we present a privacy enhancement system MIST to achieve the goal of execution footprint expunging of Android apps. MIST adopts a comprehensive footprint detecting and expunging policies, and works with real-world Android devices. We evaluate MIST with popular Android apps and demonstrate that MIST can eliminate most execution footprints compared with regular Android OS.

References

1. What if the FBI tried to crack an Android phone? We attacked one to find out. https://theconversation.com/what-if-the-fbi-tried-to-crack-an-android-phone-we-attacked-one-to-find-out-56556
2. White Paper: Red Hat Crash Utility. http://people.redhat.com/anderson/crash_whitepaper/

3. Aggarwal, G., Bursztein, E., Jackson, C., Boneh, D.: An analysis of private browsing modes in modern browsers. In: USENIX Security Symposium, pp. 79–94 (2010)
4. Albano, P., Castiglione, A., Cattaneo, G., De Santis, A.: A novel anti-forensics technique for the android os. In: 2011 International Conference on Broadband and Wireless Computing, Communication and Applications (BWCCA), pp. 380–385. IEEE (2011)
5. Cai, L., Chen, H.: Touchlogger: inferring keystrokes on touch screen from smartphone motion. HotSec **11**, 9 (2011)
6. Chen, J., Chen, H., Bauman, E., Lin, Z., Zang, B., Guan, H.: You shouldnt collect my secrets: thwarting sensitive keystroke leakage in mobile IME apps. In: 24th USENIX Security Symposium (USENIX Security 15), pp. 657–690 (2015)
7. Djoko, J.B., Jennings, B., Lee, A.J.: Tprivexec: private execution in virtual memory. In: Proceedings of the Sixth ACM on Conference on Data and Application Security and Privacy, pp. 285–294. ACM (2016)
8. Dunn, A.M., et al.: Eternal sunshine of the spotless machine: Protecting privacy with ephemeral channels. In: Presented as part of the 10th USENIX Symposium on Operating Systems Design and Implementation (OSDI 12), pp. 61–75 (2012)
9. Fawaz, K., Feng, H., Shin, K.G.: Anatomization and protection of mobile apps location privacy threats. In: 24th USENIX Security Symposium (USENIX Security 15), pp. 753–768 (2015)
10. Halderman, J.A., et al.: Lest we remember: cold-boot attacks on encryption keys. Commun. ACM **52**(5), 91–98 (2009)
11. Jana, S., Narayanan, A., Shmatikov, V.: A scanner darkly: protecting user privacy from perceptual applications. In: 2013 IEEE Symposium on Security and Privacy (SP), pp. 349–363. IEEE (2013)
12. Kollár, I.: Forensic ram dump image analyser. Master's Thesis, Charles University in Prague (2010)
13. Li, L., Zhao, X., Xue, G.: Unobservable re-authentication for smartphones. In: NDSS, pp. 1–16 (2013)
14. Lin, C.C., Li, H., Zhou, X.Y., Wang, X.: Screenmilker: how to milk your android screen for secrets. In: NDSS (2014)
15. Lin, Z., Rhee, J., Wu, C., Zhang, X., Xu, D.: Dimsum: discovering semantic data of interest from un-mappable memory with confidence. In: Proceedings of NDSS (2012)
16. Michalevsky, Y., Boneh, D., Nakibly, G.: Gyrophone: recognizing speech from gyroscope signals. In: 23rd USENIX Security Symposium (USENIX Security 14), pp. 1053–1067 (2014)
17. Nan, Y., Yang, M., Yang, Z., Zhou, S., Gu, G., Wang, X.: Uipicker: user-input privacy identification in mobile applications. In: 24th USENIX Security Symposium (USENIX Security 15), pp. 993–1008 (2015)
18. Onarlioglu, K., Mulliner, C., Robertson, W., Kirda, E.: Privexec: private execution as an operating system service. In: 2013 IEEE Symposium on Security and Privacy (SP), pp. 206–220. IEEE (2013)
19. Peters, T.M., Gondree, M.A., Peterson, Z.N.: Defy: a deniable, encrypted file system for log-structured storage (2015)
20. Reardon, J., Marforio, C., Capkun, S., Basin, D.: User-level secure deletion on log-structured le systems. In: Proceedings of the 7th ACM Symposium on Information, Computer and Communications Security, pp. 63–64. ACM (2012)
21. Saltaformaggio, B., Bhatia, R., Gu, Z., Zhang, X., Xu, D.: Guitar: piecing together android app guis from memory images. In: Proceedings of the 22nd ACM SIGSAC Conference on Computer and Communications Security, pp. 120–132. ACM (2015)

22. Saltaformaggio, B., Bhatia, R., Gu, Z., Zhang, X., Xu, D.: VCR: app-agnostic recovery of photographic evidence from android device memory images. In: Proceedings of the 22nd ACM SIGSAC Conference on Computer and Communications Security, pp. 146–157. ACM (2015)
23. Saltaformaggio, B., Bhatia, R., Zhang, X., Xu, D., Richard III, G.G.: Screen after previous screens: spatial-temporal recreation of android app displays from memory images. In: USENIX Security Symposium, pp. 1137–1151 (2016)
24. Saltaformaggio, B., Gu, Z., Zhang, X., Xu, D.: Dscrete: automatic rendering of forensic information from memory images via application logic reuse. In: 23rd USENIX Security Symposium (USENIX Security 14), pp. 255–269 (2014)
25. Shu, J., Zhang, Y., Li, J., Li, B., Gu, D.: Why data deletion fails? a study on deletion flaws and data remanence in android systems. ACM Trans. Embed. Comput. Syst. (TECS) 16(2), 61 (2017)
26. Simon, L., Anderson, R.: Security analysis of android factory resets. In: 4th Mobile Security Technologies Workshop (MoST) (2015)
27. Skillen, A., Mannan, M.: On implementing deniable storage encryption for mobile devices (2013)
28. Tang, Y., Ames, P., Bhamidipati, S., Bijlani, A., Geambasu, R., Sarda, N.: Cleanos: limiting mobile data exposure with idle eviction. In: Presented as part of the 10th USENIX Symposium on Operating Systems Design and Implementation (OSDI 12), pp. 77–91 (2012)
29. Xu, M., Jang, Y., Xing, X., Kim, T., Lee, W.: Ucognito: private browsing without tears. In: Proceedings of the 22nd ACM SIGSAC Conference on Computer and Communications Security, pp. 438–449. ACM (2015)
30. Yajin, Z., Kapil Singh, X.J.: Appshell: making data protection practical for lost or stolen android devices. In: IEEE/IFIP Network Operations and Management Symposium. IEEE (2016)
31. Zhang, N., Yuan, K., Naveed, M., Zhou, X., Wang, X.: Leave me alone: app-level protection against runtime information gathering on android. In: 2015 IEEE Symposium on Security and Privacy, pp. 915–930. IEEE (2015)
32. Zhang, X., Ying, K., Aafer, Y., Qiu, Z., Du, W.: Life after app uninstallation: are the data still alive? data residue attacks on android. In: Proceedings of the Network and Distributed System Security Symposium (NDSS), San Diego, California, USA(2016)
33. Zhou, X., et al.: Identity, location, disease and more: inferring your secrets from android public resources. In: Proceedings of the 2013 ACM SIGSAC Conference on Computer & Communications Security, pp. 1017–1028. ACM (2013)

A Comprehensive Study of Permission Usage on Android

Yemian Lu[1]([✉]), Qi Li[2], Purui Su[3], Juan Pan[1], Jia Yan[3], Pengyi Zhan[1], and Wei Guo[1]

[1] China Academy of Information and Communications Technology, Beijing 100191, China
{luyemian,panjuan,zhanpengyi,guowei1}@caict.ac.cn
[2] Graduate School at Shenzhen, Tsinghua University, Shenzhen 518055, China
qi.li@sz.tsinghua.edu.cn
[3] Institute of Software, Chinese Academy of Sciences, Beijing 100190, China
{supurui,yanjia}@tca.iscas.ac.cn

Abstract. Nowadays, redundant permissions and probing permissions are common in Android applications and third-party libraries, which may cause massive security threats to their users. Existing tools used for permission analysis may introduce incorrect detection results, due to their regardless of the relationships between permissions and the values of function parameters and fields. In order to extract the exact used permissions in Android applications and third-party libraries, we propose a Dalvik register-based data flow analysis technique (DARFA) to get the parameter values of function parameters and fields. By leveraging DARFA, we design and implement PermHunter, a static analysis tool, to detect redundant permissions and probing permissions in Android apps and third-party libraries. We have evaluated PermHunter by analyzing 45 third-party libraries and 653 applications. These results indicate that nearly half of these third-party libraries have redundant permissions and probing permissions, and the proportions in Android applications are even higher.

Keywords: Permission analysis · Redundant permissions
Probing permissions · Android

1 Introduction

Android is the most popular operating system for mobile phones, more and more developers began to design various kinds of Android applications. Android applications (we use "apps" for short) have to ask for correct permissions to access the protected resources of the system or other apps. Google, which is the development team of Android, has advocated the principle of least privilege for app developers, that is, Android apps should only apply for the permissions they actually used to avoid redundant permissions and security risks. However,

M. H. Au et al. (Eds.): NSS 2018, LNCS 11058, pp. 64–79, 2018.
https://doi.org/10.1007/978-3-030-02744-5_5

many developers have redundant permissions in their apps, because they are not familiar with the permission mechanism or they deliberately apply for the permissions for future use or attacks. If the attacker take control of these kind of apps, he/she can use the redundant permissions to perform more sensitive operations. In apps that use the same *sharedUserId*, an app can probe and use the permissions that applied by the other apps to perform sensitive behaviors, these kinds of permissions can be called probing permissions. In this case, the user cannot realize these sensitive behaviors from the permissions list of the current app, which may put him/her into danger.

There are also some redundant permissions and probing permissions in the third-party libraries used in Android apps, which will lead to even more security threats. For example, third-party libraries can abuse the permissions applied by the host apps to perform sensitive behaviors. Since all the permissions applied by the host app and third-party library will be listed in the file *AndroidManifest.xml*, and there are no differences between these two parts, it's hard to point out either the library or the app should be blamed for the sensitive behaviors. The problems brought by the existing redundant and probing permissions will be even more severe, for a third-party library may be used in many apps.

In order to find the redundant permissions and probing permissions in Android apps and third-party libraries, we should find the actually used permissions as accurately as possible. There are two jobs should be undertaken, one is the construction of an accurate permission map, the other is an analysis tool that detects the permission related API calls, Content URIs, Intent actions and others items used in the apps and libraries. There have been some tools. PScount [2] and Axplorer [3] can be used to construct the permission maps, and Stowaway [1] can be used to construct the permission-API map for Android 2.2 and detect the permission related items used in Android apps. However, all these works ignore the impact of function parameters and fields introduced for the permission usage, which will generate many false positives and false negatives in the results. For example, VIBRATE permission will be used only when the filed defaults of a Notification object is set as Notification.DEFAULT_VIBRATE or Notification.DEFAULT_ALL. There are also some cases that the used permission can only be determined by the subsequent use of the returned object of a certain method, for example, the method that uses the return value of Uri.parse("content://com.android.contacts") is query() or insert() will determine the used permission is READ_CONTACTS or WRITE_CONTACTS. However, existing tools missed this kind of permission used information.

In order to extract the exact used permissions in Android apps and third-party libraries, we have done some work in two aspects. First, we construct a custom permission map which includes the mappings between permissions and the values of function parameters and fields. With more accurate permission mapping information, the accuracy of detection results can be improved effectively. Second, we propose a static analysis tool, PermHunter, to detect the permission related items used in Android apps and third-party libraries. We propose a Dalvik register-based data flow analysis technique (DARFA) to get both the function parameter and field values. With DARFA, PermHunter can get the exact permissions used by the parameters and the fields, and improve the accuracy of the detection results.

Contributions. In summary, we make the following contributions in this paper:

- We construct a custom permission map, which includes the permission mapping information introduced by function parameters and fields that are missing in the existing work.
- We propose a Dalvik register-based data flow analysis technique (DARFA) to get the value of function parameters and files. Using DARFA, we design and implement PermHunter, a static analysis tool, to detect the improper used permissions in Android apps and libraries.
- We analyze 653 Android apps whose target SDK version is 19, and find redundant permissions and probing permissions in a lot of apps. We also analyze 45 commonly used third-party libraries and find more than a half of these libraries have redundant permissions or probing permissions.

2   Background

Permission mechanism is one of the significant features of Android. Android apps must apply for the appropriate permissions to access the network, Bluetooth, contacts or other resources of the system or other apps. Most of the permissions applied by an app are bound to the app's UID. When a number of apps are set up with the same *sharedUserID* and one of the apps is given a permission, the other apps will also be granted with the same permission automatically and can access the resources protected by this permission.

The control granularity of the Android permission mechanism remains at the application level, and there are no boundaries between the codes of different parts of the same application. The third-party libraries used in apps share all the granted permissions with the host apps. Malicious third-party libraries can abuse the permissions which they haven't declared in their documents but the host app applied, so that they can perform sensitive behaviors silently.

The used permissions in apps and libraries can be divided in the following categories:

- A particular function is called.
- A particular field is used. This kind of fields include the Content URI stored in the Uri object, such as the field CONTENT_URI of the Bookmarks class.
- A particular Content URI string is used. That is, if the app uses the string as the parameter of the function Uri.parse(), it may need to apply for the appropriate permissions to use the returned Uri object. And the permissions used may be different depending on the subsequent read or write operations.
- A particular Intent action string is used. That is, if a particular string is used in the inter-component communication, the app should apply for the

appropriate permissions. The Intent action strings can be divided into two cases: the strings used in the inter-component communication APIs and the strings used in the intent filters of the components in the manifest file.

- A particular parameter value of a function is used. For example, if the app calls the function TelephonyManager.listen() with the second parameter set to 32 (the value of PhoneStateListener.LISTEN_CALL_STATE), permission READ_PHONE_STATE should be applied.
- A field is set to a particular value. For example, if the app set the field defaults of a Notification object with an integer value 2 (the value of Notification.DEFAULT_VIBRATE), then permission VIBRATE should be applied.

In addition, the functions and fields accessed through Java reflection code may also cause the use of permissions, which should also be considered in the analysis.

Existing tools such as Stowaway [1] can detect some of the above, but they all ignore the permissions used with the function parameters and fields, which may introduce errors in the detection results. In order to get the actually used permissions in Android apps and libraries as accurately as possible, we need a data flow analysis scheme to check whether the target function parameters and fields are set to particular values. Both Flowdroid [4] and Androbugs [5] provide data flow analysis. Flowdroid checks whether the return value of a source function is used as a parameter of a sink function in some way. If flows of this kind are found, there may be some privacy data leaks. In our case of permission detection, what we want to get is the value used by a function parameter or a field, not only how a return value of a function is used, so we cannot directly use the functions provided by Flowdroid. Androbugs provides data flow analysis for data of basic types (such as int, Boolean, String etc.) throughout the codes within a function, and then detect whether a function uses a particular value as a parameter. Androbugs is closer to our analysis targets, but it cannot trace the data flow passing through the function call chains. In addition, Androbugs has not yet provide the data analysis for the return objects of functions such as Uri.parse(). So we propose a Dalvik register-based data flow analysis technique (DARFA) to do the job, and use DARFA to design and implement PermHunter, a static analysis tool, to detect the improper used permissions in Android apps and third-party libraries.

3   Framework of PermHunter

We propose a tool, PermHunter, to detect the permissions actually used in Android apps and third-party libraries. The framework of PermHunter is shown in Fig. 1. There are three phases in PermHunter: pre-processing, permission detection and result analysis.

Pre-processing. We use Androbugs to decompile the apks and third-party libraries. Androbugs requires the dex file as input, so we should first convert the

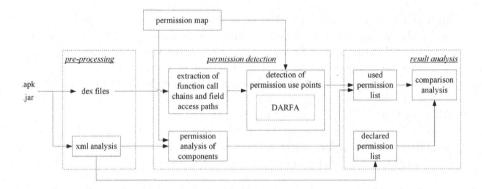

Fig. 1. Framework of PermHunter

jar files to dex files when we analyze the third-party libraries. There are also some dex files stored in the assets directory or somewhere else in an apk file, so we should go through all the possible folders in the tested app or library to get all the dex files.

We analyze the manifest file to get the declared permission list of the app or library. We also get the information of the used components listed in the manifest file, including permissions and Intent actions. All these information will be used to find the permissions actually used by the components.

Permission Detection. PermHunter uses Androbugs to get the function call chains and field access paths in the app or library, and uses DARFA we proposed to get the value of the target function parameters and fields that we care about. Then PermHunter extracts the permissions that are actually used based on the permission map and constructs the used permission list.

Result Analysis. In this process, PermHunter compares and analyzes the two lists extracted from the up two processes and extracts the redundant permissions and probing permissions in the app or third-party library. We take the permissions that exist only in the declared permission list as redundant permissions, and take the permissions that exist only in the used permission list as probing permissions.

There are two challenges in the design and implementation of PermHunter. One is how to construct a permission map that includes the permission mapping information introduced by the value of function parameters and fields as much as we can. The other is the design and implementation of DARFA. We will address them in the following sections.

4 Custom Permission Map

In order to get the permission mapping information introduced by function parameters and fields, we adds the following information into our custom permission map:

Fields with Fixed Values. We found that in the documents of Android APIs, fields in some classes have fixed values. They can be used as the value of function parameters or fields. And the use of this kind of fields will results in the use of related permissions. For example, if we use the code notification.default |= Notification.DEFAULT_VIBRATE, then permission VIBRATE will be used. The description of the field DEFAULT_VIBRATE in the Android document is shown in Fig. 2, in which the "See Also" region lists the field that can use DEFAULT_VIBRATE as its value and the "Constant Value" region gives the value of DEFAULT_VIBRATE.

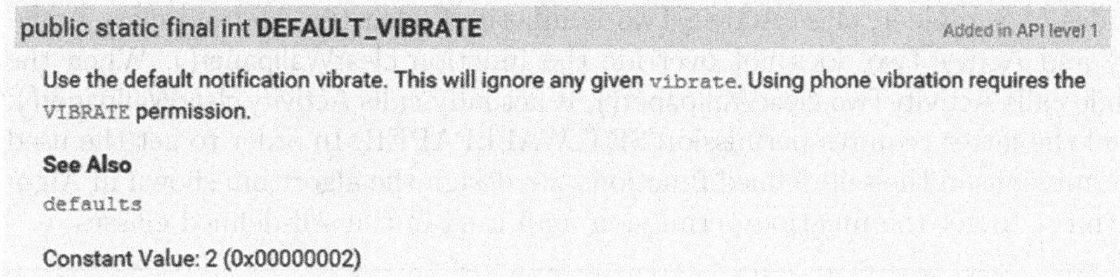
public static final int **DEFAULT_VIBRATE** Added in API level 1

Use the default notification vibrate. This will ignore any given `vibrate`. Using phone vibration requires the `VIBRATE` permission.

See Also

`defaults`

Constant Value: 2 (0x00000002)

Fig. 2. Description of DEFAULT_VIBRATE

This kind of fields will be compiled into the corresponding values when a java file is compiled into a class file. Therefore, if the related function uses the particular value as its parameter value or the related field is set to this value, the related permissions are used. We extract this kind of permission mapping from the descriptions of these fields.

Fields Related to Permission SYSTEM_ALERT_WINDOW. Android developers can create a window with custom priority by setting the field LayoutParams.type to different values. The window with a higher priority will always overlap the window with a lower priority. There are more than 20 kinds of window types, and some require permission SYSTEM_ALERT_WINDOW when they are used. But this kind of information is not included in the documents of Android APIs or the permission map of existing works. So we extracted the information manually. We find that all these types have a fixed integer value, so we put the values of different window types and permission SYSTEM_ALERT_WINDOW into our custom permission map.

Functions Related to Permission WRITE_SETTINGS and Permission WRITE_SECURE_SETTINGS. In Android, the system and apps can store some global configuration data into the Settings database provided by the system, and the write operation requires permission WRITE_SETTINGS or WRITE_SECURE_SETTINGS. This kind of information is also missing in the documents of Android APIs and the permission map of existing works.

The Android system packages the operations on the Settings database into different subclasses named System, Secure and Global in the class of android.provider.Settings, and the functions named putFloat, putInt, putLong, etc. in these classes require permission WRITE_SETTINGS or WRITE_SECURE_SETTINGS. We put these functions and their related permissions into the custom permission map.

Permission Mapping Introduced by Tested App or Third-Party Library. There may be some permissions used in the self-defined functions when their class inherits from an original Android class, and the functions with the same name in the Android class require the permissions. For example, in the codes of Sample 1, class ActivityTwo is inherited from the Android class Activity and ActivytTwo does not override the function clearWallpaper(). When the code calls ActivityTwo.clearWallpaper(), it actually calls Activity.clearWallpaper(), and the latter requires permission SET_WALLPAPER. In order to get the used permissions in the self-defined functions, we design the algorithm shown in Algorithm 1 to get the function-permission map used in the self-defined classes.

```
1  //Sample 1
2  public class ActivityTwo extends Activity
3  {
4      @Override
5      protected void onCreate (Bundle savedInstanceState)
6      {
7          super.onCreate(savedInstanceState);
8          setContentView(R.layout.test);
9          try{
10             clearWallpaper();
11         } catch (IOException e) {
12             e.printStackTrace();
13         }
14     }
15 }
```

5   Dalvik Register-Based Data Flow Analysis

We use Dalvik register-based data flow analysis (DARFA) to get the values of target function parameters and target fields. In order to achieve our analysis targets, we have to choose appropriate analysis objects and analysis process.

5.1   Data Flow Analysis Objects

According to our analysis of the permissions used by function parameters and fields, we found that the target parameters and fields are all with basic data types such as int, Boolean, String, etc. Then the analysis objects of DARFA can be divided into three cases:

- Data of basic types such as int, float, Boolean, String, etc.
- The return objects of target functions such as Uri.parse().
- Objects whose data type is Class. This kind of objects are used to find the classes of functions and parameters used in the Java reflection codes.

Algorithm 1. Get the function-permission map in self-defined classes

---

Input: *aosp_perm_list*: permission map extracted from Android system; *method_list*: the list of implemented methods in the app or third-party library; *class_list*: the list of defined classes in the app or third-party library

Output: *extended_perm_list*

1: **function** "GETEXTENDEDPERMLIST"
2:     *extended_perm_list* = {}
3:     *superclass_list* = {}
4:     **for** each *class* in *class_list* **do**
5:         *classname* = the name of *class*
6:         *supername* = the name of the parent class
7:         **if** *supername* is not instance of "Ljava/lang/Object;" **then**
8:             *superclass_list* += (*classname*, *supername*)
9:         **end if**
10:     **end for**
11:     **for** each *classname* in *superclass_list*.keys() **do**
12:         *supername* = the parent class of *classname* in *superclass_list*
13:         **while** *superclass_list*.haskey(*supername*) **do**
14:             *supername* = the parent class of *supername* in *superclass_list*
15:         **end while**
16:         **if** there are methods in the class of *supername* exist in *aosp_perm_list* **then**
17:             *method_perm_list* = the corresponding method-permission map of *supername* in *aosp_perm_list*
18:             **for** *method* in *method_perm_list* **do**
19:                 *method_perms* = the used permission list of *method*
20:                 **if** method in the class of *classname* doesn't exist in *method_list* **then**
21:                     *extended_perm_list* += (method with the class name *classname*, *method_perms*)
22:                 **end if**
23:             **end for**
24:         **end if**
25:     **end for**
26:     **return** *extended_perm_list*
27: **end function**

5.2   Analysis Processes

The codes in a dex file is called Dalvik bytecode. Dalvik bytecode instructions use registers to identify the source and destination operands of the current operation. Therefore, the data flow analysis in DARFA is performed by tracking the data in registers used by the Dalvik bytecode instructions. The analysis can be divided into three processes: forward data flow analysis, backward parameter analysis and return object analysis.

Forward Data Flow Analysis. DARFA takes data of basic types and objects whose data type is Class as the analysis objects in this process. Each instruction of the function which uses the target functions or fields will be analyzed in order. DARFA records the Dalvik registers with the analysis objects in a list during the analysis. Each item in the list keeps the register number, the value and the type of the current data. Some examples can be seen in Fig. 3. Types of the data include basic type (such as int, float, Boolean, string), param (which means that data stored in the current register is the parameter of the current function, and the value filed in the record gives the index of this parameter) and Class. When the analysis arrives the instruction that uses the target function or field, DARFA gets the value stored in the register that are used by the target function parameter or field from the register list it records.

In order to get the real type of a Class object, all the instructions which can be used to get a Class object should be analyzed. For example, DARFA records the parameter and return object of the function Class.forName(), and then use the record data to get the class type of the object used by reflection codes.

If the value DARFA gets is of basic data types, PermHunter can use the information in permission map to determine which permissions are used here. If the value is a class object, it will be used to get the function or field used by the reflection codes. If the register used by target function parameter or target field stores the parameter of the current function, DARFA will use backward parameter analysis to perform the following analysis.

Backward Parameter Analysis. If the value obtained from the process of forward data flow analysis is the parameter of the caller, then backward parameter analysis should be used. As shown in Fig. 3, Uri.parse() is the target function, and the forward data flow analysis (①) shows that the parameter of the target function is the first parameter of the caller (createUri()). So we go back to the function which calls the caller, and then undertake another forward data flow analysis (②). The result shows that the first parameter of createUri() is "content://com.android.contacts", which means that the parameter of the target function Uri.parse() is also "content://com.android.contacts".

Forward data flow analysis and backward parameter analysis may be alternately repeated many times during the entire data flow analysis.

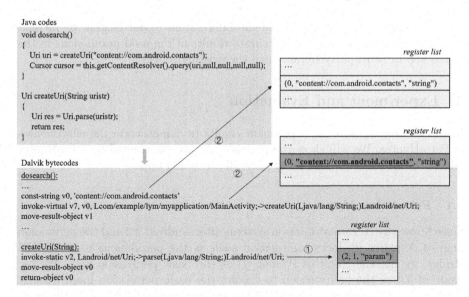

Fig. 3. An example to show the analysis of different process. Uri.parse() is the target function.

Return Object Analysis. Sometimes, we need to know the subsequent use of the return objects of target functions, and then find the exact used permissions. This kind of analysis can be divided into three cases: (1) There are sink functions (Android APIs that use the return object of the target function and require permissions to run the codes) in the caller of the target function. (2) The caller of the target function calls the self-defined functions which calls the sink functions. (3) The return object is returned directly by the caller of the target function.

The process of the return object analysis is shown as following:

step 1 First, we use backward parameter analysis to get the list of self-defined functions that call the sink functions and use their own parameters as the parameters of the sink functions.
step 2 Second, we use forward data flow analysis to find whether the return object of the target function is used as the parameter of the sink functions or the functions in the list extracted from step 1.
step 3 If the return object of the target function is directly returned by the caller, we use the return object of the caller as the analysis object and the caller as the target function, and then repeat the operation in step 2.

In the example of Fig. 3, the return object of the target function (Uri.parse()) is used as the return object of the caller (createUri()). So we can use the return object of createUri() as the analysis object and undertake a forward data flow analysis in the function dosearch(), and finally find it is used by ContentResolver.query(), which means only permission READ_CONTACTS is used.

Using the result of DARFA and the information in our custom permission map, PermHunter can get more accurate results of the used permissions in the tested app or third-party library than the existing tools.

6   Experiment and Evaluation

In this section, we will use experiment results to demonstrate the effectiveness of PermHunter. We will show the permission map constructed by PermHunter and the permission usage in third-party libraries and apps.

6.1   Permission Map

Since Stowaway [1] cannot work on systems after Android 2.2 and the permission map of Axplorer [6] lacks information such as the permissions used by URI strings, we use the result of PScout [7] as the basic permission map. We use Android 4.4 as the base version to extract the basic permission map, because PScout doesn't work well on the higher versions and version 4.4 is the most widely used version in the previous versions. We have added 232 additional permission mapping information into the result of PScout. In addition, we found that the mappings between permission READ_PROFILE and many functions are not accurate, so we remove some inaccurate mapping information.

6.2   Permission Analysis

Analysis Result of Third-Party Libraries. We have collected 45 widely used third-party libraries from appbrain.com [8] and some famous service providers in China, such as Baidu [9], Tencent [10], Umeng [11], DevStore [12] and so on. Results of PermHunter running on these libraries are shown in Fig. 4.

Among all the permissions, READ_EXTERNAL_STORAGE and WRITE_EXTERNAL_STORAGE cannot be easily separated, because the permission map considers the use of the function getExternalStorageDirectory() is associated with both permissions, and it is difficult to obtain all the subsequent operations on the return value of this function. So we simply classify these two permissions in the result of PermHunter as permission EXTERNAL_STORAGE. Similarly, permission ACCESS_FINE_LOCATION and ACCESS_COARSE_LOCATION are classified as permission LOCATION.

The results show that, a total of 26 third-party libraries have at least one redundant permission, accounting for 57.78%, and of which 7 libraries have more than 4 redundant permissions, accounting for 15.56%. There are 26 third-party libraries have at least one probing permission, accounting for 57.78%, and of which 2 libraries have more than 4 probing permissions.

In order to show how much the missing permission information introduced by function parameters or fields can affect the analysis results, we run PermHunter in two cases. We use the custom permission map we construct in this paper

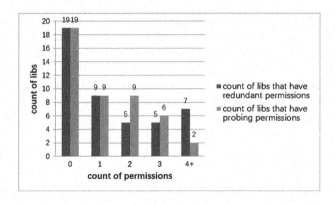

Fig. 4. Permission analysis result of third-party libraries.

in case1, and use the original permission map constructed by PScout in case 2. Some of the differences in the results are shown in Table 1. We manually analyzed the code that uses these permissions in these libraries, and confirmed the use of these permissions. The result shows that the analysis using our custom permission map has a higher detection rate for the actual used permissions and can effectively reduce the false positives of the result for redundant permissions.

Table 1. The differences in the results of case 1 and case 2. The second column and the third column give the count of libs that are considered to have used the listed permissions in the analysis. The fourth column and fifth column give the count of libs that are considered to probe the permissions during their running in the analysis. The sixth column and seventh column give the count of libs that are considered to apply for the permissions but never use them in the code.

Permission	Total result		Result for probing permission		Result for redundant permission	
	case 1	case 2	case 1	case 2	case 1	case 2
VIBRATE	17	3	4	0	4	14
WRITE_SETTINGS	21	1	7	1	2	16
SYSTEM_ALERT_WINDOW	2	0	1	0	4	5
LOCATION	21	19	6	5	0	1

Analysis Result of Android Apps. We have collected 653 apps with *targetS-dkVersion* set to 19 from Google Play and another two app stores in China (Anzhi and Wandoujia). The analysis results of these apps are shown in Fig. 5. Compared with the results of third-party libraries, the proportions of apps with redundant permissions and probing permissions are significantly increased. An important reason is the use of third-party libraries in these apps. We have found that 324 of these 653 apps use the 45 third-party libraries we analyzed above. Some of the redundant permissions in 186 apps come from the third-party libraries they use, and some of the probing permissions in 254 apps come from the libraries. The results show that, the use of unsecure third-party libraries may have a significant impact on the security of the entire application. The 45 libraries we chose cannot cover all the libraries used in the tested apps, so the impact of the third-party libraries would be even more severe in practice.

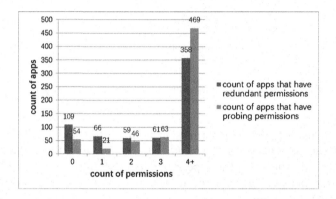

Fig. 5. Permission analysis result of Android apps.

7   Limitation

DARFA directly uses the function call chains extracted from the dex file analysis class, VMAnalysis, in Androbugs to get the caller of each function. Therefore, inter-process analysis and inter-component analysis are not supported, and some false negatives may exist. There may also be some dead codes that are difficult to identify by static analysis tool like DARFA, which may introduce some false positives. In addition, PermHunter is an static analysis tool, which may also be limited in processing the obfuscated apps.

8   Related Work

Permission Analysis. Researchers found that the Android documents for permissions are confused for application developers to apply for proper permissions in their apps. Some of them extracted the permission map by manually analyzing the Android documents, and then proposed Permission Check Tool [13] to help developer find the redundant permissions in their apps. Felt et al. proposed Stowaway [1] to construct the permission map of Android 2.2 and then detect the redundant permissions in Android apps. They use unit testing and API fuzzing to get the permission map, which is difficult to guarantee the API coverage. PScout [2] extracts the permission map from Android source code by building the call graph of the framework and finding the reachable APIs which can reach a permission check function in the call graph. By using static analysis techniques, PScout can extract permission maps from different versions of Android system. Similar to PScout, COPES [14] also uses static analysis to extract permission map from the Android framework. But the result contains only the mapping between permissions and Android API calls. Backes et al. [3] found that there are many calls in the CFG of PScout that could not exist in practice, because PScout constructs the CFG based on class inheritance relationships. So they build a more accurate call graph by using object sensitive pointer analysis technology. Their work is called Axplorer.

However, all these tools ignore the relationship between permission use and function parameters or fields. When a function call requires a permission in one situation, these tools add the mapping to their permission map, which will introduce false positives in the result map. This paper deals with this issue, extracts the missing permission mapping information as much as possible, and proposes the appropriate analysis tool to detect the permissions used in the Android apps and third-party libraries.

Static Analysis. AdRisk [15] uses the execution path analysis to detect the risk behaviors in ads libraries. AdRisk takes the sensitive APIs used in the ad libraries as the target APIs, analyzes the path reachability, and takes the path reachable API calls as the dangerous behaviors that actually occurs. SCanDroid [16] analyzes the inter-component and inter-app data flow to make security-relevant decisions automatically. FlowDroid [4] is a static taint analysis tool for detecting privacy data leakage in Android apps. Flowdroid creates a complete model of Android application lifecycle to build the inter-procedural control-flow graph as completely as possible, and also includes the callback functions and taint propagation in the UI components during the analysis process. Androbugs [5] uses static analysis to detect the existing security vulnerabilities in Android apps. Since some vulnerabilities occur only when certain parameters are used by the target Android API, Androbugs takes a data flow analysis for the data of basic types within the range of the detected method, in order to obtain the parameter value of the target API.

Both Flowdroid and Androbugs provide data flow analysis functions. But Flowdroid cannot get the value used by a function parameter or a field, and Androbugs can only perform the data flow analysis within the scope of one method. We extend Androbugs to do our analysis. In addition to the existing data flow analysis within a method used by Androbugs, we also propose backward parameter analysis and return object analysis, and then use the detected parameter values and field values to get the used permissions as accurately as possible.

9   Conclusion

Permission Analysis is an important field of the security analysis for Android apps and third-party libraries. Existing tools may introduce incorrect detection results due to the regardless of the relationships of permission use and

the values of function parameters and fields. This paper deals with this issue
and extracts the missing permission mappings as much as possible. Then we
propose Dalvik register-based data flow analysis technique to get the values of
target function parameters and fields in an Android app or a third-party library.
With this technique, we propose a novel permission analysis tool, PermHunter,
which detects the permissions that are actually used in an Android app or a
library, and then extracts the redundant permissions and probing permissions.
It has been confirmed that using our custom permission map, PermHunter can
get more accurate results than using the original permission map of PScout.
These results indicate that nearly half of the tested third-party libraries have
redundant permissions and probing permissions, and the proportions in tested
Android apps are even higher. Further analysis shows that many of the improper
used permissions in apps are imported by the used third-party libraries.

References

1. Felt, A.P., Chin, E., Hanna, S., et al.: Android permissions demystified. In: Proceedings of the 2011 ACM Conference on Computer and Communications Security (CCS), pp. 627–638. ACM, New York (2011)
2. Au, K.W.Y., Zhou, Y.F., Huang, Z., et al.: PScout: analyzing the android permission specification. In: Proceedings of the 2012 ACM Conference on Computer and Communications Security (CCS), pp. 217–228. ACM, New York (2012)
3. Backes, M., Bugiel, S., Derr, E., et al.: On demystifying the android application framework: re-visiting android permission sepecification analysis. In: Proceedings of the 25th USENIX Security Symposium (USENIX Security), pp. 1101–1118. USENIX Association, Berkeley (2016)
4. Arzt, S., Rasthofer, S., Fritz, C., et al.: Flowdroid: precise context, flow, field, object-sensitive and lifecycle-aware taint analysis for android apps. In: Proceedings of the 35th ACM SIGPLAN Conference on Programming Language De-sign and Implementation (PLDI), pp. 259–269. ACM, New York (2014)
5. AndroBugs_Framework. https://github.com/AndroBugs/AndroBugs_Framework. Accessed 4 Apr 2017
6. axplorer demystifying the Android Application Framework. http://www.axplorer. org/. Accessed 11 Oct 2017
7. PScout. http://pscout.csl.toronto.edu/downloads.php. Accessed 15 Apr 2017
8. AppBrain-Android library statistics. http://www.appbrain.com/stats/libraries. Accessed 4 Feb 2017
9. Baidu developer. http://developer.baidu.com/platform/catalog/navigation-c/ node/n301. Accessed 4 Feb 2017
10. Weixin Developer. https://open.weixin.qq.com. Accessed 4 Feb 2017
11. Umeng. http://www.umeng.com/codecenter.html. Accessed 4 Feb 2017
12. DevStore. http://www.devstore.cn/service/newproductList/sta3-cla4.html. Accessed 4 Feb 2017
13. Vidas, T., Christin, N., Cranor, L.: Curbing android permission creep. In: Proceedings of the Web 2.0 Security and Privacy 2011 Workshop (W2sp) (2011)
14. Bartel, A., Klein, J., Traon, Y. L., et al.: Automatically securing permission-based software by reducing the attack surface: an application to Android. In: Proceedings of the 27th IEEE/ACM International Conference on Automated Software Engineering (ASE), pp. 274–277. ACM, New York (2012)

15. Grace, M.C., Zhou, W., Jiang, X., et al.: Unsafe exposure analysis of mobile in- app advertisements. In: Proceedings of the 5th ACM Conference on Security and Privacy in Wireless and Mobile Networks (WiSec), pp. 101–112. ACM, New York(2012)
16. Fuchs, A.P., Chaudhuri, A., Foster, J. S.: SCanDroid: automated security certification of android applications. In: Proceedings of the 2010 IEEE Symposium on Security and Privacy (S&P). IEEE, Piscataway (2010)

Performance Analysis of Searchable Symmetric Encryption Schemes on Mobile Devices

Dennis Y. W. Liu[1]([⊠]), Chi Tsiu Tong[1], and Winnie W. M. Lam[2]

[1] Department of Computing, The Hong Kong Polytechnic University,
Kowloon, Hong Kong
csdennis@comp.polyu.edu.hk, tony.ct.tong@connect.polyu.hk
[2] Department of Mathematics and Information Technology,
The Education University of Hong Kong, Tai Po, Hong Kong
winnielam@eduhk.hk

Abstract. In the age of cloud computing, it is common for individuals to store their digital documents to the cloud so that they can access them anytime and anywhere. While the demand of cloud storage continues to grow, the associated security threat has caught attention of the public. Searchable encryption (SE) attempts to ensure confidentiality of data in public storage while offering searching capability to the end users. Previous studies on SE focused on the security and performance on desktop applications and there were no discussions of those on mobile devices, where their memory, computational and network capabilities are limited. In this paper, we implemented three recent SE schemes and evaluated their performance in Android mobile devices in terms of indexing time and searching time, under (1) exact-match, (2) partial search, and (3) multi-keyword queries. We realize that each of the schemes has its performance advantages and disadvantages. Since user experience is one of the major concerns in mobile App, our findings would help App developers to choose the appropriate SE schemes in their applications.

Keywords: Searchable encryption schemes · Android devices
Encryption scheme performance

1 Introduction

These days, it is common for mobile device users to outsource their data to cloud storage providers (CSP). By utilizing the managed service provided by CSPs, data owners can minimize the cost and efforts of hosting storage servers and accessing their data from virtually everywhere. Despite the fact that the storage outsourcing approach sounds attractive, there are increasing number of people worrying about data security and user privacy issues. Common cloud settings often operate in a black-box manner and require the data owners to trust the service providers. If inadequate security measures are adopted, sensitive

© Springer Nature Switzerland AG 2018
M. H. Au et al. (Eds.): NSS 2018, LNCS 11058, pp. 80–94, 2018.
https://doi.org/10.1007/978-3-030-02744-5_6

data could be leaked to unauthorized parties. Furthermore, the rise of big data analytics has made personal data unprecedentedly valuable. Malicious CSPs can monitor user activities and look into users' data anytime without notifying the data owner. As a result, cloud users' privacy is compromised. We believe aforementioned security threats are the major barriers that prevent individuals, businesses, and government from migrating sensitive data to the cloud.

To ensure data secrecy in a cloud environment, the most straightforward method is to encrypt the data before sending it to the cloud. By transforming data into a scrambled format, the secret key holder remains the only one who can access the original information. To instantiate a search, the client must download the documents, decrypt them and perform searching. If the document is lengthy or the document collection is large, it could be time-consuming and wasting network bandwidth, which are particular the major concerns for mobile device users. The idea of searchable encryption emerged and the primary goal is to make searching feasible on encrypted data while retaining data confidentiality and eliminates the need for downloading entire document to local storage first. In the past decades, numerous researchers [3–5,8,15] have contributed to the topic and proposed different constructs to achieve the goal. Prior studies focus on improving the searching efficiency and enhancing the data security, and less effort has been put on exploring the impact of these schemes on mobile devices, where their memory, computational and network capabilities are limited, which compared with their desktop/laptop counterparts. Given that searchable encryption schemes usually involve complicated computations, it would place a burden on the mobile devices and eventually lead to an undesired user experience.

In this paper, we propose a software implementation of three recent searchable encryption schemes [2,10,12] and benchmark their performances in Android mobile devices, in terms of (1) exact-match, (2) partial search, and (3) multi-keyword queries. We believe that our findings could give insights to mobile App developers the impact of adopting SSE schemes in applications of mobile devices.

2   Related Work

2.1   Symmetric Searchable Encryption

The development of symmetric searchable encryption (SSE) can be traced back to 1996 when Oblivious RAMs (ORAM) [8] were first proposed. ORAM is a computing technique that was originated for software protection, but the concept can also be applied to searchable encryption. By using ORAM, one can modify a function's memory access pattern without changing its input and output behavior. Recall that the key objectives of SSE are retaining data secrecy and protecting user privacy, ORAM can hide the underlying data structure and access pattern so that an optimal level of privacy can be achieved. The drawback is that it requires $O(log\ n)$ rounds per read/write, which is not an efficient approach. Since ORAM-based searching algorithms are computational expensive in nature, researchers started to explore other feasible methods in addressing the efficiency problem. One of the research direction is relaxing certain security attributes (e.g., leaking the search pattern) in return for better performance. Song et al. [15] proposed an SSE scheme that can secure the data being outsourced, together with substantial queries and corresponding result. Their scheme can be classified into two phases: the setup phase and the search phase. During the setup phase, each document is tokenized into words. Every word is encrypted into "search token" using a combination of deterministic encryption with random factor (pseudorandom number generated by the word position within that document). The client concludes the setup phase by pushing encrypted documents and the "search tokens" to the server. When performing searches, the client first encrypts the search term into token and send the token to the server. The server performs matching with saved search tokens and returns the document(s) accordingly. As the server does not have access to any plaintext, nor the encryption key, the data remains confidential. This scheme requires $O(n)$ operations for encryption and search for a document with length n. It is comparatively faster and more efficient.

The method from [15] enjoys a significant efficiency improvement over ORAM based schemes. But the performance remains a problem when the documents are large. To resolve this problem, they suggested to use keyword-as-key hash tables to store pointers to documents (a.k.a. inverted indexes to documents). Goh [7] argues that this method could leak partial information of the encrypted documents when the hash table is being updated. Adversaries can perform chosen-ciphertext attacks (CCA) and deduce the encrypted content by analyzing the update pattern of the indexes. As an alternative, Goh suggested using Bloom Filter can fix this update loophole. In Goh's Z-IDX construction, it does not store the keyword directly, but it runs each keyword through multiple hash functions and maps the output into an arbitrary number of bits (e.g., m-bit array). When performing a search, we just need to run the search phase with the same procedure again. By comparing the result with the stored m-bit array, then we can easily determine whether the document contains the keyword. Because of hash collisions, the use of Z-IDX could bring false positive to the search result. But the actual index size is much smaller and it allows quick comparison when perform searching.

Another interesting topic under SSE is about the capability to perform partial searches on encrypted data. When searching, it is common for us to enter only certain part of the keyword and ask the search engine to return all matched results. The previous SSE schemes mentioned does not address the substring searching problem explicitly. To facilitate substring searching in these SSE schemes, a simple method is to include all substrings when constructing the index, but this generally brings drawbacks that could outweigh the benefits in return. For example, in Song et al.'s [15] construction, this would dramatically increase the index size and computation rounds per keyword (for a string with length n, there will be an extra $n*(n+1)/2-1$ substrings to be stored/processed). This also means that there will be more computations during the search phase. As for Goh's [7] Z-IDX scheme, it can amplify the false positive rate in the search result and the extra overhead could slow down the index-building process.

2.2 Profiling Methods Under Android Platform

There exist many profiling tools in Java that allow us to gain insights into applications under different aspects. While the Java profilers for the desktop platform are well-developed, the story is totally different for the Android platform. Despite both platforms can be coded with Java, the internal architecture of two platforms are different. Android is designed to run on power-constrained devices, it is equipped with a specialized virtual machine called Dalvik Virtual Machine (DVM). Different from the Java Virtual Machine (JVM), DVM is characterized by its register based design and its proprietary format of bytecode (.dex). In addition, the Dalvik VM supports a subset of the standard Java library only, in which some useful benchmarking packages (e.g. the *java.lang.instrumentation* package) are missing or have limited functionalities. For these reasons, most of the existing Java profiling tools and frameworks are not compatible with Android.

At present, the most effective way to profile an Android App is using the built-in Android Monitor [1] under Android Studio. It provides a graphical representation of key aspects (e.g., CPU, memory, and GPU usage) of the DVM runtime and includes several tools which can capture and save information while the App is running. The Android Monitor is useful in analyzing an App, but it does not provide a structured way to store the profiled data for later inspection.

Another approach in profiling Android App is to introduce extra code to the App. For instance, one could create two variables to store the time before and after the invocation of methods. By calculating the elapsed time, developers can get the actual processing time of that method. This approach allows customizable code measurement, but it requires modification of existing code. Practically, it is not well suited for Apps that have complex structure because it can cause more confusion with the code base. Some developers have spotted this problem and introduced AspectJ [6]. AspectJ is an open source library that supports Compile Time Weaving (CTW). During compilation, it modifies existing Java code behind the scene and introduces extra behavior to existing functions. Recent AspectJ development on Android platform allows us to benchmark and monitor function calls easily. In the Hugo plugin [17], Jake Wharton consolidated the AspectJ library into a Gradle plugin which can be easily integrated with existing Android Apps. Through this plugin, developers can "annotate" their Java methods and get the parameters and execution time printed to the console. In our analysis, we employ similar techniques in capturing function calls as well as measuring the execution time.

Our Results. In this paper, we give our results of performance analysis of three SSE schemes on Android devices in terms of indexing time and searching time, under (1) exact-match, (2) partial search, and (3) multi-keyword queries. The three schemes are implemented in Java so that it is completely compatible and testable in Android devices.

3   Analysis Approach

3.1   Introduction

Our analysis is divided into several phases. In the initial phase, a library skeleton, an Android client App and a web service are created. At the beginning, these three objects contain only a few classes and simple user interface. Then, three SSE schemes are chosen and implemented in Java. We integrate the newly implemented schemes into the library skeleton. Performance tests are conducted to test the actual impact when running on our Android phone. We made use the AspectJ library in measuring CPU time. In the next phase, we proceed to develop the corresponding Android App (client) and the supportive web service (server). The client allows users to upload documents stored in their phone to cloud storage in an encrypted format. It also provides the interface for searching uploaded documents. As for the web service, it mainly supports three primary functions: (1) document indexes storage; (2) search request handling; (3) statistics (for both client/server) recording for evaluation. To ensure the maximum degree of compatibility and promote code reuse, both the client and server applications are written in Java.

3.2   Software Architecture

As searchable encryption schemes assume a client-server setting, we followed this design when implementing our system. The system can be spitted into two logical parts - the **Client** and the **Server**. The **Client** consists of four components. Our **Android App** uses the Android API for the user interface and other built-in functions. The **SSE Client Library** contains a subset of the logics and functions that would be used in SSE schemes. Our App employs the **Google Play Service API** to authenticate Google accounts and storing encrypted documents to the cloud. These encrypted documents were stored at user's own Google Drive storage. We target on Android API level 19 as the minimum API because it supports both Dalvik and Android Runtime (ART). We could switch between ARTs and compare the performance difference efficiently. The **Server** part contains four components. The **Web Service** runs a Java Web application and utilizes Tomcat API for HTTP service. The **SSE Server Library** contains utility functions which allows the Web Service to perform comparison between search tokens and stored search indexes. Taking into account that the search indexes could be large in size, the Web Service stores the search indexes at the database server to facilitate near-constant time of retrieval. The **JDBC Library** were used for database related operations.

3.3   Hardware Architecture

Similar to our software design, we adopt client-server approach in hardware architecture. There are three servers: (1) **Query Server**, (2) **Database Server** and (3) **Cloud-based Storage Server**. When the end user uploads a document, the **Android Client** sends both the encrypted document and search indexes to the network. The search indexes will be forwarded to the **Query Server**. The **Query Server** stores the received search indexes into the **Database Server** for later search operations. As for the encrypted document, it will be routed to and stored into the **Cloud-based Storage Server**. In this paper, we are referring Google Drive as the **Cloud-based Storage Server**. For search queries, they are issued by the **Android Client**. The **Android Client** passes the query to the **Query Server**. The **Query Server** processes the query and performs retrieval with the **Database Server**. **Database Server** returns matched information to the **Query Server**. The **Query Server** returns formatted result to the **Android Client**. Based on search result, documents are retrieved from the **Cloud-based Storage Server** to **Android Client**.

3.4 Experiment Design

Our experiments on SSE schemes are coded with Java. Experiments on client device are conducted on an LG G2 D802 (Snapdragon 800 with 2 GB RAM, Android 4.4.2). This model was publicly available in 2013 and comes with a quad-core CPU. Given most of the Android phones nowadays usually come with 4+ core CPU and few GBs of RAM, we believe the capability of D802 can reflect the performance of mainstream Android phone in the current market. For the experiments on the server, they are conducted on a laptop computer (i7 2620M Dual Core 2.7 GHz, 8 GB RAM, Windows 7 x64), which hosts the web service and the database server on the same machine. In our settings, both the Android phone (WiFi) and the laptop (wired) are connected to the same LAN, so network latency is minimized. To offer a common ground for evaluation, we have selected the alt.atheism from the 20 Newsgroup Data Set [16] as the testing data. It consists of 1000 ASCII encoded documents which sized from 438 bytes to 51 kilobytes. Detailed information about this dataset can be found below (Table 1).

Table 1. Statistical information of "alt.atheism" document set

	File Size (Bytes)	Word Count per Document	Word Count per Document (Normalized)	Word length (No. of Characters)
Max	51425	11513	2524	313
Average	2558.28	403.55	212.1	6.04
Min	438	29	29	1

These 1000 text-based documents are stored in the internal storage of the client device. For each document, the client parses the content and tokenizes every line into keywords. The extracted keywords were then converted into lowercase and duplicates are removed (or "normalized"). The client processes each unique keywords (the actual method varies for different SSE schemes) and transmits the search indexes to the server. Since mobile devices usually have memory constraints, the search indexes will be uploaded to the search server upon creation and purged from the memory immediately. This approach keeps the memory usage to the minimum. As for the document files, the client performs encryption on each document and tranfers them to the cloud storage. Same as the method we used in creating search indexes, the encrypted documents will be discarded immediately once they have been uploaded to the cloud storage. Note that three implemented SSE schemes share a common method for encrypting documents, so the performance differences in file-encryption can be neglected. We use 128-bit AES in CBC mode for file-based encryption and PKCS7 padding is used to fill up empty bytes within ending block so the resulting encrypted documents would be slightly larger. All of the aforementioned tasks are carried in single-threaded, sequential approach. We have implemented three schemes which vary in terms of search index construction and query processing. In order to provide a comprehensive comparison of each scheme, our analysis also covered the performance of server side. We developed automated tests for simulating client/server communication. The test metrics include the search time of implemented SSE schemes and the required storage for storing the search indexes. Since all three implemented SSE schemes support multi-keyword searching (either implicitly or explicitly), we would also evaluate the extra overhead when more than one keyword is submitted. For our server environment, we host a single instance PostgreSQL 9.5 as our database server. We choose PostgreSQL over other RDBMS product mainly due to two reasons: (1) it is open-source and does not incur any additional cost, (2) it supports extensions which allow developers to extend database features with their favorable programming language. In our case, we developed a PostgreSQL extension using the PL/Java [16] library. This allows us to facilitate database level matching so that we do not need to fetch all indices from the database for searching. We can obtain reasonable performance while avoid using excessive memory.

3.5   Experiment Implementation

For the client-side experiments, we make use of AspectJ library in measuring the actual CPU time of the testing subject. To minimize confusion on existing classes, we have created a separate Android module for storing AspectJ related code. This module contains three Java classes StopWatch, PrefMon, and TraceAspect. The StopWatch class is a Java bean which contains two variables, one for storing the start time and the other one stores the end time of method execution. The PrefMon class is a marker interface which is used to annotate methods to be tested. In our experiments, information will be captured from the annotated methods only. During compilation, methods annotated by PrefMon will have additional code "injected". The code injection process is done behind the scene and does not require intervention by the developer. The injected code exposes runtime information to the TraceAspect class. Through the TraceAspect class, we can learn runtime information about the method being invoked (e.g., method name, signature, parameters and their data type) or manipulate the parameters on the fly.

Since our goal is to measure the execution time, we create a StopWatch variable for storing the timestamp before/after the function calls. By computing the delta between two timestamps, we get the elapsed time of each function call. The TraceAspect class consolidates captured information (e.g., execution time, method name, input size, and number of keywords) and uploads to the remote server for further analysis and evaluation. Similar to the way we handled the search indexes, these key information will be pushed to the server and discarded immediately at the client device.

For the server side experiments, we used the JUnit [13] library and Apache HttpComponents [11] for our tests. We first extracted all unique keywords (around 350 K keywords, extracted with the same logic as search indexes construction) from our testing dataset and put them into one set, S. During our tests, we randomly sampled one thousand keywords from S, created and submitted the search token to the server. We used the *org.apache.http.impl.client.CloseableHttpClient* to submit POST requests to the server. Then, we counted the duration starting from the time that the client issues a request to the point when the server returns the result to the client. All the above tasks were handled in single-threaded sequential order, in which a single-client environment is simulated.

4 Our SSE Code Implementations

4.1 SUISE

We adopted the SSE scheme suggested by Hahn and Kerschbaum [10] and implemented SUISE as our first SSE scheme. SUISE is IND-CCA2 secure. It consists of six operations and most computationally intensive operations such as index construction and file encryption are handled by the client. In contrast, the server side does not involve many complex operations apart from the search operations. SUISE features dynamic secure index and efficient query processing. The client is allowed to change the document contents after initial outsourcing and alter the search index accordingly. Hash table is used in inverted indexing to facilitate quick searches. Another key design is the use of caching on improving substantial query performance. In their proposal, the client is the only one who possesses the keys. Any other parties including the storage and search server do not have access to the keys. The scheme makes use of the keyed hash function and random salt in creating search index that is "blind". Therefore, even the communication channel or servers are compromised, attackers still cannot access to the original information. In our implementation, we use *javax.security.SecureRandom* class to generate the random salt. This class is commonly used in Java cryptography applications. HMAC-MD5 is used to construct search indexes and generating search tokens. Using SHA family algorithms can result in larger search indexes, and of course, the incurred memory overhead is also higher. Therefore, MD5 is used in our final implementation.

Moreover, there is possibility of enabling substring searching for this scheme by enumerating all substrings when building index and then we can match it during the search phase. On the basis of this idea, we further extended SUISE to support substring search and named them as SUISE2. SUISE2 supports prefix-based partial search (e.g., uses "t","ta", "tax","taxi" to match "taxi") and requires additional $n - 1$ storage for indexing where n is length of the keyword.

4.2   VASST16

For the second SSE scheme, we implemented the scheme by Vasudha Arora and Tyagi [2] (VASST16). Unlike other traditional Boolean-based SSE schemes, the document sorting feature is incorporated into this scheme. The relevancy sorting feature is essential to any retrieval system, especially when searching through a large document collection. The scheme uses TF-IDF (Term Frequency and Inverse Document Frequency) as weighting method, where TF refers to how many times the keyword occurred within a single document, and IDF refers to the number of documents containing a particular keyword. Every document is sorted by their TF-IDF scores in descending order, and Top-K (where K is the desired number of result) results are returned to the client. In their construction, the generation of search index is a twofold encryption process. The client first generates a secret key and large random number x. Each extracted keywords are encrypted into a token using a deterministic encryption algorithm, and then further encrypted. The final value could be extremely large if the token is long. To reduce the token size, we selected AES128 in CTR mode with no padding for 1st round encryption. Taking into account the final value can be large, Java's primitive data types (e.g. long, double) are not sufficient to store the value without losing precision. Therefore, the *java.math.BigDecimal* class is used when implementing this scheme. Since the TF-IDF method does not only cater the individual term occurrences but also looking into the overall document frequency within the whole document collection, the system is designed to scan through whole document collection to compute the IDF component. Therefore, it can take a considerable amount of RAM and it does not fit well in memory constrained settings. In addition, if any new documents are being added to the document collection, the TF-IDF score would become inaccurate because the total number of document (IDF) has changed. In other words, we need to rebuild the search index and update the server again. To address this problem, we have modified the original scheme to fit our settings. In our implementation, we delegated the IDF calculation to the server. When creating search index, we computed only the term frequency of the keywords only. We used the tuple T = (SearchToken, Frequency) to store the encrypted index accompany with its term frequency.

Because we skipped the IDF component during the index phase, we computed it at search time instead. The search server is responsible for computing the IDF component upon request. We first retrieved (1) the number of matched documents, (2) the total number of documents including those unmatch items and (3) matched index entries and their frequency from the database. Based on this information, we calculated the TF-IDF score of each document and sorted them in descending order. All these calculation were done at the server side. In the end, the top-10 most relevant documents are returned.

Similar to SUISE2 which supports substring searching. We have implemented another version, called VASST16-2, that supports prefix-based partial search, so that the performance of the schemes chosen can be properly compared.

4.3   CHLH15

When searching is performed, it is common for us to enter only certain parts of keyword for searching. From the user perspective, these kinds of partial search method are intuitive and helpful in locating relevant documents. And it is widely used in some popular search engines such as Google and Bing. While these partial search method can bring users great convenience, they also come with a cost. A classic example is that database queries with partial search components generally run slower than exact-match. In the field of searchable encryption, the same concept applies. Encryption attempts to transform user data into scrambled and randomized message to secure data secrecy, but the process itself also breaks the relationship between character and word. In our first implementation, we tried a way to retain the character-word relationship by enumerating all possible substrings within a word. The drawback of this approach is that it can take a considerable amount of index storage, and is inefficient for both index construction and search.

To solve this problem, Changhui Hu and Lidong Han [12] proposed a new scheme (CHLH15). In their proposal, they feed each individual characters of keyword plus its position into a Bloom Filter (Index BF) and then store this filter to the cloud. During the search phase, they use the same method to create another Bloom Filter (Trapdoor BF) and submit to the server. The server side performs bitwise AND operation with the Index BF and Trapdoor BF. If the bitwise result does not equal to the keyword filter, the document does not contains the keyword; if the bitwise result matches with the keyword filter, this document *may* contain the keyword. Originally in our CHLH15 implementation, we attempted to use the Bloom Filter (BF) from the Guava library [9]. However, we encountered an "Android Dex Over 64K Methods" error when compiling it with Android Studio. This is because Guava contains too many classes and methods that cannot be compiled into Android's Dex format. Eventually, we chose Magnus Skjegstad's Bloom Filter [14] as our concrete BF implementation. Magnus's implementation contains only one class and it depends on the Java/Android API only, which is relatively easy to integrate into existing code. In addition, Magnus's implementation provides sophisticated control over several performance-critical parameters, such as expected false positive rate and number of expected elements.

Back to our CHLH15 implementation details. Due to the memory constraints, we have modified CHLH15 to fit into mobile device settings. In original construct, only single Index BF is created and the whole document collection will share the same BF. In our implementation, we will create a separate set of Bloom Filter for each individual document. In other words, for a collection of m documents, we will get m Bloom Filter entries instead of one. After our modification, the required index space is now having a linear relation with the total number of document, so there will be a performance penalty if the document collection is large. On the other hand, our modification also comes with some benefits. As comparatively less keyword is being added to the same Bloom Filter, it helps to maintain the false positive rate at a low level. In addition, the index update cost is reduced when changing document contents. For any changes made on a single document, we just need to recreate the Bloom Filter for that particular document and update the server.

5   Performance Comparison

In this section, we evaluate the three schemes in terms of indexing and search speed under single keyword and multi-keyword queries (Table 2).

Table 2. Security and Functional Comparisons of the Three Schemes

	SUISE	VASST16	CHLH15
Security	IND-CCA2	IND-CPA	IND-CCA2
Partial Search	Support[a]	Support[a]	Native
Multi-keyword	Support	Support	Support
Index-Length	Fixed	Variable	Fixed

[a] via all-substring enumeration index approach

5.1   Performance Comparison for Single Keyword Exact-Match Queries

For single keyword exact-match queries, SUISE has the fastest indexing speed among all implemented schemes. On average, it takes 100ms to compute, which is 20% of CHLH15 and 10% of VASST16. CHLH15 has the medium performance. It takes 0.5 ms by average to process a single document. VASST16 has the worst indexing performance, which takes 1s because of the computational expensiveness in the 2nd round encryption (Table 3).

Table 3. Average Index Building and Searching Time of SUISE/VASST16/CHLH15 (per file, in milliseconds)

	SUISE	VASST16	CHLH15
Index Building Time (ms)	99.767	1054.253	506.72
Searching Time (ms)	1781.547	544.447	909.503

From the searching point of view, VASST16 has the fastest response time. On average, it takes half a second to process a single-keyword query. The second rank belongs to CHLH15, where it takes nearly 1 s to return the search result. For the slowest scheme, SUISE takes 1.8 s to process.

To understand why SUISE performs significantly less efficient in searching, it is essential to understand the differences between their index designs. In VASST16 and CHLH15, the information stored at the index are static. The search token received are in the same form as the one stored at the search server. During searching, the token is submitted to the server for one-to-many equality test. There are no additional steps to compute. In contrast, SUISE's index design is dynamic. For every token received, the server needs compute a new HMAC digest before using it for equality test. Therefore, the searching speed is significantly slower.

5.2 Performance Comparison for Single Keyword Partial Search Queries

After including all prefixes during the indexing phase, SUISE2 remains the fastest schemes in indexing documents. Its performance is slightly better than CHLH15, with approximately 100 ms faster. VASST16-2's indexing speed remains the last, which takes around 4 s to index a document (Table 4).

Table 4. Average Index Build Time of SUISE2/VASST16-2/CHLH15 (per file, in Milliseconds)

	SUISE2	VASST16-2	CHLH15
Index Building Time (ms)	384.235	3957.9	506.72
Searching Time (ms)	6890.219	2105.675	909.503

For the search time of partial search queries, CHLH15 has the best performance in terms of prefix-based queries. It requires 900 ms to process, which is around 50% of VASST16-2 and 14% of SUISE2. As the number of index entries increase, more comparisons have to be done at the server side. From these tests, we can identify the competitive advantages of CHLH15 over other schemes. Because the number of index of CHLH15 is linear to the document count, it prevents an excessive amount of index entries from slowing down the processing time of searching. We did not further test our VASST16 implementation against the all-substring indexing method. But given the poor performance of indexing method (SUISE2 and VASST16-2), we expect the resulting speed is even worst.

5.3 Performance Comparison of Multi-keyword Exact-Match Queries

We consolidate the searching time information of three schemes in Table 5. The searching performance of SUISE scales with the number of the keyword used.

For any new keyword added, the search time of SUISE is increased by 1000 ms. In contrast, VASST16 and CHLH15 are less sensitive to the keyword count. The performance of these schemes does not deteriorate much when additional keywords submitted.

Table 5. Average Searching Time for Multi-Keywords of SUISE/VASST16/CHLH15 (in Milliseconds)

No. of Keywords	2	3	4	5	6	7	8	9	10
SUISE	2774	4361	5695	6399	7957	8638	10709	12195	13753
VASST16	459	448	393	443	414	475	516	498	522
CHLH15	672	670	780	645	648	638	651	649	630

6   Performance Analysis

For SUISE, preliminary test results show that file-based encryption is reasonably efficient at the client side, but the index construction could be a problem when the document is large. The construction time is linear to the number of words, which is not desirable for lengthy documents. Moreover, we have explored the possibility of enabling partial search in SUISE without extensive modification on the scheme. Results show that it is feasible, but at the cost of heavy processing at both the client and server sides. Prolonged indexing time and query response time can lead to an undesirable user experience. For VASST16, the document sorting feature from VASST16 has caught our attention, but we have experienced difficulties in realizing it due to memory constraints. In addition, it is observed that Android's "big number" constructs are fairly computationally expensive. Accordingly, the 2nd level encryption of the VASST16 has suffered performance penalty at the client side. Despite its usefulness in finding a needle in a haystack, it seems that our Android implementation needs further optimization before it reaches an acceptable performance. As for our 3rd SSE scheme, test results show that CHLH15 have satisfactory index creation speed and quick response time. Nevertheless, its sensitiveness to the false positive rate and immutable nature have restricted the use cases. For instance, developers must be aware of the number of items to be indexed or the underlying data structure will get saturated. This limited the scalability and extensibility when deploying on a real application. In the light of our comparison result, it is observed that SUISE has the best indexing performance under exact match queries, and has minimal impact on the client devices. Nevertheless, due to the complexity of the search token-index comparison, it requires the longest process time for searching. Application users may not feel comfortable with the prolonged search time. For functional reasons, VASST16 requires the most computational time at the client side but the scheme does not show advantages that could overweight the cost in return. Yet, the existence of VASST16 proves that document relevancy sorting under SSE is feasible, though further development and optimization is necessary. CHLH15 balanced the indexing time and searching time under partial search queries. Users can obtain a reasonable response time in searching while having minimal computation overhead on their devices.

7 Conclusion

The rise of cloud data outsourcing brings us convenience and cost saving, but it also leads to security and privacy problems. Existing proposal of searchable encryption schemes attempts to strike a balance between usability and data privacy, but at the cost of high computational requirement. While this may be acceptable in the desktop/laptop environment, the actual impact on mobile devices remains unanswered. In an effort to answer the question, we have chosen three recent SSE schemes from literature, implemented them and compare their performance in Android mobile devices. We explored several existing Java profiling tools and found that most of them are not compatible with the Android platform due to structural differences in the runtime environment. We developed a new module for capturing and storing the benchmarking results. We performed an analysis on the indexing time and searching time, under (1) exact-match, (2) partial search, and (3) multi-keyword queries. We believe that our research provides insights to mobile App developers about the computational requirements of various SSE schemes for applications in mobile devices.

References

1. Android. Android monitor basics (2018). https://developer.android.com/studio/profile/am-basics. Accessed 4 May 2018
2. Arora, V., Tyagi, S.: An efficient multi-keyword symmetric searchable encryption scheme for secure data outsourcing. Int. J. Comput. Netw. Inf. Secur. **8**(11), 65–71 (2016)
3. Bellare, M., Boldyreva, A., O'Neill, A.: Deterministic and efficiently searchable encryption. In: Menezes, A. (ed.) CRYPTO 2007. LNCS, vol. 4622, pp. 535–552. Springer, Heidelberg (2007). https://doi.org/10.1007/978-3-540-74143-5_30
4. Boldyreva, A., Chenette, N., Lee, Y., O'Neill, A.: Order-preserving symmetric encryption. In: Joux, A. (ed.) EUROCRYPT 2009. LNCS, vol. 5479, pp. 224–241. Springer, Heidelberg (2009). https://doi.org/10.1007/978-3-642-01001-9_13
5. Boneh, D., Sahai, A., Waters, B.: Functional encryption: definitions and challenges. In: Ishai, Y. (ed.) TCC 2011. LNCS, vol. 6597, pp. 253–273. Springer, Heidelberg (2011). https://doi.org/10.1007/978-3-642-19571-6_16
6. Eclipse Foundation. The aspectj project (2018). http://www.eclipse.org/aspectj/. Accessed 4 May 2018
7. Goh, E.: Secure indexes. IACR Cryptology ePrint Archive 2003, 216 (2003)
8. Goldreich, O., Ostrovsky, R.: Software protection and simulation on oblivious rams. J. ACM **43**(3), 431–473 (1996)
9. Google: google/guava (2018). https://github.com/google/guava. Accessed 4 May 2018

10. Hahn, F., Kerschbaum, F.: Searchable encryption with secure and efficient updates. In: Proceedings of the 2014 ACM SIGSAC Conference on Computer and Communications Security, Scottsdale, AZ, USA, 3–7 November 2014, pp. 310–320 (2014)
11. Hc.apache.org. Apache httpcomponents (2018). https://hc.apache.org/. Accessed 4 May 2018
12. Hu, C., Han, L.: Efficient wildcard search over encrypted data. Int. J. Inf. Sec. **15**(5), 539–547 (2015)
13. Junit.org: Junit - about (2018). https://junit.org/junit4/. Accessed 4 May 2018
14. Skjegstad, M.: Magnuss/java-bloomfilter (2018). https://github.com/magnuss/java-bloomfilter. Accessed 4 May 2018
15. Song, D.X., Wagner, D.A., Perrig, A.: Practical techniques for searches on encrypted data. In: 2000 IEEE Symposium on Security and Privacy, Berkeley, California, USA, vol. 14–17, pp. 44–55, May 2000
16. Tada.github.io: Postgresql pl/java pl/java: stored procedures, triggers, and functions for postgresql (2018). https://tada.github.io/pljava/. Accessed 4 May 2018
17. Wharton, J.: Hugo (2018). https://github.com/jakeWharton/hugo. Accessed 4 May 2018

Anonymous Attribute-Based Conditional Proxy Re-encryption

Xianping Mao[1], Xuefeng Li[1], Xiaochuan Wu[1], Chuansheng Wang[2],
and Junzuo Lai[2(✉)]

[1] ZhongAn Information Technology Service Co., Ltd., Shanghai, China
xpmoore@gmail.com, {linco.li,wuxiaochuan}@zhongan.io
[2] Jinan Univesity, Guangzhou, China
chueng0828@126.com, laijunzuo@gmail.com

Abstract. Attribute-based conditional proxy re-encryption (AB-CPRE) enables ciphertext owners to carry out fine-grained decryption delegation control. In AB-CPRE schemes, we observe that the attributes associated with ciphertexts are explicitly stored along with the ciphertexts. This property is not appropriate for certain applications where attributes contain sensitive information.

We consider a new requirement for AB-CPRE: *anonymity*. Specifically, anonymity guarantees that no one, except users with corresponding secret keys, can gain any knowledge about the attributes related to a ciphertext. We give the formal model of anonymous AB-CPRE and propose a concrete construction. We prove that our proposed scheme is both secure and anonymous, without relying on random oracles.

Keywords: Proxy re-encryption · Attribute-based encryption
Anonymity

1 Introduction

In 1998, Blaze et al. introduced the notion of Proxy Re-encryption (PRE) [5]. In a PRE system, a ciphertext forwarded to Alice can be transformed into an encryption under Bob's public key by a semi-trust proxy. The security requirement is that the privacy of the involved plaintext messages should be preserved throughout the transformation, that is, the proxy learns no knowledge from the involved ciphertexts. PRE has many practical applications, such as encrypted email forwarding [5], secure distributed file storage systems [2], digital rights management (DRM) [26,28], privacy preserving in anonymity revocation [27].

It is worth noting that, in traditional PRE, the proxy is able to transform *all* the ciphertexts under Alice's public key into ones for Bob, once the re-encryption key has been received. This might be undesirable because it involved some Alice's personal files that should remain secret from Bob. In order to solve this problem, Tang proposed a type-based PRE scheme [29] and Weng et al. introduced conditional PRE system [31], respectively. Although different

M. H. Au et al. (Eds.): NSS 2018, LNCS 11058, pp. 95–110, 2018.
https://doi.org/10.1007/978-3-030-02744-5_7

in naming, type-based PRE and conditional PRE are essentially the same. In such systems, each ciphertext is generated along with a certain attribute, and the re-encryption key is related to a condition, which is a specific value. The proxy is able to convert a ciphertext only if the condition in the re-encryption key is equal to the attribute associated with this ciphertext. Although, compared with traditional PRE, conditional PRE implements delegation of decryption rights to some extent, the condition expression is not flexible enough for practical applications. For instance, Alice is on business trip from 10/04/2018 to 20/04/2018, and she wants Bob to process the emails from Company D during this period of time, i.e. Alice wants the proxy to transform her ciphertexts received between "10/04/2018–20/04/2018" from Company D into the ciphertexts under Bob's public key. Apparently, conditional PRE cannot support such expressive conditions. To address this issue of expressiveness on condition, Zhao et al. [32] proposed an attribute-based conditional proxy re-encryption scheme (AB-CPRE) by combining key-policy attribute-based encryption with conditional PRE. In their scheme, each ciphertext is associated with attributes featuring this file, and the re-encryption key is related to a policy. With a re-encryption key, the proxy is able to transform the ciphertexts whose associated attributes satisfy the policy embedded in the re-encryption key. We observe that the associated attributes are explicitly stored along with the ciphertext in their scheme. This property is not appropriate for certain applications where attributes contain sensitive information. We illustrate this important property of hiding ciphertexts' associated attributes with the following example.

Imagine that a department manager, Alice, is away for vacation and she wants to delegate Bob to process the received emails sent by Company E or Company F. A number of emails with different attribute sets were sent to Alice during her vacation. They contained ones sent by her friends, by hospitals, by some magazine companies whose products Alice has subscribed to, and so on. They were encrypted before transmitting in order to preserve the data's privacy. For flexible access control on decryption delegation, every encrypted email was associated with certain attributes that can describe the corresponding ciphertext. Alice specified a policy describing that only emails from Company E or Company F can be handled by Bob. With this policy, her own secret key and Bob's public key, Alice generated by herself a re-encryption key from Alice to Bob. With a corresponding re-encryption key generated by Alice, the email server can transform the ciphertexts satisfying the policy embedded in the re-encryption key into the encrypted emails under Bob's public key. Note that in a system with plain emails' attributes, the email server might learn that Alice probably went to hospital to take some disease testing, and what kinds of magazines that Alice was interested in. The inference about Alice's disease history might have an impact on her daily life, and the magazine subscriptions may expose Alice's hobby and disposition for recreation. Additionally, it could possibly result in leaking some sensitive information to some commercial cooperations, even though the complete and exact content remains secret from the server (refer to Fig. 1). Obviously, this is not the situation that Alice expects to be. These personal and sensitive data should be completely shrouded (i.e., guaranteeing *payload-hiding* and *attribute-hiding* simultaneously).

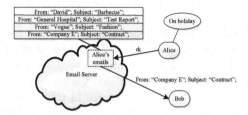

Fig. 1. Attribute-based conditional proxy re-encryption

The above observations show the necessity of hiding ciphertexts' attributes from prying eyes in certain applications. Therefore, it motivates us to study attribute-based conditional proxy re-encryption scheme (AB-CPRE) supporting attribute-hiding in this paper.

1.1 Our Contributions

In this paper, we first modify the model of AB-CPRE in [32] to allow for anonymity of the original ciphertexts. After describing the formal definition of anonymous AB-CPRE, we construct a concrete anonymous AB-CPRE scheme based on this new model. Finally, we prove our proposed scheme in the sense of both security and anonymity, without relying on random oracles.

1.2 Related Work

In this section, we summarize the major related works in the areas of attribute-based encryption and proxy re-encryption.

Attribute-Based Encryption. The notion of ABE was first introduced by Sahai and Waters as an application of their fuzzy identity-based encryption (IBE) scheme [25]. In such an ABE system, both ciphertexts and secret keys are associated with attributes. The decryption on a ciphertext will succeed if and only if the attribute set for the ciphertext and the one for the secret key overlap by at least a fixed threshold value k. In 2006, Goyal et al. [14] formalized two complimentary forms of ABE: KP-ABE and CP-ABE. In a CP-ABE scheme, decryption keys are associated with attribute sets and ciphertexts are associated with access structures, while, in a KP-ABE, the situation is reversed (i.e., decryption keys are associated with access structures and ciphertexts are associated with attribute sets). Later, Goyal et al. [13] proposed a general method for transformation from KP-ABE to CP-ABE.

In terms of the expressive power of access structures, Goyal et al. [14] presented the first KP-ABE supporting monotonic access structures. To enable more flexible access control policy, Ostrovsky et al. [24] proposed a KP-ABE system that can support the expression of non-monotone formulas in key policies. The problem of building KP-ABE systems with multiple authorities was investigated in [9,10,22]. Recently, Lewko and Waters [20] proposed a KP-ABE scheme which is "unbounded" in the sense that the public parameters do not impose additional limitations on the functionality of the scheme.

On the other hand, Bethencourt et al. [4] proposed the first concrete CP-ABE construction and proved it secure under the generic group model. Later, Cheung and Newport [11] proposed an CP-ABE scheme that is secure under the standard model; however, the access structures in this scheme are restricted to AND operation of different attributes. Recently, secure and expressive CP-ABE schemes [18,30] were proposed. CP-ABE schemes with multiple authorities were also studied in [19,23].

Proxy Re-encryption. In 1998, Blaze et al. [5] introduced the concept of proxy re-encryption. Such proxy re-encryption system allows a proxy, using a re-encryption key, to transform an encryption of m under Alice's public key into an encryption of the same m under Bob's public key without the proxy learning anything about the encrypted message m. Blaze et al. classified PRE schemes into two types: one is *multi-hop*, i.e., the ciphertext can be transformed from Alice to Bob, then to Charlie and so on; the other one is *single-hop*, i.e., the ciphertext can only be transformed once. According to the direction of transformation, PRE schemes can also be categorized into two types: one is *bidirectional*, i.e., the proxy can convert from Alice to Bob and vice versa; the other one is *unidirectional*, i.e., the proxy can only convert in one direction. Until now, many different PRE schemes and different variants of PRE with different security properties have been proposed [1,2,5,7,12,15,16,21,31] since the advent of PRE [5].

In 2010, Zhao et al. [32] combined key-policy attribute-based encryption with conditional proxy re-encryption to propose an attribute-based conditional PRE scheme. Since then, because of its fine-grained delegation control, AB-CPRE has attracted much more attention. But in these schemes, they do not take account of attribute-hiding.

1.3   Organization

The rest of paper is organized as follows. In Sect. 2, we review some standard notations and cryptographic definitions. In Sect. 3, we describe the basic definition of anonymous attribute-based conditional proxy re-encryption and the corresponding models for it. Then a concrete construction of anonymous AB-CPRE is presented in Sect. 4. Details of the security proofs of the proposed construction follows. In Sect. 5, we state our conclusion.

2   Preliminaries

If S is a set, then $s \xleftarrow{\$} S$ denotes the operation of picking an element s uniformly at random from S. Let $\mathbb{N}$ denote the set of natural numbers. If $\lambda \in \mathbb{N}$ then 1^λ

denotes the string of λ ones. Let $z \leftarrow \mathsf{A}(x, y, \ldots)$ denote the operation of running an algorithm A with inputs $(x, y, \ldots)$ and output z. A function $f(\lambda)$ is *negligible* if for every $c > 0$ there exists a λ_c such that $f(\lambda) < 1/\lambda^c$ for all $\lambda > \lambda_c$.

2.1 Access Structures

Definition 1 (Access Structure [3]). *Let* $\{P_1, \ldots, P_n\}$ *be a set of parties. A collection* $\mathbb{A} \subseteq 2^{\{P_1, \ldots, P_n\}}$ *is monotone if* $\forall B, C :$ *if* $B \in \mathbb{A}$ *and* $B \subseteq C$, *then* $C \in \mathbb{A}$. *An access structure (respectively, monotone access structure) is a collection (respectively, monotone collection)* $\mathbb{A}$ *of non-empty subsets of* $\{P_1, \ldots, P_n\}$, *i.e.,* $\mathbb{A} \subseteq 2^{\{P_1, \ldots, P_n\}} \backslash \{\emptyset\}$. *The sets in* $\mathbb{A}$ *are called authorized sets, and the sets not in* $\mathbb{A}$ *are called unauthorized sets.*

In our context, attributes play the role of parties and we restrict our attention to monotone access structures. It is possible to (inefficiently) realize general access structures using our techniques by treating the negation of an attribute as a separate attribute.

2.2 Linear Secret Sharing Schemes

Our construction will employ linear secret-sharing schemes. We use the definition adapted from [3]:

Definition 2 (Linear Secret-Sharing Schemes (LSSS)). *A secret sharing scheme* Π *over a set of parties* $\mathcal{P}$ *is called linear (over* $\mathbb{Z}_p$*) if*

1. *The shares for each party form a vector over* $\mathbb{Z}_p$.
2. *There exists a matrix* $\mathbf{A}$ *with* ℓ *rows and* n *columns called the share-generating matrix for* Π. *For all* $i = 1, \ldots, \ell$, *the* i^{th} *row of* $\mathbf{A}$ *is labeled by a party* $\rho(i)$ *(* ρ *is a function from* $\{1, \ldots, \ell\}$ *to* $\mathcal{P}$*). When we consider the column vector* $v = (s, r_2, \ldots, r_n)$, *where* $s \in \mathbb{Z}_p$ *is the secret to be shared, and* $r_2, \ldots, r_n \in \mathbb{Z}_p$ *are randomly chosen, then* $\mathbf{A}v$ *is the vector of* ℓ *shares of the secret* s *according to* Π. *The share* $(\mathbf{A}v)_i$ *belongs to party* $\rho(i)$.

It is shown in [3] that every linear secret-sharing scheme according to the above definition also enjoys the linear reconstruction property, defined as follows. Suppose that Π is an LSSS for the access structure $\mathbb{A}$. Let $S \in \mathbb{A}$ be any authorized set, and let $I \subset \{1, \ldots, \ell\}$ be defined as $I = \{i | \rho(i) \in S\}$. Then there exist constants $\{\omega_i \in \mathbb{Z}_p\}_{i \in I}$ such that, if $\{\lambda_i\}$ are valid shares of any secret s according to Π, then $\sum_{i \in I} \omega_i \lambda_i = s$. Let A_i denotes the ith row of $\mathbf{A}$, we have $\sum_{i \in I} \omega_i A_i = (1, 0, \ldots, 0)$. These constants $\{\omega_i\}$ can be found in time polynomial in the size of the share-generation matrix $\mathbf{A}$ [3]. Note that, for unauthorized sets, no such constants $\{\omega_i\}$ exist.

Boolean Formulas. Access structures might also be described in terms of monotonic boolean formulas. Using standard techniques [3] one can convert any monotonic boolean formula into an LSSS representation. We can represent the boolean formula as an access tree. An access tree of ℓ nodes will result in an LSSS matrix of ℓ rows. We refer the reader to the appendix of [19] for a discussion on how to perform this conversion.

2.3 Composite Order Bilinear Groups and Complexity Assumptions

We will construct our scheme using both prime order bilinear groups and composite order ones whose order is the product of four distinct primes.

Let $\mathcal{G}$ be an algorithm that takes as input a security parameter λ and outputs a tuple $(p, \mathbb{G}, \mathbb{G}_T, e)$, where $\mathbb{G}$ and $\mathbb{G}_T$ are multiplicative cyclic groups of prime order p, and $e : \mathbb{G} \times \mathbb{G} \rightarrow \mathbb{G}_T$ is a map such that:

1. **Bilinearity:** $e(g^a, h^b) = e(g, h)^{ab}$ for all $g, h \in \mathbb{G}$ and $a, b \in \mathbb{Z}_p^*$.
2. **Non-degeneracy:** $e(g, h) \neq 1$ whenever $g, h \neq 1_\mathbb{G}$.
3. **Computability:** efficient computability for any input pair.

We refer to the tuple $(p, \mathbb{G}, \mathbb{G}_T, e)$ as a *prime order bilinear group*.

Composite order bilinear groups were first introduced in [6]. They have similar property to that of prime order bilinear groups. $\mathbb{G}$ and $\mathbb{G}_T$ are cyclic groups of order $N = p_1 p_2 p_3 p_4$ and e is a bilinear map $\mathbb{G} \times \mathbb{G} \rightarrow \mathbb{G}_T$, where p_1, p_2, p_3, p_4 are distinct primes. Bilinearity, Non-degeneracy and Computability all work for $g, h \in \mathbb{G}, a, b \in \mathbb{Z}_N$. We refer to the tuple $(p_1, p_2, p_3, p_4, \mathbb{G}, \mathbb{G}_T, e)$ as a *composite order bilinear group*. Additionally, we use $\mathbb{G}_{p_1}, \mathbb{G}_{p_2}, \mathbb{G}_{p_3}, \mathbb{G}_{p_4}$ to denote the subgroups of $\mathbb{G}$ having order p_1, p_2, p_3, p_4, respectively. Observe that $\mathbb{G} = \mathbb{G}_{p_1} \times \mathbb{G}_{p_2} \times \mathbb{G}_{p_3} \times \mathbb{G}_{p_4}$. Note also that if $g_1 \in \mathbb{G}_{p_1}$ and $g_2 \in \mathbb{G}_{p_2}$ then $e(g_1, g_2) = 1$. A similar rule holds whenever e is applied to elements in distinct subgroups.

Definition 3. *3-weak Decision Bilinear Diffie-Hellman Inversion assumption. Given* $(g, g^a, g^{a^2}, g^{a^3}, g^b, T)$ *with unknown* $a, b \in \mathbb{Z}_p^*$, *a* (t, ϵ)-*distinguisher* $\mathcal{B}$ *breaks the assumption if it runs in time* t *and*

$$\left| \Pr[\mathcal{B}(g, g^a, g^{a^2}, g^{a^3}, g^b, e(g,g)^{b/a}) = 1] - \Pr[\mathcal{B}(g, g^a, g^{a^2}, g^{a^3}, xg^b, T) = 1] \right| \leq \epsilon.$$

3 Formal Model of Anonymous AB-CPRE

According to the definition of AB-CPRE in [32], the resulting ciphertext output by algorithm $\mathsf{Encrypt}(\mathsf{PK}, m, D = (d_1, \ldots, d_n))$ is generated along with $(d_1, \ldots, d_n)$ explicitly. On the contrary, anonymous AB-CPRE requires that no plain $D = (d_1, \ldots, d_n)$ would appear in the ciphertext. Generally, considering unidirectional type, an anonymous AB-CPRE scheme consists of the following six algorithms:

Setup(1^λ): Taking as input a security parameter λ, it generates the global parameters *params*. (For brevity, we assume that *params* is implicitly included in the input to the rest algorithms.)

KeyGen(i): Taking as input user identity i, it generates the public/secret key pair $(\mathsf{PK}_i, \mathsf{SK}_i)$ for user i.

Encrypt($\mathsf{PK}, m, D = (d_1, \ldots, d_n)$): Taking as input a public key PK, a plaintext $m \in \mathcal{M}$ and a set of attributes $D = (d_1, \ldots, d_n)$, it outputs ciphertext CT associated with D under pk (note that, unlike the AB-CPRE scheme in [32], this resulting CT does not contain plain attribute set D).

RKeyGen($\mathsf{SK}_i, \mathsf{PK}_j, \mathcal{P}$): Taking as input user i's secret key SK_i, j's public key PK_j and a policy structure $\mathcal{P}$, it outputs a re-encryption key $\mathsf{RK}_{i\leftarrow j}$. This algorithm is run by user i.

ReEncrypt($\mathsf{RK}_{i\rightarrow j}, CT_i$): Taking as input a re-encryption key $rk_{i,j}$ associated with policy structure $\mathcal{P}$ and a ciphertext CT_i labeled by attribute set D under public key PK_i, it outputs a re-encrypted ciphertext CT_j under public key pk_j if D satisfies the policy structure $\mathcal{P}$ (i.e., $\mathcal{P}(D) = 1$).

Decrypt(CT, SK): Taking as input a original/re-encrypted ciphertext CT and a secret key SK, it outputs a plaintext $m \in \mathcal{M}$ or a symbol $\perp$ indicating failure on decryption.

We now describe the security (i.e. *payload-hiding*) and anonymity (i.e. *attribute-hiding*) for AB-CPRE, respectively. Firstly, by security, it means that we guarantee the privacy on plaintext. We consider the *replayable* CCA security introduced in [8] where a harmless mauling of the challenge ciphertext is tolerated.

Security of Original Ciphertexts. At the beginning of this security game, the challenger chooses keys for corrupt and honest parties, and the challenge user key is among the honest parties. The RCCA security for AB-CPRE on original ciphertexts is defined using the following game, Game_O, between a challenger and an adversary:

Setup. The challenger $\mathcal{B}$ runs $\mathsf{Setup}(1^\lambda)$ to obtain the public parameters *params*. It gives the public parameters *params* to the adversary $\mathcal{A}$.

Phase 1. $\mathcal{A}$ adaptively issues queries $q_1, \ldots, q_m$ to the challenger $\mathcal{B}$, where query q_i is one of the following:

- Uncorrupted key generation query(i): $\mathcal{B}$ first runs algorithm $\mathsf{KeyGen}(i)$ to obtain a public/secret key pair $(\mathsf{PK}_i, \mathsf{SK}_i)$, and then sends PK_i to $\mathcal{A}$.
- Corrupted key generation query(j): $\mathcal{B}$ first runs algorithm $\mathsf{KeyGen}(j)$ to obtain a public/secret key pair $(\mathsf{PK}_j, \mathsf{SK}_j)$, and then gives $(\mathsf{PK}_j, \mathsf{SK}_j)$ to $\mathcal{A}$.
- Re-encryption key generation query($\mathsf{PK}_i, \mathsf{PK}_j, \mathcal{P}$): $\mathcal{B}$ runs algorithm $\mathsf{RKeyGen}(\mathsf{SK}_i, \mathsf{PK}_j, \mathcal{P})$ to generate a re-encryption key $\mathsf{RK}_{i\leftarrow j}$ and returns it to $\mathcal{A}$. Here SK_i is the secret key corresponding to PK_i, and it is required that PK_i and PK_j were generated beforehand by algorithm KeyGen.
- Re-encryption query($\mathsf{PK}_i, \mathsf{PK}_j, CT_i, \mathcal{P}$): $\mathcal{B}$ runs algorithm $\mathsf{ReEncrypt}$ ($\mathsf{RKeyGen}(\mathsf{SK}_i, \mathsf{PK}_j, \mathcal{P}), CT_i$) and returns the resulting ciphertext CT_j to $\mathcal{A}$, if the attribute set D associated with CT_i satisfies the policy $\mathcal{P}$. It is required that PK_i and PK_j were generated beforehand by algorithm KeyGen.
- Decryption query(CT_i, PK_i): $\mathcal{B}$ returns the output of $\mathsf{Decrypt}(CT_i, \mathsf{SK}_i)$ to $\mathcal{A}$, where SK_i is corresponding to PK_i. It is required that PK_i was generated beforehand by algorithm KeyGen.

Challenge. The adversary $\mathcal{A}$ submits a target public key PK_{i^*}, a target attribute set D^* and two (equal length) messages m_0, m_1. The challenger $\mathcal{B}$ selects a random bit $\eta \in \{0, 1\}$, sets $CT^* = \mathsf{Encrypt}(\mathsf{PK}_{i^*}, m_\eta, D^*)$ and sends CT^* to $\mathcal{A}$ as its challenge ciphertext.

Phase 2. $\mathcal{A}$ continues to adaptively query the challenger $\mathcal{B}$ as in Phase 1., and $\mathcal{B}$ answers them as above, except that Decryption query(CT, PK) outputs $\perp$ if the recovered plaintext $M \in \{m_0, m_1\}$.

Guess. $\mathcal{A}$ outputs its guess $\eta' \in \{0, 1\}$ for η and wins the game if $\eta = \eta'$.

During this game, adversary $\mathcal{A}$ is subject to the following restrictions:

1. $\mathcal{A}$ cannot issue Corrupted key generation query on (i^*) to attain the target secret key SK_{i^*}.
2. $\mathcal{A}$ cannot issue Decryption query on neither $(CT^*, \mathsf{PK}_{i^*})$ nor (ReEncrypt $(\mathsf{RK}_{i^* \to j}, CT^*), \mathsf{PK}_j)$.
3. If $\mathcal{A}$ has obtained the secret key SK_j, $\mathcal{A}$ cannot issue Re-encryption query on $(\mathsf{PK}_{i^*}, \mathsf{PK}_j, CT^*, \mathcal{P})$, and vice versa.

The advantage of adversary $\mathcal{A}$ in this game is defined as

$$\mathrm{Adv}_O = \left| \Pr[\eta = \eta'] - \frac{1}{2} \right|,$$

where the probability is taken over the random bits used by the challenger and the adversary.

Definition 4. *An AB-CPRE scheme achieves RCCA security on original ciphertexts if all polynomial time adversaries have at most a negligible advantage in* Game$_O$.

Security of Transformed Ciphertexts. In this security game, for *single-hop* PRE schemes, the adversary $\mathcal{A}$ is granted access to all re-encryption keys. Since transformed cannot be re-encrypted further, there is no reason to keep adversaries from obtaining all honest-to-corrupt re-encryption keys. As all the re-encryption keys are available to $\mathcal{A}$, the re-encryption oracle becomes useless; so does the Decryption query on original ciphertexts. Therefore, the RCCA security for AB-CPRE on transformed ciphertexts is defined as follows, Game$_T$, between a challenger and an adversary:

Setup. The same as that in Game$_O$.

Phase 1. $\mathcal{A}$ adaptively issues queries $q_1, \ldots, q_m$ to the challenger $\mathcal{B}$, where query q_i is one of the following:
  - Uncorrupted key generation query(i): The same as that in Game$_O$.
  - Corrupted key generation query(j): The same as that in Game$_O$.
  - Re-encryption key generation query$(\mathsf{PK}_i, \mathsf{PK}_j, \mathcal{P})$: The same as that in Game$_O$.
  - Decryption query(CT, PK): The same as that in Game$_O$, except that it only accepts the requests on transformed ciphertexts.

Challenge. The adversary $\mathcal{A}$ submits a target delegatee public key PK_{j^*}, a target attribute set D^* and two (equal length) messages m_0, m_1. The challenger $\mathcal{B}$ selects a random bit $\eta \in \{0, 1\}$ and a delegator public key PK_i, and then sets $CT_i = \mathsf{Encrypt}(\mathsf{PK}_i, m_\eta, D^*)$. $\mathcal{B}$ proceeds to compute $\mathsf{RK}_{i \to j^*}$. After that, $\mathcal{B}$ performs $\mathsf{ReEncrypt}(\mathsf{RK}_{i \to j^*}, CT_i)$ to attain the challenge ciphertext CT^*, and sends CT^* to $\mathcal{A}$ as its challenge ciphertext.

Phase 2. The same as that in Game$_O$.

Guess. $\mathcal{A}$ outputs its guess $\eta' \in \{0,1\}$ for η and wins the game if $\eta = \eta'$.

During this game, adversary $\mathcal{A}$ is subject to the following restrictions:

1. $\mathcal{A}$ cannot issue Corrupted key generation query on (j^*) to attain the target secret key SK_{j^*}.
2. $\mathcal{A}$ cannot issue Decryption query on neither $(CT^*, \mathsf{PK}_{j^*})$.

The advantage of adversary $\mathcal{A}$ in this game is defined as

$$\mathrm{Adv}_T = \left| \mathsf{Pr}[\eta = \eta'] - \frac{1}{2} \right|,$$

where the probability is taken over the random bits used by the challenger and the adversary.

Definition 5. *An AB-CPRE scheme achieves RCCA security on transformed ciphertexts if all polynomial time adversaries have at most a negligible advantage in* Game$_T$.

Next, we describe the anonymity ensuring that an $\mathsf{Encrypt}(\mathsf{PK}, m, D)$ does not reveal any information about the associated attribute set D unless $\mathsf{RK}_{i \to j}$ with $\mathcal{P}(D) = 1$ is available. The formal game for anonymity, Game$_A$, between a challenger and an adversary is defined as follows:

Setup. The same as that in Game$_O$.

Phase 1. $\mathcal{A}$ adaptively issues queries $q_1, \ldots, q_m$ to the challenger $\mathcal{B}$, where query q_i is one of the following:

 - Uncorrupted key generation query(i): The same as that in Game$_O$.
 - Corrupted key generation query(j): The same as that in Game$_O$.
 - Re-encryption key generation query$(\mathsf{PK}_i, \mathsf{PK}_j, \mathcal{P})$: The same as that in Game$_O$.
 - Re-encryption query$(\mathsf{PK}_i, \mathsf{PK}_j, CT_i, \mathcal{P})$: The same as that in Game$_O$.
 - Decryption query(CT, PK): The same as that in Game$_O$.

Challenge. The adversary $\mathcal{A}$ submits a target public key PK_{i^*}, a target message m^* and two attribute sets D_0, D_1, subject to the restriction that neither D_0 nor D_1 can satisfy any of the queried access structures. The challenger $\mathcal{B}$ selects a random bit $\eta \in \{0,1\}$, sets $CT^* = \mathsf{Encrypt}(\mathsf{PK}_{i^*}, m^*, D_\eta)$ and sends CT^* to $\mathcal{A}$ as its challenge ciphertext.

Phase 2. $\mathcal{A}$ continues to adaptively query the challenger $\mathcal{B}$ as in Phase 1., and $\mathcal{B}$ answers them as above, except that, if $\mathcal{A}$ wants to obtain a valid re-encrypted ciphertext CT_j^* of CT^*, $\mathcal{A}$ can issue Re-encryption query on $(\mathsf{PK}_{i^*}, \mathsf{PK}_j, CT^*, -)$, where $-$ represents a non-specified policy structure.

Guess. $\mathcal{A}$ outputs its guess $\eta' \in \{0,1\}$ for η and wins the game if $\eta = \eta'$.

During this game, adversary $\mathcal{A}$ is subject to the following restrictions:

1. $\mathcal{A}$ cannot issue Corrupted key generation query on (i^*) to attain the target secret key SK_{i^*}.

2. $\mathcal{A}$ cannot issue Decryption query on neither $(CT^*, \mathsf{PK}_{i^*})$ nor $(\mathsf{ReEncrypt}$ $(\mathsf{RK}_{i^* \to j}, CT^*), \mathsf{PK}_j)$.
3. $\mathcal{A}$ cannot issue Re-encryption key generation query on $(\mathsf{PK}_{i^*}, \mathsf{PK}_j, \mathcal{P})$, where $\mathcal{P}$ can be satisfied either by D_0 or D_1.
4. If $\mathcal{A}$ has obtained the secret key SK_j, $\mathcal{A}$ cannot issue Re-encryption query on $(\mathsf{PK}_{i^*}, \mathsf{PK}_j, CT^*, -)$, and vice versa.

In Phase 2, the slight modification indicates that $\mathcal{A}$ can always attain a valid re-encrypted ciphertext CT_j^* without knowing a policy $\mathcal{P}^*$ that satisfies either D_0 or D_1, as long as the secret key SK_j hasn't been issued before. Note that this operation is totally legal and reasonable for $\mathcal{A}$, because the adversary should always be able to obtain valid re-encrypted ciphertexts of challenge ciphertext without learning the attribute set of CT^*, and the received transformed ciphertext CT_j^* doesn't provide any help for the adversary in winning this game.

The advantage of adversary $\mathcal{A}$ in this game is defined as

$$\mathrm{Adv}_A = \left| \Pr[\eta = \eta'] - \frac{1}{2} \right|,$$

where the probability is taken over the random bits used by the challenger and the adversary.

Definition 6. *An AB-CPRE scheme achieves anonymity if all polynomial time adversaries have at most a negligible advantage in* Game_A.

4   Proposed Anonymous AB-CPRE Construction

Suppose Alice encrypts a file with keywords $(d_1, \ldots, d_n)$ and stores it on the cloud server, where n is the number of keyword fields (For example, if files were emails, we could define 4 keyword fields, such as "From","To", "Subject" and"Date"). For notational purpose, let i denote the i-th keyword field. We express an monotone boolean predicate by an LSSS $(\mathbf{A}, \rho, \mathcal{T})$, where $\mathbf{A}$ is an $l \times m$ share-generating matrix, ρ is a map from each row of matrix $\mathbf{A}$ to a keyword field (i.e., ρ is a function from $\{1, \ldots, l\}$ to $\{1, \ldots, n\}$), $\mathcal{T}$ can be parsed as $(t_{\rho(1)}, \ldots, t_{\rho(l)})$ and $t_{\rho(l)}$ specified by the predicate.

Using this notation, a file with keywords $(d_1, \ldots, d_n)$ satisfies a predicate $(\mathbf{A}, \rho, \mathcal{T})$ if and only if there exist $\mathcal{I} \subseteq \{1, \ldots, l\}$ and constants $\{w_i\}_{i \in \mathcal{I}}$ such that $\sum_{i \in \mathcal{I}} w_i A_i = (1, 0, \ldots, 0)$ and $d_{\rho(i)} = t_{\rho(i)}$ for $\forall i \in \mathcal{I}$.

Before presenting our AB-CPRE scheme, we give some intuitions of our construction. Based on Lai et al.'s searchable public key encryption scheme [17], we bind several ciphertext components altogether using a strongly unforgeable one-time signature, like the way they did in [7,21]. The ciphertext's keywords $(d_1, \ldots, d_n)$ will be encrypted using the encryption algorithm of Lai et al.'s S-PKE scheme, and the token keys in Lai et al.'s S-PKE scheme will be included in the re-encryption key of our AB-CPRE scheme. The proposed AB-CPRE scheme is specified as follows:

Setup(1^λ) Given security parameter λ, this algorithm runs $\mathcal{G}(1^\lambda)$ to obtain $(p, \mathbb{G}_1, \mathbb{G}_2, e_1)$, where $\mathbb{G}_1$ and $\mathbb{G}_2$ are cyclic groups of order p and e_1 is a bilinear map $\mathbb{G}_1 \times \mathbb{G}_1 \rightarrow \mathbb{G}_2$. Then, this algorithm chooses a collision-resistant hash function $H_0 : \mathbb{G}_2 \rightarrow \mathbb{Z}_p^*$ and a strongly unforgeable one-time signature scheme $\mathcal{S} = (\mathcal{S}_{gen}, \mathcal{S}_{sign}, \mathcal{S}_{ver})$. Finally, this algorithm randomly picks $g_{pub}, u_{pub}, v_{pub}, h_{pub} \in \mathbb{G}_1$ and sets the public parameters as

$$params = \{\mathbb{G}_1, \mathbb{G}_2, g_{pub}, u_{pub}, v_{pub}, h_{pub}, e_1, H_0, \mathcal{S}\}.$$

KeyGen$(1^\lambda, params, i)$ Given the security parameter λ, the public parameters $params$ and user identity i, this algorithm performs as follows:
1. Run $\mathcal{G}(1^\lambda)$ to attain $(N, \mathbb{G}_N, \mathbb{G}_T, e_2)$ with $\mathbb{G}_N = \mathbb{G}_{p_1} \times \mathbb{G}_{p_2} \times \mathbb{G}_{p_3} \times \mathbb{G}_{p_4}$, where $\mathbb{G}_N$ and $\mathbb{G}_T$ are cyclic groups of order $N = p_1 p_2 p_3 p_4$.
2. Choose $\alpha, \alpha' \in \mathbb{Z}_N$, $g_1, u, h_1, \ldots, h_n \in \mathbb{G}_{p_1}$ uniformly at random.
3. Choose $X_3 \in \mathbb{G}_{p_3}$ and $X_4, Z, Z_0, Z_1, \ldots, Z_n \in \mathbb{G}_{p_4}$ uniformly at random.
4. Pick a random $y_i \in \mathbb{Z}_p^*$, and compute $Y_i = g_{pub}^{y_i}$.
5. Set user i's public key as

$$\mathsf{PK}_i = (e_2(g_1, g_1)^\alpha, g_1 Z, U = u Z_0, \{H_j = h_j \cdot Z_j\}_{1 \le j \le n}, X_4, Y_i)$$

and user i's secret key as

$$\mathsf{SK}_i = (\alpha, g_1, u, h_1, \ldots, h_n, X_3, y_i).$$

Note that $(\mathbb{G}_1, \mathbb{G}_2)$ are of the different orders from $(\mathbb{G}_N, \mathbb{G}_T)$. On the other hand, e_1 is a bilinear map for prime order groups $(\mathbb{G}_1, \mathbb{G}_2)$, while e_2 is one for composite order groups $(\mathbb{G}_N, \mathbb{G}_T)$.

Enc$(params, \mathsf{PK}_i, M, D = (d_1, \ldots, d_n) \in \mathbb{Z}_N^n)$ Given public parameters $params$, user i's public key PK_i, a message M and a set of attributes D, this algorithm performs as follows:
1. Choose $r_1, r_2 \in \mathbb{Z}_p^*$, $s \in \mathbb{Z}_N$ and $Z_{1,0}, \{Z_{1,i}\}_{1 \le i \le n} \in \mathbb{G}_{p_4}$ uniformly at random.
2. Generate a one-time signature pair $(ssk, svk) \leftarrow \mathcal{S}_{gen}$.
3. Set $D_1 = svk$ and $D_1' = r_2$.
4. Compute $D_2 = Y_i^{r_1}$, $D_3 = e_1(g_{pub}, g_{pub})^{r_1} \cdot M$, $D_4 = (u_{pub}^{H_0(D_3)} \cdot v_{pub}^{r_2} \cdot h_{pub})^{r_1}$, $\hat{C} = e_2(g_1, g_1)^{\alpha \cdot s}$, $C_0 = (g_1 Z)^s \cdot Z_{1,0}$ and $C_i = (U^{d_i} H_i)^s \cdot Z_{1,i}$.
5. Perform $\sigma = \mathcal{S}_{sign}(ssk, (D_1', D_3, D_4, \hat{C}, C_0, \{C_i\}_{1 \le i \le n}))$ to obtain a one-time signature.
6. Set the ciphertext as

$$CT = (D_1, D_1', D_2, D_3, D_4, \hat{C}, C_0, \{C_i\}_{1 \le i \le n}, \sigma).$$

It is worth noting that the one-time signature σ is just on $(D_1', D_3, D_4, \hat{C}, C_0, \{C_i\}_{1 \le i \le n})$.

RKeyGen$(\mathsf{SK}_i, \mathsf{PK}_j, \mathcal{P} = (A, \rho, \mathcal{T}))$ Given user i's secret key SK_i, user j's public key PK_j and a policy structure $\mathcal{P}$, where A is an $l \times m$ matrix, ρ is a map from each row A_x of A to $\{1, \ldots, n\}$ and $\mathcal{T} = (t_{\rho(1)}, \ldots, t_{\rho(l)}) \in \mathbb{Z}_N^l$, this algorithm performs as follows:

1. Randomly pick two vectors $v \in \mathbb{Z}_N^m$ such that $\mathbf{1} \cdot v = \alpha$. (Here $\mathbf{1}$ denotes $(1, 0, \ldots, 0)$).
2. Choose random elements $z_x \in \mathbb{Z}_N$ and $R_{1,x}, R_{2,x} \in \mathbb{G}_{p_3}$ for each row A_x of $\mathbf{A}$.
3. Compute $rk_0 = Y_j^{1/y_i} = g_{pub}^{y_j/y_i}$, $rk_{1,x} = g_1^{A_x \cdot v} \cdot (u^{t_{\rho(x)}} \cdot h_{\rho(x)})^{z_x} \cdot R_{1,x}$ and $rk_{2,x} = g_1^{z_x} \cdot R_{2,x}$.
4. Set the re-encryption key

$$\mathsf{RK}_{i \to j} = ((A, \rho, \mathcal{T}), rk_0, \{rk_{1,x}, rk_{2,x}\}_{1 \le x \le l}).$$

Note that the only component of user j's public key PK_j we use is Y_j in the construction of rk_0, and the construction of rest parts $\{rk_{1,x}, rk_{2,x}\}_{1 \le x \le l}$ just involves SK_i and $\mathcal{P}$.

Re-Enc$(\mathsf{RK}_{i \to j}, CT)$ Given a re-encryption key $\mathsf{RK}_{i \to j}$ and a ciphertext CT, this algorithm performs as follows:

1. Parse the re-encryption key as $\mathsf{RK}_{i \to j} = ((A, \rho, \mathcal{T}), rk_0, \{rk_{1,x}, rk_{2,x}\}_{1 \le x \le l})$ and the ciphertext as $CT = (D_1, D_1', D_2, D_3, D_4, \hat{C}, C_0, \{C_i\}_{1 \le i \le n}, \sigma)$.
2. Check whether the following conditions hold

$$e_1(D_2, u_{pub}^{H_0(D_3)} \cdot v_{pub}^{D_1'} \cdot h_{pub}) = e_1(Y_i, D_4), \tag{1}$$

$$\mathcal{S}_{ver}(D_1, \sigma, (D_1', D_3, D_4, \hat{C}, C_0, \{C_i\}_{1 \le i \le n}) = 1. \tag{2}$$

Output $\perp$ if either of them falls; otherwise, go to the next step.
3. Calculate $I_{A,\rho}$ from (A, ρ).
4. Check if there exists an $\mathcal{I} \in I_{A,\rho}$ that satisfies

$$\hat{C} = \prod_{x \in \mathcal{I}} \frac{e_2(C_0, rk_{1,x})^{w_x}}{e_2(C_{\rho(x)}, rk_{2,x})^{w_x}},$$

where $\sum_{x \in \mathcal{I}} w_x A_x = (1, 0, \ldots, 0)$. Output $\perp$ if no such subset was found; otherwise, go to the next step.
5. Randomly pick $k \in \mathbb{Z}_p^*$, then compute $E_1 = Y_i^k$, $E_2 = rk_0^{1/k} = g_{pub}^{y_j/(y_i k)}$ and $E_3 = D_2^k = Y_i^{r_1 k}$.
6. Output the transformed ciphertext as

$$CT' = (D_1', D_3, D_4, E_1, E_2, E_3).$$

Dec There exist two situations:

– To decrypt an original ciphertext CT, with the secret key SK_i, this algorithm first checks whether both relations (1) and (2) are satisfied. If so, it derives the plaintext M by computing

$$\frac{D_3}{e_1(D_2, g_{pub})^{1/y_i}};$$

otherwise, the algorithm outputs $\perp$.

– To decrypt a re-encrypted ciphertext CT', with the secret key SK_j, this algorithm checks whether all the following conditions hold

$$e_1(E_1, E_2) = e_1(Y_j, g_{pub}), \tag{3}$$

$$e_1(E_3, u^{H_0(D_3)} \cdot v_{pub}^{D'_1} \cdot h_{pub}) = e_1(E_1, D_4). \tag{4}$$

If so, it then derives the plaintext M by computing

$$\frac{D_3}{e_1(E_2, E_3)^{1/y_j}};$$

otherwise, the algorithm outputs $\bot$.

In our proposed AB-CPRE scheme, a ciphertext involves a part: $(\hat{C}, , C_0, \{C_i\}_{1 \le i \le n})$. This part is used to decide which attribute set of a ciphertext satisfies the access structure associated with a re-encryption key which has a part:$((A, \rho, \mathcal{T}), \{rk_{1,x}, rk_{2,x}\}_{1 \le x \le l})$. If a satisfied ciphertext is found, then the proxy is able to transform this ciphertext with the corresponding re-encryption key. These parts $(\hat{C}, , C_0, \{C_i\}_{1 \le i \le n})$ and $((A, \rho, \mathcal{T}), \{rk_{1,x}, rk_{2,x}\}_{1 \le x \le l})$ can be viewed as components of a KP-ABE scheme. The KP-ABE construction in [18] uses composite order bilinear groups whose order is a product of three distinct primes, while the counterpart in our construction is of order of four distinct primes. Note that, in our construction, most of the components of an user's public key $(g_1 Z, U = u Z_0, \{H_i = h_i \cdot Z_i\}_{1 \le i \le n}, X_4)$ have an element from $\mathbb{G}_{p_4}$ as a factor. This formation allows us to prove that the access structures of our KP-ABE related components are partially hidden (namely, the attribute set of ciphertexts are anonymous).

4.1   Confidentiality Security

We firstly state a 3-wDBDHI assumption's variant which we are going to use in our security proof, we then state two confidentiality theorems of our AB-CPRE scheme, where we use the 3-wDBDHI problem in. We omit the proof of these two theorems due to the limited space.

Lemma 1. *The 3-wDBDHI problem is equivalent to decide whether T equals $e(g, g)^{b/a^2}$ or a random value, given $(g, g^{1/a}, g^a, g^{a^2}, g^b)$ as input.*

This lemma has been proved by Libert et al. in [21]. Like Libert et al. did, we prove the confidentiality security of our AB-CPRE scheme under this variant for the purpose of being convenient.

Theorem 1. *Assuming the strong unforgeability of the one-time signature, our AB-CPRE scheme is RCCA-secure on original ciphertexts under the 3-wDBDHI assumption.*

Theorem 2. *Assuming the strong unforgeability of the one-time signature, our AB-CPRE scheme is RCCA-secure on transformed ciphertexts under the 3-wDBDHI assumption.*

4.2 Anonymity

Next, we state the anonymity theorem of our AB-CPRE scheme. We also omit the proof of these two theorems due to the space limitations.

Theorem 3. *Suppose the searchable public key encryption by Lai et al. [17] is secure, then our AB-CPRE scheme achieves anonymity on original ciphertexts.*

5 Conclusions

In this paper, we considered a new requirement, anonymity, for AB-CPRE. First, we modified the original model of AB-CPRE proposed by [32] to include anonymity. Based on this modified model, we proposed a concrete anonymous AB-CPRE scheme, and we presented the proofs for security and anonymity without replying on random oracles. One open problem would be to devise secure anonymous AB-CPRE schemes in a fully adaptive corruption model using bilinear groups of prime order. Also, it would be interesting to construct a secure *multi-hop* anonymous AB-CPRE scheme. Under the circumstance of *multi-hop*, another property, termed *master secret security* [2], would seem desirable.

References

1. Ateniese, G., Benson, K., Hohenberger, S.: Key-private proxy re-encryption. In: Topics in Cryptology - CT-RSA 2009 The Cryptographers' Track at the RSA Conference 2009, San Francisco, CA, USA, 20–24 April 2009. Proceedings, pp. 279–294 (2009)
2. Ateniese, G., Fu, K., Green, M., Hohenberger, S.: Improved proxy re-encryption schemes with applications to secure distributed storage. ACM Trans. Inf. Syst. Secur. **9**(1), 1–30 (2006)
3. Beimel, A.: Secure schemes for secret sharing and key distribution. Ph.D. thesis, Israel Institute of Technology (1996)
4. Bethencourt, J., Sahai, A., Waters, B.: Ciphertext-policy attribute-based encryption. In: IEEE Symposium on Security and Privacy, pp. 321–334 (2007)
5. Blaze, M., Bleumer, G., Strauss, M.: Divertible protocols and atomic proxy cryptography. In: Nyberg, K. (ed.) EUROCRYPT 1998. LNCS, vol. 1403, pp. 127–144. Springer, Heidelberg (1998). https://doi.org/10.1007/BFb0054122
6. Boneh, D., Goh, E.-J., Nissim, K.: Evaluating 2-DNF formulas on ciphertexts. In: Kilian, J. (ed.) TCC 2005. LNCS, vol. 3378, pp. 325–341. Springer, Heidelberg (2005). https://doi.org/10.1007/978-3-540-30576-7_18
7. Canetti, R., Hohenberger, S.: Chosen-ciphertext secure proxy re-encryption. In: ACM Conference on Computer and Communications Security, pp. 185–194 (2007)
8. Canetti, R., Krawczyk, H., Nielsen, J.B.: Relaxing chosen-ciphertext security. In: Boneh, D. (ed.) CRYPTO 2003. LNCS, vol. 2729, pp. 565–582. Springer, Heidelberg (2003). https://doi.org/10.1007/978-3-540-45146-4_33
9. Chase, M.: Multi-authority attribute based encryption. In: Vadhan, S.P. (ed.) TCC 2007. LNCS, vol. 4392, pp. 515–534. Springer, Heidelberg (2007). https://doi.org/10.1007/978-3-540-70936-7_28

10. Chase, M., Chow, S.S.M.: Improving privacy and security in multi-authority attribute-based encryption. In: ACM Conference on Computer and Communications Security, pp. 121–130 (2009)
11. Cheung, L., Newport, C.C.: Provably secure ciphertext policy ABE. In: ACM Conference on Computer and Communications Security, pp. 456–465 (2007)
12. Chu, C.-K., Tzeng, W.-G.: Identity-based proxy re-encryption without random oracles. In: Garay, J.A., Lenstra, A.K., Mambo, M., Peralta, R. (eds.) ISC 2007. LNCS, vol. 4779, pp. 189–202. Springer, Heidelberg (2007). https://doi.org/10.1007/978-3-540-75496-1_13
13. Goyal, V., Jain, A., Pandey, O., Sahai, A.: Bounded ciphertext policy attribute based encryption. In: Aceto, L., Damgård, I., Goldberg, L.A., Halldórsson, M.M., Ingólfsdóttir, A., Walukiewicz, I. (eds.) ICALP 2008. LNCS, vol. 5126, pp. 579–591. Springer, Heidelberg (2008). https://doi.org/10.1007/978-3-540-70583-3_47
14. Goyal, V., Pandey, O., Sahai, A., Waters, B.: Attribute-based encryption for fine-grained access control of encrypted data. In: ACM Conference on Computer and Communications Security, pp. 89–98 (2006)
15. Green, M., Ateniese, G.: Identity-based proxy re-encryption. In: Katz, J., Yung, M. (eds.) ACNS 2007. LNCS, vol. 4521, pp. 288–306. Springer, Heidelberg (2007). https://doi.org/10.1007/978-3-540-72738-5_19
16. Ivan, A.A., Dodis, Y.: Proxy cryptography revisited. In: NDSS (2003)
17. Lai, J., Zhou, X., Deng, R., Li, Y., Chen, K.: Expressive search on encrypted data. In: ACM Symposium on Information, Computer and Communications Security (2013)
18. Lewko, A., Okamoto, T., Sahai, A., Takashima, K., Waters, B.: Fully secure functional encryption: attribute-based encryption and (hierarchical) inner product encryption. In: Gilbert, H. (ed.) EUROCRYPT 2010. LNCS, vol. 6110, pp. 62–91. Springer, Heidelberg (2010). https://doi.org/10.1007/978-3-642-13190-5_4
19. Lewko, A., Waters, B.: Decentralizing attribute-based encryption. In: Paterson, K.G. (ed.) EUROCRYPT 2011. LNCS, vol. 6632, pp. 568–588. Springer, Heidelberg (2011). https://doi.org/10.1007/978-3-642-20465-4_31
20. Lewko, A., Waters, B.: Unbounded HIBE and attribute-based encryption. In: Paterson, K.G. (ed.) EUROCRYPT 2011. LNCS, vol. 6632, pp. 547–567. Springer, Heidelberg (2011). https://doi.org/10.1007/978-3-642-20465-4_30
21. Libert, B., Vergnaud, D.: Unidirectional chosen-ciphertext secure proxy re-encryption. In: Cramer, R. (ed.) PKC 2008. LNCS, vol. 4939, pp. 360–379. Springer, Heidelberg (2008). https://doi.org/10.1007/978-3-540-78440-1_21
22. Lin, H., Cao, Z., Liang, X., Shao, J.: Secure threshold multi authority attribute based encryption without a central authority. In: Chowdhury, D.R., Rijmen, V., Das, A. (eds.) INDOCRYPT 2008. LNCS, vol. 5365, pp. 426–436. Springer, Heidelberg (2008). https://doi.org/10.1007/978-3-540-89754-5_33
23. Müller, S., Katzenbeisser, S., Eckert, C.: Distributed attribute-based encryption. In: Lee, P.J., Cheon, J.H. (eds.) ICISC 2008. LNCS, vol. 5461, pp. 20–36. Springer, Heidelberg (2009). https://doi.org/10.1007/978-3-642-00730-9_2
24. Ostrovsky, R., Sahai, A., Waters, B.: Attribute-based encryption with non-monotonic access structures. In: ACM Conference on Computer and Communications Security, pp. 195–203 (2007)
25. Sahai, A., Waters, B.: Fuzzy identity-based encryption. In: Cramer, R. (ed.) EURO-CRYPT 2005. LNCS, vol. 3494, pp. 457–473. Springer, Heidelberg (2005). https://doi.org/10.1007/11426639_27
26. Smith, T.: Dvd jon: buy DRM-less tracks from apple itunes. http://code.google.com/p/libfenc (2005)

27. Suriadi, S., Foo, E., Smith, J.: Conditional privacy using re-encryption. In: IFIP International Conference on Network and Parallel Computing, NPC 2008, pp. 18–25. IEEE (2008)
28. Taban, G., Cárdenas, A.A., Gligor, V.D.: Towards a secure and interoperable DRM architecture. In: Proceedings of the ACM workshop on Digital Rights Management, pp. 69–78. ACM (2006)
29. Tang, Q.: Type-based proxy re-encryption and its construction. In: Chowdhury, D.R., Rijmen, V., Das, A. (eds.) INDOCRYPT 2008. LNCS, vol. 5365, pp. 130–144. Springer, Heidelberg (2008). https://doi.org/10.1007/978-3-540-89754-5_11
30. Waters, B.: Ciphertext-policy attribute-based encryption: an expressive, efficient, and provably secure realization. In: Catalano, D., Fazio, N., Gennaro, R., Nicolosi, A. (eds.) PKC 2011. LNCS, vol. 6571, pp. 53–70. Springer, Heidelberg (2011). https://doi.org/10.1007/978-3-642-19379-8_4
31. Weng, J., Deng, R.H., Ding, X., Chu, C.K., Lai, J.: Conditional proxy re-encryption secure against chosen-ciphertext attack. In: ASIACCS, pp. 322–332 (2009)
32. Zhao, J., Feng, D., Zhang, Z.: Attribute-based conditional proxy re-encryption with chosen-ciphertext security. In: GLOBECOM, pp. 1–6 (2010)

A Provably-Secure Two-Factor Authenticated Key Exchange Protocol with Stronger Anonymity

Xiaoyan Yang[1], Han Jiang[1(✉)], Mengbo Hou[1], Zhihua Zheng[2],
Qiuliang Xu[1], and Kim-Kwang Raymond Choo[3]

[1] School of Software, Shandong University, Jinan 250101, China
{xyyang, jianghan, houmb, xql}@sdu.edu.cn
[2] College of Information Science and Engineering,
Shandong Normal University, Jinan 250358, China
zhengzhihua@sdnu.edu.cn
[3] Department of Information Systems and Cyber Security,
University of Texas at San Antonio, San Antonio, TX 78249, USA
raymond.choo@fulbrightmail.org

Abstract. Authentication is an effective mechanism for determining whether a user is unauthorized to access to the device and/or online account. In addition, users may also be concerned about preserving their online privacy (e.g. identity, and individual preferences). Conventional anonymous two-factor authenticated key exchange (AKE) protocols only guarantee user anonymity against an external adversary, although user identity may be easily learned by a malicious insider (e.g. server), and the latter may also trace the user's activities and analyze the user's individual preferences for illicit financial gains. To address this problem, we propose a novel anonymous two-factor AKE protocol, which achieves stronger anonymity in the sense that no useful information about the user's identity is revealed to either an adversary or the server. We then give a formal security proof of the protocol in the random oracle model.

Keywords: Anonymous authentication · Authenticated key exchange
Two-factor authentication

1 Introduction

Authentication is an effective mechanism for determining whether a user is unauthorized to access to the device and/or online account. An additional property is anonymity, where a user would not be easily identified if his/her personal information, such as identity and individual preferences, are exposed (e.g. due to security breaches). Anonymous authentication [1] can achieve both authentication and privacy requirements at the same time. For example, anonymous authenticated key exchange (AKE) protocols can also generate a secret key between two participants, which can be used to establish a secure channel for their subsequent communication.

There has been extensive study on AKE protocols in the literature. In a two-party AKE protocols, two communication parties must share some secret information, such

M. H. Au et al. (Eds.): NSS 2018, LNCS 11058, pp. 111–124, 2018.
https://doi.org/10.1007/978-3-030-02744-5_8

as some cryptographically-strong information [2–6] or a low entropy password [7–12]. In practice, password is typically used. However, there are known weaknesses in using passwords. For example, passwords are often chosen from a very small set of possible candidates which are subject to dictionary attacks [8]. Moreover they may be recovered via social engineering, shoulder surfing and keyboard wiretapping etc. Single factor authentication does not meet the goal of providing stronger security protection in some specific application.

A number of two-factor authentication AKE protocols using smart card and password [13–16] have been proposed in the literature, and such protocols are designed to provide a higher level of security. AKE protocols can also be extended to support anonymity and untraceability, i.e. anonymous two-factor authentication/AKE protocols [17–21].

Anonymity implies that the identity of the user who communicates with the server cannot be determined, and untraceability means the adversary cannot distinguish whether two transcripts of a protocol execution are initiated by the same user. Conventional anonymous two-factor AKE protocols achieve anonymity only against an external adversary, and only a few of these protocols also achieve untraceability [18], since the server can learn the identity of the registered users. That is to say, the honest-but-curious server may identify the user, trace the user's activities, and analyze the user's individual preferences for financial benefits (e.g. selling of user shopping behavior or profile to advertisers). Such protocols generally use dynamic ID technique [17], where the identity of the user is concealed in an encryption of his/her identity or a one-way hash function. The connection between the identity and dynamic ID can be found by the server. Moreover, such protocols generally require an additional synchronization mechanism to maintain the consistency of the one-time identity between the user and the server. These protocols are vulnerable to de-synchronization attacks.

To address this problem, we present an anonymous two-factor AKE (ATAKE) protocol that reveals no valuable information concerning the user's identity to the server or an external adversary. The server only learns that it is interacting with a user that belongs to a trusted group, and nothing more about this user. Our idea of achieving stronger anonymity comes from the classic method in anonymous password-based AKE protocols [22], that is a 1-out-of-n oblivious transfer (OT) protocol [23] is embedded in the scheme, where the server S has n secret values and the user C_i can get only one of these values without revealing his/her choices. S transfers i-th message to C_i using the OT protocol. Since only authorized users can retrieve the Diffie-Hellman component Y, this in turn proves C_i is authorized and only C_i can computer the session key (assuming that the key has not been compromised). We then give a formal security proof of the scheme in the random oracle model.

To the best of our knowledge, this is the first provably-secure anonymous two-factor authenticated protocol that achieves anonymity against both the adversary and the server.

2 Related Work

A number of AKE protocols have been proposed, such as dynamic ID-based remote user authentication protocol that uses smart card of Das et al. [17]. This protocol allow users to freely choose and change their passwords and the server does not maintain any password list. Other similar protocols include those presented in [24–32], although many of these protocols only have heuristic security arguments. The protocols were subsequently found to be insecure and a new solution was introduced, and in some cases these new schemes were also found to be insecure. To break this "attack-fix" cycle, it is vital to give a formal proof of the security in a security model.

Liu et al. [18] showed that Sun et al.'s scheme [32] lacks untraceability, and proposed a new robust anonymous PAKE scheme using smart card. They also presented a security proof of their scheme in the random oracle model. A new set of design goals for fairly evaluating anonymous two-factor AKE schemes was presented in [19]. Wang et al. [20] investigated the inner relationships of evaluation criteria for anonymous two-factor authentication, which offers us a better understanding of the design criteria for two-factor protocols. Xie et al. [21] proposed an anonymous two-factor AKE protocol based on dynamic ID, which is secure against attacks such as offline dictionary and lost-smart-card attacks.

As mentioned above, the design idea of our scheme is analogous with that of anonymous password-based AKE protocols. The first anonymous password-based AKE scheme was proposed by Viet et al. [22], which combines a two-party PAKE scheme with an oblivious transfer (OT) protocol. Yang et al. [33] proposed another APAKE protocol, NAPAKE, which was subsequently included in a draft of ISO/IEC 20009-4 which specifies anonymous entity authentication mechanisms based on weak secrets. Recently, Yang et al. [34] proposed a verifier-based anonymous password-authenticated key exchange protocol using smooth projective hash function (SPHF) [12] and gave a security proof of the protocol in the standard model.

3 Preliminaries and Security Model

We will now describe Computational Diffie-Hellman (CDH) assumption, Smooth Projective Hashing Function on ElGamal ciphertext and the security model.

3.1 Computational Diffie-Hellman Assumption

Let $\mathbb{G} = \langle g \rangle$ be a finite cyclic group of order prime q. A (t, ε)-CDH attacker is a probabilistic machine A running in time t such that

$$\text{Succ}_{\mathbb{G}}^{\text{cdh}}(A) = \Pr_{x,y}[\Delta(g^x, g^y) = g^{xy}] \geq \varepsilon$$

where the probability is taken over the random values x and y. The CDH-Problem is (t, ε)-intractable if there is no (t, ε)-attacker in $\mathbb{G}$.

3.2   Smooth Projective Hashing Function on ElGamal Ciphertext

Smooth Projective Hashing Function. Let X denotes the domain of the functions and L be a language with $L \subset X$. For words $C \in L$ there exists a witness w for C. A SPHF [12] for L is defined by four algorithms:

- HKGen (L) generates a hashing key hk for the language L
- ProjKGen (hk, L, C) derives the projection key hp, possibly depending on the word C
- Hash (hk, L, C) outputs the hash value h from the hashing key hk, for any word $C \in X$;
- ProjHash (hp, L, C, w) outputs the hash value h from the projection key hp and the witness w for any $C \in L$.

A SPHF is correct if for all $C \in L$ with witness w: Hash (hk, L, C) = ProjHash (hp, L, C, w). A SPHF is smooth if for all $C \notin L$, the hash value h is statistically indistinguishable from a random element in $\mathbb{G}$.

ElGamal Encryption. We will recap the concept of ElGamal encryption. Let $\mathbb{G}$ be a group of prime order q, and $g \in \mathbb{G}$ be a generator. The key generation algorithm chooses a random $x \leftarrow Z_q$ and computes $h \leftarrow g^x$. The public key is $<\mathbb{G}, q, g, h>$ and the private key is x. For a message $m \in \mathbb{G}$, chooses a random $y \leftarrow Z_q$, the ciphertext is $\langle g^y, h^y m \rangle$. To decrypt a ciphertext $\langle c_1, c_2 \rangle$ using the private key $sk = x$, computes $m := c_2 / c_1^x$.

SPHF on ElGamal Ciphertext. We will now give the description of SPHF on ElGamal ciphertext: the hashing key $hk = (\alpha, \beta) \in_R Z_q^2$; the projection key $hp = g^\alpha h^\beta$. Then, one can compute the hash values in two different ways as below:

$$\text{Hash}(hk, L, C) = g^{y\alpha}(h^y m / m)^\beta = g^{y\alpha} h^{y\beta}$$

$$\text{ProjHash}(hp, L, C, w) = hp^y = (g^\alpha h^\beta)^y = g^{\alpha y} h^{\beta y}$$

3.3   Security Model

We extend the security model of APAKE [34] where password is the single authentication factor to support two-factor authentication.

PARTICIPANTS. The participants include a predefined user group $\Gamma = \{C_1, \ldots, C_n\}$ and the server S which is assumed to be honest-but-curious. Participant U is denoted either as C_i in Γ or the server S. The user $C_i \in \Gamma$ choose a password pw_i and the minimum of password entropy is β, and S has a long-term secret key s. In the phase of user registration, S stores V_i in the smart card and V_i is a transformation of pw_i and s.

We let $\mathcal{A}$ denote a probabilistic polynomial adversary, which take full control of the communication between C_i and S. Many concurrent instances of participant U can be invoked by the adversary and $\prod_U^i$ denotes an instance i of participant U.

QUERIES. The adversary interact with the protocol participants via oracle queries

- Execute (U, i, U', j): This query models passive attack, where the adversary eavesdrops on honest execution. The output is the transcript of the execution between $\prod_U^i$ and $\prod_{U'}^j$.
- Send (U, i, m): This query models active attack. Specifically, the adversary sends m to $\prod_U^i$ and obtains the response that $\prod_U^i$ would generate upon receiving m.
- Reveal (U, i): This query models the misuse of the session key, and is only available to the adversary if it has been set.
- Corrupt (S): This query models server corruption. The output of this query is the server's private key, but the adversary can not get any internal data of S.
- Corrupt (C_i, a): This query models user corruption. If $a = 1$, then the output is the password pw_i of the user C_i. If $a = 2$, then the query outputs the information contained in the smart card. The adversary does not obtain any internal data of C_i.
- Test (U, i): This query captures the adversary's ability of distinguishing a real session key from a random key. This query is only available to the adversary if $\prod_U^i$ is fresh and can be asked only once. A coin b is flipped, outputs the session key if $b = 1$ or a random value if $b = 0$.

PARTNERING. We say that $\prod_U^i$ and $\prod_{U'}^j$ are partnered, only when both oracles accept and the following hold: (1) $sid_U^i = sid_{U'}^j$; (2) $sk_U^i = sk_{U'}^j$; (3) $pid_U^i = U'$ and $pid_{U'}^j = U$; (4) $U \in \Gamma$ and U' is the server, or $U' \in \Gamma$ and U is the server.

FRESHNESS. An instance is fresh, only when the session key has been established and is not trivially known to the adversary. More precisely, $\prod_U^i$ with $pid_U^i = U'$ is fresh if: (1)Π_U^i has accepted and hold a session key; (2) no Reveal(U', j) query has been asked where Π_U^i and $\Pi_{U'}^j$ are partnered; and (3) no Corrupt query has been made by the adversary before the session key is accepted.

AKE Security. An adversary $\mathcal{A}$ should issue the Test query to a fresh instance Π_U^i only once, outputs a bit b'. $\mathcal{A}$ succeeds if $b' = b$. This event is denoted as *Succ*, and the advantage of $\mathcal{A}$ in attacking the protocol P is defined by $\mathrm{Adv}_{P,\mathcal{A}}^{\mathrm{ake}} = 2\Pr[Succ] - 1$.

A protocol is AKE security if $\mathrm{Adv}_{P,\mathcal{A}}^{\mathrm{ake}} \leq q_s/2^\beta + negl()$ for some negligible function *negl*, where q_s is the number of Send queries and β is the minimum of password entropy.

AUTHENTICATION. The adversary violates server-to-user authentication if a user instance terminates but has no partner server instance, and the probability is defined by $Succ_P^{S-auth}$. The adversary violates user-to-server authentication if a server instance terminates but has no an instance of a user in Γ, and the probability is defined by $Succ_P^{C-auth}$. The protocol P is said to be *S-auth-secure* (resp. *C-auth-secure*) if the adversary's success probability for breaking server-to-user authentication (resp. user-to-server authentication) is negligible.

ANONYMITY. A protocol achieves anonymity if neither the server nor the adversary can determine the real identity of the user communicating with the server. They only know that the user belongs to a predefined set of authorized users but not the user's actual identity.

We define user anonymity using the below experiment $\text{Expt}_{P,A,n}^{\text{anon}}$, which follows that of [1]. We assume that A is an adversary or an honest-but-curious server seeking to compromise user anonymity.

1. The public parameters are identical with the protocol description;
2. An index i is chosen uniformly at random from the set $\{1,\ldots,n\}$;
3. The adversary A interacts with C_i by running the protocol P;

At the end of the experiment, A outputs $j \in \{1,\ldots,n\}$. The output of the experiment is defined to be 1 if $j = i$, that is $\text{Expt}_{P,A,n}^{\text{anon}} = 1$.

If $\Pr[\text{Expt}_{P,A,n}^{\text{anon}} = 1] \leq 1/n$ for every adversary , then the protocol P is said to achieve perfect anonymity. If for every adversary , there exists a negligible function such that $\Pr[\text{Expt}_{P,A,n}^{\text{anon}} = 1] \leq 1/n + negl()$, then protocol P is said to achieve computational anonymity.

4 Proposed ATPAKE Protocol

In this section, we present our anonymous two-factor authenticated key exchange protocol ATPAKE, and prove its security in the random oracle model

Given a finite cyclic group $\mathbb{G} = \langle g \rangle$ of order a ℓ-bit prime number q, where the operation is denoted multiplicatively. Hash functions from $\{0,1\}^*$ to $\{0,1\}^{\ell_i}$ are denoted $\mathcal{H}_i$, for $i = 0,1,2,3,4$ where $\ell_0, \ell_1 = \ell$.

4.1 User Registration

Consider a predefined user group $\Gamma = \{C_1,\ldots,C_n\}$ and an server S which is assumed to be honest-but-curious. The messages are transferred between user $C_i \in \Gamma$ and a server S via a secure channel.

1. C_i chooses the identity $ID_i \in \{0,1\}^l$ and the password pw_i, sends them to S for registration. S holds a long-term secret key $s \in [1, q-1]$.
2. S randomly selects $N_i \in [1, q-1]$ for C_i, and computes $V_i = \mathcal{H}_0(ID_i\|N_i\|s) \oplus \mathcal{H}_0(pw_i)$. The value V_i is written in the smart card.

4.2 Authentication and Establishing the Session Key

As illustrated in Fig. 1, the protocol consists of three flows:

1. C_i chooses uniformly at random $a, b, x \in_R Z_q$ and computes $X = g^x, u = g^a, v = g^b$, $c = ab$, $z_i = V_i \oplus \mathcal{H}_0(pw_i)$, $d = g^{c-z_i}$. Then, C_i sends (Γ, X, u, v, d) to S.
2. S chooses uniformly $y, r_1,\ldots,r_n, t_1,\ldots,t_n \in_R Z_q$ and computes $Y = g^y$. For $1 \leq j \leq n$, compute $s_j = \mathcal{H}_0(ID_j\|N_j\|s)$, $w_j = u^{t_j}g^{r_j}$, $k_j = (dg^{s_j})^{t_j}v^{r_j}$ and $\beta_j = \mathcal{H}_1(k_j, j) \oplus Yg^{s_j}$. Then, S generates $K_S = X^y$, $Trans = \Gamma\|S\|u\|v\|d\| \{w_j, \beta_j\}_{1 \leq j \leq n}\|X\|Y$ and the authenticator $Auth_S = \mathcal{H}_2(Trans, K_S)$. Finally S sends $(S, \{w_j, \beta_j\}_{1 \leq j \leq n}, Auth_S)$ to C_i.

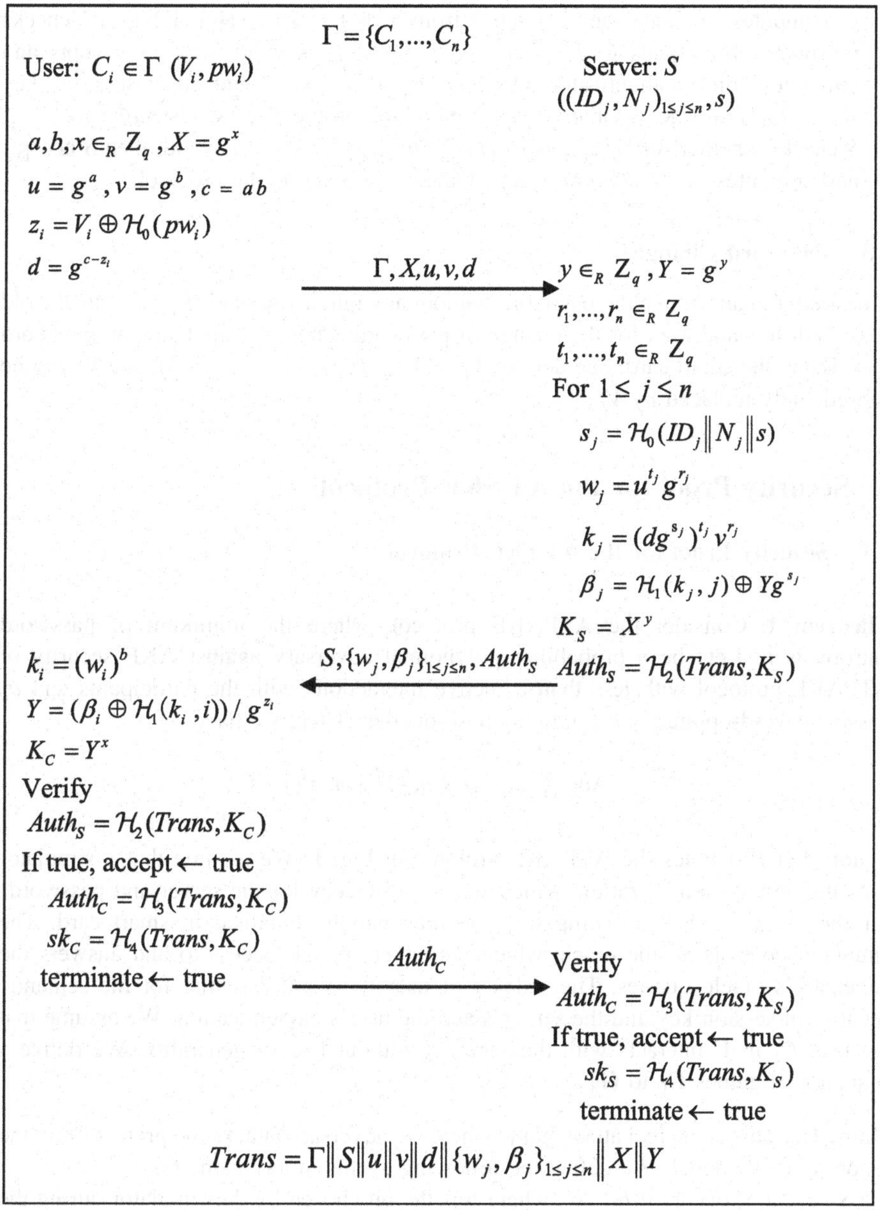

$$\Gamma = \{C_1, ..., C_n\}$$

User: $C_i \in \Gamma$ (V_i, pw_i)

Server: S
$$((ID_j, N_j)_{1 \le j \le n}, s)$$

$a, b, x \in_R Z_q$, $X = g^x$

$u = g^a$, $v = g^b$, $c = ab$

$z_i = V_i \oplus \mathcal{H}_0(pw_i)$

$d = g^{c-z_i}$

$\xrightarrow{\quad \Gamma, X, u, v, d \quad}$

$y \in_R Z_q$, $Y = g^y$

$r_1, ..., r_n \in_R Z_q$

$t_1, ..., t_n \in_R Z_q$

For $1 \le j \le n$

$\quad s_j = \mathcal{H}_0(ID_j \| N_j \| s)$

$\quad w_j = u^{t_j} g^{r_j}$

$\quad k_j = (dg^{s_j})^{t_j} v^{r_j}$

$\quad \beta_j = \mathcal{H}_1(k_j, j) \oplus Yg^{s_j}$

$K_S = X^y$

$k_i = (w_i)^b$

$\xleftarrow{\quad S, \{w_j, \beta_j\}_{1 \le j \le n}, Auth_S \quad}$ $Auth_S = \mathcal{H}_2(Trans, K_S)$

$Y = (\beta_i \oplus \mathcal{H}_1(k_i, i)) / g^{z_i}$

$K_C = Y^x$

Verify

$Auth_S = \mathcal{H}_2(Trans, K_C)$

If true, accept $\leftarrow$ true

$\quad Auth_C = \mathcal{H}_3(Trans, K_C)$

$\quad sk_C = \mathcal{H}_4(Trans, K_C)$

terminate $\leftarrow$ true

$\xrightarrow{\quad Auth_C \quad}$

Verify

$Auth_C = \mathcal{H}_3(Trans, K_S)$

If true, accept $\leftarrow$ true

$\quad sk_S = \mathcal{H}_4(Trans, K_S)$

terminate $\leftarrow$ true

$$Trans = \Gamma \| S \| u \| v \| d \| \{w_j, \beta_j\}_{1 \le j \le n} \| X \| Y$$

Fig. 1. An execution of the protocol ATAKE.

3. C_i computes $k_i = (w_i)^b$ and extracts Y from β_i as $Y = (\beta_i \oplus H(k_i, i))/g^{z_i}$. C_i checks whether $Auth_S$ equals to $\mathcal{H}_2(Trans, K_C)$. If $Auth_S$ is valid, then C_i accepts and computes the authenticator $Auth_C = \mathcal{H}_3(Trans, K_C)$ and the session key $sk_C = \mathcal{H}_4(Trans, K_C)$. Otherwise, C_i aborts the protocol. C_i sends $Auth_C$ to S.
4. S checks whether $Auth_C$ equals to $\mathcal{H}_3(Trans, K_S)$. If $Auth_C$ is valid, then S accepts and computes $sk_S = \mathcal{H}_4(Trans, K_S)$. Otherwise, S aborts the protocol.

4.3 Password Change

If desired, C_i can change the password without any interaction with S. C_i inputs the old password pw_i, and asks for the change of password. Then, C_i inputs a new password pw_i^*. Using the smart card, one derives $V_i^* = V_i \oplus \mathcal{H}_0(pw_i) \oplus \mathcal{H}_0(pw_i^*)$, and V_i will be subsequently replaced by V_i^*.

5 Security Proof for the ATAKE Protocol

5.1 Security Proof for the ATAKE Protocol

Theorem 1. Consider the ATPAKE protocol, where the minimum of password entropy is β. Let be a probability polynomial adversary against AKE security of ATPAKE protocol with less than q_s active interactions with the participants and q_p passive eavesdropping, and asking q_h hash-queries. Then, we have

$$\text{Adv}^{\text{ake}}_{\text{ATAKE}}(\mathcal{A}) \leq q_s/2^\beta + negl()$$

Proof: Let P denotes the ATPAKE protocol in Fig. 1. We assume that a simulator runs the protocol initialization, which selects secret key for the server and passwords for the users, as well as computing the information contained in smart card. The simulator controls all the oracle which the adversary has access to and answers the adversary's oracle queries. The index i of user C_i is not essential for the semantic security of session key and the server's and the user's authentication. We assume that the user C_1 in Γ interacts with the server S without loss of generality. We define a sequence of games $\mathbf{G_0}$ to $\mathbf{G_8}$.

Game $\mathbf{G_0}$: This is the real attack game where the adversary attacks the protocol P in the random oracle model. We define the following events in any game $\mathbf{G_i}$:

S_i: event S_i occurs if $b = b'$, where b is the bit chosen by the simulator during the Test query, and b' is the output of the adversary.

Auth_i^C: event Auth_i^C occurs if an server instance $\prod_S^i$ accepts with no partner user instance $\prod_C^i$.

Auth_i^S: event Auth_i^S occurs if an user instance $\prod_C^i$ accepts with no partner server instance $\prod_S^i$.

$$\text{Adv}_{\mathbf{G_0}} = 2\Pr[S_0] - 1$$

Game $\mathbf{G_1}$: In this game, we simulate the hash oracles ($\mathcal{H}_0, \mathcal{H}_1, \mathcal{H}_2, \mathcal{H}_3$ and $\mathcal{H}_4$, but also additional hash functions $\mathcal{H}'_i : \{0,1\}^* \to \{0,1\}^{\ell_i}$ for $i = 0, 1, 2, 3, 4$, that will appear in the Game $\mathbf{G_5}$) as usual by maintaining hash lists Λ_h. We also simulate all the instances, as the real players would do, for the Send queries and for the Execute, Reveal and Test-queries. From this simulation, we easily see that the game is perfectly indistinguishable from the real attack.

Game $\mathbf{G_2}$: In this game, we cancel games in which collisions on the transcripts $((\Gamma, X, u, v, d), (S, w_1, \beta_1))$ appear and collisions on the output of $\mathcal{H}_0$:

$$|\Pr[S_2] - \Pr[S_1]| \leq (q_p + q_s)^2/2q + q_h^2/2q$$

Game $\mathbf{G_3}$: We modify the way Execute queries are answered. We replace d by a value chosen uniformly and randomly from Z_q. We can look d as an ElGamal ciphertext. Because the CPA security of ElGamal encryption, we have:

$$|\Pr[S_3] - \Pr[S_2]| \leq negl()$$

Game $\mathbf{G_4}$: We modify the way Execute queries are answered. We replace k_1 by a value chosen uniformly and randomly from Z_q. Due to d is not a valid ElGamal ciphertext, k_1 is statistically close to uniform in $\mathbb{G}$ thanks to the smooth of SPHF, we have:

$$|\Pr[S_4] - \Pr[S_3]| \leq negl()$$

Game $\mathbf{G_5}$: The way Execute queries are answered is modified again. We compute β_1, authenticator $Auth_S$ and $Auth_C$ and the session key sk_C and sk_S using the private oracles $\mathcal{H}'_1, \mathcal{H}'_2, \mathcal{H}'_3$ and $\mathcal{H}'_4$, thus $sk_C, sk_S, Auth_S$ and $Auth_C$ are completely independent from Y, K_C and K_S. We use the following rules:

Compute $\beta_1 = \mathcal{H}'_1(k_1, 1)$

Compute the authenticator $Auth_S = \mathcal{H}'_2(\Gamma\|S\|u\|v\|d\|(w_1, \beta_1)\|X)$ and $Auth_C = \mathcal{H}'_3(\Gamma\|S\|u\|v\|d\|(w_1, \beta_1)\|X)$.

Compute the session key $sk = sk_C = sk_S = \mathcal{H}'_4(\Gamma\|S\|u\|v\|d\|(w_1, \beta_1)\|X)$.

The games $\mathbf{G_5}$ and $\mathbf{G_4}$ are indistinguishable unless the event AskH happens: $\mathcal{A}$ queries the hash functions $\mathcal{H}'_2, \mathcal{H}'_3$ and $\mathcal{H}'_4$ on $\Gamma\|S\|u\|v\|d\|(w_1, \beta_1)\|X\|Y\|K_C$ or on $\Gamma\|S\|u\|v\|d\|(w_1, \beta_1)\|X\|Y\|K_S$, that is on common value $\Gamma\|S\|u\|v\|d\|(w_1, \beta_1)\|X\|Y\|CDH(X, Y)$. By a random self-reducibility property of the CDH-problem, we have

$$|\Pr[S_5] - \Pr[S_4]| \leq q_h \text{Succ}_{\mathbb{G}}^{\text{cdh}}()$$

Game $\mathbf{G_6}$: The way Send queries are answered is modified. We abort the executions if the adversary may have been guessed the authenticator $Auth_S$ without asking the corresponding hash oracles. The two games $\mathbf{G_6}$ and $\mathbf{G_5}$ are indistinguishable unless the user rejects a valid $Auth_S$. This happens only if d and $Auth_S$ had been correctly guessed by the adversary, we have

$$|\Pr[S_6] - \Pr[S_5]| \leq q_s/2^{l_1}$$

Game G_7: The way Send queries are answered is modified. We abort the executions if the adversary may have been guessed the authenticator $Auth_C$ without asking the corresponding hash oracles. The two games G_7 and G_6 are indistinguishable unless the user rejects a valid $Auth_C$. This happens only if $Auth_C$ had been correctly guessed by the adversary, we have

$$|\Pr[S_7] - \Pr[S_6]| \leq q_s/2^{l_1}$$

Game G_8: The way Send queries are answered is modified again. As in Game G_5, We compute β_1, authenticator $Auth_S$ and $Auth_C$ and derives the session key sk_C and sk_S using the private oracles $\mathcal{H}'_1, \mathcal{H}'_2, \mathcal{H}'_3$ and $\mathcal{H}'_4$, thus sk_C, sk_S, $Auth_S$ and $Auth_C$ are completely independent from Y, K_C and K_S. We use the same rules in G_5 to compute the authenticator and the session key.

If asks Corrupt $(C_i, 2)$ query and do not ask Corrupt $(C_i, 1)$ query, that is corrupted the information contained in smart card. Then the adversary only test one password in each transcript. We have:

$$|\Pr[S_8] - \Pr[S_7]| \leq q_s/2^{\beta} \quad \Pr[S_8] = \frac{1}{2}$$

Games 1–8 imply $\text{Adv}^{\text{ake}}_{\text{ATAKE}}(\mathcal{A}) \leq q_s/2^{\beta} + negl()$. $\square$

5.2   Proof for Anonymity and Untraceability

Theorem 2. The ATAKE protocol P achieves perfect anonymity and untraceability.

Proof. We assume that $\mathcal{A}$ is a server or an external adversary who eagers to detect the identity of the user who participants the execution of the protocol. Because a, b and x are selected uniformly at random in Z_q, the first message (Γ, X, u, v, d) sent by the user C_i is uniformly distributed from the view of the adversary. Therefore, for any index i chosen in the experiment $\text{Expt}^{\text{anon}}_{P,\mathcal{A},n}$ the view of the adversary $\mathcal{A}$ is identical. This implies that the probability that $j = i$ is at most $1/n$. The ATAKE protocol P achieves perfect anonymity and untraceability.

6   Security and Performance Comparison

6.1   Security: A Comparative Summary

In our comparative summary of the security properties, we focus on anonymity regarding to the server and the adversary, untraceability, the ability to withstand offline dictionary attack without smart card, not requiring clock synchronization, key exchange and mutual authentication, and no password table. Table 1 presents the comparative summary between our scheme and the related schemes described in [18, 21, 27, 30–32].

Table 1. Security: a comparative summary

	[18]	[27]	[31]	[32]	[21]	[30]	Ours
Anonymity regarding to the server and the adversary	N	N	N	N	N	N	Y
Untraceability	Y	N	N	N	Y	Y	Y
Withstanding the offline dictionary attack without smart card	Y	N	Y	N	Y	Y	Y
Not requiring clock synchronization	Y	Y	Y	Y	N	Y	Y
Key change and mutual authentication	Y	Y	Y	Y	Y	Y	Y
No password table	Y	Y	Y	Y	Y	Y	Y

6.2 Performance: A Comparative Summary

We evaluate the computational cost in the phases of authentication and establishing session key of our scheme and the related schemes [18, 21, 27, 30–32] – see Table 2, where E represents block encryption/decryption, M represents modular exponentiation, H represents cryptographic hash operation, and S represents the elliptic curve scalar multiplication.

Table 2. Computation cost: a comparative summary.

	Smart Card	The server	Total
[18]	$S + 3H$	$2S + 4H$	$3S + 7H$
[27]	$2S + 5H + 3E$	$S + 5H + 6E$	$3S + 10H + 9E$
[31]	$2S + 7H$	$S + 7H$	$3S + 14H$
[32]	$2S + 6H$	$2S + 6H + 2E$	$4S + 12H + 2E$
[21]	$3S + 6H$	$3S + 5H + 2E$	$6S + 11H + 2E$
[30]	$2M + 1E + 8H$	$M + E + 5H$	$3M + 2E + 13H$
Ours	$7M + 5H$	$(6n + 2)M + (2n + 4)H$	$(6n + 9)M + (2n + 9)H$

The computational cost of our protocol is $O(n)$, where n is the number of users in the user group. This is higher than other anonymous two-factor AKE protocols in Table 2. However, our protocol achieves stronger anonymity and this is a trade-off between performances and secure properties.

7 Conclusion

In this paper, we proposed a novel anonymous two-factor AKE protocol, which achieves anonymity against both the server and an external adversary and achieves two-way authentication. We also proved the security of the protocol in the random oracle model.

Future research includes implementing a prototype of the proposed scheme and evaluating its performance in a real-world setting.

References

1. Lindell, Y.: Anonymous authentication. J. Priv. Confidentiality **2**, 4 (2007)
2. Bellare, M., Rogaway, P.: Entity authentication and key distribution. In: Stinson, D.R. (ed.) CRYPTO 1993. LNCS, vol. 773, pp. 232–249. Springer, Heidelberg (1994). https://doi.org/10.1007/3-540-48329-2_21
3. Blake-Wilson, S., Johnson, D., Menezes, A.: Key agreement protocols and their security analysis. In: Darnell, M. (ed.) Cryptography and Coding 1997. LNCS, vol. 1355, pp. 30–45. Springer, Heidelberg (1997). https://doi.org/10.1007/BFb0024447
4. Canetti, R., Krawczyk, H.: Analysis of Key-Exchange Protocols and Their Use for Building Secure Channels. In: Pfitzmann, B. (ed.) EUROCRYPT 2001. LNCS, vol. 2045, pp. 453–474. Springer, Heidelberg (2001). https://doi.org/10.1007/3-540-44987-6_28
5. LaMacchia, B., Lauter, K., Mityagin, A.: Stronger security of authenticated key exchange. In: Susilo, W., Liu, J.K., Mu, Y. (eds.) ProvSec 2007. LNCS, vol. 4784, pp. 1–16. Springer, Heidelberg (2007). https://doi.org/10.1007/978-3-540-75670-5_1
6. Choo, K.-K.R.: Secure key establishment. Springer Science & Business Media, Boston (2008). https://doi.org/10.1007/978-0-387-87969-7
7. Bellovin, S.M., Merritt, M.: Encrypted key exchange: password-based protocols secure against dictionary attacks. In: Proceedings of the 1992 IEEE Computer Society Symposium on Research in Security and Privacy, pp. 72–84. IEEE (1992)
8. Bellare, M., Pointcheval, D., Rogaway, P.: Authenticated key exchange secure against dictionary attacks. In: Preneel, B. (ed.) EUROCRYPT 2000. LNCS, vol. 1807, pp. 139–155. Springer, Heidelberg (2000). https://doi.org/10.1007/3-540-45539-6_11
9. Katz, J., Ostrovsky, R., Yung, M.: Efficient password-authenticated key exchange using human-memorable passwords. In: Pfitzmann, B. (ed.) EUROCRYPT 2001. LNCS, vol. 2045, pp. 475–494. Springer, Heidelberg (2001). https://doi.org/10.1007/3-540-44987-6_29
10. Gennaro, R., Lindell, Y.: A framework for password-based authenticated key exchange. In: Biham, E. (ed.) EUROCRYPT 2003. LNCS, vol. 2656, pp. 524–543. Springer, Heidelberg (2003). https://doi.org/10.1007/3-540-39200-9_33
11. Katz, J., Vaikuntanathan, V.: Round-optimal password-based authenticated key exchange. In: Ishai, Y. (ed.) TCC 2011. LNCS, vol. 6597, pp. 293–310. Springer, Heidelberg (2011). https://doi.org/10.1007/978-3-642-19571-6_18
12. Benhamouda, F., Blazy, O., Chevalier, C., Pointcheval, D., Vergnaud, D.: New techniques for SPHFs and efficient one-round PAKE protocols. In: Canetti, R., Garay, J.A. (eds.) CRYPTO 2013. LNCS, vol. 8042, pp. 449–475. Springer, Heidelberg (2013). https://doi.org/10.1007/978-3-642-40041-4_25
13. Yang, W.-H., Shieh, S.-P.: Password authentication schemes with smart cards. Comput. Secur. **18**, 727–733 (1999)

14. Juang, W.-S.: Efficient password authenticated key agreement using smart cards. Comput. Secur. **23**, 167–173 (2004)

15. Yang, G., Wong, D.S., Wang, H., Deng, X.: Two-factor mutual authentication based on smart cards and passwords. J. Comput. Syst. Sci. **74**, 1160–1172 (2008)

16. Wei, F., Zhang, R., Ma, C.: Two factor authenticated key exchange protocol for wireless sensor networks: formal model and secure construction. In: Sun, X., Liu, A., Chao, H.-C., Bertino, E. (eds.) ICCCS 2016. LNCS, vol. 10039, pp. 377–388. Springer, Cham (2016). https://doi.org/10.1007/978-3-319-48671-0_34

17. Das, M.L., Saxena, A., Gulati, V.P.: A dynamic ID-based remote user authentication scheme. IEEE Trans. Consum. Electron. **50**, 629–631 (2004)

18. Liu, C., Ma, C.-G.: An efficient and provable secure PAKE scheme with robust anonymity. In: Liu, B., Ma, M., Chang, J. (eds.) ICICA 2012. LNCS, vol. 7473, pp. 722–729. Springer, Heidelberg (2012). https://doi.org/10.1007/978-3-642-34062-8_94

19. Madhusudhan, R., Mittal, R.: Dynamic ID-based remote user password authentication schemes using smart cards: a review. J. Network Comput. Appl. **35**, 1235–1248 (2012)

20. Wang, D., He, D., Wang, P., Chu, C.-H.: Anonymous two-factor authentication in distributed systems: certain goals are beyond attainment. IEEE Trans. Dependable Secure Comput. **12**, 428–442 (2015)

21. Xie, Q., Wong, D.S., Wang, G., Tan, X., Chen, K., Fang, L.: Provably secure dynamic id-based anonymous two-factor authenticated key exchange protocol with extended security model. IEEE Trans. Inf. Forensics Secur. **12**, 1382–1392 (2017)

22. Viet, D.Q., Yamamura, A., Tanaka, H.: Anonymous password-based authenticated key exchange. In: Maitra, S., Veni Madhavan, C.E., Venkatesan, R. (eds.) INDOCRYPT 2005. LNCS, vol. 3797, pp. 244–257. Springer, Heidelberg (2005). https://doi.org/10.1007/11596219_20

23. Naor, M., Pinkas, B.: Efficient oblivious transfer protocols. In: Proceedings of the Twelfth Annual ACM-SIAM Symposium on Discrete Algorithms, pp. 448–457. Society for Industrial and Applied Mathematics, Washington, D.C. (2001)

24. Chien, H.-Y., Chen, C.-H.: A remote authentication scheme preserving user anonymity. In: 19th International Conference on Advanced Information Networking and Applications. AINA 2005, pp. 245–248. IEEE (2005)

25. Fan, C.-I., Chan, Y.-C., Zhang, Z.-K.: Robust remote authentication scheme with smart cards. Comput. Secur. **24**, 619–628 (2005)

26. Liao, I.-E., Lee, C.-C., Hwang, M.-S.: Security enhancement for a dynamic ID-based remote user authentication scheme. In: International Conference on Next Generation Web Services Practices. NWeSP 2005, p. 4. IEEE (2005)

27. Juang, W.-S., Chen, S.-T., Liaw, H.-T.: Robust and efficient password-authenticated key agreement using smart cards. IEEE Trans. Industr. Electron. **55**, 2551–2556 (2008)

28. Li, X., Qiu, W., Zheng, D., Chen, K., Li, J.: Anonymity enhancement on robust and efficient password-authenticated key agreement using smart cards. IEEE Trans. Industr. Electron. **57**, 793–800 (2010)

29. Khan, M.K., Kim, S.-K., Alghathbar, K.: Cryptanalysis and security enhancement of a 'more efficient & secure dynamic ID-based remote user authentication scheme'. Comput. Commun. **34**, 305–309 (2011)

30. Wang, D., Wang, N., Wang, P., Qing, S.: Preserving privacy for free: Efficient and provably secure two-factor authentication scheme with user anonymity. Inf. Sci. **321**, 162–178 (2015)

31. Li, X., Zhang, Y.: A simple and robust anonymous two-factor authenticated key exchange protocol. Secur. Commun. Netw. **6**, 711–722 (2013)

32. Sun, D.-Z., Huai, J.-P., Sun, J.-Z., Li, J.-X., Zhang, J.-W., Feng, Z.-Y.: Improvements of Juang's password-authenticated key agreement scheme using smart cards. IEEE Trans. Industr. Electron. **56**, 2284–2291 (2009)
33. Yang, J., Zhang, Z.: A new anonymous password-based authenticated key exchange protocol. In: Chowdhury, D.R., Rijmen, V., Das, A. (eds.) INDOCRYPT 2008. LNCS, vol. 5365, pp. 200–212. Springer, Heidelberg (2008). https://doi.org/10.1007/978-3-540-89754-5_16
34. Yang, X., Jiang, H., Xu, Q., Hou, M., Wei, X., Zhao, M., Choo, K.-K.R.: A provably-secure and efficient verifier-based anonymous password-authenticated key exchange protocol. In: Trustcom/BigDataSE/ISPA 2016 IEEE, pp. 670–677. IEEE (2016)

Multi-user Forward Secure Dynamic Searchable Symmetric Encryption

Qiao Wang[1], Yu Guo[2], Hejiao Huang[1(✉)], and Xiaohua Jia[2]

[1] Department of Computer Science, Harbin Institute of Technology
Shenzhen Graduate School, Shenzhen, China
huanghejiao@hit.edu.cn
[2] Department of Computer Science, City University of Hong Kong,
Kowloon, Hong Kong

Abstract. Searchable Symmetric Encryption (SSE) makes it possible to privacy-preserving search over encrypted data stored on an untrusted server. Dynamic SSE schemes add the ability for the user to support secure update of encrypted data records. However, recent attacks show that update information can be exploited to recover the underlying values of ciphertexts. To improve the security, the notion of forward security is proposed, which aims to thwart those attacks by adding new documents without revealing if they match previous search queries. Unfortunately, existing forward secure SSE schemes are mostly for single-user settings, and cannot be easily extended to multi-user settings.

In this paper, we propose a multi-user forward secure dynamic SSE scheme with optimal search complexity. By introducing a semi-trusted proxy server who does not collude with the cloud server, we take a nice method to solve multi-user queries problem in most forward secure SSE schemes. With the help of proxy server who maintains keywords' state information, our scheme achieves forward security. Our experimental results demonstrate the efficiency of the proposed scheme.

Keywords: Multi-user · Forward security
Dynamic searchable symmetric encryption

1 Introduction

Searchable encryption is a popular approach which protects plaintext information from the compromised server while preserving the search functionality at the server side. Considering security, efficiency, and functionality, a line of work on searchable encryption schemes have been proposed, such as fully-homomorphic encryption and Oblivious RAM (ORAM). However, these techniques are usually too expensive to be used in practical systems. Searchable Symmetric Encryption (SSE) is a class of structured encryption technique, which enables a client to perform the keyword search on the encrypted database efficiently while preserving the privacy of the data and queries. In order to perform efficient keyword search, many SSE solutions construct their search structures such as invert

© Springer Nature Switzerland AG 2018
M. H. Au et al. (Eds.): NSS 2018, LNCS 11058, pp. 125–140, 2018.
https://doi.org/10.1007/978-3-030-02744-5_9

indexes, trees, graphs and so on. Static SSE scheme does not consider to handle the updates in the encrypted dataset. Sometimes, new data records are added and some old data records are removed from the dataset. To serve the above updates, dynamic SSE schemes [4,7,10,11,14,16,18,20] have been developed.

Recent attacks have shown that update information can be exploited to recover the underlying values of ciphertexts [3,8,22]. Specifically, the file-injection attack introduced by Zhang et al. [22] shows that it is possible to recover the contents of previous search queries of dynamic SSE schemes by injecting just a few documents. Hence, it is desirable to achieve forward security for dynamic SSE. Forward security is defined as that the cloud server cannot know the newly-added document that contains the keywords queried before. Stefanov et al. propose the first forward secure dynamic SSE scheme [5]. Yet, their design relies on an ORAM-like index with the hierarchical structure, which incurs a high bandwidth overhead. To achieve better performance, Bost et al. [2] propose an add-only dynamic SSE scheme, which achieves optimal search and update complexity by using trapdoor permutations. However, most of them only support the single-user setting, and is not suitable in the multi-user setting. This is because these schemes ask the client to maintain the state information locally and later re-encrypt the query results with a fresh key. Such treatment restricts the other users to access the updated state unless requesting from the data owner. Therefore, it requires that the data owner should always stay online.

In this paper, we propose MFS, a multi-user forward secure dynamic SSE scheme with optimal search complexity. First, we solve the key sharing problem by using bilinear pairing. Then, by introducing a semi-trusted proxy server, which serves as a network middlebox to store and manage state, we can ensure that authorized users can perform forward-privacy update operations without the interaction with the data owner. Finally, a system prototype is designed to evaluate and demonstrate the effectiveness and efficiency of our proposed scheme. The main contributions of this paper can be summarized as follows:

(1) Our MFS scheme achieves forward security with optimal search complexity. We introduce a proxy server that can help the data owner to maintain the keywords' state information and generate search trapdoors for authorized users. It can reduce not only data owner's storage overhead but also the time cost of generating search trapdoors.

(2) We propose the non-interactive multi-user access control scheme and integrate it into our design. In this scheme, we solve the problem of key sharing by using bilinear pairings. And the data owner can dynamically and efficiently authorize users to query the encrypted database (EDB) or revoke users authorization.

(3) We design a system prototype and evaluate the performance of our proposed scheme. Experimental results show that both the query performance and the update efficiency are improved when comparing to the interactive scheme.

The rest of this paper is organized as follows. Section 2 presents our system architecture, design requirements, and primitives. Then we present our multi-user forward secure dynamic SSE construction in Sect. 3. Sections 4 and 5 give the security analysis and performance evaluation, respectively. Finally, we discuss the related work in Sect. 6 and conclude this work in Sect. 7.

2 Overview

2.1 System Architecture

Considering a cloud data hosting service involving four different entities, as illustrated in Fig. 1: data owner, data user, proxy server, and cloud server. Data owner has a collection of documents $\mathcal{F} = (f_1, f_2, ..., f_n)$ to be outsourced to the cloud server in encrypted form while keeping the capability to search over them. Before outsourcing, data owner will build an encrypted searchable index T and an encrypted keyword state information table W from $\mathcal{F}$. Besides, in order to mitigate the risk of key exposure, the data owner selects a distinct encryption key ek_f for each document f. Finally, it stores both the index T and the encrypted documents on the cloud server, and stores the keyword state information table W on the proxy server. To grant query capabilities to the other authorized users, the data owner selects a query key qk_u and a decryption key dk_u for each registered user, and computes his complementary query key qk_c and complementary decryption key dk_c. Finally, the data owner transmits these keys to the proxy server and the cloud server respectively.

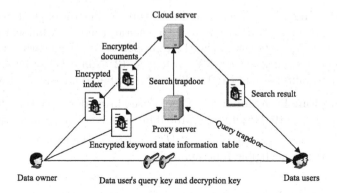

Fig. 1. Multi-user searchable encryption system model.

To search documents for a given keyword w, the authorized user u first generates a query trapdoor $Tr_u(w)$ and submits it to the proxy server. Upon receiving $Tr_u(w)$, the proxy server forms a search trapdoor by using the user u's complementary query key qk_u and w's state information stored in W, and sends it to the cloud server. Then, the cloud server is responsible to search on the index T, and locates each matching document f's complementary decryption secret, and returns the matching documents and complementary decryption secrets to the user u. Finally, u computes the decryption key dk_f from the returned secret and obtains the final result set.

2.2 Security Requirements

In this paper, we consider cloud server and proxy server to be honest-but curious, which means that they execute out proposed protocol while also trying to find more secret information. Besides, we assume that the proxy server will never collude with the cloud server. The proposed multi-user forward secure dynamic SSE scheme should satisfy the following security requirements.

- **Data confidentiality:** It requires that the owners' data and queries must be protected from both cloud servers and unauthorized users. It is the most basic security requirement in general searchable encryption schemes.
- **Forward security:** It means that the cloud server cannot know the newly-added document that contains the keywords queried before. Forward security is a stronger security definition of dynamic SSE schemes.
- **Query unforgeability:** Query unforgeability ensures the adversary cannot even produce a valid query on behalf of an authorized user.
- **Revocability:** User revocation is a necessary operation in the multi-user setting. A revoked user may attack the system by performing a search due to personal goals, which may lead to privacy exposure. Hence, it is essential to permit data owner to revoke the query capabilities of revoked users.

2.3 Cryptographic Primitives

Bilinear Pairings: Let G_1, G_2 and G_T be three bilinear groups of prime order p. Let g_1 be a generator of G_1 and g_2 be a generator of G_2. A bilinear pairing is a map $\hat{e} : G_1 \times G_2 \to G_T$ with the three properties: (1) Bilinearity: for all $u \in G_1$, $v \in G_2$ and $a, b \in Z_p$, $\hat{e}(u^a, v^b) = \hat{e}(u, v)^{ab}$. (2) Non-degeneracy: $\hat{e}(g_1, g_2) \neq 1$. (3) Computability: $\hat{e}(u, v)$ can be efficiently computed for any $u \in G_1$, $v \in G_2$.

Pseudo-random Functions: Let F be a pseudo-random function defined as: $\{0,1\}^\lambda \times \{0,1\}^m \to \{0,1\}^n$, if for all probabilistic polynomial-time distinguishers D, $|Pr[D^{F(k,\cdot)} = 1 | k \xleftarrow{\$} \{0,1\}^\lambda] - Pr[D^g = 1 | g \xleftarrow{\$} \{\mathsf{Func}[m,n]\}]| < negl(\lambda)$, where $negl(\lambda)$ is a negligible function in λ.

3 Multi-user Forward Secure Dynamic SSE

In this section, we start from giving solutions to the two problems—forward security and multi-user queries—in our proposed scheme. Then we give a detail description of our multi-user forward secure dynamic SSE construction.

3.1 Achieving Forward Security

Forward security in dynamic SSE schemes requires that cloud server cannot know whether the newly-added document contains the keywords queried before. It can be achieved when the newly-added keyword is not associated with the encrypted keywords stored in the cloud server. Instead of taking ORAM technique that

Table 1. The structure of the chaining index table T

Storage address	The form of encrypted keyword/document(e_1, e_2)
0	null
$addr(w, ind_c)$	$< addr(w, ind_j) \| k(w, ind_k) > \oplus <$ $Tr(w) \| F(k(w, ind_c), addr(w, ind_c)) >, ind_c \oplus F(k(w, ind_c), i_w)$
...	...
$addr(w, ind_j)$	$< addr(w, ind_k) \| k(w, ind_k) > \oplus <$ $Tr(w) \| F(k(w, ind_j), addr(w, ind_j)) >, ind_j \oplus F(k(w, ind_j), i_w)$
...	...
$addr(w, ind_k)$	$< 0^\mu \| s \in 0, 1^\lambda > \oplus < Tr(w) \| F(k(w, ind_k), addr(w, ind_k)) >$ $, ind_k \oplus F(k(w, ind_k), i_w)$

using computationally heavy cryptographic primitives, in this paper we combine keyword state information stored on the proxy server and a chaining structure of index T stored on the cloud server, and utilizes the lightweight cryptographic primitives to achieve forward security, which is explained as follows.

For each keyword/document pair in the database (DB), data owner generates an encryption key, and a non-collision storage address for it. Besides, data owner associates every inserted keyword w an identifier i_w. Each keyword w's latest state information is denoted as a tuple $(addr(w, ind_c), k(w, ind_c), i_w)$ indexed by its trapdoor $Tr(w)$, where $addr(w, ind_c) = H_1(sk_1, w \| ind_c)$ is currently the latest storage address of added pair that contains keyword w, $k(w, ind_c) = H_2(sk_2, w \| ind_c)$ is an encryption key of the pair, $i_w = F(k_s, w)$ is an identifier of keyword w, and sk_1, sk_2, k_s are private keys owned by the data owner. All keywords' latest state information is stored in keyword state information table W, which is maintained by the proxy server. Now, we introduce the two main data structures W and T, and then explain why our scheme achieves forward security. As mentioned before, W maps every inserted keyword w to its latest state information, which is indexed by its trapdoor $Tr(w)$. We denote the current search trapdoor for a keyword w as a tuple $(Tr(w), addr(w, ind_c), k(w, ind_c), i_w)$. Given the current search trapdoor for keyword w, the cloud server can retrieve all documents' identifiers that match w from the chaining index table T. Each entry of T stores an encrypted keyword/document pair, and contains two elements e_1, e_2 as shown in Table 1, where e_1 stores information about previous pair that contain the same keyword, and e_2 is expressed as an encrypted identifier of a certain document. When data owner wants to find documents that contains a keyword w, he generates query trapdoor $Tr(w)$ by using keyword encryption key wk, and sends it to the proxy server. Upon receiving the query trapdoor from the proxy server, the proxy server obtains w's latest state information from keyword state information table W and then forms current search trapdoor $(Tr(w), addr(w, ind_c), k(w, ind_c), i_w)$, which sent to the cloud server. Upon receiving keyword w's current search trapdoor, the cloud server utilizes the search trapdoor to obtain current matching

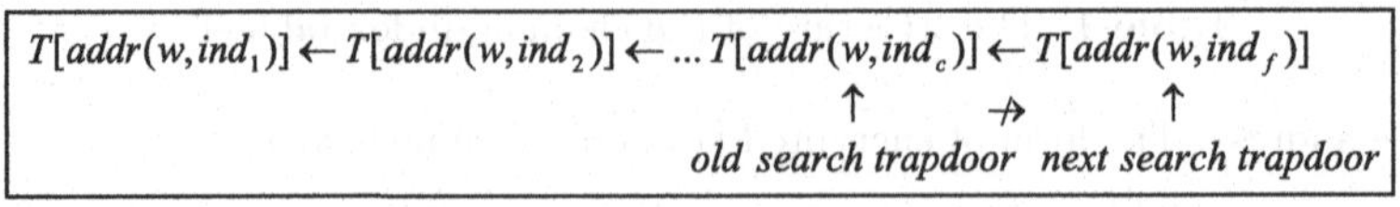

$$T[addr(w,ind_1)] \leftarrow T[addr(w,ind_2)] \leftarrow ... T[addr(w,ind_c)] \leftarrow T[addr(w,ind_f)]$$
$$\uparrow \qquad \nrightarrow \qquad \uparrow$$
$$\text{old search trapdoor} \quad \text{next search trapdoor}$$

Fig. 2. An index chain of the keyword w after adding a keyword/document pair.

document's identifier ind_c by calculating $T[addr(w,ind_c)].e_2 \oplus F(k(w,ind_c),$ $i_w)$ = $ind_c \oplus F(k(w,ind_c),i_w) \oplus F(k(w,ind_c),i_w)$, and get previous pair's information by calculating $T[addr(w,ind_c)].e_1 \oplus \langle Tr(w)||F(k(w,ind_c),$ $addr(w,ind_c))\rangle$. Repeat search operations until the previous pair's address equals 0^μ. Therefore, the cloud server can retrieve all documents' identifiers that contain keyword w.

When a new document f with identifier ind_f is added, for each keyword $w \in W(f)$, data owner computes and sends the addition tuple $(Tr(w), addr(w,ind_f), k(w,ind_f), i_w, e_2)$ to the proxy server, where e_2 equals $ind_f \oplus F(k(w,ind_f), i_w)$. Upon receiving the addition tuple, the proxy server forms the addition trapdoor $(addr(w,ind_f), e_1, e_2)$, where e_1 is computed as follows: $\langle addr(w,ind_c)||k(w,ind_c)\rangle \oplus \langle Tr(w)||F(k(w,ind_f), addr(w,ind_f))\rangle$, where $addr(w,ind_c)$ and $k(w,ind_c)$ are currently w's latest state information. Note that if the added pair is the first one that contains keyword w, $addr(w,ind_c)$ and $k(w,ind_c)$ would be set as 0^μ and a random string s of λ bits respectively. Then, the proxy server sends the addition trapdoor to the cloud server and updates w's state information in W according to the addition tuple. Given the addition trapdoor, the cloud server stores (e_1, e_2) at $T[addr(w,ind_f)]$. The cloud server does not know $k(w,ind_f)$ until next query for the same keyword w. Without knowing $k(w,ind_f)$, the cloud server cannot recover the ind_f stored at $T[addr(w,ind_f)]$. Meanwhile, without knowing private key sk_1, the cloud server cannot know whether $addr(w,ind_f) = H_1(sk_1, w||ind_f)$ is generated from the same keyword as that of $addr(w,ind_i)$, $1 \leq i \leq c$ shown in Fig. 2. Hence, this solution achieves forward security.

3.2 Supporting Multi-user Queries

We solve the problem of key sharing in multi-user setting by adopting bilinear pairings. In more detail, data owner not only generates a distinct symmetric encryption key for each document, but also selects a distinct query key and decryption key for each registered user. In this way, the risk of key exposure is mitigated. To support multi-user queries, it refers to two questions: (1) how to grant query capabilities to authorized users; (2) how to revoke authorized user's query capability if necessary. Besides, we require that the approach supporting multi-user queries should be efficient, which means that authorization and revocation should be handled without extensive interaction between the data owner and authorized users. It should be also secure so that illegal and revoked users cannot query the EDB. The solution is described as follows. The data owner randomly selects a keyword encryption key $wk \in Z_p^*$, which used to encrypt keywords and generate keyword trapdoors. Besides, the data owner also randomly chooses a data encryption master key $ek \in Z_p^*$, and generates a distinct symmetric encryption key ek_f for each document f by calculating $ek_f = h_3(\hat{e}(r_f, g_2)^{ek})$, where r_f is a random number selected in G_1. Then, the data owner sends the encrypted document and corresponding random numbers to the cloud server.

Query Capability Enforcement: To enable a new user u to query the EDB and decrypt the returned ciphertexts, the data owner proceeds as follows: (1) Selecting a unique identity uid for the user u. (2) Randomly choosing a query key $qk_u \in Z_p^*$ and a decryption key $dk_u \in Z_p^*$ for the user u. (3) Calculating the user u's complementary query key $qk_c = g_2^{wk/qk_u}$ and complementary decryption key $dk_c = g_2^{ek/qk_u}$ (4) Transmitting the tuple (uid, qk_u, dk_u) to the user u, and sending the tuples (uid, qk_c) and (uid, dk_c) to the proxy server and the cloud server respectively. An authorized user u can generate a query trapdoor $Tr_u(w)$ for a keyword w by calculating $Tr_u(w) = h_1(w)^{qk_u}$, where qk_u is the user u's query key. Then, the user u transmits $Tr_u(w)$ to the proxy server. Upon receiving the query trapdoor $Tr_u(w)$, the proxy server utilizes the user u's complementary query key qk_c to reconstruct keyword trapdoor $Tr(w)$ by calculating $Tr(w) = h_2(\hat{e}(Tr_u(w), qk_c))$. Then, the proxy server forms search trapdoor for keyword w as we described in the previous subsection, and send it to the cloud server. The cloud server can retrieve all documents' identifiers that match w from the chaining index table T. Before returning the corresponding encrypted documents to the user u, the cloud server will compute each document f's complementary decryption secret cds_f by calculating $cds_f = \hat{e}(r_f, dk_c)$, where r_f is the random number related to the document f, and dk_c is the user u's complementary decryption key. Upon receiving the search results from the cloud server, the user u obtains each document f's decryption key dk_f by calculating $dk_f = h_3(cds_f^{dk_u})$, where dk_u is the user u's private decryption key. Finally, the user u can decrypt all returned encrypted documents.

User Revocation: To revoke an authorized user u, the data owner sends the user u's identity uid to both the proxy server and the cloud server. Then, the proxy server deletes u's complementary query key qk_u from his storage, and the cloud server deletes u's complementary decryption from his storage as well. The revoked user u is no longer able to query the EDB in that the proxy server cannot compute keyword trapdoor and form search trapdoor for him without knowing his complementary query key. Besides, the revoked user u cannot decrypt the ciphertexts anymore without knowing corresponding complementary decryption secrets computed by using his complementary decryption key.

3.3   The MFS Design

The above approaches demonstrate the way to achieve forward security and support multi-user queries in our MFS scheme. In this subsection, we will present our MFS construction and corresponding query protocols.

Algorithm 1. SE.Setup(λ, $\perp$) $\rightarrow$ (SK, st_q, EDB)

Data owner(λ, $\perp$) $\rightarrow$ (SK, PK, st_q, EDB)

1: $(p, g_1, g_2, G_1, G_2, h_1, h_2, h_3) \leftarrow$ PublicSystemParamGen(1^λ)
2: $wk \xleftarrow{\$} Z_p^*$; $ek \xleftarrow{\$} Z_p^*$; $sk_1 \xleftarrow{\$} \{0,1\}^\lambda$; $sk_2 \xleftarrow{\$} \{0,1\}^\lambda$; $k_s \xleftarrow{\$} \{0,1\}^\lambda$
3: W, T = empty map; SK = $(wk, ek, sk_1, sk_2, k_s)$
4: $st_q \leftarrow$ W ; EDB $\leftarrow$ T

MFS.Setup: The Algorithm 1 takes as input a security parameter λ, sets up the public system parameters $(p, g_1, g_2, G_1, G_2, h_1, h_2, h_3)$, and selects a keyword encryption key wk, a data encryption master key ek from Z_p^*, and three private keys sk_1, sk_2, $k_s \in \{0,1\}^\lambda$. And the algorithm also initializes an empty table W and an empty table T for the proxy server and the cloud server respectively.

MFS.Add: To add a new document f with identifier ind_f into the EDB, for each keyword $w \in W(f)$, the Algorithm 2 proceeds the following operations: (1) Data owner computes addition tuple of the pair (w, ind_f), and sends it to the proxy server; (2) Proxy server generates addition trapdoor by using w's state and the addition tuple, and then sends it to the cloud server. Finally, he updates w's state information according to the addition tuple. (3) Cloud server stores the encrypted keyword/document pair in T according to the addition trapdoor.

MFS.Register: In Algorithm 3, the data owner first chooses a unique identity uid, and generates a query key qk_u and a decryption key dk_u for the user u. Then, he computes the user u's complementary query key qk_c and complementary decryption key dk_c. Finally, he transmits the tuple (uid, qk_u, dk_u) to the user u, transmits the tuple (uid, qk_c) to the proxy server, and transmits (uid, dk_c) to the cloud server. And the cloud server and proxy update the key tables respectively.

MFS.Search: Given a keyword w, a data user u computes query trapdoor $Tr_u(w)$ by using his query key qk_u, and transmits it to the proxy server. Upon receiving $Tr_u(w)$ from the user u, the proxy server reconstructs keyword trapdoor $Tr(w)$ by using the user u's complementary query key qk_c, and forms the search trapdoor for keyword w by looking up w's state information in W. Then, the proxy server sends the search trapdoor to the cloud server. Given the search trapdoor, the cloud server retrieves all documents' identifiers that match keyword w from the chaining index T.

MFS.Decrypt: Upon receiving search results from the cloud server, the data user u computes each document f's decryption key dk_f by using his decryption key dk_u and corresponding complementary decryption secrets cds_f. Then, the user u can decrypt the ciphertext C_f by using the symmetric encryption algorithm with decryption key dk_f.

Algorithm 2. MFS.Add((SK, f), st_q, EDB) $\rightarrow$ $(st'_q$, EDB$')$

Data owner(SK, (w, ind_f)) $\rightarrow$ (AddTuple)

1: AddTuple $\leftarrow \emptyset$
2: **for** each $w \in W(f)$ **do**
3:     $addr(w, ind_f) = H_1(sk_1, w\|ind_f)$
4:     $k(w, ind_f) = H_2(sk_2, w\|ind_f)$
5:     $i_w = F(k_s, w)$
6:     $Tr(w) = h_2(\hat{e}(h_1(w), g_2)^{wk})$
7:     $e_2 = ind_f \oplus F(k(w, ind_f), i_w)$
8:     AddTuple $\leftarrow (Tr(w), addr(w, ind_f), k(w, ind_f), i_w, e_2)$
9:     send AddTuple to the proxy server
10: **end for**
11: $r_f \xleftarrow{\$} G_1$; $ek_f \leftarrow h_3(\hat{e}(r_f, g_2)^{ek})$
12: $C_f = AES.Encrypt(ek_f, f)$
13: send the ciphertext (C_f, r_f) to the cloud server

Proxy server(AddTuple, st_q) $\rightarrow$ (AddTrapdoor, st'_q)

1: parse AddTuple as $(Tr(w), addr(w, ind_f), k(w, ind_f), i_w, e_2)$
2: AddTrapdoor $\leftarrow \emptyset$
3: **if** W$[Tr(w)]\neq\perp$ **then**
4:     $(addr(w, ind_c), k(w, ind_c), \emptyset) \leftarrow W[Tr(w)]$
5:     $e_1 = \langle addr(w, ind_c)\|k(w, ind_c)\rangle \oplus \langle Tr(w)\|F(k(w, ind_f), addr(w, ind_f))\rangle$
6:     AddTrapdoor $\leftarrow (addr(w, ind_f), e_1, e_2)$
7: **else**
8:     $s \xleftarrow{\$} \{0,1\}^\lambda$; $e_1 = \langle 0^\mu\|s\rangle \oplus \langle Tr(w)\|F(k(w, ind_f), addr(w, ind_f))\rangle$
9:     AddTrapdoor $\leftarrow (addr(w, ind_f), e_1, e_2)$
10: **end if**
11: W$[Tr(w)] \leftarrow (addr(w, ind_f), k(w, ind_f), i_w)$
12: send AddTrapdoor to the cloud server

Cloud server(AddTrapdoor, EDB) $\rightarrow$ (EDB$'$)

1: parse AddTrapdoor as $(addr(w, ind_f), e_1, e_2)$
2: T$[addr(w, ind_f)] \leftarrow (e_1, e_2)$

Algorithm 3. MFS.Register(u, Ucqt, Ucdt) $\rightarrow$ $(uid, qk_u, dk_u, qk_c, dk_c)$

Data owner(u) $\rightarrow$ $(uid, qk_c, qk_u, dk_c, dk_u)$

1: generate a unique identity uid for a new user u
2: $qk_u \xleftarrow{\$} Z_p{}^*$; $dk_u \xleftarrow{\$} Z_p{}^*$
3: $qk_c = g_2{}^{wk/qk_u}$; $dk_c = g_2{}^{ek/dk_u}$
4: send (uid, qk_c) to the proxy server
5: send (uid, dk_c) to the cloud server
6: send (uid, qk_u, dk_u) to the new user u

Algorithm 4. MFS.Search$((w,qk_u), (qk_c,st_q), (dk_c,\text{EDB})) \rightarrow \text{rst}$

Data user u$(w, qk_u) \rightarrow (Tr_u(w),\ uid)$

1: $Tr_u(w) = h_1(w)^{qk_u}$
2: send $Tr_u(w)$ to the proxy server together with his identity uid

Proxy server$(Tr_u(w),\ uid,\ qk_c,\ st_q) \rightarrow (\text{SearchTrapdoor})$

1: SearchTrapdoor $\leftarrow \emptyset$
2: **if** Ucqt$[uid] \neq \bot$ **then**
3:　　$qk_c \leftarrow$ Ucqt$[uid]$
4: **else**
5:　　the algorithm stops, return "unauthorized user"
6: **end if**
7: $Tr(w) = h_2(\hat{e}(Tr_u(w), qk_c))$
8: **if** W$[Tr(w)] \neq \bot$ **then**
9:　　$(addr(w, ind_c), k(w, ind_c), i_w) \leftarrow$ W$[Tr(w)]$
10:　　SearchTrapdoor $\leftarrow (Tr(w), addr(w, ind_c), k(w, ind_c), i_w)$
11:　　send SearchTrapdoor and uid to the cloud server
12: **else**
13:　　send "none" to the data user u
14: **end if**

Cloud server(SearchTrapdoor, uid, dk_c, EDB) $\rightarrow$ (rst)

1: parse SearchTrapdoor as $(Tr(w), addr(w, ind_c), k(w, ind_c), i_w)$
2: $ResultSet \leftarrow \emptyset;\ rst \leftarrow \emptyset$
3: **while** $addr(w, ind_c) \neq 0^\mu$ **do**
4:　　$ind =$T$[addr(w, ind_c)].e_2 \oplus F(k(w, ind_c), i_w)$
5:　　$\langle addr(w, ind_c) || k(w, ind_c) \rangle \leftarrow$ T$[addr(w, ind_c)].e_1$
　　　　$\oplus \langle Tr(w) || F(k(w, ind_c), addr(w, ind_c)) \rangle$
6:　　$ResultSet \leftarrow ResultSet \cup ind$
7: **end while**
8: $dk_c \leftarrow$ Ucdt$[uid]$
9: **for** each $ind \in ReturnSet$ **do**
10:　　$cds_{ind} = \hat{e}(r_{ind}, dk_c);\ rst \leftarrow rst \cup (cds_{ind}, C_{ind})$
11: **end for**
12: return rst to the data user u

Algorithm 5. MFS.Decrypt(rst, dk_u) $\rightarrow$ F

Data user(rst, dk_u) $\rightarrow$ F

1: $F = \emptyset$
2: **for** each $(cds_{ind}, C_{ind}) \in rst$ **do**
3:　　$dk_i = h_3(cds_{ind}^{dk_u});\ f = AES.Decrypt(dk_i, C_{ind})$
4:　　$F \leftarrow F \cup f$
5: **end for**

Table 2. Comparison of search and update complexity between MFS and Sophos

Scheme	Computation			Communication	
	Search	Add	Delete	Search	Add/Delete
Sophos	$O(a_w + d_w)$	$O(1)$	$O(1)$	$O(n_w)$	$O(1)$
MFS	$O(n_w)$		$O(1)$	$O(n_w)$	$O(n_w)$	$O(1)$

4   Security Analysis

Our above construction optimizes the query and update complexity while preserving the expected security strengths. That is, our design ensures that either of the two servers learns nothing about the sensing values. Such security guarantees provided by our improved construction also based on the security framework for search over encrypted data [3]. Due to the space limit, here we discuss how our scheme can achieve forward security strengths and leave a formal security analysis to our extended version.

Data Confidentiality: The outsourced documents are encrypted with the secure symmetric encryption algorithm (e.g., AES) with different secret keys. Their confidentiality is ensured by the secure symmetric encryption. Likewise, each index entry is encrypted with the secure pseudo-random function F. Therefore, the server cannot learn the underlying content without the secret key.

Forward Security: As described in Sect. 3, we combine keyword state information table W stored on the proxy server and a chaining index table stored on the cloud server to preserve our scheme to achieve forward security. Because the search trapdoor for keyword w is generated from the entry of W associated with w and this entry updates once when a keyword/document pair (w, ind) is added to the EDB. The cloud server does not know newly-updated search trapdoor for keyword w until next query of keyword w. As illustrated in Fig. 2, the cloud server cannot recover the document's identifier stored at newly-added entry in T without the newly-updated search trapdoor, neither know whether the newly-added entry is generated from the same keyword as that of those previous added entries that contain the same keyword w without knowing secrete key sk_1.

5   Implementation and Evaluation

In this section, we evaluated and compared the performance of our MFS scheme with Sophos's (Bost et al. [2]) in three aspects: EDB creation, EDB search and EDB update. We implemented our MFS scheme in Java. The pseudo-random function F and the (keyed) hash function are using HMAC. W is implemented as a hash table. And the chaining index table T is stored using Redis [1]. We ran our experiments on a desktop computer a single Intel Core i5 4590K 3.30 GHz CPU, 4 GB of RAM, running on Windows 7.

Table 3. Comparison with EDB creation using different size of the dataset

Scheme	Times (ms)	Pairs of k/doc
MFS	798,261	500k
	2,319,001	1.4M
Sophos(with RSA-2048)	5,103,634	500k
	16,201,916	1.4M
Sophos(with RSA-1024)	921,278	500k
	2,858,560	1.4M

To better explain our experience results, we first give the comparison of search and update complexity between our MFS scheme and Sophos as shown in Table 2. The complexities are based on retrieving documents that contain a keyword w, or updating a keyword/document pair. n_w is the size of result set for searching keyword w, and a_w (resp. d_w) is the number of times the keyword w was historically added to (resp. deleted from) the encrypted database.

EDB Evaluation: Table 3 shows the time of EDB creation using different size of the dataset. For Sophos, we also used 1024 bits RSA instead of 2048 bits to improve the performance because the RSA decryption in Sophos may be a delayed factor. It shows that our scheme takes less time to create the EDB than Sophos with the same size of the dataset. Because our scheme mainly utilizes symmetric-key based operations, such as pseudo-random functions and secure hash functions. In contrast, Sophos requires heavy public key operations, i.e., RSA encryption. As we can see from Table 3, the time cost decreased greatly when we use 1024 bits RSA instead of 2048 bits, which confirms that the RSA decryption is a delayed factor.

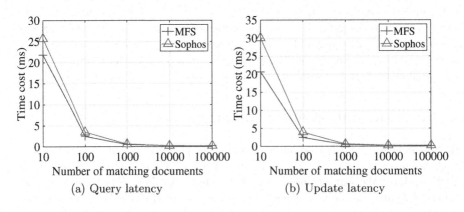

(a) Query latency   (b) Update latency

Fig. 3. Performance evaluation

Table 4. Comparison of performance during add-delete operations (units: ms)

Iterations	MFS		Sophos	
	Add	Delete	Add	Delete
Init(1.4M)	2,319,001	—	16,201,916	—
100k	170,721	283,193	1,364,744	1,096,763
200k	349,233	512,660	2,583,204	2,016,892
400k	676,272	1,263,036	4,767,194	4,594,459

Query Evaluation: To compare the speed of our search algorithm and Sophos's just after EDB creation, we searched for a set of keywords with different frequency in our dataset. Figure 3(a) presents the performance of search algorithm of our scheme and Sophos. Here, the cost time equals the time taken to search divided by the number of matching documents. As illustrated in Fig. 3(a), we can notice that the larger the result set, the faster the search algorithm based on the search time per matching entry, for both our scheme and Sophos. Our scheme is superior in search speed than Sophos especially in the case where the number of matched documents is relatively small. Because our scheme just uses simple cryptographic primitives to generate search trapdoors, while Sophos highly relies on RSA encryption.

Update Evaluation: To measure the performance of update algorithm, we selected 100k, 200k, 400k keyword/document pairs for add operations. And we randomly selected 100k, 200k, 400k pairs of keyword/document from previously added pairs for delete operations. Note that our design can simply support delete operation by removing the entry directly from the chain index. Due to the space limit, we leave a detailed update protocol to future work. In terms of Sophos, we make it to support delete operations by creating two EDB instances for storing add pairs and deleted pairs respectively. And the search result is the difference between the matched documents in both EDB instances.

As shown in Table 4, both of our add algorithm and delete algorithm are faster than Sophos, although our delete operations' complexity is higher than Sophos shown in Table 2. This is because the RSA decryption takes relatively more time than simple cryptographic primitives operations. Besides, the efficiency of delete algorithm in MFS is lower than the add algorithm, because it operates on the original EDB and updates it, which preserves that the deleted entries would never be searched in subsequent queries. For Sophos, delete operations perform the same as add operations so that the efficiency of its add and delete algorithm is almost the same.

To measure the effect of update operations to the EDB, we also compared the search speed after add-delete operations to the EDB, as shown in Fig. 3(b). We can observe that our search algorithm still performs better than Sophos's. Compared with Fig. 3(a), our searching speed almost had no change after add-delete operations to the EDB, while Sophos's search algorithm performs slightly worse than before. As shown in Table 2, our searching computation complexity is optimal, which is lower than Sophos's. In our scheme, deleted pairs are removed from the EDB by our delete algorithm, and thus the search speed is almost the same as before. However, for Sophos, delete operations performed the same as the add's, and deleted pairs would also be searched if they matched the query keyword. Therefore, the search speed gradually decreases where updates operation are frequent for Sophos.

6   Related Works

Dynamic Searchable Encryption: Searchable symmetric encryption (SSE) had first been introduced by Song et al. [17], in which search complexity is linear with the size of the data. Curtmola et al. [6] had proposed an index-based SSE scheme for the first time, which achieves sublinear search complexity, but in static setting. Kamara et al. [11] were the first to introduce both dynamic and sublinear scheme, but would leak the hashes of updated keyword in the newly added documents. Forward security was highlighted by Zhang et al. [22], in which show us that the powerful file-injection attacks can break the user's query privacy severely in dynamic SSE systems. Stefanov et al. [18] presented an ORAM-like forward private SSE construction. In [2], Bost built a formal definition for forward private and proposed an insertion-only SSE scheme, which achieved optimal update complexity. Ocansey et al. [15] proposed a dynamic searchable encryption scheme that achieving forward security by maintaining an increasing counter for each keyword at an IoT gateway.

Multi-client Access in Searchable Encryption: Another line of related work [6,9,12,13,19,21] (just to list a few) is multi-client access in searchable encryption. Curtmola et al. [6] proposed the first construction for multi-user SSE based on broadcast encryption, which enables a basic access control policy. In [9], Jarecki et al. presented another multi-user SSE construction with a more strict and refined access policies. By leveraging oblivious PRF for the generation of keyword trapdoors, authorized users can query the authorized keywords.

Lin et al. [13] proposed a multi-client searchable encryption settings over the distributed key-value stores. They utilize a homomorphic signature mechanism to authorize the users, where the search trapdoors can be signed by the data owner and verified by the server via a per-query blinding factor. Sun et al. [19] proposed a non-interactive multi-client scheme, where an authorized user only needs to communicate with the data owner one time to obtain the necessary search keys for authorized keywords. In [12], Shabnam Kasra et al. proposed a multi-user SSE scheme based on the single-user Oblivious Cross Tags (OXT) protocol. The scheme allows any user to perform a search query by interacting with the server and any θ-1 'helping' users. Yuan et al. [21] proposed a multi-client SSE scheme with boolean queries in distributed key-value stores, where further adapt a secure non-interactive multi-user scheme proposed in [19].

7 Conclusion

This paper introduces a multi-user dynamic SSE scheme, called MFS, with forward security data protection. We combine the keyword state information table W and chaining index table T to make our scheme to achieve forward security. To support secure multi-user queries, we further integrate the multi-user searchable encryption scheme into our design. In addition, we conduct security analysis to demonstrate the strong security strength of this design. Finally, the evaluation results show that MFS is more efficient than the previous work.

Acknowledgment. This work is financially supported by National Science and Technology Major Project under Grant No. 2016YFB0800804 and No. 2017YFB0803002, National Natural Science Foundation of China under Grant No. 61672195 and No. 61732022.

References

1. Redis: A key-value store. http://redis.io/download
2. Bost, R.: Sophos - forward secure searchable encryption. In: Cryptology ePrint Archive, Report 2016/728 (2016)
3. Cash, D., Grubbs, P., Perry, J., Ristenpart, T.: Leakage-abuse attacks against searchable encryption. In: Proceedings of ACM CCS (2015)
4. Cash, D., et al.: Dynamic searchable encryption in very large databases: data structures and implementation. In: Proceedings of NDSS (2014)
5. Chang, Y.-C., Mitzenmacher, M.: Privacy preserving keyword searches on remote encrypted data. In: Ioannidis, J., Keromytis, A., Yung, M. (eds.) ACNS 2005. LNCS, vol. 3531, pp. 442–455. Springer, Heidelberg (2005). https://doi.org/10.1007/11496137_30
6. Curtmola, R., Garay, J., Kamara, S., Ostrovsky, R.: Searchable symmetric encryption: improved definitions and efficient constructions. In: Proceedings of ACM CCS (2006)
7. Hahn, F., Kerschbaum, F.: Searchable encryption with secure and efficient updates. In: Proceedings of ACM CCS (2014)
8. Islam, M., Kuzu, M., Kantarcioglu, M.: Access pattern disclosure on searchable encryption: ramification, attack and mitigation. In: Proceedings of NDSS (2012)
9. Jarecki, S., Jutla, C., Krawczyk, H., Rosu, M., Steiner, M.: Outsourced symmetric private information retrieval. In: Proceedings of ACM CCS (2013)
10. Kamara, S., Papamanthou, C.: Parallel and dynamic searchable symmetric encryption. In: Sadeghi, A.-R. (ed.) FC 2013. LNCS, vol. 7859, pp. 258–274. Springer, Heidelberg (2013). https://doi.org/10.1007/978-3-642-39884-1_22
11. Kamara, S., Papamanthou, C., Roeder, T.: Dynamic searchable symmetric encryption. In: Proceedings of ACM CCS (2012)
12. Kasra Kermanshahi, S., Liu, J.K., Steinfeld, R.: Multi-user cloud-based secure keyword search. In: Pieprzyk, J., Suriadi, S. (eds.) ACISP 2017. LNCS, vol. 10342, pp. 227–247. Springer, Cham (2017). https://doi.org/10.1007/978-3-319-60055-0_12
13. Lin, W., Yuan, X., Li, B., Wang, C.: Multi-client searchable encryption over distributed key-value stores. In: Proceedings of SMARTCOMP (2017)
14. Naveed, M., Prabhakaran, M., Gunter, C.: Dynamic searchable encryption via blind storage. In: Proceedings of IEEE S&P (2014)

15. Ocansey, S.K., Ametepe, W., Li, X.W., Wang, C.: Dynamic searchable encryption with privacy protection for cloud computing. Int. J. Commun. Syst. **31**(1), e3403 (2018)
16. Pappas, V., et al.: Blind seer: a scalable private DBMS. In: Proceedings of IEEE S&P (2014)
17. Song, D., Wagner, D., Perrig, A.: Practical techniques for searches on encrypted data. In: Proceedings of IEEE S&P (2000)
18. Stefanov, E., Papamanthou, C., Shi, E.: Practical dynamic searchable symmetric encryption with small leakage. In: Proceedings of NDSS (2014)
19. Sun, S.-F., Liu, J.K., Sakzad, A., Steinfeld, R., Yuen, T.H.: An efficient non-interactive multi-client searchable encryption with support for boolean queries. In: Askoxylakis, I., Ioannidis, S., Katsikas, S., Meadows, C. (eds.) ESORICS 2016. LNCS, vol. 9878, pp. 154–172. Springer, Cham (2016). https://doi.org/10.1007/978-3-319-45744-4_8
20. Yavuz, A.A., Guajardo, J.: Dynamic searchable symmetric encryption with minimal leakage and efficient updates on commodity hardware. In: Dunkelman, O., Keliher, L. (eds.) SAC 2015. LNCS, vol. 9566, pp. 241–259. Springer, Cham (2016). https://doi.org/10.1007/978-3-319-31301-6_15
21. Yuan, X., Yuan, X., Li, B., Wang, C.: Secure multi-client data access with boolean queries in distributed key-value stores. In: Proceedings of CNS (2017)
22. Zhang, Y., Katz, J., Papamanthou, C.: All your queries are belong to us: the power of file-injection attacks on searchable encryption. In: Proceedings of USENIX Security (2016)

Towards Security Authentication for IoT Devices with Lattice-Based ZK

Jie Cai[1], Han Jiang[2(✉)], Qiuliang Xu[2], Guangshi Lv[1], Minghao Zhao[3], and Hao Wang[4]

[1] School of Mathematics, Shandong University, Ji'nan, Shandong, China
caijie0318@mail.sdu.edu.cn, gslv@sdu.edu.cn
[2] Software College, Shandong University, Ji'nan, Shandong, China
{jianghan,xql}@sdu.edu.cn
[3] School of Software, Tsinghua University, Beijing, China
mh-zhao17@mails.tsinghua.edu.cn
[4] School of Information Science and Engineering, Shandong Normal University, Ji'nan, Shandong, China
wanghao@sdnu.edu.cn

Abstract. In recent years, IoT devices have been widely used in the newly-emerging technologized such as crowd-censoring and smart city. Authentication among each IoT node plays a central role in secure communications. Generally, zero-knowledge identification scheme enables one party to authenticate himself without disclosing any additional information. However, a zero-knowledge based protocol normally involves heavily computational or interactive overhead, which is unaffordable for lightweight IoT devices. In this paper, we propose a modified zero-knowledge identification scheme based on that of Silva, Cayrel and Lindner (SCL, for short). The security of our scheme relies on the existence of a commitment scheme and on the hardness of ISIS problem (i.e., a hardness assumption that can be reduced to worst-case lattice problems). We present the detail construction and security proof in this paper.

Keywords: Lattice-based cryptography · Identification
Hash function · SIS problem · Zero-knowledge

1 Introduction

As an emerging technology, Internet of Things (IoT) provides a promising opportunity to build powerful industrial systems and applications by leveraging the growing ubiquity of radio-frequency identification (RFID), and wireless, mobile, and sensor devices. It is the core technology in constructing smart city and intelligent transportation etc. In the wireless sensor networks (i.e., networks composed by interconnection of IoT devices), authentication and identification among the sensor nodes serves as a central part in IoT network security insurance, as it is the basic functionality in enforcing access control policy.

© Springer Nature Switzerland AG 2018
M. H. Au et al. (Eds.): NSS 2018, LNCS 11058, pp. 141–150, 2018.
https://doi.org/10.1007/978-3-030-02744-5_10

Specifically, an identification (ID) scheme consists of two protocols called *registration* and *identification*. These schemes are two-party (*prover* and *verifier*) interactive protocols. In purely cryptographic identification schemes, the purpose is demonstrating that a successful prover knows some secret which is associated with his identity. There are many basic cryptographic constructions of ID schemes (challenge-response schemes), such as using symmetric or asymmetric encryption, authentication and zero-knowledge protocols. To withstand cheating verifier attacks, usually the asymmetric encryption scheme and the digital signature scheme must withstand adaptive chosen-ciphertext attacks and adaptive chosen-massage attacks, respectively. As is known to all, the costs of the above two schemes are quite high. And some of ID schemes based on number theoretic problems, e.g., [1,15], do not resist quantum attacks using Shor's algorithm [14]. The fact that lattice-based zero-knowledge identification schemes can resist against quantum adversaries is well known.

The reason why we keen on research of these schemes is that any ID scheme can be efficiently transformed into a signature scheme, in the random oracle model, with the same hardness assumption [1]. Hence, getting an efficient signature construction, one must design a similarly efficient ID scheme first. In our ID scheme, we consider the short integer solution ($SIS_{n,q,\beta,m}$) problem which is the same as SCL construction. One is given an average case instance $\mathbf{A} \in \mathbb{Z}_q^{n \times m}$, $m = \Omega(n(logn))$, and a norm bound β. Then it is hard to find a non-zero vector $\mathbf{v} \in \mathbb{Z}^m$ such that $\mathbf{Av} \equiv \mathbf{0}(\text{mod } q)$ and $\|\mathbf{v}\| \leq \beta$. And for any $m = poly(n)$, any $\beta > 0$, and any sufficient large $q \geq \beta \cdot poly(n)$, solving $SIS_{n,q,\beta,m}$ with non-negligible probability is at least as hard as solving the decisional approximate shortest vector problem $GapSVP_\gamma$ on arbitrary $n-$dimensional lattices (i.e., in the worst case) with overwhelming probability, for some $\gamma = \beta \cdot poly(n)$ [9]. See [2,7,8] for more results of this problem.

In lattice-based ID schemes, the construction of Lyubashevsky's ID schemes (see [4,6]) was based on a witness-indistinguishable proof of knowledge. Although, it had no soundness error, its completeness error of $1 - 1/e$, unavoidably leads to increased communication costs and an honest prover might be rejected by the verifier which was an unexpected scenario. Another efficient ID scheme, named CLRS, based on SIS was proposed by Cayrel et al. [12] which possessed a soundness error of $(q + 1)/2q$ per round. Then Silva et al. improved CLRS scheme in [13]. It achieves lower communication costs compared with previous lattice-based zero-knowledge identification schemes. The contribution of SCL scheme was reflected in two aspects. The one was the nonces that were used in conjunction with the *Com* functions generated in a way that only one of the three values $\mathbf{r}_i$ was chosen uniformly at random. The other was the computation of a blinding vector $\mathbf{u}$ was obtained by using a seed of a permutation σ, $\mathbf{u} \leftarrow \sigma^{-1}(\mathbf{u}^*)$.

Our Contribution. By observing the SCL, we find that one of the three nonces $\mathbf{r}_2$ and the blinding vector $\mathbf{u}$ can be left out in our scheme to reduce the communication costs. First of all, in SCL, c_1 and c_2 which both contain random numbers play an equivalent role. Hence we hold only one for the proof of our scheme. Three commitment values of the original scheme are reduced to two values. Then, our design has lower computation (for the verifier) and communication costs. Secondly, we take the seed $\mathbf{u}^*$ which is the same as SCL instead of $\mathbf{u}$ itself. The main reason why we do that is $\sigma(\mathbf{u}) = \mathbf{u}^*$ having the same Hamming weight and randomness. Thus, we optimize the parameter selection. Thirdly, our scheme satisfies security properties. We give a better process of proving according to article [12].

2 Preliminaries

Notation. In this paper, we use bold capital letters to denote matrices and bold small letters to indicate vectors, while normal fonts for integers and reals. All vectors are column-vectors unless otherwise noted. We use $\|$ to show that multiple inputs of a function are concatenated. For example, let $h{:}\{0,1\}^* \to \{0,1\}^m$ be a hash function, and $\mathbf{a}, \mathbf{b}$ be vectors, then we write $h(\mathbf{a}\|\mathbf{b})$ to denote the evaluation of h, where implicit binary encodings of vectors $\mathbf{a}$ and $\mathbf{b}$ are concatenated.

Security Model. Our identification scheme applies a string commitment scheme that satisfies computationally binding and statistically hiding, and we also assume that a trusted party honestly sets up the system parameters for both the prover and verifier, which are the same as CLRS and SCL.

Zero-Knowledge. Given a language L and one of its words x, we call zero-knowledge proof of knowledge that x belongs L a protocol with the following properties:

- Completeness: if the statement is true, the honest verifier (i.e., one following the protocol properly) will be convinced of this fact by an honest prover.
- Soundness: if the statement is false, no cheating prover can convince the honest verifier that it is true, except with some small probability.
- Zero-knowledge: if the statement is true, no cheating verifier learns anything other than the fact that the statement is true. In other words, just knowing the statement (not the secret) is sufficient to imagine a scenario showing that the prover knows the secret.
  Comparing the distributions produced by simulator and the real communication tapes (see [3]), they provided three kinds of zero-knowledge, i.e. perfect, statistical and computational zero-knowledge.

Lattice. Lattices are formally defined as discrete additive subgroups of $\mathbb{R}^m$. We often represented them as $\mathcal{L} = \mathbf{B}\mathbb{Z}^n$, $n \leqslant m$, where $\mathbf{B}$ is a basis. In cryptography, integral lattices, i.e. subgroups of $\mathbb{Z}^m$ are usually considered. An important parameter denoted by λ_1 is the length of the shortest nonzero vector in a lattice. It is usually equivalently shown that it is the smallest r such that the lattice points inside a ball of radius r span a space of dimension 1. For $i \in \{1,\ldots,n\}$, the ith successive minimum is $\lambda_i = \inf\{r \mid dim(span(\mathcal{L} \cap \bar{\mathbf{B}}(0,r))) \geq r\}$, where $\bar{\mathbf{B}}(0,r) = \{\mathbf{x} \in \mathbb{R}^m \mid \|\mathbf{x}\| \leq r\}$ is the closed ball of radius r round 0.

It is easy to see that the successive minimum is the generation of λ_1 such that $\lambda_i \leq \lambda_j, i \leq j(i, j \in \{1, \ldots, n\})$.

There are some lattice-based computational problems whose hardness can be used as security assumption when building cryptographic applications. Next, we will list several necessary problems relevant for our scheme.

Definition 1 (Search) SVP *Given a basis* **B** *of n-dimensional lattice find* $\mathbf{v} \in \mathcal{L}(\mathbf{B})$ *such that* $\|\mathbf{v}\| = \lambda_1$.

In fact, there are two other variants of SVP, depending on whether find its length (optimization SVP), or decide if it is shorter than some given number (decisional SVP). And the three obove variants are essentially equivalent.

Definition 2 GapSVP$_\gamma$ *Given a basis* **B** *of n-dimensional lattice* $\mathcal{L} = \mathcal{L}(\boldsymbol{B})$ *where either* $\lambda_1(\mathcal{L}) \leq 1$ *or* $\lambda_1(\mathcal{L}) > \gamma(n)$.

Definition 3 SIVP$_\gamma$ *Given a basis* **B** *of full-rank n-dimensional lattice* $\mathcal{L} = \mathcal{L}(\boldsymbol{B})$, *output a set* $\mathbf{S} = \mathbf{s}_i \subset \mathcal{L}$ *of n linearly independent lattice vectors where* $\|\mathbf{s}_i\| \leq \gamma(n) \cdot \lambda_n$ *for all i.*

Definition 4 SIS *Given a prime q, a positive real number* β, *m uniformly random vectors* $\boldsymbol{a}_i \in \mathbb{Z}_q^n$, *forming the columns of a matrix* $\mathbf{A} \in \mathbb{Z}_q^{n \times m}$, *find a nonzero integer vector* $\mathbf{z} \in \mathbb{Z}^m$ *of norm* $\|\mathbf{z}\| \leq \beta$ *such that* $\mathbf{Az} = \mathbf{0} \pmod{q}$.

With the same conditions above, given a random vector $\mathbf{u} \in \mathbb{Z}_q^n$, one need to find a nonzero integer vector $\mathbf{z} \in \mathbb{Z}^m$ of norm $\|\mathbf{z}\| \leq \beta$ such that $\mathbf{Az} = \mathbf{u} \pmod{q}$, which is called ISIS problem. Notice that, it is an inhomogeneous version of SIS problem. And it's not hard to show that the homogeneous and inhomogeneous problems are essentially equivalent for typical parameters. The security of our scheme is based on the average-case hard problem SIS which can be reduced to some worst-case problems.

Theorem 1 *[11] For any* $m = poly(n)$, *any* $\beta > 0$, *and any sufficiently large* $q \geq \beta \cdot poly(n)$, *solving* $SIS_{n,q,\beta,m}$ *with non-negligible probability is as least as hard as solving the decisional approximate shortest vector problem GapSVP$_\gamma$ and the approximate shortest independent vector problems SIVP$_\gamma$ (among others) on arbitrary n-dimensional lattices (i.e., in the worst case) with overwhelming probability, for some* $\gamma = \beta \cdot poly(n)$.

Definition 5 Commitment scheme *Let Commit:* $\{0,1\}^k \times \{0,1\}^* \longrightarrow \{0,1\}^*$ *be a deterministic polynomial time, where k is a security parameter. A (non-interactive) commitment scheme consists of two phases between a sender and a receiver:*

Commit Phase. *The sender commits to a value* $r \in \{0,1\}^*$ *by computing* $C = Commit(x, r)$, *where* $x \in_R \{0,1\}^k$, *and sending C to the receiver. The receiver stores C for later use.*

Reveal Phase. *The sender opens commitment* $C = Com(x, r)$ *by sending x and r to the receiver. The receiver computes Com(x,r) and verifies that it is equal to the stored commitment value.*

The commitment scheme generally satisfies two properties, one is hiding, which means for any adversary $\mathcal{A}$, $Pr[Com(x_1, r_1) = Com(x_2, r_2)|x_1, x_2 \in_R \{0,1\}^k, r_1 \neq r_2, r_1, r_2 \in \{0,1\}^*] \leq negl$. The other is binding which means the distributions between $Com(x_1, r_1)$ and $Com(x_1, r_2)$ are indistinguishable.

3 Our Identification Scheme

3.1 Description

We use the same definitions of ID scheme as SCL. Our scheme consists of two algorithms: keygen and identification protocol. Firstly, we uniformly chose matrix $\mathbf{A} \in \mathbb{Z}_q^{n \times m}$ and random κ binary vectors with length m, Hamming weight p and disjoin support. The corresponding public keys are obtained by the private key multiplying the chosen matrix $\mathbf{A}$. More precisely, this process corresponds to the ISIS problem. To instantiate the algorithm, we need to select a family of commitment functions $\mathcal{F}$ which are statistically hiding and computationally binding. In addition, several valid private keys are necessary to establish the security of our scheme. The details are in Table 1.

Table 1. Keygen algorithm, parameters n, m, q are public

Keygen:
$\mathbf{x}_i \leftarrow_R \{0,1\}^m$ s.t. wt $(\mathbf{x}_i) = p, 1 \leq i \leq \kappa$
$\mathbf{A} \leftarrow_R \mathbb{Z}_q^{n \times m}$
$\mathbf{y}_i \leftarrow \mathbf{A}\mathbf{x}_i \pmod{q}$, let $\mathbf{X} = (\mathbf{x}_1, \cdots, \mathbf{x}_\kappa)$, $\mathbf{Y} = (\mathbf{y}_1, \cdots, \mathbf{y}_\kappa)$
$Com \leftarrow_R \mathcal{F}$, suitable family of commitment functions
Output $(sk, pk) = (\mathbf{X}, (\mathbf{Y}, \mathbf{A}, Com))$

Secondly, we show our improved identification protocol in Table 2 which is more efficient than SCL. To compare with SCL scheme, we continue to use the original symbols $\mathbf{u}^*$, a random permutation σ and nonces $\mathbf{r}_i (i = 1, 2)$. S_m is a set of all m dimension vectors permutations. In original scheme, there are three $\mathbf{r}_i (i = 1, 2, 3)$, two random number $\mathbf{u}, \mathbf{u}^*$ and it produces three commitment values $\mathbf{c}_i (i = 1, 2, 3)$. Although they utilize the relationships of those random parameters to reduce the communication costs, it is not optimal. And the proof of the soundness property is better than [13].

3.2 Security

We consider our protocol in Table 2 as a zero-knowledge interactive proof of knowledge of some predicate. We firstly define the predicate $P(I, \mathbf{X})$, where $I = \{\mathbf{A}, \mathbf{Y}, m, q\}$ is the public data shared by the parties prover and verifier, and $\mathbf{X}$ satisfying the equation $\mathbf{A}\mathbf{X} = \mathbf{Y} \pmod{q}$.

Table 2. Identification protocol

Prover$\mathcal{P}$(sk,pk)		Verifier$\mathcal{V}$(pk)
$\mathbf{u}^* \leftarrow_R \mathbb{Z}_q^m$,		
$\sigma \leftarrow_R S_m$		
$\mathbf{r}_2 \leftarrow_R \{0,1\}^m$		
$\mathbf{r}_1 \leftarrow \sigma(\mathbf{r}_2)$		
$c_1 \leftarrow Com(\sigma \| \mathbf{A}\mathbf{u}^*, \mathbf{r}_1)$	$\xrightarrow{\quad c_1 \quad}$	
	$\xleftarrow{\quad s,t \quad}$	$s,t \leftarrow_R \{1,\cdots,\kappa\}$
$c_2 \leftarrow Com(\sigma(\mathbf{x}_s + \mathbf{x}_t) + \mathbf{u}^* \pmod q), \mathbf{r}_2)$	$\xrightarrow{\quad c_2 \quad}$	
	$\xleftarrow{\quad b \quad}$	$b \leftarrow_R \{0,1\}$
If$b = 0$	$\xrightarrow{\sigma, \mathbf{u}^* + \mathbf{x}_s + \mathbf{x}_t \pmod q), \mathbf{r}_2}$	check
		$\mathbf{r}_1 \leftarrow \sigma(\mathbf{r}_2), \sigma \overset{?}{\in} S_m$
		$c_1 \overset{?}{=} Com(\sigma \| \mathbf{A}(\mathbf{u}^* + \mathbf{x}_s + \mathbf{x}_t) - \mathbf{y}_s - \mathbf{y}_t, \mathbf{r}_1)$
Else	$\xrightarrow{\mathbf{u}^*, \sigma(\mathbf{x}_s + \mathbf{x}_t), \mathbf{r}_2}$	check
		$c_2 \overset{?}{=} Com(\sigma(\mathbf{x}_s + \mathbf{x}_t) + \mathbf{u}^* \pmod q), \mathbf{r}_2)$
		$\mathrm{wt}(\sigma(\mathbf{x}_s + \mathbf{x}_t)) = 2p$

We prove the security of our scheme from the following three aspects: completeness, soundness and zero-knowledge.

Completeness. Our scheme is perfect completeness. Suppose an honest prover has knowledge of the private keys $\mathbf{x}_i$, the blending mask $\mathbf{u}^*$, and the permutation σ, he must be able to derive the commitments c_1, c_2 and reveal to the verifier necessary information to check whether they are right or not. Also he can show the appropriate Hamming weights of his private keys. Therefore, the verifier will always accept the honest prover's identity in each round.

Zero $-$ knowledge. In this aspect, we require the protocol Com is statistically hiding, i.e., $Com(\mathbf{x}, \mathbf{r})$ is indistinguishable from uniform for a random uniform $\mathbf{r} \in \{0,1\}^n$.

Theorem 2 *Let q be prime. The described protocol is a statistically zero- knowledge proof of knowledge if the employed commitment scheme is statistically hiding.*

Proof. To prove the zero-knowledge property, we construct a simulator S that output a protocol view V_S without knowing the secret $\mathbf{x}$, such that V_S is indistinguishable from the real interaction V of an honest prover with an honest verifier.

We require the simulator can access to a cheating verifier V^*, who sends s, t and b. Thus S generates $\mathbf{r}_1, \mathbf{r}_2$ corresponding to protocol and obtains $(\mathbf{A}, \mathbf{y}, Com)$ as input. The main challenge for simulator is guessing b before talking to V^*. For convenience of proving, we suppose the guess is correct.

If $b = 0$, S selects $\mathbf{u}^*$ and σ as per protocol and solves the equation $\mathbf{A}\mathbf{x}_i = \mathbf{y}_i$ (mod q) for $\mathbf{x}_i$ which dose not need to be short, where $i = s, t$. Then it computes

c_1 and c_2 corresponding to the protocol. Because commitment value Com is statistically hiding, the deviation in c_2 cannot be recognized. Therefore, S reveals the values $\{\sigma, \mathbf{u}^* + \mathbf{x}_s + \mathbf{x}_t \pmod{q}, \mathbf{r}_2\}$ to the verifier.

If $b=1$, S needs to play against the second verifier branch. It selects $\mathbf{u}^*$ and σ as per protocol and computes c_1 to the verifier. After getting the values s, t, it picks $\mathbf{x}_s$ and $\mathbf{x}_t$ uniformly as a binary vectors of dimension m, Hamming weight p and disjoint support, without satisfying the equations $\mathbf{A}\mathbf{x}_i = \mathbf{y}_i \pmod{q}$, $i = s, t$. Then S computes c_2 and sends it to the verifier. Also, such deviation is hidden by Com.

In consequence, S outputs a correct view with probability $1/2$. Since the simulator can access to V^*, it is able to restart the scheme whenever the guessed b was incorrect.   ∎

Soundness. In article [10], the author gave an idea of tree to model the probability space. It can be applied to our scheme directly. Their method makes us find a node with two sons with overwhelming probability in the execution tree associated with the protocol between a cheating prover and a verifier, according to the reception of two possible values for challenge b.

Theorem 3 *For any $\epsilon > 0$, a positive integer κ, after r rounds of protocol execution, a cheating prover is accepted with probability at least $(1/2+1/\kappa^2)^r + \epsilon$, then there exists a polynomial time probabilistic machine M which breaks the binding property of the commitment or solves the ISIS problem with non-negligible probability.*

Proof. To simulate the adversary's environment, we need to input the SIS problem instance $(n, m, q, \mathbf{A})$ and a challenge commitment Com. This process is usually divided into two steps: a verification step and an impersonation step. In addition, we choose $\mathbf{x}_i$ and $\mathbf{y}_i (i = \{1, \cdots, \kappa\})$, as in Keygen protocol and run the adversary $\mathcal{A}$ on public parameters each round.

In the first step, since the protocol is statistically zero-knowledge which have been proved above, we are able to simulate the prover perfectly. Therefore, the adversary's output distribution is the same as for all alternative secret keys $\mathbf{x}_i \neq \mathbf{x}_j, i \neq j$.

In the second step, we let $\mathcal{A}$ play the role of the cheating prover. For simplicity, we note $\mathbf{x}_s + \mathbf{x}_t = \bar{\mathbf{x}}$, $\mathbf{y}_s + \mathbf{y}_t = \bar{\mathbf{y}}$, $\mathbf{u}^* = \bar{\mathbf{u}}$. By rewinding the adversary and using Véron's technology, we can get several equations below.

For $b = 0$, there are two views $(\sigma, \bar{\mathbf{u}} + \bar{\mathbf{x}}, \mathbf{r}_2)$ and $(\sigma', \bar{\mathbf{u}}' + \bar{\mathbf{x}}', \mathbf{r}_2')$. Since Com is binding, we infer that $\mathbf{r}_2 = \mathbf{r}_2'$, $\mathbf{r}_1 = \mathbf{r}_1'$ we obtain equation:

$$\sigma \| \mathbf{A}(\bar{\mathbf{u}} + \bar{\mathbf{x}}) - \bar{\mathbf{y}} = \sigma' \| \mathbf{A}(\bar{\mathbf{u}}' + \bar{\mathbf{x}}') - \bar{\mathbf{y}}' \tag{1}$$

which implies $\sigma = \sigma'$.

For $b = 1$, we get $(\bar{\mathbf{u}}, \sigma(\bar{\mathbf{x}}), \mathbf{r}_2)$ and $(\bar{\mathbf{u}}', \sigma'(\bar{\mathbf{x}}'), \mathbf{r}_2')$. Then we obtain equation:

$$\sigma(\bar{\mathbf{x}}) + \bar{\mathbf{u}} \pmod{q} = \sigma'(\bar{\mathbf{x}}') + \bar{\mathbf{u}}' \pmod{q} \tag{2}$$

We define $\Delta\bar{\mathbf{u}} = \bar{\mathbf{u}}' - \bar{\mathbf{u}}$, $\Delta\bar{\mathbf{x}} = \bar{\mathbf{x}}' - \bar{\mathbf{x}}$ and $\Delta\bar{\mathbf{y}} = \bar{\mathbf{y}}' - \bar{\mathbf{y}}$ respectively. Now, we turn to extracting $\mathcal{A}'s$ secret key by rearranging parts of Eqs. (1) and (2). Furthermore, we get

$$\mathbf{A}(\Delta\bar{\mathbf{u}} + \Delta\bar{\mathbf{x}}) = \Delta\bar{\mathbf{y}}(\bmod q) \tag{3}$$

$$-\sigma(\Delta\bar{\mathbf{x}}) = \Delta\bar{\mathbf{u}}(\bmod q) \tag{4}$$

which implies $max(wt(\Delta\bar{\mathbf{x}})) = 4p = max(wt(\Delta\bar{\mathbf{u}}(\bmod q)))$. Hence, we get max $(wt(\Delta\bar{\mathbf{u}} + \Delta\bar{\mathbf{x}})) = 8p$. We let $8p \leq \sqrt{m}$, namely $p \leq \sqrt{m}/8$ which means we can find a solution of the ISIS problem in probabilistic polynomial time. That is contradictory with our assumption. ∎

3.3   Efficiency and Security Considerations

We assume that the seeds used to generate random elements $\mathbf{u}^*$ in our scheme is 128 bits and that the output of commitment function is 256 bits, the same as SCL. Clearly, there are two basic differences between our and SCL. One is that, when the prover answers to the second challenge $b = 0$, $(\sigma, \mathbf{u}^* + \mathbf{x}_s + \mathbf{x}_t(\bmod q), \mathbf{r}_2)$ communication cost is $m + 256$ bits instead of $mlogq + 256$ bits. The other is that we only use two Com (i.e., c_1, c_2) instead of three (see Table 3 for details). As a result, our scheme outweighs the SCL in term of efficiency. Total communication costs is 11275 bits in the SCL. Obviously, our scheme requires much less communication overhead.

Table 3. Parameters for 100 bits security.

Parameters	Relationship	Value (bits)
q	Prime	257
n	–	64
m	–	2048
κ	–	24
Com	$c_1 + c_2$	512
s, t	$2log\kappa$	10
b	–	1
Answer to challenge $b = 0$	$m + 256$	2304
Answer to challenge $b = 1$	$m + 256$	2304
Total communication costs	$2log\kappa + m + 769$	2827

Ideal lattices can be used in the identification scheme to improve performance and reduce the amount of public data. It's important to note two points: (a) irreducibility of the polynomial that characterizes the ring where the lattice is defined; (b) Its expansion factor must be observed, as recommended in [5]. Our scheme is also secure against concurrent attacks. Because of a public key corresponding to multiple secret keys, the protocol is witness indistinguishable. More details are in [14].

4 Conclusion and Further Work

In this paper, we improve the SCL scheme to reduce the communication costs and make the form of ID scheme simpler. At the same time we give a more formal proof about soundness property compared with SCL. As further work, we will conduct elaborate experiment to evaluate the real-world performance in large scale deployed IoT devices environment.

Acknowledgement. This work is supported by the National Natural Science Foundation of China under grant No. 61572294, 61602287 and 11771252, Natural Science Foundation of Shandong Province under grant No. ZR2017MF021, State Key Program of National Natural Science of China under grant No. 61632020, the Fundamental Research Funds of Shandong University under grant No. 2017JC019 and 2016JC029, and the Primary Research & Development Plan of Shandong Province under grant No. 2018GGX101037. We thank the reviewers for their constructive suggestions. Special thanks for Chuan Zhao at University of Jinan for his generous help and discussion.

References

1. Fiat, A., Shamir, A.: How to prove yourself: practical solutions to identification and signature problems. In: Odlyzko, A.M. (ed.) CRYPTO 1986. LNCS, vol. 263, pp. 186–194. Springer, Heidelberg (1987). https://doi.org/10.1007/3-540-47721-7_12
2. Gentry, C., Peikert, C., Vaikuntanathan, V.: Trapdoors for hard lattices and new cryptographic constructions. In: ACM Symposium on Theory of Computing, pp. 197–206 (2008). https://doi.org/10.1145/1374376.1374407
3. Goldwasser, S., Micali, S., Rackoff, C.: The knowledge complexity of interactive proof systems. J. Comput. **18**(1), 186–208 (1989). https://doi.org/10.1137/0218012
4. Lyubashevsky, V.: Lattice-based identification schemes secure under active attacks. In: Cramer, R. (ed.) PKC 2008. LNCS, vol. 4939, pp. 162–179. Springer, Heidelberg (2008). https://doi.org/10.1007/978-3-540-78440-1_10
5. Lyubashevsky, V., Micciancio, D.: Generalized compact knapsacks are collision resistant. In: Bugliesi, M., Preneel, B., Sassone, V., Wegener, I. (eds.) ICALP 2006. LNCS, vol. 4052, pp. 144–155. Springer, Heidelberg (2006). https://doi.org/10.1007/11787006_13
6. Lyubashevsky, V., Micciancio, D.: Asymptotically efficient lattice-based digital signatures. In: Canetti, R. (ed.) TCC 2008. LNCS, vol. 4948, pp. 37–54. Springer, Heidelberg (2008). https://doi.org/10.1007/978-3-540-78524-8_3
7. Micciancio, D., Peikert, C.: Hardness of SIS and LWE with small parameters. In: Canetti, R., Garay, J.A. (eds.) CRYPTO 2013. LNCS, vol. 8042, pp. 21–39. Springer, Heidelberg (2013). https://doi.org/10.1007/978-3-642-40041-4_2
8. Micciancio, D., Regev, O.: Worst-case to average-case reductions based on gaussian measures. In: IEEE Symposium on Foundations of Computer Science, pp. 372–381, October 2004. https://doi.org/10.1109/FOCS.2004.72
9. Miklós, A.: Generating hard instances of lattice problems. Electron. Colloq. Comput. Complex. **3**(7) (1996). http://eccc.hpi-web.de/eccc-reports/1996/TR96-007/index.html
10. Véron, P.: Cryptanalysis of harari's identification scheme. In: Boyd, C. (ed.) Cryptography and Coding 1995. LNCS, vol. 1025, pp. 264–269. Springer, Heidelberg (1995). https://doi.org/10.1007/3-540-60693-9_28

11. Peikert, C.: A decade of lattice cryptography. Found. Trends Theor. Comput. Sci. **10**(4), 283–424 (2016). https://doi.org/10.1561/0400000074
12. Cayrel, P.-L., Lindner, R., Rückert, M., Silva, R.: Improved zero-knowledge identification with lattices. In: Heng, S.-H., Kurosawa, K. (eds.) ProvSec 2010. LNCS, vol. 6402, pp. 1–17. Springer, Heidelberg (2010). https://doi.org/10.1007/978-3-642-16280-0_1
13. Rosemberg, S., Pierre-Louis, C., Richard, L.: Zero-knowledge identification based on lattices with low communication costs. XI Simpósio Brasileiro de Segurança da Informaçao e de Sistemas Computacionais **8**, 95–107 (2011)
14. Shor, P.W.: Polynomial-time algorithms for prime factorization and discrete logarithms on a quantum computer. SIAM Rev. **41**(2), 303–332 (1999). https://doi.org/10.1137/S0036144598347011
15. Uriel, F., Amos, F., Adi, S.: Zero-knowledge proofs of identity. J. Cryptol. **1**(2), 77–94 (1988). https://doi.org/10.1007/BF02351717

Secure Semantic Search Based on Two-Level Index Over Encrypted Cloud

Lili Xia[✉] and Zhangjie Fu

Nanjing University of Information Science and Technology, Nanjing, China

Abstract. With the rapid development of the IoT and the mobile applications, users are tending to outsource the data to the cloud servers. Thus, the encrypted data search on the cloud is very important. Now there are a lot existed keyword search schemes in which the relationship between the size of the file set and the search time is linear. In order to solve this problem, we propose a semantic retrieval framework for central word expansion based on two-level index. In this paper, we have taken a new approach for index construction - the two-level index to ensure that the retrieval time is not affected by the file size. In order to better meet the semantic requirements of user queries, we introduced the central word expansion technology to further improve the accuracy of the search. The main idea of central keyword extension semantic search (CKESS) based on two-level index is that match the expanded central keyword with index firstly, then compute the similarity between the query and the index under the first matching result, and finally return the result with the highest similarity. Our proposed solution meets the privacy protection requirements under two different threat models. Through the experiment of the real data set, we prove that our scheme is efficient, accurate and secure.

Keywords: Two-level index · Central word expansion · Semantic search

1 Introduction

For the reason that IoT and mobile applications are widely used, more and more data is being generated all the time. In order to save local storage space, storing these data in the cloud server has become a popular trend. However, cloud servers are considered "honest but curious". In order to ensure data security and user privacy, users usually encrypt the sensitive data first and then store the ciphertext data in the cloud server. The encrypted data is no longer searchable, so how to retrieve the content the user needs in the ciphertext environment is a challenging problem.

To improve the performance of the searchable schemes, many researchers do a lot study on the construction of the index. Goh et al. [1] defined a security index model based on pseudo-random function and Bloom filter, which can resist adaptive chosen keyword attack (IND-CKA) and improve the security of the scheme, but this scheme cannot support the sort of results. Sun et al. [2] proposed a searchable encryption scheme (MRSE) that can solve multi-keyword search. The scheme replaced the inner product with cosine similarity, and used TF/IDF algorithm to sort the results and improve the retrieval accuracy. However, the search efficiency is too low to suit the big

© Springer Nature Switzerland AG 2018
M. H. Au et al. (Eds.): NSS 2018, LNCS 11058, pp. 151–159, 2018.
https://doi.org/10.1007/978-3-030-02744-5_11

data processing. Katz et al. [3] proposed a ciphertext search scheme based on predicate encryption, which realized the functions of polynomial equality query and extraction query. Fu et al. [4] proposed a ciphertext search scheme based k-d tree to improve efficiency.

In this paper, we propose a central keyword extension semantic search based on two-level index (CKESS). Different from the existing multi-keyword search scheme, a naive two-level index structure is adopted in the index construction. The index structure combines the existing forward index and inverted index structure. Our scheme does search by using the central keyword of the query keywords, so the complexity is only determined by the size of the file set which related to the keyword. This paper uses the central keyword expansion method to improve the semantic relevance and retrieval accuracy of the search results. Our work first gives the basic framework of central keyword extension semantic search based on two-level index. Then, two specific ciphertext search schemes are given for the privacy protection requirements under different threat models. Our main contributions are as follows:

- We propose the central keyword extension semantic search based on two-level index (CKESS) to make the search time independent from the size of the file set. The independence is mainly reflected that we use query keywords to locate the index keyword, rather than using keywords to match the file set one by one. Compared with the general ciphertext search schemes, our search efficiency has great improvement;
- We propose a two-level matching technique based on central keyword expansion to optimize the precision and semantic relevance of ciphertext search. Our scheme makes use of the method of two-level matching, the first matching uses the expansion of the central query keyword to match the keywords of file with the first-level index, and the second level matches the obtained result from the first matching with the non-central word of the query to achieve the Top-k files with highest similarity. Compared with the general semantic search scheme, our scheme is more accurate in terms of semantic relevance;
- Based on the privacy protection requirements of data, we utilize the two techniques of two-level index and central keyword semantic extension, and design two secure and specific search schemes to solve the problem of privacy leakage under different threat models. The experimental analysis under the real database proves that our schemes are efficient, accurate and security.

The rest of the paper is organized as follows. In the second part, we introduce the system model, the threat model and the design goals. In the third part, we describe the two-level index, the central word expansion and describe the specific retrieval schemes under different threat models in detail. In the fourth part, we conducted a detailed analysis of the experimental results. The fifth part introduces the related work of this article, and we conclude the full text in the last part.

2   Problem Formulation

2.1   System Model

There are three entity in our system model as shown in Fig. 1: Data Owner, Data User, and Cloud Server.

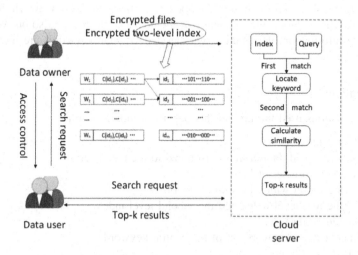

Fig. 1. The framework of the system model

Data Owner. The data owner is responsible for uploading the fileset F to the cloud. Because these files contain many sensitive private information, the data owner needs to encrypt the data before outsourcing. In order to better utilize the encrypted data, the data owner needs to extract the keyword W of the plain text file F and construct the index I. The data owner needs to outsource the built index I to the cloud server.

Data User. After receiving the authorization from the data owner, the data user generates a trapdoor according to the search keyword and sends a search request to the cloud server, and decrypts the returned result of the cloud server.

Cloud Server. The cloud server receives and stores the encrypted files and indexes uploaded by the data owner and processes the data user's search request and returns encrypted files related to the trapdoor.

2.2   Threat Model

Our default that data owners and authorized users are trustworthy, but the cloud server is semi-trustworthy. According to the different information that the cloud server can obtain and the difference of the privacy requirement, this part considers two different threat models.

Known Ciphertext Model. The cloud server can only obtain encrypted filesets and secure index structures from data owners (DO), encrypted trapdoors from data users (DU), and secure search results. The cloud server cannot understand the meaning of the fileset and query keywords.

Known Background Model. Based on the known ciphertext model, the cloud server can obtain some additional background information. The background information includes the statistical information of the document, the relationship between the query keyword and the trapdoor, the frequency of the query keywords, and so on. With this background information, the cloud server can deduce what keywords are included in the encrypted file.

2.3   Notations

The main notations used throughout this paper are shown as follows.

F — the plaintext fileset.
C — the encrypted dataset that outsourced to the cloud server.
W — the keyword set of F.
F(w) — the fileset which have the keyword w.
I_1, I_2 — the first level index and the second level index.
Q — the query datasets.
E — the extended keyword set of the central keyword.
Bf — the bloom filter.
R — the importance of the semantic relationship.
n — the number of keywords in the dataset W.
t — the number of query keyword.

3   Secure Search Scheme

3.1   Central Keyword Extension

In the real world, people input a number of keywords as a query key words to search. According to the different intentions of people, the importance of each keyword is also different. Our early work [9] was mainly to build a personal user interest model for each user based on the user's search history. However, when users input unconventional keywords, the user model needs to be re-established. In this paper, we use the grammatical relationship between keywords as a measure for the importance of keywords. This approach allows the cloud server to search documents based on the user's interests. Actually, the grammatical relationship between the keywords is the reflection of the preference information of the user search. To some extent, the grammatical relations between keywords can be regarded as the connection between words and words in the grammatical relation tree. Stanford parser can convert the input keywords into the syntax parse tree, and output the grammatical relations of the keywords and the tree. For example, the phrase tree of "black shirt made in silk" is shown in Fig. 2, in which "NP" is the noun phrase, "NN" is the noun, "JJ" is represented an adjective or a number, and so on.

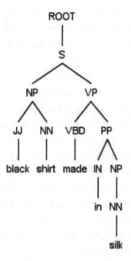

Fig. 2. The phrase tree of "black shirt made in silk"

In fact, many keywords have the same meaning, if the query keyword which the user entered is "shirt", but the index keyword only contains "blouse", the cloud server will not return correct results to the user. Therefore, in this paper, we use Wordnet for keyword expansion. WordNet is a large vocabulary database of the English corpus [8]. By using it, when the user queries the keyword "shirt", the cloud server returns files not only containing "shirt" but also files having "blouse". We use the central keyword to calculate the semantic score of each expanded keyword. The semantic score is the weight of each extended keyword.

We use Lin's measure [10] to calculate the similarity between two words.

$$Sim(w_1, w_2) = [2 \times I(F(W_1) \cap F(W_2))]/[I(F(W_1) + F(W_2))] \tag{1}$$

Where $F(w)$ is the feature set owned by w. $I(S) = -\sum_{f \in S} \log P(f)$ is the amount of information contained in a set of features S, where $P(f)$ is the probability of feature f.

3.2 Two-Level Index Framework

Traditional index construction usually only uses the forward index or the inverted index simply. The construction methods of these indexes have limitations in terms of efficiency or accuracy. In order to improve our search efficiency and accuracy, our paper uses a new index construction method — the two-level index. This naive index we build contains different files and keywords. In the first-level index, we treat each keyword in the lexicon as a label, and this label points to all the file IDs that contain this keyword. The second-level index is exactly the opposite. It considers each file ID in the first-level index as the tag, and each tag points to all the keywords contained in the file.

In the consideration of privacy, each of our file IDs is encrypted. In the framework of this two-level index, the task of first-level index is to perform keyword matching effectively, locate the trapdoor and shrink the search range in multi-keyword searches. The second index mainly calculates the similarity between the file set in the shrink range and the trapdoor, and obtains the similarity ranking result of the file.

The specific two-level index search process is mainly containing two match process. First, keyword search is performed in the first-level index to get the shrink file set. Then, according to this file set, the cloud server calculates the similarity between each file and the trapdoor to obtain the most relevant files.

As shown in Fig. 3, according to the user's keywords, we first determine the central keyword and extend the central keyword. After the cloud server gets the encrypted index, files, and trapdoor, it first matches the extended keyword set (w_1, w_3) with the keywords in the first level index. With the first match, the scope of the file set is reduced $(i.e. C(id_1), C(id_2), C(id_5), C(id_6))$. Then, during the second match, the file IDs are decoded and the Bloom filter is used to verify that the keywords contained in the file match the keywords in the query. As shown in Fig. 3, S_1, S_2, S_3 and S_4 are the inner products between the first match results and the query. More bigger the score is, the higher semantic relevance the file has.

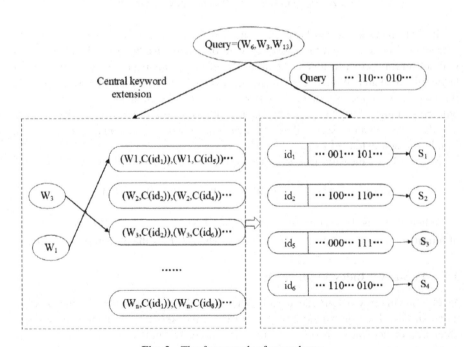

Fig. 3. The framework of our scheme

4 Performance Analysis

In this section, we implement the proposed scheme to evaluate the overall performance. The experiment is realized on Windows 7 server which with Core 2 CPU 2.93 GHz by using Java language.

4.1 Precision

In our schemes, we add some keywords in order to achieve the semantic search. For evaluating the accuracy of the experiment, we used two probabilities pr1 and pr2, in which pr1 means the two keywords only have one different character and pr2 means two keywords have multiple different characters. As the Fig. 4 shown, when the number of hash functions in F becomes large, pr1 decreases, and when c increases, pr1 is get larger. However, pr2 is exactly the opposite of pr1. As the number of hash functions in F increases, pr2 increases and pr2 decreases as c increases. Thus, it is significant to make pr1 and pr2 trade-off.

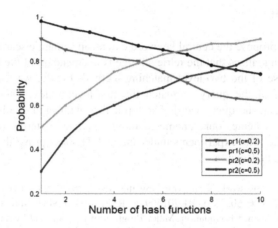

Fig. 4. Precision of scheme

4.2 Index Construction

The time of index construction is mainly composed of the time of building index vector and the time of encrypting index vector. The time cost of these two processes is affected by the vector dimension. As shown in Fig. 5, we can see that our scheme is better than MRSE, because we use high dimension submatrices to generate the secret matrices for reducing the time of encryption. Because the dimension of $CKESS_2$ is more than $CKESS_1$, the $CKESS_2$ is better than $CKESS_1$. And the size of the file sets is also the main factor that affects the time of index construction, we can see that the time cost of index construction increases with the number of file sets.

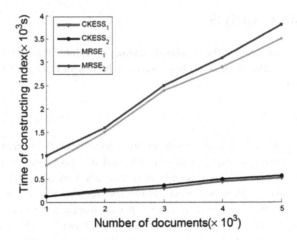

Fig. 5. The time of Index construction

5   Conclusion

In this paper, we propose the central keyword extension semantic search based on two-level index, which realizes that the retrieval time is independent of the file set size. Our scheme makes use of the two-level matching method. Firstly, we use the expansion central keywords of the query to match the first-level index. Then, matching the obtained results and the query word. The top-k files with high similarity. Compared with the general scheme, our scheme is more accurate in terms of accuracy and semantic relevance. The experiments under the real database prove that our scheme is efficient, accurate and secure.

Acknowledgment. This work is supported by the NSFC (61772283, 61672294, U1536206, 61502242, U1405254, 61602253), BK20150925, R2017L05, PAPD fund, Project funded by China Postdoctoral Science Foundation, Major Program of the National Social Science Fund of China (17ZDA092), Qing Lan Project, and Meteorology Soft Sciences Project.

References

1. Goh, E.J.: Secure indexes. Submission (2003)
2. Sun, W., Wang, B., Cao, N., Li, M., Lou, W., et al.: Verifiable privacy-preserving multi-keyword text search in the cloud supporting similarity-based ranking. IEEE Trans. Parallel Distrib. Syst. **25**(11), 3025–3035 (2014)
3. Katz, J., Sahai, A., Waters, B.: Predicate encryption supporting disjunctions, polynomial equations, and inner products. J. Cryptol. **26**(2), 192–224 (2013)
4. Fu, Z., Sun, X., Liu, Q., Zhou, L., Shu, J.: Achieving efficient cloud search services: multi-keyword ranked search over encrypted cloud data supporting parallel computing. IEICE Trans. Commun. **98**(1), 190–200 (2015)
5. Cao, N., Wang, C., Li, M.: Privacy-preserving multi-keyword ranked search over encrypted cloud data. IEEE Trans. Parallel Distrib. Syst. **25**(1), 222–233 (2014)

6. Har-Peled, S., Indyk, P., Motwani, R.: Approximate nearest neighbor: towards removing the curse of dimensionality. In: ACM Symposium on Theory of Computing, pp. 604–613 (1998)
7. Bloom, B.H.: Space/time trade-offs in hash coding with allowable errors. Commun. ACM **13** (7), 422–426 (1970)
8. Miller, G.A., Beckwith, R., Fellbaum, C., Gross, D., Miller, K.J.: Introduction to WordNet: an on-line lexical database*. Int. J. Lexicogr. **3**(4), 235–244 (1990)
9. Fu, Z., Ren, K., Shu, J., Sun, X., Huang, F.: Enabling personalized search over encrypted outsourced data with efficiency improvement. IEEE Trans. Parallel Distrib. Syst. **27**(9), 2546–2559 (2016)
10. Lin, D.: An information-theoretic definition of similarity. In: Fifteenth International Conference on Machine Learning. Morgan Kaufmann Publishers Inc., pp. 296–304 (1998)
11. Wong, W.K., Cheung, D.W., Kao, B., Mamoulis, N.: Secure kNN computation on encrypted databases. In: ACM SIGMOD International Conference on Management of Data. ACM, pp. 139–152 (2009)
12. Yang, J., Liu, Z., Li, J., Jia, C., Cui, B.: Multi-key searchable encryption without random Oracle. In: International Conference on Intelligent NETWORKING and Collaborative Systems. IEEE, pp. 79–84 (2015)
13. Chen, X., Huang, X., Li, J., et al.: New algorithms for secure outsourcing of LargeScale systems of linear equations. IEEE Trans. Inf. Forensics Secur. **10**(1), 69–78 (2014)
14. Wang, B., Li, M., Wang, H., Li, H.: Circular range search on encrypted spatial data. In: Communications and Network Security, pp. 182–190. IEEE (2015)
15. Li, J., Wang, Q., Wang, C., Cao, N., Ren, K., Lou, W.: Fuzzy keyword search over encrypted data in cloud computing. In: Conference on Information Communications, pp. 441–445. IEEE Press (2010)
16. Chuah, M., Hu, W.: Privacy-aware BedTree based solution for fuzzy multi-keyword search over encrypted data. In: International Conference on Distributed Computing Systems Workshops. IEEE Computer Society, pp. 273–281 (2011)
17. Kuzu, M., Islam, M.S., Kantarcioglu, M.: Efficient similarity search over encrypted data. In: IEEE International Conference on Data Engineering, pp. 1156–1167. IEEE (2012)
18. Wang, J., Yu, X., Zhao, M.: Privacy-preserving ranked multi-keyword fuzzy search on cloud encrypted data supporting range query. Arab. J. Sci. Eng. **40**(8), 2375–2388 (2015)
19. Fu, Z., Wu, X., Guan, C., Sun, X., Ren, K.: Toward efficient multi-keyword fuzzy search over encrypted outsourced data with accuracy improvement. IEEE Trans. Inf. Forensics Security **11**(12), 2706–2716 (2017)
20. Sun, X., Zhu, Y., Xia, Z., et al.: Secure keyword-based ranked semantic search over encrypted cloud data. In: The International Conference on Multimedia, Computer Graphics and Broadcasting, pp. 271–283 (2013)

Fast QuadTree-Based Pose Estimation
for Security Applications
Using Face Biometrics

Paola Barra[1], Carmen Bisogni[1], Michele Nappi[1],
and Stefano Ricciardi[2(✉)]

[1] Department of Informatics, University of Salerno, Fisciano, Italy
barra90@gmail.com, {cbisogni,mnappi}@unisa.it
[2] Department of Biosciences, University of Molise, Campobasso, Italy
stefano.ricciardi@unimol.it

Abstract. Face represents a convenient contactless biometric descriptor, currently exploited in a wide range of security applications, though its performance may be considerably affected by subject's pose variations with respect to enrolment pose. This issue is particularly challenging whether the face image is acquired in uncontrolled conditions, or it is extracted from video sequence, the latter representing a more and more frequent case given the huge diffusion of audiovisual content on the internet. To this regard, in this paper, a pose estimation method aimed at rapidly evaluating face rotations is presented. The proposed approach exploits a novel adaptation of quad-tree data structure to achieve an approximate estimate of face's yaw/pitch angles, enabling to select the face image most compliant to the stored template. Preliminary results confirm the efficiency of the proposed method, that provides a more than halved computing time with respect to the state of the art with further improvement margins.

1 Introduction

Nowadays, the use of biometrics as a reliable way to authenticate a person based on the "something you are" paradigm, has spread from typical access control applications to a growing number of transaction authorization procedures, part of which performed through the internet. In this context, face notoriously represents one of the most diffused biometric descriptors, thanks to its good distinctiveness along with high acceptability resulting from its contactless acquisition. Nevertheless, face's reliability may be undermined by ample posing variations, typically induced by acquisition performed under uncontrolled or loosely controlled conditions. The more the angular distance (measured with regard to three degrees of freedom) between the captured face and the reference template, the more the expected impact on the verification accuracy. This performance degradation can be somewhat mitigated by specifically designed feature extraction/matching algorithms, but as the rotation increases the recognition error increases as well. This situation may easily happen whenever a mobile device camera, either in still or video mode, is used for face capture, a kind of person-authentication

© Springer Nature Switzerland AG 2018
M. H. Au et al. (Eds.): NSS 2018, LNCS 11058, pp. 160–173, 2018.
https://doi.org/10.1007/978-3-030-02744-5_12

modality that is becoming more and more common given the large number of apps requiring some form of user authorization. Another typical context To this regard, the growing networks of surveillance cameras diffused throughout buildings and cities provide multiple face capture opportunities from different perspectives which could be used for this purpose. Paradoxically, face capture performed in video mode provide a large number of frames in which subject's face is recorded in slightly different poses (depending on the frame-rate and the subject's head motion with respect to the camera's frustum) some of which could be close to the neutral pose captured during enrollment. Being able to rapidly detect which frame in a sequence is the best match (rotation-wise) to the template image would minimize the posing issue, thus increasing the verification accuracy. To this regard, this paper describes a pose estimation method aimed at rapidly evaluating face rotations, to determine the frame in a video sequence which is the best candidate for subject authentication or identification. The proposed approach exploits a specifically designed adaptation of well-known quad-tree data structure to achieve an approximate estimate of face's yaw/pitch angles, enabling to select the face image most compliant to the stored template. Experiments confirm both the effectiveness and the efficiency of the proposed method, that is able to estimate face rotations in a fraction of the computing time required by the state of the art.

The remainder of the paper is organized as follows. Section 2 resumes main works and methods related to the topic of face pose estimation and normalization. Section 3 describes the proposed system in detail. Section 4 presents the results of the experiments conducted so far. Finally, Sect. 5 concludes, providing directions for future research.

2 Related Works

The problem of head/face pose estimation and the related topic of face "frontalization" (i.e. face normalization according to its rotation axes) have been investigated by a number of works [1], both combined together and dealt with separately. Among the methods treating pose estimation and frontalization as a single problem, some makes use of 3D models, as in [2], in which a dense grid of 3D facial landmarks is projected to each 2D face image, enabling feature extraction in a pose adaptive fashion. In the subsequent step, for the local patch around each landmark, an optimal warp is estimated through homography, to correct texture deformation caused by pose variations.

The authors of [3] focus their attention to the role of occlusions in frontalization, by using Facial Feature Detection to obtain a set of landmarks to be compared to 3D model's landmarks. Other works exploit the distances between key points in face [4], though, these metrics could be affected by considerable angular error which should not be underestimated in pose estimation.

Methods aimed uniquely at pose estimation are more specific and they may be applied in several different contexts. A single face's range-image is sufficient to estimate the 3D pose of a previously unseen subject, in [5]. This approach is based on a novel shape signature to identify noses in range images. The GPU based algorithm generates candidates for their positions, and then generates and evaluates many pose hypotheses in parallel. A novel error function that compares the input range image to precomputed pose images of an average face model is also proposed.

Face depth data, captured through a depth sensing device, are used in [6] to achieve pose estimation as a regression problem through a random forest framework. Since the regressor needs to be trained on labeled data, the method solves this problem by training only on synthetic data, generating an arbitrary number of training examples without the need of laborious and error-prone annotations.

In [7], a 3D pose-estimate algorithm based on central profile is proposed. The central profile is a unique curve on a 3D face surface that starts from forehead center, goes down through nose ridge, nose tip, mouth center, and ends at a chin tip. Based on the properties of the central profile, Hough transform is applied to determine the symmetry plane by invoking a voting procedure. An objective function maps the central profile to an accumulator cell with the maximal value. It detects the nose tip on the central profile and estimates the pitch angle.

The authors of [8] propose a pose classification framework based on dictionary-learning and sparse representation-based classifier (SRC). They implemented a Gabor feature vector after Gaussian weighted pre-processing as the face pose images' feature and used factors analysis in dictionary training. A specifically built dictionary of face occlusion helps solving the estimation problem when a face is occluded.

In [9], the aim of precisely estimating face rotation angles is achieved by means of a multi-level structured hybrid forest. The head contour is derived from patches, which are either head region or the background. Subsequently, randomly selected patches sub-regions are used to develop the MSHF for head pose estimation. This approach features an average head detection and pose estimation time of about 0.44 s.

Another relevant category of methods focuses on head pose estimation in uncontrolled environments and rely on neural networks.

A convolutional network is used in [10] to map images of faces to points on a low-dimensional manifold parametrized by pose, and images of non-faces to points far away from that manifold. Given an image, detecting a face and estimating its pose is viewed as minimizing an energy function with respect to the face/non-face binary variable and the continuous pose parameters.

Four different convolutional neural networks architectures are described in [11] and compared to evaluate the best pose estimate performance on in-the-wild face datasets. They investigate the use of dropout and adaptive gradient methods and show that the results achieved joining CNNs and adaptive gradient methods lead to the best results.

A method called Hyperface, for simultaneous face detection, landmarks localization, pose estimation and gender recognition, is proposed in [12]. The method works by fusing the intermediate layers of a deep CNN using a separate CNN followed by a multi-task learning algorithm operating on the fused features. This architecture exploits the synergy among the tasks which boosts up their individual performances.

In [13] a multi-task learning deep neural network is applied to a small grayscale face image. The network jointly detects multi-view faces and estimates head pose even under poor environment conditions such as illumination change, vibration, large pose change, and occlusion. The method performs face detection, bounding box refinement, and head pose estimation by using shared features learned through multi-task learning. Other methods focus on the problem of face pose estimation in uncontrolled conditions.

The authors of [14] address this challenge as a continuous regression problem on real images with large variations in background, illumination and expression. To this aim, they propose a probabilistic framework with a general representation not based on locating facial features. Face is represented with a non-overlapping grid of patches, instead. This representation is used in a generative model for automatic estimation of head pose in images taken in uncontrolled environments.

Finally, in [15] a unified model for face detection, pose estimation, and landmark estimation in cluttered images is proposed. This approach is based on a mixture of trees with a shared pool of parts each model by a facial landmark and it uses global mixtures to capture topological changes due to viewpoint.

Compared to the approaches resumed above, the pose estimation method proposed in this paper provides the following contributions:

1. It does not have any of the practical issues involved with 3D models.
2. It does not require neural networks and the related training.
3. It is fast since it is simply based on face landmarks accumulation through the efficient quad-tree data structure [16], disregarding illumination, color or background and returning discrete estimates for both for yaw and pitch angles and it could also estimate the roll (though this third face's degree of freedom is statistically less relevant and would significantly increase computing time).
4. Finally, it can be applied regardless of the context, since it is not dependent on any training set or database.

3 Method Description

The proposed method involves the use of facial landmarks and quad-tree decomposition to estimate face's pose and is structured in three main steps resumed below and depicted in Fig. 1:

- Step 1, *Face detection and facial landmarks localization*;
- Step 2, *Quad-tree decomposition* to obtain a sparse matrix representing the facial features;
- Step 3, *Pose estimation*, transforming the sparse matrix in a tree-array and comparing it to 35 angular references procedurally generated from a 3D synthetic face model through Hamming distance metric.

More in detail, given an input image a face localization algorithm is applied to detect key facial structures on the region of interest. Viola-Jones algorithm [17] is used to detect the presence and the location of the face in the image, resulting in a square region containing the face, referenced through the coordinates of the upper left corner and the size of the sides. After the face detection stage, facial landmarks are used to localize and represent salient regions of the face, such as eyes, nose, eyebrows, mouth and jawline.

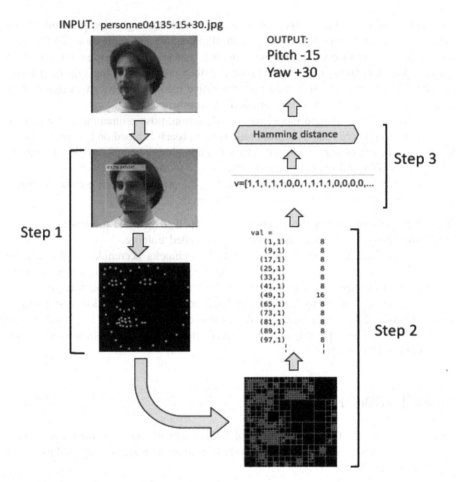

Fig. 1. Steps of the proposed method.

This procedure, based on [18] requires:

1. a training set of labeled facial landmarks on an image, these images are manually annotated, specifying 2D coordinates of regions surrounding each main facial feature.
2. the probability of distance between pairs of input pixels.

Given this training data, an ensemble of regression trees is trained to estimate the facial landmark positions directly from pixel intensity values. The final result of this process is a facial landmark detector that can be used to find facial landmark in a small time with high accuracy. More precisely, this landmarks detector is used to estimate the location of 68 2D coordinates referencing relevant facial features (shown in Fig. 2) and resulting in a 68 × 2 array organized as follow:

- rows [1–17] contains jawline landmarks coordinates;
- rows [18–22] contains left eyebrow landmarks coordinates;
- rows [23–27] contains right eyebrow landmarks coordinates;
- rows [28–36] contains nose landmarks coordinates;
- rows [37–42] contains left eye landmarks coordinates;
- rows [43–48] contains right eye landmarks coordinates;
- rows [49–68] contains mouth landmarks coordinates.

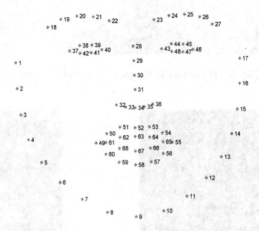

Fig. 2. The indexes of the 68-coordinates corresponding to the facial landmarks selected.

For the sake of balancing efficacy and efficiency, it is crucial to choose the right number of landmarks. A number of landmarks too small, indeed, may lead to insufficient precision in determining the pose angles. On the other hand, using too many landmarks may be counterproductive in terms of computing time, considerably impacting the practical usefulness of the whole approach.

Whenever landmarks have been identified (refer to Fig. 3 for examples), other details as background, color, illumination, hair, makeup and glasses, are no longer relevant for pose estimation and there is no need to consider them in the following steps. This makes possible working on more compact and manageable data further increasing the efficiency of the proposed algorithm. The image is cropped around the outermost landmarks and then converted to black and white to obtain a binary matrix (see Fig. 4). Quad-tree decomposition is then applied to this matrix to obtain the quad-tree. A quad-tree is a very specific tree in which every parent node may have four child nodes or none, and consequently it is a complete tree if every node has four child nodes except leaf nodes. In this case the binary matrix of landmark is the root of the tree and each decomposition makes a child node of the previous node, in other words on each near pass, image is split into four equally-sized smaller sections.

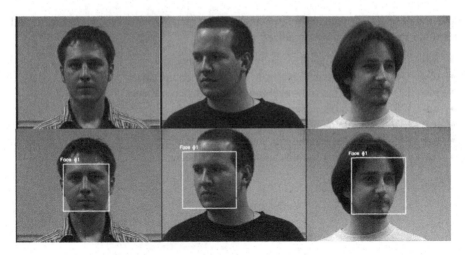

Fig. 3. The output of the facial landmarks algorithm.

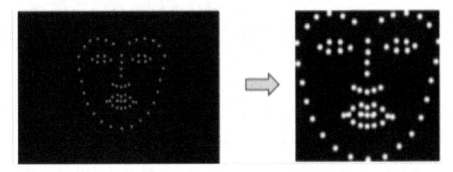

Fig. 4. Face-landmarks image cropping and binarization.

At each step, quad-tree decomposition tests each block to see if it meets some criterion of homogeneity. If a block meets the criterion, it is not divided any further. If it does not meet the criterion, it is subdivided again into four blocks, and the test criterion is applied to those blocks. This process is repeated iteratively until each block meets the criterion or equals the minimum set size. The decomposition process described above represents the region quad-tree, typically used for image processing applications such as image union, intersection and connected component labelling. In this work, the potential advantages of this technique have been brought to the problem of pose estimation by conveniently modifying its parameters and imposing some constraints. In this case, indeed, a block is split if the maximum value of the block elements minus the minimum value of the block elements is greater than the median of the binary landmarks matrix. Moreover, a minimum size has been chosen to avoid generation of blocks smaller than four pixels on each side. This criterion has been preferred to limit decomposition, this threshold can be further increased to make decomposition as quickly as possible, provided that the minimum size must be a power of 2. By proceeding in this way, the final result of quad-tree decomposition is the original image split into various block of different sizes. The method resizes always the original face-landmarks image in 256 × 256 pixels, consequently, the block size must be between 4 pixels and 256 pixels on each side. In our case there won't be any block bigger than 32 × 32 pixels, because decomposition will be done at least twice.

As it is visible in the Fig. 5, the higher the number of blocks, the closer are the landmarks. The numerical result of this procedure is a sparse matrix which contains in the upper left corner of each block its size, and zeros in the pixels that make up the block. This data structure is particularly suited to create a tree in the form of a binary array, which is computationally inexpensive. The algorithm transforms the sparse matrix resulting from the quad-tree decomposition into an array representing a tree (Fig. 6).

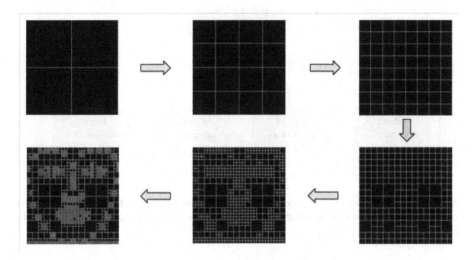

Fig. 5. The consecutive steps in quad-tree decomposition, from the upper left-hand corner to lower left corner: first decomposition, block of size 128 × 128; second decomposition, block of size 64 × 64; third decomposition, block of size 32 × 32; fourth decomposition, block of size 16 × 16; fifth decomposition, block of size 8 × 8; sixth decomposition, block of size 4 × 4.

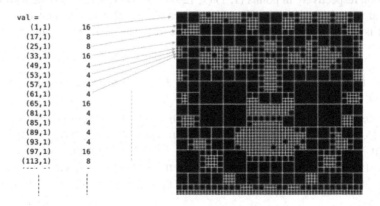

Fig. 6. Sparse matrix with coordinates and size of each block, ordered by column.

This tree is a complete tree of depth 6, in which each node has 4 children, accounting for 1365 nodes in total. Consequently, the array representing the tree has 1365 elements and each element corresponding to a node has value 1 if the node exists, 0 otherwise. Initially, the array is initialized with all values equal to 0. The tree is built with the recursive algorithm summarized in Fig. 7 below:

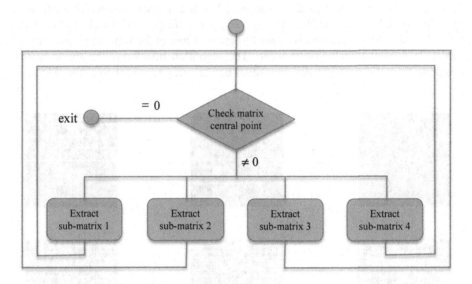

Fig. 7. Given an nxn matrix, if the central point has a value other than 0 then it means that the node has four children and therefore the four matrices originating from that point are recursively processed.

For instance, the first matrix, with 256 × 256 dimension that originates at point (1, 1) represents the root of the tree. To understand if the root has children, a check for a value other than 0 in the central point of the matrix, i.e. the point at (129,129) is performed. If so, then this means that the root has 4 children with 128 × 128 dimension respectively in points (1, 1) (1, 129) (129, 1) (129.129) and the algorithm is executed recursively in each submatrix. For each node that has generated children, a value 1 is assigned to the array representing the tree. The new tree is compared to each

Table 1. Rotation values (pitch, yaw) for all the 35 poses considered. Angular range: pitch [−30°, 30°], yaw [−45°, 45°]

(30, −45)	(30, −30)	(30, −15)	(30, 0)	(30, 15)	(30, 30)	(30, 45)
(15, −45)	(15, −30)	(15, −15)	(15, 0)	(15, 15)	(15, 30)	(15, 45)
(0, −45)	(0, −30)	(0, −15)	(0, 0)	(0, 15)	(0, 30)	(0, 45)
(−15, −45)	(−15, −30)	(−15, −15)	(−15, 0)	(−15, 15)	(−15, 30)	(−15, 45)
(−30, −45)	(−30, −30)	(−30, −15)	(−30, 0)	(−30, 15)	(−30, 30)	(−30, 45)

of the 35 trees corresponding to 35 reference poses featuring the rotation values (pitch, yaw) indicated in Table 1. These 35 reference poses were obtained by renderings of a 3D face model created through MakeHuman [17], an open source application designed for parametric modeling of humanoid figures (see Fig. 8).

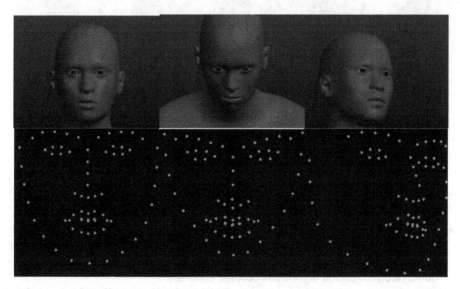

Fig. 8. Examples of synthetic face renderings (top half) and the corresponding landmarks (bottom half) for pitch and yaw values of (0, 0) (−30, 0) (15, −30)

Finally, a comparison is performed through the Hamming distance metric. The input tree is compared with each of the 35 poses. The tree corresponding to the lowest Hamming distance determines the pose of the input tree with regard to a couple of pitch and yaw values.

4 Experiments

The proposed method has the advantage of not having a training phase, therefore it can be applied to any image source. All the experiments conducted have been performed on the public database Pointing '04 [19] consisting of 16 sets of images (samples shown in Fig. 9).

The first set contains 30 frontal images of 15 people, with/without glasses and different ethnicity/skin-color. The remaining sets contain each one a person in different poses. The database contains image with varies head pose, determined by 2 angles (pitch, yaw) varying from −90° to +90°, including the combination of angles. That accounts for 93 images of the same person at different poses, for a total of 2790 image.

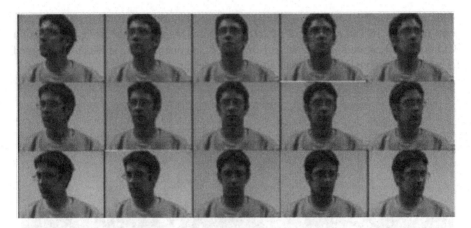

Fig. 9. Example of a subject in different poses from Pointing '04 database.

In this work a subset of the original database has been selected for the experiments according to the following criteria:

- The final aim of the method is to be part of a face recognition pipeline aimed at security applications, therefore, rotation angle exceeding 30° for pitch and 45° for yaw have not been considered. The simple reason is that in case of extreme rotations, face recognition algorithms become unreliable.
- Since the proposed method is based on facial landmarks not affected by variations such as makeup, glasses, hair, etc., images featuring these variations have been discarded.

In the end, the final gallery included 30 frontal images of 15 person, and 15 sets of 35 images each from 15 different subjects, for a total of 555 images. However, 37 images (6% of gallery) with maximum pitch and/or values have been excluded due to some inconsistency with actual rotation values (refer to Fig. 10), resulting in 518 valid images on which the pose estimation method has been applied to.

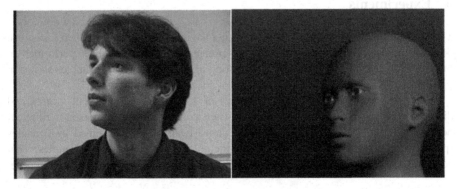

Fig. 10. subject 162 (+15, +45) compared to synthetic reference with corresponding angular values. It is possible to note an inconsistency between the actual subject's head pose and the annotated rotation values.

For each of the faces in the database pitch and yaw rotations were correctly esti-mated with a maximum angular error within 15°, that represents the discretization step adopted for the synthetic reference dataset used for comparison. With regard to pro-posed method's efficiency, the overall time required for pose estimate since input image is provided amounts to approximately 0.22 s on average. More in detail, landmarks detection required the greatest fraction of total processing time (74% accounting for 0.16 s), quad-tree decomposition only required 8% and 0.017 s, while pose estimation was performed in 0.04 s on average (18%).

In other terms, most of the time is used for the landmarks detection step. This could mean that an improvement of this step can make the algorithm substantially faster. For example, the number of landmark required to ensure an accurate (application-wise) estimate of the face pose, could possibly be reduced. Nevertheless, the proposed method results twice as fast as the state of the art [6], though its angular accuracy appears to be lower (Fig. 11).

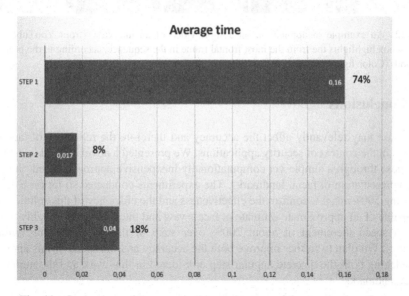

Fig. 11. Comparison of time required by main steps of the proposed method.

However, for the main application context to which this method is targeted, this lower accuracy could be negligible, since the main purpose is to determine which frame results the most promising for face recognition in the shortest possible amount of time. This is particularly true for the frequent case of video sequences which are becoming even more diffused than still images for security applications. As shown in Fig. 12, we successfully tested the proposed algorithm on video content in order to rapidly determine the best candidate (i.e. the most frontal frame) for face recognition.

Fig. 12. An example of application on a short video of an interview (from YouTube). The yellow box highlights the from the most frontal frame in the sequence, according to the proposed method. (Color figure online)

5   Conclusions

Face pose may relevantly affect the accuracy and therefore the reliability of face biometrics in the context of security applications. We presented a novel method to estimate face pose through a simple yet computationally inexpensive approach based on quadtree representation of facial landmarks. The experiments conducted so far on a dataset featuring 500+ images, confirm the effectiveness and the efficiency of this solution, that is capable of an approximate estimate of face's yaw and pitch angles in roughly 0,22 s, with a speed increment of about 200% over state of the art algorithms (without training). We plan to further improve both the accuracy and the speed of this approach by reducing both the discrete angular step considered in this work and the number of facial landmarks.

References

1. Murphy-Chutorian, E., Trivedi, M.M.: Head pose estimation in computer vision: a survey. IEEE Trans. Pattern Anal. Mach. Intell. **31**(4), 607–626 (2009)
2. Ding, C., Tao, D.: Pose-invariant face recognition with homography-based normalization. Pattern Recogn. **66**, 144–152 (2017)
3. Çelik, A., Arica, N.: Occlusion analysis for face frontalization. In: 2016 4th International Symposium on Digital Forensic and Security (ISDFS)
4. Kavitha, J., Mirnalinee, T.T.: Automatic frontal face reconstruction approach for pose invariant face recognition. Procedia Comput. Sci. **87**, 300–305 (2016)

5. Breitenstein, M.D., Kuettel, D., Weise, T., Van Gool, L., Pfister, H.: Real-time face pose estimation from single range images. In: IEEE Conference on Computer Vision and Pattern Recognition, CVPR 2008, pp. 1–8. IEEE, June 2008
6. Fanelli, G., Gall, J., Van Gool, L.:. Real time head pose estimation with random regression forests. In: 2011 IEEE Conference on Computer Vision and Pattern Recognition (CVPR), pp. 617–624. IEEE, June 2011
7. Lia, D., Pedrycz, W.: A central profile-based 3D face pose estimation. Pattern Recogn. **47**(2), 525–534 (2014)
8. Liao, H., Shejie, L., Wang, D.: Tied factor analysis for unconstrained face pose classification. Optik Int. J. Light Electron Opt. **127**(23), 11553–11566 (2016)
9. Liu, Y., Xie, Z., Yuan, X., Chen, J., Song, W.: Multi-level structured hybrid forest for joint head detection and pose estimation. Neurocomputing **266**, 206–215 (2017)
10. Osadchy, M., Cun, Y.L., Miller, M.L.: Synergistic face detection and pose estimation with energy-based models. J. Mach. Learn. Res. **8**(May), 1197–1215 (2007)
11. Patacchiola, M., Cangelosi, A.: Head pose estimation in the wild using Convolutional Neural Networks and adaptive gradient methods. Pattern Recognit. **71**, 132–143 (2017)
12. Ranjan, R., Patel, V.M., Chellappa, R.: Hyperface: a deep multi-task learning framework for face detection, landmark localization, pose estimation, and gender recognition. IEEE Trans. Pattern Anal. Mach. Intell. (2017)
13. Ahn, B., Choi, D.-G., Park, J., Kweon, I.S.: Real-time head pose estimation using multi-task deep neural network. In: Robotics and Autonomous Systems, vol. 103, pp. 1–12, May 2018
14. Aghajanian, J., Prince, S.: Face pose estimation in uncontrolled environments. In: BMVC, vol. 1, no. 2, p. 3, September 2009
15. Zhu, X., Ramanan, D.: Face detection, pose estimation, and landmark localization in the wild. In: 2012 IEEE Conference on Computer Vision and Pattern Recognition (CVPR), pp. 2879–2886. IEEE, June 2012
16. Samet, H.: The quadtree and related hierarchical data structures. ACM Comput. Surv. (CSUR) **16**(2), 187–260 (1984)
17. Viola, P., Jones, M.: Rapid object detection using a boosted cascade of simple features. In: Proceedings of the 2001 IEEE Computer Society Conference on Computer Vision and Pattern Recognition, CVPR 2001, vol. 1, pp. I-I. IEEE (2001)
18. Kaemi, V., Sullivan, J.: One millisecond face alignment with an ensemble of regression trees. In: 2014 IEEE Conference on Computer Vision and Pattern Recognition (CVPR)
19. http://www.makehuman.org
20. Gourier, N., Hall, D., Crowley, J.L.: Estimating face orientation from robust detection of salient facial features. In: Proceedings of Pointing 2004, ICPR, International Workshop on Visual Observation of Deictic Gestures, Cambridge, UK

Walking on the Cloud: Gait Recognition, a Wearable Solution

Aniello Castiglione[1], Kim-Kwang Raymond Choo[2],
Maria De Marsico[3]([✉]), and Alessio Mecca[3]

[1] University of Salerno, Salerno, Italy
[2] The University of Texas at San Antonio, San Antonio, TX 78249, USA
[3] Sapienza University of Rome, Rome, Italy
demarsico@di.uniroma1.it

Abstract. Biometrics and cloud computing are converging towards a common application context aiming at deploying biometric authentication as a remote service (Biometrics as a Service - BaaS). The advantages for the final user is to be relieved from the burden related to acquire/maintain specific software, and to gain the ability of building personalized applications where biometric services can be embedded through suitable cloud APIs. Gait is one of the promising biometric traits that can be investigated in this scenario. In particular, this paper deals with the processing techniques based on wearable sensors, e.g., accelerometers. These sensors are nowadays ubiquitous in mobile devices, and allow the acquisition of lightweight signals that can be sent remotely for processing. As an example of possible applications, a positive recognition may automatically allow access to restricted zones without an explicit action by the user, that has just to approach the entrance walking normally.

Keywords: Gait recognition · Wearable sensors · Cloud services
Biometrics as a Service · BaaS

1 Introduction

Modern mobile devices are not only ubiquitous, but also embed an increasing number of sensors. The original aim of those sensors is, basically, to provide an increasingly "natural" interaction (e.g., triggering functions just by shacking the device), and advanced features (e.g., sending directly a captured image). Thanks to them, the equipped smartphones, tablets and wearables can further lend themselves to unanticipated uses. It is worth noticing that the variety of tasks that are performed nowadays trough them, especially for some user groups, often overcomes the use of traditional desktop computers. However, for some specific applications, either storage or computational capabilities may still be not sufficient. This is the typical, if not main, context where cloud computing may represent an effective and efficient solution. Among the mobile applications gaining popularity, biometric authentication is one that can take significant advantage from the mobile+cloud architectural schema. The biometric community

© Springer Nature Switzerland AG 2018
M. H. Au et al. (Eds.): NSS 2018, LNCS 11058, pp. 174–186, 2018.
https://doi.org/10.1007/978-3-030-02744-5_13

usually classifies the biometric traits into two main categories, namely hard and soft. The hard ones better meet the conditions for a sufficient accuracy and reliability of subject recognition, e.g., universality, uniqueness, permanence, and ubiquitousness [19]. Popular examples, which are consolidated also in everyday practice, are face, fingerprint, and iris. Hard traits are basically static ones, i.e., bound to subject appearance and physical features. Thanks to good levels of discriminating power and permanence they can achieve good performance in terms of accurate recognition, especially in controlled conditions. However their strict relation to physical/appearance features makes systems based on "strong" traits suffer from the problems that typically affect pattern recognition based on visual characteristics, and that are caused by uneven illumination, different orientation with respect to a capture device, special trait configurations (e.g., expression in face). Moreover, just because they are "visible", they are easier to "copy" and are subject to spoofing. As a consequence, for those traits it is especially important to verify the liveness of the presented sample, in order to distinguish a real user from a photo or a video used for a presentation attack.

The biometric traits classified as soft, instead, lack to meet one or more of the required conditions mentioned above. Nevertheless, they can be useful at least to delimit specific classes of persons, and to reduce the search space in recognition operations. Some examples are represented by either physical traits bound to subject (static) appearance, e.g., face shape, height, skin or hair color, or demographic features (gender, age, ethnicity), that can be in turn inferred from physical appearance and identify groups of subjects rather than a single one. Several traits in the "soft" category are related to subject behavior instead: gait time progression, dynamics of signature, writing behavior in general, and keystroke dynamics are only some examples. The idea underlying the use of these traits to identify people is that, while humans are not very good at remembering passwords, they are quite good at simply being (and behaving as) themselves. But the same traits can be affected by behavioral as well as emotional factors, so that they may lack permanence. Moreover, they may still lack a completely reliable/accurate processing. Notwithstanding their limitations, those traits can be used in controlled conditions, or can further enforce recognition accuracy of strong ones. In addition, they are more difficult to forge and/or replicate.

This contribution deals with gait recognition, which is included among soft biometrics. There are different approaches tackling this problem, that can be divided into three classes. The earliest ones used for user recognition rely on machine vision-based techniques, that exploit visual models for both the static and dynamic aspects of the gait pattern of a subject. Gait analysis for medical applications traditionally exploits floor sensors-based techniques, that capture features of subject gait through special sensors equipping an ambient floor, e.g., pressure and/or weight sensors. Finally, wearable sensors-based techniques move sensors from the ambient to the subject body, therefore achieving an ubiquitous recognition ability. This latter class of techniques is the object of the present proposal. While verification (1:1 matching with a claimed identity) might be carried out locally, both security and privacy issues claim for a remote processing when identification (1:N matching) is requested. Moreover, the possible application of wearable sensor-based gait recognition as a cloud-related service is investigated, sketching a possible architecture. In fact, cloud computing offers an efficient storage/processing infrastructure to exploit mobile user authentication also with large scale populations.

2   Wearable Sensors: A Possible Solution for Gait Recognition?

The errors of a biometric recognition system occur either when a subject is confused with another due to inter-personal similarities, or when a subject is not recognized due to intra-personal differences. Both problems are related to the discriminative power of adopted traits and related approaches. In addition, both intrinsic and external variations can modify the appearance or, more generally, the characteristics of a biometric trait. This holds at a different level for hard and soft biometrics. For example, A-PIE variations (age, pose, illumination, and expression) affect face recognition. Gait is not an exception in the biometric scenario. Walking speed is the main factor affecting gait dynamics, but also the kind of shoes (e.g., heels for women shoes, or heavy working shoes [17,18]), the irregular ground slope, and also some temporary illness (e.g., leg contusions or other problems related to articulation or feet) can cause variations of the individual gait pattern. Gait recognition techniques that are based on processing silhouettes extracted from video sequences, can further suffer from common image processing problems, e.g., illumination, occlusion or self-occlusion, pose, and perspective with respect to the camera. The last two raise similar issues, but the first one is intrinsic to the user while the second is an extrinsic factor acting notwithstanding the user absolute position. Finally, clothes and carried objects can also affect the reliable extraction of silhouette features. In practice, each class of approaches may present specific problems, besides those that characterize this biometric trait (see Fig. 1). Gait recognition also presents some positive aspects. As for the other behavioral traits, it is quite difficult to copy or forge a gait pattern. In approaches based on machine vision, it can be carried out at a distance of 10 m or more, therefore the user is not necessarily aware of the recognition. In wearable sensor-based approaches distance is not a problem since the acquisition devices are located on user body, and in this case the user is usually cooperative. Floor sensor-based approaches are a special case, since the acquisition devices are inside the floor. In all cases, gait recognition is non-intrusive and does not require a strong cooperation from the user. Moreover, it is non-invasive because it does not require the user to do any specific action but walk, except for very limited cases. The following analysis focuses on wearable sensor-based techniques, in particular on advantages and issues characterizing sensors built in modern smartphones and other personal mobile devices [8,9]. The use of mobile devices to carry out biometric recognition is gaining increasing interest in scientific community. The wearable sensors embedded in smartphones, tablets and smart watches. e.g., accelerometers and gyroscopes, allow exploring new

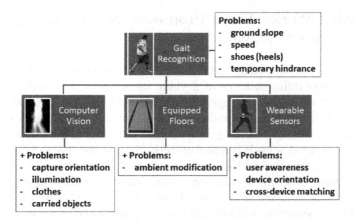

Fig. 1. Gait recognition methodologies and specific problems raised.

research topics that go beyond biometric recognition based on traditional traits, such as face and fingerprints. In general, a gait template acquired by an inertial sensor is made up by 3 time series. When an accelerometer is used, these are the acceleration values from the 3 axes over which the signal is captured. When a gyroscope is exploited too, there is a further triplet of signals, synchronized with the accelerometer ones, and acquired over the same 3 axes. Figure 2 shows an example from the BWR MultiDevice dataset [7] of the data recorded by an embedded accelerometer in a commercial smartphone, namely a OnePlus One.

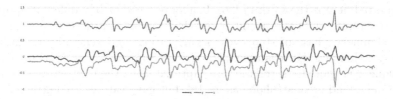

Fig. 2. An example of walking signal from the BWR Dataset.

Besides gait recognition, new behavioral patterns are also being investigated, whose analysis exploits ubiquitous and cheap user equipment. For instance, Google is developing the Abacus project [21], in the context of Google's Advanced Technology and Projects group (ATAP). This is a team and in-house technology incubator created by former DARPA. Abacus explores the use of the phone sensors to gather data about their user.

3 Related Works: Some Proposals for Gait Recognition via Wearable Devices

Works in literature addressing the topic of gait recognition via wearable devices report the use of different kinds of devices, sometimes not readily available in an everyday context. From an operational point of view, it is possible to sketch a rough classification into two main categories, out of which some examples follow. The first category includes proposals that rely on a preliminary step/cycle detection (in general, a cycle is a pair of steps). In this way, instead of comparing the full signals, "chunks" of them are matched, either choosing the best representative subset or fusing results from matching each chunk on its own. Two examples of this category are [17,18]. They exploit a Motion Recording Sensor (MRS), which measures acceleration in three orthogonal directions, namely up-down, forward-backward and sideways, with a sampling frequency of 100 Hz. The MRS includes an internal memory to record the signal and a port to transfer it. The device is attached to the ankle. Walking cycles are detected and normalized in time, so that each cycle contains 100 acceleration values. Matching is carried out by Euclidean distance, either between the average steps of each walk, or between each pair of steps respectively in the two works. The work in [15] exploits the accelerometer embedded in Google G1 phone. During gait signal recording, the phone is placed in a pocket attached to the belt of the subject on the right-hand side of the hip. The phone is positioned horizontal, the screen points to the body, the upper part of the phone points in walking direction. Matching exploits the classical Dynamic Time Warping (DTW) algorithm. This is also common to other methods. The use of DTW allows, up to a certain extent, to avoid constraining cycles to be of the same size. The last example reported here is the work in [26]. It adopts a completely different approach using signature points and neighbor search. Proposals in the second group lack the preliminary phase of step/cycle segmentation, and generally use machine learning techniques. For example, [22] exploits Support Vector Machine (SVM) technique. The gait characteristics are captured using the built-in accelerometer of the same kind of smartphone as in [15], but gait features are extracted from the times-series data from a selected time window without a preliminary identification of the contained gait cycles. Various features are extracted from the measured accelerations and used to train a SVM. It is interesting to notice that the extracted features include the Mel- and Bark-frequency cepstral coefficients (MFCC, BFCC) which are commonly used in speech and speaker recognition. As a further example, still capturing data by Google G1 phone, [23] exploits Hidden Markov Models (HMM) for modeling the time series data corresponding to the gait signal. A modified version of Viterbi algorithm is used for matching. The works in [24,25] both rely on k-NN algorithm, but the second one takes again cycles into consideration, and moreover exploits the addition of gyroscope signal. Finally, [31] is an evolution of the system proposed in [26], that fuses the use of the signature points with a preliminary clustering phase to increase the final performances.

4   From Wearable Sensors to the Cloud

In few words, the cloud model and its solutions especially address the needs of companies or consumers needing to exploit specific technologies, but lacking the necessary software/hardware/technical resources, or preferring an outsourcing strategy. Therefore, many major stakeholders started providing cloud services, also in the form APIs to be embedded in proprietary software (e.g., Microsoft Azure [30]).

Biometric applications are becoming more and more widespread and sophisticated [1]. Moreover, the last trend of the market is to make them available even on devices, e.g. personal mobiles, that may not be equipped with the necessary storage/computational resources. The Biometrics-as-a-Service (BaaS) model can be considered similar to the Software-as-a-Service (SaaS) model, because it provides software tools (in this case related to biometric recognition tasks) in the cloud and makes it available to customers. An example of prototypical consumer application that uses Cognitive Services included in Microsoft Azure is presented in [13,14].

The cloud paradigm raises new challenges, both related in general to cloud computing and Software-as-a-Service, and in particular to Biometrics-as-a-Service [5]. As for any cloud-based model, anomalous behavior from the application can be raised by misconfigurations, non-fatal hardware errors or by programming mistakes. These problems can derive, for example, from the virtualization layer, e.g., from the Virtual Machine (VM) Monitor, and they "*may cause failures, ranging from simply detectable crashes to unpredictable and erratic runtime behaviors*" [6]. Of course, problems in such level will propagate upwards the above levels. Moreover, software failures can also happen at higher levels, for example they can regard the hosted Web server or databases. The causes can be manifold, spacing from natural disasters, human errors, application bugs, erroneous configurations. Notwithstanding the possible cause(s) of rising issues, the service must be maintained available on a continuous basis (resilient). Otherwise a degradation of the quality of service (QoS) can be perceived by the users and practically represent a violation of the Service Level Agreement (SLA) contract. This may ultimately rise possible legal actions. In order to increase fault-tolerance, the cloud-based services tend to duplicate resources, e.g., physical servers in possibly different locations and more hosting per service. Interested reader can find more detailed information about cloud services in [27], while [16] provides an exhaustive description of structure, approaches and issues for systems dealing with mobile cloud computing. Finally, [29] provides information about security issues risen in this field.

The use of mobile devices for biometric gait recognition raises specific issues. First of all, capture of the reference sample to use for the future recognition operations (enrollment) may be carried out by the user without the assistance of an operator. This calls for user interaction features implementing a robust protocol, in order to support the acquisition of good quality signals even by non-expert users [2,10–12]. After capture and local processing of the biometric sample, this must be secured in order to avoid its theft. Recognition operations can be carried out either through a verification procedure, that entails an identity claim and a 1:1 matching, or an identification procedure. In this case the matching is 1:N, and requires to compare the new incoming sample (probe) with all enrolled ones (gallery). Of course, it is hard to hypothesize that this latter kind of operation can be carried out locally. One of the reasons that is often mentioned is the lack of sufficient computing power on present mobile devices. Actually, though being a real possible problem, this is not the main one. In order to carry out identification locally, any single personal device should store the complete gallery of samples of enrolled subjects. Besides being hardly feasible, both privacy and security issues advise against this solution. Notwithstanding any securing and/or anonymizing procedure, the replication on poorly attended/secured devices of potentially sensible data can create a serious flaw. Therefore, a secure transmission protocol must be devised, that submits a probe to recognize to a dedicated cloud service. The latter both includes storing facilities for possibly large size galleries, and enough computing resources to carry out recognition in real time even against massive amounts of data. In order to ensure data protection, the modeling of cryptographic protocols [3, 4] and distributed ledger might be deployed to ensure the exclusive use of sensitive data, either local or distributed. Being the gait signal quite cheap in terms of storage (with respect to images) both storage and processing can be especially efficient.

Of course, a real market deployment requires to address problems specifically related to the gait signal. It is important to consider that the accelerometers present inter-device differences [7], that can be relevant even in the case of the same sensor model exiting from the same production line and built in identical conditions. Calibrations and systematic errors can especially happen when the sensor is built in a smartphone. This is because in this case the required accuracy is generally not especially high. In addition, the data might be either read with a constant frequency or on "significant" value changes, as for Android standard for accelerometer signal. This causes relevant differences in the "shape" of the captured signal. The acceleration values are not even independent from the sensor orientation and this creates further significant problems when the device in which the sensor is built-in can freely rotate. Different kinds of approaches are studied in literature in order to reduce these problems. These topics are addressed by ongoing research [15, 21, 24, 31]. However, it is interesting to notice the possibility of significant improvement even with simple preliminary solutions. Tables 1 and 2 show results from a set of experiments carried out to validate the feasibility of a signal normalization procedure that can be carried out by the user when the application is installed on the telephone. Three smartphones of different brands were used to test cross-device performances, each with a different accelerometer model embedded, namely a OnePlus One (with a LIS3DH Accelerometer, by ST Microelectronics), a Samsung Galaxy S4 Active (with a K330 3-axes Accelerometer), and a Sony Xperia S (with a Bosch Sensortec BMA250 accelerometer). Walk signals belong to 25 subjects in two acquisition sessions with an average time distance of about 15 days. The subjects wore different kinds of shoes but no high heels. Each single session is composed by 6 acquisitions, 2 for each smartphone, for a total of 300 walk signals. The adopted procedure [7] allows to increase the accuracy of both intra- and inter-device (cross-device) matching. In Tables 1 and 2, the performance are measured in terms of Recognition Rate (RR) for closed set identification (the most popular 1:N matching modality in literature: the probe subject is always present in the system gallery): the higher the RR, the better; Equal Error Rate (EER) is used instead for both verification (1:1 matching with identity claim) and open set identification (1:N, but the probe user may not be an enrolled one): the lower the EER, the better. Two different matching algorithms are used, one applying Dynamic Time Warping (DTW) to the whole gait signal (WHOLE WALK), whose results are reported in Table 1, and the second one using a segmentation procedure to match single steps (SEPARATE STEPS), whose results are reported in Table 2. In the figure, AllDevices refers to a situation where the matched gait signal may be either captured by the same device or not. Device_vs_Device represents the average performance achieved by matching a probe captured with one device with a gallery sample captured by a different device. SameDevice represents the average performance achieved by matching only signals coming from the same device. O.D. stands for Original Dataset, while N.D. denotes the Normalized Dataset.

Table 1. Example of performance achieved by accelerometer-based gait recognition in a cross-device setting with a complete walk.

Closed Set Identification - WHOLE WALK			
Test	RR - O.D.	RR - N.D.	Improv.
AllDevices	52.0%	54.5%	4.81%
Device_vs_Device	35.3%	49.3%	39.62%
SameDevice	50.3%	52.0%	3.31%

Verification - WHOLE WALK			
Test	ERR - O.D.	ERR - N.D.	Improv.
AllDevices	31.8%	29.6%	7.43%
Device_vs_Device	31.4%	29.5%	6.23%
SameDevice	28.8%	29.0%	-0.69%

Open Set Identification - WHOLE WALK			
Test	ERR - O.D.	ERR - N.D.	Improv.
AllDevices	31.8%	29.6%	7.43%
Device_vs_Device	79.2%	72.3%	9.45%
SameDevice	25.2%	25.0%	0.67%

Once the above problems are addressed, the combination of mobile gait recognition and cloud storage/computing can create a kind of transparent authentication, e.g., to access protected areas. The user has no need to either claim an identity or carry out a specific operation. A pair of very small Bluetooth emitting sources (beacons) suitably positioned along the controlled pathway drives the

Table 2. Example of performance achieved by accelerometer-based gait recognition in a cross-device setting with segmented steps.

Closed Set Identification - SEPARATE STEPS			
Test	RR - O.D.	RR - N.D.	Improv.
AllDevices	22.5%	34.5%	53.33%
Device_vs_Device	15.2%	26.7%	47.06%
SameDevice	22.0%	29.0%	106.67%

Verification - SEPARATE STEPS			
Test	ERR - O.D.	ERR - N.D.	Improv.
AllDevices	50.0%	50.0%	0.00%
Device_vs_Device	47.2%	42.5%	11.17%
SameDevice	44.9%	43.1%	4.26%

Open Set Identification - SEPARATE STEPS			
Test	ERR - O.D.	ERR - N.D.	Improv.
AllDevices	83.3%	71.3%	16.83%
Device_vs_Device	92.2%	88.7%	3.95%
SameDevice	65.8%	47.7%	38.11%

start and stop of the sample acquisition. In general, the only function of beacons is to broadcast their IDs. Once they are registered within a specific application, capture of the broadcasted ID can trigger the start of signal acquisition as well as its termination and sending to the remote authentication/storage service. In this way, the user is free from the duty to start and stop capture and send the data. All operations happen according to the model of implicit interaction [28]. No cooperation is required by the user except for turning on Bluetooth on the mobile device and walk to reach the interested area (see Fig. 3).

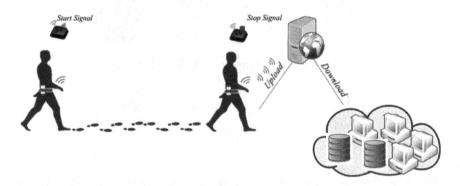

Fig. 3. A possible architecture for gait recognition via mobile devices and cloud resources.

From the point of view of privacy protection and robustness to spoofing, it is to say that these two aspects are both less critical when gait is involved. As for the former, acquiring the gait signal of a person does not allow to recover its identity, as it may happen for example with face images seen by chance in other contexts. As for the latter, mimicking the walking pattern of another person has been found to be very hard [20]. From the communication security point of view, the new standards, such as HTTPS with TLS 1.2[1] or the new 1.3 version, are increasing more and more their encryption/protection capabilities, allowing a secure data transfer between a mobile device and the recognition server/cloud service. Moreover, it is possible to include in the acquisition application the requirement for a specific "fingerprint" on the Certification Authority (CA) TLS certificate, effectively blocking rogue CA, possibly used in Man in the Middle (MITM) attacks.

This kind of architecture can also be adapted to other biometric traits. However, the only one that can be captured via mobile without any user explicit action is gait, and this makes related features particularly appealing. Figure 4

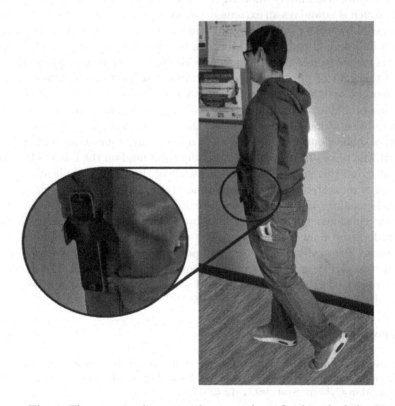

Fig. 4. The user simply carries the smartphone fixed to the belt.

---

[1] https://tools.ietf.org/html/rfc5246.

shows a possible use of the technology, with the smartphone simply fixed to the belt. There will be no need for pushing buttons, issuing commands, or whatever.

It is to say that for other biometric traits the combined use of biometric recognition and cloud computing is already a concrete possibility. An example is represented by Microsoft Cognitive Services[2], which are part of the Azure framework and include face, voice and emotion recognition services that can be called via provided APIs. Actually other service providers have also embraced the strategy of Biometrics as a Service (BaaS) or "Biometric security in the Cloud" to provide services to companies (see for example Fujitsu[3] and AWARE[4]). The next challenge is to widen the use of these technologies from company to user applications.

5   Conclusions

Gait recognition by wearable sensors is a promising approach that tries to solve problems related to computer vision-based techniques. The entailed signal capture procedure is definitely unobtrusive, since the user has only to wear a smartphone, which is nowadays an extremely common practice. Automatic capture can be triggered by small Bluetooth radio transmitters, according to the paradigm of implicit interaction. Authorized users can be free to move along the places where access is granted without needing to provide smartcards or passwords. However, even if the kind of produced signals (temporal series from accelerometers and other sensors) is lightweight if compared to images, large scale processing can still pose cost problems for in-house large scale applications. In this scenario, BaaS is a possible solution. BaaS may follow the same growth, from company to consumer, of other cloud-based services. Two issues are to be considered: price and privacy. The price of the service is normally computed on the basis of bunches of API calls, and therefore depends on the scale of the hosting application, and on the level of requested service. An extension to consumer applications calls for a reasonable scaling of present service costs for a more limited scope. For example, a private consumer might be attracted by the idea of automatically identifying on the doorstep only a small set (order of ten) of trusted subjects allowed to enter home. Privacy and safe storing of personal data have to be addressed too. A biometric service provider would become a critical collector of sensible data to be strongly protected. Once costs and security issues will be addressed, BaaS may really become a part of everyday life.

References

1. Abate, A.F., Nappi, M., Ricciardi, S.: I-am: implicitly authenticate me person authentication on mobile devices through ear shape and arm gesture. IEEE Trans. Syst. Man Cybern. Syst. **99**, 1–13 (2017)

---

[2] https://docs.microsoft.com/en-us/azure/cognitive-services/welcome.

[3] http://www.fujitsu.com/us/services/application-services/saas/biometrics-as-a-service/.

[4] https://www.aware.com/category/biometrics-as-a-service-baas/.

2. Barra, S., De Marsico, M., Nappi, M., Narducci, F., Riccio, D.: A hand-based biometric system in visible light for mobile environments. Inf. Sci. (2018)
3. Castiglione, A., Santis, A.D., Masucci, B., Palmieri, F., Castiglione, A., Huang, X.: Cryptographic hierarchical access control for dynamic structures. IEEE Trans. Inf. Forensics Secur. **11**(10), 2349–2364 (2016). https://doi.org/10.1109/TIFS.2016. 2581147
4. Castiglione, A., et al.: Hierarchical and shared access control. IEEE Trans. Inf. Forensics Secur. **11**(4), 850–865 (2016). https://doi.org/10.1109/TIFS.2015. 2512533
5. Castiglione, A., Choo, K.K.R., Nappi, M., Narducci, F.: Biometrics in the cloud: challenges and research opportunities. IEEE Cloud Comput. **4**(4), 12–17 (2017)
6. Cinque, M., Russo, S., Esposito, C., Choo, K.K.R., Free-Nelson, F., Kamhoua, C.A.: Cloud reliability: possible sources of security and legal issues? IEEE Cloud Comput. **5**(3), 31–38 (2018)
7. De Marsico, M., De Pasquale, D., Mecca, A.: Embedded accelerometer signal normalization for cross-device gait recognition. In: 2016 International Conference of the Biometrics Special Interest Group (BIOSIG), pp. 1–5. IEEE (2016)
8. De Marsico, M., Mecca, A.: Biometric walk recognizer. In: Murino, V., Puppo, E., Sona, D., Cristani, M., Sansone, C. (eds.) ICIAP 2015. LNCS, vol. 9281, pp. 19–26. Springer, Cham (2015). https://doi.org/10.1007/978-3-319-23222-5_3
9. De Marsico, M., Mecca, A.: Biometric walk recognizer. Multimedia Tools Appl. **76**(4), 4713–4745 (2017)
10. De Marsico, M., Nappi, M., Narducci, F., Proença, H.: Insights into the results of miche I-mobile iris challenge evaluation. Pattern Recogn. **74**, 286–304 (2018)
11. De Marsico, M., Nappi, M., Proença, H.: Results from miche II-mobile iris challenge evaluation II. Pattern Recogn. Lett. **91**, 3–10 (2017)
12. De Marsico, M., Nappi, M., Riccio, D., Wechsler, H.: Mobile iris challenge evaluation (miche)-I, biometric iris dataset and protocols. Pattern Recogn. Lett. **57**, 17–23 (2015)
13. De Marsico, M., Nemmi, E., Prenkaj, B., Saturni, G.: A smart peephole on the cloud. In: Battiato, S., Farinella, G.M., Leo, M., Gallo, G. (eds.) ICIAP 2017. LNCS, vol. 10590, pp. 364–374. Springer, Cham (2017). https://doi.org/10.1007/ 978-3-319-70742-6_34
14. De Marsico, M., Nemmi, E., Prenkaj, B., Saturni, G.: House in the (biometric) cloud: a possible application. IEEE Cloud Comput. **5**(4), 58–69 (2018)
15. Derawi, M.O., Nickel, C., Bours, P., Busch, C.: Unobtrusive user-authentication on mobile phones using biometric gait recognition. In: 2010 Sixth International Conference on Intelligent Information Hiding and Multimedia Signal Processing (IIH-MSP), pp. 306–311. IEEE (2010)
16. Dinh, H.T., Lee, C., Niyato, D., Wang, P.: A survey of mobile cloud computing: architecture, applications, and approaches. Wirel. Commun. Mobile Comput. **13**(18), 1587–1611 (2013)
17. Gafurov, D., Snekkenes, E.: Towards understanding the uniqueness of gait biometric. In: 8th IEEE International Conference on Automatic Face & Gesture Recognition, FG 2008, pp. 1–8. IEEE (2008)
18. Gafurov, D., Snekkenes, E., Bours, P.: Improved gait recognition performance using cycle matching. In: 2010 IEEE 24th International Conference on Advanced Information Networking and Applications Workshops (WAINA), pp. 836–841. IEEE (2010)
19. Jain, A.K., Ross, A., Prabhakar, S.: An introduction to biometric recognition. IEEE Trans. Circ. Syst. Video Technol. **14**(1), 4–20 (2000)

20. Muaaz, M., Mayrhofer, R.: Smartphone-based gait recognition: from authentication to imitation. IEEE Trans. Mobile Comput. **16**(11), 3209–3221 (2017)
21. Neverova, N., et al.: Learning human identity from motion patterns. IEEE Access **4**, 1810–1820 (2016)
22. Nickel, C., Brandt, H., Busch, C.: Classification of acceleration data for biometric gait recognition on mobile devices. BIOSIG **11**, 57–66 (2011)
23. Nickel, C., Busch, C., Rangarajan, S., Möbius, M.: Using hidden markov models for accelerometer-based biometric gait recognition. In: 2011 IEEE 7th International Colloquium on Signal Processing and Its Applications (CSPA), pp. 58–63. IEEE (2011)
24. Nickel, C., Wirtl, T., Busch, C.: Authentication of smartphone users based on the way they walk using K-NN algorithm. In: 2012 Eighth International Conference on Intelligent Information Hiding and Multimedia Signal Processing (IIH-MSP), pp. 16–20. IEEE (2012)
25. Nowlan, M.F.: Human identification via gait recognition using accelerometer gyro forces. Yale Computer Science (2009). http://www.cs.yale.edu/homes/mfn3/pub/mfngaitid.pdf. Accessed 12 Nov 2013
26. Pan, G., Zhang, Y., Wu, Z.: Accelerometer-based gait recognition via voting by signature points. Electr. Lett. **45**(22), 1116–1118 (2009)
27. Rimal, B.P., Choi, E., Lumb, I.: A taxonomy and survey of cloud computing systems. In: Fifth International Joint Conference on INC, IMS and IDC, NCM 2009, pp. 44–51. IEEE (2009)
28. Schmidt, A.: Implicit human computer interaction through context. Pers. Technol. **4**(2–3), 191–199 (2000)
29. Subashini, S., Kavitha, V.: A survey on security issues in service delivery models of cloud computing. J. Netw. Comput. Appl. **34**(1), 1–11 (2011)
30. Wilder, B.: Cloud Architecture Patterns: Using Microsoft Azure. O'Reilly Media Inc., Sebastopol (2012)
31. Zhang, Y., Pan, G., Jia, K., Lu, M., Wang, Y., Wu, Z.: Accelerometer-based gait recognition by sparse representation of signature points with clusters. IEEE Trans. Cybern. **45**(9), 1864–1875 (2015)

EMA-LAB: Efficient Multi Authorisation Level Attribute Based Access Control

Nesrine Kaaniche[1], Sana Belguith[2($\boxtimes$)], and Giovanni Russello[2]

[1] SAMOVAR, Telecom SudParis, University Paris-Saclay, Paris, France
nesrine.kaaniche@telecom-sudparis.eu
[2] The Cyber Security Foundry, The University of Auckland, Auckland, New Zealand
sbel452@aucklanduni.ac.nz, g.russello@auckland.ac.nz

Abstract. Recent years have witnessed the trend of increasingly relying on remote and distributed infrastructures. This increases the complexity of access control to data, where access control policies should be flexible and distinguishable among users with different privileges. In this paper, we present **EMA-LAB**, a novel Multi Authorisation Level Attribute Based Access Control with short ciphertexts size. It relies on the usage of a constant-size threshold attribute based encryption scheme. The **EMA-LAB** scheme is multifold. First, it ensures a selective access to encrypted data with respect to different security levels. Second, the proposed construction protects the secrecy of enciphered contents against malicious adversaries, even in case of colluding users. Third, **EMA-LAB** relies on low computation and communication processes, mainly for resource-constrained devices, compared to most closely related schemes.

Keywords: Multi-level threshold scheme
Attribute based encryption with short ciphertext · Access control

1 Introduction

Nowadays, data sharing is gaining an expanding interest, mainly with the development of remote services and distributed infrastructures. It allows data owners to share their outsourced data among groups of users. However, many security concerns arise, as the outsourced data should be protected from unauthorized access. Thus, fine grained access privileges should be ensured, while preventing malicious access.

The increasing need and complexity of access control to outsourced data lead to the emergence of several encrypted access control schemes. Among these techniques, Attribute based Encryption (ABE) has appeared as a promising cryptographic technique which provides fine grained access control for outsourced data. ABE is used to encrypt data files with respect to an access policy associated with a set of attributes.

However, sharing data contents between different involved actors is often an issue, due to the complexity of access control policies' management. This issue

M. H. Au et al. (Eds.): NSS 2018, LNCS 11058, pp. 187–201, 2018.
https://doi.org/10.1007/978-3-030-02744-5_14

becomes more complex when involved actors do not share the same access privileges to each part of the data file. Hence, different access levels need to be defined to allow authorized users to access different sub-parts of enciphered data. The translation of an access control structure into an equivalent multi-level policy remains the main challenging issue of encrypted access control mechanisms.

To protect some parts of data from unauthorised access, *redaction* techniques are applied to black out or remove these parts. Several redaction techniques have been proposed such as sanitizing schemes for digitally signed document, content extraction algorithms, redactable signatures and sanitizable signatures [1,11]. These schemes rely on malleable cryptographic primitives such as chameleon hash functions to allow redactors having their own secret key to modify some parts of the originally encrypted or signed data file. Although these techniques allow selective access to some parts of data, they are not efficient with multi-level access privileges.

The multi level access control policies in ABE schemes have been recently explored [12]. In these schemes, data files are encrypted using a multi level access policy where users can access parts of these data w.r.t. their access level. Although these proposals ensure multi level access control, the communication and computation overhead as well as the bandwidth consumption increase exponentially with the number of attributes required in the aggregated access structure.

To save the storage cost of ciphertext and processing overhead of encryption, attribute based encryption schemes with constant ciphertext size have been introduced [2,7,9]. In these schemes, the size of the generated ciphertext does not depend on the number of attributes used on the threshold access policies, which presents an interesting feature mainly for resource-constrained devices.

Contributions—In this paper, we propose EMA-LAB, a new multi-threshold attribute based encryption scheme. First, it permits a selective access to enciphered data with respect to different threshold levels. Second, the size of the resulting ciphertext does not depend on the number of attributes involved in the access policy, which makes our scheme more suitable for bandwidth-limited applications. Third, it is proven secure under standard assumptions. Finally, EMA-LAB provides interesting performances compared to most closely related schemes.

Paper organization—The remainder of this paper is organized as follows. First, Sect. 2 clarifies the problem statement and highlights security and functional requirements and Sect. 3 discusses related works. Then, Sect. 4 introduces EMA-LAB system and threat models. Section 5 presents complexity assumptions and mathematical background, and details EMA-LAB concrete construction. The security analysis of EMA-LAB is discussed in Sect. 6. Finally, performances analysis is detailed in Sect. 7 before concluding in Sect. 8.

2   Motivating Scenario

Publish and subscribe (pub/sub) systems have been widely bared to ensure dissemination of data contents from publishers to interested subscribers [14]. Similar to most of existing outsourcing mechanisms, pub/sub systems raise serious security concerns, mainly related to published data access control. It is commonly agreed that emerging encryption techniques are good alternatives to protect data from unauthorised access, namely Attribute Based Encryption (ABE) schemes [3,5].

Let us consider the following example depicted by Fig. 1, where a company subscribing its employees to a finance news service. That is, each publication P is composed of several sub-parts p_i related to k different authorization levels such that each access level corresponds to l sub-parts of data (i.e., $P = \{\{p_i\}_{i \in [1,l]}\}_{l \in [1,k]}$).

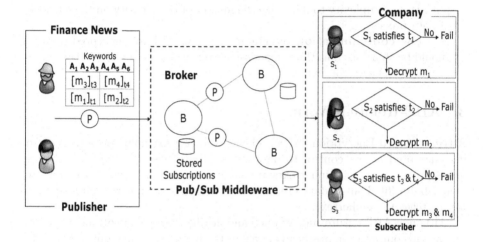

Fig. 1. Publish-subscribe system architecture

The subscribed employees can access received publications with respect to their authorisation level. Indeed, an employee who has only two interests can access a small amount of published data while a manager can access more sub-parts of data contents of the same publication. Obviously, the company's CEO can access the full publication. Thus, a multi level access control is defined as depicted by Fig. 1. As mentioned above, publications should be encrypted before forwarding to the pub/sub middleware.

A naive solution[1] is to divide publications into several parts and encrypt them separately with respect to different security levels. However, this solution presents several drawbacks. First, it contradicts the decoupled feature of pub-/sub system as the publisher will be aware of the interests of the subscribers. Second, this solution incurs huge computation and communication overheads

---

[1] Note that the security of publications' keywords and subscribers' interests at the broker side while performing the matching feature is above the scope of this paper.

due to performing the encryption of the same data content several times, as well as defining several access structures, depending on redundant attributes (i.e., company's employees may share several attributes). Third, it removes the multi authorisation level feature as each subscriber will receive her related publication.

To support all these features with efficiency, we propose to design a multi threshold level ABE scheme. Thus, the proposed scheme EMA-LAB must fulfill the following properties:

- **R1. data confidentiality** – the proposed scheme has to protect the secrecy of encrypted data contents against malicious users, even in case of collusions.
- **R2. multi level access control** – our proposal should ensure flexible security policies among dynamic groups of users with different granted privileges.
- **R3. low processing cost** – the encryption algorithm should have a low computational complexity to minimize the impact of the security on the efficiency of data processing.
- **R4. low communication overhead** – our multi-level encrypted data file should be short-sized as the transmission overhead is important in the emerging infrastructure context.

3   ABE-Related Work

Attribute based Encryption (ABE) schemes are cryptographic primitives ensuring encrypted access control to data. In attribute based encryption schemes, user's private keys and ciphertexts are associated with an access policy or a set of attributes [6]. Thus, a data user is able to decrypt the ciphertext if his private key matches the ciphertext.

Although ABE ensures fine grained and flexible access control, the communication and computation overhead as well as the bandwidth consumption increase exponentially with the number of attributes required in the access policies. To countermeasure this limit, several ABE schemes with short or constant ciphertexts have been proposed [4,7,9]. Herranz et al. [9] have proposed the first constant size threshold attribute based encryption scheme. Indeed, the ciphertext size is constant and does not depend on the number of attributes involved in the threshold access policies. Later, Waters et al. [16] proposed an efficient attribute based encryption scheme with short ciphertext. However, the ciphertext size, the encryption and the decryption times increase linearly with the number of attributes involved in the access structure. Ge et al. [7] have proposed a constant size threshold attribute based encryption scheme. The authors used a different design strategy scheme in order to achieve security against chosen ciphertext attacks (CCA) in the standard model unlike Herranz et al. [9] scheme which is secure against chosen plaintext attacks (CPA). In [17], the authors propose a generic attribute-based data sharing system based on a hybrid mechanism of CP-ABE and a symmetric encryption scheme. This scheme ensures efficient computation costs as well as reduced ciphertext size.

Although these schemes propose efficient solutions to protect outsourced data from unauthorized access, they are still inefficient with multi-level access policies, where users have to share the same data content with different access rights to distinct parts of the data file.

Wang et al. [15] have proposed an efficient file hierarchy attribute-based encryption scheme in cloud computing. The layered access structures are integrated into a single access structure, and then, the hierarchical files are encrypted with the integrated access structure. Kaaniche et al. [12] have introduced an encryption scheme based on attribute based mechanisms for multi-level access policies. This scheme ensures a selective access to data based on users' granted privileges. Practically, when a party encrypts a data file, she specifies an access structure and a certain number of security levels. Thus, a user is able to decrypt a sub-set of data blocks related to a security level k that user's private keys satisfy the sub-set of attributes related to the k-security level (Table 1).

Table 1. A comparison of ABE schemes.

Schemes	R1	R2	R3	R4
Herranz et al. [9]	✓	×	✓	✓
Waters et al. [16]	✓	×	✓	✓
Ge et al. [7]	✓	×	✓	✓
Zhang et al. [17]	✓	×	✓	✓
Wang et al. [15]	✓	✓	×	×
Kaaniche et al. [12]	✓	✓	×	×
EMA-LAB	✓	✓	✓	✓

✓ and × indicate that the requirement is achieved or not, respectively

The communication and computation overhead as well as the bandwidth consumption in the existing multi level ciphertext policy attribute based encryption [4,12] schemes increase exponentially with the number of attributes required in the multi level access policies. This motivates us to address the problem of constructing a multi level attribute based encryption scheme which introduces a short ciphertext size cost for multi level access control and data confidentiality.

4   Model Description

In this section, we first present the system model of EMA-LAB scheme. Then, we detail the security model.

4.1   System Model

We suppose that the encrypting entity $\mathcal{E}$ chooses a subset S from the attribute universe $\mathbb{U}$ and a set of thresholds $\{t_j\}$ such that $1 \leq t_j \leq l \leq |S|$, and $l \leq |\mathbb{T}|$

(i.e., $\mathbb{T}$ is the threshold universe supported by the system) to define his multi-threshold $(\{t_j\}_{\{1,\cdots,l\}}, S)$ access policy. Then, $\mathcal{U}$ encrypts the message $M \in \mathcal{M}$ (i.e., $\mathcal{M}$ is the message space), where $M = \{m_j\}_{\{1,\cdots,l\}}$ with respect to the policy $(\{t_j\}_{\{1,\cdots,l\}}, S)$.

Our multi-threshold attribute based encryption mechanism consists of four randomized algorithms: setup, keygen, encrypt and decrypt, defined as follows:

setup(ξ) $\rightarrow$ (pp, msk) – the setup algorithm is performed by the central trusted authority. It takes as input a security parameter ξ. The setup algorithm outputs the public parameters pp and the master secret key msk.

encrypt(pp, $(\{t_j\}_{\{1,\cdots,l\}}, S), M)$ $\rightarrow$ C – the encryption algorithm is performed by an encrypting entity $\mathcal{E}$. It takes as inputs the public parameters pp, the $(\{t_j\}_{\{1,\cdots,l\}}, S)$ multi level threshold access policy and the message M, defined as a set of sub-messages $M = \{m_j\}_{\{1,\cdots,l\}}$. This algorithm outputs an encrypted message referred to as C.

keygen(pp, msk, $A_{\mathcal{U}}$) $\rightarrow$ $sk_{\mathcal{U}}$ – this randomized algorithm is executed by the trusted authority to derive the secret keys of the user $\mathcal{U}$ related to his set of attributes $A_{\mathcal{U}}$. Given the public parameters pp, the master secret key msk and an attribute set $A_{\mathcal{U}} \subset \mathbb{U}$ (i.e., $\mathbb{U}$ is the attribute universe) of the user $\mathcal{U}$. The algorithm outputs the user's secret key $sk_{\mathcal{U}}$ associated to the attribute set $A_{\mathcal{U}}$.

decrypt(pp, $sk_{\mathcal{U}}, A_{\mathcal{U}}, (\{t_j\}_{\{1,\cdots,l\}}, S), C)$ $\rightarrow$ m_j – the decryption algorithm is executed by the user $\mathcal{U}$. It takes as inputs the public parameters pp, the user's private key $sk_{\mathcal{U}}$, the access policy $(\{t_j\}_{\{1,\cdots,l\}}, S)$ and the encrypted message C. The algorithm returns the message m_j if the user $\mathcal{U}$ has successfully obtained the secret key related to the t_j required attributes for deciphering the encrypted message, with respect to the threshold t_j. Otherwise, the algorithm outputs a reject symbol $\perp$.

Our EMA-LAB multi-threshold attribute based encryption scheme has to satisfy the **correctness property** defined hereafter as follows.

The correctness property requires that for all security parameter ξ, all attribute universe descriptions $\mathbb{U}$, all threshold universe $\mathbb{T}$, all (pp, msk) $\in$ setup(ξ), all domain entities $\mathcal{E}$, all $A_{\mathcal{E}} \subseteq \mathbb{U}$, all $sk_{\mathcal{E}} \in$ keygen(pp, msk, $A_{\mathcal{E}}$), all $M \in \mathcal{M}$ defined as a set of sub-messages $M = \{m_j\}$, all $(\{t_j\}_{\{1,\cdots,l\}}, S) \in \mathcal{G}$ ($\mathcal{G}$ is the access policy space) and all $C \in$ encrypt(pp, $(\{t_j\}_{\{1,\cdots,l\}}, S), M)$, if the decrypting entity $\mathcal{E}$ has successfully obtained the secret key related to the t_j required attributes for deciphering the encrypted message such that $|A_{\mathcal{E}} \cap S| \geq t_j$, the derypt(pp, $sk_{\mathcal{U}}, A_{\mathcal{E}}, (\{t_j\}_{\{1,\cdots,l\}}, S), C)$ outputs m_j with respected to the satisfied threshold t_j.

4.2   Security Model

For designing a secure multi-threshold attribute based encryption scheme, we consider malicious users (i.e.; subscribers in our motivating scenario (Sect. 2)), with respect to the indistinguishability property. The indistinguishability property means that if an adversary has some information about the plaintext, he should not learn about the ciphertext. This security notion requires the computational impossibility to distinguish between two messages chosen by the adversary with a probability greater than a half. Indeed, in ABE schemes, the adversary may lead an attack against the indistinguishability property either on his own or through a collusion attack.

EMA-LAB is said to be indistinguishable against non-adaptive chosen ciphertext attacks if there is no probabilistic polynomial time (PPT) adversary that can win the Exp^{conf} security game with non-negligible advantage. The Exp^{conf} game is formally defined, between an adversary $\mathcal{A}$ and a challenger $\mathcal{C}$ as follows:

INITIALISATION – $\mathcal{A}$ selects a set of encryption attributes S^* (i.e., S^* corresponds to the set of attributes specified for the general access policy) to be used for encrypting the challenge ciphertext, as a set of threshold values $\{t^*_j\}_{\{j \in [1,m]\}}$, where m is the number of threshold values. $\mathcal{A}$ sends $(\{t^*_j\}_{\{j \in [1,m]\}}, S^*)$ to $\mathcal{C}$.

SETUP – the challenger $\mathcal{C}$ runs the setup(ξ) algorithm of the encryption scheme and sends the public parameters pp to the adversary $\mathcal{A}$.

DECRYPTION QUERY PHASE – the adversary $\mathcal{A}$ can request, as many times as he wants, the following queries:

- keygen – the adversary $\mathcal{A}$ queries, for each session i, an encryption attribute set $A_{\mathcal{A},i}$ with respect to a threshold $t^*_{k,i} \in \{t^*_j\}_{\{j \in [1,m]\}}$ where $|A_{\mathcal{A},i} \cap S^*| < t^*_{k,i}$. The challenger $\mathcal{C}$ answers by running the keygen(pp, msk, $A_{\mathcal{A},i}$) algorithm and sends the resulting secret key to the adversary $\mathcal{A}$, with respect to the required threshold $t^*_{k,i}$. The secret key is referred to as $sk_{\mathcal{A},i}$.
- decrypt – the adversary $\mathcal{A}$ requests the decryption of C with respect to a threshold $t^*_{k,i}$, while considering the encryption attribute set $A_{\mathcal{A},i}$. The challenger $\mathcal{C}$ executes the keygen algorithm to generate the secret key $sk_{\mathcal{C},i} = $ keygen(pp, msk, $A_{\mathcal{A},i}$), such that $|A_{\mathcal{A},i} \cap S^*| < t^*_{k,i}$. Finally, the challenger $\mathcal{C}$ answers the query by running the decrypt(pp, $sk_{\mathcal{C},i}$, $A_{\mathcal{C},i}$, $(t^*_{k,i}, S^*)$, C) algorithm that outputs a message m_j or a reject symbol $\perp$.

CHALLENGE PHASE – during the challenge phase, $\mathcal{A}$ picks two equal length cleartexts M_0^* and M_1^* and a threshold encrypting attribute set (t_k^*, S^*) (i.e; t_k^* has never been queried during the DECRYPTION QUERY PHASE) and sends them to $\mathcal{C}$. This latter chooses a random bit b from $\{0, 1\}$ and computes the challenge encrypted message $C_b^* = $ encrypt(pp, (t_k^*, S^*), M_b^*). Then, the challenger sends C_b^* to $\mathcal{A}$.

GUESS – $\mathcal{A}$ tries to guess which message M_i, where $i \in \{0, 1\}$ corresponds to the enciphered data C_b^*. Thus, $\mathcal{A}$ outputs a bit b' of b and wins the game if $b = b'$. The advantage of the adversary $\mathcal{A}$ in the above game is defined as $Adv_{\mathcal{A}}[Exp^{Conf}(1^\xi)] = |Pr[b = b'] - \frac{1}{2}|$.

5   EMA-LAB: Multi-threshold ABE Scheme

In this paper, we develop a new multi-threshold level attribute based encryption scheme, denoted by EMA-LAB with short ciphertext size. Our proposal is based on the constant size attribute based encryption proposed by Herranz et al. [9], which has been extended to support multi-level access to data.

5.1 Complexity Assumptions

In our short ciphertext size multi level attribute based encryption construction, we rely on the Computational Diffie Hellman Assumption (CDH) and the augmented multi-sequence of exponents computational Diffie-Hellman $((\tilde{l}, \tilde{m}, \tilde{t})$-aMSE-CDH) [2,9]. These assumptions are defined as follows:

Computational Diffie Hellman (CDH) Assumption—Let $\mathbb{G}$ be a group of a prime order p, and g is a generator of $\mathbb{G}$. The CDH problem is, given the tuple of elements (g, g^a, g^b), where $\{a, b\} \xleftarrow{R} \mathbb{Z}_p$, there is no efficient probabilistic algorithm $\mathcal{A}_{CDH}$ that computes g^{ab}.

Bilinear Diffie-Hellman (BDH) Assumption—Let $\hat{e} : \mathbb{G}_1 \times \mathbb{G}_1 \to \mathbb{G}_T$ be an efficiently computable bilinear map. Let $a, b, c \in \mathbb{Z}_p^*$ are random numbers and g be a generator of $\mathbb{G}_1$. No probabilistic polynomial-time algorithm is able to compute $\hat{e}(g, g)^{abc}$ with non-negligible advantage if the tuple $\{g, g^a, g^b, g^c\}$ is known.

$(\tilde{l}, \tilde{m}, \tilde{t})$**-augmented multi-sequence of exponents computational Diffie-Hellman** $((\tilde{l}, \tilde{m}, \tilde{t})$**-aMSE-CDH**$)$ – The $(\tilde{l}, \tilde{m}, \tilde{t})$-aMSE-CDH problem related to the group pair $(\mathbb{G}, \mathbb{G}_\mathbb{T})$ is to compute $T = e(g_0, h_0)^{k \cdot f(\gamma)}$. It takes as **input**: the vector $\boldsymbol{x}_{\tilde{l}+\tilde{m}} = (x_1, \cdots, x_{\tilde{l}+\tilde{m}})^\top$ whose components are pairwise distinct elements of $\mathbb{Z}_p$ which define the polynomials f(X) and g(X) as follows:

$$f(X) = \prod_{i=1}^{\tilde{l}}(X + x_i); \qquad g(X) = \prod_{\tilde{l}+1}^{\tilde{l}+\tilde{m}}(X + x_i) \qquad (1)$$

where the values x_i are random and pairwise distinct of $\mathbb{Z}_p^*$, and the values:

$$\begin{cases} g_0, g_0^\gamma, \cdots, g_0^{\gamma^{\tilde{l}+\tilde{t}-2}}, g_0^{k \cdot \gamma \cdot f(\gamma)} \\ g_0^{\omega\gamma}, \cdots, g_0^{\omega\gamma^{\tilde{l}+\tilde{t}-2}} \\ g_0^\alpha, g_0^{\alpha\gamma}, \cdots, g_0^{\alpha\gamma^{\tilde{l}+\tilde{t}}} \\ h_0, h_0^\gamma, \cdots, h_0^{\gamma^{\tilde{m}-2}} \\ h_0^\omega, h_0^{\omega\gamma}, \cdots, h_0^{\omega\gamma^{\tilde{m}-1}} \\ h_0^\alpha, h_0^{\alpha\gamma}, \cdots, h_0^{\alpha\gamma^{2(\tilde{m}-\tilde{t})+3}} \end{cases}$$

Where $k, \alpha, \gamma, \omega$ are unknown random elements of $\mathbb{Z}_p$ and g_0 and h_0 are generators of $\mathbb{G}$. We can solve the problem if we get an **output** $b \in \{0, 1\}$ where $b = 1$ if $T = e(g_0, h_0)^{k \cdot f(\gamma)}$ or $b = 0$ when T is a random value from $\mathbb{G}_T$.

5.2 Aggregate Algorithm

Our scheme relies on the aggregate algorithm **aggreg** introduced by Delerablee et al. [9]. Let us consider a list of values $\{g^{\frac{r}{\gamma+x_i}}, x_i\}_{1 \leq i \leq n}$, where $r, \gamma \in \mathbb{Z}_p^*$ and $x_1, \cdots, x_n$ are pairwise different. Then, the algorithm proceeds as follows:

$$\mathbf{aggreg}(\{g^{\frac{r}{\gamma+x_i}}, x_i\}_{1 \leq i \leq n}) = g^{\frac{r}{\prod_{i=1}^{n}(\gamma+x_i)}}$$

Concretely, the **aggreg** algorithm defines $P_{0,m} = g^{\frac{r}{\gamma + x_m}}$ for each $m \in \{1, \cdots, n\}$. Afterwards, the algorithm computes sequentially $P_{i,m}$ for $i = 1 \cdots n - 1$ and $m = i + 1, \cdots, n$ using the induction:

$$P_{i,m} = \left(\frac{P_{i-1,i}}{P_{i-1,m}}\right)^{\frac{1}{x_m - x_i}} \tag{2}$$

Then, we get $P_{i,m} = g^{\frac{r}{(\gamma + x_m)\prod_{k=1}^{i}(\gamma + x_k)}}$ where $1 \leq i \leq m \leq n$. Therefore, since the elements $x_1, \cdots, x_n$ are pairwise different [2] and using the Eq. 2, we can compute $P_{i,m}$ for $i = 1 \cdots n - 1$ and $m = i + 1 \cdots n$ such as $P_{n,n-1} = g^{\frac{r}{\prod_{i=1}^{n}(\gamma + x_i)}}$.

5.3   Concrete Construction

EMA-LAB relies on four algorithms defined as follows:

- **setup** – the trusted authority selects a bilinear group $(\hat{e}, p, \mathbb{G}_1, \mathbb{G}_2, \mathbb{G})$ of prime order p, such that $\hat{e} : \mathbb{G}_1 \times \mathbb{G}_2 \rightarrow \mathbb{G}$. It selects random generator $g \in \mathbb{G}_1$ and a set of $\mathbb{G}_2$ generators $\{h_j\}_{j=1,\cdots,m}$, such that $m = |\mathbb{T}|$ is the cardinal of the threshold universe $\mathbb{T}$, supported by the system. In addition, it defines an encoding function τ such that $\tau : \mathbb{U} \rightarrow (\mathbb{Z}/p\mathbb{Z})^*$, where $|\mathbb{U}| = n$ and $\mathbb{U}$ is an attribute universe. For each attribute $a \in \mathbb{U}$, the encoded attribute values $\tau(a_i) = x_i$ are pairwise different, where $i \in [1, n]$.
  Then, the **setup** algorithm selects a set $\mathcal{D} = \{d_1, ..., d_{n-1}\}$ consisting of $n - 1$ pairwise different elements of $(\mathbb{Z}/p\mathbb{Z})^*$ (i.e., dummy users), which must also be different to the values $\tau(a_i)$, for all $a_i \in \mathbb{U}$. Note that for any integer i lower or equal to $n - 1$, we denote as $\mathcal{D}_i$ the set $\{d_1, ..., d_i\}$. Finally, the **setup** algorithm computes u defined as $u = g^{\alpha \cdot \gamma}$ and outputs the global public parameters **pp** as follows:

$$\text{pp} = \{\mathbb{G}_1, \mathbb{G}_2, \mathbb{G}, \hat{e}, u, \{h_j^{\alpha \gamma^i}\}_{\{i=0,\cdots,2n-1;j=1,\cdots,m\}}, \mathcal{D}, \tau, \{\hat{e}(g^\alpha, h_j)\}_{\{j=1,\cdots,m\}}\}$$

  We note that the master key of the trusted authority is referred to as $\text{msk} = (g, \alpha, \gamma)$ where α, γ are two random values from $(\mathbb{Z}/p\mathbb{Z})^*$.
- **encrypt** – let $(\{t_j\}_{\{j=1,\cdots,l\}}, S)$ be the access policy where $\{t_j\}$ is the set of defined threshold values, l is the cardinal of $\{t_j\}$, $S \subset \mathbb{U}$ is an attribute set of size $s = |S|$ such that for all $j \in [1, l]$, $1 \leq t_j \leq |S|$.
  To encrypt the message M defined as $M = \{m_j\}_{\{j=1,\cdots,l\}}$ with respect to $(\{t_j\}_{\{j=1,\cdots,l\}}, S)$, the encrypting entity $\mathcal{E}$ picks at random $\kappa \in \mathbb{Z}/p\mathbb{Z}$ and generates the ciphertext $C = (C_1, C_{2,j}, C_{3,j})_{\{j=1,\cdots,l\}}$ defined as:

$$\begin{cases} C_1 = g^{-\kappa\alpha\gamma} \\ C_{2,j} = h_j^{\kappa\alpha \prod_{a \in S}(\gamma + \tau(a)) \prod_{d \in D_{n+t_j-1-s}}(\gamma + d)} \\ C_{3,j} = m_j \hat{e}(g^\alpha, h_j)^\kappa = m_j K_j \end{cases}$$

Finally, the encrypting entity outputs the encryption of the message M such that $C = (C_1, C_{2,j}, C_{3,j})_{\{j=1,\cdots,l\}}$.

- **keygen** – for any subset $A_{\mathcal{U}} \subset \mathbb{U}$ of attributes associated with the decrypting user $\mathcal{U}$, the trusted authority chooses a random value $r_{\mathcal{U}} \in (\mathbb{Z}/p\mathbb{Z})^*$ and computes the related secret key as follows:

$$sk_{\mathcal{U}} = (\{g^{\frac{r_{\mathcal{U}}}{\gamma+\tau(a)}}\}_{a \in A_i}, \{h_j^{r_{\mathcal{U}}\gamma^i}\}_{i=0,\cdots,n-2,j=1\cdots m}, \{h_j^{\frac{r_{\mathcal{U}}-1}{\gamma}}\}_{j=1\cdots m})$$
$$= (sk_{\mathcal{U}_1}, sk_{\mathcal{U}_2}, sk_{\mathcal{U}_3})$$

- **decrypt** – the decrypting entity $\mathcal{U}$ having a set of attributes $A_{\mathcal{U}}$ where $|A_{\mathcal{U}} \cap S| = t_j$ can decrypt the enciphered message m_j under the access policy $(\{t_j\}_{j=1,\cdots,l}, S)$, with respect to the t_j threshold level.
  For this purpose, for all $a \in A_{\mathcal{U}}$, $\mathcal{U}$ firsts aggregates the required attributes, with respect to t_j satisfied by his certified attributes, such as:

$$A = \mathtt{aggreg}(\{g^{\frac{r_{\mathcal{U}}}{\gamma+\tau(a)}}, \tau(a)\}_{a \in A_{\mathcal{U}}}) = g^{\frac{r_{\mathcal{U}}}{\prod_{a \in A_{\mathcal{U}}}(\gamma+\tau(a))}}$$

Afterwards, $\mathcal{U}$ uses the aggregated secret key A and the ciphertext element $C_{2,j}$, related to the satisfied threshold t_j, to compute:

$$L_j = \hat{e}(g^{\frac{r_{\mathcal{U}}}{\prod_{a \in A_{\mathcal{U}}}(\gamma+\tau(a))}}, C_{2,j}) \tag{3}$$
$$= \hat{e}(g, h_j)^{r_{\mathcal{U}}\kappa\alpha \prod_{a \in S \setminus A_{\mathcal{U}}}(\gamma+\tau(a)) \prod_{d \in D_{n+t_j-1-s}}(\gamma+d)}$$

Then, $\mathcal{U}$ defines the polynomial $P_{(A_{\mathcal{U}},t_j,S)}(\gamma)$ such as:

$$P_{(A_{\mathcal{U}},t_j,S)}(\gamma) = \frac{1}{\gamma}(\prod_{a \in S \cup D_{n+t_j-1-s} \setminus A_S}(\gamma+\tau(a)) - \prod_{a \in S \cup D_{n+t_j-1-s} \setminus A_U}\tau(a)) \tag{4}$$

Afterwards, $\mathcal{U}$ uses the aggregated secret key A and the $sk_{\mathcal{U}_2}$ key elements to compute:

$$[\hat{e}(C_1, h_j^{r_{\mathcal{U}}P_{(A_{\mathcal{U}},t_j,S)}(\gamma)}) \cdot L_j]^{\frac{1}{\prod_{a \in S \cup D_{n+t_j-1-s} \setminus A_U}\tau(a)}} \tag{5}$$
$$= e(g, h_j)^{\kappa \cdot \alpha \cdot r_{\mathcal{U}}}$$

Then, from Eq. 5 and the secret key element the $sk_{\mathcal{U}_3}$, related to t_j, the decrypting entity $\mathcal{U}$ deduces the deciphering key K_j such as:

$$K_j = \hat{e}(C_1, sk_{\mathcal{U}_3}) \cdot \hat{e}(g, h_j)^{\kappa \cdot r_{\mathcal{U}} \cdot \alpha}$$
$$= \hat{e}(g, h_j)^{\alpha \cdot \kappa}$$

Finally, $\mathcal{U}$ recovers the sub-message m_j, with respect to related access level t_j, by computing $m_j = \frac{C_{3,j}}{K_j}$.

6   Security Analysis

To ensure multi-level threshold encryption scheme, our EMA-LAB construction mainly relies on the constant size attribute based encryption scheme proposed by Herranz et al. [9]. As such, the data confidentiality preservation is tightly related to the security of the used attribute based encryption algorithm. Our EMA-LAB scheme is secure against selective non-adaptive chosen ciphertext attacks in the standard model, under the CDH, BDH and $(\tilde{l}, \tilde{m}, \tilde{t})$-aMSE-CDH assumptions, with respect to the Exp^{conf} experiment.

Sketch of proof—As presented in Sect. 4.2, the adversary may lead an attack against the indistinguishability property either on his own or through a collusion attack.

First, the design of our EMA-LAB scheme was motivated by preventing collusion attacks among users. Thus, as our scheme relies on the constant size threshold ABE construction of Herranz et al. [9], it randomizes, in the same way, users' private keys such that they cannot be combined. In fact, each private key element contains a random value $r_{\mathcal{U}}$ related to the user $\mathcal{U}$, which prevents colluding users to override their rights and successfully perform a collusion attack. Consequently, our EMA-LAB mechanism is resistant against collusion attacks.

Second, in order to decrypt a ciphertext with respect to a threshold level t^*_j, an adversary $\mathcal{A}$ may conduct, on his own, an attack against the indistinguishability property. That is, he must recover $K_j = \hat{e}(g, h_j)^{\kappa\alpha}$, where the secret κ is embedded in the ciphertext. For this purpose, $\mathcal{A}$ has to retrieve the corresponding K_j, based on the related private key associated with t^*_j.

To prove that our scheme is secure against selective, non-adaptive chosen ciphertext attacks, we first distinguish two different cases, based on the number of defined threshold values during the INITIALISATION phase of Exp^{conf} experiment, introduced in Sect. 4.2:

Case 0: we set only one threshold level t_j^*, such as the public parameter m selected by the adversary is equal to 1. That is, all queried private keys are related to the set of attributes S^* that decrypt ciphertexts, encrypted with respect to t_j^*, for each session i. This first sub-case simulates a selective CCA-1 security game for [9] scheme.

Case 1: for this case, the challenger defines different threshold levels, during the INITIALISATION phase, such as $m > 1$. For each session i, we suppose that $\mathcal{A}$ has access to $C_i = \{C_{k,i}\}_{l \in [1, m^*]}$, where $C_{k,i}$ is an encrypted data block $m_{k,i}$ under a threshold $t^*_{k,i}$.

For **Case 0**, one single threshold level is set. Thus, EMA-LAB scheme follows the construction proposed by Attrapadung et al. in [2]. That is, the SETUP, DECRYPTION QUERY PHASE and CHALLENGE phases are based on one single threshold level, where the challenge message M_b contains one single data block related to the threshold t_j^*. The main difference consists in the derivation of the ciphertext element C_{3, t_j^*} corresponding to a pre-defined threshold level t_j^*, and relying on the public parameter $\hat{e}(g, h_j)^{\alpha}$. Indeed, unlike the [2] scheme relying the `aggreg` algorithm and based on the $(\tilde{l}, \tilde{m}, \tilde{t})$-aMSE-CDH assumption, in our construction, the generation of ciphertexts depends on different public elements, mainly for C_{3,t_j*}. More precisely, the main difference mainly consists in $K_j = \hat{e}(g, h_j)^{\alpha\kappa}$, where $\hat{e}(g, h_j)^{\alpha}$ is a public parameter generated by the challenger $\mathcal{C}$, generated with respect to each different threshold level t_j^*. As such, similarly to [2], the advantage of the Exp^{conf} adversary is at most equal to advantage of an algorithm resolving the $(\tilde{l}, \tilde{m}, \tilde{t})$-aMSE-CDH assumption.

For **Case 1**, the INITIALISATION phase is executed similarly as for **Case 0**. In fact, the challenger $\mathcal{C}$ sends the public parameters pp defined as:

$$\text{pp} = \{\mathbb{G}_1, \mathbb{G}_2, \mathbb{G}, \hat{e}, u, \{h_j^{\alpha\gamma^i}\}_{\{i=0,\cdots,2n-1;j=1,\cdots,m\}},$$
$$\mathcal{D}, \tau, \{\hat{e}(g^{\alpha}, h_j)\}_{\{j=1,\cdots,m\}}\}.$$

For ease of presentation, we do not show the progress of SETUP and DECRYPTION QUERY PHASE between $\mathcal{C}$ and $\mathcal{A}$, where the outputs of keygen and decrypt are closely similar to **Case 0**, considering m^* encrypted sub-messages $\{m_i\}_{\{i\in[1,m^*]\}}$ related to m^* threshold levels. During the challenge phase, when $\mathcal{A}$ asks for the encryption of the challenge message with respect to a challenge access structure $(\{t^*_j\}_{\{j\in[1,m]\}}, S^*)$, $\mathcal{C}$ does the following. $\mathcal{C}$ first chooses a random $\kappa \in \mathbb{Z}/p\mathbb{Z}$ and outputs the encryption of the challenge message such that: for each threshold level t_j, we have $C_j = \hat{e}(g, h_j)^{\kappa\alpha}$. These values are then sent to the adversary. We state that if $\mathcal{A}$ asks for a decryption key for a set of attributes such that $|A_{\mathcal{A}} \cap S^*| > t^*_k$, then $\mathcal{C}$ does not issue the key. Similarly, if $\mathcal{A}$ asks for S^*, with respect to any threshold value, such that one of the keys is already issued then the simulation aborts. In the sequel, the advantage of the adversary is at most equal to **Case 0**, due to the randomness of the choice of variable values in the simulation, based on the CDH and BDH assumptions. Indeed, $\mathcal{A}$' view in this simulation is identically distributed for all threshold levels. In fact, the encryptions of data blocks of the challenge message M_b are completely independent, thanks to the use of different $\hat{e}(g, h_j)$ functions. As such, **Case 1** can be considered as m^* random repetitions of **Case 0** simulation, with respect to m^* threshold levels.

As such, we prove that EMA-LAB scheme is secure against selective non-adaptive chosen ciphertext attacks in the standard model, under the CDH, BDH and $(\tilde{l}, \tilde{m}, \tilde{t})$-aMSE-CDH assumptions, with respect to the Exp^{conf} experiment.

7   Performance Analysis

In most ciphertext policy attribute based encryption schemes, the size of an encrypted data file increases with the number of attributes involved in the access policy used in the encryption phase [2,4]. As detailed in Table 2, in [10,13], the ciphertext size increases with the number of attributes defined in the access structure used to encrypt data. Similarly, the encryption and decryption costs depend on the number of attributes. To countermeasure this limit, attribute based encryption schemes with constant ciphertext size have been introduced. Herranz et al. [9] designed a threshold attribute based encryption scheme where ciphertext size does not depend on the number of attributes. In addition, the

Table 2. Computation and storage costs of multi level attribute based encryption schemes

Scheme	Access policy	Multi-level	Ciphertext size	$\mathcal{E}$ Computation overhead	$\mathcal{U}$ Computation overhead
[12]	Monotone	Yes	$2n + 2m$	$mE + \tau_p + (m + 2n)E_1$	$mE + 2\tau_p$
[15]	Monotone	Yes	$2m + 3n$	$(2n + m)E + (2n + m)E_1$	$(2n + m)\tau_p + (n + m)E$
[13]	Monotone	No	$3n + 1$	$E + (2n + 1)E_1 + \tau_P$	$(2 + n)\tau_P + nE$
[10]	Monotone	No	$2n + 2$	$(2n + 1)E + (3n + 3r)E_1 + \tau_P$	$(n + r)E + 2(n + r)\tau_P$
[9]	Threshold	No	3	$E_1 + E_2 + E$	$(t + 1)E_1 + 3\tau_p + E_2 + E$
EMA-LAB	Threshold	Yes	$2m + 1$	$E_1 + mE_2 + mE$	$(t_j + 1)E_1 + 3\tau_p + E_2 + E$

encryption overhead is constant while varying the size of the used threshold access predicate. Nevertheless, the aforementioned schemes [9,10,13] do not provide the multi level access feature. In [12,15], the authors have extended a ciphertext-policy attribute based encryption scheme to ensure multi authorisation level access control to data. Although the practicability of their schemes in several domains, they are lacking for more efficiency especially related to storage and computation costs. Indeed, the ciphertext size and the computation overheads in the encryption and decryption phases increase with both the number of attributes in the access policies and the number of security levels (thresholds). To bring both the practicability and the efficiency features, EMA-LAB introduces a more efficient ABE scheme with short ciphertext. Indeed, as shown by Table 2, our contribution introduces a ciphertext size which only depends on the number of thresholds used in the multi level access policy unlike state of the art multi level ABE schemes which depend on both the number of attributes and the number of thresholds. Similarly, the computation overheads at the encrypting and the decrypting entities sides only depend on the number of thresholds. In other words, the decryption overhead and the ciphertext size are constant for each threshold level.

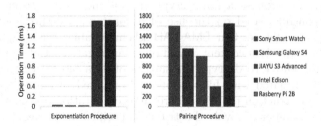

Fig. 2. Elementary functions computation costs

Several research works have been proposed to evaluate the computation overhead of attribute based encryption schemes [5,8]. Our ongoing implementation of the EMA-LAB's Proof of Concept (PoC) consists in evaluating the impact of elementary cryptographic operations on different resource-constrained devices as detailed in Table 3. As our EMA-LAB framework relies on the use of bilinear maps as well as mathematical operations in a multiplicative group, we investigate the impacts of these operations (c.f. Fig. 2) on the performance of different IoT devices, based on the results introduced in [5].

In our ongoing implementation, we only consider the computational cost in terms of time in our encryption and decryption algorithms. Indeed, for a single threshold level, the encryption time is constant while varying the number of attributes. Moreover, the decryption overhead increases linearly with the number of attributes in the threshold level. This is due to the aggregation (c.f., Sect. 5.2) of the decrypting entity's secret keys performed in the decryption phase.

Table 3. Selected devices [5]

Device	Type	Processor
Sony SmartWatch 3 SWR50	Smart Watch	520 MHz Single-core Cortex-A7
Samsung I9500 Galaxy S4	Smartphone	1.6 GHz Dual-Core Cortex-A15
Jiayu S3 Advanced	Smartphone	1.7 GHz Octa-Core 64bit Cortex A53
Intel Edison	IoT Development Board	500 MHz Dual-Core Intel AtomTM CPU, 100 Mhz MCU
Raspberry Pi 2 model B	IoT Development Board	900 MHz Quad-Core ARM Cortex-A7

8   Conclusion

In this paper, we propose a novel cryptographic mechanism to ensure multi-level access control, based on the use of a constant size threshold attribute based encryption scheme. Our EMA-LAB scheme enables the enciphering user to encrypt the same data content, based on an aggregated set of attributes, and the deciphering entity to decrypt the subsets of data blocks with respect to a threshold t_j, associated with his attributes. Compared to most-closely related schemes, our construction provides interesting computation costs, as it does not depend on the number of involved attributes specified in the aggregated access predicate.

References

1. Ateniese, G., Chou, D.H., de Medeiros, B., Tsudik, G.: Sanitizable signatures. In: di Vimercati, S.C., Syverson, P., Gollmann, D. (eds.) ESORICS 2005. LNCS, vol. 3679, pp. 159–177. Springer, Heidelberg (2005). https://doi.org/10.1007/11555827_10

2. Attrapadung, N., Herranz, J., Laguillaumie, F., Libert, B., De Panafieu, E., Ràfols, C.: Attribute-based encryption schemes with constant-size ciphertexts. Theor. Comput. Sci. **422**, 15–38 (2012)
3. Belguith, S., Kaaniche, N., Jemai, A., Laurent, M., Attia, R.: PAbAC: a privacy preserving attribute based framework for fine grained access control in clouds. In: 13th IEEE International Conference on Security and Cryptography (Secrypt), pp. 133–146 (2016)
4. Belguith, S., Kaaniche, N., Laurent, M., Jemai, A., Attia, R.: Constant-size threshold attribute based signcryption for cloud applications. In: SECRYPT 2017: 14th International Conference on Security and Cryptography, vol. 6, pp. 212–225 (2017)
5. Belguith, S., Kaaniche, N., Laurent, M., Jemai, A., Attia, R.: PHOABE: securely outsourcing multi-authority attribute based encryption with policy hidden for cloud assisted IoT. Comput. Netw. **133**, 141–156 (2018)
6. Bethencourt, J., Sahai, A., Waters, B.: Ciphertext-policy attribute-based encryption. In: IEEE Symposium on Security and Privacy (2007)
7. Ge, A., Zhang, R., Chen, C., Ma, C., Zhang, Z.: Threshold ciphertext policy attribute-based encryption with constant size ciphertexts. In: Susilo, W., Mu, Y., Seberry, J. (eds.) ACISP 2012. LNCS, vol. 7372, pp. 336–349. Springer, Heidelberg (2012). https://doi.org/10.1007/978-3-642-31448-3_25
8. Guo, L., Zhang, C., Yue, H., Fang, Y.: PSaD: a privacy-preserving social-assisted content dissemination scheme in DTNs. IEEE Trans. Mobile Comput. **13**(12), 2903–2918 (2014)
9. Herranz, J., Laguillaumie, F., Ráfols, C.: Constant size ciphertexts in threshold attribute-based encryption. In: Nguyen, P.Q., Pointcheval, D. (eds.) PKC 2010. LNCS, vol. 6056, pp. 19–34. Springer, Heidelberg (2010). https://doi.org/10.1007/978-3-642-13013-7_2
10. Horváth, M.: Attribute-based encryption optimized for cloud computing. In: Italiano, G.F., Margaria-Steffen, T., Pokorný, J., Quisquater, J.-J., Wattenhofer, R. (eds.) SOFSEM 2015. LNCS, vol. 8939, pp. 566–577. Springer, Heidelberg (2015). https://doi.org/10.1007/978-3-662-46078-8_47
11. Johnson, R., Molnar, D., Song, D., Wagner, D.: Homomorphic signature schemes. In: Preneel, B. (ed.) CT-RSA 2002. LNCS, vol. 2271, pp. 244–262. Springer, Heidelberg (2002). https://doi.org/10.1007/3-540-45760-7_17
12. Kaaniche, N., Laurent, M.: Attribute based encryption for multi-level access control policies. In: SECRYPT 2017: 14th International Conference on Security and Cryptography, vol. 6, pp. 67–78. Scitepress (2017)
13. Li, L., Chen, X., Jiang, H., Li, Z., Li, K.C.: P-CP-ABE: parallelizing ciphertext-policy attribute-based encryption for clouds. In: 2016 17th IEEE/ACIS International Conference on Software Engineering, Artificial Intelligence, Networking and Parallel/Distributed Computing (SNPD), pp. 575–580. IEEE (2016)
14. Onica, E., Felber, P., Mercier, H., Rivière, E.: Confidentiality-preserving publish-/subscribe: a survey. ACM Comput. Surv. (CSUR) **49**(2), 27 (2016)
15. Wang, S., Zhou, J., Liu, J.K., Yu, J., Chen, J., Xie, W.: An efficient file hierarchy attribute-based encryption scheme in cloud computing. IEEE Trans. Inf. Forensics Secur. **11**(6), 1265–1277 (2016)
16. Waters, B.: Ciphertext-policy attribute-based encryption: an expressive, efficient, and provably secure realization. In: Catalano, D., Fazio, N., Gennaro, R., Nicolosi, A. (eds.) PKC 2011. LNCS, vol. 6571, pp. 53–70. Springer, Heidelberg (2011). https://doi.org/10.1007/978-3-642-19379-8_4
17. Zhang, Y., Zheng, D., Chen, X., Li, J., Li, H.: Efficient attribute-based data sharing in mobile clouds. Pervasive Mob. Comput. **28**, 135–149 (2016)

SCARA: A Framework for Secure Cloud-Assisted RFID Authentication for Smart Building Access Control

Ahmed Raad Al-Sudani[1]([⊠])(iD), Wanlei Zhou[1], Sheng Wen[2],
and Ahmed Al-Mansoori[1]

[1] School of Information Technology, Faculty of Science,
Engineering and Built Environment, Deakin University, Geelong, Australia
{aralsuda,wanlei.zhou,ajalma}@deakin.edu.au
[2] School of Information Techonolgy, Swinburne University, Hawthorn, Australia
swen.works@gmail.com

Abstract. Managing security in an RFID system is a complex activity considering that it is imperatively challenging to implement trust among tags and readers. There is always the chance that an unauthorized individual might assume the identity of a trusted tag and manage to gain confidential data in an RFID system. The situation becomes worse in systems that use a backend server and a private Internet connection. In such a system, there is no comprehensive mechanism for authenticating a tag into the system. It is thus essential to consider the implementation of a robust framework that improves the trust and the authentication levels in an RFID system. In this paper, a system known as Secure Cloud-Assisted RFID Authentication (SCARA) is proposed, which uses cloud-assisted RFID authentication to reap benefits of cloud-like scalability, availability and fault tolerance. It has three parties such as a cloud server, RFID reader and issuer involved. Issuer provides system parameters to other parties through a secure channel. Server and RFID reader are included in the authentication process with the help of information obtained from the issuer. The proposed system is secure even if the private keys associated with server and RFID tag are compromised. It does mean that it can prevent server-side insider attack in addition to external attacks. Amazon EC2 is used to have experiments. We built a prototype application to demonstrate proof of the concept. The empirical results revealed that the proposed system is able to withstand various kinds of attacks and provides a more efficient solution with less overhead.

Keywords: Cloud-assisted RFID authentication · Smart building
Hash · Encryption

1 Introduction

Radio frequency identification (RFID) is a technology that uses radio signals for the identification, tracking, sorting and detecting objects through an automatic and non-contact environment. RFID technology is used for tracking objects

© Springer Nature Switzerland AG 2018
M. H. Au et al. (Eds.): NSS 2018, LNCS 11058, pp. 202–211, 2018.
https://doi.org/10.1007/978-3-030-02744-5_15

among people, buildings, vehicles, and any moving objects [3]. Because RFID uses radio or electromagnetic signals, its applicability is limited to a line of sight contact and within a short distance that spans a few meters.

RFID tags are commonly used in enforcing security measures and access controls in buildings and internal installations. Identification badges are placed in strategic places in buildings and vehicles whereby they are able to detect signals from moving objects. In many security installations, RFID tags are strategically installed and configured using a smart security system [9]. In such a scenario, the security system is capable of identifying and storing personal information, which is later used for future identifications.

RFID tags are associated with various security concerns especially in matters of privacy. Unauthorized access from the use of an unidentified tag might consequently pose a threat to confidential information. Additionally, there is a possibility that RFID tags might be exposed to various security vulnerabilities such as spoofing, jamming, denial of service attacks, and eavesdropping among others. The vulnerability of a security system based on RFID technology is mainly dependent on the existing security tools [3, 8]. Weak security tools present issues of trust and accountability in a system backed by RFID tags.

The maintenance of trust in security systems based on RFID technologies is an issue that elicits significant research. Security concerns associated with RFID technology have a strong bearing on the efficiency and reliability of the underlying security system [2]. Despite the implementation of robust security mechanisms, there is the likelihood that attackers will exploit various weaknesses in RFID security system. Consequently, it is paramount to have an efficient mechanism that will culminate in the implementation of a comprehensive security system based on the use of RFID technology [11].

This paper proposes a methodology that is used to mitigate trust issues in a security system backed by RFID technology. Managing trust issues is a gruesome activity especially considering that it is imperatively challenging to control access and privacy in a security setting. There is a need to have a mechanism that will ensure that trust is effectively maintained within RFID backed security system to minimize any possible security threats [12]. A variety of approaches are applicable in a typical security system but the focus of the paper is based on the implementation of an optimal solution that not only reduce the security threat, but that will also utilize minimal resources and reduce authentication time.

In this paper, we propose a system whereby the intention is to build an authentication system that is based on two different server-based systems. The plan is to have a locally based server that hosts the RFID identification and authorization system, which can be easily accessed and controlled by a customized program interface [4, 5]. An additional identification and authorization system should be located in the dedicated cloud-server and be equipped with the same capabilities as the local instance. The proposed mechanism is found on the premise that it is difficult to have simultaneous control of both the local and cloud-based RFID program interface. Even if an attacker is able to gain control of the locally based instance of security controls, the system should be able to perform computational comparisons to determine the eligibility and the authenticity of the access mechanism. This way, it is possible to enforce trust-based rules in the underlying RFID-based security system.

The proposed methodology consists of the development of a robust framework aimed at determining the distinct values upon which to use when providing access control in an RFID-based security system. An algorithm will be developed, which will be used to compute a checksum value that will be passed to the system and consequently used to identify a prospective user of the security system. The algorithm should be able to compare the checksum values form the local and the cloud-based server instance before granting access control to any user of the security system. The paper is organized in the following sections. Section 2 is dedicated towards the overview and description of main concepts associated with RFID technology. Section 3 is dedicated to the sections of the related work whereby the RFID technology is described together with the respective applications and security features. Section 4 is the proposed methodology whereby the functionality of the proposed system is thoroughly analyzed as well as the exploration and the description of the algorithm to be used for the identification process. Section 5 provides a detailed description of the experimental analysis as well as the respective results from the experimental procedure. The evaluation of the effectiveness and usefulness of the checksum algorithm is described in Sect. 6. An overview containing the conclusion, recommendation, and a mention of future works and threats to validity is found in the last two sections.

2   Related Work

A variety of methodologies and solutions has been developed, and others proposed aimed at addressing trust based problems in RFID. Majority of the existing or proposed solutions are based on improving the authentication process between an RFID tag and a smart label. The works described in this paper are restricted to cloud-based authentication solutions for RFID systems. Lehtonen, Michahelles, and Fleisch [10] proposed an authentication process used for detecting fraud in products in a distribution store. The approach utilizes the use of tags that contains authentication information. The approach described by Lehtonen et al. uses the object-specific information to generate the authentication data. Another approach described by Lehtonen et al. is the use of location-based authentication, which makes it challenging to perpetrate an attack when in non-prescribed location [10]. The methodology proposed by Lehtonen et al. is mainly designed to address the cloning problem in product forgery.

Bingol et al. [7] delve significantly into the aspect of trust maintenance in a cloud-based platform whereby authentication is enhanced by RFID tags. The proposed approach uses private keys to implement secure but anonymous access to a cloud-based server. Additionally, RFID tags are used to improve cloud-based trust using mutual authentication protocols. The strength of this approach is replicated in the fact that authentication can still occur even if the private keys are lost.

Juels and Pappu [6] advocates for the development of an authentication system that utilizes public keys cryptosystem. Additionally, a private key is a private key that is only known by a specific reader. The authentication system must be accomplished using both public and private keys. Because the combination of public and private keys (Pk, Sk) might be a complicated and resource-oriented activity, Xiao, Alshehri, and Christianson [13] propose another RFID authentication mechanism that is based on an insecure communication channel. Cloud-RAPIC as the methodology is known to maintain the privacy between the tags and the cloud server. The model protects the data during the transmission time from the reader to the cloud server. Xia et al. have managed to analyze the cloud-RAPIC protocol using UPriv and verified by AVISPA tool. Abughazalah, Markantonakis, and Mayes [1] serve to propose a solution that is an extension of the model developed by Xie et al. The proposed solution is found on the premise that the model developed by Xie et al. is prone to identity theft and impersonation attacks and thus cannot adequately guarantee the privacy of tag data. The solution proposed by Abughazalah et al. ensures that tag data is anonymous and any access attempt should be preceded by mutual authentication between the tag, cloud-server, and the reader. Having analyzed the proposed protocol using the CasperFDR, the solution proposed by Abughazalah et al. is capable of improving the privacy of tags data. The review of related works provides a clear picture of various solutions used for the implementation of RFID security. The maintenance of trust in RFID is based on the authentication protocol being used. The works proposed by Xie et al. and Abughazalah et al. are particularly important because they have a similar resemblance to the proposed solution. Consequently, the proposed framework will be found in the operational principles of cloud-based RFID authentication.

3   Proposed Framework

3.1   Overview of Our Framework

In the proposed framework, There are three parties involved in the RFID based cloud-assisted authentication. They are known as Tag Reader, Cloud Server and Issuer. The security primitives are based on threshold encryption known as ElGamal encryption. Each party involved in the communication holds only one unique decryption share that is generated by an issuer and distributed to all parties (Fig. 1).

A cloud server is the server location in the public cloud which plays a vital role in the authentication scheme. The scheme does not assume any trustworthiness of cloud server unlike some of the schemes found in the literature. Even if the owners of cloud servers leak private keys or the private keys are leaked due to corrupted RFID tags, the proposed scheme provides security and ensures non-disclosure of private information. The scheme can address all kinds of internal attacks in the server. The server can have a large set of pre-computed encryption keys to make it more efficient and reduce overhead in the server. The issuer is responsible for generating the required prime numbers, generator, secret polynomials, and

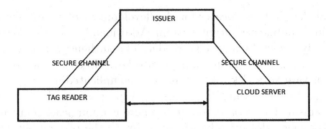

Fig. 1. Proposed secure cloud-assisted RFID authentication scheme (SCARA)

unique secret shares required by other entities. The issuer has a secret channel to communicate with other two parties. Tag reader deals with understanding RFID tags and cooperates in getting the tags authentication in the proposed cloud-assisted RFID authentication scheme. An RFID tag is associated with a single object. Each tag holds its own share and public share of a server. The following subsection provides the steps involved in the proposed scheme.

3.2 Description of Secure Cloud-Assisted RFID Authentication

The cloud assisted RFID authentication scheme is described here. The communication is between tag reader and server (Table 1).

- Every server (s) has its own share key(x^s, y^s). This is maintained and used in encryption and decryption for authentication purpose.
- Every object has one single tag. We represent this tag as i. This can be useful in computation of object own share key(x^i, y^i).
- After computing server and object share keys we have to encrypt object information and stored in cloud server.
- For encryption and decryption keys first object tag select a random number $r^i \in_R \{0,1\}^l$ and sends it to the server where l is a security parameter.
- The server also selects one random number$R^s \in_R \{0,1\}^l$ and calculates an ElGamal encryption of message $m = r^s \parallel r^i$.
- To encrypt the message m, we pick a random prime value $r \in Z_q$. Using this random prime value we compute encryption pair C $= (h^r m, g^r)$ and also compute the decryption share $\sigma = g^r y^s$. Then server sends C and σ to the i-th tag of object.
- After receiving the message σ, C from server the tag of object first completes the decryption share of the server as $\sigma_s = \frac{x^i}{\sigma x^i - x^s}$.
- Then, it computes its decryption share as $\sigma_i = g^{ryi} \frac{x^s}{x^s - x^i}$.
- Finally, it recovers the original message as $r^{\sim s} \parallel r^{\sim i} = \frac{h^r m}{\sigma_s \sigma_i}$.
- If the $r^{\sim i}$is equal to the original random value r^i. $r^{\sim s}$ is assigned to $\hat{r}$ and its sends to server. Server checks the $\hat{r}$ to originalr^s.
- If the $r^{\sim i}$is not equal to the original random value r^i. It selects one random value, assigned to $\hat{r}$ and its sends to server. Server checks the $\hat{r}$ to original.

Table 1. Notations used in the proposed authentication scheme

Notation	Description
f(x)	Secret curve
a_0	The private key
h	Public key.
(x^s, y^s)	Server own key share
(x^i, y^i) $i^t h$ tag of object	Unique secret share of
i	Object tag
$m = r^s \parallel r^i$	ElGamal encryption of message
Zq	Primary numbers set
C	Encrypted message pair
σ	Decryption share
σ_s	Decryption share of the server
σ_i	Decryption share of tag i
q	Prime number
m	Message
r	Random prime number
R	Random parameter set with 0,1
l	Security parameter
S	Server
G	Generator

4 Experimental Setup

Experiments are done with the three parties involved. We implemented three software components that encapsulate the functionality of the server, RFID reader and Issuer. The server and issuer components are deployed in Amazon EC2 compute engine. The RFID reader component runs on the local machine. The communication among the three parties is made as per the proposed scheme. Amazon EC2 is the compute engine that provides an environment for execution of the server and issuer components. The tag reader program runs on the local machine. The RFID tag information is stored in the server and gets authenticated with the proposed scheme.

Each piece of software implemented to show the performance of the proposed scheme is evaluated practically. The proposed scheme is able to provide secure cloud-assisted RFID authentication which can be used in controlling access to smart homes. This scheme is meant for improving our baseline authentication scheme whose overview is shown in Fig. 3.

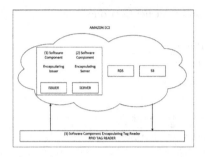

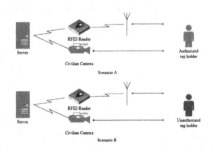

Fig. 2. Experimental setup with the three software components

Fig. 3. Smart building authentication system model

5   Experimental Results

Experiments are done with a synthetic dataset containing different scenarios in which the number of tags and number of tag readers differs. The dataset is visualized as shown in Fig. 4. There are 12 scenarios, and in each scenario, a different number of tags and readers are used for the experiments. As per the dataset, the experiments are carried out with the experimental setup presented in Fig. 2.

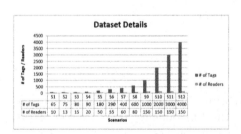

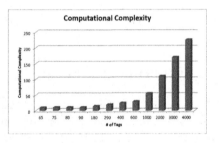

Fig. 4. Dataset used to help experiments

Fig. 5. Computational complexity

In the first scenario that is S1, the number of tags used is 65 and the number of readers used is 10. In the last scenario, the number of tags is 4000, and the number of readers is 150. The computational complexity of the proposed scheme is computed and evaluated. The results are as shown in Fig. 5.

With the 12 scenarios, experiments are made to understand the computational complexity. The results revealed that the computational complexity depends on the number of tags and the number of tag readers. The results revealed the linear computational complexity.

6 Evaluation

6.1 Security and Complexity Analysis

The proposed scheme is able to provide both privacy and security as required by cloud-assisted RFID authentication. Even when the server is compromised and the Tag Reader compromised the authentication scheme to ensure privacy (non-disclosure of identity information) and security. Here is the analysis of how it works. Assume that an adversary has already compromised server which contains security keys. There are two possible attacks now. The first one is that the adversary mimics like a semi-honest party by following underlying protocol rules, but he aims to capture the identity of the tag. Since the identity of the tag is sensitive information, the disclosure leads to a privacy issue. As per the proposed scheme the adversary cannot obtain tag information as it is random. The adversary can only find that the tag is a numeric value found in the database but cannot get the true identity of it. The second behaviour of the adversary is that he does not mimic like an honest party. As in the first case, the adversary cannot get the identity of the tag though he is able to decrypt secret shares with the help of server's compromised keys. However, still, authentication fails as the tag reader sends random bits.

6.2 Forward and Backward Secrecy

Even when the server is compromised, and security keys are known, an adversary is not able to distinguish tag data based on the observed communications. Therefore the proposed scheme achieves both forward secrecy and backward secrecy.

6.3 Unlinkability of Tags

It does mean that the adversaries will not be able to distinguish tag information based on the observed communications. Stated differently, the messages generated by tags as per the protocol do not leak any information to adversary related to identity. As the scheme is using an only random number in step 1 and step 3, the sensitive information related to tag identity is not disclosed. As the second step makes use of encryption, the messages obtained by the adversary cannot be linked to a specific tag.

6.4 Complexity Analysis

The security primitives used in the proposed scheme are entirely secure in the presence of server-side attacks. The computations involved for each tag include one multiplication, three inversion operations and three exponentiation operations. Moreover, the inversion operations can be done offline on the TagReader side. With respect to the server, one multiplication and three exponentiation operations are required. In addition to this, all encryptions and partial decryption to be performed by the server can be done offline. Even adding a new tag does not add to the overall complexity of the system. A new user gets new share pertaining to secret key and computations are the same as other tags. This does not cause any additional overhead to a server. Nevertheless, overall linear complexity is found as presented in Fig. 5.

7   Conclusion and Future Work

In this paper, we have proposed a framework for secure cloud-assisted RFID authentication (SCARA) to gain access to a smart home. Smart homes need 24x7 service availability and authentication services. Cloud computing is the technology that provides on-demand computing resources without the time and geographical restrictions in pay per use fashion. It is characterized by the scalability of resources, round the clock and 365 days of service availability. The proposed scheme has three parties involved. They are Issuer, Server and RFID Reader. Issuer provides necessary keys to other parties through a secure channel. Afterwards, there is mutual authentication between the RFID reader and server. The salient feature of the proposed scheme is that even if the server side private keys or RFID reader private keys are compromised for any reason, the secure authentication will not fail. Amazon EC2 is the cloud used for experiments. We built three software components to encapsulate the functionalities of the three parties as mentioned earlier. Out of them, we keep the Server and Issuer parties in the EC2 managed environment while the RFID Tag Reader runs in the local machine. The interactions among them take place as discussed in the proposed methodology. The application is tested and evaluated. The proposed scheme is not only secure but also reduces complexity besides providing security against compromises of Tag Reader and Server due to insider attacks. It can handle both insider and outsider attacks and provide secure cloud-assisted RFID authentication to gain access to smart homes. An important direction for future work is to investigate the resistance mechanism against tag tampering to be part of the framework. There is another exciting direction for future work that is to consider Internet of Things scenario while performing RFID authentication.

References

1. Abughazalah, S., Markantonakis, K., Mayes, K.: Secure improved cloud-based RFID authentication protocol. In: Garcia-Alfaro, J., et al. (eds.) DPM/QASA/SETOP -2014. LNCS, vol. 8872, pp. 147–164. Springer, Cham (2015). https://doi.org/10.1007/978-3-319-17016-9_10
2. Alabrah, A., Bassiouni, M.: A tree-based authentication scheme for a cloud toll/traffic RFID system. In: 2015 IEEE Vehicular Networking Conference (VNC), pp. 108–111. IEEE (2015)
3. Bu, K., Weng, M., Zheng, Y., Xiao, B., Liu, X.: You can clone but you cannot hide: a survey of clone prevention and detection for RFID. IEEE Commun. Surv. Tutor. **19**(3), 1682–1700 (2017)

4. Dong, Q., Tong, J., Chen, Y.: Cloud-based RFID mutual authentication protocol without leaking location privacy to the cloud. Int. J. Distrib. Sens. Netw. **11**(10), 937198 (2015)
5. Fan, K., Luo, Q., Li, H., Yang, Y.: Cloud-based lightweight RFID mutual authentication protocol. In: 2017 IEEE Second International Conference on Data Science in Cyberspace (DSC), pp. 333–338. IEEE (2017)
6. Juels, A., Pappu, R.: Squealing euros: privacy protection in RFID-enabled banknotes. In: Wright, R.N. (ed.) FC 2003. LNCS, vol. 2742, pp. 103–121. Springer, Heidelberg (2003). https://doi.org/10.1007/978-3-540-45126-6_8
7. Kiraz, M.S., Bingöl, M.A., Kardaş, S., Birinci, F.: Anonymous RFID authentication for cloud services. Int. J. Inf. Secur. Sci. **1**(2), 32–42 (2012)
8. Lehtonen, M., Staake, T., Michahelles, F.: From identification to authentication- a review of RFID product authentication techniques. In: Cole, P., Ranasinghe, D. (eds.) Networked RFID Systems and Lightweight Cryptography, pp. 169–187. Springer, Heidelberg (2008). https://doi.org/10.1007/978-3-540-71641-9_9
9. Lehtonen, M.O., Michahelles, F., Fleisch, E.: Trust and security in RFID-based product authentication systems. IEEE Syst. J. **1**(2), 129–144 (2007)
10. Lin, I.C., Hsu, H.H., Cheng, C.Y.: A cloud-based authentication protocol for RFID supply chain systems. J. Netw. Syst. Manag. **23**(4), 978–997 (2015)
11. Rahman, M., Sampangi, R.V., Sampalli, S.: Lightweight protocol for anonymity and mutual authentication in RFID systems. In: 2015 12th Annual IEEE Consumer Communications and Networking Conference (CCNC), pp. 910–915. IEEE (2015)
12. Weber, R.H.: Internet of things-new security and privacy challenges. Comput. Law Secur. Rev. **26**(1), 23–30 (2010)
13. Xiao, H., Alshehri, A.A., Christianson, B.: A cloud-based RFID authentication protocol with insecure communication channels. In: 2016 IEEE Trustcom/BigDataSE/I SPA, pp. 332–339. IEEE (2016)

Continuous Authentication on Smartphone by Means of Periocular and Virtual Keystroke

Silvio Barra$^{(\boxtimes)}$, Mirko Marras, and Gianni Fenu

Department of Mathematics and Computer Science, University of Cagliari,
Via Universita' 40, 09124 Cagliari, Italy
{silvio.barra,mirko.marras,fenu}@unica.it

Abstract. Nowadays, biometric recognition and verification methods are everywhere, trying to face the security issues that constantly affect our digital-every day life. In addition, many special-purpose applications, also need a constant (continuous) verification of the user in order to avoid that a sensitive operation is executed by an impostor; as an example let think to banking operations. In this paper, a continuous authentication method on mobile device is presented, which uses smartphone gestures data for the constant verification of the user and periocular data for a second step verification module. The results executed over two datasets show a verification accuracy of 83% and 94% approximately, respectively for smartphone touch features and periocular data.

Keywords: Continuous authentication · Smartphone gesture data
Periocular recognition

1 Introduction

Nowadays, biometric systems are able to provide very high levels of security, both in stand-alone applications [1,2] and in cloud environments [3–5]. Mainly thanks to their flexibility and universality, these are currently present in many security environments: video surveillance systems provided with biometric recognition modules [6–8] are not a novelty and nowadays also on e-learning platforms for educational purposes we can find continuous authentication modules for assessing the identity of the students [9]. Surely, the smartphone security is one of the trend topic of the last ten years, due to the big amount of sensitive data which day-by-day we store on such devices. This is the main reason why many recognition and feature extraction methods which were supposed to work on laptops or ad-hoc systems, have been migrated on portable devices [10,11]. This paper aims at proposing an fast method for the continuous authentication on mobile while a user is performing actions on his phone.

© Springer Nature Switzerland AG 2018
M. H. Au et al. (Eds.): NSS 2018, LNCS 11058, pp. 212–220, 2018.
https://doi.org/10.1007/978-3-030-02744-5_16

2   Related Work

Continuous authentication is a challenging problem that has been actively researched for more than two decades. The objective is to regularly check the user's identity throughout the session. Existing applications include monitoring whether an unsuspected impostor has hijacked a genuine user's session on a device [12] or, more specifically, on an online website [13] as well as identifying whether an authorized user willingly share their credentials with others in remote e-learning exams [14], etc. In addition, there has been a growing interest in continuous authentication for access control security in cloud environments [15].

Existing techniques for continuous authentication have extracted physiological and behavioral biometrics by leveraging built-in sensors. Physiological biometrics, such as those of the face, have been captured using front-facing cameras and analyzed to get distinctive user's features [16]. Furthermore, sensors such as mouse, keyboard, microphone, touchscreen, and inertial measurement unit (i.e., gyroscope, accelerometer, magnetometer) have been used to measure behavioral biometrics, such as gait [17], typing [18], touching [19], mouse movements [20], and hand movements [21]. Unimodal continuous authentication methods have had to deal with noise, intraclass variation, spoof attack, etc. More recent multimodal systems, such as face and touch [22], touch and inertial measurement units [23], mouse and keystroke [24], linguistic style together with application usage and location [25], have mitigated the impact of the mentioned issues.

In this continuous multi-biometric setting, the trade-off among computation, processing speed, and accuracy becomes even more essential [26]. Existing physiological methods tend to provide higher accuracy, but require higher computational resources. In contrast, behavioral methods often do their work with few computational resources, but provide lower accuracy. Existing multi-modal systems fuse biometrics in parallel, reaching good accuracy, but loosing efficiency. Our approach plays with the trade-off by operating in serial mode (i.e., only if the touch-based system does not recognize the user, their face is analyzed) and by operating only on the periocular area when needed. This makes our approach lighter, getting the advantages of multi-biometric fusion while limiting computationally-expensive tasks to cases when they are really needed.

3   The Proposed Method

The proposed method aims at providing a fast continuous authentication process for mobile environments. Both periocular and touch features have been used for this purpose. In particular, for the authentication based on the touch, the features are collected every time an event

$$TouchDown - Move - TouchUp$$

is detected. The TouchDown event describes the action of the user in which the finger press on the display. Similarly, the TouchUp event describes the finger rising up off the screen. In the middle several Move events are described, each of which is described with the X and Y coordinates of the position of the finger, the pressure and the contact size on the display. As regards the periocular area acquisition, this step starts as soon a certain number of rejects has happened over the touch features. Let T_{touch} be the threshold identified as the maximum number of rejection allowed for the system. As the $(T_{touch} + 1)$th rejection happens, a photo of the user face is caught.

The Viola-Jones [27] object detection method is applied in order to detect and acquire the periocular pair area. Due to the advanced camera mounted on the smartphones nowadays, the output of the acquisition results in a high resolution image. If from one side, the high resolution allowed the extraction of many features, on the other side, the feature extraction methods can take many seconds for the processing of the image. For this reason, a normalization is achieved. The periocular image is first resized to $100X400$, without any kind of distortion introduced, since the area extracted by Viola Jones as a *row/column* factor of $1/4$. Then the image is posterized, i.e. the details of the image are reduced. In Fig. 1, the posterization process is shown.

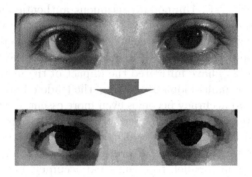

Fig. 1. The effect of the posterization process, applied to a typical periocular image.

3.1   Touch Features Reduction Method

Since many *Move* events may be acquired, a reduction of the features is needed to keep the number of features limited, in order to both simplify and speed up the authentication process. The features reduction method is based on the computation of the centroid among the data, as following. For each *Move* event m composed of N points in a 4D space (considering x and y coordinate, touch pressure infos p and contact size s), the Euclidean distance $ED(xyz(i), xyz(i + 1))$ between pairs of consecutive 4D points is measured. If ED is lower than a threshold t, then $xyps(i)$ and $xyps(i + 1)$ are added to a set P. As soon as a point $j + 1$ following a point j is found, such that $ED > t$, the centroid c of points in P is computed by averaging their components. Hence, all points in P are substituted by the single point p_1 whose distance from the centroid c is the minimum; the process restarts with an empty P until the whole signal has been processed. The authentication phase is achieved by using the new sets of points.

3.2   Subject Authentication

In Fig. 2 the overview of the system is presented; as the user accesses the system, the detection of the touch events starts to collect data. In particular, the acquisition of the data starts as a *TouchDown* event is detected and ends with a *TouchUp* event. The data about the movement (*Move* event) are acquired each 20ms and are rejected if less than 10 acquisitions are collected. On the contrary, the touch features reduction method, explained in Sect. 3.1 is applied, in order to reduce the data to the proper dimension. Hence, the features are sent to the Touch Authentication Module, which consists of an aggregation of Decision Trees, trained on the data of the user u. If the score of the authentication overcome a threshold (which for the application is set to 65%), the system keeps to collect data for the next authentication phase. If the threshold is not passed, the timestamp in which the rejection has taken place is stored in a structure called REL (Reject Event List), if within 20 s, more than 4 authentication rejects happen, the control is transfered to the Periocular Verification Module, which achieves the matching between the template stored and the one acquired in live mode from the front camera of the smartphone. For this step, a classifier based on the Subspace Discriminant Analysis is trained over the LBP code extracted from the samples of the user; this is invoked when the verification is needed.

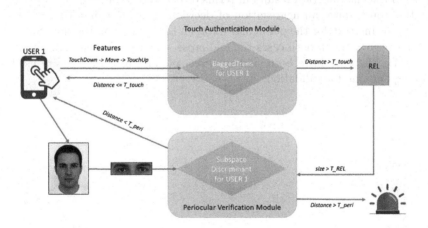

Fig. 2. Overview of the continuous authentication system.

4   Experimental Results

In the following section, the experimental results are shown. In order to test the proposed system, the construction of a Chimeric Dataset has been necessary, since datasets containing both face/periocular images and smartphone touch data are not publicly available. Therefore, an extended test set has been constructed by combining two existing datasets: the *H-MOG Dataset* [28] and the *MICHE Face Dataset*, respectively for Touch Event data and face image.

4.1   The Construction of the *Chimeric* Subjects

The construction of a chimeric dataset is a very popular practice, above all when dealing with multibiometric recognition/verification. Usually, the correctness of this practice is tied to the non-dependency between the data. Cases in which the dataset may be correlated do not allow the construction of chimeric dataset. In [29] is shown the construction of a chimeric dataset bu merging EEGs from a dataset and ECGs from another one. The H-MOG dataset and the MICHE Face dataset consist respectively of 94 and 64 subjects. Therefore, a Chimeric Dataset consisting of up to 64 subjects is possible to construct. Even if it is not realistic to think that a single smartphone may be used by so many subjects, we decided to test the application over all the possible set of subjects. Therefore, starting from the H-MOG dataset and the MICHE Face dataset, in order to properly test the proposed biometric trait, 64 *chimeras* have been created. Given a Touch Event data $touch_i$, belonging to the HMOG dataset and a face image $face_j$, belonging to the MICHE Face dataset, a *chimera* subject c_{ij} is defined as follows:

$$c_{ij} = (touch_i, face_j); \tag{1}$$

4.2   The Results

In Fig. 3 the classification results in terms of percentage of accuracy are shown. For the Touch data, an aggregation of decision trees (Bagging Trees) [30] has been built. Instead, for the periocular data, an LDA based on Random Subspace [31] has been used. In both cases the fold-cross-validation has been applied with $k = 3$, i.e. the data have been split in three sets and in turn, two are used for training and one for validation.

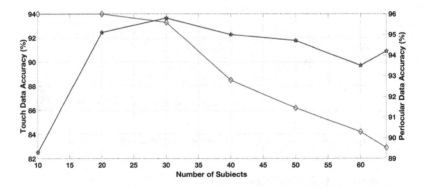

Fig. 3. In the figure, the results in terms of accuracy are shown, by varying the number of subjects in the Gallery (x-axis). In blue and in orange, respectively the accuracies over the touch and the periocular data

For the following experiments, the widest set has been used. Therefore, 64 subjects are considered.

The results are shown in terms of EER (Equal Error Rate), AUC (Area Under ROC Curve) and DEC (Decidability). Also ROC curve, CMS Curve, Genuins/Impostors distribution and FAR/FRR intersection (used for the estimation of the EER) is shown. The first experiment aimed at proving the reliability of the touch features: in Fig. 4 the plots related to FAR/FRR plot, ROC curve, CMS curve and GI (Genuins/impostors) distribution are shown. From the image it's possible to appreciate the EER lower than 0.05% and an AUC (Area Under Roc Curve) of 96%. Beside this, the Genuins/Impostors intersection area is below the 1%. Decidability of 2.9 shows that in terms of verification, the touch features is much discriminant (if related to the subset we considered).

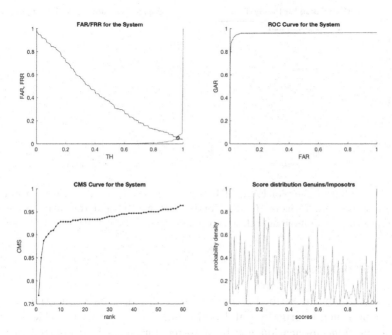

Fig. 4. In the figure, the plot FAR/FRR (top-left image), the ROC Curve (top-right), the Cumulative Match Score (CMS) Curve (bottom-left) and the distribution Genuins/Impostors (bottom-right) related to the touch features over 64 subjects

The second experiment tested the discriminative abilities of the periocular area. With respect to the *touch* features, the periocular is known to be a pretty strong hard biometric trait. As a consequence the results are extremely better than those obtained with the *touch* features. In fact, we obtained a quite low Genuines/Impostors distribution (0.002%) as well as an AUC value of 99.16%. Also an EER of 0.01 is obtained. These results can also be inferred by watching the plots in Fig. 5.

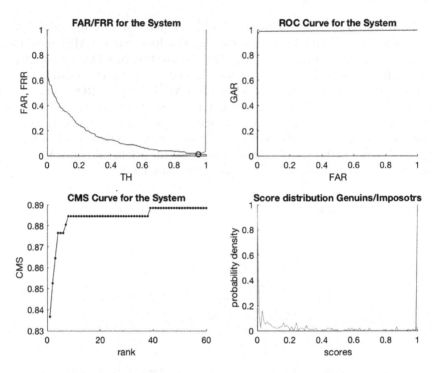

Fig. 5. In the figure, the plot FAR/FRR (top-left image), the ROC Curve (top-right), the Cumulative Match Score (CMS) Curve (bottom-left) and the distribution Genuins/Impostors (bottom-right) related to the periocular LBP features over 64 subjects

5   Conclusion

The proposed work described a continuous authentication application by using smartphone touch information and periocular area, in order to achieve subject verification. The application has been tested for being incorporated in the e-learning platform presented in [9], which currently only considered laptops and PC devices. Nowadays smartphone gestures data have been revealed to be very useful, and the research in this sense is growing ever more. On the other side, the presence of strongest and more reliable features is still needed, in order to overcome behavioral limitations encountered by the soft biometrics. In this work we preferred to use periocular data rather than face, since in real applications it's quite difficult to obtain a clear image of the face during the use of the smartphone, due to the fact that people look at the device in different ways and not always a clear (and complete) image of a face can be acquired. The results obtained are promising for applicative extensions and further investigations above this topic.

Acknowledgments. Mirko Marras gratefully acknowledges Sardinia Regional Government for the financial support of his PhD scholarship (P.O.R. Sardegna F.S.E. Operational Programme of the Autonomous Region of Sardinia, European Social Fund 2014–2020, Axis III "Education and Training", Thematic Goal 10, Priority of Investment 10ii, Specific Goal 10.5). The Italian Ministry of University, Education and Research (MIUR), partially supported this work, under the project ILEARNTV (announcement 391/2012, SMART CITIES AND COMMUNITIES AND SOCIAL INNOVATION).

References

1. Shen, H., Gao, C., He, D., Wu, L.: New biometrics-based authentication scheme for multi-server environment in critical systems. J. Ambient. Intell. Humaniz. Comput. **6**(6), 825–834 (2015)
2. Liu, Y., Ling, J., Liu, Z., Shen, J., Gao, C.: Finger vein secure biometric template generation based on deep learning. Soft Comput. **22**(7), 2257–2265 (2018)
3. Chen, Z., Wu, J., Castiglione, A., Wu, W.: Human continuous activity recognition based on energy-efficient schemes considering cloud security technology. Secur. Commun. Netw. **9**(16), 3585–3601 (2016)
4. Castiglione, A., Choo, K.K.R., Nappi, M., Narducci, F.: Biometrics in the cloud: challenges and research opportunities. IEEE Cloud Comput. **4**(4), 12–17 (2017)
5. Castiglione, A., Choo, K.K.R., Nappi, M., Ricciardi, S.: Context aware ubiquitous biometrics in edge of military things. IEEE Cloud Comput. **4**(6), 16–20 (2017)
6. Neves, J.C., Moreno, J.C., Barra, S., Proença, H.: Acquiring high-resolution face images in outdoor environments: a master-slave calibration algorithm. In: 2015 IEEE 7th International Conference on Biometrics Theory, Applications and Systems (BTAS), pp. 1–8, September 2015
7. Neves, J., Narducci, F., Barra, S., Proença, H.: Biometric recognition in surveillance scenarios: a survey. Artif. Intell. Rev. **46**(4), 515–541 (2016)
8. Neves, J.C., Santos, G., Filipe, S., Grancho, E., Barra, S., Narducci, F., Proença, H.: *Quis-Campi*: extending *in the Wild* biometric recognition to surveillance environments. In: Murino, V., Puppo, E., Sona, D., Cristani, M., Sansone, C. (eds.) ICIAP 2015. LNCS, vol. 9281, pp. 59–68. Springer, Cham (2015). https://doi.org/10.1007/978-3-319-23222-5_8
9. Fenu, G., Marras, M., Boratto, L.: A multi-biometric system for continuous student authentication in e-learning platforms. Pattern Recognit. Lett. (2017)
10. Barra, S., Marsico, M.D., Galdi, C., Riccio, D., Wechsler, H.: Fame: face authentication for mobile encounter. In: 2013 IEEE Workshop on Biometric Measurements and Systems for Security and Medical Applications, pp. 1–7, September 2013
11. Abate, A.F., Barra, S., Gallo, L., Narducci, F.: Kurtosis and skewness at pixel level as input for som networks to iris recognition on mobile devices. Pattern Recogn. Lett. **91**, 37–43 (2017). Mobile Iris CHallenge Evaluation (MICHE-II)
12. Dasgupta, D., Roy, A., Nag, A.: Advances in User Authentication. Springer, Heidelberg (2017)
13. Schiavone, E., Ceccarelli, A., Bondavalli, A.: Continuous biometric verification for non-repudiation of remote services. In: Proceedings of the 12th International Conference on Availability, Reliability and Security, p. 4. ACM (2017)
14. Sanna, P.S., Marcialis, G.L.: Remote biometric verification for elearning applications: where we are. In: Battiato, S., Gallo, G., Schettini, R., Stanco, F. (eds.) ICIAP 2017. LNCS, vol. 10485, pp. 373–383. Springer, Cham (2017). https://doi.org/10.1007/978-3-319-68548-9_35

15. Fenu, G., Marras, M.: Leveraging continuous multi-modal authentication for access control in mobile cloud environments. In: Battiato, S., Farinella, G.M., Leo, M., Gallo, G. (eds.) ICIAP 2017. LNCS, vol. 10590, pp. 331–342. Springer, Cham (2017). https://doi.org/10.1007/978-3-319-70742-6_31

16. Fathy, M.E., Patel, V.M., Chellappa, R.: Face-based active authentication on mobile devices. In: 2015 IEEE International Conference on Acoustics, Speech and Signal Processing (ICASSP), pp. 1687–1691. IEEE (2015)

17. Muaaz, M., Mayrhofer, R.: An analysis of different approaches to gait recognition using cell phone based accelerometers. In: Proceedings of International Conference on Advances in Mobile Computing & Multimedia, p. 293. ACM (2013)

18. Ali, M.L., Monaco, J.V., Tappert, C.C., Qiu, M.: Keystroke biometric systems for user authentication. J. Signal Process. Syst. **86**(2–3), 175–190 (2017)

19. Teh, P.S., Zhang, N., Teoh, A.B.J., Chen, K.: A survey on touch dynamics authentication in mobile devices. Comput. Secur. **59**, 210–235 (2016)

20. Rahman, K.A., Moormann, R., Dierich, D., Hossain, M.S.: Continuous user verification via mouse activities. In: Dziech, A., Leszczuk, M., Baran, R. (eds.) MCSS 2015. CCIS, vol. 566, pp. 170–181. Springer, Cham (2015). https://doi.org/10.1007/978-3-319-26404-2_14

21. Shen, C., Chen, Y., Guan, X.: Performance evaluation of implicit smartphones authentication via sensor-behavior analysis. Inf. Sci. **430**, 538–553 (2018)

22. Zhang, H., Patel, V.M., Chellappa, R.: Robust multimodal recognition via multitask multivariate low-rank representations. In: 2015 11th IEEE International Conference and Workshops on Automatic Face and Gesture Recognition (FG), vol. 1, pp. 1–8. IEEE (2015)

23. Sitová, Z., Šeděnka, J., Yang, Q., Peng, G., Zhou, G., Gasti, P., Balagani, K.S.: Hmog: new behavioral biometric features for continuous authentication of smartphone users. IEEE Trans. Inf. Forensics Secur. **11**(5), 877–892 (2016)

24. Mondal, S., Bours, P.: A study on continuous authentication using a combination of keystroke and mouse biometrics. Neurocomputing **230**, 1–22 (2017)

25. Fridman, L., Weber, S., Greenstadt, R., Kam, M.: Active authentication on mobile devices via stylometry, application usage, web browsing, and GPS location. IEEE Syst. J. **11**(2), 513–521 (2017)

26. Patel, V.M., Chellappa, R., Chandra, D., Barbello, B.: Continuous user authentication on mobile devices: recent progress and remaining challenges. IEEE Signal Process. Mag. **33**(4), 49–61 (2016)

27. Viola, P., Jones, M.: Rapid object detection using a boosted cascade of simple features. In: Proceedings of the 2001 IEEE Computer Society Conference on Computer Vision and Pattern Recognition, CVPR 2001, vol. 1, p. I. IEEE (2001)

28. Sitová, Z., et al.: Hmog: new behavioral biometric features for continuous authentication of smartphone users. IEEE Trans. Inf. Forensics Secur. **11**(5), 877–892 (2016)

29. Barra, S., Casanova, A., Fraschini, M., Nappi, M.: EEG/ECG signal fusion aimed at biometric recognition. In: Murino, V., Puppo, E., Sona, D., Cristani, M., Sansone, C. (eds.) ICIAP 2015. LNCS, vol. 9281, pp. 35–42. Springer, Cham (2015). https://doi.org/10.1007/978-3-319-23222-5_5

30. Meinshausen, N.: Quantile regression forests. J. Mach. Learn. Res. **7**, 983–999 (2006)

31. Zhang, X., Jia, Y.: A linear discriminant analysis framework based on random subspace for face recognition. Pattern Recognit. **40**(9), 2585–2591 (2007)

Real-Time IoT Device Activity Detection in Edge Networks

Ibbad Hafeez[1]([✉]), Aaron Yi Ding[2,3], Markku Antikainen[1,4],
and Sasu Tarkoma[1,4]

[1] University of Helsinki, Helsinki, Finland
{ibbad.hafeez,markku.antikainen,sasu.tarkoma}@helsinki.fi
[2] Technical University of Munich, Munich, Germany
aaron.ding@tum.de
[3] Delft University of Technology, Delft, Netherlands
[4] Helsinki Institute of Information Technology, Helsinki, Finland

Abstract. The growing popularity of Internet-of-Things (IoT) has created the need for network-based traffic anomaly detection systems that could identify misbehaving devices. In this work, we propose a lightweight technique, IoTGUARD, for identifying malicious traffic flows. IoTGUARD uses semi-supervised learning to distinguish between *malicious* and *benign* device behaviours using the network traffic generated by devices. In order to achieve this, we extracted 39 features from network logs and discard any features containing redundant information. After feature selection, fuzzy C-Mean (FCM) algorithm was trained to obtain clusters discriminating *benign* traffic from *malicious* traffic. We studied the feature scores in these clusters and use this information to predict the type of new traffic flows. IoTGUARD was evaluated using a real-world testbed with more than 30 devices. The results show that IoTGUARD achieves high accuracy ($\geq$98%), in differentiating various types of *malicious* and *benign* traffic, with low false positive rates. Furthermore, it has low resource footprint and can operate on OpenWRT enabled access points and COTS computing boards.

Keywords: Network · Security · Traffic monitoring · Classification
Anomaly detection · Semi-supervised learning

1 Introduction

The Internet-of-Things (IoT) trend has significantly increased the number devices connected to the Internet. Predictions forecast this number to exceed 20 billion by year 2020 [22]. Despite its benefits, a number of security concerns have been raised about the connected devices themselves. Majority of smart devices operate on limited power and computational resources and hence do not support host-based security software such as anti-malware. Also, IoT products are mostly developed by product development teams who have limited resources

© Springer Nature Switzerland AG 2018
M. H. Au et al. (Eds.): NSS 2018, LNCS 11058, pp. 221–236, 2018.
https://doi.org/10.1007/978-3-030-02744-5_17

and who may not follow standard security practices e.g. reusing code snippets, weak encryption keys, lack of security-by-design etc. [2, 23, 24].

IoT devices are lucrative targets for attackers who want to obtain user-related information or to perform large scale network attacks. Due to the poor security of many IoT devices, network-based security solutions are often the only line of defence against incoming attacks that target these devices.

Unfortunately, traditional network security solutions, such as network intrusion detection/prevention systems (NIDS/NIPS) and firewalls, fall short in distinguishing and filtering malicious traffic generated by these smart devices for a number of reasons. Firstly, it is infeasible to collect signatures for all possible network interactions for these devices, due to heterogeneity in devices and firmware versions. In practice, a device's network behaviour may vary significantly in different firmware releases. Secondly, the costs of deploying and maintaining traditional NIDS/NIPS and firewall solution is high for small-office and home networks. Lastly, amount of network traffic data that needs to be processed may overwhelm the NIDS/NIPS systems that perform traffic analysis. Therefore, it is necessary to research new solutions for traffic monitoring and classification, which are self-adaptive, cost efficient and do not require specialized hardware.

In this work, we propose a self-adaptive semi-supervised learning based classification scheme named as IoTGUARD, which predicts traffic class (i.e. *malicious* or *benign*) based on the network activity of the device generating the traffic.

Our technique primarily uses the data extracted from network logs that are obtained from access-points (APs) and gateways. IoTGUARD does not specifically rely on specialized logs obtained from domain-controllers, firewalls or NIDS, because smaller networks (i.e. small-office and home networks, aka. SOHO networks) rarely have these. However, if available, our technique can use data also from such specialized logs to further improve the efficiency and accuracy of the system. All this data is combined to identify network-level patterns for different kinds of traffic the devices generate, and use these patterns to identify any malicious activities in the network. We resolved data imbalance issues by oversampling and under-sampling data from minority and majority class respectively. Our choice of unsupervised learning is motivated by the reason that class labels for most network logs are not available and classification scheme should be able to learn from various patterns observed in network traffic.

Our work demonstrates that a simple, yet effective, clustering technique combined with in-depth feature analysis enables real-time traffic classification, without requiring dedicated hardware. Our key contributions are:

- We propose a pipeline detailing feature extraction, analysis and reduction techniques, to develop the set of most useful features for performing clustering on network data.
- We propose traffic classification scheme using fuzzy C-Mean clustering and fuzzy interpolation scheme, which is able to determine the degree of maliciousness, therefore, giving more information for taking appropriate measures to handle different types of malicious traffic.

– We evaluate the performance of IOTGUARD in real-world environment with off-the-shelf consumer-grade devices. IOTGUARD boasts high prediction accuracy ($\geq$98%) for both *binary* and *multi-class* problems with low false-positive-rate ($\simeq$0.01).

In the rest of paper, Sect. 2 discuss our threat model outlining the types of attacks in IoT edge networks, followed by methodology in Sect. 3. The data set and evaluation results are discussed in Sects. 4 and 5 respectively. Section 6 gives a comparison of IOTGUARD with existing approaches. Section 7 discusses the some limitations of IOTGUARD, followed by concluding remarks.

2 Threat Model

This work focuses on small-office and home networks. These networks usually have a star topology where all devices are connected to an access point that also provides Internet connectivity. IoT devices in such networks are often mismanaged and not hardened. Thus, while the devices are intrinsically benign, an attacker can easily compromise and use these devices for various follow-up attacks. The list of attacks, which can be launched in a SOHO networks with an aid of an already compromised device, is given as:

Network-scanning attacks, where an adversary tries to find any device on the network, running services with open, unguarded ports. Network scanning commonly include *port-scan*, *port-sweep* and *address-sweep* attacks.

Flooding attacks, where a (compromised) device participates in a large scale Distributed Denial-of-Services (DDoS) attack. DDoS attacks are often used as a smoke-screen to divert attention off dedicated attacks occurring in parallel.

Infection attacks, where a compromised or infected device actively tries to infect to other devices in the network. For example, an attacker may try to make repeated login attempts to services discovered by *network-scanning*, in order to download malware on other devices in the network.

Spying attacks, where a device collects user data without explicit consent and sends it to untrusted third party.

This work uses network-level semantics of these attacks to predict type of traffic in the network. It does not individually profile each device's behaviour as *benign* or *malicious*. Instead, it uses feature scores observed in various traffic types, to identify traffic, irrespective of what device generated it.

3 Methodology

3.1 Design Challenge

A key limitation in using supervised learning algorithms for network traffic classification is the unavailability of labelled data covering all traffic classes seen in real-world environments. With a huge variety of IoT devices and their heterogeneous mode of operations, it is expensive and infeasible to label all data collected by monitoring network traffic. To overcome this challenge, unsupervised learning provides a better alternative, as it does not require nor depend on labelled data. Clustering can partition large volumes of network traffic data into small number of clusters based on similar patterns observed in data.

Any new data point will be added to a cluster based on its similarity with existing data points in the cluster. Meanwhile, these clusters can be rearranged, divided or combined depending on number of classes of data.

3.2   Feature Extraction

IOTGUARD uses features collected from the access point and, if available, from individual device logs. With an assumption of unique IP address per device, we use the source and destination IP addresses together with timestamps (3-tuple identifier) from each traffic flow, for identifying the feature vector for that flow. Each feature vector consists of a total of 39 discrete and continuous features, listed in Table 1.

Table 1. Discrete and continuous features extracted from network connections

	Type	Feature
Discrete	L2 Protocol	ARP, LLC
	L3 Protocol	IP, ICMP, ICMPv6, EAPoL
	L4 Protocol	TCP, UDP
	L5 protocol	HTTP, HTTPS, DHCP, BOOTP, SSDP, (M)DNS, NTP
	IP Options	Padding, Router Alert
Continuous	Src and dest	# unique destination IP addresses
		# unique source and destination ports
	Counters	# total connections, # connections to/from unique dest/src
		Connection lengths, SYN packets & errors, REJ errors, URG packets
	Data	Total data transferred
		Total data from source to destination
		Total data from destination to source
		Packet sizes, payload signatures
	Auth	Total login attempts (inc. SSH connection, using default credentials, failed login attempts)

For some features (e.g. authentication and network discovery), we need accurate time synchronization among all devices. In case if network does not use time synchronization mechanisms such as NTP, we have to manually account for the time differences between network and device logs.

We aggregate the same-host, same-service features over n latest connections instead of using time-based aggregation. Time-based aggregation (used in KDD-Cup99 dataset [1]) aggregates the features over a definite time e.g. number of connections made in last two seconds between *Device-A* and *Device-B*. This scheme falls short in detecting attacks where attacker introduces a time-delay between successive connection attempts. In contrast, connection-based aggregation techniques aggregate features over last n connections i.e. out of last n connections made by *Device-A*, how many terminated at *Device-B*. This technique accommodates the time-delay added to successive connections. However, if n is small and device connects to several destinations simultaneously i.e. behaviour not observed commonly in compromised devices targeting certain destination, connection-based aggregation may not work effectively.

3.3 Feature Analysis

The value distributions of the features was studied in order to identify relative importance of features, based on variance and modality. Any features with low variance across different samples are discarded because they do not substantially contribute to clustering. This dimensionality reduction also helps speed up the clustering process.

Figure 1 shows cumulative distribution functions for three (of 39) extracted features. The distributions in the figures are not Gaussian, but heavy tailed with majority of probability mass lying in smaller values. For example Fig. 1a shows that $\geq 70\%$ devices connect to ≤ 20 unique destinations but there are some devices which connect to ≥ 6000 unique destinations. The tail of these distributions is particularly interesting because it encapsulates events where a device may be exhibiting anomalous behaviour. The knowledge from feature value distributions is used to choose the features that will most likely result in clusters with well defined boundaries and outliers.

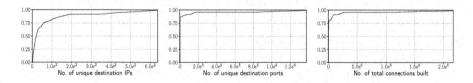

Fig. 1. CDF plots for a subset of connection metadata

3.4 Feature Reduction

Feature reduction decreases the model complexity, reduces resource consumption, and improves generalization. Therefore, *correlation-based feature selection* (CFS), *deviation method*, and feature value distributions are used to identify and remove any features that do not significantly contribute to clustering process.

Pearson coefficient provides fairly accurate results with bounded feature value ranges when size of the dataset is large [8]. We use Pearson correlation coefficient R to measure the linear dependencies of strongly correlated features. One of any two strongly correlated features (i.e. $R \geq 0.99$) can be discarded as redundant.

With deviation method, we first mine 1-length items from each feature to obtain 39 feature vectors that contain frequent items for each of the seven activity types listed in Table 2. The frequent items for binary features can be found with algorithms such as Apriori [3] or FP-Growth [20]. For continuous variables, 1-length items are found by comparing the frequency of a continuous variable against a specified minimum support. If the deviation range for a feature overlaps across all traffic types, we do not expect it to significantly contribute in clustering and, therefore, remove it.

The normalized feature scores is studied for every feature in all clusters and any features with similar values across different clusters are removed. To ensure that no feature over-influences clustering, all feature values are normalized to range $[0, 1]$. It was observed that the use of *principal component analysis* (PCA) for dimensionality reduction prior to clustering does not benefit to our approach because PCA fails to capture outliers (tail of distribution) in its principal components and those outliers can be particularly useful for identifying anomalies.

3.5   Clustering

Fuzzy C-mean (FCM) clustering algorithm is used to separate data points based on their self similarity. Our choice of FCM is based on its ability to maintain weighted association of any point not only for the cluster which it is assigned to, but for neighbouring clusters as well, where it is weakly associated [27]. These weak associations are useful in predicting labels for unknown traffic flows since *all* cluster associations are considered when assigning assigning a label. This approach helps in reducing the number of false-positives.

Using FCM, initially a random membership value is assigned to each data point X_j $(j = 1, 2, ..., n)$ for every cluster C_i $(i = 1, 2, ..., c)$. Each data point X_j is represented as $\left(f_j^{(1)}, f_j^{(2)}, ..., f_j^{(k)}, ..., f_j^{(h)} \right)$ where $f_j^{(k)}$ is value for k^{th} feature in X_j and $1 \leq k \leq 39$ (i.e. 39 features).

The membership value μ_{ij}, $(0 \leq \mu_{ij} \leq 1)$ for a data point X_j assigned to cluster C_i is such that $\sum_{i=1}^{c} \mu_{ij} = 1$ for $1 \leq i \leq c$ and $1 \leq j \leq n$. The membership values μ_{ij} and cluster centres V_i are optimized using Eq. 1, to minimize objective function in Eq. 2.

$$\mu_{ij} = \left(\sum_{d=1}^{c} \left(\frac{\|V_i - X_j\|}{\|V_d - X_j\|} \right)^{\frac{2}{m-1}} \right)^{-1} \quad ; \quad V_i = \frac{\sum\limits_{j=1}^{n} (\mu_{ij})^m \times X_j}{\sum\limits_{j=1}^{n} (\mu_{ij})^m} \quad ; \quad \substack{1 \leq i \leq c \\ 1 \leq j \leq n} \quad (1)$$

$$J_m = \sum_{i=1}^{c} \sum_{j=1}^{n} \mu_{ij}^m \|V_i - X_j\|^2 \quad (2)$$

where m is fuzziness index [32] and $\|V_i - X_j\|$ is the Euclidean distance between cluster center V_i for cluster C_i and data point X_j.

Clusters labels are assigned based on feature value distribution for each cluster. The labels can be manually verified using dataset ground truth. Each of these clusters is translated to a fuzzy rule, used by *fuzzy interpolation scheme* (FIS) for predicting type of given traffic flow.

3.6 Parameter Optimization

The optimal number of clusters i is determined by examining the degree of cohesion among data points in a cluster, *fuzzy partition coefficient* [30] (FPC), and trade-off between sensitivity, specificity and accuracy of our prediction.

The process is initialized with a range of possible values for i. Then, FCM algorithm runs for $n = 3000$ iterations to calculate FPC and *within-cluster-sums-of-distances* (WCSD) for each value of i. i with minimum WCSD is chosen, to remove any initialization bias and prevent the output to reside in local minima [8]. WCSD is calculated using Eq. 3, where c is the number of clusters, S_i is the set of data points belonging to i^{th} cluster, and x_{ki} is the kth variable of V_i.

$$WCSD = \sum_{i=1}^{c} \sum_{j \in S_i} \sum_{k=1}^{p} \|x_{ki} - x_{ji}\| \tag{3}$$

Silhouette values [5] (using Eq. 4) are calculated for all data points x_k and verify our choice of i by studying how well a given data point belongs to the cluster it is assigned to. The optimal choice for i will have minimum WCSD and maximum average silhouette value.

$$s(x) = \frac{b(x) - a(x)}{\max(a(x), b(x))} \tag{4}$$

3.7 Prediction Algorithm

IOTGUARD uses *fuzzy interpolation scheme* (FIS) to predict the type of traffic using the rules obtained from clustering. FIS allows us to deduce a conclusion using a sparse fuzzy rule base. Let us consider an sparse fuzzy rule set such as

Rule 1: if $f_1 \in A_{11}, f_2 \in A_{21}, \ldots, f_k \in A_{k1}, \ldots, f_h \in A_{h1} \implies y \in O_1$

Rule 2: if $f_1 \in A_{12}, f_2 \in A_{22}, \ldots, f_k \in A_{k2}, \ldots, f_h \in A_{h2} \implies y \in O_2$

$$\vdots$$

Rule Q: if $f_1 \in A_{1q}, f_2 \in A_{2q}, \ldots, f_k \in A_{kq}, \ldots, f_h \in A_{hq} \implies y \in O_q$

Observation: $f_1 \in A_1^*, f_2 \in A_2^*, \ldots, f_k \in A_k^*, \ldots, f_h \in A_h^*$

Conclusion: $y = O^*$

where R_i $(1 \le i \le Q)$ is i^{th} rule in sparse fuzzy rule base generated from cluster C_i.

A_{ki} and O_i are triangular fuzzy sets for k^{th} antecedent feature $f_k, 1 \le k \le h$ and consequent variable y respectively. For any new observation, A_k^* and O^* are triangular fuzzy sets for antecedent and consequent variable obtained as a result of interpolation of spare fuzzy rule base.

The classification rules obtained from clusters generate the rule base such that R_i is generated from C_i with h antecedent features and one consequent label assigned to the given cluster.

$$R_i: if\ f_1 \in A_{1i}, f_2 \in A_{2i},\ ...\ , f_k \in A_{ki},\ ...\ , f_h \in A_{hi} \implies y \in B_i$$

The characteristic points a_{ki}, b_{ki}, c_{ki} for triangular fuzzy set are calculated for all antecedents A_{ki} and consequent B_i in R_i. The weight W_i of given rule R_i $(i = 1, 2, ..., c)$ is calculated on the basis of input observations $x_1 = f_j^{(1)}, x_2 = f_j^{(2)}, ..., x_h = f_j^{(h)}$ as:

$$W_i = \left(\sum_{d=1}^{c} \left(\frac{\|r^* - r_i\|}{\|r^* - r_d\|} \right)^2 \right)^{-1}, \tag{5}$$

where r^* is the input feature vector $\left(f_j^{(1)}, f_j^{(2)}, ..., f_j^{(h)} \right)$ and r_i is set of de-fuzzified values[1] of antecedent fuzzy sets in R_i. The final inferred output is calculated as

$$O_j^* = \sum_{i=1}^{c} W_i \times D_f (B_i) \tag{6}$$

where $D_f (B_i)$ is the de-fuzzified value of consequent fuzzy variables B_i with $0 \le W_i \le 1$ and $\sum_{i=1}^{c} W_i = 1$. The type for the traffic is assigned on the basis of inferred output.

4   Dataset

The data set was collected using a real-world testbed with 30+ typical user devices. These devices include smartphones, tablets, smart appliances and personal computing devices etc., running popular operating systems including iOS, Android, Windows, MAC OS, Tizen and webOS. All devices support wireless connectivity with 32 devices supporting Bluetooth as well.

Testbed setup: The testbed represents a typical SOHO network, where all user devices connected to an AP through wired/wireless medium and the AP is connected to Internet. Data was collected by connecting all devices to an AP setup running wireless and wired networks, with one interface connected to the Internet. All traffic over wireless and wired interfaces in both LAN and WAN networks was collected.

Scenarios: Table 2 shows seven different scenarios used for data collection. These scenarios represent *benign* and (commonly expected) *malicious* device activity. Data collection for each scenario was repeated for $n = 20$ times to

---

[1] $d : D \mid d(A_{ki}) = (1/4)(a_{ki} + 2 \times b_{ki} + c_{ki})$ for triangular set A_{ki}.

avoid any discrepancies and peculiarities in the data. For each iteration, a set of devices (may vary depending on scenario) was connected to the network and data was collected from both WiFi and Ethernet interfaces, to record all traffic within and across the network, including the traffic among wireless clients. After each iteration, the testbed (including devices) was reset to get a clean-slate for next iteration. Non-overlapping set of devices was used for data collection in similar scenarios, to minimize any redundancy and remove any device specific behaviors from the dataset. Any duplicate data points were removed from the dataset to prevent any bias in the learning algorithm.

Table 2. Scenarios for data collection, representing network activity types

Scenario	Description
Auth. attack (A)	A compromised host makes multiple login attempts to other host(s)
Botnet activity (B)	A compromised host opens many connections to one or more usually remote destination hosts
Normal (N)	Typical, non-malicious, usage pattern
Port Sweep (P-Sweep)	A compromised host scans all ports on a destination host
Port Scan (P-Scan)	A compromised host scans a subset of all ports of a target
Spying (S)	A compromised host tries to send user data to a remote destination
Worm (W)	A compromised host scans the network for access to other hosts and tries to copy malicious content on destination host(s)

Due to real-world testbed setting, dataset imbalance issues result in *benign* traffic becoming *majority* class and *malicious* traffic becoming *minority* class. It is because devices rarely exhibit *malicious* behavior [15,16]. In order to prevent the imbalanced data problem, data points from *majority* class are undersampled. The experiments showed that under-sampling does not affect the accuracy of prediction because the *majority* class data is correlated and under-sampling does not result in loss of significant traits in the data. Meanwhile, *minority* class data points were over-sampled using SMOTE [9] to get 7 : 3 ratio for *benign:malicious* class data points. All six sub-classes in *minority* class contain equal data points.

5   Evaluation

Feature extraction, feature analysis, clustering and prediction scheme was implemented with Python using `dpkt`, `imbalanced-learn` and `scikit-learn` libraries. After feature reduction, clustering was performed to groups all the data points into clearly differentiable clusters based on self-similarity. Figure 2a shows the clusters obtained by performing FCM clustering on our dataset. The figure was plotted by mapping 22 dimensional feature space to 2 dimensional surface using *multi-dimensional scaling* (MDS) [26]. Figure 2a shows that our technique produces clearly differentiable clusters with distinct boundaries. Moreover, the figure shows that the clustering algorithm can also easily among distinguish different sub-classes of *malicious* traffic. After clustering, the feature value distributions in each of the clusters are shown in Fig. 2a.

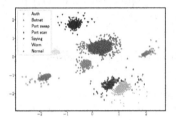 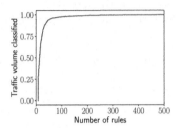

Fig. 2. (a): Clusters obtained as a result of applying FCM clustering algorithm. (b): CDF plot for the number of classification rules required to predict traffic class

Figure 3 show clearly distinguishable normalized features scores for each of the clusters. Out of the 39 features extracted from network metadata (see Sect. 3.2), the normalized feature scores of 18 features was studied. Features f1-f9 correspond to connection-related data (e.g. connection count, unique IPs), f10-f13 correspond to flagged packets (e.g. urgent, SYN, REJ), f14-f18 correspond to data (e.g. SRC2DST, DST2SRC), and f19-f22 correspond to authentication related features (e.g. SSH connections, login attempts).

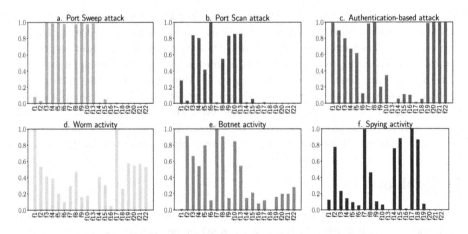

Fig. 3. Normalized feature averages for distinguishing features representing clusters for each attack scenario.

Table 3 shows the prediction accuracy for binary-class problem, where IoT-GUARD achieves 98.61% accuracy with a *precision* of 0.985 and 0.99 score for both *sensitivity* and *specificity*, giving us an overall F1-score of 0.986.

Table 3. Confusion matrix for binary-class problem

		Predicted		
		benign	*malicious*	**Total**
Actual	*benign*	533	7	540
	malicious	8	532	540
	Total	541	539	1080

The decision to preserve information in outliers (tail of distribution) helped in clearly differentiating between otherwise overlapping classes, resulting in good prediction accuracy. By removing the features containing redundant information, FCM algorithm was able to generate clusters with distinct boundaries, resulting in low false positives and false negatives. The choice of FCM algorithm was also helpful in improving accuracy because it allowed us to use the weighted association with neighbouring clusters to predict class labels for new traffic flows.

Table 4a shows the prediction accuracy for detecting individual attack types. It shows that, on average, IoTGUARD achieved 98% accuracy with 0.94 F1-score in multi-class prediction.

Although IoTGUARD was able to predict P-Sweep and P-Scan with high accuracy, the highest number of inaccurate predictions have been made for these two classes. Figure 3a and b show that this behaviour is due to overlapping the feature scores of these classes e.g., the instances of P-Scan attack over a large range of ports will result in so many connections that it is predicted as P-Sweep attack. Similarly, a P-Sweep attack over a limited range of ports may be predicted as P-Scan attack.

6   Comparison with Existing Approaches

A number of researchers have used machine learning (ML) algorithms to detect malicious traffic [7,21]. Their proposals use data mining [12], supervised ML [4], and unsupervised ML techniques [8,28] to build network intrusion detection systems (NIDS). Bekerman et al. [7] used 942 features to identify malware by analysing network traffic. Strayer et al. [29] and Lu et al. [14] studied network behaviour and application classification to identify bots in networks. BotMiner [11] used clustering technique for detecting botnets independent of underlying command-and-control protocol and strategy. Bohara et al. [8] used unsupervised learning to predict class labels for unlabelled network.

IoT Sentinel [19] uses device type information to limit the network access of vulnerable devices whereas PorfilIoT [18] uses a multi-stage classification technique for differentiating IoT from non-IoT devices and then finding the actual

Table 4. (a): Confusion matrix for the *malicious* activity types. A = Actual, P = Predicted; (b): Prediction performance for subclasses of *malicious* traffic

(a)

P A	A	B	PS	Ps	S	W
A	**86**	0	0	0	0	3
B	0	**83**	0	2	2	0
PS	0	0	**81**	9	0	0
Ps	3	0	3	**84**	0	0
S	0	0	0	0	**86**	1
W	3	2	0	0	0	**84**

(b)

Measure/	A	B	PS	Ps	S	W	Mean
Accuracy	0.98	0.98	0.98	0.96	0.98	0.98	0.98
Precision	0.93	0.95	0.96	0.87	0.95	0.95	0.94
Specificity	0.96	0.92	0.90	0.93	0.96	0.93	0.94
Sensitivity	0.99	0.99	0.99	0.97	0.99	0.99	0.99
F1-score	0.95	0.94	0.93	0.90	0.95	0.94	0.94

type of IoT device. IoT Sentinel and ProfilIoT rely on fingerprints generated from devices' network activity to train classification models, and thus fail to detect impersonation attacks. Roux et al. [13] propose the use of RSSI using radio probes to detect an attacker trying to hijack user devices. Cheng et. al [10] propose running time patching of access points to block malicious traffic flows in the network. Barrera et al. [6] proposed a security policy enforcement framework for restricting IoT devices communication to necessary interactions.

Table 5. Qualitative comparison of anomaly detection techniques

System	Feature count	Learning algorithm	Functionality
Strayer et al. [29]	16	supervised	Botnet detection
IoT Sentinel [19]	23	supervised	Device identification
Beckerman et al. [7]	972	supervised	Malware detection
Yi et al. [31]	5	supervised	Anomaly detection
Median et al. [17]	274	supervised	Device identification
IoTGUARD	18–39	semi-supervised	Anomaly detection

Meidan et al. [18] used machine learning approach for detecting device types for 17 IoT devices with 99.4% accuracy. Ran et al. [25] proposed a self-adaptive technique for traffic classification based on semi-supervised machine learning, which dynamically choose optimal system parameters to achieve high accuracy. Yi et al. [31] proposed an algorithm using decision trees (DT) and co-training to detect abnormal/botnet traffic generated by a webcam.

Table 5 presents a qualitative comparison of IOTGUARD with current state of the art in traffic classification and IoT security research. IOTGUARD is considered *semi-supervised* only because the labels assigned to the clusters are manually verified.

7 Discussion

The evaluation of IOTGUARD shows that our approach allows us to successfully accurately predict the various type of traffic, discussed in our threat model.

The ability to use unlabelled data can be useful in improving the traffic classification schemes for a number of reasons. It will save the effort of labelling all traffic data used for model training and makes the system more flexible to adapt.

This work mainly use the data extracted from network and device logs. Therefore, our technique can be used in various network settings irrespective of what devices are connected to the network. Our model allows us to extend the classification to identify more types of *malicious* traffic seen in the network e.g. crypto-jacking attacks, which usually exhibit traffic patterns as seen in spying attacks. IOTGUARD can also be extended further to classify the sub-types of normal user traffic. This information could then be used for on-demand bandwidth provisioning and dynamic traffic management based on the traffic patterns.

A possible limitation of IOTGUARD is that it can only identify a device's malicious activity if it communicates over the network. That is, IOTGUARD cannot tell if an attacker physically accessed a device e.g. smart door-bell, and extracted information by directly connecting to it over physical, serial connection. However, IOTGUARD will be able to identify the (misbehaving) tampered device as soon as it connects to the network, and prevents it from executing any attacks against local or remote destinations.

IOTGUARD has been evaluated using devices with both wireless and wired network connection. However, its performance is not analysed for lower power communication protocols such as Zigbee, Z-Wave, Bluetooth LE etc. The process of verifying labels assigned to clusters can be automated, by cross-referencing the information from other sources. We expect the future research to explore new set of features to extend the types of attacks this approach can classify.

Finally, software updates in devices may change their network behaviour, which can initially be detected as malicious. However, IOTGUARD can adapt to this new network behaviour quickly, to stop prevent any false-positives. This behaviour was intentional, as it can be used to detect firmware versions of devices connected to the network.

8 Conclusion

This paper present a lightweight semi-supervised learning based technique, IOT-GUARD, for identifying *benign* and several types of *malicious* traffic in edge networks. This paper introduces a threat model based on the most common attacks in IoT landscape and a real-world testbed setup for collecting network data and device level logs. Our proposed pipeline for feature extraction, analysis, and reduction identifies the set of features that yield most value to the IoT device activity detection. Evaluation results for IOTGUARD show that using clustering and FIS, various types of *malicious* and *benign* traffic can be predicted with high accuracy in real-time.

In specific, IOTGUARD is able to predict traffic class in 250 ms, without requiring specialized hardware. IOTGUARD can be extended to identify more attack types, other than the ones considered in this paper. The technique can also be re-purposed for detecting devices, firmware versions and improving network bandwidth management, traffic routing problem based on the traffic patterns observed in the networks.

Acknowledgements. The work was supported in part by the Business Finland PraNA research project.

References

1. Kdd cup 1999 data. http://kdd.ics.uci.edu/databases/kddcup99/kddcup99.html. Accessed 18 July 2016
2. Senrio. 400,000 publicly available IoT devices vulnerable to single flaw. https://bit.ly/2Ieghvu. Accessed 5 May 2016
3. Agrawal, R., Srikant, R.: Fast algorithms for mining association rules in large databases. In: Proceedings of the 20th International Conference on Very Large Data Bases, VLDB 1994, pp. 487–499 (1994)
4. Akbar, S., et al.: Improving network security using machine learning techniques. In: 2012 IEEE International Conference on Computational Intelligence and Computing Research, pp. 1–5 (2012)
5. Aranganayagi, S., Thangavel, K.: Clustering categorical data using silhouette coefficient as a relocating measure. In: International Conference on Computational Intelligence and Multimedia Applications (ICCIMA 2007), vol. 2, pp. 13–17 (2007)
6. Barrera, D., Molloy, I., Huang, H.: IDIoT: securing the Internet of Things like it's 1994. CoRR abs/1712.03623 (2017)
7. Bekerman, D., et al.: Unknown malware detection using network traffic classification. In: 2015 IEEE Conference on Communications and Network Security (CNS), pp. 134–142 (2015)
8. Bohara, A., Thakore, U., Sanders, W.H.: Intrusion detection in enterprise systems by combining and clustering diverse monitor data. In: Proceedings of the Symposium and Bootcamp on the Science of Security, HotSos 2016, pp. 7–16 (2016)
9. Chawla, N.V., Bowyer, K.W., Hall, L.O., Kegelmeyer, W.P.: Smote: synthetic minority over-sampling technique. J. Artif. Int. Res. **16**(1), 321–357 (2002)
10. Cheng, S.M., et al.: Traffic-aware patching for cyber security in mobile IoT. IEEE Commun. Mag. **55**(7), 29–35 (2017)

11. Gu, G., Perdisci, R., Zhang, J., Lee, W.: Botminer: clustering analysis of network traffic for protocol- and structure-independent botnet detection. In: Proceedings of the 17th Conference on Security Symposium, SS 2008, pp. 139–154 (2008)
12. Jeyakumar, V., Madani, O., ParandehGheibi, A., Yadav, N.: Data driven data center network security. In: Proceedings of the 2016 ACM on International Workshop on Security And Privacy Analytics, IWSPA 2016, p. 48 (2016)
13. Roux, J., et al.: Toward an intrusion detection approach for IoT based on radio communications profiling. In: 13th European Dependable Computing Conference, Geneva, Switzerland, p. 4p. (2017)
14. Lu, W., et al.: Automatic discovery of botnet communities on large-scale communication networks. In: Proceedings of the 4th International Symposium on Information, Computer, and Communications Security, ASIACCS 2009, pp. 1–10 (2009)
15. Martindale, J.: Nearly 30 percent of all web traffic is sent by malicious bots. https://www.digitaltrends.com/web/bad-bots-intrnet/. Accessed 6 Apr 2018
16. McMillan, R.: Up to three percent of internet traffic is malicious, researcher says. https://www.csoonline.com/article/2122506/data-protection/up-to-three-percent-of-internet-traffic-is-malicious-researcher-says.html. Accessed 6 Apr 2018
17. Meidan, Y., et al.: Detection of unauthorized IoT devices using machine learning techniques. CoRR abs/1709.04647 (2017). http://arxiv.org/abs/1709.04647
18. Meidan, Y., et al.: Profiliot: a machine learning approach for IoT device identification based on network traffic analysis. In: Proceedings of the Symposium on Applied Computing, SAC 2017, pp. 506–509 (2017)
19. Miettinen, M., et al.: IoT sentinel: automated device-type identification for security enforcement in IoT. In: 2017 IEEE 37th International Conference on Distributed Computing Systems (ICDCS), pp. 2177–2184 (2017)
20. Narvekar, M., Syed, S.F.: An optimized algorithm for association rule miningusing FP tree. Procedia Comput. Sci. 45(Supplement C), 101–110 (2015). http://www.sciencedirect.com/science/article/pii/S1877050915003336. International Conference on Advanced Computing Technologies and Applications
21. Nguyen, T.T.T., Armitage, G.: A survey of techniques for internet traffic classification using machine learning. IEEE Commun. Surv. Tutor. 10(4), 56–76 (2008)
22. Nordum, A.: Popular internet of things forecast of 50 billion devices by 2020 is outdated. https://bit.ly/2K2Tk3Z. Accessed 7 May 2017
23. Patton, M., et al.: Uninvited connections: a study of vulnerable devices on the Internet of Things (IoT). In: 2014 IEEE Joint Intelligence and Security Informatics Conference, pp. 232–235 (2014)
24. Pauli, D.: 414,949 d-link cameras, IoT devices can be hijacked over the net. https://www.theregister.co.uk/2016/07/08/414949_dlink_cameras_iot_devices_can_be_hijacked_over_the_net/. Accessed 7 May 2017
25. Ran, J., Kong, X., Lin, G., Yuan, D., Hu, H.: A self-adaptive network traffic classification system with unknown flow detection. In: 2017 3rd IEEE International Conference on Computer and Communications (ICCC), pp. 1215–1220 (2017)
26. ur Rehman, Z., Idris, A., Khan, A., : Multi-dimensional scaling based grouping of known complexes and intelligent protein complex detection. Comput. Biol. Chem. 74, 149–156 (2018). https://doi.org/10.1016/j.compbiolchem.2018.03.023
27. Shanmugam, B., Idris, N.B.: Improved intrusion detection system using fuzzy logic for detecting anamoly and misuse type of attacks. In: 2009 International Conference of Soft Computing and Pattern Recognition, pp. 212–217 (2009)
28. Shanmugavadivu, R., Nagarajan, N.: Network intrusion detection system using fuzzy logic. Indian J. Comput. Sci. Eng. (IJCSE) 2(1), 101–111 (2001)

29. Strayer, W.T., Lapsely, D., Walsh, R., Livadas, C.: Botnet detection based on network behavior. In: Lee, W., Wang, C., Dagon, D. (eds.) Botnet Detection. Advances in Information Security, vol. 36, pp. 1–24. Springer, Boston (2008). https://doi.org/10.1007/978-0-387-68768-1_1
30. Trauwaert, E.: On the meaning of dunn's partition coefficient for fuzzy clusters. Fuzzy Sets Syst. **25**(2), 217–242 (1988)
31. Yi, L., Shi, Y.: Research on abnormal traffic classification of web camera based on supervised learning and semi-supervised learning. In: 2017 3rd IEEE International Conference on Computer and Communications (ICCC), pp. 547–551 (2017)
32. Zhou, K., et al.: Fuzziness parameter selection in fuzzy c-means: the perspective of cluster validation. Sci. China Inf. Sci. **57**(11), 1–8 (2014)

Enhanced Keystroke Recognition Based on Moving Distance of Keystrokes Through WiFi

Chen Yunfang[1], Zhu Yihong[1], Zhou Hao[2], Chen Wei[1],
and Zhang Wei[1,3(✉)]

[1] Nanjing University of Posts and Telecommunications, Nanjing, China
zhangw@njupt.edu.cn
[2] The Hong Kong Polytechnic University, Hongkong, China
[3] Jiangsu High Technology Research Key Laboratory for Wireless Sensor
Networks, Nanjing, China

Abstract. The increasing credit card consumption makes the security of keypad input become a problem that cannot be ignored. We propose a novel keystroke recognition system called WiKey. When the user enters the password on the keypad with his/her fingers, the posture and position of different keystrokes will introduce a unique interference to the multi-path signals, which can be reflected by the Channel State Information. After analysis of the fluctuation of the CSI waveform between two keystrokes, we find that there is a strong correlation between the distance of finger movement and the shape of the waveform. We exploit the association to infer the user's number input. Compared with the previous approaches of keystroke inference, the use of auxiliary information improves their cognition accuracy. We implemented the WiKey in the normal Point Of Sale. The results of experiment show that the average accuracy rate is about 90%, which are 5–10% higher than the rate of the previous keystroke inference approaches.

Keywords: Channel state information · Wireless security
Keystroke recognition · Auxiliary information

1 Introduction

Keystroke privacy is becoming ever more important in our daily lives. There are three methods to recognize keystrokes in the past, which are acoustic emission, electromagnetic emission and vision. The use of small radio equipment to perceive the surrounding environment is emerging in recent years. Compared to the previous professional equipment, small radio equipment is easy to carry and low cost, and CSI-based keystroke recognition has also become a research hotspot. Since Daniel Halperin [1] introduced the method of acquiring the channel state information (CSI) with Commercial Off-The-Shelf (COTS) WiFi devices, the technology of perception with WiFi devices has been considerably developed. For example, we can use the WiFi signal for more accurate indoor positioning [2–5], human gestures recognition [6–8] or even hearing someone's speaking [9].

© Springer Nature Switzerland AG 2018
M. H. Au et al. (Eds.): NSS 2018, LNCS 11058, pp. 237–250, 2018.
https://doi.org/10.1007/978-3-030-02744-5_18

Imagining that when we are in banks or supermarkets with WiFi, attackers place WiFi devices in a hidden place previously, and only rely on the information collected by these devices to easily recognize the passwords we enter on the point of sale (POS) machine. It is a magical and horrible thing. Now this technology has been implemented, and it is likely to be gradually applied to the factual scenario.

When typing on a keypad, the different posture and position of keystroke can disturb the electromagnetic wave and produce a unique time-series of channel state information. WiFi transceivers can provide enough CSI values to generate CSI waveforms for each keystroke. In the previous research [10, 11], they have exploited CSI to recognize keystroke. The method they used focuses on the waveform of each keystroke, and achieves a high keystroke recognition accuracy, but they ignore fluctuations of the waveform which caused by the finger movement between two keystrokes. If we can take full advantage of it, the keystroke recognition accuracy can be further improved.

In this paper, we examine how to exploit the auxiliary information of the keystroke to improve recognition accuracy. First, we collect and preprocess channel state information, and then we design a keystroke extraction algorithm to extract the keystroke waveform. At the same time, the waveform between two keystrokes will also be recorded. A new keystroke recognition model will be constructed. In the model we will extract the keystroke features to build supported vector machine (SVM) multi-classifier [12] for keystroke recognition. When we have difficulty in recognizing keystroke, the change rule of the CSI waveform caused by finger movement between two keystrokes can be exploited, according to the last keystroke has been recognized, to select the most likely decision by the SVM recognition results. We present a novel system, WiKey.

In the first section, we present a novel keystroke recognition system called WiKey. In the second section, we propose the framework and the process of the system. In the third section, we introduce the CSI acquisition and preprocessing, as well as the extraction of the keystroke features. In the fourth section, we propose an enhanced keystroke recognition algorithm that uses the change rule of the waveform between two keystrokes. In fifth section, the evaluation and real-world experiment are introduced. Finally, the conclusions and future work are given in section six.

2 Framework and Process

Pressing the key in the WiFi environment will have a unique influence on the multi-path signals and generate different CSI time series due to posture and position of different keystrokes. In order to receive all these valuable information, we use the receiver to connect WiFi and receive CSI. The specific environment is shown in Fig. 1.

After receiving the data, we begin to recognize the keystrokes. WiKey system is mainly composed of three parts, as shown in Fig. 2.

The first step is the acquisition and preprocess of CSI signal data. After collecting the channel state information, a series of preprocess operations are performed, including noise removal, anomaly handling and dimension reduction based on principal component analysis. The following step is the extraction of keystroke features. We should extract the keystrokes from the channel state information time series one by one.

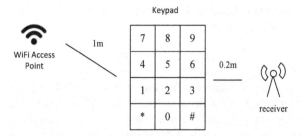

Fig. 1. Logical scene of keystroke recognition

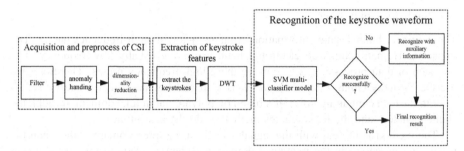

Fig. 2. System architecture of WiKey

Wavelet transform is mainly used to reduce the dimension. The last step is the recognition and identification of the keystroke waveform. Depending on the characteristics of the keystroke waveform, we establish the SVM multi-classifier model to predict the keystroke. When we are in the continuous keystrokes, the finger moves to different areas. Because the movement distance of the finger is different, the keystroke waveform is also different. Through continuous exploration and summary, we found that there are some change rules in the CSI waveform between the two keystrokes, and call it the auxiliary information of the keystroke. When it is very difficult for the classifier to recognize keystrokes, we can use the change rules of waveform caused by the finger movement between the two keystrokes. According to the last keystroke has been recognized, and then we select the most likely keystroke from the identification results of SVM.

3   Preprocess Before Keystroke Recognize

3.1   Collection and Filtering of Signal Data

(1)   Collection of CSI signal

Now WiFi devices supporting IEEE 802.11 standards are mostly composed of multiple antennas. The MIMO channel between each pair of transmitting and receiving antennas comprises a plurality of subcarriers [13]. We can obtain detailed amplitude and phase information of different subcarriers in the form of channel state information. At time t CSI can be accessed as a vector.

$$C = [C_1 \quad C_2 \quad \cdots \quad C_S \quad \cdots C_{30}] \tag{1}$$

C_S is CSI value for subcarriers. The Intel 5300 WiFi NIC can be used to record channel state information. Now the commercial wireless signals transceiver equipment sometimes may lose data packet. The most intuitive result is that the amplitude of CSI signals waveform suddenly changes. After observing the anomalies, they usually occur at the beginning and ending of the CSI waveform. When collecting data for a long time, we can remove abnormal points directly.

(2) Savitzky-Golay filter

The original channel state information contains a lot of high-frequency noise. The impact of Human actions on electromagnetic waves are usually low-frequency. The first step of data processing is to remove these high-frequency noises. Therefore, we use the Savitzky-Golay filter [14], which is a special low-pass filter, mainly used to smooth the data containing noise. It's based on polynomial in time domain, through the sliding window and the least squares method to do the best fitting.

The method is to deal with the signal directly in the time domain, rather than the usual filter processes in the frequency domain and then converts to the time domain, and it can accelerate the signal processing. Compared with other similar smoothing methods, Savitzky-Golay filter can preserve the distribution of the relative maximum, minimum and width.

(3) Dimensionality reduction based on PCA

The data after filtering contain 30 subcarriers. These waveforms are similar and contain noise that low-pass filter cannot remove. Therefore, principal component analysis (PCA) [15] are used. It is mainly used for data dimensionality reduction, through a linear transformation to eliminate the correlation between variables, with fewer variables to explain most of the original data variables. Before PCA, the data need to be standardized, so that each CSI waveform with zero mean and unit variance. According to the experiment, we found that the first four principal components contain major information of sub-carriers, probably more than 90%. The remaining principal components could be considered noise, which we do not need. When the surrounding noise is weak, the first principal component does contain most of the channel state information changes, but when the surrounding noise is strong, the first principal component contains a lot of noise, which is the result we do not want to see. Therefore, we select from the second to the forth component, and these three principal components can replace the original 30 subcarriers. Not only remove the non-stationary noise, but also greatly reduce the amount of data and achieve the purpose of reducing the dimension.

3.2 Extraction of Keystroke Features

(1) extraction of keystroke waveform

In order to extract the CSI waveform of the keystrokes, the channel state information time series need to be split. After applying PCA on the CSI time series, the principal components from the second to the forth between each pair of transmitting and receiving antennas can be expressed as $C^{2:4}$.We use a moving window approach, calculate MAD and make modifications to find the starting and ending points. The algorithm [11] based on MAD is used to extract the keystroke waveform from the CSI time series.

(2) feature extraction based on DWT

After the keystroke waveform is extracted, each waveform is about 500 samples. Select these keystroke waveforms as the appropriate features for keystroke recognition. But if we use them directly, the quantity of data will be huge and inevitably affect the efficiency of the algorithm. Therefore, we will use discrete wavelet transform (DWT). DWT can not only effectively compress the data, but also get rid of high-frequency noise. DWT decomposes the signal at different scales. We use the DWT based on Daubechies D4 wavelet three times, and only keep the approximate component. Appling DWT three times, not only retain enough keystroke information that can be used to recognize the keystroke, but also greatly compress the amount of data.

4 Enhanced Keystroke Recognition and Inference

In the process of keystroke recognition, the CSI time series waveforms of different keystrokes are used as the characteristics, and establish the classifier model with SVM multi-classifier. SVM multi-classifier training is carried out by the keystroke waveform in the training set and tries to find the most optimal parameter δ and the best penalty factor c; Data in the testing set are used to test the accuracy of the classification device. The total 18 waveforms from each keystroke can be used to identify the keystroke. We can select majority of the results as the result. Sometimes SVM multi-category identification may occur two or more keys are evenly matched so that we cannot accurately determine the result. Then, we can use the enhanced keystroke recognition for further inference.

4.1 The Observation of the Waveform Between Two Keystrokes

When we strike on the keypad continuously, the entire process of keystroke can actually be expressed as "strike key - move hand - next strike" continuous cycle. The waveform of the continuous keystroke changes as showed in Fig. 3, not only the waveforms of the keystroke in slice 1, 3, 5 are obvious, but also the waveforms between the two keystrokes in slice 2, 4 are clear as well. In the past, the keystroke waveform was viewed as a research object and we often overlooked the waveform which is caused by finger movement between two keystrokes.

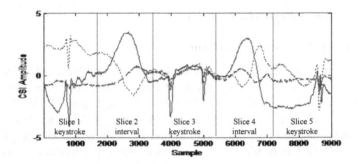

Fig. 3. CSI waveforms of continuous keystrokes

After several experiments, it was found that the difference in the distance of the finger movement would also lead to different changes in the waveform, and the finding would help identify keystroke better. By observing the waveforms generated by the different distance of finger movement, we gradually find some rules.

4.2   Keystroke Waveform Characteristics Based on Moving Distance

Between the two keystrokes, due to the different distance of finger movement, it will cause the waveform to change differently. In order to further observe its changes, we utilize the number 1 as the starting key, and then strike the other keys. After studying hundreds of the interval of the two keystrokes, we find some rules. Based on the distance between each key and the number key 1, the keypad is divided into three areas, as showed in Fig. 4, yellow, green and blue areas. Finger moves from the number key 1 to the button in three areas and the waveform changes have their own characteristics.

7	8	9
4	5	6
1	2	3
*	0	#

7	8	9
4	5	6
1	2	3
*	0	#

7	8	9
4	5	6
1	2	3
*	0	#

Fig. 4. The different areas of keystrokes (Color figure online)

- If the two keystrokes are same, pressing the number 1 twice: the waveform between the two keystrokes changes gently, as showed in Fig. 5(a) and (b).
- If the next key is the number 2 or 4 in the yellow area, which is a short distance movement: waveform changes as shown in Fig. 5(c) and (d). The waveform directly goes up or down, and then tends to smooth which is similar to the letter l and is called l-type.

- If the next key is the number 0, 3, 5 or 7 in the green area, which is the middle distance movement: the waveform changes are shown in Fig. 5(e) and (f). At least one principal component waveform goes up or down and generates an observable peak. The shape is similar to the letter u or n, called the U-type.
- If the next key is the number 6, 8 or 9 in the blue area, that is, the long distance movement: the waveform changes are shown in Fig. 5(g) and (h). At least one principal component waveform will have two or more obvious peaks, which is similar to the transverse letter s or z, called the S-type.

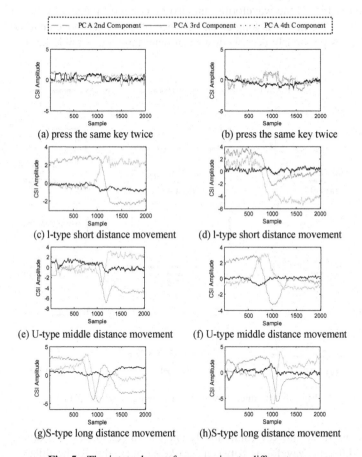

Fig. 5. The interval waveform moving to different areas

Using the number key 1 as the start key, and press the other keys. On the keypad, number 2, 4 are the closest to 1, number 0, 3, 5, 7 are rank second, and number 6, 8, 9 farthest. These three kinds of different distance length, respectively, corresponding to the three different shapes of the waveform. It can be obviously seen from these three types that the more distant the finger moving, the waveform changes are more complex.

So there is a problem, since the number keys from the number 1 to other numbers have this law, will this law apply to other keys?

For the waveform changes generated by the movement of the equivalent distance on the keypad, we identify and make statistics. Each kind of distance has approximately 100 keystroke intervals to be identified, with an average accuracy rate of 92.5%. For example, 1 to 2, 4 to 5, 7 to 8, the moving distance of the finger is the same, and they are all short distance movement. In Fig. 6(a), (b), (c), we can clearly see that the waveform changes can be judged as l-type. We also compare the waveform of the middle-distance and long-distance movement in the Fig. 6(d), (e), (f) and (h), (i), (j). As showed in Fig. 6, the waveforms can also be correctly judged. So this rule can be extended to all the keys. As long as the distance of the finger movement meets one of the three cases previously described, we can determine the possible keys.

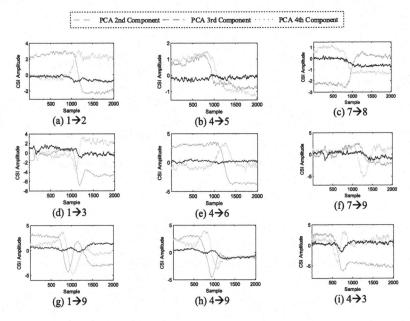

Fig. 6. The interval waveform moving different distance

When we strike the key continuously and the finger moves to a different area, it produces different waveforms between two keystrokes, due to the different distance. The rule of waveform between two keystrokes is called the auxiliary information of keystroke.

4.3   Enhanced Keystroke Recognition with Auxiliary Information

After using SVM multi-classifier identification, the results of keystroke recognition have their own probability. According to the last key, we can re-select the most likely button with auxiliary information as the final keystroke recognition results. The key recognition method with the auxiliary information can be used to identify the keystroke more accurately.

We can simply determine the type of waveform with its shape. By further observation, we can see that S-type waveform has at least two significant peaks, U-type waveform has only one, and l-type does not have. Then we can quickly determine the type of waveform through the number of peaks.

As is showed in Fig. 7, (a) and (d) show the U-type and S-type waveform between two keystrokes. Firstly, we find the local maximum or minimum points A from the waveforms. Extend the fixed length (we use 150 sample points) from A to the left and right, and intersect the waveforms with point B and C. We respectively calculate the difference between B, C and A on the vertical axis, and denoted as $\Delta y1$ and $\Delta y2$. Compare the smaller difference with threshold k. If the difference exceeds k, local extreme points can be determined as the peak. The reason for setting the threshold k is that some points are local extreme points, but $\Delta y1$ and $\Delta y2$ are not all greater than threshold k. It is possible that the left or right fluctuation of the extreme point is not obvious. The point 1 in Fig. 7(a) is a local extreme point, but the left fluctuation of the extreme point $\Delta y1$ is significantly small. Therefore, it cannot be seen as a peak. All local extreme points should be further judged to determine the type of waveform according to the number of peaks.

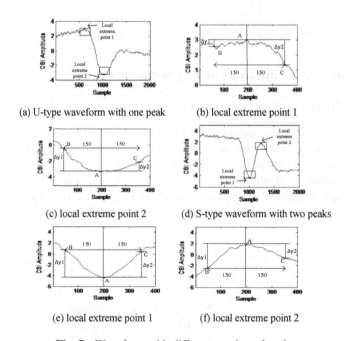

(a) U-type waveform with one peak

(b) local extreme point 1

(c) local extreme point 2

(d) S-type waveform with two peaks

(e) local extreme point 1

(f) local extreme point 2

Fig. 7. Waveform with different number of peaks

In the enhanced keystroke recognition method, the CSI time series waveforms of different keystrokes are extracted as the feature of keystroke, and we use the SVM multi-classifier for the initial recognition. If the result of SVM multi-classification is not ideal and cannot be correctly identified, we will re-select the probable likely number key with auxiliary information. The use of auxiliary information cannot have precise identification results, but can effectively narrow the scope of possible keys, and improve the accuracy of keystroke recognition. The flow chart of enhanced keystroke recognition is shown in Fig. 8.

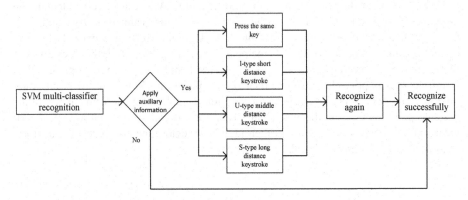

Fig. 8. The flow chart of enhanced keystroke recognition

5   Results and Evaluation of Experiments

5.1   The System Environment Setup

WiKey uses WiFi hardware devices, which is a Lenovo X200 laptop with an Intel 5300 wireless network card. The wireless network card is used as a receiver and connected to three antennas of the laptop. The system operation of the X200 laptop is Ubuntu 11.04, and it is installed the modified wireless driver to receive channel status information. The X200 laptop is placed on the right side of the keypad at a distance of 20 cm, and the distance between router and keypad is about 1 m, as showed in Fig. 9.

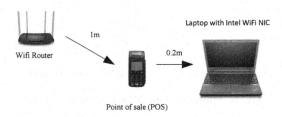

Fig. 9.   Scene of keystroke recognition

WiKey uses the WiFi router to send internet control message protocol(ICMP) ping packet, and makes the sample rate of CSI is about 800 packets/s. Our experiment requires 10 volunteers, and they all use their right hand to press the button. Each volunteer will enter the disrupted 0 to 9 digital sequence for 10 times.

5.2 Preprocessing and Feature Extraction

(1) Preprocess of CSI

After receiving CSI, we use a filter to remove noise. The initial CSI waveform has 30 subcarriers. Figure 10(a) shows the original CSI time series of the first subcarrier, and Fig. 10(b) shows the waveform after using the filter. By comparing the initial waveform with the waveform after filtering, the filter removes most of the high frequency noise. The initial 30 subcarriers are showed in Fig. 10(c). We use PCA to decrease the dimension, and select 3 principal components to replace the original 30 subcarriers. Figure 10(d) shows the three principal component waveforms after PCA.

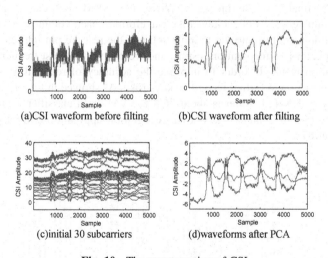

(a)CSI waveform before filting   (b)CSI waveform after filting

(c)initial 30 subcarriers   (d)waveforms after PCA

Fig. 10. The preprocessing of CSI

(2) Feature extraction

It is necessary to extract the waveform of the individual keystroke from the CSI time series. We calculate the MAD of the time series, and use the keystroke extraction algorithm to find out the approximate start and end points of each keystroke. The length of keystroke waveform is about 500 sample points, and the keystroke waveform is shown in Fig. 11(a). After the keystroke waveform is extracted, we use the DWT based on Daubechies D4 (four coefficients per filter) wavelet three times. The transformed waveform is showed in Fig. 11(b).

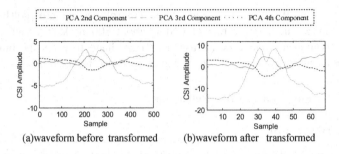

(a)waveform before transformed   (b)waveform after transformed

Fig. 11. Discrete wavelet transform before and after

5.3 Result Analysis of Keystroke Recognition

We build classifier with the transformed keystroke waveform. In the past paper, the KNN (k-nearest neighbor) classifier model is utilized and obtains a decision from each classifier in the example. The majority voting on the decisions of KNN classifier is selected as the final result. In this paper, WiKey uses SVM multi-classifier model. We recruit 10 volunteers and collect keystroke waveform of each volunteer from number 0 to 9. Half of data are put into the training set, and the rest are put into the testing set. Each keystroke has 18 recognition results, and we choose the most frequent key value as a recognition result. In order to improve the accuracy of recognition, we use the auxiliary information to further recognize keystroke. As showed in Fig. 12, the average accuracy rate of KNN classifier is about 76.8%, SVM multi-classifier is about 82.5%. The accuracy rate of enhanced keystroke recognition applying auxiliary information reaches about 87.1%.

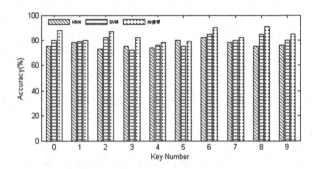

Fig. 12. The accuracy rate of keystroke recognition

5.4 Keystroke Recognition Towards POS Machine

The conventional protection for keystroke only uses shelters, but the spread of wireless signals has a strong ability of penetration. WiFi has the natural advantages that the visual method does not have. We apply this system to the POS machine in the bank, and make the system more practical and flexible. When hearing the indication voice, volunteers begin pressing the key and CSI is collected at the same time. We choose 6-digit password and use the enhanced keystroke recognition model. WiKey lists the possible 6-digit keystroke sequence.

The more the training data we have, the higher the accuracy rate of keystroke recognition is. We press the number key from 0–9 as a training loop. Figure 13 shows the relationship between the training loop and the accuracy of the keystroke recognition. When the training loop is 10, the average accuracy of the keystroke recognition reaches 88.5%.

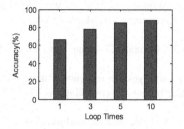
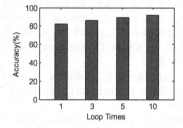

Fig. 13. Accuracy rate and training loop   **Fig. 14.** Accuracy rate and test loop

If we can get enough training data and user's 6-digit password keystroke sequences which can be called test loops, WiKey will predict the keystroke based on possibility. Figure 14 shows the accurate rate with the test loop increasing.

If WiKey can get enough training and test data, the accuracy rate of keystroke recognition reaches 90.1%.

6   Conclusion and Future Work

In this paper, we design the WiKey for the keystroke recognition of the ordinary POS machine. Experiment shows that WiKey can have a great performance with adequate training and testing data. Compared with the previous method that utilizes CSI waveform to recognize keystroke, the enhanced keystroke recognition helps us further improve the accuracy rate. We not only make full use of the keystroke waveform, but also the waveform between two keystrokes which caused by the finger movements. Now the WiKey only recognizes the keystroke for a single person. Because the CSI waveform is very sensitive for the change of action, it is necessary not to do additional action when collecting CSI. In future we will examine how to further improve the accuracy rate of keystroke recognition when there is interference in the surrounding environment.

Acknowledgements. The authors would like to thank the reviewers for their insight and comments on this paper. This work was supported by the National Natural Science Foundation of China (Grant No. 61272422 and 61202353).

References

1. Halperin, D., Wenjun, H., Shethy, A., Wetherall, D.: Tool release: gathering 802.11n traces with channel state information. ACM SIGCOMM Comput. Commun. Rev. **41**(1), 53 (2011)
2. Wang, Y., Liu, J., Chen, Y., Gruteser, M., Yang, J., Liu, H.: E-eyes: device-free location-oriented activity identification using fine-grained WiFi signatures. In: MobiCom 2014, September 7–11, 2014, Maui, Hawaii, USA, pp. 617–628. ACM (2014)
3. Zeng, Y., Pathak, P.H., Xu, C., Mohapatra, P.: Your AP knows how you move: fine-grained device motion recognition through WiFi. In: HotWireless 2014, September 11, 2014, Maui, Hawaii, USA (2014)
4. Wang, W., Liu, A.X., Shahzad, M., et al.: Understanding and modeling of WiFi signal based human activity recognition. In: International Conference on Mobile Computing and NETWORKING, pp. 65–76. ACM (2015)
5. Adib, F., Katabi, D.: See through walls with WiFi! Comput. Commun. Rev. **43**(4), 75–86 (2013)
6. Pu, Q., Gupta, S., Gollakota, S., et al.: Whole-home gesture recognition using wireless signals. In: International Conference on Mobile Computing & Networking, pp. 27–38. ACM (2013)
7. Wang, W., Liu, A.X., Shahzad, M., Ling, K., Lu, S.: Understanding and modeling of WiFi signal based human activity recognition. In: MobiCom 2015, September 7–11, 2015, Paris, France, pp. 65–76. ACM (2015)
8. Abdelnasser, H., Harras, K.A., Youssef, M.: WiGest demo: a ubiquitous WiFi-based gesture recognition system. In: IEEE Infocom 2015 Live/Video Demonstration, pp. 17–18 (2015)
9. Wang, G., Zou, Y., Zhou, Z., Wu, K., Ni, L.M.: We can hear you with Wi-Fi! In: MobiCom 2014, September 7–11, 2014, Maui, Hawaii, USA, pp. 593–604 (2014)
10. Li, M., Meng, Y., Liu, J., et al.: When CSI meets public WiFi: inferring your mobile phone password via WiFi signals. In: ACM SIGSAC Conference, pp. 1068–1079. ACM (2016)
11. Ali, K., Liu, A.X., Wang, W., et al.: Keystroke recognition using WiFi signals. In: International Conference on Mobile Computing and Networking, pp. 90–102. ACM (2015)
12. Chen, P.H., Lin, C.J., Scholkopf, B.: A tutorial on v-support vector machines. Appl. Stoch. Models Bus. Ind. **21**(2), 111–136 (2005)
13. Halperin, D., Wenjun, H., Sheth, A., Wetherall, D.: 802.11 with multiple antennas for dummies. ACM SigComm. Comput. Commun. Rev. **40**(1), 19–25 (2010)
14. Schafer, R.W.: What is a Savitzky-Golay filter? IEEE Signal Process. Mag. **28**(4), 111–117 (2011)
15. Shlens, J.: A tutorial on principal component analysis. **51**(3), 219–226 (2014)

Analyzing the Communication Security Between Smartphones and IoT Based on CORAS

Motalib Hossain Bhuyan, Nur A. Azad, Weizhi Meng[(✉)], and Christian D. Jensen

Department of Mathematics and Computer Science, Technical University of Denmark, Lyngby, Denmark
{s155372,s162426}@student.dtu.dk, weme@dtu.dk

Abstract. The exponential growth of Internet-of-Things (IoT) devices and applications may expose tremendous security vulnerabilities in practice, as there are different protocols in the application layer to exchange sensor data, e.g., MQTT, AMQP, CoAP. For the MQTT protocol, IoT devices would publish a plain message that could potentially cause loss of data integrity and data stealing. Motivated by this, we first present a risk assessment on the communication channel between smartphones and IoT using the method of CORAS, which is a model-based security risk analysis framework. Then the paper analyzes several known cryptographic methods and mechanisms to identify which cryptography solution best fits resource constrained IoT devices. Further, we discuss appropriate cryptographic algorithms that can help protect data integrity between smartphones and IoT.

Keywords: Network security · Risk assessment · CORAS
Internet-of-Things · Smartphone security · Data integrity

1 Introduction

The current cyber-physical world is building on top of IoT devices and the relevant applications in healthcare, military, and environmental monitoring. Regarding IoT, lots of devices, sensors, actuators are connected through complex networks. They continuously collect and exchange a huge amount of data over the cloud and public network. There exist a lot of challenges such as routing, data transmission, data aggregation and tempering, resource utilization and so on. As a result, the security has become more demanding and challenging due to the heterogeneous nature of IoT devices.

In IoT, there are different techniques may be employed to fulfill the security requirements in sensing applications, and each of them has advantages and drawbacks. In general, the particularities and limitations of IoT sensor networks will dictate what the most appropriate approaches for security protection are. The primary defense mechanism is often based on cryptographic algorithms, but

M. H. Au et al. (Eds.): NSS 2018, LNCS 11058, pp. 251–265, 2018.
https://doi.org/10.1007/978-3-030-02744-5_19

IoT nodes suffer from resource constraints in the aspects of processor, memory and energy consumption. These constraints provide enormous challenges for IoT applications. On the other hand, in a short-distance environment, there are many other kinds of threats such as spoofing, message altering, replay attack, flooding, etc.

To protect nodes from these threats and vulnerabilities, cryptography is the fundamental solution [6,9]. There are two kinds of cryptography algorithms: symmetric and asymmetric. Both approaches have their pros and cons; thus, the use of cryptographic approaches depends on the application and infrastructure of the deployed network or system.

Focusing on this issue, in this work, we conducted a risk assessment to identify critical assets, threats, the likelihood of attack, and the consequences on the communication channel between smartphones and IoT, based on CORAS. It is a model-based security risk analysis framework for risk assessment. It also provides a UML-based tool to document, maintain and report the result from the risk modeling. After identifying all possible risks, we prioritized them and selected the most important one (i.e., plain-text data publishing) for effective treatment in this paper. Also, we developed an Android application where the cryptographic method is deployed to secure the communication channel between smartphones and IoT, which can work with SSL/TLS. Then, we provided a comparative analysis of several symmetric and asymmetric key algorithms, based on encryption time, decryption time and throughput. In particular, the symmetric approach was used for payload encryption; whereas asymmetric approach was used for key exchange. To provide data integrity, hash-based message authentication code (HMAC) was used along with encryption.

Paper Organization. In Sect. 2, we introduce the basic concept of risk management and analyze our target system using CORAS, which is a model-based security risk analysis framework. Section 3 details our experimental settings and results on different cryptography algorithms. We make a discussion in Sect. 4 and review some related work in Sect. 5. Finally, we conclude our work in Sect. 6.

2 Risk Management

The risk management helps make a balance between the operative cost and financial costs of defensive measures and the gain achieved by protecting the IT systems. According to [2,3], risk management consists of three processes such as risk assessment, risk mitigation, and evaluation-assessment. IT-security risk assessment is a process that identifies critical assets, threats, the likelihood of attack, and the consequences on the IoT system. There are a few methods or standards out there for risk assessment (discussed in related work section), but we assess risk in our project based on CORAS. It is a model-based security risk analysis framework for risk assessment. The CORAS also provides a UML-based tool to document, maintain and report the result from the risk modeling.

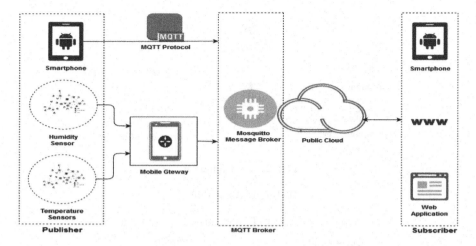

Fig. 1. High level system overview

2.1 Introductory Meeting

The method of the security analysis and the scope of the assessment are presented in the introductory meeting. The goal is to define the scope and the high-level overview of the system. The limitation of the assessment is also discussed and agreed upon the focus of the assessment. In this paper, we mainly focus on performing a risk assessment on our target system (see Fig. 1) and discussing several common attacks against particular vulnerabilities. Our risk assessment targets on the communication channel between smartphone (publisher) to message broker and message broker to a smartphone (subscriber). Another communication channel between two smartphones is also considered. It is worth noting that the rest of communication channels, e.g., from sensors to gateway and gateway to the broker, are out of the scope.

2.2 High-Level Analysis

The purpose of the second step is to classify assets (direct and indirect) and get an outline of the main risks. We identify our assets as shown in Fig. 2. There are six assets in our system in total, four out of them are direct and the rest two are indirect assets.

The direct assets are sensor data, cryptographic key, mobile device, and sensor nodes. On the other hand, indirect assets are IoT service and trust on IoT service. An unwanted incident has a direct effect on direct asset whereas indirect assets are harmed only if one of the direct assets is affected. For example in Table 1, the attacker can temper or sniff the plaintext message which directly affects the sensitive sensor data. Thus the users lose the trust in IoT service which is our indirect asset.

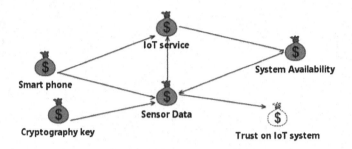

Fig. 2. Asset diagram

Table 1. Asset table

Asset	Importance	Type of asset
Sensor data	1	Direct
Cryptographic key	1	Direct
IoT service	2	Indirect
Mobile device	2	Direct
Trust on IoT	2	Indirect
Sensor node	3	Direct

2.3 Approval of Risk Analysis

As per our target system and identified assets, we agree on the common understanding of risk analysis of the system. All identified asset that is in the scope of the risk assessment should be ranked according to the importance of the system. The consequence and likelihood scale of each asset is set. There are different ways to calculate likelihood and consequence, but in this paper, we define the likelihood based on the group discussion as shown in Tables 2 and 3. We also discuss and set risk evaluation criteria for each asset.

In this step, we categorize risks that are acceptable and those need further evaluation. To do so, we rank all the assets according to their significance in Table 1. Here we rank all the risks between 1 to 5 based on their importance: 1 means the most important assets whereas 5 means the least important

Table 3 shows the defined likelihood scale that will be used for all scenarios and cases in this paper. The combined likelihood values can also be derived based on this scale (which will be discussed later).

We identify all the incidents in Fig. 3 that are not desired in the target system which includes the following:

- Unwanted data publishing (UP)
- Integrity loss of message (IM)
- Data stealing (DS)
- Confidentiality of Data CD)
- Service Interruption (SI)

Table 2. Consequence scale for 'sensor data'

Level of consequences	Descriptions
Catastrophic	10000+ sensor data (SDs) are affected
Major	1000–10000 SDs are affected
Moderate	100–1000 SDs are affected
Minor	1–100 SDs are affected
Insignificant	No SD is affected

Table 3. Likelihood scale

Level of likelihood	Descriptions
Certain	Fifty times or more per year
Likely	Thirty to fifty times per year
Possible	Ten to thirty times per year
Unlikely	Less than ten per year
Rare	Less than ten per ten year

As discussed earlier, our focused threats in this paper are human deliberate as illustrated in Fig. 3. We can argue that weak authentication, poor key management, the absence of encryption/access control and low bandwidth may compromise the data confidentiality and integrity.

2.4 Risk Identification

In this step, we populate threat diagram in Fig. 3 by depicting two main threats: hacker and eavesdropper. A hacker can get access to the system and steal data, while an eavesdropper may listen and gather information from users' smartphones. If the system has no robust authentication mechanism, an attacker can introduce malicious devices in the network which may result in unwanted data publishing or denial-of-service (DoS) attack. The unwanted data publishing or DoS attack may also happen as a consequence of unauthorized access in the absence of access control. If the devices publish/send a message without encryption, a hacker can temper with data to compromise data confidentiality and integrity. There are also non-human threats like system failure due to power constraint in IoT devices and low bandwidth of internet. These may interrupt data transmission, and as consequence integrity of message could be lost.

2.5 Risk Estimation

In this step, estimation of likelihood values and their consequences should be accomplished. These values determine the risk value which dictates whether the risk is acceptable or not.

For each threat scenario, the likelihood is estimated based on historical data or personal experience. In our case, we have estimated likelihood and consequence by group discussion. This likelihood of the threat scenarios is used to derive the combined likelihood of unwanted incidents. For each unwanted incident-asset relation, consequences are projected. This consequence value is used from the consequence scale of the asset from Sect. 2.3. Figure 3 shows likelihood and consequence for different attack scenarios.

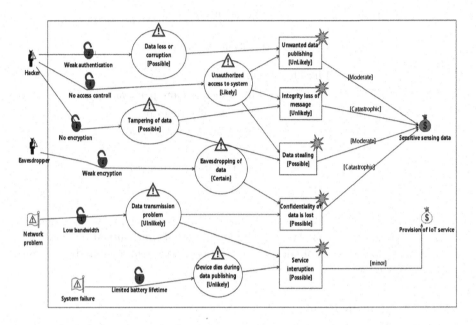

Fig. 3. Threat diagram with likelihood and consequence

2.6   Risk Evaluation

The primary task of the risk evaluation step is to formulate risk matrix. In our case, Table 4 shows the risk evaluation matrix with risk consequence.

There are five unwanted incidents and five risks in our threat diagram model. Since the interruption of service is within the acceptable risk levels, it will not be assessed in the treatment identification. Only SI is acceptable in our case, and the rest require further consideration. This paper mainly focuses on "Integrity loss of Message" and "Data Stealing" for treatment. Due to time and space limitation, our scope is only one of the vulnerabilities (i.e., No Encryption) that causes these incidents. Implementation details of our evaluation are discussed in the subsequent section of this paper.

2.7   Risk Treatment

The final step in security risk analysis is the treatment documentation. The unacceptable risks need to be further evaluated and come up with ideas on

Table 4. Risk evaluation matrix with risks consequence

		Consequence				
		Insignificant	Minor	Moderate	Major	Catastrophic
Likelihood	Rare					
	Unlikely			UP		IM
	Possible		SI	DS		CD
	Likely					
	Certain					

how to minimize them. Before a final treatment plan is made, the cost/benefit analysis should be performed in advance as the treatment can be expensive. The risk treatment procedure mitigates risk by identifying the unacceptable threat and minimizes the value of asset loss. According to the priority of assets and the impact by cost/benefit, we can make a trade-off and choose which risk needs to be mitigated first.

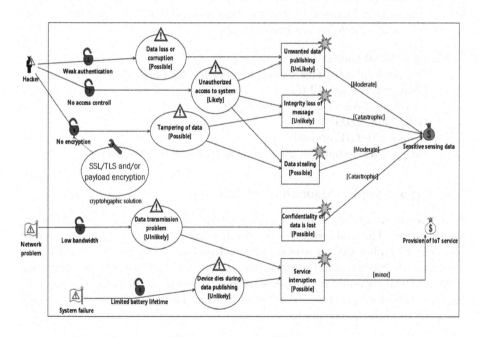

Fig. 4. Treatment diagram

In our scenario, the integrity of sensor data is the most critical asset for the IoT system. The integrity of data can be compromised due to weak authentication and authorization, and the absence of end-to-end encryption. Thus, in our risk treatment scenario, we try to establish a secure channel by implementing the cryptographic algorithms in a proper way. The MQTT can also ensure secure channel using SSL/TLS, but it is expensive for resource constraint IoT devices.

So payload encryption is another choice to establish a secure channel between smartphones and IoT. The overall treatment plan is shown in Fig. 4.

3   Result Analysis

To provide cryptographic solution to ensure data confidentiality and integrity, we firstly have to analyze different algorithms. This experiment focuses on how much time is required to encrypt plaintext to ciphertext for the smartphone we have chosen. Then based on the experimental result, we calculate the throughput for each individual cryptographic algorithms. For competitive performance analysis, the throughput is calculated as follow: dividing the data-size by required-time for operation (encryption and decryption).

3.1   Experimental Setup

The experiment is carried out to find an efficient algorithm for payload encryption and hash-based message authentication code (HMAC). We use the android smartphone with the following configurations:

1. Samsung I9300 Galaxy S III
   - OS: Android 4.0.4 (Ice Cream Sandwich), 4.3 (Jelly Bean)
   - Chipset:Exynos 4412 Quad
   - CPU:Quad-core 1.4 GHz Cortex-A9
   - GPU:Mali-400MP4
   - Memory:16 GB internal
   - Sensor: Accelerometer, gyro, proximity, compass, barometer

3.2   Cryptography Algorithms of Interest

In this work, we mainly consider some well-known cryptographic algorithms in the literature. The evaluation is based on how much time is required to encrypt plaintext to ciphertext on a smartphone. In contrast, the time needed for an algorithm to extract plaintext from the ciphertext is considered as decryption time. The throughput for an operation is calculated dividing the data-size by required time for encryption/decryption action. This derived value is used for competitive performance analysis.

3.3   Symmetric Cryptography Algorithms

The symmetric cryptography is simple and widely used encryption/decryption technique. It is also known as shared key cryptography. For such kinds of algorithms, both sender and receiver would use the identical key.

The performance comparison of symmetric algorithms for encryption operation is shown in Fig. 5. The graph shows that ARC4 performed the best and DES-64 performed the worst in the aspect of encryption operation. The size of

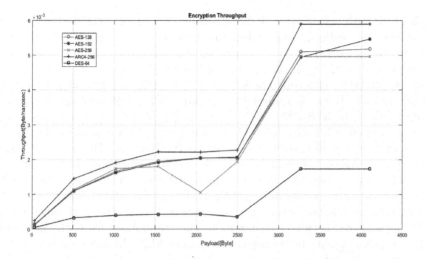

Fig. 5. Encryption throughput

payload varies from 32 bytes to 4096 bytes. The algorithms AES-128, AES-192, and AES-256 also performed close to ARC4 with 256-bit key size. In Fig. 5, it is clear that the encryption throughput of ARC4-256 is the best among other symmetric algorithms.

In the aspect of decryption operation, the performance comparison is made among five different algorithms: AES-128, AES-192, AES-256, ARC4-256, and DES-64. The number on the right indicates the key size. The decryption through-

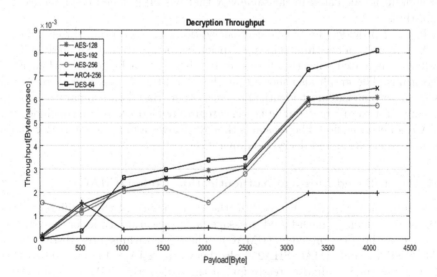

Fig. 6. Decryption throughput

put is linear with data size for all five algorithms (in Fig. 6). The decryption time drastically rises with data size when the data size gets more than 2500 bytes. We need to do further research to get the possible explanation for this behavior. In general ARC4 with the key size of 256 bit reveals the lowest throughput compared to AES with different key sizes (128, 192 and 256 bit). The graph depicts that the decryption throughput is the best for DES with 64-bit key size, which is similar to AES-192.

In a nutshell, DES with a 64-bit key size performed the best for decryption only, and ARC4 performed the best for encryption only. However, AES-128, AES-192, and AES-256 provide moderately steady performance for both encryption and decryption operation. Furthermore, DES and ARC4 are vulnerable to different crypto attacks because of their weak key generation. According to our experimental results and several research papers [15, 16], AES performs the best regarding security, resource-consumption, and throughput for both encryption and decryption operation. We could choose only AES with different key sizes to secure messages, but our another interest is to evaluate the actual performance of ARC4 and DES on a smartphone.

3.4   Asymmetric Encryption

The public key infrastructure is considered to be secured but complex and resource consuming. Asymmetric cryptography solves the problem of secure communication without exchanging private key. Analysis of performance (see Fig. 7) is based on throughput of RSA and ECC (only these two are available in Android API 19) public key cryptography algorithms. The figure illustrates that RSA performs significantly better than ECC (for both encryption and decryption). The throughput is calculated in the same way that has been done for symmetric key algorithms.

Figure 7 provides the behavior of encryption and decryption throughput for RSA and ECC algorithm. The encryption throughput of RSA and ECC is gradually increased with the data size, but RSA has a higher rate than ECC algorithms. The graph also shows that the decryption throughput of RSA and ECC algorithms is almost identical to each other. Based on comparative analysis between two different public key cryptography algorithms, we conclude that RSA is a better choice. The reason is that RSA gives a more stable performance for both encryption and decryption operation.

3.5   Hash-Based Message Authentication Code (HMAC)

To ensure data integrity, we analyze the performance of three different algorithms to calculate hash-based message authentication code or keyed-hash message authentication code (HMAC). These algorithms are: HMAC-MD5, HMAC-SHA1, and HMAC-SHA256 also known as SHA-2. Figure 8 shows that the hashing time is almost steady for all three algorithms. We experiment for different data size ranging from 32 bytes to 4094 bytes. The figure clearly shows that HMAC-256 takes the lowest and HMAC-MD5 takes the highest time for

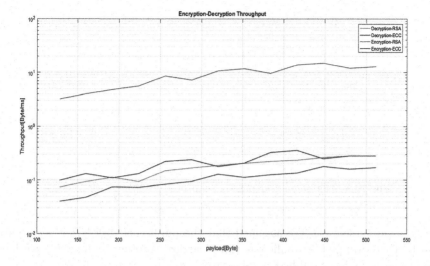

Fig. 7. Throughput: encryption and decryption

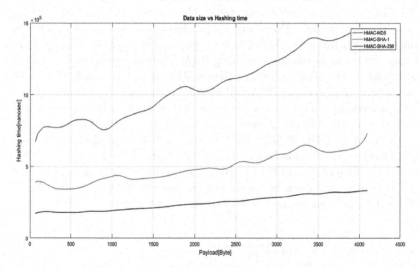

Fig. 8. Hashing times for different data sizes

hashing. Furthermore, due to the collisions detected in MD5 and SHA-1 [5], we suggest to deployed HMACSHA-256 together with payload encryption.

4 Discussion

To ensure data integrity and secure channel between mobile devices, we have tested our proposed solution on a resource-constrained Android phone that acted as an IoT device. This device can sense and transmit data through the public

```
> Internet Protocol Version 4, Src: 192.168.2.3, Dst: 192.168.2.2
> Transmission Control Protocol, Src Port: 43120, Dst Port: 1883,
∨ MQ Telemetry Transport Protocol, Publish Message
   > Header Flags: 0x32 (Publish Message)
     Msg Len: 28
     Topic Length: 6
     Topic: health
     Message Identifier: 3
     Message: HR: 90, BP: 80/110
```

Fig. 9. MQTT plain text message captured by Wireshark software

network infrastructure. We assumed that the public network is not secure and can be eavesdropped by malicious third parties. Another assumption we have made that the proper public key infrastructure (PKI) is in place. We also do not want to deploy SSL/TLS due to limited resource of the device.

To achieve our goal, we need to deploy the cryptographic solution to protect our sensitive sensor data. Based on our previous experiment, we decided to use symmetric algorithms, i.e., AES-256 is for payload encryption. So for secure key exchange, we strongly recommend using RSA. The RSA requires extra resources which could be challenging for IoT device. However, for a smartphone, this is not a massive issue because RSA will be used only once to exchange the key.

The smartphone publishes sensitive sensor data, e.g., heart rate (HR) and blood pressure (BP). Figure 9 shows that the MQTT publish message was captured as plaintext (HR: 90, BP: 80/110) during the transmission. After implementing payload encryption by the symmetric algorithm (AES-256), we observed that the eavesdropper could not be able to get plaintext data anymore. Figure 10 shows that an attacker has to obtain the encryption key to extract information as the MQTT publish message is encrypted (ciphertext).

```
> Internet Protocol Version 4, Src: 192.168.2.3, Dst: 192.168.2.2
> Transmission Control Protocol, Src Port: 36217, Dst Port: 1883, Seq: 61, Ack: 15, Len: 117
∨ MQ Telemetry Transport Protocol, Publish Message
   > Header Flags: 0x32 (Publish Message)
     Msg Len: 115
     Topic Length: 6
     Topic: health
     Message Identifier: 3
     Message: mac: SyOI1VF4vwtLguYejuFR+gnyT5o+/jNVLx8H6ZtgPh0=\n payload: miWgAHvySBKYuOldCN4zV1FUzEvcNDvLY/GG32OJfPg=\n
```

Fig. 10. MQTT encrypted message preceded by mac: captured by Wireshark

For the message integrity, we choose HMAC-SHA-256 that calculates the hash value which is sent along with the encrypted payload. The receiver decrypts the payload and recalculates the hash value. If the two hash values are the same, the receiver assumed the payload is original; otherwise, the message is altered or manipulated by an intruder. Figure 10 shows that the message contains two parts: the first part is a hash value (mac) and the second part is an encrypted payload.

5 Related Work

This section discusses some relevant studies and results that have been done by other researchers. The related efforts are discussed in three subsections as cryptography, IoT protocol and security risk analysis.

5.1 Cryptography

There are various papers available which present a variety of aspects of cryptography. Evaluation of RSA, ElGamal, and Pallier asymmetric encryption algorithms is illustrated in [13]. They showed that the overall performance of RSA is better than ElGamal and Paillier in terms of encryption time, decryption time, throughput, and file size for encryption/decryption.

Another paper [4] has shown an evaluation of several commonly used symmetric key algorithms, e.g., AES, DES, 3DES, RC2, Blowfish, and RC6. The authors of the paper [14] conducted performance evaluation in terms of encryption time and throughput for AES, DES, and 3DES. Their study showed that AES needs less time for execution as compared to the other two.

5.2 Application Layer Protocol

There are a couple of application layer protocols available for communication between IoT devices. In [10], the authors provided a survey on different protocols, e.g., CoAP, MQTT, XMPP, RESTFUL Services, AMQP and WebSockets, and discussed the pros and cons of each protocol.

The authors of the paper [11] claimed that MQTT requires low bandwidth and a small footprint which results in less traffic in network and battery. This is why it is a better choice for smartphone messaging. The paper [12] has researched the performance of MQTT and CoAP. They showed that MQTT experiences smaller delays than CoAP due to lower packet losses.

5.3 Risk Assessment

We got inspiration from [1] to use CORAS for risk assessment in IoT. Risk assessment using the OCTAVE Allegro method has been carried out (in [7]) for security vulnerabilities on IoT-based smart-home environments. The author focused on risk and vulnerabilities of different home appliance IoT system. The risk assessment provides guidelines to mitigate and improve the security baseline of IoT device used at smart-home environments.

6   Conclusion and Future Work

In this paper, we analyze different cryptographic techniques for end-to-end encryption and data integrity. We validated that single cryptographic solution is not suitable for all applications and network infrastructures. Generally, it depends on the design and application of IoT network, as well as the priority of the organization. It is known that encryption can ensure confidentiality and the use of digital signature and hash-based message authentication code (HMAC) can help preserve data integrity. However, if the sensor is collecting and transmitting personal sensitive health data, then it needs a higher level of data privacy and integrity.

If the solution demands a higher level of security, compensation on the resource is obvious. In our experimental settings, payload encryption is recommended, and data exchange in plaintext should be avoided. We also demonstrated a case on how the payload encryption can be used in IoT. When considering security for a controlled environment, the system can use a symmetric algorithm to reduce power consumption, memory load and processing time. To design a secure system in practice, there is a need to consider public key cryptography. However, a proper key management infrastructure is required for both symmetric and asymmetric approaches, especially for key exchange.

In future, we plan to analyze the performance of payload encryption on different application layer protocols in IoT. Through comprehensive evaluation, we will define the most appropriate protocol to build a secure communication channel between smartphones and IoT.

References

1. den Braber, F., Hogganvik, I., Lund, M.S., Stølen, K., Vraalsen, F.: Model-based security analysis in seven steps - a guided tour to the CORAS method. BT Technol. J. 1(25), 101–117 (2007)
2. Stoneburner, G., Goguen, A.Y., Feringa, A.: SP 800–30. Risk management guide for information technology systems. National Institute of Standards & Technology. Gaithersburg, MD, United States (2002)
3. National Standards Authority of Ireland, Risk Management: Risk Assessment Techniques (IEC/ISO 31010:2009 (EQV). Irish standard. National Standards Authority of Ireland (2009)
4. Elminaam, D.S.A., Kader, H.M.A., Hadhoud, M.M.: Performance evaluation of symmetric encryption algorithms. IJCSNS Int. J. Comput. Sci. Netw. Secur. 8(12), 280–286 (2008)
5. Aggarwal, S., Goyal, N., Aggarwal, K.: A review of comparative study of MD5 and SHA security algorithm. Int. J. Comput. Appl. 104(14), 1–4 (2014)
6. Gaubatz, G., Kaps, J.-P., Sunar, B.: Public key cryptography in sensor networks-revisited. Worcester Polytechnic Institute, USA (2004)
7. Ali, B., Awad, A.I.: Cyber and physical security vulnerability assessment for IoT-based smart homes. Sensors 18, 817 (2018)
8. MQTT Security Fundamentals: MQTT Message Data Integrity. https://www.hivemq.com/blog/mqtt-security-fundamentals-mqtt-message-data-integrity

9. IBM, Securing IoT data over the network. https://www.ibm.com/developerworks/library/iot-trs-secure-iot-solutions2/index.html
10. Yassein, M.B., Shatnawi, M.Q., Al-zoubi, D.: Application layer protocols for the Internet of Things: a survey. In: 2016 International Conference on Engineering MIS (ICEMIS), pp. 1–4 (2016)
11. MQTT used by Facebook Messenger. http://mqtt.org/2011/08/mqtt-used-by-facebook-messenger
12. Thangavel, D., Ma, X., Valera, A., Tan, H.X., Tan, C.K.Y.: Performance evaluation of MQTT and CoAP via a common middleware. In: 2014 IEEE Ninth International Conference on Intelligent Sensors, Sensor Networks and Information Processing (ISSNIP) (2014)
13. Farah, S., Javed, M.Y., Shamim, A., Nawaz, T.: An experimental study on performance evaluation of asymmetric encryption algorithms. In: WSEAS 3rd European Conference of Computer Science (WSEAS ECCS 2012) (2012)
14. Mittal, M.: Performance evaluation of cryptographic algorithms. J. Comput. Appl. **41**(7), 1–6 (2012). (0975 – 8887)
15. Ebrahim, M., Khan, S., Khalid, U.B.: Symmetric algorithm survey: a comparative analysis. Int. J. Comput. Appl. **61**(20) (2013)
16. Elbaz, L., Bar-El, H.: Strength assessment of encryption algorithms, pp. 1–14 October 2000

Vulnerability Assessment for Unmanned Systems Autonomy Services Architecture

Yu Li[1], Ivan Frasure[1], Ademola Ayodeji Ikusan[2], Junjie Zhang[1(⊠)], and Rui Dai[2]

[1] Wright State University, Dayton, USA
{li.137,frasure.9,junjie.zhang}@wright.edu
[2] University of Cincinnati, Cincinnati, USA
{ikusanaa,dairi}@ucmail.uc.edu

Abstract. Unmanned Systems Autonomy Services (UxAS) is a set of networked software modules that collaboratively automate mission-level decision making for unmanned systems. Proposed, developed, and publicized by United States Air Force Research Laboratory (U.S. AFRL), UxAS has strong and promising implications in practice and it can be easily extended to support emulation and practical deployment of unmanned aerial vehicles (UAVs). Therefore, performing vulnerability assessment for UxAS is of significant importance. In this project, we first leveraged the threat-driven method to identify security requirements that focus on UxAS' confidentiality, integrity, and availability. Next, we designed and developed fuzz tests to evaluate whether UxAS satisfies these requirements. Our experiments have shown that the current version of UxAS is vulnerable to a variety of attacks such as denial of service, message injection/replay, service self-destruct, and timing-based side-channel attacks. Finally, we studied the root-causes for these vulnerabilities and proposed mitigation strategies.

1 Introduction

Unmanned Systems Autonomy Services (UxAS) [1] is a set of networked software modules that collaboratively automate mission-level decision making for unmanned systems. One of UxAS' design objectives is to enable the testing and integration of new services that enhance the autonomy of unmanned systems. Its bus-based communication backbone (via ZeroMQ) enables the easy integration of new services. However, security threats become a significant concern considering the possibility that untrusted services might be brought into UxAS and the communication between UxAS and unmanned systems is subject to attacks.

Proposed, developed, and publicized by United States Air Force Research Laboratory (U.S. AFRL), UxAS has strong and promising implications in practice considering its open-source nature, a rich body of control and planning algorithms, and its built-in extensibility to incorporate third-party services and tasks. Although it is currently mainly used for simulation and verification, it can be easily extended to support emulation and practical deployment of unmanned

© Springer Nature Switzerland AG 2018
M. H. Au et al. (Eds.): NSS 2018, LNCS 11058, pp. 266–276, 2018.
https://doi.org/10.1007/978-3-030-02744-5_20

aerial vehicles (UAVs). Therefore, performing vulnerability assessment for UxAS is of significant importance. It does not only demonstrate the security flaws in the current implementation of UxAS, but also reveal the general trade-off between security and performance for control systems used in unmanned vehicles.

In this project, we focused on three tasks. First, we leveraged the threat-driven method to identify security requirements that focus on UxAS' confidentiality, integrity, and availability. Next, we designed and developed fuzz tests to evaluate the satisfaction of these requirements. Experimental results have shown these requirements are not met in current UxAS. Specifically, the current version of UxAS is vulnerable to a variety of attacks such as denial of service, message injection/replay, service self-destruct, and timing-based side-channel attacks. Finally, we studied the root-causes for these vulnerabilities and proposed mitigation strategies.

2 Related Work

Security of unmanned control systems is of fundamental importance. Examples include the loss of an RQ-170 Sentinel to Iranian military forces on December 2011 [15] and a keylogging" virus that compromised an U.S. UAV fleet at Creech Air Force Base in Nevada in 2011 [11]. Both practical examples demonstrate that UAV vulnerability can cause a wide range of operation failures.

With the increasing awareness of the UAV security, many intrusion detection approaches have been proposed [2,3,10,14]. These methods focus on monitoring and analyzing UAV behaviors in real-time to detect the hardware failures and anomalies that can impede the accomplishment of pre-defined missions. While these methods are mainly focusing on detecting data injection or manipulation attacks, they cannot detect stealthy attacks such as side-channels and host-based attacks. Other methods focus on enhancing UAV security from a specific aspect. For example, encryption has been introduced to protect communication channels [16]. Researchers have also explored the threat model of a military unmanned aerial vehicle smart device ground control station [9].

Some researchers also proposed simulation testbeds to evaluate the effectiveness of attacks on UAV systems. For example, Javaid et al. [6] designed a UAV simulation platform based onOMNeT++ and used this platform to test jamming attacks and DoS attacks. Rodday et al. [12] demonstrated how to perform man-in-the-middle attacks, and how to inject control commands to interact with the compromised UAV. He et al. [4] reported a low-cost implementation of GPS spoofing attacks or WiFi attacks, together with potential mitigation solutions. Hooper et al. [5] used a fuzzing technique to discover that the Parrot Bebop UAV is vulnerable to buffer overflow attacks during its connection process.

Our work differs from these methods in various ways. First, our work focuses on a novel, collaborative, and cooperative unmanned autonomous system (UAS) control system (i.e., UxAS). It has new features such as a bus-based communication backbone and it can be easily extended to integrate new components. Second, we leverage a systematic solution to identify security requirements, perform fuzz testing, and analyze root causes. Third, we analyze the new attacks such as logic bombs and side-channel attacks to reveal the number of UAVs deployed in the certain area.

3   Background

Unmanned Systems Autonomy Services (UxAS) is a net-centric collection of interacting software modules that aim to collaboratively and cooperatively automate mission-level decision making for unmanned systems such as unmanned aerial vehicles (UAVs). UxAS is developed by United States Air Force Research Laboratory (U.S. AFRL) to evaluate the design of unmanned systems in various aspects such as task assignment, cooperative control, and sensor steering. UxAS has successfully demonstrated its usage in cooperative control, human-machine teaming, and system agility analysis.

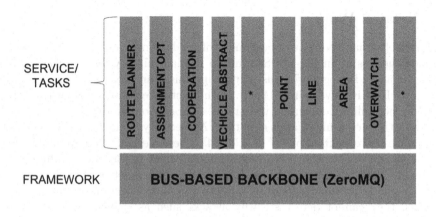

Fig. 1. The architectural overview of UxAS

As illustrated in Fig. 1, UxAS features a bus-based architecture. Specifically, all components interact with each other by sending and receiving messages through a bus-based communication backbone, which is currently implemented using ZeroMQ. Components can be classified into two categories including services and tasks. Services expose common functionalities such as planning, vehicle coordinating, and tracking necessary data; they are designed to be independent and stateless when possible. Tasks represent specific scenarios of using one or multiple services, where popular examples include area search, line search, and blockade. UxAs supports the integration of third-party tasks to enrich its capabilities. In other words, new services and tasks can be easily integrated into this framework thanks to the bus-based communication backbone.

While UxAS focuses on control and planning, the actual unmanned vehicle is currently based on a simulator named the AVTAS Multi-Agent Simulation Environment (a.k.a. AMASE). AMASE interacts with UxAS using messages exchanged through ZeroMQ. It is capable of simulating various factors of UAS such as navigation, sensing, target tracking, and visualization.

4   Security Requirement Analysis

Threat Model: Since UxAS is designed to integrate third party services and tasks, our threat model considers the possibility that a third party module is malicious. In addition, the communication channel between UxAS and the UAV, despite its current dependency on host-based ZeroMQ implementation, will be most likely to leverage existing network infrastructures such as the WiFi, local area networks, and even Internet. As a result, it is extremely challenging for UxAS to verify the trustworthiness of its communication channel. In other words, our threat model considers attackers' attempts to eavesdrop, inject, and jam the communication channel. However, we assume all built-in components and the underlying communication infrastructures are trustworthy. Figure 2 visualizes the threat model.

Threat-Driven Security Requirement Analysis: We use the attack tree [13] to model how security properties could be contaminated in UxAS. Figure 3 visualizes the attack tree we have derived. We traverse this attack tree to identify the security requirements. Specifically, the effective countermeasure against the attack in each node becomes a requirement. When closer to the root, the requirement is more generic and abstract; a requirement for a leaf node represents a concrete and implementable requirement. Table 1 presents the security requirements that will ensure the availability of the UxAS ZeroMQ backbone. The first column of the table is the requirement ID, the second is the requirement ID of the upper-level identification (i.e., to trace back to a more generic requirement), and the third column is the requirement statement. Specifically, the "SR3" requirement is the general requirement to protect the availability of the ZeroMQ backbone. The "SR4" and "SR5" requirements represent the specific requirements to detect injected messages and detect replayed messages, respectively.

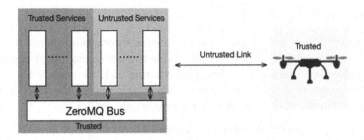

Fig. 2. Threat model

5   Security Testing

In order to evaluate the extent to which UxAS meets the proposed security requirements, we have developed a series of fuzz tests. These tests target at all three aspects of security properties including availability, integrity, and confidentiality.

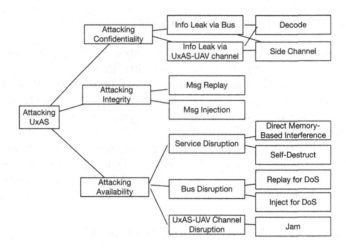

Fig. 3. Attack tree

Table 1. Security requirements for the availability of the ZeroMQ channel

ID	Trace	Requirement
SR3	[Problem]	UxAS communication channels shall always be available to intended users
SR4	SR3	UxAS shall filter out noisy data from communication channels
SR5	SR3	UxAS shall detect the authenticity of incoming messages
SR6	SR5	UxAS shall detect if an actor resends an old message

5.1 Availability Test

As the availability of UxAS relies on the proper interaction among all components, disrupting critical resources that enable the inter-component communication will effectively paralyze UxAS. Towards this end, we designed and implemented two types of attacks including a DoS attack against the bus-based communication channel and a self-destructing malicious service.

DoS Against The Bus-Based Backbone. UxAS employs ZeroMQ to build its bus-based inter-service network backbone. Specifically, each service or task will establish a TCP connection with the ZeroMQ component and subscribe to certain types of messages. Once a service (or a task) publishes a message to the ZeroMQ component, ZeroMQ will first cache this message and then push this message to all services that subscribe to this type of this message. Therefore, the ZeroMQ backbone represents a single point of failure for the entire system. We hence test the availability of the ZeroMQ backbone when a large number of messages are published in a short time period. Specifically, we have implemented a malicious service to perform such attack. We have tested two types of messages including (i) ill-formatted messages and (ii) legitimate messages compatible with pre-defined formats.

The ZeroMQ backbone should immediately discard *ill-formatted messages*. However, ZeroMQ, as a generic, application-agnostic communication channel, relies on end points to verify the correctness of messages. As a consequence, the ZeroMQ component caches all messages regardless of the correctness of their formats. The test shows that the ZeroMQ-based communication channel crashes when it receives a large number of ill-formatted messages from the malicious service. In addition, the ZeroMQ channel is also vulnerable to a large amount of *well-formatted messages* sent during a very short time period (e.g., a DoS attack based on well-formatted messages).

Self-destructing Logic Bomb. A malicious service might self-destruct in order to introduce collateral damage to the entire UxAS. Such self-destruction could be comprised of sophisticated programs/conditions (a.k.a. logic bombs) to intro-duce significant challenges to detection such as impeding static and dynamic program analysis. We have designed a self-destructing logic bomb. The self-destruction capability of this logic bomb is materialized by memory segmenta-tion faults and the logic condition is a combination of timing and the number of messages observed through the bus-based communication. These two conditions may introduce great challenges to static and dynamic analysis.

This attack exploits the fact that all services, tasks, and other libraries are executed in the same memory address space. As a result, the abortion of a maliciously- or poorly-engineered service will terminate the entire system. Figure 4 presents the consequence of this attack.

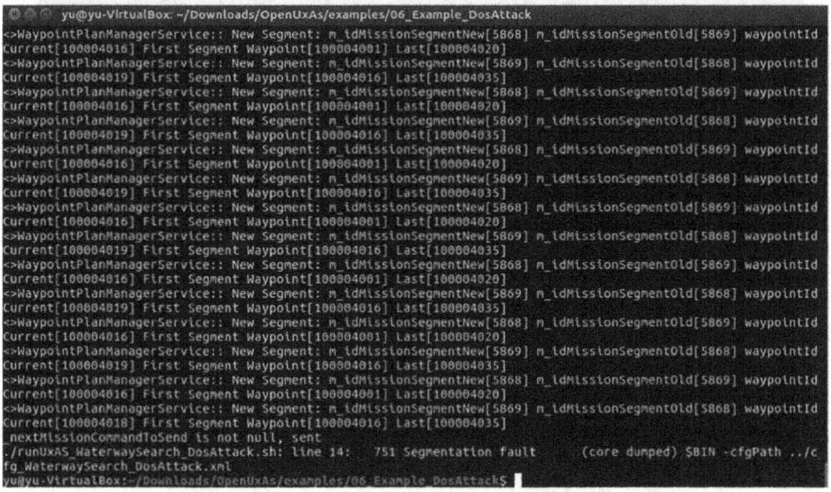

Fig. 4. Self-destructing logic bomb terminates UxAS using segmentation fault

5.2 Integrity Test

A malicious service can replay a captured message (without decrypting or decoding it); it can also fabricate a new one and inject it into the communication channel. All these activities compromise system integrity. We designed two tests to evaluate how UxAS reacts to such attacks.

Message Replay. We design a malicious service to sniff MissionCommand Messages, where MissionCommand messages are used to carry segments of paths an UAV should follow. Once a MissionCommand Message arrives, our malicious service will immediately replay it to the ZeroMQ channel. Since the next authentic MissionCommand message is sent at the completion of current one, the replayed message will arrive before the authentic one. Our testing results show that the replayed message can successfully mislead the UAV. Specifically, the UAV repeats the path that is contained in the original route indicated in the original MissionCommand Message.

Message Injection. We have designed a malicious service capable of fabricating MissionCommand messages and then injecting them into the ZeroMQ backbone. The fabricated MissionCommand message contains waypoints of a manipulated path. Our testing results show that once the fabricated message is received and processed by the UAV, the UAV deviates from the expected path and starts to follow the path indicated in the fabricated message. As indicated in Fig. 5, the green line represents a river that the UAV is expected to traverse along; the blue line represents the actual path the UAV follows after it is misled.

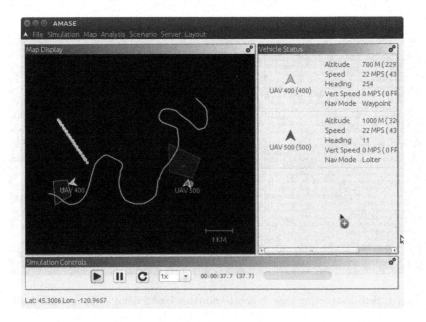

Fig. 5. The UAV misled by fabricated messages

5.3   Confidentiality Test

UxAS should never leak sensitive information to untrusted parties. However, since UxAS has not adopted any encryption method to protect its messages, all messages are exchanged in plaintext. As a result, anyone who has access to messages can extract sensitive information. Examples include malicious services that subscribe to messages and attackers who sniff on the communication channel between UxAS and the UAV, where they can extract sensitive information. Nevertheless, we expect leakage through plaintext can be addressed by encryption. Therefore, our test focuses on side-channel-based information leakage. We consider the scenario in which attackers can sniff messages exchanged between UxAS and the UAV. While the plaintext is unavailable because of encryption, packets' timing information is readily accessible to attackers [8].

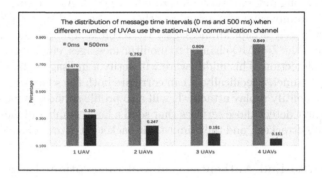

Fig. 6. Correlation between inter-packet delays and the number of UAVs

Our test explores the correlation between inter-packet delays and the number of UAVs controlled by UxAS. Specifically, we consider the distribution of time intervals between two consecutive packets when different numbers of UAVs are under control. We have experimentally derived the distribution of time intervals in two bins including [0 ms, 500 ms) and [500 ms, ∞) when the number of UAVs grows from 1 to 4, which is presented in Fig. 6. The experimental results demonstrate a high level of correlation between packets' timing and the number of UAVs. It's a strong indication that attackers can easily infer the number of UAVs from the timing-based side channel.

6   Root-Cause Analysis and Mitigation Strategies

Based on the analysis of the test results, we have concluded the root causes of UxAS vulnerabilities and proposed the mitigation solutions. The architecture with built-in mitigation solutions is presented in Fig. 7.

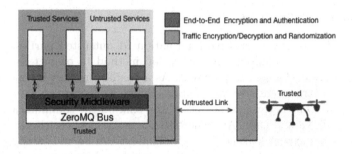

Fig. 7. UxAS with mitigation strategies

Incomplete Mediation: UxAS lacks a mechanism to monitor and mediate the interactions among different services through ZeroMQ. As a result, an arbitrary service can send any type of message to other services and the ZeroMQ channel will indiscriminately accept all messages. We recommend a middleware between all services and the ZeroMQ channel to monitor messages, enforce access control, and perform detection. This middleware will verify a message before it is sent to the ZeroMQ channel. Specifically, it can correlate both the source and the type of a message to identify replay attacks. It will also profile services' message-sending activities to first detect those services that send a large number of messages (e.g., a possible DoS attacker), and then limit their packet rates to protect the ZeroMQ channel.

Lack of End-to-End Authentication and Encryption: There is no mechanism currently in UxAS to support the verification of the authenticity and integrity of messages. While the aforementioned middleware can partially solve the authentication challenge, a fundamental solution is to integrate public/private keys in UxAS to assure authentication, encryption, and integrity for all messages.

No Inter-Service Isolation: All services operate in the same address space currently in UxAS. Therefore, the malfunction of one service, no matter intentionally or accidentally, will directly affect the operation of other services. The complete isolation of memory space for services should be enforced. For example, each service could be implemented as an individual process and it therefore has separated memory space. A more ambitious solution is to run each service in a dedicated operating system (e.g., a virtual machine) to mitigate the possible exploitation of OS kernels by malicious services.

Side Channels: The timing information of the UxAS communication channel is strongly correlated with sensitive internal states such as the number of UAVs. Two potential solutions could be employed. On the one hand, UxAS could randomize packets' timing information such as generating redundant packets at random time intervals. Although this solution can eliminate sensitive information leaked from the communication channel, it in turn might reveal the presence of the UxAS communication channel, thereby making possible other attacks such as signal jamming. On the other hand, UxAS can use traffic morphing [7] to make UxAS traffic patterns statistically indistinguishable from traffic patterns of popular network applications such as web clients or messengers.

7 Conclusion

This paper presents our security analysis for UxAS, a net-centric collection of interacting software modules that aim to collaboratively and cooperatively automate mission-level decision making for unmanned systems. We leveraged a threat-driven method to identify security requirements of UxAS and developed fuzz tests to evaluate whether UxAS satisfies these requirements. Our testing reveals all proposed security requirements are violated by the current implementation of UxAS.

References

1. Air Force Research Laboratory, Aerospace System Directorate, Power and Control Division: OpenUxAS (2017). https://github.com/afrl-rq/OpenUxAS
2. Birnbaum, Z., Dolgikh, A., Skormin, V., O'Brien, E., Muller, D., Stracquodaine, C.: Unmanned aerial vehicle security using behavioral profiling. In: 2015 International Conference on Unmanned Aircraft Systems (ICUAS), pp. 1310–1319. IEEE (2015)
3. Birnbaum, Z., Dolgikh, A., Skormin, V., Oâ Brien, E., Muller, D., Stracquodaine, C.: Unmanned aerial vehicle security using recursive parameter estimation. J. Intell. Robot. Syst. **84**(1–4), 107–120 (2016)
4. He, D., Chan, S., Guizani, M.: Communication security of unmanned aerial vehicles. IEEE Wirel. Commun. **24**(4), 134–139 (2017)
5. Hooper, M., et al.: Securing commercial Wifi-based UAVs from common security attacks. In: MILCOM 2016–2016 IEEE, pp. 1213–1218. IEEE (2016)
6. Javaid, A., Sun, W., Alam, M.: A cost-effective simulation testbed for unmanned aerial vehicle network cyber attack analysis. In: Safe & Secure Systems & Software Symposium S5, pp. 9–11 (2015)
7. Li, Y., Dai, R., Zhang, J.: Morphing communications of cyber-physical systems towards moving-target defense. In: 2014 IEEE ICC, pp. 592–598, June 2014. https://doi.org/10.1109/ICC.2014.6883383
8. Luo, X., Zhou, P., Zhang, J., Perdisci, R., Lee, W., Chang, R.K.: Exposing invisible timing-based traffic watermarks with BACKLIT, pp. 197–206. ACM (2011)
9. Mansfield, K.M., Eveleigh, T.J., Holzer, T.H., Sarkani, S.: Dod comprehensive military unmanned aerial vehicle smart device ground control station threat model. Technical report, DEFENSE ACQUISITION UNIV FT BELVOIR VA (2015)
10. Mitchell, R., Chen, R.: Adaptive intrusion detection of malicious unmanned air vehicles using behavior rule specifications. IEEE Trans. Syst. Man Cybern. Syst. **44**(5), 593–604 (2014)
11. Noah Shachtman, W.: Exclusive: computer virus hits U.S. drone fleet (2011)
12. Rodday, N.M., Schmidt, R.O., Pras, A.: Exploring security vulnerabilities of unmanned aerial vehicles. In: 2016 IEEE/IFIP Network Operations and Management Symposium (NOMS), pp. 993–994. IEEE (2016)
13. Schneier, B.: Attack trees. Dr. Dobb's J. **24**(12), 21–29 (1999)

14. Schumann, J., Moosbrugger, P., Rozier, K.Y.: R2U2: monitoring and diagnosis of security threats for unmanned aerial systems. In: Bartocci, E., Majumdar, R. (eds.) RV 2015. LNCS, vol. 9333, pp. 233–249. Springer, Cham (2015). https://doi.org/10.1007/978-3-319-23820-3_15
15. CNN Wire Staff: Obama says US has asked Iran to return drone aircraft (2011)
16. Yoon, K., Park, D., Yim, Y., Kim, K., Yang, S.K., Robinson, M.: Security authentication system using encrypted channel on UAV network. In: IEEE International Conference on Robotic Computing (IRC), pp. 393–398. IEEE (2017)

LA^3: A Lightweight Accountable and Anonymous Authentication Scheme for Resource-Constrained Devices

Wensheng Zhang$^{1(\boxtimes)}$ and Chuang Wang^2

^{1} Iowa State University, Ames, IA, USA
wzhang@iastate.edu
^{2} Microsoft Inc., Seattle, WA, USA
chuwang@microsoft.com

Abstract. In order to provide a lightweight accountable and anonymous authentication solution for resource-constrained devices, we propose LA^3, a variant of group signature scheme. The design is based on the assumptions of the DDH, q-SDH, q-DDHI and LRSW problems, as well as the knowledge of exponent assumption. A security model has been formally defined, and proofs have been provided to show that, LA^3 achieves the security properties of non-frameability, traceability and selfless anonymity in the random oracle model. LA^3 has also been implemented and compared to a few classic group signature schemes. The results show that LA^3 achieves much higher computational efficiency.

1 Introduction

More and more services are provided over the Internet, mobile ad hoc networks, sensor networks, or body-area networks. To ensure a service accessed only by authorized clients, it is common for a client to authenticate itself before is served. If service requests could leak the client's private information, the authentication algorithm is further demanded to keep anonymity for the client; meanwhile, accountability must be achieved to prevent the anonymity mechanisms from being exploited maliciously.

Resource-constrained devices may be used in the client or server side. For example, it is popular for people to access Internet services with mobile phones, smart watches or other tiny terminals, which typically have low computational capacity and prefer to run in low CPU cycles for the sake of power saving. As another example, a network of wireless sensors deployed in battlefield for surveillance may allow soldiers to access them, where the service devices (i.e., sensors or sensor gateways) and the client devices (i.e., mobile devices carried by soldiers) could be resource-constrained. In these scenarios, lightweight accountable and anonymous authentication algorithms are desired.

Many accountable and anonymous authentication schemes have been proposed for controlled access to online services. These schemes are mainly built

© Springer Nature Switzerland AG 2018
M. H. Au et al. (Eds.): NSS 2018, LNCS 11058, pp. 277–287, 2018.
https://doi.org/10.1007/978-3-030-02744-5_21

upon classic group signature algorithms such as [2, 6, 7, 9, 10], which provide provable anonymity and traceability. However, the computational costs introduced by these schemes may be too high for thin devices, as they were not designed for resource-constrained devices. Most of classic group signature primitives employ bilinear pairing, which are usually implemented over Elliptic curves. As shown by the works [12, 13, 21, 23, 25] on implementing Elliptic curve based cryptography on resource-constrained devices, bilinear pairing is much more complex and computationally expensive than the point addition and multiplication operations over Elliptic curve. Also, recent advances in group signature [3, 8, 11, 15] have been focused on developing the primitives that are secure post-quantum, which are even more costly in terms of computational and communication overheads than the classic group signature primitives. Based on the above observations, we develop LA^3, in which each authentication transaction requires only a few efficient operations over cyclic groups and finite fields.

LA^3 assumes three types of entities in the system: a service provider (called verifier) that needs to verify whether a client has the privilege to access its service, a group of clients (called provers) that need to prove their access privileges, and a trusted authority responsible for choosing system parameters and initializing the verifier and provers. Following the protocol of LA^3, a prover and the verifier can interact with each other in an authentication transaction; the scheme can also be used for clients to anonymously generate signatures for messages, and for the verifier to verify the signatures. The prover can keep anonymous to the verifier; but the authority is able to trace out the prover based on the authentication transcript when needed.

The security of LA^3 relies on the hardness assumptions of the Decisional Diffie-Hellman (DDH) [5], q-Strong Diffie-Hellman (q-SDH) [6], q-Decisional Diffie-Hellman Inversion (q-DDHI) [22] and LRSW problems [16], as well as the Knowledge of Exponent Assumption [4]. Intuitively, LA^3 has the following security properties: The first is *non-frameability*. It is hard for the verifier and any coalition of provers to impersonate any innocent prover (i.e., any prover not belonging to the coalition) in an authentication transaction. The second is *traceability*. It is hard for any coalition of provers to succeed in an authentication transaction without revealing any of their IDs to the authority. The third is *selfless anonymity*. It is hard for the verifier and any coalition of provers to determine which of two or more innocent provers involves in an authentication transaction.

Note that, LA^3 is a variant of classic group signature schemes, which have full traceability and selfless anonymity. Similar to the classic schemes, LA^3 provides selfless anonymity for provers and the tracing and revocation capabilities for the trusted authority, and it enables verifier local revocation. LA^3 differs from the classic group signature schemes in two main aspects. First, the classic schemes publish public group keys to allow everyone knowing the public key to perform verification, but LA^3 only allows the verifier to do so; this is the cost paid to achieve the simplicity and lightweight. However, this not a serious limitation to our target application scenarios of authentication for resource access, where only some resource manager (not all group members) needs to perform verification. Second, LA³ provides a weaker traceability than classic schemes in that, the authority can trace an authentication transcript to a prover only if the verifier is not malicious; that is, a malicious verifiable is able to forge a transcript that the authority cannot trace to any prover that it has initialized. However, this is not a problem to our target application scenario, because if an untraceable transaction is found, the verifier must be the only entity responsible for it; hence, this feature can deter a verifier from forging signatures. More over, LA³ has the feature of non-frameability; that is, even the verifier can forge a transaction, it (even colluding with some clients) cannot frame an innocent client by forging a transaction tracing to the innocent client.

We have implemented LA³, and compared its performance to that of a few classic group signature schemes. The results show that, as operations needed in the authentication process are simpler, the computational efficiency of LA³ is much higher than that of the compared ones; particularly, it is more than 10 times faster than the group signature scheme proposed by Boneh and Shacham [7], which has wide applications.

In the rest of the paper, Sect. 2 formally defines the problem. Section 3 presents our design. Section 4 reports the performance evaluation results, and Sect. 5 concludes the paper. Interested readers are referred to our technical report [24] for security proofs and more discussion of related works.

2   Problem Definition

Notations and Assumptions. Let $\mathbb{Z}_p$ denote a finite prime field, where $p > 2^\kappa$ and κ is a security parameter; $\mathbb{G}$ be a multiplicative cyclic group of p elements, with g as a generator. Our design is based on the following hard problems and assumptions:

Decisional Diffie-Hellman (DDH) Problem [5]: given g, g^a, g^b and g^c in $\mathbb{G}$, determine if $c = ab$.

q-Strong Diffie-Hellman (q-SDH) Problem [6]: given g, g^x, g^{x^2}, $\cdots$, g^{x^q} in $\mathbb{G}$ find $(c, g^{1/(c+x)})$ where $c \in \mathbb{Z}_p$.

q-Decisional Diffie-Hellman Inversion (q-DDHI) Problem [22]: Given g, g^x, g^{x^2}, $\cdots$, g^{x^q} and $g^{1/(x+y)}$ in $\mathbb{G}$, determine if $y = 0$.

LRSW Problem [16]: Given g, g^x and g^y in $\mathbb{G}$ and oracle O which on input s returns $(g', (g')^{sy}, (g')^{x+sxy})$ where $g' = g^z$ for some $z \in \mathbb{Z}_p$, compute $(b, t, b^{ty}, b^{x+txy})$ where $b \neq g^0 \in \mathbb{G}$ and t is not one of the s that has been queried.

Knowledge of Exponent Assumption (KEA) [4]: We use the following general form. For any adversary **A** that takes input (g_i, g_i^s) for $i = 1, \cdots, n$ and returns group element (C, Y) such that $Y = C^s$, there exists an "extractor" **Ā** which, given the same inputs as **A**, returns $x_i \in \mathbb{Z}_p$ for $i = 1, \cdots, n$ such that $C = \prod_{i=1}^n g_i^{x_i}$.

Scheme Overview. We consider a system that is composed of a verifier, a set of provers, and an off-line trusted authority which is responsible for initializing the verifier and provers as well as tracing the provers. Our proposed scheme includes the following algorithms.

System Initialization, with which the trusted authority initializes system secrets. It is formally denoted as $SystemInit(1^\kappa) \rightarrow \mathbb{SS}$, where κ is a security parameter and $\mathbb{SS}$ is a set of system secrets.

Verifier Initialization, with which the authority initializes the *verifier*. It is formally denoted as $VerifierInit\ (\mathbb{SS}) \rightarrow \mathbb{VK}$, where $\mathbb{VK}$ is the verification key.

Prover Initialization, with which the authority initializes a prover. It is formally denoted as $ProverInit\ (\mathbb{SS}, u) \rightarrow (u, \mathbb{PK}_u, T_u)$, where u is the ID of the new prover, $\mathbb{PK}_u$ is the proof key and T_u is the tracing token. The authority gives the prover u and $\mathbb{PK}_u$, but keeps T_u for tracing or revoking the prover when needed.

Authentication Protocol, with which prover u authenticates itself with the verifier. It includes the following two algorithms:

- $Prove(\mathbb{PK}_u, \tilde{c}) \rightarrow (\tilde{r})$. This algorithm is used by prover u, who holds proof key $\mathbb{PK}_u$, takes challenge $\tilde{c}$ from the verifier, and outputs response $\tilde{r}$.
- $Verify(\mathbb{VK}, \mathbb{RT}, \tilde{c}, \tilde{r}) \rightarrow 1/0$. This algorithm is used by the verifier. It holds verification key $\mathbb{VK}$, takes as inputs the revocation token set $\mathbb{RT}$ (i.e., the set of tokens of all revoked provers) and the authentication transcript $(\tilde{c}, \tilde{r})$, and outputs 1 if the verification is a success or 0 otherwise.

Prover Tracing, with which the authority traces the identity of a prover based on an authentication transcript. It is formally denoted as $Trace(\mathbb{T}, \tilde{c}, \tilde{r}), \rightarrow u$, which takes as inputs the set $\mathbb{T} = \{T_u | \forall u\}$ of all provers' tokens and an authentication transcript $(\tilde{c}, \tilde{r})$, and outputs the ID u of the prover who generated response $\tilde{r}$.

Correctness. The correctness of the scheme is defined as follows.

Definition 1. *The scheme is correct if: the authentication transcript generated by the verifier and a prover u that has not been revoked, must be verified successfully. Formally, $(Prove(\mathbb{PK}_u, \tilde{c}) \rightarrow \tilde{r}) \Rightarrow [(Verify(\mathbb{VK}, \mathbb{RT}, \tilde{c}, \tilde{c}) \rightarrow 1) \vee (T_u \in \mathbb{RT})]$.*

Non-frameability. Non-frameability defines the property that, the verifier and any set of collusive provers cannot impersonate any innocent prover.

Definition 2. *A scheme is (t, q_A, ϵ) non-frameable if no adversary can win the following* Non-frameability Game *with a probability greater than ϵ, in time t with no more than q_A authentication queries on each prover.*

Non-frameability Game. The game is between an adversary and a challenger, and composed of the following phases.

- **Phase I: Initialization.** The challenger initializes one verifier and a set of n provers.

- **Phase II: Queries.** The adversary can issue the following types of queries and the challenger should respond accordingly.
  - *Corruption of the verifier:* The adversary issues a corruption query on the verifier. In response, the challenger returns the verification key.
  - *Corruption of a prover u:* The adversary issues a corruption query on a prover u. The challenger responds with the proof key of the prover.
  - *Authentication for a prover v:* The adversary issues an authentication query for a prover v, and provides a challenge $\tilde{c}$. In response, the challenger returns a valid response $\tilde{r}$ on behalf of prover v.
  - *Hash:* The adversary issues a hash query, and the challenge responds with an element of $\mathbb{Z}_p$ randomly and consistently.
- **Phase III: Adversary's Response.** The adversary provides transcript $\tilde{c}'$ and $\tilde{r}'$.

The adversary wins if the response satisfies the following conditions: (i) The authentication is successful; i.e., $Verify(\mathbb{VF}, \emptyset, \tilde{c}', \tilde{r}') = 1$. (ii) The authentication transaction traces to a prover. (iii) If the authentication transcript traced to prover w, then no authentication query has been made for w with challenges $\tilde{c}'$, and no corruption query has been made on prover w.

Traceability. Traceability defines the property that, authentication transcripts forged by any coalition of collusive provers must trace to one of these provers; note that, the verifier is not part of the coalition.

Definition 3. *A scheme is (t, ϵ) traceable if no adversary can win the following* Traceability Game *with a probability greater than ϵ in time t.*

Traceability Game. The game is between an adversary and a challenger, and composed of the following phases.

- **Phase I: Initialization.** The challenger initializes one verifier and a set of provers.
- **Phase II: Pre-challenge Queries.** The adversary can issue three types of queries, namely, *corruption of a prover*, *authentication for a prover*, and *hash*. and the challenger responds accordingly as in the *Non-frameability Game*.
- **Phase III: Challenge.** The challenger provides a challenge $\tilde{c}'$.
- **Phase IV: Post-challenge Queries.** This is the same as Phase II.
- **Phase V: Adversary's Response.** The adversary responds with $\tilde{r}'$.

The adversary wins if the response satisfies the following conditions: (i) $Verify(\mathbb{VK}, \emptyset, \tilde{c}', \tilde{r}') = 1$. (ii) The authentication transcript cannot trace to any prover which has been corrupted or has been queried for authentication; i.e., if $\mathbb{P}$ denotes such set of provers, then $Trace(\mathbb{T}, \tilde{c}', \tilde{r}') \rightarrow u$ where $u \in \mathbb{P}$.

Selfless Anonymity. Selfless anonymity defines the property that, the verifier and any coalition of collusive provers cannot determine which innocent prover involve in an authentication process; thus, the anonymity of prover is achieved.

Definition 4. *A scheme is (t, q_A, ϵ) selfless anonymous if no adversary can win the following* Selfless Anonymity Game *with a probability greater than ϵ, in time t with less than q_A authentication queries on each prover.*

Selfless Anonymity Game. The game is between an adversary and a challenger, and composed of the following phases.

- **Phase I: Initialization.** A verifier and a set of provers.
- **Phase II: Pre-Challenge Queries.** The adversary can issue four types of queries, namely, *corruption of the verifier*, *corruption of a prover*, *authentication for a prover*, and *hash*, which are responded by the challenger as in the *Non-frameability Game*.
- **Phase III: Challenge.** The adversary selects two provers u_0 and u_1 from $\mathbb{P}$ that have not been compromised. The challenger randomly picks i from 0 or 1, and presents a response generated by u_i.
- **Phase IV: Post-Challenge Queries.** The same as Phase II except that corruption queries cannot be made on provers u_0 or u_1.
- **Phase V: Adversary's Response.** The adversary returns $i' \in \{0,1\}$.

The adversary wins if $i' = i$.

3   Our Construction

The **intuition** of the proposed construction is as follows: The authority randomly picks numbers k_1, d and l and a polynomial $C(x)$ from $\mathbb{Z}_p$. Each prover in the system is associated with a unique set of randomly selected numbers and polynomials including (i) ID u, (ii) numbers λ_u, s_u and e_u, and (iii) polynomial $B_u(x)$; based on the above, prover u is also associated with polynomial $F_u(x)$ such that

$$\lambda_u(k_1 + k_2 s_u + 1)C(x) + B_u(x)d + e_u l + F_u(x) = 0, \text{ where } k_2 = 1 - k_1. \quad (1)$$

The authority initializes each prover u by assigning to it a proof key that encodes λ_u, s_u, $B_u(x)$, e_u and $F_u(x)$, and initializes the verifier by assigning to it a verification key that encodes k_1, d, l and $C(x)$. Note that, some of these numbers and polynomials are not given in plain text, but *encoded* into the exponents of group elements in order to achieve the afore-defined security properties. In every authentication transaction, the verifier provides some challenge that is never reused. The prover generates response based on the challenge and its proof key, to prove its knowledge of the key without exposing its identity or the key. The verifier can determine if the prover has the required key through some test derived from Eq. (1). The scheme is presented in detail as follows.

3.1   System Initialization

The trusted authority initializes the system by selecting c_0, c_1, d, k_1 and l randomly from $\mathbb{Z}_p$ where $p \geq 2^\kappa$, and let $k_2 = 1 - k_1$. Formally, the procedure of system initialization can be specified as $SystemInit(1^\kappa) \rightarrow \mathbb{SS} = \{c_0, c_1, d, k_1, k_2, l\}$.

3.2   Verifier Initialization

The authority provides the following secrets to the verifier: k_1, k_2, l, $C(x)$, and $\hat{d} = g^d$. The procedure of verifier initialization can be formally specified as $VerifierInit(\mathbb{SS}) \rightarrow \mathbb{VK} = \{k_1, k_2, l, c_0, c_1, \hat{d}\}$.

3.3   Prover Initialization

Each prover is given a unique ID u and the following secrets:

- $\hat{k}_{u,0} = g^{\lambda_u}$ and $\hat{k}_{u,1} = \hat{k}_{u,0}^{k_1}$, where $\lambda_u \xleftarrow{R} \mathbb{Z}_p$;
- $s_u \xleftarrow{R} \mathbb{Z}_p$; $b_u \xleftarrow{R} \mathbb{Z}_p$; $\hat{e}_u = g^{e_u}$ where $e_u \xleftarrow{R} \mathbb{Z}_p$;
- $\hat{F}_{u,1} = g^{f_{u,1}}$, $\hat{F}'_{u,1} = g^{f'_{u,1}}$, $\hat{F}_{u,0} = g^{f_{u,0}}$ and $\hat{F}'_{u,0} = g^{f'_{u,0}}$, where $f_{u,1}, f'_{u,1}, f_{u,0}, f'_{u,0} \in \mathbb{Z}_p$ and $F_u(x) = (f_{u,1} + f'_{u,1})x + (f_{u,0} + f'_{u,0})$ satisfies Eq. (1).

Formally, the procedure of initializing prover u is specified as $ProverInit(\mathbb{SS}, u) \rightarrow (\mathbb{PK}_u, T_u)$, where $\mathbb{PK}_u = \{\hat{k}_{u,0}, \hat{k}_{u,1}, s_u, B_u(x), \hat{e}_u, \hat{F}_{u,1}, \hat{F}'_{u,1}, \hat{F}_{u,0}, \hat{F}'_{u,0}\}$ and $T_u = \{\lambda_u, s_u, b_u\}$. Note that T_u is not provided to prover u but is kept by the authority for the purpose of tracing or revoking a prover.

3.4   Authentication Protocol

The authentication protocol runs as follows.

1. When a prover u sends a verification request to the verifier.
2. The verifier randomly picks a challenge $r'_1 \in \mathbb{Z}_p$ and sends it to the prover.
3. The prover works as follows to generate a response.
   (a) It picks $r'_2 \xleftarrow{R} \mathbb{Z}_p$, and computes $r = h(r'_1 | r'_2)$, where $h()$ is a hash function mapping arbitrary strings to $\mathbb{Z}_p$.
   (b) It picks $\alpha, \beta, \xi \xleftarrow{R} \mathbb{Z}_p$, and computes and sends the following to the verifier:

$$a_{u,1,r} = 2\alpha + \xi - 1, \quad a_{u,2,r} = \alpha(s_u + 1) + \xi - 1, \quad B_{u,r} = \alpha\beta B_u(r), (2)$$

$$\hat{k}_{u,0,r} = \hat{k}_{u,0}^{\beta}, \quad \hat{k}_{u,1,r} = \hat{k}_{u,1}^{\beta}, \quad \hat{k}_{u,2,r} = (\hat{k}_{u,0})^{-\xi}, \quad \hat{k}_{u,3,r} = (\hat{k}_{u,1})^{-\xi}, (3)$$

$$\hat{e}_{u,r} = (\hat{e}_u)^{\alpha\beta}, \quad \hat{F}_{u,r} = [(\hat{F}_{u,1}\hat{F}'_{u,1})^r(\hat{F}_{u,0}\hat{F}'_{u,0})]^{\alpha\beta}. (4)$$

4. The verifier tests if

$$\hat{k}_{u,1,r} = \hat{k}_{u,0,r}^{k_1}, \quad \hat{k}_{u,3,r} = \hat{k}_{u,2,r}^{k_1}, (5)$$

and

$$(\hat{k}_{u,0,r}^{k_1 a_{u,1,r} + k_2 a_{u,2,r} + 1} \hat{k}_{u,2,r})^{C(r)} \hat{d}^{B_{u,r}} \hat{e}_{u,r}^{l} \hat{F}_{u,r} = g^0. (6)$$

If the above tests are successful, the verifier will check if the prover has been revoked as detailed in Sect. 3.6. If the prover is not revoked, the verification succeeds.

Hence, the authentication protocol can be formally expressed as

$$Prove(\mathbb{PK}_u, \tilde{c}) \to \tilde{r}, \tag{7}$$

$$Verify(\mathbb{VK}, \tilde{c}, \tilde{r}) \to 1/0, \tag{8}$$

where $\tilde{c} = \{r'_1\}$ and $\tilde{r} = \{r'_2, a_{u,1,r}, a_{u,2,r}, \hat{k}_{u,0,r}, \hat{k}_{u,1,r}, \hat{k}_{u,2,r}, \hat{k}_{u,3,r}, B_{u,r}, \hat{e}_{u,r}, \hat{F}_{u,r}\}$.

3.5   Tracing Algorithm

The authority keeps $T_i = \{s_i, \lambda_i, b_i\}$ for each prover i that it has initialized. Given $\hat{k}_{u,0,r}$, $a_{u,1,r}$, $a_{u,2,r}$ and $B_{u,r}$ responded by a prover during authentication, the authority traces the prover as follows. For each prover ID i,

$$\alpha' = (a_{u,2,r} - a_{u,1,r})/(s_i - 1). \tag{9}$$

Then, if

$$\hat{k}_{u,0,r}^{\alpha' B_i(r)/(\lambda_i B_{u,r})} = g, \tag{10}$$

the prover involved in the authentication transaction is traced to prover i.

Formally, the tracing procedure can be formally expressed as $Trace(\mathbb{T}, \tilde{c}) \to i$, where $\mathbb{T} = \{T_i | \forall \text{ prover } i\}$.

3.6   Revocation

For each revoked prover v, revocation token T_v is provided to the verifier. After a prover has passed the test expressed in Eq. (6), formula (9) is computed and then Eq. (10) is tested to find if the prover in the verification procedure has been revoked.

4   Implementation and Evaluation

We implement LA^3 based on an elliptic cyclic group. More specifically, we use the elliptic cryptographic primitives contributed by FlexiProvider [14], and adopt the recommended elliptic curve parameters specified by secp160r1 [20]. We compare the performance of LA^3 with that of the group signature scheme proposed by Boneh and Shacham [7], denoted as the BS scheme in this paper. We implement BS based on java paring-based cryptographic (jPBC) library to enable the operations on the bilinear maps [1], and adopted the type A curve. Note that, the above settings make both LA^3 and BS to have the same 80-bit level of security.

Performance Comparison with the BS Scheme [7]. We measure the performance of LA^3 and BS on a laptop computer with 1.83 GHz Genuine Intel (R) processor and 3 GB of RAM. The experimental results reported below are the averaged results of over 100 experimental runs.

Table 1. Checking time (millisecond) vs. number of revoked provers

Number of revoked provers	10	20	30	40	50	60	70	80
Time for checking revoked provers (BS Scheme)	2965	5878	8859	11754	14772	17660	20910	23932
Time for checking revoked provers (LA³ Scheme)	132	262	401	522	655	785	926	1061

BS spends about 1611 ms to generate a group signature and about 1807 ms to verify a group signature. In contrast, LA³ spends only about 66 ms at the prover and the verifier side, respectively, for each authentication transaction. LA³ outperforms BS because BS needs pairing operations while LA³ does not, and also the exponential and pairing operations over groups support bilinear mapping are much more expensive than the exponential operation over elliptic cyclic group. Particularly, for bilinear map $e : G \times G \to G_T$ that we use on type A curve, an exponentiation computation on group G takes 115 ms and a pairing computation takes 150 ms, while an exponential computation on elliptic curve secp160r1 only takes 12 ms. To check whether a prover has been revoked or not, both BS and LA³ require only the verifier to check a revocation list. Table 1 compares the revocation cost between the two schemes: LA³ is more efficient than BS; particularly, LA³ needs only 4.4% of the time needed by BS.

In terms of bandwidth consumption for each verification transaction, BS needs to transmit 2 elements from the bilinear group and 5 elements from $\mathbb{Z}_p$. Based on the type A curve that we use in the experiment, each element from $\mathbb{Z}_p$ takes 20 bytes and each element from the bilinear group takes 128 bytes. Hence, the total signature size is 356 bytes. As the element from the bilinear group can be denoted as compressed version, which is 65 bytes, the total length of a group signature in BS is 230 bytes in the compressed format.

With LA³, the prover needs to submit 6 points from the elliptic curve and 4 elements from $\mathbb{Z}_p$. As the secp160r1 elliptic curve we used in the experiment is 160-bit elliptic curve, each element from $\mathbb{Z}_p$ takes 20 bytes and each point from elliptic curve can be represented by 41 bytes. Hence, the total bandwidth consumption of LA³ is 326 bytes. Note that, each point from elliptic curve can also be represented by the compressed version, which takes 21 bytes. Hence, by using the compressed representation, the bandwidth consumption of LA³ is 206 bytes.

Performance Comparison with Other VLR Group Signature Schemes. As LA³ is a verifier-local revocation (VLR) group signature scheme, we also analyze the computational costs of other VLR group signature schemes such as [17–19] and compare their costs with that of LA³ in Table 2. As we can see, $LA³$ is much more efficient than all these schemes because (i) LA³ needs no pairing operation and smaller number of exponential operations, and (ii) the exponential operation over a regular multiplicative group is much more efficient than that in a group support pairing operations.

Table 2. Comparison of computational costs among group signature schemes [7, 17–19]

Schemes	Signing	Verification
LA^3	$6E$	$(6 + |RL|)E$
BS Scheme [7]	$8E+2P$	$6E+(3 + 2|RL|)P$
Scheme [17]	$10E+1P$	$6E+(2 + |RL|)P$
Scheme [18]	$6E+1P$	$3E+(2 + 2|RL|)P$
Scheme [19]	$(6 + 8|RL|)E$	$(9 + 8|RL|)E + 3|RL|P$

E and P: exponential and pairing operations, respectively; $|RL|$: number of revoked users.

5   Conclusions

The paper presents LA^3, a lightweight accountable and anonymous authentication scheme for resource-constrained devices. The proposed design is based on the hardness of the DDH, q-SDH, q-DDHI and LRSW problems, as well as the knowledge of exponent assumption. We proved that the LA^3 scheme has the security properties of non-frameability, traceability and selfless anonymity in the random oracle model. The LA^3 scheme has also been implemented and compared to several classic group signature schemes. The results showed that the LA^3 achieves much higher computational efficiency, which makes it more applicable to resource-constrained devices.

References

1. Java pairing-based cryptography library. http://gas.dia.unisa.it/projects/jpbc/, http://gas.dia.unisa.it/projects/jpbc/
2. Ateniese, G., Song, D., Tsudik, G.: Quasi-efficient revocation of group signatures. In: Blaze, M. (ed.) FC 2002. LNCS, vol. 2357, pp. 183–197. Springer, Heidelberg (2003). https://doi.org/10.1007/3-540-36504-4_14
3. Bansarkhani, R., Misoczki, R.: G-merkle: a hash-based group signature scheme from standard assumptions. IACR Cryptology ePrint Archive (2018)
4. Bellare, M., Palacio, A.: The knowledge-of-exponent assumptions and 3-round zero-knowledge protocols. In: Franklin, M. (ed.) CRYPTO 2004. LNCS, vol. 3152, pp. 273–289. Springer, Heidelberg (2004). https://doi.org/10.1007/978-3-540-28628-8_17
5. Boneh, D.: The decision Diffie-Hellman problem. In: Buhler, J.P. (ed.) ANTS 1998. LNCS, vol. 1423, pp. 48–63. Springer, Heidelberg (1998). https://doi.org/10.1007/BFb0054851
6. Boneh, D., Boyen, X., Shacham, H.: Short group signatures. In: Franklin, M. (ed.) CRYPTO 2004. LNCS, vol. 3152, pp. 41–55. Springer, Heidelberg (2004). https://doi.org/10.1007/978-3-540-28628-8_3
7. Boneh, D., Shacham, H.: Group signatures with verifier-local revocation. In: CCS, pp. 168–177 (2004)
8. Boneh, D., Eskandarian, S., Fisch, B.: Post-quantum EPID group signatures from symmetric primitives. IACR Cryptology ePrint Archive (2018)

9. Camenisch, J., Lysyanskaya, A.: Dynamic accumulators and application to efficient revocation of anonymous credentials. In: Yung, M. (ed.) CRYPTO 2002. LNCS, vol. 2442, pp. 61–76. Springer, Heidelberg (2002). https://doi.org/10.1007/3-540-45708-9_5

10. Camenisch, J., Lysyanskaya, A.: Signature schemes and anonymous credentials from bilinear maps. In: Franklin, M. (ed.) CRYPTO 2004. LNCS, vol. 3152, pp. 56–72. Springer, Heidelberg (2004). https://doi.org/10.1007/978-3-540-28628-8_4

11. Chase, M., et al.: Post-quantum zero-knowledge and signatures from symmetric-key primitives. In: ACM CCS, pp. 1825–1842 (2017)

12. Cheng, Z.: Implementing pairing-based cryptosystems in USB tokens. IACR Cryptology ePrint Archive (2014)

13. Gouvêa, C.P.L., López, J.: Software implementation of pairing-based cryptography on sensor networks using the MSP430 microcontroller. In: Roy, B., Sendrier, N. (eds.) INDOCRYPT 2009. LNCS, vol. 5922, pp. 248–262. Springer, Heidelberg (2009). https://doi.org/10.1007/978-3-642-10628-6_17

14. Group, F.R.: Flexiprovider. http://www.cdc.informatik.tu-darmstadt.de/flexiprovider/

15. Ling, S., Nguyen, K., Wang, H., Xu, Y.: Lattice-based group signatures: achieving full dynamicity with ease. In: Gollmann, D., Miyaji, A., Kikuchi, H. (eds.) ACNS 2017. LNCS, vol. 10355, pp. 293–312. Springer, Cham (2017). https://doi.org/10.1007/978-3-319-61204-1_15

16. Lysyanskaya, A., Rivest, R.L., Sahai, A., Wolf, S.: Pseudonym systems. In: Heys, H., Adams, C. (eds.) SAC 1999. LNCS, vol. 1758, pp. 184–199. Springer, Heidelberg (2000). https://doi.org/10.1007/3-540-46513-8_14

17. Nakanishi, T., Funabiki, N.: Verifier-local revocation group signature schemes with backward unlinkability from bilinear maps. In: Roy, B. (ed.) ASIACRYPT 2005. LNCS, vol. 3788, pp. 533–548. Springer, Heidelberg (2005). https://doi.org/10.1007/11593447_29

18. Nakanishi, T., Funabiki, N.: A short verifier-local revocation group signature scheme with backward unlinkability. In: Yoshiura, H., Sakurai, K., Rannenberg, K., Murayama, Y., Kawamura, S. (eds.) IWSEC 2006. LNCS, vol. 4266, pp. 17–32. Springer, Heidelberg (2006). https://doi.org/10.1007/11908739_2

19. Nakanishi, T., Funabiki, N.: A short anonymously revocable group signature scheme from decision linear assumption. In: ASIACCS, pp. 337–340 (2008)

20. Research, C.: Sec 2: recommended elliptic curve domain parameters. In: Standards for Efficient Cryptography (2000). http://www.secg.org/download/aid-386/sec2-final.pdf

21. Unterluggauer, T., Wenger, E.: Efficient pairings and ECC for embedded systems. IACR Cryptology ePrint Archive (2014)

22. Vercautern, F.: Main computational assumptions in cryptography (2010). http://www.ecrypt.eu.org/documents/D.MAYA.3.pdf

23. Xiong, X., Wong, D., Deng, X.: TinyPairing: a fast and lightweight pairing-based cryptographic library for wireless sensor networks. In: IEEE Wireless Communication and Networking Conference (2010)

24. Zhang, W., Wang, C.: La^3: a lightweight accountable and anonymous authentication scheme for resource-constrained devices (full version). Technical report in Computer Science Department at ISU (2018). http://www.cs.iastate.edu/~wzhang/la3full.pdf

25. Zhu, Y., Ma, D., Wang, S., Feng, R.: Efficient identity-based encryption without pairings and key escrow for mobile devices. In: Ren, K., Liu, X., Liang, W., Xu, M., Jia, X., Xing, K. (eds.) WASA 2013. LNCS, vol. 7992, pp. 42–53. Springer, Heidelberg (2013). https://doi.org/10.1007/978-3-642-39701-1_4

An Efficient Privacy Preserving Batch Authentication Scheme with Deterable Function for VANETs

Jinhui Liu[1], Yong Yu[1(✉)], Yanqi Zhao[1], Jianwei Jia[2], and Shijia Wang[3]

[1] School of Computer Science, Shaanxi Normal University, Xi'an 710119, China
yuyong@snnu.edu.cn
[2] Computer School of Wuhan University, Wuhan 430072, Hubei, China
[3] Department of Statistics and Actuarial Science,
Simon Fraser University, Burnaby, Canada

Abstract. With the rapid development of Internet of Things (IoT), intelligent transportation systems (ITS) brings more and more intelligent and convenient services to people's daily lives. Vehicular Ad hoc Networks (VANETs), as a typical application of ITS, is becoming an effective approach to manage traffic systems. However, VANETs still have to face to different security challenges in practice. In this paper, we develop a new identity-based double authentication preventing signature using bilinear pairings and then adopt it to propose a novel privacy preserving authentication scheme with deterable function based on our proposed identity-based double authentication preventing signature. This scheme provides secure authentication process for messages transmitted between vehicles and RSUs. A batch message verification mechanism is also supported by the proposed scheme to increase the message processing throughput of RSUs. And the security proof and performance analysis are presented. By comparing with other IBCPPA scheme in terms of the total time of pseudo identity generation and message signing phase and the execution times of batch verification, our proposed scheme is more efficient.

Keywords: Vehicular ad-hoc networks · Authentication protocol
Double authentication preventing signature · Bilinear pairing
Elliptic curve

1 Introduction

In the 21st century, one of the emerging trends is the constant movement of people towards more metropolitan areas, where a better living environment with social security benefits, medical support and sufficient job market can be found. In anticipation of this, governments in various nations have already started (or completed) planning for their metropolitan areas to accommodate a larger population and increase economic strength on these areas. As a consequence, it has

© Springer Nature Switzerland AG 2018
M. H. Au et al. (Eds.): NSS 2018, LNCS 11058, pp. 288–303, 2018.
https://doi.org/10.1007/978-3-030-02744-5_22

become a very important and urgent topic for metropolitan cities to manage their traffic systems effectively. To manage traffic systems, the intelligent transportation systems (ITS) is one of the most promising directions.

VANETs are a promising approach for facilitating ITS that aims at providing a platform for various applications including traffic safety and efficiency, transportation regulation, driver assistance, infotainment, etc. In a typical VANET which is shown in Fig. 1, each vehicle is assumed to have an onboard unit (OBU) and there are road-side units (RSU) installed along the roads. A trusted authority (TA) and maybe some other application servers are installed in the back end. There are three kinds of communication patterns: inter-roadside communication, vehicle-to-roadside communication and inter-vehicle communication. An on-board unit (OBU) is fixed in each vehicle. The vehicle broadcasts a message every 100–300 ms to a roadside unit (RSU) and other vehicles with the help of OBU, where the message includes information about its status (e.g. speed, location, and traffic jam). Other vehicles could respond in advance with the received message when unexpected cases (e.g. accidents and traffic jams) emerge. Upon receiving a message, the RSU check whether it could be dealt with locally. If so, the RSU will process it according to pre-defined rules. otherwise, the RSU will send the message to the traffic control center. With received messages, the traffic control center could monitor the traffic in real-time and take action in time to improve traffic environment and enhance the traffic safety. Besides main functions in public transport system, VANETs could also provide many value-added services such as digital advertisement, online movie and local information acquisition.

While the tremendous benefits expected from vehicular communications and the huge number of vehicles are strong points of VANETs, security and privacy in VANET is a challenging problem for researchers in the era of cyber threats. security is a crucial requirement for messages transmitted in VANETs. Because

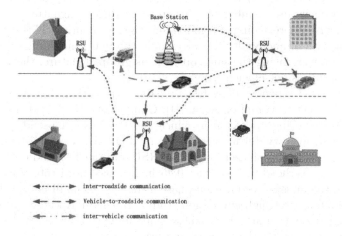

Fig. 1. A typical structure of VANET

of the wireless communication mode, it is easy for an adversary to take control of communication links and manipulate, delete, and replay messages. Privacy is another key issue in VANETs. A driver's travelling routes must be kept secret and inaccessible to others. However, it might be possible to capture a vehicle's traveling routes by capturing its messages. To address this issue, anonymous communication is essential. Simultaneously, traceability is also required because a trusted authority must be able to identify a vehicle for issues of liability when crimes or accidents occur. Security design should guarantee authentication, non-repudiation, integrity, and in some specific application scenarios, confidentiality, identity and location privacy to protect the network against unlawful tracing and attacks.

Related Works. In the field of VANETs, a bulk of research works has concentrated on improving authentication to guarantee the security in the recent past. A majority of these schemes make use of pseudonyms [1–4] or anonymous credentials [5,6]. An approach is to use a signature-based technique to achieve anonymous authentication [7,8].

In 2010, Wu et al. proposed a batch-verification system based on a group signature in which the OBU no longer needs to store more private data and the TA can effectively track the true identity of an attacker based on the revocation list without incurring the overheads caused by the retrieval of the revocation list. They achieved this goal by drawing on the novel technology of MLGSs and they also realized a context-aware threshold-authentication scheme for V2V communications in which the threshold can adaptively change in light of the context of messages, rather than having to be preset during the system-design stage. However, the verification cost in group-signature-based schemes [9–11] is too expensive for devices in VANETs which may require very fast verification time.

Similar to a group signature, ring signatures [12–14] can also be used to provide privacy preserving capability. Ring signatures are a cryptographic protocol designed to allow any member of a group to produce a signature on behalf of the group, without revealing the individual signers identity. This offers group members a level of anonymity not attainable through generic digital signature schemes. However, facing the same obstacle as group signature, the verification of ring signature is not efficient enough.

Identity-based schemes allow fast or batch verification that is particularly suitable for vehicular communications [1]. Chim et al. [15] provided a software-based bilinear pairing operation in which the RSU uses a pseudo identity to protect its true identity during message communication by establishing a shared key in the handshaking phase between the RSU and the TA. And they proposed lower message overhead and at least 0.45 higher successful rate than previous solutions in the message verification phase using the bloom filter and the binary search techniques (through simulation study). But later Horng et al. [16] overcome an impersonation attack weaknesses of Chim et al. and provided a secure scheme that can achieve the security and privacy requirements.

Zhang et al. [17] designed an identity-based conditional privacy-preserving authentication (IBCPPA) scheme for VANETs based on a novel identity-based digital signature (IBDS) scheme. To improve performance, Zhang [18] also proposed an IBCPPA scheme for VANETs using bilinear pairing. However, Lee et al. [19] claimed that Zhang et al.'s IBCPPA scheme cannot provide non-repudiation and is vulnerable to the reply attack. Lee et al. also designed a new IBCPPA scheme with improved security.

To reduce the computation overhead of the RSU when the number of messages is large, later Shim [20] proposed an ID-based CPPA scheme in which the RSU supports batch authentication of messages. However, the TA must consume more time in retrieving the entire revocation list, and it does not address the additional authentication overheads caused by illegal information.

To optimize the computation overheads in the message signature and authentication process, Zhang et al. [21] proposed another ID-based CPPA scheme which supports batch authentication in order to improve the efficiency of identity authentication. However, Liu et al. [22] pointed out that the scheme cannot resist a modification attack and Lee et al. [23] showed that the scheme cannot achieve the function of non-repudiation. Bayat et al. [24] also found that Lee et al.'s IBCPPA scheme cannot withstand the impersonation attack.

To achieve better performance and reduce computational complexity of information processing in VANETs, He et al. [25] proposed an efficient and fast signature scheme that does not use bilinear paring and demonstrated that their scheme could supports both the mutual authentication and the privacy protection simultaneously.

To reduce the computation overhead based on the scheme proposed by He et al., Zhong et al. [26] proposed a CPPA scheme to optimize the computation process. However, the schemes proposed by He et al. [25] and Zhong et al. [26] include several security assumptions which are difficult to equip each vehicle with a TPD in practice. To address this issue, Zhong et al. [27] proposed a novel and practical ID-based CPPA scheme based on invocating the registration list to reflect the role of the revocation list, which improves communication efficiency under the premise of reducing the demands in the security hypothesis.

To prevent fraud by discouraging users from submitting (signing) duplicates, we use double authentication preventing signatures (DAPS) instead of conventional signatures, where the address a (or its associated space respectively) can be given some application dependent semantics. DAPS are stronger signatures in the sense that they reveal the secret key of the signer to the public [28]. Revealing the secret key as discouragement to behave fraudulent is related to PKI-assured non-transferability approach in anonymous credential systems. Many instances are shown that a signer double signed may not be enough of a penalty but only deterable function. Consequently, we propose a novel and practical conditional privacy protection scheme based on DAPS for VANETs.

Our Contributions. The main contributions of this paper are summarized as follows.

1. We propose an efficient privacy preserving authentication scheme for VANETs to verify the authenticity of OBUs without revealing their real identities for V2V communications.
2. We present an efficient authentication scheme to verify the authenticity for a batch of vehicles when a batch of messages received from the vehicles.
3. We provide a self-enforcement mechanism that anyone can know the misbehaving vehicle. Thus, the misbehaving vehicles can be deterable and TA can revoke the misbehaving vehicles from causing any further damage.

The remainder of the paper is organized as follows. Section 2 introduces the related research of CPPA schemes in VANETs. The background knowledge and system model are introduced in Sect. 3. Section 4 describes our proposed scheme in detail and Sect. 5 presents the security analysis of the proposed scheme. Section 6 presents the performance evaluation. Finally, Sect. 7 discusses the conclusion and future research.

2 Preliminaries and System Model

2.1 Notations

The main symbols and their definitions in this paper are illustrated in Table 1.

Table 1. Notations.

Notation	Descriptions
p	A large prime number
G_1	An additive group of order q
G_2	A multiplicative group of order q
P	A generator of the group G_1
e	A bilinear map $e : G_1 \times G_1 \to G_2$
h	A secure hash functions $h : \{0,1\}^* \to Z_q$
$\overline{h}$	A secure hash functions $\overline{h} : \{0,1\}^* \to Z_q$
$\|$	The concatenation process
$\oplus$	The exclusive of OR process
RSU	A road side unit
OBU	An on board unit
TA	A trust authority
V_i	The i vehicle
TPD_i	A temper proof device of V_i

2.2 Bilinear Pairing and Hard Problem Assumption

Let G_1 and G_2 be a additive group and a multiplicative group of large prime order q separately. Bilinear map $e : G_1 \times G_1 \to G_2$ satisfies three properties:

(1) **Bilinear:** The mapping $e : G_1 \times G_1 \to G_2$ is said to be bilinear if $e(g_1 + g_2, g_3) = e(g_1, g_3)e(g_2, g_3)$ and $e(g_1, g_2 + g_3) = e(g_1, g_2)e(g_1, g_3)$ for any $g_1, g_2, g_3 \in G_1$.
(2) **Non-degeneracy:** For some point $g \in G_1$, $e(g, g) \neq 1_{G_2}$.
(3) **Computability:** Any two random points $g_0, g_1 \in G_1$, $e(g_0, g_1)$ could be calculated efficiently in polynomial time.

Definition 1 (ECDLP:) For two random points $P, Q \in G_1$, it is difficult to calculate the integer $x \in Z_q$ by the equation $P = xQ$.

2.3 System Model

The system model for VANETs scenarios consists of three entities: the trust authority TA, a vehicle equipped with an on-board units OBU and a roadside unit RSU.

TA: TA registers OBU and RSU. It initializes them with the public system information or private keys and has powerful computation ability and its responsibility is for generating the master key and system parameters. It is also responsible for registering $OBUs$ and $RSUs$. Besides, TA is the only one who could reveal the user's real identity.

OBU: OBU is a stationary wireless access point. Through executing DSRC protocol, it could receive vehicles' messages, verify their validity and send them to the traffic control center (TCC).

RSU: RSU is a tamper-proof device and issued by the TA. Through preloaded system parameters and private keys, it generates a temporary private key and uses it to sign a message.

2.4 Security Requirements

The major goal of our proposed scheme is to provide an efficient privacy preserving anonymous authentication to satisfy the following security requirements:

(1) **Message integrity and authentication:** When a vehicle enters into the region of an RSU, it should be authenticated by the RSU in an anonymous manner before it issues the safety related messages. On the other hand, a vehicle should authenticate other vehicles before it receives messages from them in an anonymous manner. Moreover, each message that is sent in the VANET system is appended with an anonymous signature to preserve the integrity of the transmitted message.
(2) **Identity privacy preserving:** The real identity of each vehicle should be kept secret from other entities in the VANET system to preserve vehicles privacy from various attacks.

(3) **Anonymity and traceability:** Even if a vehicle's real identity is hidden from entities in the network, the TA has the capability to get a vehicle's real identity of malicious vehicles that are sending bogus messages to other vehicles to disrupt traffic.

(4) **Deterable-iff-double signature by one signer:** If an user signs on colliding message (a, p_1) and (a, p_2), he can be linked and his signature keys can be extracted by anyone.

3   A New IBDAPS Scheme

Based on He et al.'s work [19] and Schnorr's work [20], we will present an IBDAPS scheme, which will be used to design our IBCPPA scheme for VANETs.

3.1   The Proposed IBDAPS Scheme

Our IBDAPS scheme consists of four algorithms: **Setup**, **Extract**$_{ID}$, **Sign**, **Verify** and **Extract**$_{sk}$ iff double signature by one signer. The details of those algorithms are presented as follows.

Setup Key Generation Center (KGC) initializes and establishes the system as follows:

(1) KGC chooses a large prime number q and generates two groups G_1 and G_2 with the same order q, where G_1 and G_2 are a additive group and a multiplicative group separately. KGC also chooses a generator P of G_1.
(2) KGC chooses a bilinear pairing $e : G_1 \times G_1 \to G_2$ and two secure hash functions $h : \{0,1\}^* \to Z_q$, $\overline{h} : \{0,1\}^* \to Z_q$.
(3) KGC selects a number s randomly as the master private key and calculates the public key $P_{pub} = s \cdot P$.
(4) KGC publishes the system parameters $(q, G_1, G_2, e, P, P_{pub}, h, \overline{h})$ and keeps the master private key s secretly.

Extract$_{ID}$. KGC generates an user U_i's private key when it receives his identity in this algorithm. The following steps are executed by KGC.

(1) KGC selects a number $t_i \in Z_q^*$ randomly and calculates $T_i = t_iP$.
(2) KGC calculates $h_i = h(ID_i\|T_i)$ and $s_i = t_i + h_is \bmod q$.
(3) KGC sends the private key $sk_i = s_i$ to U_i over security channel and publishes T_i.

Sign. The user U_i generates a signature when he receives a message M_i in this algorithm. The following steps are executed by U_i.

(1) U_i selects a number $r_i \in Z_q^*$ randomly and calculates $R_i = r_iP$.
(2) U_i calculates $k_i = \overline{h}(ID_i\|T_i\|R_i\|p_i)$ and $l_i = s_i + a \cdot k_ir_i \bmod q$.
(3) U_i outputs $\sigma_i = (T_i, R_i, k_i, l_i)$ as the signature of $M_i = (a, p_i)$.

Verify. A verifier check the validity of the message M_i's signature $\sigma_i = (T_i, R_i, k_i, l_i)$ in this algorithm. The following steps are executed by the verifier.

(1) The verifier calculates $h_i = h(ID_i\|T_i)$, $k_i = \overline{h}(ID_i\|T_i\|R_i\|p_i)$.
(2) The verifier checks whether the equation

$$e(T_i + h_i P_{pub} + a \cdot k_i R_i, P_{pub}) = e(l_i P_{pub}, P).$$

If the above equations hold, the verifier confirms that the signature is valid; otherwise, the verifier rejects the signature.

Batch Verification: Given a group signature $\sigma_1 = (T_1, R_1, k_1, l_1), \cdots, \sigma_n = (T_n, R_n, k_n, l_n)$ generated by $U_1, \cdots, U_n$ respectively. The verifier checks whether the equation

$$e(\sum_{i=1}^{n} T_i + \sum_{i=1}^{n} h_i P_{pub} + \sum_{i=1}^{n} a \cdot k_i R_i, P_{pub}) = e(\sum_{i=1}^{n} l_i P_{pub}, P)$$

holds.

Extract$_{sk}$ iff Double Signature by One Signer: Any user U_j can extract the signature key when he receives two signatures from colliding messages $M_{i1} = (a, p_{i1})$ and $M_{i2} = (a, p_{i2})$ from one user in this algorithm. The following steps are executed by every U_j.

According to $\sigma_{i1} = (M_{i1}, k_{i1}, T_i, R_i, l_{i1})$ and $\sigma_{i2} = (M_{i2}, k_{i2}, T_i, R_i, l_{i2})$, any user can output the private key s_i. Because $R_i = r_i P$, $k_{i1} = \overline{h}(ID_i\|T_i\|R_i\|p_{i1})$, $k_{i2} = \overline{h}(ID_i\|T_i\|R_i\|p_{i2})$ and $l_{i1} = s_i + a \cdot k_{i1} r_i$, $l_{i2} = s_i + a \cdot k_{i2} r_i$, any one can compute

$$s_i = \frac{k_{i1} l_{i2} - k_{i2} l_{i1}}{k_{i1} - k_{i2}}.$$

3.2 Security Model for IBDAPS Schemes

In this section, we will present the IBDAPS scheme's security model, in which all hash functions are modeled as random oracles. The unforgeability of an IBDAPS scheme is defined through a formal game executed between a challenger $\mathcal{C}$ and an adversary $\mathcal{A}$. The formal game consists of four phases.

A IBDAPS is EUF-CMA secure, if for all adversaries $\mathcal{A}$ there is a negligible function $\varepsilon(\cdot)$ such that

$$\Pr[\mathbf{Exp}_{\mathcal{A}, IBDAPS}^{EUF-CMA}(\kappa) = 1] \leq \varepsilon(\kappa),$$

where the corresponding experiment is given as follows:

$\mathbf{Exp}_{\mathcal{A}, IBDAPS}^{EUF-CMA}(\kappa):$
  $(sk_D, pk_D) \leftarrow KGen_D(1^\kappa)$

$$\mathcal{Q} \leftarrow \emptyset', \mathcal{R} \leftarrow \emptyset'$$
$$(m^*, \sigma^*, ID^*) \leftarrow \mathcal{A}^{Sign'_D(sk_D, \cdot)}(pk_\Sigma)$$

where oracle $Sign'_D$ on input m:
$(a, p) \leftarrow m$
if $a \in \mathcal{R}$, return $\perp$
$\sigma \leftarrow Sign_D(sk_D, m)$
$\mathcal{Q} \leftarrow \mathcal{Q} \cup \{m\}, \mathcal{R} \leftarrow \mathcal{R} \cup \{a\}$
return σ
return 1, if $Verify_D(pk_D, ID^*, m^*, \sigma^*) = 1 \wedge m^* \notin \mathcal{Q}$
return 0

For IBDAPS, one needs a restricted standard notion of unforgeblility, where $\mathcal{A}$ can adaptively query signatures for messages but only on distinct a.

Define 3. An IBDAPS scheme is existential unforgeability against adaptive chosen messages attacks if there is no adversary who could win the above game with non-negligible probability in polynomial time.

3.3   Security Analysis of the Proposed IBDAPS Scheme

In this subsection, we show that the proposed IBDAPS scheme is existential unforgeability against adaptive chosen messages attacks.

Theorem 1. *Our identity-based double authentication preventing signature scheme is existential unforgeability against adaptive chosen messages attacks if the CDH problem in G_1 is hard.*

Proof. A detailed discussion on the proof will appear in a full version.

4   The Proposed IBCPPA Scheme

According to the proposed IBDAPS scheme, we will construct a new IBCPPA scheme for VANETs, which consists of four phases: the key generation and pre-distribution (KGPD) phase, pseudo identity generation and message signing (PIDGMS) phase, message verification (MV) phase and signature key extraction (SKE) phase. Details of those phases are presented in the following.

4.1   Key Generation and Pre-distribution (KGPD) Phase

In this phase, as is shown in Fig. 2, the trust authority TA generates system parameters, its master private key and its public key. After that, TA also pre-loads them in a tamper-proof device, which is equipped in each vehicle. The following steps are executed by TA.

(1) TA picks a large prime number q and generates two groups G_1, G_2 with the same order q, where G_1 is an additive group and G_2 is a multiplicative group. TA also chooses a generator P of G_1.

(2) TA chooses a bilinear pairing $e : G_1 \times G_1 \to G_2$ and two secure hash functions $h : \{0,1\}^* \to Z_q, \overline{h} : \{0,1\}^* \to Z_q$.

(3) TA selects a number s randomly as the master private key and calculates the public key $P_{pub} = s \cdot P$ and pre-loads s in each vehicles tamper-proof device.

(4) TA preloads system parameters $(q, G_1, G_2, e, P, P_{pub}, h, \overline{h})$ in each road side unit and vehicle.

(5) TA choose a real identity $RID_i \in Z_q$ and a password $PW_i \in Z_q$ for the i th vehicle $ID_i^2 = RID_i \oplus h(r \cdot P_{pub})$ and stores them in its tamper-proof device TPD_i.

4.2 Pseudo Identity Generation and Message Signing (PIDGMS) Phase

In this section, the ith vehicle V_i generates its pseudo identity and an authentication message. The following steps are executed by V_i.

(1) V_i inputs its real identity $RID_i \in Z_q$ and password $PW_i \in Z_q$ into its tamper-proof device TPD_i. TPD_i checks whether both of them are equal to ones stored in it. If either of them is not equal, TPD_i rejects the requirement.

(2) TPD_i generates a random number $t_i \in Z_q^*$, computes $ID_i^1 = t_i P, ID_i^2 = RID_i \oplus h(t_i \cdot P_{pub}), h_i = h(ID_i \| T_i), s_i = t_i + h_i s \bmod q$, where $ID_i = \{ID_i^1, ID_i^2\}$. Then TPD_i sends (s_i, ID_i) to V_i.

(3) Given a message $M_i = (a, p_i)$, V_i chooses an integer $r_i \in Z_q^*$ at random, calculates $R_i = r_i P, k_i = \overline{h}(ID_i \| T_i \| R_i \| p_i \| a), l_i = s_i + a \cdot k_i r_i \bmod q$. At last, V_i sends $\sigma_i = (M_i, ID_i, T_i, R_i, k_i, l_i)$ to the nearest road side unit RSU.

4.3 Message Verification Phase

In this phase, as shown in Fig. 2, the road side unit RSU verifies the validity of received messages. The following steps are executed by RSU.

(1) Upon receiving $\sigma_i = (M_i, ID_i, T_i, R_i, k_i, l_i)$, RSU calculates $h_i = h(ID_i \| T_i)$, $k_i = \overline{h}(ID_i \| T_i \| R_i \| p_i)$ and checks whether the equation $e(ID_i + h_i P_{pub} + a \cdot k_i R_i, P_{pub}) = e((s_i + a \cdot k_i r_i) P_{pub}, P)$ holds. If it holds, RSU rejects the requirement; otherwise, V_i is authenticated.

4.4 Batch Verification Phase

Given a group signature $\sigma_1 = (M_1, ID_1, T_1, R_1, k_1, l_1), \cdots, \sigma_n = (M_n, ID_n, T_n, R_n, k_n, l_n)$ generated by $U_1, \cdots, U_n$.

The verifier checks whether the equation

$$e(\sum_{i=1}^n ID_i + \sum_{i=1}^n h_i P_{pub} + \sum_{i=1}^n a \cdot k_i R_i, P_{pub}) = e(\sum_{i=1}^n l_i P_{pub}, P)$$

holds.

4.5 Deterable Iff Double Signature Phase

In this section, if the i th vehicle V_i generates a pair colliding messages $M_{i1} = (a, p_{i1})$ and $M_{i2} = (a, p_{i2})$ to confuse RSU. The following steps can be executed by any vehicle V_j.

Given $\sigma_{i1} = (M_{i1}, ID_i, T_i, R_i, k_{i1}, l_{i1})$ and $\sigma_{i2} = (M_{i2}, ID_i, T_i, R_i, k_{i2}, l_{i2})$. Any one can compute

$$s_i = \frac{k_{i1}l_{i2} - k_{i2}l_{i1}}{k_{i1} - k_{i2}}.$$

5 Security Analysis

Based on the provable security of the proposed IBDAPS scheme, we give detailed analysis on the security of the IBCPPA scheme.

5.1 Message Integrity and Authentication

Due to the process of the proposed IBCPPA scheme, we get that an generates a temporary private key $\{ID_i, s_i\}$ and uses it to generate a signature of the message $M_i = (a, p_i)$. According to the security analysis, there is no adversary could generate a legal signature σ_i. So RSU could authenticate OBU and could find any modification of the received signature by checking whether the equation $e(ID_i^1 + h_iP_{pub} + ak_iR_i, P_{pub}) = e((s_i + ak_ir_i) \cdot P_{pub}, P)$ holds. Therefore, the proposed IBCPPA scheme for VANETs is able to provide message integrity and authentication.

5.2 Identity Privacy Preserving

The user's real identity RID_i is included in an element ID_i of the signature $(M_i, ID_i, T_i, R_i, S_i)$ generated by the OBU. If an adversary wants to get RID_i, he has to calculates t_iP_{pub} from $ID_i^1 = t_iP$ and $P_{pub} = sP$. According to the difficulty of the CDH problem, any adversary without the master key s cannot get the user's real identity. Therefore, the proposed IBCPPA scheme for VANETs is able to provide identity privacy preserving.

5.3 Traceability

Suppose TA intercepts a signature $(M_i, ID_i, T_i, R_i, S_i)$ generated by an OBU. By the description of the proposed IBCPPA scheme, the master key s is generated and saved by TA. So TA could calculate the user's identity RID_i by $RID_i = ID_i^2 \oplus h(t_i \cdot P_{pub}) = ID_i^2 \oplus h(t_i \cdot s \cdot P) = ID_i^2 \oplus h(s \cdot ID_i^1)$. Therefore, TA could trace a user's action and the proposed IBCPPA scheme for VANETs is able to provide traceability.

5.4 Deterable-iff-double Signature by One Signer

If the i th vehicle V_i generates a pair signatures on colliding messages $M_{i1} = (a, p_{i1})$ and $M_{i2} = (a, p_{i2})$ to confuse RSU. According to the two signatures σ_{i1} and σ_{i2}, signature key $s_i = \frac{k_{i1}l_{i2} - k_{i2}l_{i1}}{k_{i1} - k_{i2}}$ is revealed to allow anyone to compute valid signatures on behalf of the signer. Therefore, the proposed IBCPPA scheme for VANETs is able to discourage signers from misbehaving.

5.5 Security Comparisons

Let $SR_1, SR_2, SR_3, SR_4, SR_5$ denote message integrity & authentication, identity privacy preserving, traceability, no inefficiency problem of the double secret key, and Deterable-iff-double signature respectively. The security comparisons among our IBCPPA scheme and three related IBCPPA schemes are list in Table 2.

Table 2. Security comparisons.

	Zhang et al.	Bayat et al.	He et al.	The proposed scheme
SR_1	√	√	√	√
SR_2	√	√	√	√
SR_3	√	√	√	√
SR_4	×	×	√	√
SR_5	×	×	×	√

√: the requirement is satisfied; ×: the requirement is not satisfied.

6 Performance Analysis

The performance of VANETs is susceptible to computation and communication overheads due to the rapid speed of the vehicles and the rapid changes in the network topology.

To give practical performance analysis, we get the execution time of different cryptographic processes using the Pairing-Based Cryptography (PBC) library, which is a famous and free Java library for implementing of pairing-based cryptosystems. The experiment was executed on a personal calculater, which is equipped with an windows 7 64 OS, intel(R) Core(TM) i5-2450M CPU 2.50 GHz, 4.00 GB RAM With JPBC library for 10000 times. A type-A elliptic curve $E : y = x^3 + x$ defined a prime field F_p, where p is a 512-bits prime filed satisfying $p + 1 = 12qr$ and $q = 2^{159} + 2^{107} + 1$.

The definition and execution time of related cryptographic operations are shown in Table 3.

Let P_1, P_2 and P_3 denote pseudo identity generation & message signing, message verification and batch verification separately. Performance comparisons among related schemes in Zhang et al.'s IBCPPA scheme [10], He et al.'s IBCPPA

Table 3. The definition and execution time of related operations.

Cryptographic operation	Definition	Execution time
T_{pair}	A bilinear pairing process	7 ms
T_{pm}	A point multiplication process	12 ms
T_{pa}	A point addition process	0.0004 ms
T_H	A map-to-G_1 hash process	27 ms
T_h	A map-to-point hash process	0.005 ms
$T_{\overline{h}}$	A map-to-point hash process	0.005 ms

Table 4. Performance comparisons of related schemes

	P_1	P_2	P_3
Zhang et al.	$6T_{pm} + 1T_h$ $+2T_{pa} + 3T_H$	$3T_{pair} + 2T_{pm}$ $+2T_{pa} + 3T_H$	$3T_{pair} + 2nT_{pm}$ $+4nT_{pa} + 3nT_H$
Bayat et al.	$5T_{pm} + 2T_h$ $+1T_{pa} + T_H$	$3T_{pair} + 1T_{pm}$ $+1T_H$	$3T_{pair} + nT_{pm}$ $+nT_H + T_{Gm}$ $+(3n-3)T_{pa} + nT_h$
He et al.	$3T_{pm} + 2T_h + T_H$	$3T_{pm} + T_h$ $+T_H + 2T_{pa}$	$(3n+2)T_{pm} + nT_h$ $+nT_H + (3n-1)T_{pa}$
Our scheme	$T_{pm} + T_h + T_{pa}$	$2T_{pair} + 3T_{pm}$ $+2T_{pa} + 2T_h$	$2T_{pair} + 3nT_{pm}$ $+4nT_{pa} + 2nT_h$

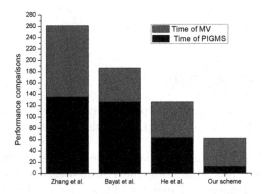

Fig. 2. Performance comparisons of the total time of PIDGMS phase and MV phase

scheme [25], Bayat's IBCPPA scheme [24] and the proposed IBCPPA scheme is depicted in Table 4.

We use Fig. 2 to show the execution time of the pseudo identity generation & message signing phase and the message verification phase to give visual comparisons of related schemes' performance. From Fig. 2, we can observe that the total time of PIDGMS phase and MV phase in our scheme is smallest.

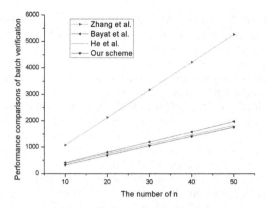

Fig. 3. Performance comparisons of batch verification

We compare the execution times of batch verification in the proposed scheme with three related schemes as shown in Fig. 3, to demonstrate the major benefit of our proposed scheme in the batch verification of multiple messages. Based on the results shown in Table 3 and Fig. 3, batch verification of the proposed scheme has lower computation cost compared to three related ID-based CPPA schemes.

7   Conclusion

In this paper, a new efficient identity-based batch double authentication preventing signature with deterable function is first introduced and then a new privacy preserving authentication scheme is developed based on the invented signature scheme for vehicular sensor network. Security analysis is conducted to show that our proposed scheme is secure against an adaptive chosen message attack under random oracle model. Besides, the proposed authentication scheme is efficient in terms of time consumption and is self-enforcement that deters mass surveillance.

Acknowledgement. This work was supported by the National Key R&D Program of China (2017YFB0802000), the National Natural Science Foundation of China (61772326, 61572303, 61872229, 61802239), NSFC Research Fund for International Young Scientists (61750110528), National Cryptography Development Fund during the 13th Five-year Plan Period (MMJJ20170216), Fundamental Research Funds for the Central Universities (GK201702004, GK201803061, 2018CBLY006) and China Postdoctoral Science Foundation (2018M631121).

References

1. Raya, M., Hubaux, J.P.: Securing vehicular ad hoc networks. J. Comput. Secur. **15**(1), 39–68 (2007)
2. Calandriello, G., Papadimitratos, P., Hubaux, J.-P., Lioy, A.: Efficient and robust pseudonymous authentication in VANET. In: Ad Hoc Networks, pp. 19–28. ACM (2007)

3. Huang, D., Misra, S., Verma, M., Xue, G.: PACP: an efficient pseudonymous authentication-based conditional privacy protocol for VANETs. IEEE Trans. Intell. Transp. Syst. **12**(3), 736–746 (2011)

4. Sun, Y., Lu, R., Lin, X., Shen, X., Su, J.: An efficient pseudonymous authentication scheme with strong privacy preservation for vehicular communications. IEEE Trans. Veh. Technol. **59**(7), 3589–3603 (2010)

5. Chim, T.W., Yiu, S.-M., Hui, L.C.K., Li, V.O.K.: OPQ: OT-based private querying in VANETs. IEEE Trans. Intell. Transp. Syst. **12**(4), 1413–1422 (2011)

6. Gonzalez-Tablas, A., Alcaide, A., de Fuentes, J., Montero, J.: Privacy-preserving and accountable on-the-road prosecution of invalid vehicular mandatory authorizations. Ad Hoc Netw. **11**(8), 2693–2709 (2013)

7. Chen, L., Ng, S.L., Wang, G.: Threshold anonymous announcement in VANETs. IEEE J. Sel. Areas Commun. **29**(3), 605–615 (2011)

8. Kounga, G., Walter, T., Lachmund, S.: Proving reliability of anonymous information in VANETs. IEEE Trans. Veh. Technol. **58**(6), 2977–2989 (2009)

9. Lin, X., Sun, X., Ho, P.H., Shen, X.: GSIS: secure vehicular communications with privacy preserving. IEEE Trans. Veh. Technol. **56**(6), 3442–3456 (2007)

10. Lin, X., Sun, X., Ho, P.H., Shen, X.: Security in vehicular ad hoc networks. IEEE Commun. Mag. **46**(4), 88–95 (2008)

11. Sun, J., Zhang, C., Zhang, Y., Fang, Y.: An identity-based security system for user privacy in vehicular ad hoc networks. IEEE Trans. Parallel Distrib. Syst. **21**(9), 1227–1239 (2010)

12. Au, M.H., Liu, J.K., Susilo, W., Yuen, T.H.: Secure id-based linkable and revocable-iff-linked ring signature with constant-size construction. Theor. Comput. Sci. **469**, 1–14 (2013)

13. Chaurasia, B.K., Verma, S.: Conditional privacy through ring signature in vehicular ad-hoc networks. Trans. Comput. Sci. **13**, 147–156 (2011)

14. Yuen, T.H., Liu, J.K., Au, M.H., Susilo, W., Zhou, J.: Efficient linkable and/or threshold ring signature without random oracles. Comput. J. **56**(4), 407–421 (2013)

15. Chim, T.W., Yiu, S.-M., Hui, L.C., Li, V.O.: SPECS: secure and privacy enhancing communications schemes for vanets. Ad Hoc Netw. **9**(2), 189–203 (2011)

16. Horng, S.-J., et al.: B-SPECS+: batch verification for secure pseudonymous authentication in vanet. IEEE Trans. Inf. Forensics Secur. **8**(11), 1860–1875 (2013)

17. Zhang, L., Wu, Q., Qin, B., Domingo-Ferrer, J.: APPA: aggregate privacy-preserving authentication in vehicular ad hoc networks. In: Lai, X., Zhou, J., Li, H. (eds.) ISC 2011. LNCS, vol. 7001, pp. 293–308. Springer, Heidelberg (2011). https://doi.org/10.1007/978-3-642-24861-0_20

18. Zhang, C., Ho, P.H., Tapolcai, J.: On batch verification with group testing for vehicular communications. Wirel. Netw. **17**(8), 1851–1865 (2011)

19. Lee, C.C., Lai, Y.M.: Toward a secure batch verification with group testing for vanet. Wirel. Netw. **19**(6), 1441–1449 (2012)

20. Shim, K.A.: An efficient conditional privacy-preserving authentication scheme for vehicular sensor networks. IEEE Trans. Veh. Technol. **61**(4), 1874–1883 (2012)

21. Jianhong, Z., Min, X., Liying, L.: On the security of a secure batch verification with group testing for vanet. Int. J. Netw. Secur. **16**(5), 351–358 (2014)

22. Lee, C.C., Lai, Y.M.: Toward a secure batch verification with group testing for vanet. Wirel. Netw. **19**(6), 1441 (2013)

23. Liu, J.K., Yuen, T.H., Au, M.H., Susilo, W.: Improvements on an authentication scheme for vehicular sensor networks. Expert Syst. Appl. **41**(5), 2559–2564 (2014)

24. Bayat, M., Barmshoory, M., Rahimi, M., Aref, M.R.: A secure authentication scheme for VANETs with batch verification. Wirel. Netw. **21**(5), 1–11 (2014)

25. He, D., Zeadally, S., Xu, B., Huang, X.: An efficient identitybased conditional privacy-preserving authentication scheme for vehicular ad hoc networks. IEEE Trans. Inf. Forensics Secur. **10**(12), 2681–2691 (2015)
26. Zhong, H., Wen, J., Cui, J., Zhang, S.: Efficient conditional privacy preserving and authentication scheme for secure service provision in vanet. Tsinghua Sci. Technol. **21**(6), 620–629 (2016)
27. Zhong, H., Huang, B., Cui, J., Xu, Y., Liu, L.: Conditional privacy-preserving authentication using registration list in vehicular ad hoc networks. IEEE Access **6**, 2241–2250 (2018)
28. Poettering, B., Stebila, D.: Double-authentication-preventing signatures. In: Kutyłowski, M., Vaidya, J. (eds.) ESORICS 2014. LNCS, vol. 8712, pp. 436–453. Springer, Cham (2014). https://doi.org/10.1007/978-3-319-11203-9_25

PrivacySearch: An End-User and Query Generalization Tool for Privacy Enhancement in Web Search

Francisco-Javier Rodrigo-Ginés[1], Javier Parra-Arnau[1], Weizhi Meng[2], and Yu Wang[3(✉)]

[1] Department of Computer Science and Mathematics,
CYBERCAT-Center for Cybersecurity Research of Catalonia,
Universitat Rovira i Virgili, 43007 Tarragona, Spain
{franciscojavier.rodrigo,javier.parra}@urv.cat
[2] Department of Applied Mathematics and Computer Science,
Technical University of Denmark, Kongens Lyngby, Denmark
[3] Department of Computer Science, Guangzhou University, Guangzhou, China
yuwang@gzhu.edu.cn

Abstract. Web search engines capitalize on, or lend themselves to, the construction of user interest profiles to provide personalized search results. The lack of transparency about what information is stored, how it is used and with whom it is shared, limits the perception of privacy that users have about the search service. In this paper, we investigate a technology that allows users to replace specific queries with more general but semantically similar search terms. Through the generalization of queries, user profile could become less precise and therefore more private, although evidently at the expense of a degradation in the accuracy of search results. In this work, we design and develop a tool of *Privacy-Search* that implements this principle in real practice. Our tool, developed as a browser plug-in for Google Chrome, enables users to generalize the queries sent to a search engine in an automated fashion, without the need for any kind of infrastructure or external databases, and in *real time*, according to simple and intuitive privacy criteria. Experimental results demonstrate the technical feasibility and suitability of our solution.

1 Introduction

Billions of queries are processed daily by Web search engines (WSEs) such as Google, Bing or Yahoo. Naturally, users of these services look for information that is relevant to their interests, and this is the fundamental reason why WSEs strive to develop increasingly sophisticated algorithms that tailor search results to meet the specific preferences of their users.

Personalization, the key enabling technology, relies on the storage of user information (e.g., the queries themselves, the search results visited, the location from which queries are submitted), the processing of such data, and the creation of a *profile* of interests and preferences. With this profile, search engines

© Springer Nature Switzerland AG 2018
M. H. Au et al. (Eds.): NSS 2018, LNCS 11058, pp. 304–318, 2018.
https://doi.org/10.1007/978-3-030-02744-5_23

Your categories	Below you can edit the interests and inferred demographics that Google has associated with your cookie:	
	Category	
	Beauty & Fitness —Fitness —Yoga & Pilates	Remove
	Hobbies & Leisure —Water Activities —Surf & Swim	Remove
	Home & Garden —Home Improvement —House Painting & Finishing	Remove
	News —Health News	Remove
	People & Society —Family & Relationships —Family —Baby Names	Remove
	People & Society —Family & Relationships —Family —Parenting —Baby Care	Remove
	Sports —Individual Sports - Cycling	Remove
	Sports —Individual Sports —Gymnastics	Remove
	Demographics —Age —25-34	Remove
	Demographics —Gender —Female	Remove

Fig. 1. The profile of a user is modeled in Google as a list of topic categories. The profile shown here reflects the user is interested in parenting-related topics, which might reveal she is pregnant.

can then adjust search results [1, 2] to provide users with more accurate links. Behind personalization, however, WSEs not only aim to offer more precise search results—the construction of profiles allows search engines to segment their users and deliver personalized ads, which have been shown to ensure conversion rates[1] that double those of geographical and contextual ads [29]. Internet companies, besides, very often obtain a direct economic benefit through the sale of this valuable information. This is the case of Yahoo, which claims to charge the US government between 30 and 40 dollars for the email address of users of its search engine [4].

Evidently, personalization techniques—and in particular the creation of interest profiles—, prompts serious privacy risks. On the one hand, the lack of transparency about what information is stored, how it is used and with whom it is shared, limits the perception of privacy that users have about the search service. On the other hand, users profiles are sensitive information per se since they may reveal health-related issues, political affiliation, salary or religion. Figure 1 shows an example of user profile and the inferences that can be drawn from it.

It is not surprising, then, that 30% of the users of these services are concerned about the fact that their behavior is scrutinized without their knowledge or consent [7]. The increasing concerns about Web-search privacy is reflected by multiple studies. From 2014 to 2015, the interest in privacy-related issues increased a five percent [8], showing the negative perception that users have about personalization technologies. Lastly, a survey by the Mozilla Foundation indicates that almost a third of users feel that they have no control over their personal information on the Internet [9].

We believe that the solution to those problems necessarily implies giving users real control over their data, and that this can only be achieved through technologies that strike a good balance privacy and personalization. However,

---

[1] In online marketing terminology, conversion usually means the act of converting Web site visitors into paying customers.

when the recipient of sensitive information (i.e., the search engine) is not fully trusted, privacy protection faces a dilemma of great practical relevance.

Contribution and Plan of this Paper. The aim of this work is to contribute to the development of privacy-enhancing technologies (PETs) that may attain a suitable trade-off between privacy and search accuracy. In particular, this paper investigates a privacy mechanism that capitalizes on the *generalization of queries*, that is to say, the replacement of specific and probably sensitive queries, into more general, albeit semantically similar, search terms.

In the literature, a couple of previous works tackle the problem of query generalization in Web search [10,30]. The major disadvantage of these few existing approaches, however, is that (i) they do not aim to protect individual queries and may reveal the actual search terms; and, more importantly, (ii) they are not intended for *end-users*, i.e., they are not designed to be used as stand-alone systems, without the need for infrastructure, and in *real time*. To the best of our knowledge, our work is the first to design and implement the principle of query generalization as a tool for end-users.

The designed tool, called *PrivacySearch*, is implemented as a Web-browser extension and allows users to generalize their search queries in an automated fashion, as they type the query, without consulting any external entity or database, and according to simple and intuitive privacy criteria. Our generalization algorithm is specifically contrived to satisfy various requirements in terms of computational overhead and storage, which enable the operation of the whole system in real-time and on the user side. The ultimate goal of our tool is to provide users with certain guarantees in terms of privacy and search experience.

The reminder of this paper is organized as follows. Sect. 2 reviews the state of the art relevant to this work. Sect. 3 describes the design principles, the system architecture and the implementation details of the proposed privacy technology. Sect. 4 evaluates different aspects of the proposed tool and shows its technical feasibility. Conclusions are drawn in Sect. 5.

2   State of the Art

Numerous approaches have been proposed to protect user privacy in the context of Web search. These approaches fundamentally suggest collaboration strategies among a group of peers, and the perturbation of user data.

An archetypical example of user collaboration is the Crowds protocol [28]. This protocol is particularly helpful to minimize requirements for infrastructure and trusted intermediaries such as anonymizers and pseudonymizers, or to simply provide an additional layer of anonymity. In the Crowds protocol, a group of users collaborate to submit their messages to a WSE, from whose standpoint they wish to remain completely anonymous. In simple terms, the protocol works as follows. When sending a message, a user flips a biased coin to decide whether to submit it directly to the recipient, or to send it to another user, who will then repeat the randomized decision.

Crowds provides anonymity from the perspective of not only the final recipient, but also the intermediate nodes. Therefore, trust assumptions are essentially limited to fulfillment of the protocol. The original proposal suggests adding an initial forwarding step, which substantially increases the uncertainty of the first sender from the point of view of the final receiver, at the cost of an additional hop. As in most ACSs, Crowds enhances user anonymity but at the expense of traffic overhead and delay.

An alternative to hinder an attacker in its efforts to precisely profile users consists in perturbing the information they explicitly or implicitly disclose when communicating with a WSE. The submission of false data, together with the user's genuine data, is an illustrative example of data-perturbative mechanism. In this kind of mechanisms, the perturbation itself typically takes place on the user side. This means that users need not trust any external entity such as the WSE, the Internet service provider or their neighboring peers. Obviously, this does not signify that data perturbation cannot be used in combination with other trusted-third solutions or mechanisms relying on user collaboration. It is rather the opposite—depending on the trust model assumed by users, this class of technologies can be synergically combined with any of other approach. In any case, data-perturbative techniques come at the cost of system functionality and data utility, which poses a trade-off between these aspects and privacy protection.

An interesting approach to provide a distorted version of a user's profile of interests is query forgery [17]. The underlying idea boils down to accompanying original queries or query keywords with bogus ones. By adopting this data-perturbative strategy, users prevent privacy attackers from profiling them accurately based on their queries, without having to trust neither the service provider nor the network operator, but clearly at the cost of traffic overhead. In other words, inherent to query forgery is the existence of a trade-off between privacy and additional traffic.

A software implementation of query forgery is the Web browser add-on TrackMeNot [12]. This popular add-on makes use of several strategies for generating and submitting false queries. Basically, it exploits RSS feeds and other sources of information to extract keywords, which are then used to generate false queries. The add-on gives users the option to choose how to forward such queries. In particular, a user may send bursts of bogus queries, thus mimicking the way people search, or may submit them at predefined intervals of time. Despite the strategies users have at their disposal, TrackMeNot is vulnerable to a number of attacks that leverage on the semantics of these false queries as well as timing information, to distinguish them from the genuine queries [13].

GooPIR [14] is another proposal aimed at obfuscating query profiles. Implemented as a software program, this approach enables users to conceal their search keywords by adding some false keywords. To illustrate how this approach works, consider a user wishing to submit the keyword "depression" to Google and willing to send it together with two false keywords. Based on this information, GooPIR would check the popularity of the original keyword and find that "iPhone" and "elections" have a similar frequency of use. Then, instead of submitting each of these three keywords at different time intervals, this approach would send them in a batch. The proposed strategy certainly thwarts attacks based on timing. However, its main limitation is that it cannot prevent an attacker from combining several of these batches, establishing correlations between keywords, and eventually inferring the user's real interest [15]. As an example, suppose that the user's next query is "prozac" and that GooPIR recommends submitting it together with the keywords "shirt" and "eclipse". In this case, one could easily deduce that the user is interested in health-related issues.

Another form of perturbation, which is the one considered in this work, is tackled in [10,30]. Given a query corresponding to an intended interest, [30] generates a set of more general, semantically-related queries that loosely correspond to that interest. Each of these queries are submitted independently to the WSE, and the level of privacy protection is determined by the least private term. Upon receiving all search results, the proposed system tries to reconstruct a ranking similar to the one that the query would have yielded. However, with the increasingly sophisticated tracking technologies available these days, it is likely that the WSE can reverse the procedure and obtain the actual interest by combining all the scrambled queries. Consequently, the submission of multiple topic-related queries may improve accuracy, but it may not protect the true specific interest from the service provider.

Similarly, [10] proposes replacing user queries with general terms. However, since the aim is not to protect each single search but the accumulated query profile, it may happen that certain individual queries are exposed to the service provider. Besides, [10] poses evident implementation and security issues, which prevent them from being put into practice as user tools. For example, the cited work relies on an external database for generalizing queries, and applies computationally-intensive natural language processing techniques. Table 1 summarizes the major conclusions of this section.

3   PrivacySearch - Local Generalization of Web Searches in Real Time

In this section, we present the main contribution of this work: a privacy system that allows users to distort their query profile by protecting each single query from the standpoint of a malicious WSE.

Our approach is based on the principle of query generalization. Although there exist *theoretical* proposals relying on this same principle of information perturbation ([10,30]), there is no practical tool available to end-users, which applies this perturbation principle and effectively protects each individual search query against WSEs. As discussed in Sect. 2, the proposals available in the literature may fail in the protection of search terms and cannot be implemented as stand-alone systems. In contrast, our technology is specifically designed to meet these two fundamental requirements:

- **Real time.** At the time of sending a query, it must be replaced automatically by a term of a higher semantic category, without the user perceiving any degradation in the search engine's response time.

Table 1. Summary of techniques that may contribute to privacy protection in the scenario of WSEs.

Approaches	Underlying mechanism	Trust model	Disadvantages
Anonymizer	TTP	Trusted	o Users must trust an external entity, o Traffic bottlenecks
Crowds [28]	User collaboration	Semi-trusted	o Numerous users must collaborate, o Vulnerable to collusion attacks, o Traffic overhead
Query forgery, TrackMeNot [12]	Data perturbation	Untrusted	o Traffic overhead, o Vulnerable to query-semantic attacks [13], o Less accurate search results
GooPIR [14]	Data perturbation	Untrusted	o An attacker can eventually learn the user's real interest [15]. o Less accurate search results
Query generalization	Data perturbation	Untrusted	o Single queries are not protected but the accumulated profile [30], o Difficult to implement as a stand-alone system [10], o Less accurate search results

- **Local mode.** The generalization algorithm, and in general the query protection tool, must perform all operations on the user side, without the help of any type of infrastructure.

The few existing proposals in the literature contemplate the use of external databases to carry out query processing and/or generalization. This is the case, for example, of [10], which uses the Open Directory Project to determine the category to which a query belongs. However, querying external databases is not an appropriate solution. An attacker, possibly the database itself, could leverage the queries to profile the user in question and compromise their privacy.

In this work, we present *PrivacySearch*, a technology that is aimed to address the issues raised in Sect. 2 and meet the requirements of real time and local-mode mentioned above. This tool is aimed at users concerned about their online privacy, who wish to prevent search engines like Google from building a precise profile based on their queries.

Our solution replaces the queries to be submitted by a user with generic terms, so that the search engine cannot find out the exact information they are

Fig. 2. Selection of the level of privacy in our tool.

looking for. How generic these terms are is determined by the users themselves through appropriate and simple privacy configurations.

Specifically, our tool allows users to configure three levels of privacy: low, medium and high (see Fig. 2). The selected privacy level indicates how generic the query generated by PrivacySearch will be from the original query[2]. As an example, consider the following use case.

Example 1 (Privacy configuration for health-related search queries). Suppose a WSE user wants to learn more about the bipolar disorder, a condition he/she has recently been diagnosed. Being aware that WSEs profile users based on their search queries, the user in question decides to install the proposed solution. Although he/she is concerned with his/her privacy, he/she may appreciate the value and usefulness of personalized search results and, hence, choose a low level of privacy protection. In this case, the specific query "bipolar disorder" typed in the Web-browser plug-in would not be changed. However, if a medium or high level of protection was selected, PrivacySearch would replace the original query automatically with "mental disorder" or "health", respectively, which would prevent the WSE from inferring the actual interest of the user, although clearly at the cost of inaccurate search results.

3.1 Implementation Details

PrivacySearch has been developed as a plug-in for the Chrome browser[3] and is currently integrated in the navigation bar. Web searches are sent through the navigation bar after typing the keyword "privacy".

It is worth emphasizing that the current implementation of our tool, available online in the Chrome Store, is based on a semantic ontology without using sophisticated natural language processing techniques or deep semantic analysis.

---

[2] Users can also choose in which search engine the processed search will be carried out.

[3] The plug-in is available at https://chrome.google.com/webstore/detail/ecippblhocppaciehgckhfboegciekkf.

As we shall describe later in this section, our aim is investigating the practical feasibility of query generalization and the performance of a tool implementing this principle.

As the user types their query, recommendations of previously processed queries may be shown to the user. The ability of our tool to operate in real time is of special relevance to conduct this task.

To generalize user queries, we capitalize on WordNet as a categorizer [18]. WordNet is a database that contains lexical relations between words in English. In particular, it has 117 798 names, 11 529 verbs, 21 479 adjectives and 4 481 adverbs. Since each WordNet entry stores its hyperonym and its hyponym, it can be construed as an ontology [19]. For example, the term "dog" has the following hypernames (note that *entity* is the common hypername to all WordNet terms):

⇒ Dog
  ⇒ Canid
    ⇒ ...
   ⇒ Animal
    ⇒ ...
     ⇒ Entity

When our plug-in receives a query, it processes it in three different steps. First, PrivacySearch pre-process the text; subsequently it performs a linguistic disambiguation; and finally it concludes by making a categorization according to the level of privacy selected by the user.

Preprocessing Queries. In this very first step, a series of tasks are conducted that aim to prepare the query for further processing by WordNet. This step is of special importance for the real-time requirement specified in the previous subsection. Essentially, queries are "simplified", although the meaning is kept, in order to diminish the workload of the following two steps.

The preprocessing done in our tool is simpler than the one suggested in [10]. In the cited work, the authors obtain the grammatical category and perform a morpho-syntactic analysis of each term using models of maximum entropy. In our case, we perform a less complex natural language processing, without taking into account neither the grammar nor the amount of information provided by each term of a query, which significantly reduces the computational overhead and notably speeds up the response time.

To preprocess a query, we perform the following tasks:

- The query is converted to lowercase, and the score is deleted. In this way, we avoid false negatives when searching for each term in WordNet.
- The so-called "stop words" of the query are removed. The stop words are words that do not contribute any meaning to the query. This is the case of articles, pronouns and prepositions. In this step, they are eliminated to reduce the execution time, without altering the meaning of the query.
- The query is *tokenized. Tokenization* is the process by which the atomic units of a text are detected and isolated.

- Plural terms become singular. With this process, we aim to prevent false negatives in the categorization phase.
- The atomic units or tokens obtained are lemmatized. The lemmatization is the linguistic process by which the motto of a given term is determined. The slogan is the form that, by agreement, is accepted as representative of all the flexed forms of the same word, that is to say, the terms that the tool will find as entries in WordNet. For this step, we use the WordNet native slogan map.
- We obtain the n-grams existing in the query. An n-gram is a contiguous sequence of n elements contained in a text. The elements can be phonemes, syllables, letters, or words. For reasons of efficiency, our categorization algorithm uses unigrams and bigrams.
- Finally, terms are eliminated in languages other than English, or that do not exist in WordNet, in order to reduce the computing time in the language disambiguation step.

Linguistic Disambiguation. Once the query has been preprocessed, we must determine the correct meaning of each term. WordNet stores the different meanings that terms can have. For example, the word "bank" can refer to a pile or mass of some material, or a company dedicated to perform financial operations, among other meanings. The only way to ascertain the correct meaning is through linguistic disambiguation [20].

Language disambiguation is currently an open problem, and there exist several approaches to tackle it. In our plug-in, we have implemented a linguistic disambiguation algorithm based on the Lesk algorithm [21]. This algorithm relies on the principle that neighboring words within a text tend to share a common theme. The concrete implementation of the algorithm is shown below by means of an example:

1. Let $A\,B\,C$ be the input query.
2. Assume each term has a set of associated meanings, denoted as follows: $A \in \{a_1, a_2, a_3\}$, $B \in \{b_1\}$, $C \in \{c_1, c_2\}$.
3. All possible permutations of meanings are formed:

$$(a_1, b_1, c_1), (a_1, b_1, c_2), (a_2, b_1, c_1), \ldots, (a_3, b_1, c_2).$$

4. A function $F(a, b)$ is defined that returns the distance between a pair of meanings:

$$F(a, b) = \sum_{i=0}^{|H_a|} \sum_{j=0}^{|H_b|} \frac{1}{|H_a|/2} + \frac{1}{|H_b|/2}, \tag{1}$$

being H_a the sequence of existing hyperonyms between a y $entity$, and H_b the sequence of existing hyperonyms between b y $entity$, where $H_{ai} \neq H_{aj}$.
5. F is evaluated for each pair of permutation meanings, and the permutation with less distance is chosen.

In the design of our tool, we have limited the number of possible permutations in the last step, since it increases exponentially with the number of terms and meanings of each term.

Below we illustrate with an example the linguistic disambiguation of the term *bass* from English. This term can refer to a musical instrument or a type of fish, among other meanings. If a user types the query "I like playing the bass guitar", our tool should return a generic query other than if the query "I like fishing sea bass" was made. With the proposed query disambiguation algorithm, our tool is able to capture these two meanings. In particular, for the low level of privacy, the algorithm returns "musical performance guitar" for the first query, and "outdoor sport saltwater fish" for the second one.

Categorization. Once the original query has been preprocessed and the correct meanings of each n-gram obtained, we proceed to conduct the categorization of the resulting terms. To carry out this step, we utilize WordNet as a categorizer. WordNet is a very popular lexical database of the English language. The proposed categorization algorithm is described in Algorithm 1.

As we discussed at the beginning of this section, WordNet can be considered an ontology. This allows us to easily access all the hypernames of a term until reaching the common hyperonym to all of them, i.e., *entity*. Accordingly, for each n-gram existing in the processed query we extract a hyperonym.

As frequently done in information retrieval and text mining, our query classifier also relies on the term frequency-inverse document frequency model. Said otherwise, we weight the resulting hyperonym/s based on the frequency of occurrence of the corresponding unigrams and bigrams.

Next, we specify the rule for choosing the depth of the hyperonym/s in the hierarchy, as a function of the level of privacy:

- For the level "low", the first hyperonym is extracted from each n-gram.
- For the privacy level "medium", we compute the depth from the n-gram to *entity*, and the hyperonym with a depth of 10% is extracted.
- For the privacy level "high", we compute the depth from the n-gram to *entity*, and the hyperonym with a depth of 20% is extracted.

A maximum depth of 20% has been configured since, for a large number of terms, experimental evidence shows that a higher percentage returns results that are too generic and, therefore, of little utility. In addition, since WordNet is not an ontology per se (it contains redundancies in its hierarchy), we proceed as follows: to avoid cycles when categorizing, when one hyperonym is detected, the following available secondary hyperonym is chosen and not the direct one.

Algorithm 1: Query categorization algorithm.

Input: Q, a sequence of terms that represents a genuine preprocessed query.

Output: $Q\_Categorized$, a sequence of terms that represents a generalized query, built from the genuine query.

1 **let** $PrivacyLevel \in \{Low, Medium, High\}$, level of privacy chosen by the user.
2 **let** $entity$, root hypername of WordNet.
3 **for** $each\ term\ t\ in\ C$ **do**
4 $\quad$ $H_t \leftarrow$ Sequence of direct hyperlinks from t until $entity$.
5 $\quad$ **if** $PrivacyLevel\ is\ Low$ **then**
6 $\quad\quad$ $|\quad Q\_Categorized \leftarrow H_{t1}$
7
8 $\quad$ **else if** $PrivacyLevel\ is\ Medium$ **then**
9 $\quad\quad$ $|\quad Q\_Categorized \leftarrow H_{t(|H_t|\cdot0.1)}$
10
11 $\quad$ **else if** $PrivacyLevel\ is\ High$ **then**
12 $\quad\quad$ $|\quad Q\_Categorized \leftarrow H_{t(|H_t|\cdot0.2)}$
13
14 **end**

---

4 Evaluation

In this section, we evaluate our tool in terms of computational efficiency and performance, with the aim of verifying whether the design requirements specified in Sect. 3 are met. Due to the relevance of showing recommended queries (i.e., generalized terms) in real time, we have performed an analysis of the execution times obtained with selected real queries from a database.

The database of queries we have employed in our experiments was published by the AOL search engine in 2006. This database contains about 37 million queries of 657 000 unique users, obtained during a period of three months (from 1 March 2006 to May 31, 2006). Other databases are available such as those of Altavista [26] and MSN database [27], but since they are rather similar in terms of user queries, we restrict just to the AOL data set.

To carry out our analysis, we run PrivacySearch on the first 100 000 records of the database. The selected subset includes searches made between March 1 to March 6, 2006. Tables 2 and 3 respectively show some statistics of the data set under study, and those of the data after the preprocessing phase.

One of the effects of the preprocessing step is an average reduction of 41.13% in the number of terms of per query. This significant reduction is essentially due to the elimination of stop words, the deletion of terms without an entry in WordNet, and the grouping of terms in n-grams. Furthermore, around 30% of queries have been omitted, since a number of them either referred to URLs, or included character names and/or terms, or were written in a language other than English; the current version of our tool only works for English searches.

Our experimental results are shown in Figs. 3 and 4. In the former figure, we observe that, in more than 85% of cases, the tasks of preprocessing, disam-

Table 2. Some statistics of the first 100 000 queries of the AOL query database.

1 term in the query:	30 603	Max.	25
2 terms in the query:	26 149	Mean	2.65
3 terms in the query:	18 750	Standard deviation	1.79
4 terms in the query:	11 195		
5 terms in the query:	6 415		
> 6 terms in the query:	6 888		

Table 3. Some statistics of the first 100 000 queries, after preprocessing.

0 terms in the query:	29 502	Max.	12
1 term in the query:	21 731	Mean	1.56
2 terms in the query:	24 859	Standard deviation	1.41
3 terms in the query:	14 939		
4 terms in the query:	6 082		
5 terms in the query:	1 925		
> 5 terms in the query:	962		

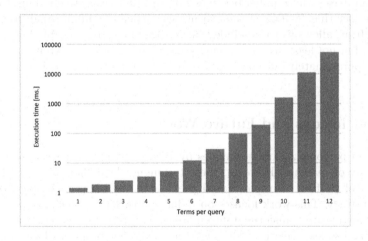

Fig. 3. Average execution time based on the number of terms.

biguation and categorization were performed in less than 3 ms. This result is of special relevance as it demonstrates that privacy protection may come at the cost of negligible processing overhead. In the latter figure, on the other hand, we can appreciate that the average running time increases exponentially with the number of terms. The reason is due to the fact that the number of computations performed by the linguistic disambiguation algorithm depends on the number of terms in the query and the number of meanings per search term.

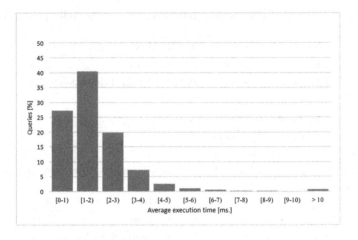

Fig. 4. Average execution time.

Despite this, if we consider only the preprocessing phase, the average number of terms per query in the selected subset of data yields 2.65; in the Altavista and BIEW databases, this number becomes 2.35 and 1.63, respectively. This, together with the fact that 99.93% of the executions carried out in our analysis did not exceed 10 ms, allows us to conclude that our tool performs suitably for real-time use. Last but not least, as far as memory use is concerned, our extension occupies 4.3 MB approximately once packaged, and 51.6 MB once installed in Chrome and in use.

5   Conclusions and Future Work

The use of personalization techniques by WSEs is a promising way to improve the quality of searches. However, these techniques lend themselves to the construction of profiles of interests and preferences, which pose serious concerns to user privacy. This work focuses on a data-perturbative mechanism by which specific queries are transformed into more general terms (although semantically similar) and so less sensitive. Although there exist few proposals based on query generalization, no solution has been designed nor developed that brings this principle into practice and is intended for end-users.

In this paper, we proposed *PrivacySearch*, a browser tool that allows users to generalize the queries sent to a search engine, automatically, without the need of any type of infrastructure or external database, and in real time. With PrivacySearch, users can control the specificity of their interest profiles in front of a search engine, through a flexible and intuitive control of the sensitivity of the information they are disclosing. In contrast to other approaches, our tool protects each individual query independently and, as such, does not make any assumption on the ability of the WSE to track all them. Experimental results show that our tool is able to categorize complex searches in real time while users are typing their queries, without affecting the performance of the system.

Future work will evaluate the proposed tool further with real users, and attempt to determine the utility loss incurred by the generalized queries (e.g., how many result pages a user must go through to find the link that best fits the original query).

Acknowledgments. Partial support to this work has been received from the European Commission (projects H2020-644024 "CLARUS" and H2020-700540 "CANVAS"), and the Spanish Government (projects TIN2014-57364-C2-1-R "Smart-Glacis" and TIN2016-80250-R "Sec-MCloud"). J. Parra-Arnau is the recipient of a Juan de la Cierva postdoctoral fellowship, IJCI-2016-28239, from the Spanish Ministry of Economy and Competitiveness.

References

1. Cao, B., Sun, J.-T., Xiang, E.W., Hu, D.H., Yang, Q., Chen, Z.: PQC: Personalized query classification. In: ACM Eighteenth Conference on Information and Knowledge Management, pp. 1217-1226 (2017)
2. Aktolga, E., Jain, A., Velipasaoglu, E.: Building rich user search queries profiles. In: Carberry, S., Weibelzahl, S., Micarelli, A., Semeraro, G. (eds.) UMAP 2013. LNCS, vol. 7899, pp. 254–266. Springer, Heidelberg (2013). https://doi.org/10.1007/978-3-642-38844-6_21
3. Ortiz-Cordova, A., Jansen, B.J.: Classifying web search queries to identify high revenue generating customers. J. Assoc. Inf. Sci. Technol. **63**(7), 426–1441 (2012)
4. Zetter, K.: Yahoo issues takedown notice for spying price list. In: Wired (2009). https://www.wired.com/2009/12/yahoo-spy-prices/
5. Pariser, E.: El filtro burbuja: Cómo la web decide lo que leemos y lo que pensamos. Penguin Random House Grupo Editorial (2017)
6. European Commission: Media pluralism and democracy: outcomes of the 2016 Annual Colloquium on Fundamental Rights. In: Annual Colloquium on Fundamental Rights, pp. 14–15 (2016)
7. Purcell, K., Brenner, J., Rainie, L.: Search engine use 2012. In: Pew Internet (2012)
8. Penn, M.: Views from Around the Globe: 2nd Annual Poll on How Personal Technology is Changing Our Lives (2015)
9. Mozilla Foundation: Online Privacy & Security Survey (2017)
10. Sánchez, D., Castellà-Roca, J., Viejo, A.: Knowledge-based scheme to create privacy-preserving but semantically-related queries for web search engines. Inf. Sci. **218**, 17–30 (2013)
11. Shen, X., Tan, B., Zhai, C.: Privacy protection in personalized search. In: ACM SIGIR Forum, vol. 41, no. 1 (2007)
12. Howe, D.C., Nissenbaum, H.: TrackMeNot: resisting surveillance in web search. Lessons Identity Trail: Priv. Anonymity Identity Netw. Soc. **290**, 417–436 (2006)
13. Chow, R., Golle, P.: Faking contextual data for fun, profit, and privacy. In: Proceedings of the 8th ACM Workshop on Privacy in the Electronic Society, pp. 105-109 (2009)
14. Domingo-Ferrer, J., Solanas, A., Castellà-Roca, J.: h (k)-Private information retrieval from privacy-uncooperative queryable databases. Online Inf. Rev. **33**(4), 720–744 (2009)

15. Balsa, E., Troncoso, C., Díaz, C.: OB-PWS: obfuscation-based private web search. In: IEEE Symposium on Security and Privacy (SP), pp. 491–505. IEEE (2012)
16. Xu, Y., Wang, K., Zhang, B., Chen, Z.: Privacy-enhancing personalized web search. In: Proceedings of the 16th International Conference on World Wide Web, pp. 591–600 (2007)
17. Rebollo-Monedero, D., Parra-Arnau, J., Forné, J.: An Information-Theoretic Privacy Criterion for Query Forgery in Information Retrieval. In: Kim, T., Adeli, H., Fang, W., Villalba, J.G., Arnett, K.P., Khan, M.K. (eds.) SecTech 2011. CCIS, vol. 259, pp. 146–154. Springer, Heidelberg (2011). https://doi.org/10.1007/978-3-642-27189-2_16
18. Miller, G.A.: WordNet: a lexical database for English. Commun. ACM **38**(11), 39–41 (1995)
19. Snasel, V., Moravec, P., Pokorny, J.: WordNet ontology based model for web retrieval. In: Web Information Retrieval and Integration, pp. 220–225 (2005)
20. Stevenson, M., Wilks, Y.: Word-sense disambiguation. In: The Oxford Handbook of Computational Linguistics, pp. 249–265 (2003)
21. Lesk, M.: Automatic sense disambiguation using machine readable dictionaries: how to tell a pine cone from an ice cream cone. In: Proceedings of the 5th Annual International Conference on Systems Documentation SIGDOC 1986, pp. 24–26 (1986)
22. Scott, S., Matwins, S.: Text classification using WordNet hypernyms. In: Usage of WordNet in Natural Language Processing Systems (1998)
23. Ganesan, P., Garcia-Molina, H., Widom, J.: Exploiting hierarchical domain structure to compute similarity. ACM Trans. Inf. Syst. (TOIS) **21**(1), 64–93 (2003)
24. Mansuy, T., Hilderman, R.J.: A characterization of WordNet features in Boolean models for text classification. In: Proceedings of the Fifth Australasian Conference on Data Mining and Analytics, vol. 61 (2006)
25. Arrington, M.: AOL proudly releases massive amounts of private data. In: TechCrunch (2006). www.techcrunch.com/2006/08/06/aol-proudly-releases-massive-amounts-of-user-search-data
26. Silverstein, C., Henzinger, M., Marais, H., Moricz, M.: Analysis of a very large web search engine query log. ACm SIGIR Forum **33**(1), 6–12 (1999)
27. Dou, Z., Song, R., Wen, J.-R.: A large-scale evaluation and analysis of personalized search strategies. In: Proceedings of the 16th International Conference on World Wide Web, pp. 581–590 (2007)
28. Reiter, M., Rubin, A.D.: Crowds: anonymity for Web transactions. ACM Trans. Inf. Syst. Secur. **I**, 66–92 (1998)
29. Beales, H.: The value of behavioral targeting, Tech. rep., Netw. Advertising Initiative, March 2010. http://www.networkadvertising.org/pdfs/Beales_NAI_Study.pdf. Accessed 15 Jan 2016
30. Avi, A., Efraimidis, P.S., Drosatos, G.: A query scrambler for search privacy on the internet. Inf. Retr. **16**(6), 657–679 (2013)

Revisiting Website Fingerprinting Attacks in Real-World Scenarios: A Case Study of Shadowsocks

Yankang Zhao[1,2], Xiaobo Ma[1,2(✉)], Jianfeng Li[1,2], Shui Yu[3], and Wei Li[1,2]

[1] Ministry of Education Key Laboratory of Intelligent Networks and Network Security, Xi'an Jiaotong University, Xi'an 710049, Shaanxi, China
[2] School of Electronic and Information Engineering, Xi'an Jiaotong University, Xi'an 710049, Shaanxi, China
xma.cs@xjtu.edu.cn
[3] School of Software, University of Technology Sydney, Sydney, Australia

Abstract. Website fingerprinting has been recognized as a traffic analysis attack against encrypted traffic induced by anonymity networks (e.g., Tor) and encrypted proxies. Recent studies have demonstrated that, leveraging machine learning techniques and numerous side-channel traffic features, website fingerprinting is effective in inferring which website a user is visiting via anonymity networks and encrypted proxies. In this paper, we concentrate on Shadowsocks, an encrypted proxy widely used to evade Internet censorship, and we are interested in to what extent state-of-the-art website fingerprinting techniques can break the privacy of Shadowsocks users in real-world scenarios. By design, Shadowsocks does not deploy any timing-based or packet size-based defenses like Tor. Therefore, we expect that website fingerprinting could achieve better attack performance against Shadowsocks compared to Tor. However, after deploying Shadowsocks with more than 20 active users and collecting 30 GB traces during one month, our observation is counter-intuitive. That is, the attack performance against Shadowsocks is even worse than that against Tor (based on public Tor traces). Motivated by such an observation, we investigate a series of practical factors affecting website fingerprinting, such as data labeling, feature selection, and number of instances per class. Our study reveals that state-of-the-art website fingerprinting techniques may not be effective in real-world scenarios, even in the face of Shadowsocks which does not deploy typical defenses.

1 Introduction

As an attack leveraging side information such as packet time and packet sizes, website fingerprinting specializes in inferring user privacy of visited websites through eavesdropping encrypted web traffic and anonymity tunnels (e.g., Tor). Before website fingerprinting was extensively studied [7,8,13,15,23], encrypted web traffic and anonymity tunnels had been commonly believed to preserve privacy by design, unless otherwise decrypted. However, recent years have

© Springer Nature Switzerland AG 2018
M. H. Au et al. (Eds.): NSS 2018, LNCS 11058, pp. 319–336, 2018.
https://doi.org/10.1007/978-3-030-02744-5_24

witnessed the prosperity of website fingerprinting methods [10,11,17], causing a significant concern about user privacy of visited websites. This concern meanwhile gave birth to a number of website fingerprinting defenses (e.g., Buflo, adaptive padding, tamarraw, etc.) [5,6,14,19,23,25], aiming at frustrating the website fingerprinting attacks. In particular, the well-known anonymity project, Tor, always releases their advanced version when new defenses are proposed.

Despite their proved success by experiments, existing website fingerprinting attacks, according to the public media, have not become a means of real-life cyber attacks as prevalent as those like worm, botnet, password theft, and vulnerability exploit. We believe that the major reason is that website fingerprinting is a sophisticated attack heavily relying on machine learning techniques, whereas learning encrypted traffic patterns in real-world scenarios have practical issues. Thus, it is necessary to consider practical factors affecting website fingerprinting in real-world scenarios. In view of this, it is desirable to revisit website fingerprinting by deploying existing website fingerprinting techniques to attack real anonymity networks or encrypted proxies with real-life users.

In this paper, we concentrate on Shadowsocks (i.e., a popular secure socks5 proxy), and deploy Shadowsocks with 20 active real-life users and collect 30 GB traces during one month. These real-life users, from their computers or smartphones, use our Shadowsocks server almost every day to access the Internet, especially for visiting those websites that are under censorship and thus blocked. The reasons that we choose Shadosocks rather than Tor are three-fold. First, Tor is a high-delay network and often blocked by local organizations. So there is less opportunities for website fingerprinting attacks on it. Second, Shadowsocks is a lightweight and easy-to-use secure socks5 proxy. It has encrypted all communications with multiple optimal algorithms (e.g, AES, IDEA, RC4 and so on), and supports all kinds of major operating systems (e.g., Windows, OS X, Android and IOS). Hence, we can deploy it, providing services for many real-life users accessing the Internet. Shadowsocks has gained its popularity these years according to Google trend [2] and GitHub star [3]. Third, the attack performance against Shadowsocks could reflect the upper bound of the attack performance against anonymity network such as Tor, because Shadowsocks does not deploy any timing-based or packet size-based defenses.

Focusing on Shadowsocks, we investigate and apply current attack techniques against Shadowsocks traffic. Meanwhile, we also perform the same attacks against Tor traffic published by Wang et al. [23]. Then, we observe attack results to compare the attack performance. Throughout our investigation, we consider the following practical factors affecting website fingerprinting.

First, recent work usually collects traffic by sending requests automatically based on tools like Webdriver that can drive a browser like a user, fed by URLs. Because the process of sending request is under control, one can easily partition packet streaming into individual websites. Therefore, each sample trace can be labeled as a website straightforwardly. However, in a real-world scenario, this is not easy to accomplish. The reason is that we can only get continuous packets captured on network, but these packets that may come from different websites might be mixed together so that we cannot separate them easily. Therefore, packet partition is key point of website fingerprinting in a real-word scenario.

Second, for attack efficiency (high classification accuracy and low time overhead), it is critical to choose a suitable classification model. Previous studies usually pay attention to overall attack performance across all classes, but considering the attack performance for each class in a multi-classification problem is also highly desirable. For example, an attack may achieve good enough overall accuracy, but fails to correctly identify the samples belonging to a class (i.e., website). Therefore, we need to consider specific performance for each class for different classification models.

Besides, previous researchers usually try different models with their own feature sets, but they do not study the possibility of feature reduction for lowering computational overhead (high overhead hinders the practical usage of website fingerprinting) while ensuring accuracy. Although Hayes et al. introduced feature selection in [9], they do not perform evaluation using the most effective feature subset. Therefore, we select the most effective feature subset by a novel feature selection method. We also find that the attack performance can be further improved by optimizing the number of instances per class (i.e., website).

Third, current attacks mostly rely on a trial-and-error paradigm to evaluate performance rather than utilizing data intrinsic distinguishability. Therefore, even if achieving a better or worse performance, we have no idea the complexity of distinguishable boundaries across different classes. It is essential to find a data complexity-based method to illustrate the underlying reasons for the attack performance.

Taking into the practical factors above, we investigate website fingerprinting against Shadowsocks, and make the following contributions.

- Following the real-world Internet censorship scenario, we label real-life Shadowsocks traces and perform website fingerprinting from the perspective of the ISP to make our attacks comply with the reality. In particular, we select unmonitored website number by the statistics of real-world traffic. We surprisingly find that the attack performance in real-world is worse than its in simulation, though the former does not deploy any website fingerprinting defenses but the latter does. Our finding suggests that website fingerprinting may not be effective as expected by the current literature in real-world scenarios.
- Unlike model selection solely based on classification accuracy, we consider not only overall attack performance, but also the performance of each class, along with a minimized time consumption for training and testing. We can obtain a better classification model (Random-Forest) based on metrics (F-score, Recall and Precision). It consumes less than 24 s for training and just 0.6 s for testing, whereas more than 10 times time is consumed by other models (e.g., KNN, SVM).
- Combining traditional information theory and data complexity, we propose a novel feature selection to find an optimal set of features, along with a data complexity metric to more comprehensively evaluate the attack performance.

We can achieve a better attack performance by less than 20% features, compared with adopting the entire set of features. Furthermore, we can improve attack performance by optimizing the number of instances per website.

Roadmap. We introduce related work and motivation in Sect. 2, and dataset in Sect. 3. We perform attack analysis in Sect. 4. Section 5 presents feature selection and Sect. 6 optimizes the number of instances. We finally conclude in Sect. 7.

2   Related Work and Motivation

2.1   Related Work

A number of website fingerprinting attack and defense methods have been proposed. The defender aims to obfuscate the traffic data so that the attacker cannot distinguish one website from another based on side information (e.g., packet sizes and ordering) of the encrypted communication. The attacker, who passively monitors the encrypted communication between an end user (whose privacy the defender wants to protect) and a private web proxy (e.g., Tor, Shadowsocks), builds the linkage between the actually visited web pages and the observed side information by selecting distinguishable features and effective classifiers.

Among all the private web proxies, Tor might be arguably the most notable one due to its second-generation onion routing mechanism with enhanced security. For example, Tor leverages cells with fixed sizes of 512 bytes for communication, removing features such as cell size distribution critical to website fingerprinting attacks. As Tor already conceals cell sizes, defenses focusing on cell (or packet) sizes, such as maximum packet padding, exponential packet padding, traffic morphing [24], and HTTPOS [18], are not applicable for Tor. Apart from the built-in defense by Tor itself, below are typical defenses that can be added to Tor for better defenses.

- Adaptive Padding(AdaP) was proposed by Shmatikov and Wang to defend against timing analysis by injecting dummy packets into statistically unlikely gaps [22].
- Decoy Pages [21]. This defense loads a randomly chosen web page (background page) simultaneously with the actually requested one. Non-monitored pages are randomly chosen as decoy pages.
- BuFLO [6]. It sends packets of a fixed size at fixed intervals for at least a fixed amount of time. If a flow goes longer than the fixed time out, BuFLO lets it conclude while still using fixed-length packets at a fixed interval.
- Tamaraw [5]. Similar to BuFLO, traffic is forwarded through MTU-size packets at fixed intervals. However, the incoming and outgoing traffic are treated differently. Outgoing packets is dispatched with a larger interval to decrease the overhead because they are less frequent.

To defeat these defenses, various attack methods, such as Naive Bayes (NB) [16], k-Nearest Neighbor (KNN) [23], Support Vector Machine (SVM) [21], k-finger-printing that combines Random Forest(RF) and KNN [9], have been proposed. We perform attacks on Tor dataset with different defenses mentioned-above in order to observe performance of different attack methods. Besides the differences in classification algorithms, these methods employ different features of their own.

Table 1. The performance of website fingerprinting attacks against different defenses.

Attack	Defense				
	No defense	AdaP [22]	Buflo [6]	Decoy pages [21]	Tamaraw [5]
NB [16]	0.5816	0.4888	0.1827	0.0407	0.0050
KNN [23]	0.9047	0.8250	0.1410	0.3428	0.0236
SVM [21]	0.9096	0.8458	0.1135	0.3112	0.0453
RF [9]	0.9188	0.8563	0.1891	0.4858	0.0421

Table 1 lists the performance of these website fingerprinting attacks against different defenses that are added to Tor, including the result without defense (i.e., there is none of extra defense). The performance is computed as the classification accuracy (i.e., the ratio of the instances correctly classified to all the instances). For the ease of comparison, the experiment was performed in a closed-world setting based on the Tor cell traces collected by Wang et al. [23], with 100 websites and 90 instances for each website.

The result indicates that Random-Forest outperforms KNN and SVM, consistent to Hayes et al. in [9]. Note that Hayes et al. use the combination of Random-Forest and k-Nearest Neighbor to attack with open-world dataset, but only Random-Forest is used in close-world. In conclusion, we will pay attention to Random-Forest model, and analysis and comparison between KNN, SVM and Random-Forest will be detailed in Sect. 4.

2.2   Motivation

Although Tor is popular in anonymous communication, it is of high-delay and might be blocked by local organizations. In this paper, we concentrate on a secure socks5 proxy, named Shadowsocks. It is very popular these years due to lightweight, easy-to-use and multiple-operating system support. In particular, Shadowsocks client has been downloaded more than 50 thousand times according to Google's Play store, and more than 112 thousand times according to ASO114 (i.e., the largest platform for mobile developer data analysis in China.). Its star number is more than 22 thousand on GitHub. Shadowsocks has become increasingly popular since 2014 according to Google trend, especially in China. Note it does not deploy any advanced defenses of traffic obfuscation like Tor.

Given the popularity of Shadowsocks, little attention has been paid to the website fingerprinting attack performance against Shadowsocks in a real-world scenario. We conjecture that people may believe that Shadowsocks does not deploy any defenses (e.g., packet padding or time modification) and thus attacking Shadowsocks are not expected to be academically challenging. Therefore, it is interesting to apply state-of-the-art website fingerprinting attacks to Shadowsocks to see to what extent Shadowsocks can protect user privacy against website fingerprinting by considering practical factors in Sect. 4.3.

3   Real-Life Shadowsocks Data Preparation

In this section, we introduce datasets including Tor and Shadowsocks traffic.

– **Tor** dataset was published by Wang et al. in [5], named as Tor-W. It contains 100 websites with 90 instances each in close-world, and 9,000 websites with one each in open-world.
– **Shadowsocks** datasets were collected in two ways. One collected 30 GB traces with 20 active real-life users during one month, named as SS, and it is also a research priority in this paper. In fairness to Tor result, two collected traffic produced by requesting Alexa's Top 10,000 websites automatically with simulation in China where many sites were blocked , named as SS-sim.

As mentioned before, SS is collected from a real-world scenario, and it is recorded in a 30 GB-sized pcap binary file How to pretreat packets captured is also the core problem of deploying website fingerprinting into real-life scenarios. Specifically, we need to split this file into individual instances. As we know, one website fetch normally triggers more than one TCP connections. Thus, we need to determine which connections belong to a specific website fetch. We use a splitting method based on 4-tuple (i.e., source ip, source port, destination ip and source port), which is simple but conforms to a real-world attacker. Note that attacker collects traffic between local and remote proxy, so the ip and port belong to the proxies and can not expose user visiting. As Fig. 1 shows, we first split a large packet sequence into some small pieces based on unique TCP port. Second, we aggregate these pieces into slightly larger pieces based on requested URLs recorded in the Shadowsocks log file. Lastly, we will receive many packet sets, and each one belongs to a website. Specifically, the log of Shadowsocks server will record requested URLs, the corresponding ports, and the timestamps. In addition, the pretreament of SS-sim is similar.

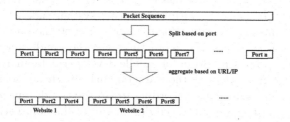

Fig. 1. The progress of splitting traffic

4 Website Fingerprinting Attack Analysis Against Shadowsocks

We propose website fingerprinting features as many as possible, and then introduce four metrics for performance evaluation.

4.1 Features Under Investigation

Features are of central importance in website fingerprinting attacks and defenses, where the attacker exploits informative features to perform attacks and the defender tries to conceal these features. Regardless of the specific encryption algorithms and anonymity tunnels, an instance of visiting a website (or webpage) can be described by a sequence of packets with various features. To facilitate our data-centric evaluation, we investigate existing features as many as possible, and categorize them into five types, namely, overall statistics, packet ordering, packet timing, head/tail statistics, and packet size.

Overall Statistics. This type of features centers around statistics regarding packet numbers and packet sizes. In the case of Tor, each cell is equally sized, thereby only statistics regarding packet numbers available. There are five specific features, including the total number of packets (*total_number*), the number of outgoing packets (*out_number*), the number of incoming packets (*in_number*), the ratio of outgoing packets to all packets (*out_fraction*), and the ratio of incoming packets to all packets (*in_fraction*). Similar statistics regarding packet sizes can be derived.

Packet Ordering. This type of features focuses on the request-response interaction ordering between the client and the server, termed as packet ordering. More precisely, this type of features reflects where each outgoing/incoming packet occurs, especially each outgoing packet. Specific features include:

- Outgoing packet index. For each outgoing packet, we count the total number of packets before it (*total_before_out_packet*). This number can represent the arrival order of the outgoing packet. The list of such numbers of all outgoing packets can be packet ordering features. We then derive two features to describe the packet ordering of outgoing packets, i.e., the mean value (*pkt_out_ordering_mean*) and the standard deviation (*pkt_out_ordering_std*) of the list of such numbers derived from all outgoing packets.
- Outgoing packet distribution. Another type of features related to packet ordering is the distribution (i.e., concentrated or dispersed) of outgoing packets along the session. To measure the distribution, packet sequence is partitioned into non-overlapping chunks of 20 packets. We then count the number of outgoing packets in each of the chunks, and calculate the mean/maximum/minimum/medium values, and the standard deviation, denoted by (*pkt_concentration_*). Note that we use * to denote the statistics such as mean, maximum, and quartiles. We also extract the list of the number of packets between two successive outgoing packets (*total_between_out_pkt*).

For incoming packets, we count the total number of packets before each incoming packet, and extract two features to describe the packet ordering of incoming packets, i.e., the mean value (*in_inter_arrival*) and the standard deviation (*pkt_in_ordering_std*) of the list of such numbers derived from all incoming packets. In addition, we also borrow the feature that combines both the outgoing packets and the incoming packets in [20]. The feature calculates the cumulative packet size in both directions (e.g., an outgoing packet with size +1, an incoming packet with size −1) as the packet number increases. We use *cumul_n* to denote the cumulative packet size at the nth packet. Since different instances differ in packet number, we use interpolation methods to sample 100 values of cumulative packet size at fixed intervals. Therefore, we have $n = 1, \ldots, 100$.

Packet Timing. Packet timing includes a set of features concerning time-related features that are mutually dependent, such as packet arrival rate, packet interarrival time, and packet transmission time.

- Packet arrival rate. The packet arrival rate is calculated every second. We then use five statistics to characterize the packet arrival rate, including the mean/maximum/minimum/medium value and the standard deviation (*number_per_second_list_*).
- Packet interarrival time. For all packets, we calculate four statistics regarding the interarrival times, namely, the mean/maximum/minimum/medium value and the standard deviation (*total_inter_arrival_*). Similar statistics can be calculated for the outgoing/incoming packets (*out_inter_arrival_*, *in_inter_arrival_*).
- Packet transmission time. For all packets, we calculate the transmission times for the nth quartiles of packets (*total_n_quartile*). Similar statistics can be calculated for the outgoing/incoming packets (*out_n_quartile, in_n_quartile*).

Head/Tail Statistics. The characteristics of the head/tail packets may also be important in distinguishing one website from another. In particular, the total sizes of the head (e.g., first 30)/tail (e.g., last 30) packets are also features used in the literature. These sizes can be derived for the outgoing packets (*first30_out_number, last30_out_number*), the incoming packets (*first30_in_number, last30_in_number*).

Packet Size. Features extracted from packet size is important in website fingerprinting. Tor project has deployed defenses to hide packet size features. We first count the number of packet size in every interval, specifically, each interval is between 2^{n-1} bytes and 2^n bytes. Then we derive the values of mean, median, std, third-quartile and sum from packet sizes of incoming, outgoing and overall respectively. In total, we can extract 27 dimension features from packet sizes.

Table 2 summarizes all the features and their definitions. In total, we obtain 776 dimensions as packet size/timing features, among which 749 dimensions are packet timing features.

Table 2. Feature description

Type	Feature name	Definition
number	total/in/out number	The number of all/incoming/outgoing packets
percentage	in/out percentage	The percentage of incoming/outgoing packets
ordering	in/out ordering mean/std	For each successive incoming and outgoing packet, the total number of packets seen before it in the sequence. Mean and std of ordering list
per second	number per second mean/std/median/ min/max/sum	Mean, std, median, min, max and sum of list of numbers per second
30 packets	first30/last30 in/out number	The number of incoming and outgoing packets in the first and last 30 packets
interval	total/in/out inter arrival max/mean/std/3 quartile	For the total, incoming and outgoing packet streams extract the lists of interarrival times between packets.For each list extract the max, mean, standard deviation, and third quartile
quartile	total/in/out 1/2/3/4 quartile	For the total, incoming and outgoing packet sequences we extract the first, second, third quartile and total transmission time
concentration	pkt concentration max/min/mean/std/ median/sum	For chunks of 20 evenly sized packets extract a list of outgoing packets number,and then extract the max, min, mean, std, median and sum on the list
cumul	cumul 1/2/3.../100	Deriving n features c1,c2,....c100 by sampling the piecewise linear interpolant.(Reference: Website Fingerprinting at Internet Scale)
before	total before out pkt 1/2/3../300	The total number of packets before each outgoing packet
between	total between out pkt 1/2/3.../300	The total number of packets between this outgoing packet and previous one
size statistics	pkt_size_in/out_1/2/ 3.../6	Count the number of packet size in every interval (the nth power of 2)
size overall	pkt_size_in/out/ overall_mean/median/std/ sum/3-quartile	Deriving mean, median, std, third-quartile and sum from packet sizes of incoming, outgoing and overall respectively

4.2 Metrics

We employ four metrics to evaluate attack performance, including Precision, Recall, F1-Score and OOB-score. These metrics demonstrate attack performance in different aspects. They are detailed below.

- **Precision** is the fraction of relevant instances among the retrieved instances. It is intuitively the ability of the classifier not to label as positive a sample that is negative.
- **Recall** is the fraction of retrieved relevant instances over the total amount of relevant instances. It reflects the ability of a classifier to find all positive samples.
- **F-score** (a.k.a. F-measure) is a weighted harmonic mean of the precision and recall, where an F-beta score reaches its best value at 1 and worst score at 0.

- **OOB-score** equals approximately 3-fold cross-validation. It uses out-of-bag samples to estimate the generalization accuracy on the process of training Random-Forest model.

4.3   Evaluation

According to Table 1, Random-Forest is a sophisticated model on website fingerprinting. To further demonstrate Random-Forest's performance, we analyze classification ability of this model in detail. Specifically, website fingerprinting attack is a multi-classification problem. Thus, we need to observe the prediction performance of each class besides the overall performance. Meanwhile, we consider time consumption of training and testing for different models. By comparing the performance in different aspects, we can obtain the best model.

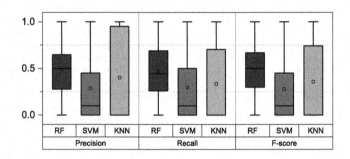

Fig. 2. Illustrating the performance of Random-Forest based on three metrics.

Table 3. Comparison of time overhead (in seconds).

Model	Train time	Test time
RF	24.09	0.62
KNN	253.79	189.59
SVM	430.82	24.08

As for SS, although we collect more than 100 instances per website in close-world, we use 70 instances each of 100 websites for training and another 20 instances for testing for fairness. Because the number of instances per website of Tao Wang's dataset is only 90. At the same time, we select randomly 2000 websites and one instance each from open-world for training. The reason why choosing 2000 is that we conclude it from statistical analysis of all requests of one group in a month. More specifically, we count all unique websites requested by all group members, and then we find only about 1800 websites have been visited, meanwhile, including only 160 websites visiting more than 100 times. Base on these settings, we perform attacks with three models (i.e., Random-Forest(RF), Support Vector Machine(SVM) and k-Nearest Neighbor (KNN)).

We utilize Precision, Recall and F-score to evaluate predictions of each class. There are 100 classes for closed-world and one class for open-world (i.e., there are 101 classes in total.) as mentioned before. In Fig. 2, it shows performance of three metrics on three models for these 101 classes. Obviously, KNN's predictions are unbalance, Because it performs better on some websites and worse on the others. In particular, there are lots of terrible predictions (i.e., predict all samples are wrong in one class.) on testing. SVM is also similar with KNN because of 25% classes with terrible predictions. Besides, Table 3 shows that the time overhead of Random-Forest is far smaller than the other two. According to three metrics and time overhead, we can conclude that Random-Forest is the best model for website-fingerprinting among the three models.

In order to observe the difference of scenarios, we perform attacks on datasets mentioned before using Rand-Forest with 500 trees and entropy criteria for tree splitting. Each result is the average value of 10 times running(all results of our experiments are calculated in the same way). For fairness, we select training and testing sets with the same way as experiment of Fig. 2 on three datasets, and extract features according to Table 2.

Table 4. Comparison based on metrics.

Dataset	Precision	Recall	F-score	OOB-score
Tor-W	0.9271	0.9041	0.913	0.9184
SS	0.5585	0.4209	0.4567	0.4871
SS-sim	0.9851	0.9766	0.9822	0.9806

The result of Table 4 shows a surprising result about Tor-W, SS and SS-sim. According to the values of metrics, SS is obviously far worse than Tor-W, but SS-sim is better than Tor-W. The difference between SS and SS-sim is just experiment settings (i.e., SS is from real life but SS-sim is from simulation), however,they get two completely different results comparing with Tor. We can conclude that attack results heavily depend on different scenarios.

Different from Tor with some advanced defenses, Shadowsocks does not deploy any defenses on packet size and timing. It only obfuscates protocol and encrypts contents, but its attack performance is confusing. The result of SS-sim conforms to the intuition because there are more distinguishable characteristics on packets. However, the result of SS is counter-intuitive. There are some possible reasons for this counter-intuitive result. In real-world scenarios, different users send requests in different ways, such as various browsers (e.g., Firefox, Chrome, Internet Explorer, etc.), various devices (e.g., Mobile Phone, Laptop, Desktop, etc.) and various networks (e.g., Wi-Fi, wired network, 4G network, etc.). As we know, different browsers have unique characteristics, different devices have their individual settings, and different networks differ in communication models.

Due to these differences, traffic patterns are hard to behave the same, even if two requests are exactly the same. In addition, the action of visiting sites may be terminated randomly at any time, so some packets do not be captured. In other words, we only get a part of website resource in this condition. In conclusion, although Shadowsocks traffic does not add any defenses like Tor, many real-world factors make traffic patterns become more complex, which hurdles good performance of website fingerprinting.

We can conclude that the performance of SS is worst on Table 4, especially for the values of Recall, F-score and OOB-socre. We then consider the possibility of performance improvement by selecting the most effective features and increase samples on training. Based on feature description of Table 2, it is not hard to find that there are some overlaps within different features. For better attack efficiency and performance, we hope to refine the entire feature set by finding the most effective feature subset.

5   Feature Refinement for Lower Overhead While Ensuring Accuracy

Feature selection not only benefits achieving a better accuracy of classification and cost minimization, but also helps to gain insight into the nature of the data. Packet size is very important for website classification intuitively in this domain, and Tor project has already hidden unique packet sizes via some effective defenses. In this section, we will compare attack performance between all features and feature subsets.

Table 5. Attacks on feature subsets

Metric	Features (749)	Features (776)	Features (50)
F-Score	0.4567	0.5269	0.6751
Precision	0.5585	0.6554	0.7457
Recall	0.4209	0.4738	0.6392
OOB-score	0.4871	0.5589	0.6763

We calculate the values of metrics based on the feature subsets. The results are shown in Table 5. We can draw two conclusions. First, features extracted from packet size is powerful on website classification. For example, the whole feature set (i.e., 776 features) is better than the only features extracted packet timing (i.e., 749 features) in terms of Random-Forest attack. Second, website fingerprinting does not benefit from more features. For example, top-50 features selected can achieve the best performance. According to the results, we can conclude that feature selection is necessary for attack performance and picking the most efficient feature subset. Besides, we discover that top-50 features include 18 features extracted from packet size (note that only 27 features extracted from packet size). This result further illustrates the importance of packet size. In other words, we can utilize a small subset of features to achieve a best result, meanwhile, the subset includes a majority of the most effective features.

Inspired by the result of Table 5, we decide to perform feature selections on website fingerprinting attack. These selections are based on information theory and data complexity respectively. We introduce feature selection methods and then evaluate them in the following subsections.

5.1 Feature Selection

We analyze the datasets from a different angle, such as the nature of data, or data complexity. We will compare feature selection methods based on entropy criteria of Random-Forest and feature efficiency we proposed, respectively.

Feature Importances of RF. The feature importance is based on the progress of building Random-Forest (RF). It is a popular method for feature ranking, since we can apply it so easily without extra feature engineering. In our experiments, we use a very popular python tool, scikit-learn [1], which implements the importance as described in [4]. It is sometimes called "gini importance" or "mean decrease impurity". Basically, the idea is to measure the decrease in accuracy on out-of-bag data when you randomly permute the values for that feature. If the decrease is low, then the feature is not important, and vice-versa. We also call this feature importance (FI).

Feature Efficiency. Inspired by series of data complexity measures [12], we will introduce a new method of feature selection based on data complexity rather than information theory. The formula is as follows and called feature efficiency.

$$F(f) = 1 - \frac{|\text{MAXMIN}_f \rightarrow \text{MINMAX}_f|}{|C_{jf} \cup C_{kf}|}$$

where

$$\text{MINMAX}_f = \min(\max(f, C_j), \max(f, C_k))$$
$$\text{MAXMIN}_f = \max(\min(f, C_j), \min(f, C_k))$$

f denotes a feature, $|\text{MAXMIN}_f \rightarrow \text{MINMAX}_f|$ denotes the number of samples between MAXMIN_f and MINMAX_f (i.e., the overlap region of two classes C_j and C_k), and $|C_j \cup C_k|$ denotes the number of samples of the set $C_j \cup C_k$.

Though F is based on the overlap region, it is measured by the ratio of the number of samples within the overlap region (rather than the size of the overlap region) to that of all the samples. F quantifies the proportion of the samples that f can distinguish between each pair of classes. Intuitively, for any feature f, larger values of F indicate stronger distinguishability of f across different class. On the contrary, smaller values of F indicate weaker distinguishability.

How does feature selection do based on measure F? Firstly, we calculate the feature efficiency for every feature over two classes and their instances, and then select the feature with the largest value of F. Next, we remove all the instances outside the overlap region of the selected single feature, and then select the second feature over the remaining instances using the same method. This procedure repeats until all the features are selected or all instances of the two classes are correctly classified. We perform the same thing for all pair of classes, and finally rank the features based on the total number of instances they can distinguish. We call this process collective feature efficiency (CFS).

5.2   Feature Evaluation

According to the selection methods above, we compute OOB-score, which is a convincing metric because of cross-validation, for two datasets in close-world. More specifically, we will use 100 websites and 90 instances each for every dataset to evaluate performance, and then we observe the change of OOB-score values as adding features (step is 10) based on selections.

In Fig. 3, selection based on CFS is better obviously, because it reaches peak with fewer features for all datasets. In addition, the peak value of OOB-score based on CFS is slightly better than its value based on FI, especially for Shadowsocks. More specifically, OOB-score reaches a maximum value with a small subset of the most effective features, and then the value will be gradually decreasing. Besides, it is obvious that difference of selections is large for different datasets. For example, the maximum value of Shadowsocks based on CFS is greater than 0.05 comparing with its value based on FI, but the maximum value of Tor-W based on CFS is just greater than 0.01 comparing with its value based on FI. Therefore, Shadowsocks has a greater improvement than Tor-W by feature selection. This result provides us a new viewpoint for attack performance optimization, and demonstrates the importance of feature selection. We therefore can further improve performance by a feature selection method like CFS.

5.3   Dataset Evaluation

In order to observe the complexity of samples from the nature, we calculate F for each feature over pair classes, and then get the max values. Formula as follows:

$$F\_max_{jk} = \max_f F(f) \tag{1}$$

where F_max_{jk} donates the max value of F for all features over class C_j and class C_k. It is also considered as the maximum distinguishability for pair class. Then, we can get the complexity of all samples given dataset by calculating F_max for each pair class.

To observe overall performance of dataset, we plot a CDF (i.e., cumulative distribution function) plot to analyze data complexity based on F_{max}. According to the definition, F_{max} indicates the maximum of F in each class pair, and thus a larger F_{max} value indicates this class pair is more distinguishable, and vice versa.

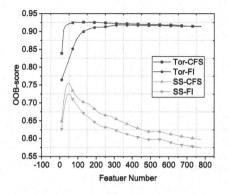

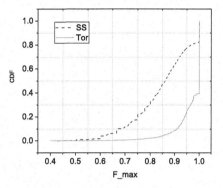

Fig. 3. The attack performance of RF as we add features.

Fig. 4. The data complexity of Tor-W and SS.

In Fig. 4, it is obvious that overall distinguishability of Shadowsocks is weaker than Tor-W's. For example, 8.5% F_{max} values are less than 0.9 on Tor-W, or 91.5% F_{max} values are greater than 0.9, which indicates most of class pairs are stronger distinguishable. However, there are 62% F_{max} values for less than 0.9 on Shadowsocks, or 38% F_{max} values are greater than 0.9, which indicates most of class pairs are weaker distinguishable. We can further demonstrate the difference of attack performance between datasets by analyzing data complexity. Although Tor-W has deployed many advanced defenses, the complexity of Shadowsocks is higher. This conclusion also explains why the attack performance of Shadowsocks is worse than that of Tor.

6 Tuning the Number of Instances for Better Attack Performance

Considering more patterns for each website in real-world scenario, the training of attack model with more samples could improve performance, because the model need lots of samples to learn to classify better. We perform website fingerprinting attacks against Shadowsocks using Random-Forest by varying the number of instances. Meanwhile, we adopt 10 websites and 1,000 instances for each website in the close-world data. The rest settings (including testing and open-world data) are the same as those in Sect. 4.

The values of Precision, Recall and F-score show different trends as varying the number of instances in Fig. 5. Because the number of instances for testing is fixed (10 websites and 20 instances for each website in close-world, and 1,000 websites in open-world), but the number of instances for training is varied (10 websites and a varying number of instances for each website in close-world, and 2,000 websites in open-world). It is not hard to understand that Recall's value will be larger and larger with increasing of proportion of instances in close-world,

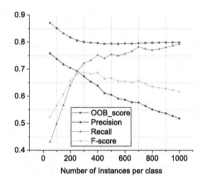

Fig. 5. The attack performance as we vary the number of instances per class.

and Precision's value is to the contrary. When the number is small (e.g., is less than 300.), the proportion of open-world instances is higher relatively and OOB-score is also not steady now. It is necessary for us to observe performance on more instances. Specifically, with the number increasing, Precision is decreasing, Recall is increasing and OOB-score is first decreasing and then keep steady. F-score value is maximum (i.e., F-score is 0.70, Recall is 0.74, Precision is 0.67 at this point) when the number of instances is 300, and OOB-score (i.e., is 0.80) is also steady here. Therefore, we conclude that the number can make an effect on attack performance.

In summary, we can achieve better performance by fine-tuning the number of instances per class when performing website fingerprinting. Because OOB-score is similar with 3-fold cross validation, it is a reliable metric. When Recall reaches OOB-score's steady value, we can choose the instance number of this point as an optimal number.

7   Conclusion

We studied website fingerprinting in a real-world scenario. We intuitively expect Shadowsocks traffic is more distinguishable due to the absence of defenses. It is surprising to find that the attack performance of real-world Shadowsocks is worse because of more complex patterns in traffic. In order to improve performance, we first select the most effective classification model for website fingerprinting attack by comparing three metrics on each class and time overhead on training and testing. Then, we introduce two feature selection methods, feature importance and feature efficiency, to select the most effective features for the performance improvement. Meanwhile, we illustrate attack results by dataset intrinsic distinguishability based on feature efficiency. Finally, in view of the complexity of traffic patterns, we further improve the performance by increasing the number of samples, and a criterion was proposed for the selection of instance number based on OOB-socre and Recall.

References

1. Scikit-learn (2017). http://scikit-learn.org/stable/
2. Google Trend of Shadowsocks, January 2018. https://trends.google.com.hk/trends/
3. Shadowsocks, January 2018. https://github.com/shadowsocks/shadowsocks
4. Breiman, L.: Random forests. Mach. Learn. **45**(1), 5–32 (2001)
5. Cai, X., Nithyanand, R., Wang, T., Johnson, R., Goldberg, I.: A systematic approach to developing and evaluating website fingerprinting defenses. In: Proceedings of the ACM CCS (2014)
6. Dyer, K.P., Coull, S.E., Ristenpart, T., Shrimpton, T.: Peek-a-boo, i still see you: why efficient traffic analysis countermeasures fail. In: Proceedings of the IEEE Security and Privacy (2012)
7. Gong, X., Kiyavash, N., Borisov, N.: Fingerprinting websites using remote traffic analysis. In: Proceedings of the ACM CCS (2010)
8. Gu, X., Yang, M., Luo, J.: A novel website fingerprinting attack against multi-tab browsing behavior. In: Proceedings of the IEEE CSCWD (2015)
9. Hayes, J., Danezis, G.: k-fingerprinting: a robust scalable website fingerprinting technique. In: Proceedings of the USENIX Security (2016)
10. Herrmann, D., Wendolsky, R., Federrath, H.: Website fingerprinting: attacking popular privacy enhancing technologies with the multinomial naïve-bayes classifier. In: Proceedings of the ACM CCSW (2009)
11. Hintz, A.: Fingerprinting websites using traffic analysis. In: Proceedings of the PET (2002)
12. Ho, T.K., Basu, M.: Complexity measures of supervised classification problems. IEEE Trans. Pattern Anal. Mach. Intell. **24**(3), 289–300 (2002)
13. Juarez, M., Afroz, S., Acar, G., Diaz, C., Greenstadt, R.: A critical evaluation of website fingerprinting attacks. In: Proceedings of the ACM CCS (2014)
14. Juárez, M., Imani, M., Perry, M., Díaz, C., Wright, M.: WTF-PAD: toward an efficient website fingerprinting defense for tor. CoRR abs/1512.00524 (2015). http://arxiv.org/abs/1512.00524
15. Li, J., et al.: Can we learn what people are doing from raw DNS queries? In: Proceedings of the IEEE INFOCOM (2018)
16. Liberatore, M., Levine, B.N.: Inferring the source of encrypted HTTP connections. In: Proceedings of the ACM CCS (2006)
17. Lu, L., Chang, E., Chan, M.C.: Website fingerprinting and identification using ordered feature sequences. In: Proceedings of the ESORICS (2010)
18. Luo, X., Zhou, P., Chan, E., Lee, W., Chang, R., Perdisci, R.: Httpos: sealing information leaks with browser-side obfuscation of encrypted flows. In: Proceedings of the NDSS (2011)
19. Nithyanand, R., Cai, X., Johnson, R.: Glove: A bespoke website fingerprinting defense. In: Proceedings of the WPES (2014)
20. Panchenko, A., et al.: Website fingerprinting at internet scale. In: Proceedings of the NDSS (2016)
21. Panchenko, A., Niessen, L., Zinnen, A., Engel, T.: Website fingerprinting in onion routing based anonymization networks. In: Proceedings of the ACM WPES (2011)
22. Shmatikov, V., Wang, M.-H.: Timing analysis in low-latency mix networks: attacks and defenses. In: Gollmann, D., Meier, J., Sabelfeld, A. (eds.) ESORICS 2006. LNCS, vol. 4189, pp. 18–33. Springer, Heidelberg (2006). https://doi.org/10.1007/11863908_2

23. Wang, T., Cai, X., Nithyanand, R., Johnson, R., Goldberg, I.: Effective attacks and provable defenses for website fingerprinting. In: Proceedings of the USENIX Security (2014)
24. Wright, C., Coulls, S., Monrose, F.: Traffic morphing: an efficient defense against statistical traffic analysis. In: Proceedings of the NDSS (2009)
25. Yu, S., Zhao, G., Dou, W., James, S.: Predicted packet padding for anonymous web browsing against traffic analysis attacks. IEEE Trans. Inf. Forensics Secur. **7**(4), 1381–1393 (2012)

User Relationship Classification of Facebook Messenger Mobile Data using WEKA

Amber Umair[1]([✉])[iD], Priyadarsi Nanda[1][iD], Xiangjian He[1][iD],
and Kim-Kwang Raymond Choo[2][iD]

[1] School of Electrical and Data Engineering, University of Technology Sydney,
Sydney, Australia
amber.umair@student.uts.edu.au
[2] Department of Information Systems and Cyber Security,
The University of Texas at San Antonio, San Antonio, TX 78249-0631, USA

Abstract. Mobile devices are a wealth of information about its user and their digital and physical activities (e.g. online browsing and physical location). Therefore, in any crime investigation artifacts obtained from a mobile device can be extremely crucial. However, the variety of mobile platforms, applications (apps) and the significant size of data compound existing challenges in forensic investigations. In this paper, we explore the potential of machine learning in mobile forensics, and specifically in the context of Facebook messenger artifact acquisition and analysis. Using Quick and Choo (2017)'s Digital Forensic Intelligence Analysis Cycle (DFIAC) as the guiding framework, we demonstrate how one can acquire Facebook messenger app artifacts from an Android device and an iOS device (the latter is, using existing forensic tools. Based on the acquired evidence, we create 199 data-instances to train WEKA classifiers (i.e. ZeroR, J48 and Random tree) with the aim of classifying the device owner's contacts and determine their mutual relationship strength.

Keywords: Mobile forensics · Social network information forensics
Weka

1 Introduction

Online social networks are a source of information, for example to profile an individual or group, to understand consumer sentiments on a particular topic, to detect an ongoing event (e.g. earthquake), to stay in touch (e.g. Facebook's Safety Check feature), etc. [13]. In other words, such information can also be useful in a forensic investigation for both criminal cases and civil litigation. However, mobile device and app forensics is constantly playing catching up due to rapid changes in mobile device technologies [3,7]. Compounding the challenge is the different formats used to store data on different devices [1,9]. Unsurprisingly,

© Springer Nature Switzerland AG 2018
M. H. Au et al. (Eds.): NSS 2018, LNCS 11058, pp. 337–348, 2018.
https://doi.org/10.1007/978-3-030-02744-5_25

mobile device and app forensics is an active research area. For example, the authors in [14] forensically examined 20 popular Android instant messaging apps and demonstrated how one can reconstruct message content, in different extent, from 16 of these 20 apps. Other researchers have also shown that a range of artifacts relating to user activities (e.g. login, uploading, downloading, deletion, and the sharing of files) can be recovered from a mobile forensic investigations [5,6,15].

Facebook messenger is another popular application (app) where a Facebook user can have text, voice or video conversations with one or more other Facebook users (e.g. one-to-one or one-to-many conversations); thus, this is the focus of this paper.

Contribution 1: Specifically, we seek to demonstrate the artifacts that can be obtained from such an app when installed on an Android device and an iOS device. We use the Digital Forensic Intelligence Analysis Cycle (DFIAC) [11] to guide the forensic investigation and use existing commercial forensic tools (i.e. FTK access data, SQLite, IPhone Analyzer) to acquire the forensic artifacts from both devices. The original DFIAC model comprises the following steps:

1. Commence (Scope/Tasking)
2. Prepare
3. Evaluate and Identify
4. Collect/Preserve/Collate
5. Analyze
6. Inference Development
7. Present, Complete/Further Tasks identified

In [11], the authors exported the metadata reports from mobile devices, and the CSV, XLS and SLSX reports were collated and manually combined into a spreadsheet. Then, the spreadsheet was converted in Pajek format for analysis. To highlight the interconnections from the acquired data, a graph (e.g. Fruchterman reingold 2D link chart) can then be created and the information analyzed, for example to identify links between individuals in seemingly disparate cases. In this paper, we limit our investigation scope to messages from only the Facebook messenger app. For example in our iOS case study, the data was acquired from a real-world suicide incident, and we were able to determine the victim's relationship strength with other contacts based on factors such as number of messages exchanged in a day or week, and time and day of the messages.

Contribution 2: We also seek to demonstrate the utility of using machine learning to classify the device owner's contacts with respect to relationship strength, from the obtained forensic artifacts. Thus, in step 6 of DFIAC (i.e. Inference Development), we train three WEKA Classifiers (i.e. ZeroR, J48 and Random tree) to efficiently classify the messenger contacts of the phone owner and determine their mutual relationship strength.

Paper's Roadmap: We will now explain how the remaining of this paper is structured. In Sect. 2, we present our case study, as well as our experimental setup along with the tools used. Section 3 explains how we can use machine learning to determine the device owner's closest contacts or friends. The last section concludes this paper.

2 Case Studies

In this section, we will describe our two case studies, namely: an Android device (see Sect. 2.1) and an iOS device (see Sect. 2.2). We also remark that our case study Sect. 2.2 used the backup image from the iPhone of a real-world victim.

2.1 Android Device Case Study

Table 1 summarizes the equipment used in this case study.

Table 1. Experimental setup

Equipment	Version	Purpose
Samsung Galaxy S3	Android Version 4.3	Test device
ADB Android Debug Bridge	Android Studio 2.3.2	Android IDE
One Root	Version 1.0	Gain super user access
Root Checker	Version 6.1.7	Verify root access
Forensic Toolkit (FTK)	FTK Imager 3.1.2.0	Disk imaging program
Dell Laptop	Intel® Core i7 Windows 10 Ent	Phone images analysis

Device Preparation: To facilitate the creation of a physical image of the Samsung Galaxy S3 device, we root the device to gain super user privileges and verify root access using the freely available One Root and Root Checker software. Android Debug Bridge (ADB) is installed on the laptop so that we can issue shell commands to the device by connecting it using a data cable.

Test Data Creation: We then create the test data by installing Facebook app on the device. We also proceed to create a test Facebook user ID and undertake the following user activities on the device:

- Sign In. (Login Id and password entered via Facebook application)
- Remove phone number
- Add Friend (Henry gray)
- Upload post (Time is flying)
- Message sent to Henry via messenger app (Hi Henry, Any Plans for the weekend.)
- Comment on own post (And I can't do anything about it.)

Imaging of Phone Memory: To examine the device's image, we acquire the physical (i.e. bit-for-bit) image of the device's storage, and we know that the device's memory partitions contain user specific data and are of potential forensic interest.

- */system - mmcblk0p9* is where read-only memory (ROM) is installed. Within the '/system' are a number of important folders that a user cannot normally access. For example, Location /system/app all where key ROM applications are located. Things like the device app and the messaging app /system/bin are where important binaries, which allow Android to execute the required commands, etc.
- */data - mmcblk0p12* contains information about the installed app, such as SMS and emails. Key directories here are /data/app and /data/data, which are generally wiped when a device is set to the factory default.
- */cache - mmcblk0p8* stores the temporary system data for everyday tasks, designed to expedite the system's access to apps.

Example artifacts of what we obtain from using FTK are depicted in Figs. 1, 2, 3, 4 and 5.

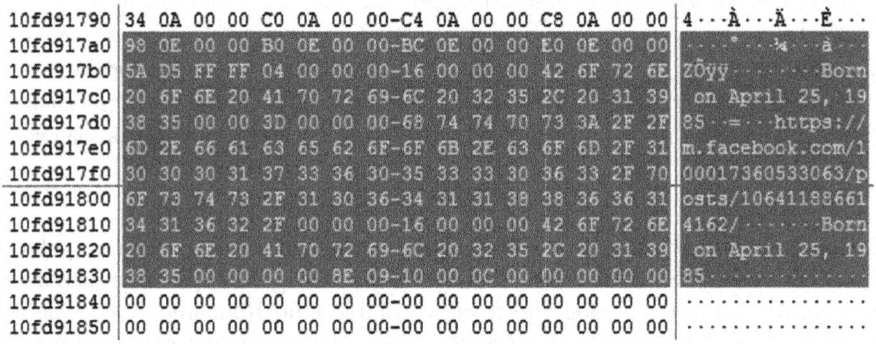

```
10fd91790  34 0A 00 00 C0 0A 00 00-C4 0A 00 00 C8 0A 00 00  4···À···Ä···È···
10fd917a0  98 0E 00 00 B0 0E 00 00-BC 0E 00 00 E0 9E 00 00  ···°···¼···à···
10fd917b0  5A D5 FF FF 04 00 00 00-16 00 00 00 42 6F 72 6E  ZÕÿÿ········Born
10fd917c0  20 6F 6E 20 41 70 72 69-6C 20 32 35 2C 20 31 39   on April 25, 19
10fd917d0  38 35 00 00 3D 00 00 00-68 74 74 70 73 3A 2F 2F  85··=···https://
10fd917e0  6D 2E 66 61 63 65 62 6F-6F 6B 2E 63 6F 6D 2F 31  m.facebook.com/1
10fd917f0  30 30 30 31 37 33 36 30-35 33 33 30 36 33 2F 70  00017360533063/p
10fd91800  6F 73 74 73 2F 31 30 36-34 31 31 38 38 36 36 31  osts/10641188661
10fd91810  34 31 36 32 2F 00 00 00-16 00 00 00 42 6F 72 6E  4162/·······Born
10fd91820  20 6F 6E 20 41 70 72 69-6C 20 32 35 2C 20 31 39   on April 25, 19
10fd91830  38 35 00 00 00 00 8E 09-10 00 0C 00 00 00 00 00  85··············
10fd91840  00 00 00 00 00 00 00 00-00 00 00 00 00 00 00 00  ················
10fd91850  00 00 00 00 00 00 00 00-00 00 00 00 00 00 00 00  ················
```

Fig. 1. User's birthday

2.2   iOS Device Case Study

The device of a teenager who had committed suicide was made available to the researchers for this research, in order to facilitate the determination of the motive and other factors relevant to the investigation. One of the evidence sources is the victim's iPhone backup files obtained from the victim's laptop. Therefore, artifacts were collected from the victim's iPhone 6 (iTunes version 12.0.1.26) backup. As the data is from an ongoing investigation, we anonymize the information to prevent the identification of the case or the individual(s) involved.

Tools used to obtain the artifacts from the iPhone are FTK Access Data, SQLite Forensic Explorer, Firefox SQLite manager and IPhone Analyzer 2.1.70. Password was not required to extract the personal data from the backup, which

```
04849ddc0  5F 66 69 65 6C 64 22 3A-7B 22 5F 5F 74 79 70 65   field":{"__type
04849ddd0  5F 5F 22 3A 7B 22 6E 61-6D 65 22 3A 22 4D 65 73   __":{"name":"Mes
04849dde0  73 65 6E 67 65 72 43 6F-6E 74 61 63 74 4E 61 6D   sengerContactNam
04849ddf0  65 22 7D 2C 22 5F 5F 74-79 70 65 6E 61 6D 65 22   e"},"__typename"
04849de00  3A 22 4D 65 73 73 65 6E-67 65 72 43 6F 6E 74 61   :"MessengerConta
04849de10  63 74 4E 61 6D 65 22 2C-22 76 61 6C 75 65 22 3A   ctName","value":
04849de20  7B 22 74 65 78 74 22 3A-22 48 65 6E 72 79 20 47   {"text":"Henry G
04849de30  72 61 79 22 7D 7D 7D 5D-2C 22 62 69 72 74 68 64   ray"}}}],"birthd
04849de40  61 79 44 61 79 22 3A 32-30 2C 22 62 69 72 74 68   ayDay":20,"birth
04849de50  64 61 79 4D 6F 6E 74 68-22 3A 31 32 2C 22 69 73   dayMonth":12,"is
04849de60  50 61 72 74 69 61 6C 22-3A 66 61 6C 73 65 2C 22   Partial":false,"
04849de70  6C 61 73 74 46 65 74 63-68 54 69 6D 65 22 3A 31   lastFetchTime":1
04849de80  35 30 35 31 39 32 36 37-37 36 31 33 2C 22 6D 6F   505192677613,"mo
04849de90  6E 74 61 67 65 54 68 72-65 61 64 46 42 49 44 22   ntageThreadFBID"
```

Fig. 2. User contact's birthday

```
0bd593e30  4F 4E 45 5F 54 4F 5F 4F-4E 45 3A 31 30 30 30 32   ONE_TO_ONE:10002
0bd593e40  32 30 38 31 38 30 31 37-35 31 3A 31 30 30 30 31   2081801751:10001
0bd593e50  37 33 36 30 35 33 33 30-36 33 06 5B 7B 22 65 6D   7360533063·[{"em
0bd593e60  61 69 6C 22 3A 6E 75 6C-6C 2C 22 75 73 65 72 5F   ail":null,"user_
0bd593e70  6B 65 79 22 3A 22 46 41-43 45 42 4F 4F 4B 3A 31   key":"FACEBOOK:1
0bd593e80  30 30 30 31 37 33 36 30-35 33 33 30 36 33 22 2C   00017360533063",
0bd593e90  22 6E 61 6D 65 22 3A 22-4A 61 6D 65 73 20 57 68   "name":"James Wh
0bd593ea0  69 74 65 22 7D 2C 7B 22-65 6D 61 69 6C 22 3A 6E   ite"},{"email":n
0bd593eb0  75 6C 6C 2C 22 75 73 65-72 5F 6B 65 79 22 3A 22   ull,"user_key":"
0bd593ec0  46 41 43 45 42 4F 4F 4B-3A 31 30 30 30 32 32 30   FACEBOOK:1000220
0bd593ed0  38 31 38 30 31 37 35 31-22 2C 22 6E 61 6D 65 22   81801751","name"
0bd593ee0  3A 22 48 65 6E 72 79 20-47 72 61 79 22 7D 5D 48   :"Henry Gray"}]H
0bd593ef0  69 20 68 65 6E 72 79 2C-20 41 6E 79 20 70 6C 61   i henry, Any pla
0bd593f00  6E 73 20 66 6F 72 20 74-68 65 20 77 65 65 6B 65   ns for the weeke
0bd593f10  6E 64 2E 7B 22 65 6D 61-69 6C 22 3A 6E 75 6C 6C   nd.{"email":null
0bd593f20  2C 22 75 73 65 72 5F 6B-65 79 22 3A 22 46 41 43   ,"user_key":"FAC
0bd593f30  45 42 4F 4F 4B 3A 31 30-30 30 31 37 33 36 30 35   EBOOK:1000173605
0bd593f40  33 33 30 36 33 22 2C 22-6E 61 6D 65 22 3A 22 4A   33063","name":"J
0bd593f50  61 6D 65 73 20 57 68 69-74 65 22 7D 01 5E 74 94   ames White}·^t·
```

Fig. 3. Private Facebook messages

```
14c7cf3d0  33 22 2C 22 74 61 67 67-65 64 5F 69 64 73 22 3A   3","tagged_ids":
14c7cf3e0  5B 5D 2C 22 73 6F 75 72-63 65 5F 74 79 70 65 22   [],"source_type"
14c7cf3f0  3A 22 6E 61 74 69 76 65-5F 74 69 6D 65 6C 69 6E   :"native_timelin
14c7cf400  65 22 2C 22 72 61 77 5F-6D 65 73 73 61 67 65 22   e","raw_message"
14c7cf410  3A 22 54 69 6D 65 20 69-73 20 66 6C 79 69 6E 67   :"Time is flying
14c7cf420  2E 22 2C 22 70 75 62 6C-69 73 68 5F 6D 6F 64 65   .","publish_mode
14c7cf430  22 3A 22 4E 4F 52 4D 41-4C 22 2C 22 6C 61 73 74   ":"NORMAL","last
14c7cf440  5F 65 72 72 6F 72 5F 64-65 74 61 69 6C 73 22 3A   _error_details":
14c7cf450  7B 22 6D 65 73 73 61 67-65 22 3A 22 22 2C 22 6C   {"message":"","l
14c7cf460  6F 67 5F 6D 65 73 73 61-67 65 22 3A 22 22 2C 22   og_message":"","
```

Fig. 4. Facebook status update and comments

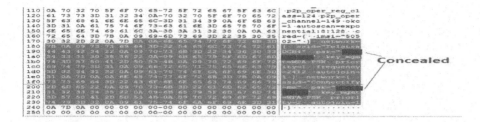

Fig. 5. WIFI and connectify details

included contact numbers, call logs, phone messages, Facebook messenger data/chats, notes, phone reminders /alarms, pictures, videos and audios. The iPhone Analyzer was able to pull out all details from the backup data, without requiring any passcode. Moreover, it was also able to export all data in the way it was organized on the victim's phone. Figures 6 and 7 are a snapshot of what could be

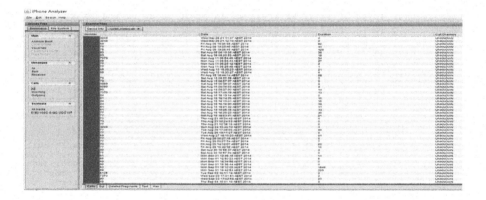

Fig. 6. iPhone analyzer

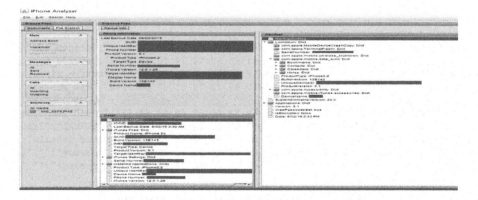

Fig. 7. iPhone Analyzer call details

obtained from the phone's backup. For example, call logs and messages could be easily seen, browsed and exported. We concealed the phone numbers to protect the identity of phone owner. For the same reason, snapshots from other messages artifacts are not shown.

Call logs and messages can be easily seen browsed and exported. The phone numbers are concealed to protect the identity of phone owner. Similarly messages artefacts snapshot is not shown.

3   Using Weka

In our case studies presented in the preceding section, one challenge we face is the difficulty in quickly pinpointing the "more important evidences" due to the different data formats, number of social apps on a device, etc. In addition, a real-world user will have possibly a number of identities for different social network accounts, a significantly larger number of contacts, etc. Thus, an investigation triage phase needs to be sufficiently robust.

We posit the importance of identifying strongly connected contacts of the device owner during a triage phase, for example by analyzing the social networking messaging app and their content. Therefore, to classify the contacts with respect to their relationship strength, we extract the data features from Facebook messenger app in our case studies. The focus is on the number of messages exchanged with a certain contact. Moreover, message exchange during certain times of the day/week (e.g. weekend) may be given a higher weight in determining relationship strength, depending on the context. In order to test the effectiveness of our approach, we analyze the message dataset of 199 instances which represent the message communication pattern of a user with his/her contacts.

Weka (Waikato Environment for Knowledge Analysis) [2] is used to determine the best performing classifiers among ZeroR [8], J48 Decision Tree [10] and Random Tree algorithms [4]. Specifically, we evaluate their performance on our dataset, based on the following key performance indicators: number of correctly identified instances, False Positive Rate (FP), Recall and F-measure.

- The correctly identified instances are the accurately classified instances, which indicate the precision of a classifier.
- FP measure denotes the number of examples predicted positive that are actually negative.
- Recall/sensitivity is the fraction of relevant instances that have been retrieved over the total amount of relevant instances.
  - Recall = True Positive/(True Positive + False Negative)
- F-measure is a measure of a test's accuracy. It is the harmonic mean of recall and precision.
  - F-measure = 2 * Recall * Precision/(Recall + Precision)

The features/attributes of our dataset are presented in Table 2. The J48 decision tree is the Weka implementation of the standard C4.5 algorithm.

Table 2. Attribute details

Attribute	Description
User	Phone owners Facebook contact/friend id. A, B, C, D, E
Wavg	Weekly messages exchanged. Can be less than or greater than 320. (64 msgs/day X 5 days = 320)
Weekend	Messages exchange on weekends 0-No messaging 1-Messaging on Saturday or Sunday 2-Messaging on both Saturday and Sunday
Relationship	Relationship type with phone owner W-Weak M-Medium S-Strong

It starts from the training data, builds a predictive model in a tree structure. Its goal is to achieve optimal classification with a minimal number of decisions. The end nodes are the targets/classes.

Random Tree Classifier is a supervised machine-learning classifier based on constructing a multitude of decision trees, choosing random subsets of variables for each tree, and using the most frequent tree output as the overall classification. We use this classifier, as it is known to correct for the J48 decision tree classifier over-fitting issue. In this method, a number of trees are grown (i.e. a forest). Variation among the trees is introduced by projecting the training data into a randomly chosen subspace before fitting each tree. Testing this algorithm on test data resulted in reduced correctly classified instances but the tree structure revealed more detailed decisions on the data attributes as shown in Fig. 8.

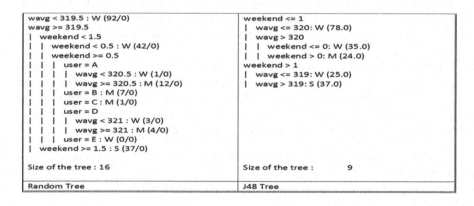

Fig. 8. Random tree and J48 tree

To evaluate performance of J48 decision tree classifier and random tree classifier, we compare their outputs to that of the ZeroR Classifier. ZeroR is the simplest classification algorithm and is based on frequency table. This classifier relies on the target/class only and ignores the features. It is useful for determining the baseline of a model. We analyze the data by using the following three test options using ZeroR, Decision Tree and Random Tree.

- Option 1: With K-fold cross validation (K = 199)
- Option 2: With 66% Split data
- Option 3: With test data

3.1 Option 1: Classifiers with K-fold cross validation (K = 100, 150, 199)

For K-fold, data is decomposed into K-blocks. Then, for K = 1 to X, the Kth block is made the test block and the rest of the data become the training data. Classifier is trained, tested, and then K is updated. Theoretically, the higher the number of folds, less biased results are achieved [12]. It is important that K <= X, where X = no. of instances. In our dataset analysis, we use three different values of K = X = 100, 150 and 199 to achieve unbiased results. ZeroR provides the baseline 69.3% accuracy for the model when used with K-fold cross validation for all three values of K (100, 150, 199). J48 classifier outperforms with a perfect correctly identified instances. Moreover, J48 classifier results remain consistent for all three values of K. The results with J48 also appears optimistic, therefore the same data are used with the random tree classifier, which results in 98.9% correctly identified instances with K = 199. Similarly, other performance indicators like FP, Recall and F-measure are more realistic when using Random Tree. The changes in K value vary between the results of Random Tree classifier from 0.5% to 1%.

Table 3 summarizes the results with K-fold cross validation for all three classifiers.

Table 3. Test Option 1: With K-fold cross validation (K = 100, 150, 199)

Classifier	K	Correctly classified	FP	Recall	F-measure
ZeroR	100	69.30%	0.693	0.693	0.568
	150	69.30%	0.693	0.693	0.568
	199	69.30%	0.693	0.693	0.568
J48	100	100%	0	1	1
	150	100%	0	1	1
	199	100%	0	1	1
Random Tree	100	98.40%	0.024	0.985	0.984
	150	99.40%	0.011	0.995	0.995
	199	98.90%	0.023	0.99	0.99

3.2 Option 2: Classifiers With Split Data (50%, 66%, 80%)

Initially, we tested the classifiers on Weka default split value of 66%. By splitting the data of 199 instances in 66% means that 66% of data (131 instances) were used as training and 34% (68 instances) as test.

In this test option, our classifiers show significantly decrease in precision as compared to the K-fold cross validation, but J48 and Random tree still performs with an above 90% accuracy rate. We also analyze the behavior of all three classifiers by splitting the data in 50% and 80%. J48 and Random tree achieve accuracy rates of 100% and 97.50% respectively, at 80% of data splitting. However, ZeroR achieves the highest accuracy (69.30%) at 66% data split and lowest accuracy (62.50%) at 80% split data. Table 4 summarizes the results of all three classifiers with 50%, 66% and 80% split data.

3.3   Option 3: Classifiers with Test Data

In the third test option, we provide a separate test data to Weka, to check the performance of our dataset. In this test option, Random tree classifier results improves by 0.5% as compared to option 1 (K-folds) and 6.8% as compared to option 2 (split data). Therefore, on an average the performance of the Random Tree classifier improves by 3.65% when a new/unknown test data is introduced. The performance of ZeroR and J48 is almost identical to the first test (K-folds) – see Table 5.

Table 4. Test Option 2: With split data (50%, 66%, 80%)

Classifier	% split	Correctly classified	FP	Recall	F-measure
ZeroR	50%	67.70%	0.677	0.677	0.546
	66%	69.30%	0.693	0.647	0.49
	80%	62.50%	0.625	0.625	0.481
J48	50%	95.95%	0.085	0.96	0.957
	66%	94.12%	0.101	0.941	0.937
	80%	100%	0	1	1
Random Tree	50%	95.95%	0.085	0.96	0.957
	66%	92.60%	0.105	0.926	0.922
	80%	97.50%	0.042	0.975	0.974

Table 5. Test Option 3: With test data

Classifier	Correctly classified	FP	Recall	F-measure
ZeroR	69.3%	0.693	0.693	0.568
J48	100%	0	1	1
Random Tree	99.4%	0.001	0.995	0.995

4 Conclusion and Future Work

In this paper, we studied the potential of using machine learning classifiers to facilitate mobile forensics, specifically in terms of Facebook messenger artifact triaging. Specifically, after acquiring forensic artifacts from an Android device and an iOS device, we created 199 data-instances and trained three WEKA Classifiers (i.e. ZeroR, J48 and Random tree). This was done so that we were able to classify the device owner's contact classification into weak, medium and strong (i.e. determine their mutual relationship strength). Our analysis with the three test options and three different classifiers revealed that J48 appeared to highly biased or overfitted to the provided dataset, and Random tree achieved optimal performance in all three test options with increased accuracy when tested with a different test dataset.

Future work includes extending this work to other classifiers as well as using a broader range of datasets.

Acknowledgments. The first author is supported by the Australian Government Research Training Program Scholarship.

References

1. Anglano, C., Canonico, M., Guazzone, M.: Forensic analysis of telegram messenger on android smartphones. Digit. Invest. **23**, 31–49 (2017)
2. Azuaje, F.: Witten IH, Frank E: data mining: practical machine learning tools and techniques 2nd edition. BioMed. Eng. OnLine **5**(1), 51 (2006). https://doi.org/10.1186/1475-925X-5-51
3. Barmpatsalou, K., Cruz, T., Monteiro, E., Simoes, P.: Current and future trends in mobile device forensics - a survey. ACM Comput. Surv. **51**, 46 (2018)
4. Breiman, L.: Random forests. Mach. Learn. **45**(1), 5–32 (2001)
5. Cahyani, N.D.W., Ab Rahman, N.H., Glisson, W.B., Choo, K.K.R.: The role of mobile forensics in terrorism investigations involving the use of cloud storage service and communication apps. Mob. Netw. Appl. **22**(2), 240–254 (2017)
6. Daryabar, F., Dehghantanha, A., Choo, K.K.R.: Cloud storage forensics: mega as a case study. Aust. J. Forensic Sci. **49**(3), 344–357 (2017). https://doi.org/10.1080/00450618.2016.1153714
7. Dezfouli, F.N., Dehghantanha, A., Eterovic-Soric, B., Choo, K.K.R.: Investigating social networking applications on smartphones detecting Facebook, Twitter, LinkedIn and Google+ artefacts on android and iOS platforms. Aust. J. Forensic Sci. **48**(4), 469–488 (2016). https://doi.org/10.1080/00450618.2015.1066854
8. Lee, K., Palsetia, D., Narayanan, R., Patwary, M.M.A., Agrawal, A., Choudhary, A.: Twitter trending topic classification. In: IEEE 11th International Conference on Data Mining Workshops, pp. 251–258, December 2011. https://doi.org/10.1109/ICDMW.2011.171
9. Marturana, F., Me, G., Berte, R., Tacconi, S.: A quantitative approach to triaging in mobile forensics. In: IEEE 10th International Conference on Trust, Security and Privacy in Computing and Communications, pp. 582–588, November 2011. https://doi.org/10.1109/TrustCom.2011.75

10. Patil, T.R., Sherekar, S.: Performance analysis of Naive Bayes and J48 classification algorithm for data classification. Int. J. Comput. Sci. Appl. **6**(2), 256–261 (2013)

11. Quick, D., Choo, K.K.R.: Pervasive social networking forensics: intelligence and evidence from mobile device extracts. J. Netw. Comput. Appl. **86**, 24–33 (2017)

12. Refaeilzadeh, P., Tang, L., Liu, H.: Cross-validation. In: Liu, L., Özsu, M.T. (eds.) Encyclopedia of Database Systems, pp. 532–538. Springer, Boston (2009). https:// doi.org/10.1007/978-0-387-39940-9_565

13. Umair, A., Nanda, P., He, X.: Online social network information forensics: a survey on use of various tools and determining how cautious Facebook users are? In: IEEE Trustcom/BigDataSE/ICESS, pp. 1139–1144, August 2017. https://doi.org/ 10.1109/Trustcom/BigDataSE/ICESS.2017.364

14. Walnycky, D., Baggili, I., Marrington, A., Moore, J., Breitinger, F.: Network and device forensic analysis of android social-messaging applications. Digit. Invest. **14**, S77–S84 (2015). https://doi.org/10.1016/j.diin.2015.05.009. http:// www.sciencedirect.com/science/article/pii/S1742287615000547. The Proceedings of the Fifteenth Annual DFRWS Conference

15. Yang, T.Y., Dehghantanha, A., Choo, K.K.R., Muda, Z.: Windows instant messaging app forensics: Facebook and skype as case studies. PLoS ONE **11**(3), 1–29 (2016). https://doi.org/10.1371/journal.pone.0150300

Using Software Visualization for Supporting the Teaching of MapReduce

Umberto Ferraro Petrillo[✉]

Dipartimento di Scienze Statistiche, Università di Roma "La Sapienza",
00185 Rome, Italy
umberto.ferraro@uniroma1.it

Abstract. The increasing number of cybersecurity threats we are facing nowadays is fueling the development of new detection and contrast techniques based on the analysis of Big Data. In such a setting, the MapReduce paradigm has quickly become the *de facto* standard for carrying out this processing. This has led to a surge in the number of job offerings involving this skill. Moreover, we are experiencing a significant increase in the number of computer science courses covering this paradigm as well as its most popular implementations, Spark and Hadoop.

In this paper, it is presented a solution for supporting the teaching of MapReduce through the use of software visualization. The proposed solution has two main goals. The first is to help students in understanding how the MapReduce paradigm succeeds in solving a complex problem by decomposing it in simpler sub problems, where each of these is solved by means of map and/or reduce operations. The second is about the capability of showing how an input dataset is partitioned in blocks and processed in parallel by the different computing units of a distributed computing system. In both cases, the use of software visualization techniques with proper graphical metaphors helps the students in understanding what is going on, by providing them with a graphical representation that, on a side, describes how the considered algorithm works on an input dataset while, on the other side, illustrates the speed-up achieved thanks to the distributed approach.

Keywords: Big data security · MapReduce · Spark
Software visualization

1 Introduction

The recent availability of unprecedented amount of data (i.e. Big Data) is calling for the development of new paradigms, methodologies and technologies allowing to efficiently store, manage, process and analyze such data. This need embraces the most disparate class of problems, varying from the extraction of relevant features from biological sequences [7] to the enumeration of the subgraphs existing

© Springer Nature Switzerland AG 2018
M. H. Au et al. (Eds.): NSS 2018, LNCS 11058, pp. 349–360, 2018.
https://doi.org/10.1007/978-3-030-02744-5_26

in a graph instance [1]. An application domain that is urging for the development and the rollout of new analysis techniques is the one related to the cybersecurity (see, e.g., [5,8]).

A popular computational approach that has gained a lot of attention in the past years is the one based on the MapReduce paradigm [10]. This paradigm has been initially developed by Google for internal purposes. Then, it has experienced a widespread adoption, mostly because of its implementation provided by the Apache Hadoop [15] and Apache Spark [19] distributed computing frameworks.

One of the main reasons behind the introduction of this paradigm was to allow users to focus on the solution of a problem in a distributed fashion while not entangling them with all the issues that typically arise when developing this kind of applications. This apparent simplicity, together with the robust market demand, made MapReduce the paradigm of choice when introducing distributed programming during computer science undergraduate courses [18].

However, teaching MapReduce to a class without any distributed programming experience poses many challenges. On a side, this paradigm relies on a very abstract programming model where complex computations are performed by means of a sequence of much simpler computations. It is not always easy for a student to grasp how a (possibly long) combination of simple or very simple operations may succeed in solving a complex problem. On the other side, the actual execution of the single operations of a MapReduce algorithm on a real dataset is typically not carried out in a sequential way on a stand-alone machine but in a parallel way leveraging the computational capabilities of a distributed system. In such a scenario, it is important -and, often, difficult to understand - the strategy adopted for partitioning the data over the nodes of the distributed system and, consequently, the achievable degree of parallelism. In this paper, we explore the possibility of using software visualization techniques to explain the basic principles of MapReduce when used to build and to run real distributed applications. The user is initially provided with a visual representation of a randomly-generated input dataset, encoded as a Spark distributed data structure. Moreover, he is given a list of standard map and reduce functions. After selecting one of these, the system runs that function on the current distributed data structure while playing a graphical animation describing the effects of that execution on the same data structure. At the end of the execution a new distributed data structure is generated and visualized, representing the result of that execution. Then, the user may choose to go on and run other functions so as requested by the algorithm being run.

Organization of the Paper. In Sect. 2, we briefly introduce the MapReduce paradigm. In Sect. 3, we focus on the issues that may arise when teaching MapReduce and point the two learning tasks we believe can be achieved with the help of software visualization. In Sect. 4, we introduce and motivate our proposal. In Sect. 5, we outline the architecture of the system we proposed. Then, in Sect. 6 we briefly review the existing literature about the usage of software visualization for supporting the teaching of algorithms, with a particular emphasis on parallel and distributed algorithms. In Sect. 7, we introduce Spark, as it is at the core of our proposal. Finally, in Sect. 8 we draw some concluding remarks for our work.

2 MapReduce

The MapReduce paradigm is a programming model developed for simplifying the processing of very large datasets, organized as a set of key-value pairs. It is based on the definition of two functions. The *map* function takes as input a key-value pair returning, as output, a (possibly empty) set of intermediate key-value pairs. The *reduce* function is used to process all the set of intermediate key-values sharing a same key, so to produce a (possibly empty) set of output key-value pairs.

Map and reduce functions are executed, as tasks, on the nodes of a distributed system. Notice that each map or reduce task is executed independently of the others. This implies the possibility to run a number of parallel map tasks equal to the number of input key-value pairs and a number of parallel reduce tasks equal to the number of intermediate pairs distinct keys. The only limitation is about the need for the reduce tasks to wait for the map tasks to be completed before being started.

All the communications occurring between map functions and reduce functions, as well as the handling of communication or execution faults, are managed by the underlying distributed computing framework, leaving the user only the task of defining map and reduce functions. Complex computations can be modeled in MapReduce by combining together several map and reduce functions.

3 Teaching MapReduce

The MapReduce paradigm is often introduced with the help of very simple distributed algorithms like word-counting or line-counting. These problems can be elegantly solved using a single pair of map and reduce functions, so they allow for a gentle approach to this topic. Then, more complex problems are often considered, like recommendation engines, graph-based algorithms and topic extraction models. The implementation of these solutions in MapReduce typically requires the execution of several consecutive map and reduce functions. This complexity shift may be problematic for students as they may have troubles in understanding how the solution to a complex problem is reached and what the cost for this solution in terms of communication overhead will be. Another issue is related to the distributed nature of the computation. While introducing a MapReduce algorithm, the emphasis is often devoted on explaining the behavior of the algorithm not on the way it is translated on a real distributed system and leverages its computational capabilities.

For these reasons, we restrict our attention to the following learning tasks:

– *Comprehension of the MapReduce paradigm.* As described in Sect. 2, all the computations implemented according to the MapReduce paradigm are expressed as a sequence of map and/or reduce functions. Complex problems may require the execution of several functions, each used to fulfill an elementary task like filtering input records according to a user-provided condition, pivoting a record around a certain attribute, summarizing variables using an aggregation functions and so on. While the purpose of a certain function may be clear, the learner may find difficult to focus on the big picture underlying all these basic operations. So, the focus of this task would be to understand how each single operation contributes to solve the starting problem in its entirety.

– *Understanding of the Implications of the Distributed Approach.* The main goal of the MapReduce paradigm is to make it possible to decompose a computation into several independent tasks, to be run on the nodes of a distributed system. This is strongly tied with how the input and intermediate data are organized in the system. Namely, the software frameworks implementing MapReduce usually partition input data in blocks, where each block is stored on one or more nodes of the system according to a configurable *replication factor*. Then, each node is usually requested to process all the data belonging to the blocks it owns (i.e., *data local computation*). For this reason, the distributed layout of input and intermediary data strongly influences the possibility of exploiting the computational capabilities of a distributed system. Indeed, by increasing the number of blocks used to store input data, it is possible to increase the parallelism level as well, because each block can be processed by a distinct computing core. However, having too many small blocks reduces the amount of time required for processing each block while increasing the amount of overhead to be paid for dealing with such a large number of tasks.

Understanding the way input data is virtually and physically partitioned in blocks, how these blocks are spread over the nodes of a distributed system and how their processing occurs is a fundamental learning task for recognizing the advantages of the MapReduce paradigm and discerning the conditions that may lead to an efficient usage of the available distributed computing resources.

4   Supporting the Teaching of MapReduce

One of the common denominators between the two learning tasks introduced in Sect. 3 is the need for the student to figure out in his mind how a distributed execution of a sequence of simple operations succeeds in solving a complex problem, while requiring a fraction of the time required to run the same computation a stand-alone machine. A possible way to support the teaching of these concepts and simplifying their comprehension is the usage of *software visualization*. Namely, we think that it would be much easier for a learner to understand the rationale of a sequence of MapReduce operations executed in a distributed setting, if these would be portrayed on screen using proper graphical metaphors and animations. In this way, the learner could "see" how the sequence of map and/or reduce operations would transform the input data in the expected output data while recognizing the execution speed-up made possible by the distributed execution.

Starting from this consideration, we designed and prototyped a software visualization system for supporting the teaching and improving the learning of MapReduce. At the start-up, our system gives the user the possibility to instantiate a randomly generated distributed input data structure while defining its size and the number of blocks used to partition it. The generated data structure, essentially a collection of values or a collection of key-value pairs, is visually partitioned in blocks so as to reflect the distributed nature of the target data structure (see, e.g., Fig. 1).

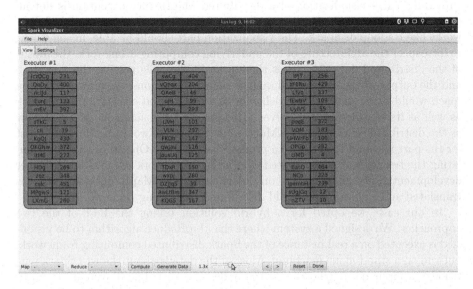

Fig. 1. A visual representation of a distributed data structure containing 45 randomly generated key-value pairs. It is partitioned over 3 executors, with each executor holding 3 blocks of 5 elements each.

Once the input data structure is ready, the user has the possibility to choose which map or reduce operation to run for processing it by choosing among a standard list of operations available through the GUI of the system. Every time a new operation is chosen then run, a graphical animation begins describing how that operation is run on each element belonging to each block of that particular input data set. The animation is played so to reflect the distributed nature of the operation. This means that, if there are several blocks of data hosted on different nodes, their respective animations are played at the same time.

Each operation being run (either map or reduce) gives rise to a new *animation stage*, where each stage starts from the output of the previous stage while its output is used as input for the subsequent stage. Moreover, the input data structure serves as input for the first stage while the output of the last stage is intended to be the output of the entire computation. At the end of each stage, the user has the possibility to visually inspect the state of the represented data structure, so to figure out the effects of the previous operation. Moreover, when the execution ends, the user has the possibility to rewind it by going back to a particular stage or by completely replaying it. By so doing, the user is given the chance of analyzing several times a particular step of the algorithm until a certain degree of confidence is reached.

5   Architecture

Providing a live visualization of a distributed MapReduce execution is not an easy task because of the inner complexity of the distributed computing frameworks like Hadoop or Spark. The visualization part should be able, in some way, to introspect the architecture of the underlying computing framework, the layout of the distributed data structures therein available while tracing the execution and the output of the distributed map or reduce operations. An alternative approach would be to simulate the behavior of a distributed computing framework as well as its MapReduce primitives. This second approach is simpler to follow as the distributed execution of a MapReduce algorithm would be simulated just for the part required to generate a proper visualization. On the other end, simulating the behavior of a distributed computing framework requires much longer development times and may fail on describing how a MapReduce algorithm is translated and ran on a real-world distributed computing framework.

In our case, we opted for a hybrid solution taking the best of the two approaches. We designed a system where the MapReduce algorithm to be visualized is executed on a real instance of the Spark distributed computing framework, but run on a stand-alone machine[1]. Most of the details about the way Spark partitions an input data structure on the nodes of a distributed system, useful to generate a proper visualization, are gathered by querying the Spark middleware. Instead, the remaining information are obtained through an emulation of the Spark framework.

In sums, our system include three modules:

- The *MapReduce algorithm module* is a generic interactive distributed Spark application. It works by instantiating an RDD distributed data structure (see Sect. 7), whose type and size is chosen by the user at the startup and whose content is randomly generated. This application implements also a standard collection of map and reduce functions, like filtering elements according to a boolean condition (map), transforming elements using a standard set of operators (map) or combining multiple elements sharing the same key using an aggregation function (reduce).

---

[1] A prototype implementation of the system is currently under development as a stand-alone Java Spark application.

- The *Orchestrator module* is a communication broker used by the visualization part for gathering information about the MapReduce algorithm to be visualized, and by the MapReduce algorithm to acquire from the GUI input parameters and other information required for its execution. Some of these information are directly fetched by the orchestrator from the underlying Spark framework. Other information, required to simulate the execution of the MapReduce algorithm on a distributed framework, are maintained internally by the orchestrator. Moreover, this module is in charge of receiving the *operation requests* issued by the visualization module for the execution of distributed operations on the current distributed data structures.
- The *Visualization module* is in charge of generating the visualization of the proposed MapReduce algorithm whose behavior is defined by the user by interacting with the application. The proposed visualization is formed by a sequence of animation stages. Each stage takes as input the current distributed data structure, processes it according to the instructions provided by the user and generates a new distributed data structure, replacing the previous one. See Fig. 2 for an example of visualization of a transformation. The selection about the distributed operator to run (either map or reduce) is done by interacting with the user interface of the application. The actual content of the visualization is generated by this module according to the information available by the MapReduce algorithm module, as provided by the orchestrator module.

6   Related Work

The increasing interest toward the teaching of topics related to Big Data motivated the publishing of several scientific results dealing with the problem of how to effectively teach these topics, like [11,12,14,16]. Most of these contributions concern the problem of designing a Big Data undergraduate course or curriculum, where typically MapReduce and its enabling technologies, Hadoop and/or Spark, play a central role. Thus, their focus is mostly on organization issues while no particular attention is put on the problem of teaching MapReduce.

As far as we know, the only scientific contribution focusing on the problem of supporting the teaching of MapReduce is [3]. Here, the authors deal with the problem of simplifying the implementation of MapReduce algorithms using the Hadoop framework. Their claim is that this framework requires a computational maturity that is often missing in students following introductory computer science courses. For this reason, they introduce a web-based framework allowing students to carry out map-reduce computations by only providing the algorithmic code while defining all the Hadoop configuration information through a simple web-based interface.

Indeed, since the pioneering work of Stasko in [17], the usage of computer graphics has been seen a potential effective medium for illustrating the behavior of an algorithm and helping a user in understanding its meaning. Apart from computer algorithms, software visualization has been used as a support tool in

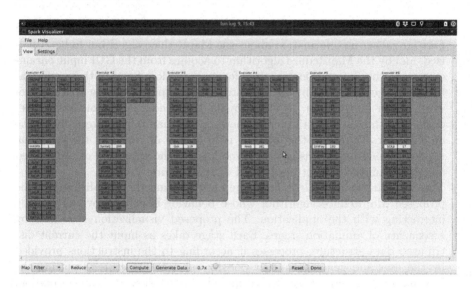

Fig. 2. A visual representation of the distributed filter action being run on a distributed data structure containing 150 randomly generated key-value pairs. The simulated distributed systems is running 6 executors. For each executor, on the left side the input data structure, partitioned in blocks containing 4 elements each. On the right side, the new data structure resulting from the execution of the filter action. The elements being considered are drawn in yellow. (Color figure online)

a variety of cases, ranging from the presentation of cryptographic protocols [6] to the teaching of the SQL database querying language [9].

This approach has been also followed for supporting the education of parallel and distributed algorithms. To name few, Naps and Chan proposed in [13] two techniques for delivering animation of parallel programs, allowing students to better comprehend a target parallel algorithm by also participating, interactively, to its construction. A similar approach has been followed by Ben Ari in [2] and by Carr *et al.* in [4], with the introduction of two systems for the implementation and the visualization of interactive parallel programs. In both cases, the user (i.e., the instructor) is provided with a programming library useful for the implementation of a parallel program. When run, the resulting code is automatically visualized using some proper graphical metaphors. The user (i.e., the instructor or the student) can visualize also the network of processes participating to the parallel execution and the workflow of the communications occurring between these processes.

All the aforementioned systems have been conceived for supporting the teaching of *explicit parallel* algorithms. In this case, the code to be run on each node of a parallel computation has to use some sort of communication primitives to explicitly exchange data with other nodes (e.g., send-to-one, send-to-may, scatter, gather). For this reason, the emphasis of these systems is most on the communication patterns occurring between the different actors of the parallel execution and not on the way data are processed.

7 Spark

Spark is one of the most popular open source software framework for Big Data processing supporting the MapReduce paradigm. It is able to leverage the computational capabilities of a cluster of computers by means of a high-level distributed programming model. The developer is required to code the driver program that, in turns, will make use of the primitives available with Spark to instantiate distributed data structures and process them using the supported distributed operations. All the aspects related to the data distribution, to the communication between the nodes of the cluster and to the managing of faults are automatically handled by the framework.

The Spark architecture is based on a master/worker model (see Fig. 3). On a side, there is a *driver program*, coded as a traditional sequential application, that is in charge of initiating and orchestrating a distributed execution. On the other side, there is a collection of *worker nodes*, carrying out the distributed computations required by the driver program. Each worker nodes hosts one or more *executors* - these are the processes that are actually responsible for the execution of the tasks issued by the driver. The communication between the driver and the worker nodes occurs with the mediation of a Spark *cluster manager*.

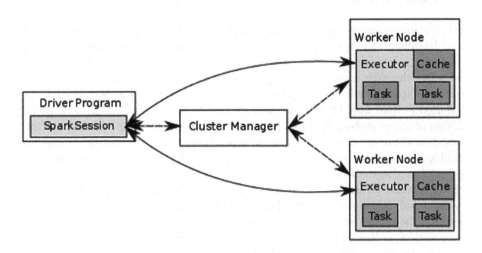

Fig. 3. An outline of the spark architecture

7.1   Resilient Distributed Datasets

The Resilient Distributed Dataset (in short, RDD) is a distributed data structure available with Spark. It is an in-memory collection of objects that can either be mono-dimensional (i.e., a collection of values) or bi-dimensional (i.e., a collection of key-value pairs). Each RDD is automatically and transparently partitioned in *blocks* and distributed over the workers of a cluster. The developer has the possibility to process the content of a distributed dataset using a high-level API provided by Spark and including two types of distributed operations:

- *Transformations.* Take as input a distributed collection of objects (mono- or bi-dimensional) and return another one (again, mono- or bi-dimensional), resulting from the application of a distributed transformation to the input.
- *Actions.* Take as input a distributed collection of objects and return a non-distributed collection of objects (or a scalar value), directly to the node running the driver program.

Among the transformations supported by Spark there are the ones implementing the map and reduce operators. The distributed part of an application run with Spark is logically divided in *stages*, where each stage corresponds to a transformation or an action. Stages related to transformations are run by Spark in a *lazy* way. This means that they are not run as soon as they are encountered during the execution of a program, but only when and if their result is needed to accomplish a subsequent step of the application.

8   Conclusions and Future Directions

Despite its apparent simplicity, the MapReduce paradigm and its applications may be difficult to understand for students when considering complex algorithms involving a long sequence of map and/or reduce operations. Similarly, understanding the way an abstract MapReduce algorithm succeeds in processing a certain dataset while fully exploiting the computational capabilities of a distributed system may be difficult as well. For these reasons, we introduced the design of a new system for supporting the teaching of the MapReduce paradigm based on the usage of software visualization. It is possible to show in a clear and intelligible way how a data structure is partitioned in blocks across the nodes of a distributed system by resorting to proper graphical representations. The same representation is also useful to illustrate how these blocks are processed in a parallel and distributed way and how a MapReduce algorithm succeeds in transforming the input data in the expected output data by a means of a sequence of map and/or reduce operations, chosen interactively by the user of the system. Among the future directions for the current work there will be, first of all, the publishing of a prototype of the proposed system. This will be assessed through the implementation of a set of reference MapReduce algorithms like, e.g., recommendation algorithms and ETL workflows. Another direction worth to be investigated is the analysis of the effectiveness of the proposed solution in a real classroom learning setting.

Acknowledgement. We are thankful to Francesco Palini for his help in developing a prototype of the proposed visualization system.

This work was supported in part by University of Rome - "La Sapienza" under project "Analisi, sviluppo e sperimentazione di algoritmi sperimentalmente efficienti".

It was also supported in part by INdAM - GNCS under project "Algoritmi e tecniche efficienti per l'organizzazione, la gestione e l'analisi di Big Data in ambito biologico" (2017) and project "Elaborazione ed analisi di Big Data modellati come grafi in vari contesti applicativi" (2018).

References

1. Afrati, F.N., Fotakis, D., Ullman, J.D.: Enumerating subgraph instances using map-reduce. In: 2013 IEEE 29th International Conference on Data Engineering (ICDE), pp. 62–73. IEEE (2013)

2. Ben-Ari, M.: Interactive execution of distributed algorithms. J. Educ. Resour. Comput. **1**(2) (2001). https://doi.org/10.1145/384055.384057

3. Brown, E.R., Garrity, P., Yates, T., Northfield, M., Shoop, E., Saint Paul, M.: Teaching map-reduce parallel computing in CS1. In: Midwest Instruction and Computing Symposium (2011)

4. Carr, S., Fang, C., Jozwowski, T., Mayo, J., Shene, C.K.: Concurrent mentor: a visualization system for distributed programming education. In: 2003 International Conference on Parallel and Distributed Processing Techniques and Applications, pp. 1676–1682 (2003)

5. Castiglione, A., Cattaneo, G., De Maio, G., De Santis, A., Roscigno, G.: A novel methodology to acquire live big data evidence from the cloud. IEEE Trans. Big Data (2017, in press)

6. Cattaneo, G., De Santis, A., Ferraro Petrillo, U.: Visualization of cryptographic protocols with GRACE. J. Vis. Lang. Comput. **19**(2), 258–290 (2008). https://doi.org/10.1016/j.jvlc.2007.05.001

7. Cattaneo, G., Ferraro Petrillo, U., Giancarlo, R., Roscigno, G.: An effective extension of the applicability of alignment-free biological sequence comparison algorithms with hadoop. J. Supercomput. **73**(4), 1467–1483 (2016). https://doi.org/10.1007/s11227-016-1835-3

8. Cattaneo, G., Ferraro Petrillo, U., Nappi, M., Narducci, F., Roscigno, G.: An efficient implementation of the algorithm by Lukáš et al. on Hadoop. In: Au, M.H.A., Castiglione, A., Choo, K.-K.R., Palmieri, F., Li, K.-C. (eds.) GPC 2017. LNCS, vol. 10232, pp. 475–489. Springer, Cham (2017). https://doi.org/10.1007/978-3-319-57186-7_35

9. Cembalo, M., Santis, A.D., Petrillo, U.F.: SAVI: a new system for advanced SQL visualization. In: Goda, B.S., Sobiesk, E., Connolly, R.W. (eds.) Proceedings of the 2011 Conference on Information Technology Education, SIGITE 2011, pp. 165–170. ACM, New York (2011). https://doi.org/10.1145/2047594.2047641

10. Dean, J., Ghemawat, S.: MapReduce: simplified data processing on large clusters. In: Proceedings of the 6th conference on Symposium on Opearting Systems Design & Implementation (OSDI), vol. 6, pp. 137–150 (2004)

11. Eckroth, J.: Teaching big data with a virtual cluster. In: Proceedings of the 47th ACM Technical Symposium on Computing Science Education, pp. 175–180. ACM (2016)

12. Eckroth, J.: Teaching future big data analysts: curriculum and experience report. In: 2017 IEEE International Symposium on Parallel and Distributed Processing Workshops (IPDPSW), pp. 346–351. IEEE (2017)

13. Naps, T.L., Chan, E.E.: Using visualization to teach parallel algorithms. In: The Proceedings of the Thirtieth SIGCSE Technical Symposium on Computer Science Education, SIGCSE 1999, pp. 232–236. ACM, New York (1999). https://doi.org/10.1145/299649.299767

14. Ngo, L.B., Duffy, E.B., Apon, A.W.: Teaching HDFS/MapReduce systems concepts to undergraduates. In: 2014 IEEE International on Parallel & Distributed Processing Symposium Workshops (IPDPSW), pp. 1114–1121. IEEE (2014)

15. O'Malley, O.: Terabyte Sort on Apache Hadoop, pp. 1–3. Yahoo (2008). http://sortbenchmark.org/YahooHadoop.pdf)

16. Shamsi, J.A., Durrani, N.M., Kafi, N.: Novelties in teaching high performance computing. In: 2015 IEEE International Parallel and Distributed Processing Symposium Workshop, pp. 772–778, May 2015. https://doi.org/10.1109/IPDPSW.2015.88

17. Stasko, J.T.: Tango: a framework and system for algorithm animation. ACM SIGCHI Bull. **21**(3), 59–60 (1990)

18. Woods, P.: The New Era of Big Data Security Analytics (2012). https://searchsecurity.techtarget.com/feature/The-new-era-of-big-data-security-analytics

19. Zaharia, M., Chowdhury, M., Franklin, M.J., Shenker, S., Stoica, I.: Spark: Cluster Computing with Working Sets. In: Proceedings of the 2nd USENIX Conference on Hot Topics in Cloud Computing, vol. 10, p. 10 (2010)

DBAF: Dynamic Binary Analysis Framework and Its Applications

Ting Chen$^{(\boxtimes)}$, Youzheng Feng, Xingwei Lin, Zihao Li, and Xiaosong Zhang

Research Center for Cybersecurity, University of Electronic Science
and Technology of China, Chengdu 611731, China
{brokendragon,johnsonzxs}uestc.edu.cn,
fengyouzheng@gmail.com, xwlin.roy@gmail.com, gforiq@qq.com

Abstract. Dynamic binary analysis is difficult and burdensome. In practice, analysts always develop dynamic binary analyzers (DBAs) based on binary instrumentation tools (BITs), which are responsible for extracting information from a binary, monitoring or altering the execution of the binary. However, existing BITs either expose machine instructions to analysts or lack user-friendly APIs. Such problems result in a steep learning curve to grasp BITs and difficulties in eliminating bugs in DBAs. This work designs DBAF, a dynamic binary analysis framework that instruments binaries dynamically, conducts an online translation from machine code into an easy-to-handle intermediate representation (IR) and provides tens of APIs for IR processing. With DBAF, analysts can process binaries in the level of IR without the troubles to interpret machine instructions. Then, we develop five DBAs on top of DBAF, which are a division-by-zero protector, an IR counter, a memory tracer, a taint analyzer and a concolic executor. It demonstrates that DBAF can reduce the development effort for DBAs, especially the ones requiring semantic interpretation of instructions. Experiments show that DBAF brings about reasonable overhead in online translation.

1 Introduction

Binary analysis is a fundamental technique in many research fields, e.g., malware analysis, obfuscation/deobfuscation, software similarity analysis, and vulnerability discovery. It can be roughly classified into three categories, static analysis, dynamic analysis and hybrid analysis which combines static and dynamic analysis. This work focuses on dynamic binary analysis. Dynamic binary analysis is difficult and burdensome which needs rich experiences and considerable coding effort. In practice, analysts often develop dynamic binary analyzers (DBAs) based on existing binary instrumentation tools (BITs). With BITs, analysts can focus on the functionalities of the DBAs rather than the low-level details about how to load binaries into memory, parse binary files, extract information (e.g., control flow graph) from binaries, monitor or alter the execution of binaries.

However, exiting BITs have several shortcomings. First, some BITs (e.g., Pin [24], Dyninst [1], DynamoRIO [2]) expose machine instructions to analysts

© Springer Nature Switzerland AG 2018
M. H. Au et al. (Eds.): NSS 2018, LNCS 11058, pp. 361–375, 2018.
https://doi.org/10.1007/978-3-030-02744-5_27

directly, leaving analysts a complicated and error-prone process of semantic interpretation. Second, some BITs (e.g., Valgrind [28]) do not provide user-friendly APIs and documents, leading to a steep learning curve for analysts to grasp the BITs. Consequently, analysts have to search for the APIs of interest from less-clear documentations, example code developed by inexperienced programmers and even the huge source code of DITs.

This work designs DBAF, a dynamic binary analysis framework that instruments binaries dynamically, translates machine instructions into an easy-to-handle intermediate representation (IR). Moreover, DBAF provides tens of APIs, enabling analysts to process binaries in the level of IR. With DBAF, analysts do not need to interpret the semantics of machine instructions, and hence considerable development effort for DBAs can be saved. The implementation of DBAF is based on Pin and hence the invocation fashion of the provided APIs is similar with Pin's APIs. Besides, DBAF selects LLVM IR [20] as its IR format and reuse some code of Mcsema [10] for translation. Therefore, people who have experiences in Pin and LLVM can use DBAF without difficulties. We do not consider the requirement is an obstacle to use DBAF because Pin and LLVM are widely-accepted in both academia and industry.

To demonstrate the utility of DBAF, we implement five DBAs on it using the provided APIs. Three out of them are simple, which are a division-by-zero protector, an IR counter and a memory tracer. The code amount of them is comparable with those DBAs implemented on Pin directly. The taint analyzer and concolic executor are two complicated DBAs because they need to interpret the semantics of IR. The code amount of them is significantly lower than those directly implemented on Pin since the semantics of LLVM LR is much simpler than the semantics of machine instructions. Finally, experiments show that the translation process of DBAF incurs reasonable overhead.

In summary, the contribution of this work is threefold.

- This work designs DBAF, which instruments binaries dynamically and translates instructions into LLVM IR.
- DBAF provides tens of APIs, allowing analysts to handle binaries in the level of IR.
- We implement five DBAs on top of DBAF, using its APIs.

This paper is organized as follows. Section 2 focuses on the design of DBAF. Section 3 concerns the implementation of DBAs. Section 4 evaluates the translation overhead of DBAF and presents two practical cases about the taint analyzer. Section 5 reviews the related studies and Sect. 6 concludes.

2   DBAF

2.1   Overview

Figure 1 illustrates the high-level architecture of DBAF which takes in a binary, instruments it and then runs the instrumented binary. The workflow of DBAF consists of six steps. Step one loads the binary into memory, parses the binary format and extracts relevant information. Then, DBAF fetches machine instructions from the binary, followed by the process of translation. The outcome of the translation step is LLVM IR. The instrumentor instruments the code of DBAs into IR and then IR is converted back to machine instruction in step five. Please note that step five is the reverse process of step three. Finally, step six runs the instrumented binary.

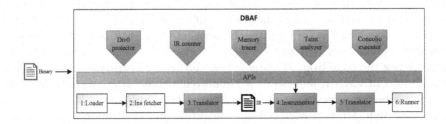

Fig. 1. High-level overview of DBAF

DBAF provides tens of APIs, allowing analysts to instrument binaries in the level of IR. Therefore, all the five DBAs invokes the proposed APIs without the troubles to interpret the semantics of machine instructions. The modules in Fig. 1 with the dark background are completely implemented by us (i.e., all DBAs and APIs) or adapted from existing BITs (i.e., translator and instrumentor), and the modules with light background directly leverage Pin. The code amount of DBAF has 6672 lines of C++, including 2258 lines for implementing the five DBAs.

2.2 Translation

The interpretation of machine instructions is burdensome and error-prone because an instruction set (e.g., x86) has hundreds of different instructions and many of them have complex semantics. Here taking a common x86 instruction cmp as an example, it has two operands which can be immediate numbers, registers and memory addresses. The bit-width of operands can be 8, 16 and 32. The execution of cmp does not change operands but affects flags. Which and how flags are affected are determined by the operands. For example, considering an instruction cmp eax, ebx where eax and ebx are two unsigned numbers, CF will be set to 1 if eax is smaller than ebx or 0 otherwise, and ZF will be set to 1 if the two operands are equal. Consequently, analysts have to spend significant effort to implement and debug complicated DBAs which requires semantic interpretation. For instance, Triton [34], a concolic execution framework that directly interpret x86/x64 instructions, has 35,120 lines of C++ code.

We propose to conduct an online translation from machine instructions into IR. An alternative is translating the binary into IR statically and then mapping instructions to IR dynamically. However, this method encounters similar challenges that exist in static disassembly, such as data embedded in the code regions, variable instruction size, indirect branches [31]. Therefore, DBAF proposes online translation that fetches an instruction right before CPU executes the instruction, and hence DBAF overcomes the aforementioned challenges.

We select LLVM IR as the IR of DBAF due to its advantages. LLVM IR is a low-level RISC-like virtual instruction set, which supports linear sequences of simple operations like add, subtract, compare, and branch [19]. Therefore, the semantics of LLVM IR is much simpler than machine instructions like x86. Besides, LLVM IR is in three address form and strongly typed which facilitates program analysis and optimization [19]. In implementation, DBAF adapts Mcsema [10], which is a library lifting binaries into LLVM IR. As a static translation tool, Mcsema suffers from the similar drawbacks with static disassembly [31]. DBAF reuses the code from Mcsema [10] for lifting an instruction rather than a binary into LLVM IR, and hence it circumvents those drawbacks. Besides, we discover a bug in Mcsema resulting in an exception during translation due to a type mismatch. Mcsema accepted our suggestion and fixed the bug soon [13].

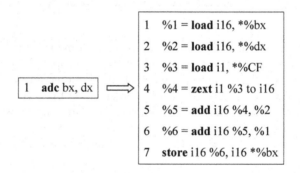

Fig. 2. Translate adc into LLVM IR

Figure 2 presents the translation of adc bx, dx into LLVM IR. The instruction adds dx to bx, and then add CF to bx. The LLVM IR after translation consists of seven statements. Statement 1 loads the value of bx into memory. %1 is actually a label representing load i16, *%bx. Therefore, one can simply think %1 is the value of bx. Similarly, statement 2 and 3 load the values of dx and CF, respectively. Statement 4 extends the 1 bit CF to 16 bits. The result of addition is represented by %6. Finally, statement seven stores the result into bx. The observation from this example is that the semantics of LLVM IR is much simpler than x86 instructions. Moreover, there are no implicit operands in LLVM IR; however, x86 instructions can have implicit operands (e.g., CF). Hence, the implementation of DBAs can be simplified after translation from machine instructions into LLVM IR.

2.3 API

Table 1 shows twenty representative APIs provided by DBAF. The APIs have similar invocation fashion with those APIs provided by Pin, so we explain some of them here. IR_AddInstrumentFunction() adds a function *func* to instrument in the level of IR, and hence *func* will be invoked after an instruction is translated into IR. Therefore, *func* can be considered as a callback function that processes each IR. IR_InsertCall() inserts a call to a function *func* before or after a specified IR, so that *func* will be called right before or after the execution of the IR. The two APIs IR_Ins() and IR_Address() map an IR to its corresponding instruction, so they bridge the gap between instruction instrumentation and IR instrumentation. IR_Opcode() and IR_Category() return the opcode and category of the IR, respectively. Please note that the opcode and category are defined in LLVM IR, rather than the instruction set.

Table 1. Twenty representative APIs provided by DBAF

API	Description
IR_AddInstrumentFunction	Add a function used to instrument at IR granularity
IR_InsertCall	Insert a call to a function relative to an IR
IR_Address	The instruction address of the IR
IR_ReadMemory	The address of the memory read by the IR
IR_WriteMemory	The address of the memory written by the IR
IR_Opcode	The opcode of IR
IR_OperandIsImmediate	Whether the specified operand of the IR is an immediate number
IR_OperandIsReg	Whether the specified operand of the IR is a register
IR_OperandIsTmp	Whether the specified operand of the IR is a temporary variable
IR_OperandTmp	Get the specific temporary variable of the IR
IR_OperandReg	Get the specific register of the IR
IR_OperandImmediate	Get the specific immediate number of the IR
IR_OperandWidth	The bit-width of the specified operand processed by the IR
IR_IsMemoryWrite	Whether the IR write memory
IR_IsMemoryRead	Whether the IR read memory
IR_Category	The category of the IR
IR_Ins	Get the instruction corresponding to the IR
syscall_entry	Call a function at the entry of a system call
syscall_exit	Call a function at the exit of a system call

LLVM IR can operate memory, registers, temporary variables and immediate numbers [23]. DBAF provides APIs to determine whether an IR read or write memory, whether an operand is an immediate number, register or a temporary variable, get the memory addresses, immediate numbers, registers or temporary variables operated by an IR. IR_OperandWidth() is responsible for obtaining the bit-width of a specific operand. Moreover, syscall_entry() and syscall_exit() allow DBAs to handle system calls without much effort. The usage of the proposed APIs is similar with the APIs provided by Pin [30], so analysts who have experiences in Pin can learn DBAF easily.

3 DBAs Based on DBAF

To demonstrate the utility of DBAF, we implement five DBAs on top of it. This section focuses on the implementation details of DBAs and shows how to use the provided APIs.

3.1 IR Counter

IR counter counts the number of executed IR, which maintains an integer representing the number of IR executed so far and increases it by one if an IR will be executed. IR counter outputs the integer when the instrumented binary finishes execution. Therefore, IR counter needs to invoke IR_InsertCall() to insert a call to a function which will be executed right before the execution of every IR. Figure 3 presents the core source code of IR counter, which uses two APIs (in bold at Line 6 and Line 12) provided by DBAF.

```
1    unsigned long long gRunInsCount = 0;

2    VOID IR_counter(ADDRINT addr) {
3        gRunInsCount += 1;
4    }

5    VOID ir_instrument_entry(IR ir, VOID* v) {
6        IR_InsertCall(ir, IPOINT_BEFORE, (AFUNPTR)IR_counter,
7            IARG_INST_PTR, IARG_END);}

8    VOID Finish(INT32 code, VOID *v) {
9        cout << "Executed IR count:" << gRunInsCount << endl;
10   }

11   int main(...){
12       IR_AddInstrumentFunction(ir_instrument_entry, 0);
13       PIN_AddFiniFunction(Finish, 0);
14       PIN_StartProgram();
15       return 0;}
```

Fig. 3. Core code of IR counter

3.2 Memory Tracer

Memory tracer records the memory address read or written by an IR and the corresponding instruction address. Figure 4 shows the core code of memory tracer. We omit the code of main() since it is the same with the main() of IR counter. Line 1 declares a file to record the trace. RecordMemRead() is responsible for recording the address read by the IR and the IR (i.e., instruction) address, which are acquired by invoking the proposed APIs IR_ReadMemory() (Line 9) and IR_Address() (Line 7), respectively. The call to RecordMemRead() is inserted before the IR (Line 10) which reads memory (Line 8). The recording of memory write is handled in a similar way.

```
1    ofstream OutFile("trace.txt");

2    VOID RecordMemRead(ADDRINT insAddr, ADDRINT memAddr) {
3        OutFile << "0x" << hex << insAddr << ": R 0x" << hex << memAddr << endl;}

4    VOID RecordMemWrite(ADDRINT insAddr, ADDRINT memAddr) {
5        OutFile << "0x" << hex << insAddr << ": W 0x" << hex << memAddr << endl;}

6    VOID ir_instrument_entry(IR ir, VOID* v) {
7        ADDRINT insAddr = IR_Address(ir);
8        if (IR_IsMemoryRead(ir)) {
9            ADDRINT irReadMemoryAddr = IR_ReadMemory(ir);
10           IR_InsertCall(ir, IPOINT_BEFORE, (AFUNPTR)RecordMemRead,
11             IARG_UINT32, insAddr, IARG_UINT32, irReadMemoryAddr, IARG_END);
12       } else if (IR_IsMemoryWrite(ir)) {
13           ADDRINT irWriteMemoryAddr = IR_WriteMemory(ir);
14           IR_InsertCall(ir, IPOINT_BEFORE, (AFUNPTR)RecordMemWrite,
15             IARG_UINT32, insAddr, IARG_UINT32, irWriteMemoryAddr, IARG_END);
     }
}
```

Fig. 4. Core code of memory tracer

3.3 Division-By-Zero Protector

Division-by-zero protector monitors the execution of a binary and halts its execution if an instruction divides zero. Figure 5 presents the core code of our division-by-zero protector (main() is omitted). The current version support unsigned integer division (UDIV_OP) and signed integer division (SDIV_OP) (Line 12). The extension for supporting floating-point division and modulo operation is straightforward. The second operand of UDIV_OP and SDIV_OP is the divisor and it can be memory (Line 16), register (Line 18) and immediate number (Line 14). The protector handles each case accordingly. The function TargetDiv() (Line 1) is responsible for checking the divisor and halting execution if the divisor is equal to zero. The call to TargetDiv() is inserted before the execution of each UDIV_OP and SDIV_OP (Line 15, 17, 19).

3.4 Taint Analyzer and Concolic Executor

Taint analysis consists of taint sources, taint propagation and taint sinks [36]. In particular, a taint analyzer marks inputs of interest (e.g., untrusted data) as taints, tracks taint propagation and takes actions (e.g., halt execution) if

```
1    void TargetDiv(int flag, void * para) {
2        bool nonzero = true;
3        if (1 == flag){//memory
4        nonzero = (*para != 0);
5        } else if (2 == flag) {//reg value or immediate number
6            nonzero = (para != 0);
        }
7        if (!nonzero) {
8            cerr << "Detected: divided by zero" << endl;
9            exit(-1);
        }
    }
10   VOID ir_instrument_entry(IR ir, VOID* v) {
11       INT opcode = IR_Opcode(ir);
12       if(opcode != UDIV_OP || opcode != SDIV_OP)
13           return;
14       if (IR_OperandIsImmediate(ir, 1)) {
15           IR_InsertCall(ir, IPOINT_BEFORE, (AFUNPTR)(TargetDiv), IARG_UINT32,
                 2, IARG_PTR, (void*)IR_OperandImmediate(ir, 1), IARG_END);
16       } else if (IR_IsMemoryRead(ir)) {
17           IR_InsertCall(ir, IPOINT_BEFORE, (AFUNPTR)(TargetDiv), IARG_UINT32,
                 1, IARG_UINT32, IR_ReadMemory(ir), IARG_END);
18       } else if (IR_OperandIsReg(ir, 1)) {
19           IR_InsertCall(ir, IPOINT_BEFORE, (AFUNPTR)(TargetDiv), IARG_UINT32,
                 2, IARG_REG_VALUE, IR_OperandReg(ir, 1), IARG_END);
     }
   }
```

Fig. 5. Core code of division-by-zero protector

taints flow into the specific place (e.g., disk files). To find taint sources and taint sinks in binaries, DBAs always instrument system calls. Our taint analyzer uses two APIs syscall_entry() and syscall_exit() to insert calls to analyst-provided functions before or after the execution of system calls. In the analyst-provided functions, taint sources are marked and actions are taken. To track taint propagation, taint analyzer conducts instrumentation in the level of IR (invoking IR_AddInstrumentationFunction()) and insert a call to a function *func* before the execution of each IR (invoking IR_InsertCall()). *func* is responsible for interpreting the semantics of IR and understand which operands should be affected by taint propagation.

Concolic execution, alias dynamic symbolic execution that runs a program concretely, tracks symbol propagation, collects constraints when encountering branches, and generates new inputs by querying a theorem prover [6]. Like taint analysis, concolic execution needs to mark symbol sources. In other words, we need to mark data of interest (e.g., test cases) as symbols. In implementation, our concolic executor instruments system calls using the provided APIs. Moreover, the concolic executor needs to track symbol propagation which is significantly difficult than tracking taint propagation. That is because concolic execution requires elaborate interpretation of IR semantics to find how (not just which) operands are affected by symbol propagation.

Therefore, our concolic executor instruments the binary in the level of IR and interprets the semantics of each IR statement. Besides, our concolic executor leverages Z3 [26] to produce new inputs. The fact is that more complicated the instruction set, more effort should be made to implement and debug a concolic executor. The code amount of our concolic executor is 1,035 lines of C++. For comparison, Triton [34] which interprets machine instruction without IR translation has 35,120 lines of C++, including 15,698 lines of code under "Triton/src/libtriton/arch/x86" are dedicated to interpret x86 semantics [33].

4   Experiments

This section presents the results of the experiments concerning the translation overhead, followed by two practical cases about our taint analyzer.

4.1   Translation Overhead

Translation overhead is a critical factor to evaluate the efficiency of DBAF because the translation process is conducted online. We select ten benchmark programs from several well-known benchmark sets. All the benchmark programs are open source and have been used to evaluate other tools. In particular, four benchmark programs are for the purpose of I/O subsystem performance testing; two aim to evaluate the performance of memory subsystem; two evaluate CPU performance; one attempts to evaluate the performance of multi-thread and the last evaluates the performance of mutex. The purpose and code amount of those benchmark programs are presented in Table 2. Please note that SysBench is an integrated benchmark, and SysBench1, SysBench2, SysBench3, SysBench4, SysBench5 indicate its different functionalities. For the same reason, we do not count the code amount of those five benchmark programs separately.

To accurately measure translation overhead, we implement two versions of NullTool (termed by NullPin and NullDBAF) which are directly built on top of Pin and DBAF, respectively. NullPin just loads the benchmark programs into memory and runs them without instrumentation. NullDBAF loads the benchmark programs, translates machine instructions into IR, then converts back to instructions and runs the programs. We measure the execution time of each benchmark program loaded by NullPin and NullDBAF, respectively and then we compute the overhead as shown in Fig. 6. The overhead averaged from the ten benchmark programs is about 4x. We need to remind that the results are conservative because NullTool does not instrument the benchmark programs. Imaging the DBAs with practical functionalities, the instrumentation overhead should be much higher than translation overhead. For example, a concolic executor often slows down the execution of analyzed programs hundreds of times. Therefore, the translation overhead incurred by DBAF is reasonable. We plan to find methods to further reduce translation overhead in our future work.

Table 2. Benchmark programs to evaluate translation overhead

Benchmark	Purpose	Code amount
Bonnie++[a]	I/O	2,919
fs_mark[b]	I/O	1,067
IOzone[c]	I/O	26,681
mbw[d]	memory	207
stress[e]	CPU	628
SysBench1[f]	CPU	7,452
SysBench2	Memory	7,452
SysBench3	Multi-thread	7,452
SysBench4	Mutex	7,452
SysBench5	I/O	7,452

https://sourceforge.net/projects/bonnie/.
https://github.com/josefbacik/fs_mark.
http://www.iozone.org/.
https://github.com/raas/mbw.
http://people.seas.harvard.edu/~apw/stress/.
https://github.com/nuodb/sysbench.

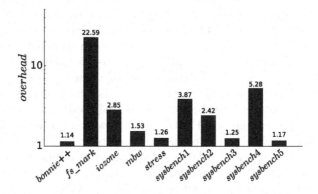

Fig. 6. Translation overhead of DBAF

4.2   Practical Cases

We evaluate the effectiveness of our taint analyzer through validating two practical vulnerabilities. To speedup the validation process, we record the memory range of the analyzed binary and restrict instrumentation in this range. In other words, we do not process the code of libraries.

CVE-2010-4051. This vulnerability exists in the function regcomp() of the GNU C library that processes untrusted inputs without preliminary checking the input for the sanity [9]. Consequently, attackers can craft an exploit containing adjacent bounded repetitions (e.g., {10,}{10,}{10,}{10,}{10,}) to trigger a stack overflow in regcomp(), resulting in a crash. To detect various kinds of control-flow hijacking attacks (including stack overflow), we enrich the taint sinks of our taint analyzer. In particular, we consider all indirect rets/jumps/calls as taint sinks, and therefore our taint analyzer detects a control-flow hijacking if the target of an indirect ret/jump/call is tainted. Please note that direct jumps/calls are not included in the taint sinks because attackers cannot subvert the jump/call targets. Our taint analyzer instruments 135,082 IR (corresponding to 21,652 instructions) and detects the vulnerability in 68 s. Before triggering the bug, 7,154,041,604 IR (corresponding to 713,671,310 instructions) are executed.

CVE-2010-0001. This vulnerability results from an integer overflow in function unlzw() of gzip before 1.4 on 64-bit platforms, allowing remote attackers to launch a DoS attack or possibly execute arbitrary code [8]. The outcome of the overflowed integer computation is used as an array index, and hence attackers control the array index and then possibly get access to arbitrary memory address. To detect memory corruption, we enrich the taint sinks of our taint analyzer. In particular, we consider all memory operations (i.e., load, store) as taint sinks, and hence our taint analyzer detects an attack for memory corruption if the binary gets access to a tainted address. Our taint analyzer instruments 109,913 IR (corresponding to 17,298 instructions) and detects the vulnerability in 170 s. Before triggering the flaw, 21,875,318,127 IR (corresponding to 2,956,988,800 instructions) are executed.

5 Related Work

This section reviews studies about binary instrumentation tools, rather than the applications based on binary instrumentation tools. Pin [24], Dyninst [1] and DynamoRIO [2] are three well-known dynamic instrumentation tools (DITs) that have been widely used in both academia and industry. Besides, new DITs usually either build on top of them or compare with them. Pin [24] is developed by Intel Corp. that is efficient and provides rich APIs and well-written documents. Dyninst [1] supports both dynamic instrumentational static instrumentation (i.e., binary rewrite) and provides unified APIs for both. DynamoRIO attempts to construct a transparent instrumentation environment because the behaviors of the instrumented binary may be changed if it is aware of the fact that it is running in an instrumentation environment [3].

To reduce the runtime overhead of the binary after instrumentating by a static instrumentation tool (SIT), PEBIL uses function level code relocation in order to insert large but fast control structures and then allows analysts to insert assembly code directly [21]. Compared with a DIT, a binary after processing by a SIT has lower runtime overhead, however, the instrumentation of SITs is easy to be bypassed. Consequently, SITs are less commonly-used to analyze malware. PSI enhances SITs by ensuring a non-bypassable instrumentation [45].

In particular, PSI enforces three properties to achieve the non-bypassability, e.g., all direct and indirect control-ow transfers made from the original code must target instructions in the original code that were validly disassembled by the disassembler [45].

EEL proposes a RISC-like IR, allowing analysts to write machine- and OS-independent applications [18]. Strata is a dynamic instrumentation framework supporting SPARK and MIPS instruction sets [37]. Unlike EEL, Strata does not translate machine instructions into IR possibly because SPARK and MIPS are RISC instructions sets. Vulcan supports both dynamic and static instrumentation, which translates instructions into MSIL (an IR designed by Microsoft Corp.) and provides APIs [11]. Hazelwood and Klauser extends Pin to support ARM instruction set [16]. Dimension is a DIT for virtual execution environments (VEEs) that has two advantages in design [44]. First, Dimension is not tightly coupled with VEE, so it can be reused easily be different VEEs. Besides, it is able to instrument both source and target binaries. HDTrans is a light-weight DIT designed for those binaries with a small and hot working set [39]. DSPInst is a SIT for Blackfin DSP processor [40], DPCL is the extension of Dyninst for supporting parallel MPI applications [22,35] and PMaCinst is a SIT supporting PowerPC instruction set [41].

Guillon proposes to instrument binary via QEMU, a cross-platform emulation tool, in order to instrument the entire software stack, including kernel modules [14]. For the similar purpose, PinOS leverages XEN, a virtual machine hypervisor to extends Pin with the ability to instrument the whole operating system [4]. Technically, PinOS runs under the guest OS to manipulate the guest OS. Feiner et al. propose a different design which implements a Linux kernel module to conduct a whole-system instrumentation [12].

Mobile devices are weaker than desktop computers in terms of processing/memory/storage capability. SIF is a selective instrumentation framework for mobile applications, enabling analysts to specify a small amount of code in applications to be instrumented, thus overhead on mobile devices can be reduced [15]. DIOTA circumvents the challenges of constructing a control flow graph and enables to instrument self-modifying code [25]. VMAD first instruments the source code of the analyzed software by LLVM and then monitors its execution in a virtual machine [17]. SecondWrite is a SIT that is able to instrument stripped binaries (i.e., without relocation information) [38]. It is a technical challenge for DITs to instrument multi-thread programs. Chung et al. apply transactional memory to enclose the data and metadata accesses within an atomic transaction, thus thread safe is maintained [7]. DIABLO is a static instrumentation framework, which translates various instruction sets into IR and provides APIs [32].

To overcome the limitation of static disassembling, BIRD combines static disassembly with an on-demand dynamic disassembly approach to guarantee that each instruction in a binary file is analyzed or transformed before it is executed [27]. SuperPin proposes to speedup instrumentation by dividing the analyzed binary into non-overlapped instruction sequences, and then starts multiple instrumentation threads to process each sequence in parallel [43]. Upton and

Cohn observe that both data collection and data analysis of binary instrumentation are time-consumption. They propose to decouple data collection from analysis and buffer the data for analysis [42]. To ease its usage for analysts, Hijacker proposes rule-based instrumentation that allows analysts to write instrumentation requirements in an xml file [29]. Our previous work designs a middleware to take care of the differences of various instrumentation tools and expose easy-to-use APIs to analysts [5]. However, the middleware does not translate instructions into IR, so analysts have to interpret instruction semantics by themselves.

6 Conclusion

Dynamic binary instrumentation is a fundamental technique for various applications. Existing DITs have their shortcomings. This study design DBAF, a dynamic binary analysis framework that translates machine instructions into LLVM IR and provides tens of Pin-like APIs enabling analysts to instrument the binary in the level of IR easily. Moreover, we present five applications based on DBAF. Experiments show that the translation overhead is reasonable. We will try to further reduce the translation overhead in our future work.

Acknowledgment. This work is supported in part by National Key R&D Program of China (2017YF-B0802903), Project 2117H14243A and Sichuan Province Research and Technology Supporting Plan, China.

References

1. Bernat, A., Miller, B.: Anywhere, any-time binary instrumentation. In: PASTE (2011)
2. Bruening, D., Duesterwald, E., Amarasinghe, S.: Design and implementation of a dynamic optimization framework for windows. In: FDDO (2001)
3. Bruening, D., Zhao, Q., Amarasinghe, S.: Transparent dynamic instrumentation. In: VEE (2012)
4. Bungale, P.P., Luk, C.K.: Pinos: a programmable framework for whole-system dynamic instrumentation. In: VEE (2007)
5. Chen, T., Xu, Y., Zhang, X.: A program manipulation middleware and its applications on system security. In: Lin, X., Ghorbani, A., Ren, K., Zhu, S., Zhang, A. (eds.) SecureComm 2017. LNICST, vol. 238, pp. 606–626. Springer, Cham (2018). https://doi.org/10.1007/978-3-319-78813-5_31
6. Chen, T., Zhang, X., Guo, S., Li, H., Wu, Y.: State of the art: dynamic symbolic execution for automated test generation. Future Gener. Comput. Syst. **29**(7), 1758–1773 (2013)
7. Chung, J., Dalton, M., Kannan, H., Kozyrakis, C.: Thread-safe dynamic binary translation using transactional memory. In: HPCA (2008)
8. CVE: Cve-2010-0001 (2011). http://cve.mitre.org/cgi-bin/cvename.cgi?name= CVE-2010-0001
9. CVE: Cve-2010-4051 (2011). http://cve.mitre.org/cgi-bin/cvename.cgi?name= CVE-2010-4051

10. Dinaburg, A., Adve, V.: McSema: static translation of x86 instructions to LLVM. In: ReCon (2014)
11. Edwards, A., Vo, H., Srivastava, A.: Vulcan binary transformation in a distributed environment (2001). https://www.microsoft.com/en-us/research/wp-content/uploads/2016/02/tr-2001-50.pdf
12. Feiner, P., Brown, A.D., Goel, A.: Comprehensive kernel instrumentation via dynamic binary translation. In: ASPLOS (2012)
13. Feng, Y.: Fixed potential LLVM value type dismatch in llvm::constantint::get. (#241) #242 (2017). https://github.com/trailofbits/mcsema/pull/2421
14. Guillon, C.: Program instrumentation with QEMU. In: International QEMU Users' Forum (2011)
15. Hao, S., Li, D., Halfond, W.G., Govindan, R.: SIF: a selective instrumentation framework for mobile applications. In: Mobisys (2013)
16. Hazelwood, K., Klauser, A.: A dynamic binary instrumentation engine for the arm architecture. In: CASES (2006)
17. Jimborean, A., Mastrangelo, L., Loechner, V., Clauss, P.: VMAD: an advanced dynamic program analysis and instrumentation framework. In: O'Boyle, M. (ed.) CC 2012. LNCS, vol. 7210, pp. 220–239. Springer, Heidelberg (2012). https://doi.org/10.1007/978-3-642-28652-0_12
18. Larus, J.R., Schnarr, E.: EEL: machine-independent executable editing. In: PLDI (1995)
19. Lattner, C.: The design of LLVMS (2012). http://www.drdobbs.com/architecture-and-design/the-design-of-llvm/240001128?pgno=1
20. Lattner, C., Adve, V.: LLVM: a compilation framework for lifelong program analysis & transformation. In: CGO (2004)
21. Laurenzano, M.A., Tikir, M.M., Carrington, L., Snavely, A.: PEBIL: efficient static binary instrumentation for Linux. In: ISPASS (2010)
22. Lee, G.L., et al.: Dynamic binary instrumentation and data aggregation on large scale systems. Int. J. Parallel Program. **35**(3), 207–232 (2007)
23. LLVM: LLVM language reference manual (2018). https://llvm.org/docs/LangRef.html
24. Luk, C.K., et al.: Pin: building customized program analysis tools with dynamic instrumentation. In: PLDI (2005)
25. Maebe, J., Ronsse, M., Bosschere, K.D.: Diota: dynamic instrumentation, optimization and transformation of applications. In: WBT (2002)
26. Moura, L.D., Bjørner, N.: Z3: an efficient SMT solver. In: TACAS (2008)
27. Nanda, S., Li, W., Lam, L.C., Chiueh, T.C.: Bird: binary interpretation using runtime disassembly. In: CGO (2006)
28. Nethercote, N., Seward, J.: Valgrind: a framework for heavyweight dynamic binary instrumentation. In: PLDI (2007)
29. Pellegrini, A.: Hijacker: efficient static software instrumentation with applications in high performance computing: poster paper. In: HPCS (2013)
30. Pin: API reference (2017). https://software.intel.com/sites/landingpage/pintool/docs/81205/Pin/html/group__API__REF.html
31. Prasad, M.: Disassembly challenges (2003). http://static.usenix.org/event/usenix03/tech/full_papers/prasad/prasad_html/node5.html
32. Put, L.V., Chanet, D., Bus, B.D., Sutter, B.D., Bosschere, K.D.: DIABLO: a reliable, retargetable and extensible link-time rewriting framework. In: ISSPIT (2005)
33. Salwan, J.: Triton source code (2018). https://github.com/JonathanSalwan/Triton/tree/master/src/libtriton/arch/x86

34. Saudel, F., Salwan, J.: Triton: concolic execution framework (2015). http:// shell-storm.org/talks/SSTIC2015_English_slide_detailed_version_Triton_Concolic_ Execution_FrameWork_FSaudel_JSalwan.pdf
35. Schulz, M., et al.: Scalable dynamic binary instrumentation for blue gene/l. In: WBIA (2005)
36. Schwartz, E.J., Avgerinos, T., Brumley, D.: All you ever wanted to know about dynamic taint analysis and forward symbolic execution (but might have been afraid to ask). In: S&P (2010)
37. Scott, K., Kumar, N., Velusamy, S., Childers, B., Davidson, J.W., Soffa, M.L.: Retargetable and reconfigurable software dynamic translation. In: CGO (2003)
38. Smithson, M., Anand, K., Kotha, A., Elwazeer, K., Giles, N., Barua, R.: Binary rewriting without relocation information (2010). http://citeseerx.ist.psu. edu/viewdoc/download?doi=10.1.1.463.3748&rep=rep1&type=pdf
39. Sridhar, S., Shapiro, J.S., Northup, E., Bungale, P.P.: HDTrans: an open source, low-level dynamic instrumentation system. In: VEE (2006)
40. Sun, E., Kaeli, D.: A binary instrumentation tool for the blackfin processor. In: WBIA (2009)
41. Tikir, M.M., Laurenzano, M., Carrington, L., Snavely, A.: PMAC binary instrumentation library for powerpc/aix. In: WBIA (2006)
42. Upton, D., Hazelwood, K., Cohn, R., Lueck, G.: Improving instrumentation speed via buffering. In: WBIA (2009)
43. Wallace, S., Hazelwood, K.: Superpin: parallelizing dynamic instrumentation for real-time performance. In: CGO (2007)
44. Yang, J., Zhou, S., Soffa, M.L.: Dimension: an instrumentation tool for virtual execution environments. In: VEE (2006)
45. Zhang, M., Qiao, R., Hasabnis, N., Sekar, R.: A platform for secure static binary instrumentation. In: VEE (2014)

Context-Aware Failure-Oblivious Computing as a Means of Preventing Buffer Overflows

Manuel Rigger[(✉)], Daniel Pekarek, and Hanspeter Mössenböck

Johannes Kepler University Linz, Linz, Austria
{manuel.rigger,daniel.pekarek,hanspeter.moessenboeck}@jku.at

Abstract. In languages like C, buffer overflows are widespread. A common mitigation technique is to use tools that detect them during execution and abort the program to prevent data leakage or the diversion of control flow. However, for server applications, it would be desirable to prevent such errors while maintaining availability of the system. To this end, we present an approach to handling buffer overflows without aborting the program. This approach involves implementing a recovery logic in library functions based on an introspection function that allows querying the size of a buffer. We demonstrate that introspection can be implemented in popular bug-finding and bug-mitigation tools such as LLVM's AddressSanitizer, SoftBound, and Intel-MPX-based bounds checking. We evaluated our approach in a case study of real-world bugs and show that for tools that explicitly track bounds data, introspection results in a low performance overhead.

Keywords: Memory safety · Reliability · Dependability
Availability · Fault tolerance

1 Introduction

Buffer overflows in C, where an out-of-bounds pointer is dereferenced, belong to the most dangerous software errors [5,32]. Unlike higher-level languages, buffer overflows invoke *Undefined Behavior* and are not prevented during execution; programmers also cannot handle them using exception or similar mechanisms, since the language lacks them. Buffer overflows allow attackers to overflow function addresses stored on the stack or heap and thus to maliciously divert execution of the program [28] and to leak sensitive data [31]. A plethora of tools exist that make their exploitation more difficult or detect them and abort execution of the program [30,32,34,36]. However, when availability of an application is important (e.g. for production servers), it would be preferable to continue

We thank Oracle Labs for funding this research. We thank Gergő Barany, Roland Yap, and Fabio Niephaus for their useful feedback on an early draft of this paper. We thank Ingrid Abfalter for proofreading and editorial assistance.

© Springer Nature Switzerland AG 2018
M. H. Au et al. (Eds.): NSS 2018, LNCS 11058, pp. 376–390, 2018.
https://doi.org/10.1007/978-3-030-02744-5_28

execution as long as security is not compromised [24]. This could, for example, make it harder to perform a denial-of-service attack where a buffer overflow is exploited to crash the program or inject code.

To safely maintain execution in the presence of buffer overflows, we have come up with the concept of *context-aware failure-oblivious computing*. Our core idea is that library writers (e.g., the libc maintainers) can query run-time data such as bounds information in library functions by using an introspection interface. This information can then be used to implement a recovery logic that can mitigate incorrect execution states instead of aborting the program. Library writers can implement a custom recovery logic that depends on each function's semantics, which is why we refer to our technique as being context-aware. For example, a libc function that processes an unterminated string could prevent an out-of-bounds access by checking for the end of the buffer to handle the fault and continue execution. We expect that this recovery logic would be used mainly in a production context, as it would be preferable that execution is aborted if an error occurs during development and testing so that programmers can fix the error.

Our work is based on a combination of *failure-oblivious computing* [25] and our previous work on an introspection interface for C to increase the robustness of libraries [23]. We show how the introspection interface can be used to implement a failure-oblivious computing mechanism. We evaluated our approach by demonstrating that introspection for preventing buffer overflows can be implemented in popular bug-finding and bug-mitigation tools such as LLVM's AddressSanitizer [27], SoftBound [15], and GCC's Pointer Bounds Checker, which is based on the Intel Memory Protection Extensions (MPX) [19]. Furthermore, we show how our approach allows execution to continue in the presence of buffer overflows found in real-world programs as described by the Common Vulnerabilities and Exposures (CVE) database [33], and demonstrate that the performance overhead for introspection implemented in approaches such as MPX is negligible.

2   Background

Failure-oblivious computing. One technique for maintaining availability in the presence of buffer overflows is *failure-oblivious computing*, where invalid writes are discarded and values for invalid reads are manufactured [25,26]. By carefully selecting a sequence of return values for invalid reads, the program can successfully continue execution in most cases. However, a drawback of this approach is that it is "blind"; that is, it cannot guess the context (i.e., a function's semantics) to return a meaningful value for all reads. In this paper, we address this aspect by making failure-oblivious computing context-aware.

Introspection for C. As part of previous work, we demonstrated how use of introspection (i.e., exposing run-time data) benefits the robustness of libraries [23]. The core idea of our approach was that bug-finding tools and runtimes for C that track additional metadata such as object bounds or object types can expose this data to library writers via an introspection interface, which programmers can use to check the input of library functions. We showed that various introspection functions can be used to detect bugs or to maintain availability of the program. For example, to detect buffer overflows by means of introspection, the _size_right() function can be applied, which expects a pointer and returns the number of allocated bytes to the right of the pointee (or zero for invalid pointers) and can therefore be used for bounds checks. In this paper, we expand on how introspection can be used to increase availability, which we define as *context-aware failure-oblivious computing*.

Evaluation of Introspection. We have previously evaluated an introspection libc using Safe Sulong [21,22], an LLVM IR interpreter on top of the Java Virtual Machine (JVM) [20] which automatically keeps track of array lengths, object sizes, and object types of C data [23]. Although the JVM tracks all relevant run-time information necessary to implement our introspection mechanism, it is not a typical environment in which to execute C code. In this paper, we address this by evaluating our approach in the context of popular bug-finding and bug-mitigation tools for buffer overflows and show that our refined introspection approach prevents real-world errors while maintaining availability.

3   Introspection Interceptors

This section explains the implementation of the introspection-based libc functions. These enhanced functions rely on the _size_right() introspection function to mitigate buffer overflows. Challenges to introducing them were that the original code not be cluttered by the introspection checks, that the effort for implementing these checks be low, and that the code behave in the same way as the original library during correct execution.

Libc Interceptors. Based on our requirements, we implemented the introspection-based libc functions as *interceptors*, which are wrappers that intercept calls to libc functions and which are used by many bug-checking and bug-mitigation tools (including ASan, GCC's Pointer Bounds Checker and SoftBound)[1]. The introspection logic was kept separate from the normal code to avoid cluttering of the original source code. The cost of adding introspection-based recovery logic was low, as for each unsafe function that we considered (e.g., strlen()), libc provides safer functions that expect an additional size argument, which we used for our implementation (e.g., strnlen()). By reusing existing libc functions from the same library, we expect correct execution to behave in the same way as without the interceptors. For example, consider our strlen() interceptor, which is based on the safer strnlen() function:

---

[1] Note that in our previous work we instead reimplemented parts of a libc to use introspection, which made the libc less readable and required programs to be compatible with this libc.

```
size_t strlen(const char *s) {
  return ORIGINAL(strnlen)(s, _size_right(s));
}
```

The `ORIGINAL` macro yields a reference to the function passed as its argument that is part of the library and prevents recursively calling interceptors. We implemented the `_size_right()` function in various memory-safety-checking tools, as described in Sect. 4. Both the original `strlen()` implementation and this interceptor behave correctly for strings that are terminated with a '\0', which is needed to determine their length. However, if an unterminated string is passed to the original `strlen()` implementation, the function results in a buffer overflow that causes bug-finding and bug-mitigation tools to abort execution. Using the introspection-based interceptor instead prevents the buffer overflow, as the string length can be computed even for strings for which the '\0' is missing, because the interceptor assumes the underlying buffer size to be the maximum length of the string. Note that application-level functions can still cause bug-finding and bug-mitigation tools to abort execution if these functions run over string bounds. However, in many cases, application-level functions process strings up to the length computed by `strlen()`, which consequently prevents an out-of-bounds access.

As another example, an introspection interceptor can address the insecure interface of `gets()`, which reads user input and writes it to a buffer whose size is unknown to the function:

```
char *gets(char *s) {
  return ORIGINAL(fgets)(s, _size_right(s), stdin);
}
```

Using introspection, `gets()` reads only as much user input as the buffer can store.

Some introspection interceptors correct invalid parameters, for instance, in `memcpy`:

```
void *memcpy(void *dest, const void *src,
             size_t n) {
  ssize_t dstsz = _size_right(dest);
  size_t len = n;
  if (dstsz < len) {
    len = dstsz;
  }
  return ORIGINAL(memcpy)(dest, src, len);
}
```

If the size of the destination buffer is smaller than the number of bytes that the function is expected to copy, the function ignores the writes that go out of bounds. Note that another check for the size of the source buffer would be applicable.

In contrast to our previous work [23], we treat the return value of `_size_right()` as a conservative estimate of the object's right bounds. This estimate can be the real size of the object, in which case the introspection interceptors work most reliably. However, it can also be at least as large as the actual allocation, which could include additional space due to alignment requirements (e.g., to accommodate approaches that track only allocation sizes). Finally, if no bounds information is available for a given pointer, returning MAX_LONG effectively disables the introspection interceptors. This is useful, since it allows execution without recompilation of the code even when no tool is used that could determine the bounds of an object.

4   Introspection in Tools

We implemented _size_right() by exposing existing bounds information in three tools, namely LLVM's AddressSanitizer [27], SoftBound [15], and GCC's Intel MPX-based Pointer Bounds Checker instrumentation. SoftBound and LLVM's AddressSanitizer (ASan) are both software-based approaches. SoftBound provides access to bounds information in constant time, and is therefore a favorable candidate for implementing introspection. ASan's representation of metadata is suboptimal for implementing introspection, because it does not explicitly maintain bounds information and finding the end of an object takes linear time. By implementing introspection in ASan, we wanted to determine a worst-case overhead for implementing introspection in existing tools. Intel MPX instrumentation allowed us to additionally evaluate a hardware-based approach.

SoftBound. SoftBound is a bounds checker that has also been enhanced by a mechanism (called CETS) to find temporal memory errors [16]. It tracks base and bounds information for every pointer as separate metadata. To propagate this metadata across call sites, SoftBound adds additional base and bounds metadata to pointer arguments of functions. To implement _size_right(), we return the right bounds of a pointee by subtracting its base address from its bounds, which are associated with the pointer. For all SoftBound experiments, we used the latest stable version 3.8.0, which is distributed together with CETS.

LLVM's AddressSanitizer. ASan is one of the most widely used bug-finding tools for C/C++ programs; it allows memory errors such as buffer overflows and use-after-free errors to be found by instrumenting the program during compile time. Its implementation is based on *shadow memory* [17], where a memory cell allocated by the program has a corresponding shadow memory cell that stores meta-information about the original allocation. To detect buffer overflows, ASan allocates space between allocations and marks the corresponding shadow memory as *redzones*; if a dereferenced pointer points to such a redzone, ASan detects the overflow and aborts the program. Shadow memory is not a favorable representation of metadata for introspection, since bounds information cannot be accessed in constant time. We implemented _size_right() in linear time by iterating over the current buffer until its associated shadow memory indicates that a redzone has been reached. For all LLVM and ASan experiments, we used the development branch of LLVM version 6.0.0 based on commit 1d871d6 in compiler-rt.

Intel MPX. Intel MPX is an instruction set extension that adds instructions for creating, maintaining, and checking bounds information. Although its performance overhead is relatively high [19], providing buffer overflow protection at the hardware level is a promising research direction [35]. To use Intel MPX, we relied on GCC's Pointer Bounds Checker instrumentation, which employs Intel MPX to verify bounds. Similarly to SoftBound's implementation, we implemented _size_right() by querying the upper bounds (using a GCC builtin function) and subtracted the pointer address from it. For all experiments, we used GCC version 7.2.0.

Using libc. To use our introspection-based libc extensions, we redefined the names of the libc functions by means of preprocessor macros. While this required recompilation of the target application, it allowed the tools to also instrument our introspection-based libc functions and did not require us to maintain bounds information, as libc calls from our interceptors invoked the tools' interceptors. Note that our approach could be extended by using the dynamic loader to load the interceptors to retain binary compatibility (e.g., using the LD_PRELOAD mechanism); however, redefining the function names was less invasive.

5   CVE Case Study

To demonstrate the applicability of our approach in real-world projects, we considered recent (i.e., less than one year old) buffer overflows in widely-used software such as Dnsmasq, Libxml2, and GraphicsMagick. We selected the first libc-related bugs that we found in the CVE database for which an executable exploit existed. For each buffer overflow, we evaluated whether our introspection-based approach could mitigate the error and whether execution could successfully continue. Our approach prevented four out of five buffer overflows while successfully continuing execution; in one case, execution was aborted due to a subsequent buffer overflow in user-level code. Note that the unmodified tools also detected those buffer overflows; however, they aborted the program instead of mitigating the error and continuing execution. Since we performed this case study on complex real-world applications, and because SoftBound is a research prototype, we could not successfully execute any of these applications with it. The unmodified SoftBound version was also unable to execute them.[2] However, we extracted the functions in which the errors occurred, which SoftBound could execute, and created a driver to trigger the bug.

Dnsmasq. Dnsmasq is a lightweight DHCP server and caching DNS server which is used in many home routers.[3] In versions prior to 2.78, a bug existed that could

---

[2] https://github.com/santoshn/softboundcets-3.8.0/issues/$x \in \{5, 6, 7, 8\}$.

[3] http://www.thekelleys.org.uk/dnsmasq/doc.html.

cause a stack-based buffer overflow that allowed attackers to execute arbitrary code or to cause denial of service by crafting a DHCPv6 request with a wrong size (see CVE-2017-14493). It occurred in `memcpy()`, to which an incorrect size argument was passed:

```
state->mac_len = opt6_len(opt) - 2;
memcpy(&state->mac[0], opt6_ptr(opt, 2), state->mac_len);
```

A similar bug could be exploited for denial of service attacks (see CVE-2017-14496). It occurred in `memset()` and was triggered by an integer overflow:

```
/* Clear buffer beyond request to avoid risk of information disclosure. */
memset(((char *)header) + qlen, 0, (limit - ((char *)header)) - qlen);
```

When using our introspection interceptors, all tools continued execution by copying or setting up to as many bytes as the destination buffer could hold. The server stayed fully functional.

Libxml2. Libxml2 is a widely used open-source XML parsing library.[4] For versions up to 2.9.4, a vulnerability in the `xmlSnprintfElementContent()` function enabled attackers to crash the application through a buffer overflow (see CVE-2017-9047). It was caused by an incorrect length validation (at another code location) followed by `strcat()`:

```
if (content->name != NULL)
  strcat(buf, (char *) content->name);
```

The introspection interceptor for `strcat()` mitigated the buffer overflow by restricting the length of the concatenated string in all tools. The application continued execution and printed the truncated string as part of an error message. Although the error message was truncated, the output appeared reasonable from the user's point of view.

GraphicsMagick. GraphicsMagick is a widely used image processing tool.[5] In version 1.3.26, its `DescribeImage()` function allowed attackers to overflow and corrupt the heap to execute arbitrary code or to cause denial-of-service attacks (see CVE-2017-16352). As shown below, the size argument in the call to `strncpy()` did not limit the number of copied bytes to the size of the buffer; instead, the number was calculated by the length of the directory name (which was determined by searching for the newline or NUL). Consequently, an overly long directory name could be used to cause an overflow:

```
for (p=image->directory; *p != '\0'; p++) {
  q=p;
  while ((*q != '\n') && (*q != '\0'))
    q++;
  (void) strncpy(image_info->filename,p,q-p);
  image_info->filename[q-p]='\0';
```

---

[4] http://xmlsoft.org/.
[5] http://www.graphicsmagick.org/.

```
p=q;
// ...
}
```

The introspection interceptor for `strncpy()` successfully restricted the length of the copied string to the length of the destination buffer `image_info->filename`. However, in the line after the call to `strncpy()`, the program attempted to write a NUL character to the end of the string, which then caused an out-of-bounds access in the user application. The introspection approach does not protect against buffer overflows that happen in code that does not use introspection; however, we intend introspection to be used together with a bounds-checking tool, which is expected to abort execution for unhandled errors and thus prevent incorrect execution. In fact, all introspection-instrumented tools prevented this buffer overflow by aborting execution.

LightFTP.   LightFTP   is   a   small   FTP   server.[6]   A   logging   function `writelogentry()` in version 1.1 of LightFTP was vulnerable to a buffer overflow that allowed denial of service or remote code execution (see CVE-2017-1000218). As shown below, the program added log entries to a buffer with a hard-coded size; as the log entries depended on user input that was restricted by another, larger constant, a buffer overflow could be triggered:

```
char _text[512];
// ...
if (logtext1)
    strcat(_text, logtext1);
if (logtext2)
    strcat(_text, logtext2);
strcat(_text, CRLF);
```

The introspection interceptor for `strcat()` mitigated the error without crashing the FTP server. Note that our mitigation truncated the log entry, but allowed subsequent requests to be handled successfully.

6   Performance Evaluation

To determine the performance of the introspection-based interceptors, we used LightFTP and Dnsmasq, which are the servers we also investigated in our CVE case study. We selected them for their high attack surface and because they are expected to be highly available. We evaluated the performance of ASan and Intel MPX both with and without the introspection interceptors; SoftBound failed to execute the servers, as explained above. Further, to establish a baseline, we measured the performance of C programs compiled with the Clang compiler [13] without using any bug-mitigation mechanisms. For all systems, we turned on compiler optimizations by using the -03 flag. We measured the throughput by

---

[6] https://github.com/hfiref0x/LightFTP/.

means of the load-testing tool JMeter version 3.3. We configured JMeter to use 4 threads, each of which each sent 250 requests to simulate multiple concurrent users using the built-in FTP sampler and the UDP Protocol Support plugin. As the Intel MPX instructions are not thread-safe [19], we also evaluated all tools using only 1 thread. We performed each measurement 10 times to account for variability. Our setup consisted of a quad-core Intel Core i7-6700HQ CPU at 2.60 GHz on Ubuntu version 17.10 (with kernel 4.13.0-32-generic) with 16 GB of memory.

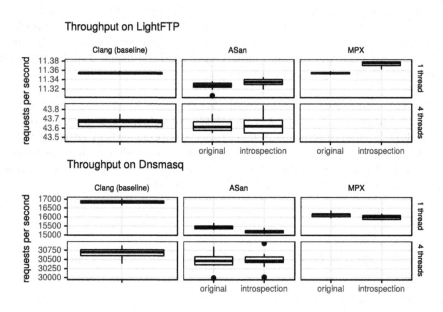

Fig. 1. Throughput on LightFTP and Dnsmasq.

Figure 1 shows boxplots of the results for LightFTP and Dnsmasq. On LightFTP, the performance overhead for using introspection was below 1% for ASan; MPX was even slightly faster when introspection was used. On Dnsmasq, employing introspection caused a slowdown of around 1% when using only one thread for both ASan and MPX. The performance difference to the baseline was negligible on LightFTP, and up to 11% on Dnsmasq (between Clang and ASan with introspection), which suggests that the applications' performance was dominated by factors other than instrumentation cost (e.g., networking overhead). Thus, our measurements cannot be generalized to CPU-bound benchmarks.

To quantify the overhead on CPU-bound benchmarks, we also evaluated the approaches on the SPEC2006 INT benchmarks, which consist of 12 benchmarks. We excluded all C++ benchmarks (471.omnetpp, 473.astar, and 483.xalancbmk), which we expected to make little use of C functions and thus of our interceptors. Further, we excluded all benchmarks in which the tools detected memory safety errors (400.perlbench and 403.gcc). ASan detected memory leaks in two benchmarks (445.gobmk and 464.h264ref), and since we investigated only buffer overflows in this work, we disabled memory leak detection to also run them. SoftBound in its original and introspection versions detected memory safety errors in all but one benchmark (458.sjeng), which were presumably false positives. MPX had an additional known false positive [19] in one benchmark (429.mcf), so we excluded this benchmark for MPX.

Figure 2 shows the execution times of the SPECInt2006 benchmarks relative to Clang -O3 as a baseline. On four of the seven benchmarks (429.mcf, 456.hmmer, 458.sjeng, 462.libquantum), the performance overhead was negligible because no interceptors were executed in code that contributed to the overall run-time performance of the respective benchmark. For SoftBound, the introspection overhead was 3% on the only benchmark that it could execute. Using introspection with ASan resulted in higher overheads, namely 140% on h264ref, 43% on bzip2, and 81% on gobmk. For MPX, the performance overhead of introspection was relatively low, with maximum overheads of 13% on bzip2 and 6% on gobmk.

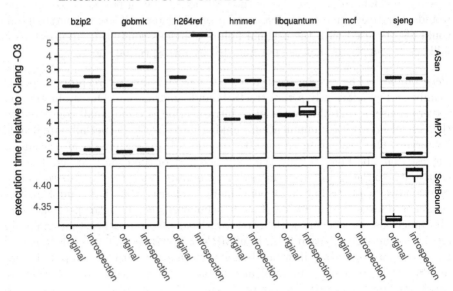

Fig. 2. Execution times on the SpecInt2006 benchmarks.

We also executed micro-benchmarks, measuring the direct overhead of interceptors. For example, we evaluated the performance of the `strlen()` interceptor, which directly relies on `_size_right()` to call the safer `strnlen()` function. For SoftBound, the overhead was not measurable. For Intel MPX, the overhead was 2× for strings with a length of 10; for longer strings (e.g., a length of 1000) the overhead was not measurable. The overhead for ASan was the highest, as our `size_right()` implementation has to traverse the shadow memory, which depends linearly on the length of the string. Its overhead varied between 2× and 10× with different string lengths.

7 Discussion

Availability. We have demonstrated that our introspection-based libc interceptors are an effective means of mitigating the effects of buffer overflows. Our main idea is to use run-time information that is tracked by existing tools to prevent buffer overflows and to increase the availability of applications. Using the introspection-based interceptors is useful only in production, because during development and testing it would be preferable to abort execution so that the programmer can fix bugs that cause errors.

Complementarity. We have designed our approach to complement existing approaches for handling buffer overflows. Our idea is that, for important functions, programmers can implement custom semantics that mitigate the effects of buffer overflows. For buffer overflows in other functions or in user-level code, existing memory tools would continue to detect out-of-bounds accesses and would abort execution in the case of an error. Alternatively, the interceptors could also be used with the original failure-oblivious computing approach as a fallback for functions that are not guarded by introspection checks.

Performance. The overhead of introspection and our interceptors depends mainly on how efficiently a tool tracks bounds information. Our evaluation on servers suggests that the overhead of introspection is often small compared to the cost of network communication, making introspection especially applicable for servers. Our evaluation on the CPU-bound SPEC benchmarks also seems to suggest that libc functions are typically not part of the code that significantly contributes to the overall performance of a program. While the MPX-based introspection overhead was low on all benchmarks, only the ASan-based implementation caused larger overheads on three benchmarks. Overall, introspection-based libc functions are feasible with a low overhead for approaches that maintain explicit bounds information (e.g., Intel MPX or SoftBound), but result in higher overheads for approaches in which bounds information must be computed (e.g., in ASan). Furthermore, our implementation could be made more efficient by using introspection directly in the libc functions.

Implementation. We have demonstrated implementations of the `_size_right()` function for three popular bug-finding and bug-mitigation approaches and believe that implementing this function in many others (e.g., libcrunch [10,11]) is also straightforward. Some tools cannot give precise estimates for all pointers, which makes our approach less effective. For example, binary-instrumentation tools such as Valgrind [18] and Dr. Memory [3] cannot reliably determine the size of buffers located on the stack. Other approaches track run-time information only for specific types of allocations (e.g., stack buffers [2]). Furthermore, some tools give rough estimates in general or round up allocation sizes [1, 2, 6]; for example, after evaluating our approach with low-fat pointer checking [6, 8], we found that rounding up allocation sizes alone mitigated several of the buffer overflows that we investigated.[7] Note that conservative estimates (e.g., the maximum integer value if no information is available) ensure correct execution, but might result in undetected errors.

8   Related Work

Failure-Oblivious Computing. Rinard et al. coined the term *failure-oblivious computing*, where illegal read accesses yield predefined values and out-of-bounds write accesses are ignored [25]. An extension of this work are *boundless memory blocks*, where out-of-bounds writes store the value in a hash map that can be returned for out-of-bounds reads to that address [4, 12, 26]. Furthermore, Long et al. extended failure-oblivious computing by also covering divide-by-zero errors and NULL-pointer dereferences [14]. In contrast to these approaches, introspection enables programmers to handle out-of-bounds accesses by taking into account the semantics of a function. However, the drawback of our approach is that library developers must implement these checks manually.

Failure-Oblivious Computing Models. Durieux et al. studied failure-oblivious computing behaviors [9]. Their findings suggest that for many failures, multiple alternative strategies exist that can mitigate the error. For example, to mitigate a NULL-pointer dereference the access could be ignored, but the pointer could also be initialized with the address of a newly-created or existing object.

Monitored Execution. Sidiroglou et al. devised a system that monitors an application for failures such as buffer overflows [29]. If a fault occurs, the current function is aborted and—based on heuristics—an appropriate value is returned. In order to avoid crashes because a pointer returns NULL, the heuristics take into account whether the parent function dereferences the pointer thereafter. While this approach takes into account the context of the fault, it lacks the ability of our introspection approach to benefit from programmer knowledge.

Libsafe. Libsafe replaces libc functions with enhanced versions that prevent buffer overflows from going beyond the stack frame [2]. It achieves this by traversing frames to determine their bounds and aborting the program if the bounds are exceeded. While we tried implementing the introspection function using the traversal logic, we found that it is based on assumptions such as the location of the stack, which no longer hold with modern mitigation techniques such as address space layout randomization. Additionally, libsafe does not handle out-of-bounds reads well, for which our approach, in contrast, can compute meaningful results, for example, by letting `strlen()` return the length of the buffer underlying the string if it is unterminated.

---

[7] EffectiveSan [7], an extension of the low-fat pointer approach, provides accurate bounds but has not been released to the public as of June 2018.

9   Conclusion

In this paper, we have presented how implementation of an introspection function that returns the length of an object can be used to implement failure-oblivious computing mechanisms. We have also shown that such a mechanism is useful in mitigating real-world errors and that the performance overhead when implemented in approaches such as Intel MPX is negligible. For reproducibility and to facilitate further research, we distribute all artifacts and experimentation scripts at https://github.com/introspection-libc/main.

References

1. Akritidis, P., Costa, M., Castro, M., Hand, S.: Baggy bounds checking: an efficient and backwards-compatible defense against out-of-bounds errors. In: Proceedings of the 18th Conference on USENIX Security Symposium, SSYM 2009, pp. 51–66. USENIX Association, Berkeley, CA, USA (2009)
2. Baratloo, A., Singh, N., Tsai, T.: Libsafe: protecting critical elements of stacks. White Paper (1999). http://www.research.avayalabs.com/project/libsafe
3. Bruening, D., Zhao, Q.: Practical memory checking with Dr. memory. In: Proceedings of the 9th Annual IEEE/ACM International Symposium on Code Generation and Optimization, CGO 2011, pp. 213–223. IEEE Computer Society, Washington, DC, USA (2011)
4. Brunink, M., Susskraut, M., Fetzer, C.: Boundless memory allocations for memory safety and high availability. In: Proceedings of the 2011 IEEE/IFIP 41st International Conference on Dependable Systems & Networks, DSN 2011, pp. 13–24. IEEE Computer Society, Washington, DC, USA (2011). https://doi.org/10.1109/DSN.2011.5958203
5. Cowan, C., Wagle, P., Pu, C., Beattie, S., Walpole, J.: Buffer overflows: attacks and defenses for the vulnerability of the decade. In: Proceedings of the DARPA Information Survivability Conference and Exposition, DISCEX 2000, vol. 2, pp. 119–129. IEEE (2000)
6. Duck, G.J., Yap, R.H.C.: Heap bounds protection with low fat pointers. In: Proceedings of the 25th International Conference on Compiler Construction, CC 2016, pp. 132–142. ACM, New York, NY, USA (2016). https://doi.org/10.1145/2892208.2892212
7. Duck, G.J., Yap, R.H.C.: EffectiveSan: type and memory error detection using dynamically typed C/C++. In: Proceedings of the 39th ACM SIGPLAN Conference on Programming Language Design and Implementation, PLDI 2018, pp. 181–195. ACM, New York (2018). https://doi.org/10.1145/3192366.3192388
8. Duck, G.J., Yap, R.H., Cavallaro, L.: Stack bounds protection with low fat pointers. In: Symposium on Network and Distributed System Security (2017)
9. Durieux, T., Hamadi, Y., Yu, Z., Baudry, B., Monperrus, M.: Exhaustive exploration of the failure-oblivious computing search space. In: Proceedings of the International Conference on Software Testing and Verification (ICST), ICST 2018, April 2018 (2018)
10. Kell, S.: Towards a dynamic object model within unix processes. In: 2015 ACM International Symposium on New Ideas, New Paradigms, and Reflections on Programming and Software (Onward!), Onward! 2015, pp. 224–239. ACM, New York (2015). https://doi.org/10.1145/2814228.2814238

11. Kell, S.: Dynamically diagnosing type errors in unsafe code. In: Proceedings of the 2016 ACM SIGPLAN International Conference on Object-Oriented Programming, Systems, Languages, and Applications, OOPSLA 2016, pp. 800–819. ACM, New York (2016). https://doi.org/10.1145/2983990.2983998

12. Kuvaiskii, D., et al.: SGXBOUNDS: memory safety for shielded execution. In: Proceedings of the Twelfth European Conference on Computer Systems. EuroSys 2017, pp. 205–221. ACM, New York (2017). https://doi.org/10.1145/3064176.3064192

13. Lattner, C., Adve, V.: LLVM: a compilation framework for lifelong program analysis transformation. In: CGO 2004, pp. 75–86 (2004)

14. Long, F., Sidiroglou-Douskos, S., Rinard, M.: Automatic runtime error repair and containment via recovery shepherding. In: Proceedings of the 35th ACMSIGPLAN Conference on Programming Language Design and Implementation, PLDI 2014, pp. 227–238. ACM, New York (2014). https://doi.org/10.1145/2594291.2594337

15. Nagarakatte, S., Zhao, J., Martin, M.M., Zdancewic, S.: Softbound: Highly compatible and complete spatial memory safety for C. In: Proceedings of the 30th ACM SIGPLAN Conference on Programming Language Design and Implementation, PLDI 2009, pp. 245–258. ACM, New York (2009). https://doi.org/10.1145/1542476.1542504

16. Nagarakatte, S., Zhao, J., Martin, M.M., Zdancewic, S.: CETS: compiler enforced temporal safety for C, pp. 31–40 (2010). https://doi.org/10.1145/1806651.1806657

17. Nethercote, N., Seward, J.: How to shadow every byte of memory used by a program. In: Proceedings of the 3rd International Conference on Virtual Execution Environments, VEE 2007, pp. 65–74. ACM, New York (2007). https://doi.org/10.1145/1254810.1254820

18. Nethercote, N., Seward, J.: Valgrind: a framework for heavyweight dynamic binary instrumentation. In: Proceedings of the 28th ACM SIGPLAN Conference on Programming Language Design and Implementation, PLDI 2007, pp. 89–100. ACM, New York (2007). https://doi.org/10.1145/1250734.1250746

19. Oleksenko, O., Kuvaiskii, D., Bhatotia, P., Felber, P., Fetzer, C.: Intel MPX explained: a cross-layer analysis of the intel MPX system stack. Proc. ACM Meas. Anal. Comput. Syst. **2**(2), 28:1–28:30 (2018). https://doi.org/10.1145/3224423

20. Rigger, M., Grimmer, M., Wimmer, C., Würthinger, T., Mössenböck, H.: Bringing low-level languages to the JVM: efficient execution of LLVM IR on truffle. In: Proceedings of the 8th International Workshop on Virtual Machines and Intermediate Languages, VMIL 2016, pp. 6–15. ACM, New York (2016). https://doi.org/10.1145/2998415.2998416

21. Rigger, M., Schatz, R., Grimmer, M., Mössenböck, H.: Lenient execution of c on a java virtual machine: Or: How i learned to stop worrying and run the code. In: Proceedings of the 14th International Conference on Managed Languages and Runtimes, ManLang 2017, pp. 35–47. ACM, New York (2017). https://doi.org/10.1145/3132190.3132204

22. Rigger, M., Schatz, R., Mayrhofer, R., Grimmer, M., Mössenböck, H.: Sulong, and thanks for all the bugs: finding errors in C programs by abstracting from the native execution model. In: Proceedings of the Twenty-Third International Conference on Architectural Support for Programming Languages and Operating Systems, ASPLOS 2018. https://doi.org/10.1145/3173162.3173174

23. Rigger, M., Schatz, R., Mayrhofer, R., Grimmer, M., Mössenböck, H.: Introspection for C and its applications to library robustness. Art Sci. Eng. Program. (2) (2018). https://doi.org/10.22152/programming-journal.org/2018/2/4

24. Rinard, M.: Acceptability-oriented computing. In: Companion of the 18th Annual ACM SIGPLAN Conference on Object-oriented Programming, Systems, Languages, and Applications, OOPSLA 2003, pp. 221–239. ACM, New York (2003). https://doi.org/10.1145/949344.949402
25. Rinard, M., Cadar, C., Dumitran, D., Roy, D.M., Leu, T., Beebee, Jr., W.S.: Enhancing server availability and security through failure-oblivious computing. In: Proceedings of the 6th Conference on Symposium on Opearting Systems Design & Implementation, OSDI 2004, vol. 6, p. 21. USENIX Association, Berkeley (2004)
26. Rinard, M.C.: Failure-oblivious computing and boundless memory blocks, Technical report (2005)
27. Serebryany, K., Bruening, D., Potapenko, A., Vyukov, D.: AddressSanitizer: a fast address sanity checker. In: USENIX Annual Technical Conference, pp. 309–318 (2012)
28. Shacham, H.: The geometry of innocent flesh on the bone: Return-into-libc without function calls (on the x86). In: Proceedings of the 14th ACM Conference on Computer and Communications Security, CCS 2007, pp. 552–561. ACM, New York (2007). https://doi.org/10.1145/1315245.1315313
29. Sidiroglou, S., Locasto, M.E., Boyd, S.W., Keromytis, A.D.: Building a reactive immune system for software services. In: Proceedings of the Annual Conference on USENIX Annual Technical Conference, ATEC 2005, p. 11. USENIX Association, Berkeley (2005)
30. Song, D., et al.: Sok: sanitizing for security. In: IEEE Symposium on Security and Privacy (S&P 2019) (2019, to Appear). Accepted
31. Strackx, R., Younan, Y., Philippaerts, P., Piessens, F., Lachmund, S., Walter, T.: Breaking the memory secrecy assumption. In: Proceedings of the Second European Workshop on System Security, EUROSEC 2009, pp. 1–8. ACM, New York (2009). https://doi.org/10.1145/1519144.1519145
32. Szekeres, L., Payer, M., Wei, T., Song, D.: Sok: eternal war in memory. In: Proceedings of the 2013 IEEE Symposium on Security and Privacy, SP 2013, pp. 48–62. IEEE Computer Society, Washington, DC (2013). https://doi.org/10.1109/SP.2013.13
33. The MITRE Corporation: Common vulnerabilities and exposures. https://cve.mitre.org/
34. van der Veen, V., dutt-Sharma, N., Cavallaro, L., Bos, H.: Memory errors: the past, the present, and the future. In: Balzarotti, D., Stolfo, S.J., Cova, M. (eds.) RAID 2012. LNCS, vol. 7462, pp. 86–106. Springer, Heidelberg (2012). https://doi.org/10.1007/978-3-642-33338-5_5
35. Watson, R.N.M., et al.: Cheri: a hybrid capability-system architecture for scalable software compartmentalization. In: 2015 IEEE Symposium on Security and Privacy, pp. 20–37, May 2015. https://doi.org/10.1109/SP.2015.9
36. Younan, Y., Joosen, W., Piessens, F.: Runtime countermeasures for code injection attacks against C and C++ programs. ACM Comput. Surv. **44**(3), 17:1–17:28 (2012). https://doi.org/10.1145/2187671.2187679

ATPG Binning and SAT-Based Approach to Hardware Trojan Detection for Safety-Critical Systems

Animesh BasakChowdhury[1(✉)], Ansuman Banerjee[2],
and Bhargab B. Bhattacharya[2]

[1] Verification and Validation Group, TCS Research, Pune, India
animeshbchowdhury@gmail.com
[2] ACMU, Indian Statistical Institute, Kolkata, India

Abstract. Combating threats and attacks imposed by Hardware Trojans that are stealthily inserted in hardware systems, has surfaced as a challenging problem in recent times. Such threats degrade the reliability and endanger security of the system. Due to scalability issues, Trojan detection remains an extremely difficult problem, especially, when the circuit size is large and Trojan sizes are small. Hardware Trojan is surreptitiously inserted into the design by selecting a few circuit nodes, where rare logic value occurs. This makes their detection probability negligibly small, thereby rendering the arrival of an input combination activating the same, an extremely rare event. Since the number of such Trojans may be exponentially large in terms of such rare nodes, almost all state-of-art techniques suffer from scalability bottlenecks and coverage issues, while generating test vectors. In this work, we propose a systematic approach to sampling in order to lessen the search space, yet preserving the diversity of population. We use binning of trigger-population based on Automatic Test Pattern Generation (ATPG), and invoke Boolean Satisfiability (SAT) solvers to generate test vectors with high Trojan coverage. Simulation results demonstrate the effectiveness and superiority of our method with respect to prior work in terms of Trojan coverage and the cardinality of the test set.

Keywords: Hardware trojan · Activation nodes · Trigger instance
Trojan instance · Trigger · Payload · ATPG binning

1 Introduction

Malicious tampering of hardware designs in a digital system with Trojans and backdoor poses a severe security threat in recent times, endangering the normal functioning of the system quite unexpectedly [21]. Hardware Trojans (HT) are additional circuit elements that are stealthily inserted into the design by adversaries. During functional operation, the design produces the correct behavior most of the time for most of the input patterns; however, when certain input

© Springer Nature Switzerland AG 2018
M. H. Au et al. (Eds.): NSS 2018, LNCS 11058, pp. 391–410, 2018.
https://doi.org/10.1007/978-3-030-02744-5_29

patterns are fed, one or more outputs produce behaviors that deviate from the expected values.

An adversary, who intends to insert Trojans for corrupting a design can attack it at different stages of the System-on-Chip (SoC) life-cycle. In [23], it has been demonstrated that the use of analog malicious hardware built with a capacitor and a few transistors may replace digital counter-based triggers and jeopardize the system. In [3,4,8,20,21], authors have discussed details of the potential stages of the SoC flow, where Trojans may be inserted. In particular, the phases where third-party Intellectual Property (IP) blocks are used or technology mapping by third-party vendors is needed, are more conducive to Hardware Trojan insertion. In general, the aim of Trojan insertion is:

(a) The erroneous functionality ought not to be easily exposed while performing conventional manufacturing testing.
(b) The triggering of the Trojan must be an unusual but valid event.

Modifications and tampering done during the pre-silicon stage for Trojan insertion are outside the scope of this discussion. Here, we are mainly focused on such tampering, that can be non-destructively effected in the post-silicon stage thereby, modifying the netlist, such that the change in functionality can escape the normal ATPG test patterns [21]. Thus, one possible way of inserting Trojans by an adversary is to identify certain states or input combinations in the given circuit, which are extremely *rare*. Whenever any such state (or input combination) is reached, the Trojan is activated and some unexpected behavior is observed at one or more primary outputs. The detection of Trojans heavily relies on how they are modeled and the techniques used to detect them.

In this paper, we explore the problem of test set generation for hardware Trojan detection, using a novel combination of ATPG and SAT. We believe that a disciplined combination of sampling, ATPG and SAT techniques can serve as an effective aid in targeting rare Trojans and detection of their insertion points. We study the shortcomings of the methods in existing literature, and present a novel approach which can generate quality test sets that increase Trojan coverage to a great extent, within reasonable CPU time. We present experimental results to demonstrate the scalability and coverage advantage our method achieves over others. The rest of the paper is organized as follows. Section 2 describes prior approaches used for the detection of hardware Trojans. Section 3 presents our main idea and the methodology proposed to solve this problem. Section 4 presents details of our experimental set-up and results. Section 5 concludes the discussion with notes on possible future directions.

2   Background and Related Work

In this section, we first present an example to illustrate the problem at hand. Figure 1a shows a simple combinational circuit free from Trojans. For node $G7$ to attain the logical value 0, $G1$ and $G2$ both have to be set at 0. Similarly for $G8 = 1$, both $G3$ and $G4$ should be having value 1, and for $G11 = 1$, all $G3$, $G4$, $G5$ and $G6$ should be set at 1.

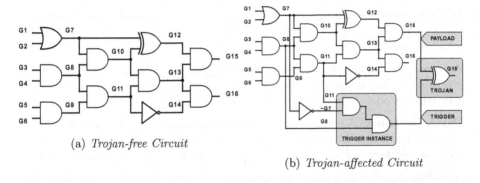

(a) *Trojan-free Circuit*

(b) *Trojan-affected Circuit*

Fig. 1. Figure showing Trojan-free and Trojan-affected circuit

Therefore, it can be concluded that the probability of occurrence of the logic value 0 at $G7$ is 0.25, i.e. out of every 4 test vectors, there exists only 1 test vector, which can activate the state $G7 = 0$. For $G8 = 1$ and $G11 = 1$, the respective probabilities of occurrence are 0.25 and 0.0625. Hence, the combination $G7 = 0, G8 = 1$ and $G11 = 1$, is expected to occur very rarely. In other words, the state having simultaneous occurrence of these three logic values is relatively uncommon. Only 1 out of 2^6 possible test vectors can drive the circuit to this state (G1 = G2 = 0 and G3 = G4 = G5 = G6 = 1). Such an occurrence can be appropriately termed as a rare event. Even though the combination is rare, it must be a valid activation, and the error must be observable at some outputs. Otherwise, the Trojan will never be triggered, thereby defeating the whole purpose of the adversarial attacker. Hence, there should exist a test input that can expose it. In most of the cases, the trigger's presence can be suitably modeled by a stuck-at fault (s-a-f). The combination of rare nodes provides a favorable location for an adversary where a Trojan instance is likely to be created. In Fig. 1b, we have created a conjunction of three nodes $G7 = 0$, $G8 = 1$ and $G11 = 1$, where the occurrence of logic 1, is a rare event. Under a particular input combination, the output of the resultant conjunction will become high and corrupt the logic value at the output node $G15$. We first define a few terminologies used frequently throughout this work.

Rareness Threshold: Using structural analysis of a given netlist, the probability of occurrence of logic values 0 and 1 at a circuit node can be determined statically. A *rareness threshold* value is set to determine the rarity of occurrence of a logic value at a particular circuit node. We denote this rareness threshold by θ.

Activation Node: A node where the probability of occurrence of a logic value is less than the *rareness threshold* can play a dominant role in creation of a trigger instance, which in turn can serve as an *activation node* for a Trojan in the netlist.

Trigger Instance: An instance formed by the conjunction of several *activation nodes* is termed a *trigger instance*. The output of the conjunction (AND gate) is the *trigger*.

Payload: A node in the netlist, whose logic value is corrupted by the trigger is a *payload*. Any internal node or a primary output is a fertile ground for such logic corruption.

Trojan Instance: A suitable trigger-payload combination is termed as a *Trojan instance*. Typically, the output of the trigger is XOR-ed with the payload to flip the expected logic value at that point, and such a modification creates a Trojan.

Q-Value: Number of activation nodes used to create a trigger instance, denoted by Q. This value determines the size of the trigger.

Controllability: Controllability of a trigger instance is a measure of hardness of trigger activation.

Observability: Observability can be defined as how hard/easy is the propagation of corrupted logic value occuring at a payload, at any Primary Output (PO).

A low-controllable low-observable trigger-payload combination, constitutes an ideal Trojan. The main challenge arises when an adversary chooses the activation nodes by setting a very small value to θ; as a sequel, a combination (AND-ing) of such nodes would become extremely rare to happen. Trojan detection has been an active area of research in recent times in the hardware security research community [2,5,6,10,15,17,22]. Significant work has been done in the field of hardware Trojans, focusing mainly on the insertion strategy and techniques for detecting them. These include, among others, observing side-channel parameters such as power surge, delay analysis, and path propagation for detecting the presence of Trojans [1,9,16]. However, most of these techniques fail to detect the Trojans, especially when there are non-uniform variations of side-channel parameters of the golden design in the design-under-test (DUT). Test-based approaches have also been extensively studied and the derivation of the MERO test pattern is an important research contribution in this direction [5]. Other techniques such as ODETTE [2], DFTT [10] and TeSR [15], are also capable of producing efficient test patterns for detecting Trojans. The authors in [17] proposed an improved version of MERO aiming to maximize Trojan coverage. Several other techniques have focused on the prevention of hardware Trojan attacks on a given design [6,22]. In a very recent work [7], authors have proposed a hybrid technique of using model checking and ATPG for Trojan detection. However, the threat model is not very generic. They have considered the output of non scan flip flops (FF) in a partial scan sequential design, as the point of attack. In our paper, we have used the same threat model as used in MERO and the improved MERO models, and hence is completely different from the one proposed in [7]. Therefore, test generation, in particular, for the threat model used in [7] is beyond the scope of our work. Nevertheless, our test generation methodology on full scan sequential circuits is an over-approximated modeling of partial scan designs and can uncover the Trojan set, based on the threat model proposed for partial scan design.

In this paper, we focus mainly on the development of a scalable test generation framework for uncovering covertly inserted Trojans. Since the number of possible Trojan instances can be exponential, determining a test set with substantial Trojan coverage suffers from severe scalability issues when circuit size is large. The authors in MERO [5] and Improved MERO [17], have described statistical and heuristic techniques for generating test pattern to detect hardware Trojans. In MERO, an N-detect test set is generated for the activation nodes. Effectively, from a set of random test patterns, test vectors are applied in an iterative manner so that each activation node is excited to the rare logic value at least N times. Increasing N effectively increase the probability of trigger activation. As the primary focus is on small sized Trojan instances, the maximum number of activation nodes that can participate in a trigger instance has been considered upto four [4,17]. In the improved MERO version, the authors have used genetic algorithm (GA) combined with payload-aware test generation and a SAT-based technique for detecting extremely hard-to-detect Trojan instances. Although the results outperform the MERO-based approach, the framework samples the trigger instances randomly only once from entire population. There are certain open issues that need to be addressed:

(a) MERO [5], and Improved MERO [17] are evaluated on the ISCAS85 and ISCAS89 circuits only. In MERO, random 100k test patterns are selected initially to derive optimized test patterns. In improved MERO, initially 100k trigger samples for ISCAS85 circuits, and 10k instances for ISCAS89 circuits are chosen randomly to generate test vectors. But, when circuit size increases, one time random sampling may result in poor sampled set of trigger population. There is a high chance that the sampled population does not contain all activation nodes, as part of trigger instances.

(b) MERO [5] is a lightweight heuristic framework, which takes care of controllability of trigger instances. It does not consider the observability of malfunctioned logic at the output. In improved MERO [17], payload aware test vector has been generated. However the process initially optimizes trigger coverage, and then based on the test vectors generated, pseudo test vectors (PTV) are created to cover feasible payloads. Thus, payload aware test vector generation gives priority to maximizing trigger coverage over feasible payload coverage.

Motivated by the above limitations, our main aim is to derive an efficient and high coverage test-set for detecting Trojans. The detection process has to be fast and efficient, and take less CPU-time. We consider hardware Trojan instances that are non-destructively inserted in a logic circuit during the post-silicon phase utilizing the rarity of activation nodes. To address the coverage problem, we introduce a well organized, judicious and cost effective sampling of trigger population. The modified sampling technique ensures that the sampled population contains all activation nodes in right proportion. The initial population plays a major role, in determining the quality of test vectors generated. More the variety amongst trigger instances in population, greater is the heterogeneity of test vectors. Again, for scaling up the process, we use a divide-and-conquer strategy called ATPG-binning, which helps in partitioning the population into disjoint sets and solve a larger problem, by solving multiple sub-problems. We then generate test patterns using classical ATPG tools for normal trigger instances and SAT-based techniques for hard-to-detect trigger instances. SAT-based methods are computationally costly, taking one trigger at a time. Owing to recent advances in SAT-solving techniques, infeasibility test of trigger activation can be done in reasonable time. However, there can still exist very few cases, where SAT-solver is unable to generate result within a specified time limit. In such cases, we call the trigger as unsolvable. Hence, it is a reasonable choice to employ the SAT tool on trigger instances declared aborted by structural ATPG tools. This three step methodology is able to detect a large number of Trojan instances within a reasonable CPU-time on large sized circuits. Our method provides a general framework for Trojan analysis that can be used to warrant certain level of trust and reliability of safety critical applications. The main contributions of this paper are as follows:

(1) A simple sampling technique to choose an initial trigger population over which the test vectors are ought to be generated. This sampling technique guarantees the presence of each activation node in right propotion and more heterogeneity.
(2) A scalable methodology of test vector generation in the form of ATPG binning, which takes as input a sampled trigger population. Sampling ensures that the population is qualitatively and quantitatively good, to generate high quality test vectors. To scale up the framework on a large trigger population, a divide and conquer strategy called ATPG binning is employed.
(3) The framework tries to improve the trigger and Trojan coverage simultaneously. Iteratively, for a given set of test vectors, trigger and payload coverage are computed, and a subset of them is chosen, ensuring high coverage of both parameters. This is done in both steps, during ATPG binning and SAT.

3 Methodology

We now present a detailed methodology of test vector generation for Hardware Trojan detection. Our discussion has been broadly divided into three main sections:

1. Static analysis and initial sampling of trigger population.
2. Test generation using ATPG binning.
3. SAT-based test generation for hard-to-detect triggers.

3.1 Static Analysis and Initial Sampling

Initially, we analyze the circuit statically, using structural analysis. For proper identification of suitable trigger candidates, we determine the probability of occurrence of logic values, 0 (P_{zero}), and 1 (P_{one}), for each node. Figure 2 shows

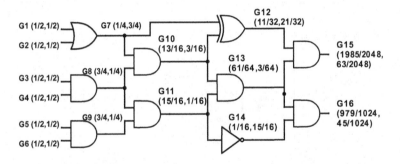

Fig. 2. The probabilities of a line being at logic 0 and 1 are shown as ($Prob_0$, $Prob_1$)

the probability values of logic 0 and 1 for all nodes in a typical netlist. We adopted the framework given in [19] to determine rarity of logic values at nodes. The rareness value has to be properly defined at the user end. Based on the rarity value, rareness threshold θ, is set, which roughly furnishes a measure of Trojan stealthiness. Suppose, Attacker 1 chooses $\theta_1 = 0.1$ and Attacker 2 chooses $\theta_2 = 0.4$, w.r.t the netlist shown in Fig. 2. For Attacker 1, creating a trigger with a combination of four such nodes would have activation probability value in the range $[(0.1)^4, 0.1]$. Whereas, for Attacker 2, the activation probability is quite high, i.e. $[(0.4)^4, 0.4]$. Higher the activation probability values, higher are the chances of Trojan getting exposed during regular test application. The detailed mathematical proof regarding the probability values associated with the activation of trigger and Trojan instances, have been shown in [5].

Once the design is statically analyzed, all nodes having either P_{zero} or P_{one} value less than θ, are identified. These nodes are called as *activation nodes*, and constitute candidates of trigger instances. We now define the parameters associated with trigger population and activation nodes.

$(\mathbf{i}, \mathbf{L_i})$: The tuple is a representation of an activation node and its associated rare logic value. i denotes the node name, and L_i denotes the rare logic value.

Activation Node Set R: Set of all activation nodes in a given netlist N. $R = \{(i, L_i), \forall i \in N \text{ and } P(L_i) < \theta\}$.

In literature, it is already established that a Trojan created from a trigger instance having a large Q-Value, is easily detectable with side channel analysis. But, when the trigger-size is small ($Q < 5$), the false positive rate is alarmingly high. Therefore, testing based approaches are tightly coupled with side channel analysis techniques to uncover more trojans. We proceed with our methodology, keeping our focus on small sized Trojans. Accordingly as in literature, we restrict our choice of Q-Value up to 4.

Even though the Q-Value is low, the search space of trigger instances is exponential in terms of the number of *activation nodes* of a circuit. For Trojan instances, it is again multiplied by another exponential factor of number of possible payloads. Hence, it is practically infeasible to generate test vectors covering the entire population. This demands the necessity of a quality sampled trigger

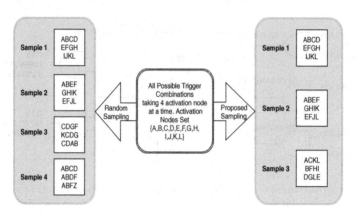

Fig. 3. Sampled sets of trigger using random sampling and proposed sampling.

population, which can ensure decent coverage over entire search space. Rather than going for random sampling, we propose a novel strategy of sampling trigger instances to generate a quality initial sampled set. We now describe, how and why our modified sampling technique is capable of generating good quality test vectors.

In Fig. 3, we have presented an example of the modified sampling approach. Initially, we have a set of 12 distinct activation nodes. Taking Q-Value = 4, there can be $\binom{12}{4}$ possible trigger instances. Now, we have the option to take all $\binom{12}{4}$ trigger instances as initial population for test vector generation. But, as circuit size increase, the number of activation nodes increases dramatically. Hence, intelligent sampling is required out of $\binom{12}{4}$, for scalability purpose. MERO [5] and Improved MERO [17] use random sampling of fixed 100k instances. For the sake of explanation, consider we are interested to sample three trigger instances out of $\binom{12}{4}$ possible combinations. Now, if we go for random sampling, each time we may end up having different samples. As shown in Fig. 3, there are 4 different samples of trigger population that we can possibly get from random sampling. After a careful observation, one can conclude that both Sample 1 and Sample 2 are quite good. They contain all 12 activation nodes distributed over 3 trigger instances, whereas, Sample 3 and Sample 4 do not cover all of them. Therefore, test vectors that are derived by ATPG targeting Sample 1 and Sample 2, would certainly yield superior coverage over those needed for testing Sample 3 and Sample 4. Upon close examination, it can be seen that test vectors generated for Sample 3 will be biased towards activation nodes A and B. Similarly, for Sample 4, it would be biased towards nodes C and D. Hence, with a very high probability, test vectors would miss any trigger created with an activation node, missing from the sampled set. In order to get quality test vectors, it is necessary that the initial sample population of trigger instances contain enough information, diversity and lesser correlation amongst trigger instances. We now introduce our modified sampling approach based on the Q-Value and the activation set R. We first define some parameters used in our sampling approach.

numCountInSample$_X$: Count of the Activation node X present in trigger instances of Sampled Trigger Population.

popCount: Minimum threshold count to be maintained for each activation node present in trigger instances of the sampled trigger population.

Initially, for all activation nodes, the numCountInSample value is initialized to 0. In the first iteration of sampling, a set *chooseSet* is initialized to R. Now, *Qvalue* number of activation nodes are chosen from the *chooseSet* without replacement. The trigger crafted out of that, is checked whether it is already present in the Sampled Trigger Population (T). If it is present, the trigger is discarded. The process of creating new trigger continues, until the new trigger is absent from T. Then, the trigger is included in T, only if there exists an activation node a for which $numCountInSample_a < popCount$. Once the trigger is included, the $numCountInSample$ value for all activation node in the trigger, is incremented by 1. Trigger creation using activation nodes from *chooseSet* continues, until the cardinality of *chooseSet* becomes less than $QValue$. After that, the *chooseSet* is again reinitialized to R, and the process is repeated. Note that, in one iteration, triggers created will not have any activation node in common. The sampling process completes when $numCountInSample$ for each activation node, is at least popCount. In Fig. 3, we have applied our sampling technique and generated the sampled trigger population, keeping popCount = 1. Such a sample automatically guarantees better test vector generation as compared to random samples. Algorithm 1 presents the relevant steps related to static analysis and the sampling mechanism.

3.2 ATPG Binning

In our methodology, our sampling criteria ensures that quality test-sets are generated. For generating test vectors for a trigger instance, we model trigger activation as a single stuck-at fault (s-a-f). We apply stuck-at 1 (s-a-1) fault at the output of the trigger, and go on to generate test vectors for the same. As the number of elements in the sampled trigger population is high, it is practically infeasible for a structural ATPG tool to generate them in one go. To make our method scalable, we divide the population into smaller disjoint bins randomly. The set, containing all the bins, is called K. The number of trigger instances in a bin depends on the maximum number of primary outputs (POs) that an ATPG tool can handle. This step ensures that we generate efficient test vectors without hitting the scalability bottleneck.

A typical modified netlist consists of all trigger instances of the bin, additional inserted as POs, in the original netlist. Now, for each modified netlist (corresponding to each bin) in set K, a structural ATPG tool is deployed. We use Deterministic Test Pattern Generation (DTPG) in our test vector generation approach using structural ATPG. As a result, testcubes are generated, consisting of $X(Don't~Care)$ terms. The output reports presence of three kinds of trigger instances: (a) *Feasible Trigger Instances*, for which test cubes have been generated, (b) *Redundant Trigger Instances*, i.e. no test vector exists to activate the trigger instance (can be safely ignored as infeasible triggers), and (c)

Algorithm 1. Creation of initial sampled trigger population

Input:

  N : Gate level netlist

  θ : Rareness threshold

  q : Q-Value

  popCount : Minimum threshold count of activation node to be present in trigger instances of Sampled Population.

Output: T : Sampled trigger population.

  1: Read gate level netlist of design.
  2: **for** $\forall$ node $i \in N$ **do**
  3:     Calculate $P_{\text{zero}}(i)$ and $P_{\text{one}}(i)$
  4:     **if** $P_{\text{zero}}(i) < \theta$ **then**
  5:         $R \leftarrow R \cup (i, 0)$
  6:     **else**
  7:         **if** $P_{\text{one}}(i) < \theta$ **then**
  8:             $R \leftarrow R \cup (i, 1)$
  9:         **end if**
 10:     **end if**
 11: **end for**
 12: Set R is reported as set of tuples (i, L_i), where i is the node and L_i is its associated Rare logic value.
 13: Initialize $T \leftarrow \phi$.
 14: **for** *each* activation node $i \in R$ **do**
 15:     Initialize $numCountInSample_i \leftarrow 0$
 16: **end for**
 17: **while** $\exists$ activation node $i \in R$, s.t. $numCountInSample_i < popCount$ **do**
 18:     Initialize $chooseSet \leftarrow R$.
 19:     **while** $|chooseSet| >= q$ **do**
 20:         Generate a trigger instance $TRIG$, choosing q tuples from chooseSet, without replacement.
 21:         **if** $TRIG \notin T$ **then**
 22:             **if** $\exists$ activation node $i \in TRIG$, s. t.$numCountInSample_i < popCount$ **then**
 23:                 $T \leftarrow T \cup TRIG$
 24:                 Increment $numCountInSample$ by 1, $\forall$ activation node $i \in TRIG$.
 25:             **end if**
 26:         **end if**
 27:     **end while**
 28: **end while**
 29: Report set T.

Aborted Trigger Instances, which can be categorized as extremely hard and rare trigger instances. Structural ATPG tool failed to report whether such instances are feasible or not. After testcubes generation, we apply a lightweight compaction methodology as described in [14] for testcube compaction. We cluster the testcubes based on similarity of skeleton structure, and then construct the parent testcube set T_x, having four logic values 0, 1, X (Don't care) and

C (Contradict). This compaction is done in order to preserve important test cubes. The test vector generated from these test cubes would be taken into the final Trojan detection test-set, based on the coverage efficiency. Let us define two types of coverages, which we have used to determine the quality of a test vector, in the rest of the paper.

Trigger Coverage of a test vector is defined as the number of trigger instances, which can be activated by the application of the test vector.

Stuck-at fault Coverage of a test vector is defined as the number of nodes in the circuit, whose stuck-at fault can be detected by the test vector.

We now present **Theorem** 1, which basically relates trigger coverage and overall *s-a-f* coverage of a test vector with Trojan coverage.

Theorem 1. *Let G be an internal node, which has been XORed by a trigger instance T. If there is a test vector t_i that activates trigger T, and detects a s-a-f at G, then t_i will be able to detect the Trojan consisting of T as trigger and G as payload.*

An illustration of this result is shown in Fig. 4.

As a consequence of Theorem 1, we can expand the parent testcube set T_x, and calculate the trigger Coverage and stuck-at fault coverage of the generated test vector. Test vectors providing coverage of unique triggers and stuck-at faults are taken into the master test-set TA. Now, for each parent testcube in the compressed testcube set T_x, test vectors are generated by randomly filling up with 0s and 1s at X bit. For every C (Contradict) bit of the test cube, a pair of test vectors should be generated, one having 0, other having 1, as shown in Fig. 5. Now, for each test vector, we check for trigger coverage in the bin, and s-a-f coverage in the entire circuit. The test vector is included in the master testset TA, if any new trigger is covered from the bin or the overall *s-a-f* coverage of the circuit is increased. After all feasible trigger instances from the bin are covered, the next p consecutive steps are checked to see if there is any increase in *s-a-f* coverage. If there is no increase in *s-a-f* coverage, we stop adding test vectors to the master test set TA. The current bin is called *explored*, and removed from set K.

Once a bin is explored, for all the test vectors in TA, we check for trigger coverage of bins already present in K. The triggers, which are covered by TA, are appropriately removed from their respective bins. Now, the bins are arranged in decreasing order, according to the number of triggers present. The bin, having highest number of triggers, is taken into consideration. The process continues until all the bins are covered. After all the steps are performed, we get the master testset TA, and the set of aborted trigger instances of all the bins. Figure 6 shows the overall workflow of our algorithm.

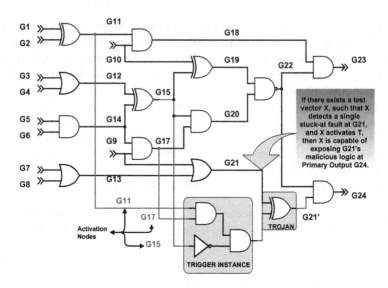

Fig. 4. A test vector covering the single s-a-f at internal node G21 and trigger T can uncover the Trojan created by the combination of G21 and T.

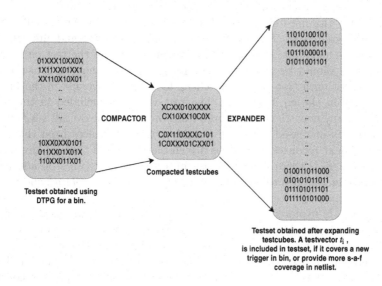

Fig. 5. Compaction and expansion of test cubes for each bin under consideration

3.3 SAT Methodology

SAT-based test generation methodology has been used in recent times, especially to report test vectors for hard-to-detect faults. A test generation problem can be suitably converted into a Boolean Satisfiability problem. Owing to efficiency of

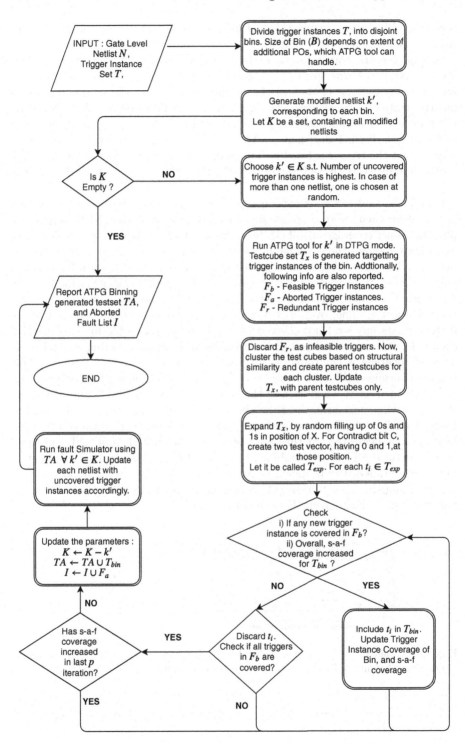

Fig. 6. Flowchart of ATPG binning algorithm

powerful SAT-solvers, we use this methodology to report test vectors for *aborted trigger instances* reported from the structural ATPG tool.

Using Tseytin transformation, the gate level netlist is converted to Conjunctive Normal Form. For each aborted trigger instance, CNF clauses are created conjuncting the clauses of the original circuit and the clause representing the trigger. The clauses are then fed to a SAT-solver to check for existence of any satisfiable assignment. Modern SAT-solvers are able to precisely arrive at two distinct decisions - SAT and UNSAT, in a reasonable time. SAT implies that the trigger is feasible. The input test vector can be fetched from the instance returned from SAT solver. UNSAT denotes no test vector exists for the trigger.

For increasing the s-a-f coverage, we try to generate M distinct satisfying instances for each aborted trigger instance, provided it is feasible. We first compute the *s-a-f* coverage of all M test vectors. Out of M, we choose a subset S_M. Figure 7 shows the coverage of M test vectors, for a typical aborted trigger instance. The subset S_M is chosen such that it provides same overall *s-a-f* coverage, as that of M vectors. We employ a simple greedy algorithm for creating S_M. Initially, we put each test vector into S_M, which covers a unique *s-a-f* of a node. Once it is done, overall coverage by S_M is computed, and checked to see if there exists any s-a-f not covered by S_M, but still coverable by M. Then, for each s-a-f still uncovered, we pick a random test vector covering it, and overall s-a-f coverage is computed again, including that test vector into S_M. This process continues, till s-a-f coverage of S_M is equal to the s-a-f coverage of M. S_M is assigned as M when each of the M test vectors provide distinct coverage. We repeat this step for each of the aborted instances. The triggers reported as UNSAT from the SAT solver can be regarded as infeasible trigger instances, and hence can be neglected. At the end, test vectors generated from SAT and those from structural ATPG are combined to report the final testset for Trojan detection. The detailed flow is shown in Algorithm 2. This 2-step methodology used for obtaining the testset ensures high confidence level of coverage of all feasible triggers and Trojans, given the value of q and θ.

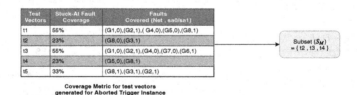

Coverage Metric for test vectors
generated for Aborted Trigger Instance

Fig. 7. Coverage for test vectors generated by SAT-solver for a typical trigger instance. S_M denotes the subset of test vectors which provide maximum coverage.

Algorithm 2. Test generation with SAT-solver

Input:
   N : Gate level netlist
   TA : Testset TA generated by ATPG binning
   I : Aborted trigger instance set
   M : Number of distinct test vectors required for each aborted trigger to find efficient test subset.
Output: $TEST_{\text{final}}$: Combined testset - Testset generated from SAT ($TEST_{\text{SAT}}$) + Testset generated from ATPG Binning (TA).
1: Read netlist N, do Tseytin transformation and generate CNF of netlist, C.
2: Initialize $TEST_{\text{SAT}} \leftarrow \phi$.
3: **for** each trigger instance $t \in I$ **do**
4:     Generate CNF for trigger instance t, C'.
5:     $C' \leftarrow C \bigwedge C'$
6:     Initialize $numTestVecGenerated \leftarrow 0$.
7:     $testSetForTrig \leftarrow \phi$
8:     **while** $numTestVecGenerated \neq M$ **do**
9:        Check for satisfiable instance for C'.
10:        **if** Instance is SAT **then**
11:           Retrieve test vector, t_{SAT}.
12:           $testSetForTrig \leftarrow testSetForTrig \cup t_{\text{SAT}}$.
13:           $C' \leftarrow C' \bigwedge \sim t_{\text{SAT}}$.
14:           Increment $numTestVecGenerated$ by 1.
15:        **else**
16:           Instance is UNSAT.
17:           **break**
18:        **end if**
19:     **end while**
20:     **if** $numTestVecGenerated == 0$ **then**
21:        Trigger instance is infeasible.
22:     **else**
23:        Generate 's-a-f' coverage metric for each test vector $\in testSetForTrig$.
24:        Choose a subset S_M from testSetForTrig, which maximise the overall 's-a-f' coverage.
25:        $TEST_{\text{SAT}} \leftarrow TEST_{\text{SAT}} \cup S_M$.
26:     **end if**
27: **end for**
28: $TEST_{\text{final}} \leftarrow TEST_{\text{SAT}} \cup TA$
29: Report testset $TEST_{\text{final}}$.

---

4   Experimental Results

We carried out simulation on combinational benchmarks from ISCAS-85, and sequential benchmarks from ISCAS-89 and ITC-99. All sequential circuits are taken in full scan mode. The framework is developed in C++ and Python and the experiment has been carried out on a Linux Workstation with Intel Xeon E5 3 GHz Processor and 32 GB RAM. We used the Transition Probability Calculation (TPC) [18] tool from trust-hub.org. The tool takes a circuit netlist as input, statically analyses the structure and reports the probability of occurrence of 0 (P_{zero}) and 1 (P_{one}) for circuit nodes. We next selected the value of the rareness threshold. For the sake of comparison with previous state-of-art techniques MERO [5], Improved MERO [17], we took $\theta = 0.1$ (for ISCAS-85 circuits) and 0.01 for full scan ISCAS-89 and ITC-99 circuits respectively. The Q-Value was taken as four, and $popCount = 5000$ for our experimental results. The values of Q-Value, θ, and $popCount$ taken in this set-up, ensure the test generation is targeted for those Trojans, which are rare and remain hidden during normal ATPG test. An appropriate $popCount$ value is taken to ensure sufficient presence of all activation nodes in the sampled population. However, increasing $popCount$ value is going to increase initial population. Depending on the need, the parameter can be suitably tuned to get enough diversity. The set of activation nodes is fed to program $genTrojanComb$, that generates sampled trigger population. The sampled population is then divided into several disjoint bins by dumping them into individual files. The Bin Size B, is determined by the limit of the ATPG tool. In order to harbour more POs, we modified the source code of the ATALANTA ATPG tool [11] to process maximum number of POs in a single run. The original netlist along with a bin are provided as input to the program $TrojanInjection$, that outputs the modified netlist. The process is repeated for all the bins and the output generated at the end contains a set of modified netlists K. Thereafter, the ATPG Binning Algorithm is deployed on the set K for end-to-end run using structural ATPG ATALANTA, compactor [14], expander and HOPE fault simulator [12]. At the end, we get testset TA, aborted trigger instances I and redundant trigger instances. All redundant triggers can be safely ignored as infeasible/false trigger instances. Aborted trigger instances can be considered as hard-to-trigger instances, owing to failure of test vector generation in a stipulated time. We used the SAT-solver to generate test vectors, for the triggers present in the aborted fault list I. For each trigger in I, the instance, along with the original netlist is fed to a $createSATInstance$ tool. The SAT-formulation for the trigger instance is then fed to the SAT-solver, $zChaff$ [13]. A Python wrapper has been used over $zChaff$, to produce M distinct input vectors for a trigger instance. In order to produce distinct test vectors in each iteration, the test vector t_{SAT} generated in the current iteration is negated and then conjuncted with existing CNF. This ensures the same test vector is not generated twice. To maintain the trade-off between computation time, number of test vectors, and s-a-f coverage over the netlist, we take value of M = 5. Once the test vectors are generated for a trigger, the coverage is computed and S_M is determined. The iteration continues till all the aborted triggers are covered. The test vectors generated by the SAT-solver are then combined with testset TA, to report the final test vector set.

The results in Tables 1 and 2 show the effectiveness of the proposed method over existing test based approaches for Trojan detection. Table 1 presents the efficacy of the approach on standard ISCAS85 and ISCAS89 benchmarks and large industrial benchmarks like ITC99. To the best of our knowledge, most of the techniques have considered only 0.1 million sampled trigger instances, with no information about quality of initial population. Our technique provides 100%

Table 1. Table showing test vectors generated by the proposed scheme. θ is 0.1 for ISCAS85 combinational circuits and 0.01 for ISCAS89 and ITC99 benchmark circuits. popCount = 5000 for initial sampled trigger population.

Benchmark circuits	No. of activation nodes	Trigger instances in sampled population	Feasible trigger instances	Testset length			CPU Time (in seconds)
				Testset generated by ATPG binning	Testset generated by SAT	Total testset generated	
c432	40	57387	56181	534	0	534	0.5
c499	48	71893	4764	1421	15	1436	23.1
c880	62	91964	86192	2097	71	2168	94.2
c1355	112	167231	1432	1876	0	1876	110.3
c1908	65	89267	82141	3387	2967	6534	3005.7
c2670	67	97129	92110	4329	1108	5437	1478.5
c3540	196	261152	193475	4126	2307	6433	9761.2
c5315	176	237084	221885	9029	5467	14496	22721.3
c7552	232	310872	289116	12674	32101	44775	57643.9
s15850	748	1002785	561038	7824	1583	9407	17298.1
s38417	1254	1622398	1209345	38762	10976	49738	68012.5
b14	711	1012654	632093	18943	6584	25527	45019.4
b15	684	1021997	731092	21721	7894	29615	52310.8
b17	879	1255612	910901	25892	9197	35089	57119.6
b20	970	1474958	877213	19373	10176	29549	84081.4
b21	1472	2040812	1484708	27174	9178	36352	77210.6
b22	1736	2480198	1806734	32023	37434	69457	96211.7

Table 2. Table showing trigger and Trojan coverage with proposed scheme. Trojan sample size - 100K for all ISCAS85, ISCAS89 and ITC99 benchmarks.

Benchmark circuits	Trigger coverage (%)	Trojan coverage (%)	Benchmark circuits	Trigger coverage (%)	Trojan coverage (%)
c432	100	93.12	c7552	79.5	69.51
c499	100	94.1	s15850	77.67	59.09
c880	100	91.87	s38417	71.42	52.8
c1355	99.31	83.67	b14	81.41	63.53
c1908	100	92.3	b17	70.28	60.58
c2670	100	89.1	b20	61.21	52.21
c3540	94.67	78.2	b21	55.78	43.71
c5315	92.81	76.7	b22	53.47	44.1

trigger coverage for most of the ISCAS85 circuits. Table 2 shows the coverage of trigger and Trojan instances, over various benchmarks. The trigger and Trojan instances over which coverage results have been shown here, are not part of

Table 3. Table showing comparison of trigger and Trojan coverage for MERO, Improved MERO, and the proposed scheme. For MERO, N = 1000. $\theta = 0.1$ (combinational), 0.01 (sequential). Trojan sample size - 100K (combinational), 10K (sequential)

Benchmark circuits	MERO		Improved MERO		Proposed scheme	
	Trigger coverage	Trojan coverage	Trigger coverage	Trojan coverage	Trigger coverage	Trojan coverage
c880	75.92	69.96	96.19	85.70	100	91.87
c2670	62.66	49.51	87.15	75.82	100	89.1
c3540	55.02	23.95	81.55	60.00	94.67	78.2
c5315	43.50	39.01	85.91	71.13	92.81	76.7
c7552	45.07	31.90	77.94	69.88	79.5	69.51
s15850	36.00	18.91	68.18	57.30	79.21	65.18
s38417	21.07	14.41	56.95	38.10	74.61	58.9

the initial Sampled Trigger Population. Our approach shows better coverage when compared to all previous state-of-art techniques, in terms of trigger and Trojan coverage, even when the circuit size increases considerably. Table 3 shows comparative results of our method with MERO [5] and Improved MERO [17]. Both the techniques suffer from poor coverage when circuit size increases.

We now present a comparative analysis for the circuit c7552, for the proposed method versus state-of-art techniques [5,17]. In Fig. 8a, it is clearly visible that for every value of θ selected, the proposed scheme provides considerable coverage than both the previous techniques. Even when θ is lowered, our scheme is able to uncover triggers almost as twice as the improved MERO version. This is because our approach considers a good initial sample trigger population. It also makes sure of the fact that test vectors are not biased towards certain activation nodes, and trigger population is heterogeneous. In Fig. 8b, Trojan coverage has been compared with already existing techniques and the proposed scheme, over a range of rareness threshold θ values. It is noticeable that even for Trojan coverage, the proposed scheme outperforms the existing techniques.

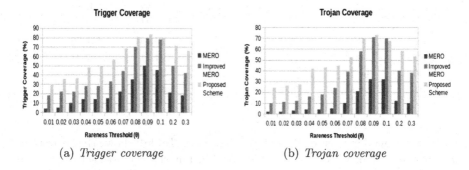

(a) *Trigger coverage*   (b) *Trojan coverage*

Fig. 8. Trigger and Trojan coverage chart for c7552

5   Conclusion

In this work, we have presented a scalable approach for producing an efficient test set that is capable of detecting stealthily-inserted hardware Trojans in a digital circuit. Our method uses a judicious sampling process followed by ATPG-binning that helps to reduce the complexity of the search process significantly, followed by SAT-solving for hard trigger instances. The proposed method can take care of both trigger coverage and feasible payload coverage simultaneously, in order to improve Trojan coverage significantly. Our technique provides a scalable framework for hardware Trojan detection over a generic threat model.

References

1. Agrawal, D., et al.: Trojan detection using IC fingerprinting. In: IEEE S&P (2007)
2. Banga, M., et al.: ODETTE: a non-scan design-for-test methodology for trojan detection in ICs. In: HOST (2011)
3. Beaumont, M., et al.: Hardware trojans-prevention, detection, countermeasures (a literature review). Technical report, DTIC Document (2011)
4. Chakraborty, R.S., et al.: Hardware trojan: threats and emerging solutions. In: HLDVT (2009)
5. Chakraborty, R.S., et al.: MERO: a statistical approach for hardware trojan detection. In: CHES (2009)
6. Chakraborty, R.S., et al.: Security against hardware trojan through a novel application of design obfuscation. In: ICCAD (2009)
7. Cruz, J., et al.: Hardware trojan detection using ATPG and model checking. In: VLSI Design (2018)
8. Jacob, N., et al.: Hardware trojans: current challenges and approaches. IET Comput. Dig. Tech. 8, 264–273 (2014)
9. Jin, Y., et al.: Hardware trojan detection using path delay fingerprint. In: HOST (2008)
10. Jin, Y., et al.: DFTT: Design for trojan test. In: ICECS (2010)
11. Lee, H., et al.: ATALANTA: an Efficient ATPG for Combinational Circuits. Virginia Polytechnic Institute and State University, Blacksburg (1993)
12. Lee, H.K., et al.: HOPE: an efficient parallel fault simulator for synchronous sequential circuits. In: IEEE TCAD (1996)
13. Mahajan, Y.S., et al.: Zchaff: an efficient SAT solver. In: Theory and Applications of Satisfiability Testing (2004)
14. Mrugalski, G., et al.: Compression based on deterministic vector clustering of incompatible test cubes. In: ITC (2009)
15. Narasimhan, S., et al.: TeSR: a robust temporal self-referencing approach for hardware trojan detection. In: HOST (2011)
16. Rad, R., et al.: A sensitivity analysis of power signal methods for detecting hardware trojans under real process and environmental conditions. In: IEEE TVLSI (2010)
17. Saha, S., et al.: Improved test pattern generation for hardware trojan detection using genetic algorithm and boolean satisfiability. In: CHES (2015)
18. Salmani, H.: TPC: Transition probability calculation (2011). https://www.trust-hub.org/

19. Salmani, H., et al.: A novel technique for improving hardware trojan detection and reducing trojan activation time. In: IEEE TVLSI (2012)
20. Tehranipoor, M., et al.: Trustworthy hardware: trojan detection and design-for-trust challenges. Computer **44**, 66–74 (2010)
21. Xiao, K., et al.: Hardware trojans: lessons learned after one decade of research. In: ACM TODAES (2016)
22. Xiao, K., et al.: A novel built-in self-authentication technique to prevent inserting hardware trojans. In: IEEE TCAD (2014)
23. Yang, K., et al.: A2: analog malicious hardware. In: IEEE S&P (2016)

Android Malware Detection Methods Based on the Combination of Clustering and Classification

Zhi Xiong[(⊠)], Ting Guo, Qinkun Zhang, Yu Cheng, and Kai Xu

Department of Computer Science and Technology, Shantou University,
243 Daxue Road, Shantou, Guangdong, China
zxiong@stu.edu.cn

Abstract. With the popularity of Android platform, Android malware detection is a challenging practical problem that needs to be resolved urgently. In this paper, we propose two static analysis methods for Android malware detection based on the combination of clustering and classification. First, we obtain original feature set from the manifest file and disassembled code of Android applications. Then, through the analysis of the category and appearance frequency of each feature, we extract some key features for malware detection so as to reduce the dimensionality of feature vector. Finally, we propose two methods based on the combination of clustering and classification to distinguish malicious and benign applications. One is mixed clustering, which clusters the malicious and benign samples together; the other is separate clustering, which clusters the malicious and benign samples separately. We choose to use the K-mean clustering algorithm and the K-Nearest Neighbor (KNN) classification algorithm. Evaluation results show that our methods outperform the common SVM-based method in detection accuracy, and outperform the KNN-based method in prediction time. In addition, the detection ability for unknown malware families of our methods is also better than that of the SVM-based method.

Keywords: Android · Malware detection · Clustering · Classification
Dimensionality reduction · Static analysis

1 Introduction

With the rapid development of mobile Internet technology, smartphones have become an indispensable part of our convenient life. Android is the mobile operating system with the highest smartphone market share. According to 2017 smartphone operating system data released by Kantar Worldpanel ComTech [1], Android smartphone sales accounted for 87.2% of all sales of mobile phones. However, Android platforms are also continuously suffering from various malware threats. According to the "China Mobile Security Risk Report 2017" [2] released by Qihoo 360 Technology Company, the 360 Internet Security Center has monitored a total of 58.127 million mobile end users infected with malicious programs in 2017, and the average number of malicious application infections per day reached 646,000. Therefore, Android malware detection is a challenging practical problem that needs to be resolved urgently.

© Springer Nature Switzerland AG 2018
M. H. Au et al. (Eds.): NSS 2018, LNCS 11058, pp. 411–422, 2018.
https://doi.org/10.1007/978-3-030-02744-5_30

The existing Android malware detection technologies can be mainly divided into two categories: static analysis and dynamic analysis. Dynamic analysis is based on the behavior of applications at run-time, and needs to monitor the running of applications. For example, [3] monitors the network traffic, [4] monitors the system call behaviors, [5] tracks the system calls of applications under different events. Although dynamic analysis can achieve high accuracy in identifying malicious activity, the run-time monitoring is very costly and cannot be deployed on mobile devices [6]. On the contrary, static analysis has lower overhead and higher code coverage, and it can be directly applied on mobile devices. Static analysis is to obtain static features information, such as permissions, components, API calls, etc., through decompiling apk installation package, and then base on these features to detect malware. For example, the detection methods proposed in [6–9] belong to this category.

Machine learning has been widely used in Android malware detection. The method of static analysis mainly contains two steps: the first step is to extract features from apk installation package, and the second step is to build classifier by using machine learning algorithm to distinguish malicious and benign applications. In the aspect of feature extraction, [6] extract 545,333 different features from the manifest file and disassembled code, and each feature is expressed as a string, but the dimensionality of its feature vector is tremendous, which may leads to huge computation overhead and low detection accuracy. It's worth mentioning that [6] opens their dataset and all extracted feature set to foster the research in the area of Android malware detection. Reference [10] simplifies and abstracts the decompiled Dalvik instructions into simpler symbolic sequences, and then uses N-Gram to extract features from these sequences. In [11], the feature set includes sensitive path features and permissions features, and the sensitive paths are extracted from the function call graph of the application. Reference [12] extracts permissions as feature set and calculates a score for each permission. Reference [13] utilizes entropy based category coverage difference and weighted mutual information to select prominent features. Reference [7] simplifies function call graph into Sensitive API call Related Graph (SARG), and then uses the frequent sub graphs of SARG as features. In the aspect of classifier, Support Vector Machine (SVM) [6, 7, 10, 12, 13], Decision Tree [7, 11, 12], Random Forest [7, 10, 12, 13], and K-Nearest Neighbor (KNN) [7, 10, 12] are common classifiers. Thereinto, SVM is the most common one.

In this paper, we use static analysis technology, and propose two methods for Android malware detection based on the combination of clustering and classification. First, we disassemble the apk installation file of an Android application and obtain original feature set from the manifest file and disassembled code. Then, through the analysis of the category and appearance frequency of each feature, we just extract some key features for malware detection so as to reduce the dimensionality of feature vector. Finally, we propose two methods based on the combination of clustering and classification to distinguish malicious and benign applications. Evaluation results show the feasibility and effectiveness of the two methods.

The rest of this paper is organized as follows. Feature analysis and dimensionality-reduction are discussed in Sect. 2. In Sect. 3, we propose our detection methods. Evaluation and analysis are given in Sect. 4. Finally, we conclude in Sect. 5.

2 Feature Analysis and Dimensionality-Reduction

2.1 Feature Acquisition

There are two main methods for feature acquisition of Android application: static reverse engineering and dynamic monitoring. Compared to dynamic monitoring, static analysis has small overhead. Therefore, the static reverse engineering method is used in this paper.

The apk, also called Android package file, is the installation package for Android applications. Through disassembling the apk file of an application, we can get two important files: AndroidManifest.xml and class.dex. The androidManifest.xml file is an essential file for each Android application, and it contains the package name, permission, version number, component information, and so on. The class.dex file is the executable file of the application. From it, we can get the API calls and strings contained in the application.

2.2 Dataset Sources

The dataset utilized in this paper comes from Drebin [14], which contains 5,560 malware and 123,453 benign applications. It also supplies the extracted feature set of each application. Through analysis, we get a total of 545,333 different features, and each feature is expressed as a string. Each feature string is divided into two parts by "::", and the first part denotes the category of the feature. Figure 1 gives the schematic diagram of the feature vector of an application. If a feature exists in the application, the corresponding position of the feature is marked as 1. Otherwise, it is marked as 0.

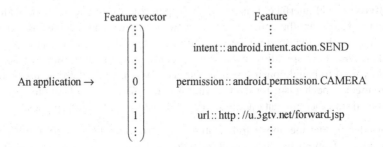

Fig. 1. The schematic diagram of feature vector

The dimensionality of the feature vector is tremendous, which may lead to huge computation overhead and low detection accuracy, so we must eliminate inessential features to decrease the dimensionality of the feature vector.

2.3   Dimensionality-Reduction of Feature

The original feature set contains some inessential features for malware detection, and we adopt two measures to reduce the dimensionality of feature vector. Below we introduce the two measures separately.

Dimensionality-Reduction Based on Feature Category. By a further analysis of the feature set, there are ten feature categories, and the name and feature number of each category is given in Fig. 2.

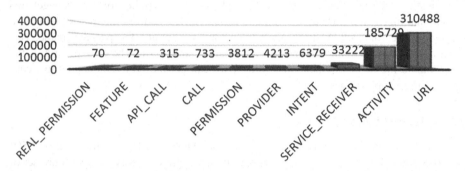

Fig. 2. The name and feature number of each category

Below is the explanation of part of the feature categories:

- **URL:** network address. Some applications need to retrieve some resources through network. The URLs has no particular rules, and the number is gigantic.
- **Activity:** visual interface. It is primarily responsible for the interactions with users.
- **Service_Receiver:** the communication between service and receiver. **Receiver** is a mechanism that focuses on receiving information sent by system and applications, and making corresponding processing according to the information. **Service** is mainly used to handle business logic that has nothing to do with the user interface.
- **Provider:** a mechanism for data sharing between Android applications. It provides a unified interface for data addition, deletion, and modification queries.

Considering that the above four feature categories contain a large number of features and these features has little effect on malware detection, we remove them from the feature vector.

Dimensionality-Reduction Based on Feature Appearance Frequency. In the dataset, the total number of applications is 5,560 + 123,453 = 129,013. If a feature occurs too often (i.e., almost all applications have the feature) or too rarely (i.e., the feature only appears in a very few applications), then it has little effect on detection results, so we can delete it. Through statistical analysis, we get the following results:

- The "feature::android.hardware.touchscreen" feature appears in 128,702 applications with a frequency of up to 99.7%.

- There are 367,895 features that appear in only one application, 81,567 features in only two applications, and 35,819 features in only three applications.

Therefore, we remove the "feature::android.hardware.touchscreen" feature and the features that occur three times or less. After the above two dimensionality-reduction measures, the dimensionality of feature vector is reduced to 2,182.

3   Detection Methods

3.1   K-means

K-means clustering is an unsupervised learning algorithm. The samples are clustered into k clusters according to the similarity degree. The similarity within a cluster is high, but the similarity between clusters is low. In K-means, the center of a cluster is called centroid. First, k samples are randomly selected as the initial centroid of the k clusters. The next step is to assign each sample to the closest cluster, and recalculate the centroid of each cluster. The second step is repeated until convergence criteria is met, for example, the positions of all centroids no longer change.

3.2   K-Nearest Neighbor

K-Nearest Neighbor (KNN) is a supervised machine learning algorithm used for classification and regression. In KNN classification, the output is a class membership. A sample is classified by a majority vote of its neighbors, with the sample being assigned to the class most common among its k nearest neighbors. The Euclidean distance is used to calculate the distance between samples.

3.3   Detection Methods Based on the Combination of Clustering and Classification

We propose two detection methods based on the combination of clustering and classification. One is mixed clustering, which clusters the malicious and benign samples together; the other is separate clustering, which clusters the malicious and benign samples separately.

Mixed-Clustering and Classification. The schematic diagram is as Fig. 3 shows. The workflow is as follows:

1. Cluster the training samples into a certain number of clusters.
2. Train a classifier for each cluster.
3. Combine the classifiers and the centroids of all clusters to build a composite model.
4. For each test sample, select a classifier according to the distance to each cluster centroid. The classifier of the nearest cluster will be selected.
5. Use the selected classifier to predict.

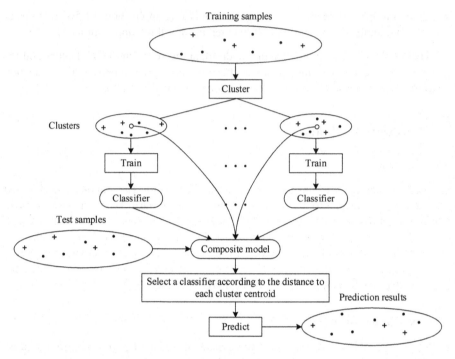

Fig. 3. The method based on the combination of mixed-clustering and classification

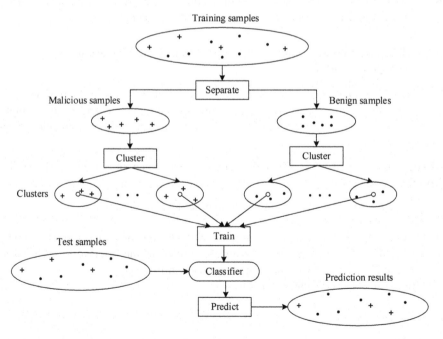

Fig. 4. The method based on the combination of separate-clustering and classification

Separate-Clustering and Classification. The schematic diagram is as Fig. 4 shows. The workflow is as follows:

1. Separate the training samples into malicious samples and benign samples according to the label of each sample.
2. Cluster the malicious samples and benign samples into a certain number of clusters, separately.
3. Train a classifier with the centroids of all clusters.
4. For each test sample, use the classifier to predict.

In our methods, we choose to use the K-mean clustering algorithm and the KNN classifier.

4   Evaluation

4.1   Evaluation Environment

We use the Python language and the machine learning package scikit-learn (namely sklearn) [15] to evaluate our malware detection methods. The evaluation environment is as Table 1 shows.

Table 1. Environment configuration

Category	Item	Configuration
Hardware	CPU	Intel(R) Core(TM) i7-4790 @3.6 GHz
	Memory	8 GB
Software	OS	Windows 7 64bit
	Python	3.6.1
	Sklearn	0.19.1
	Numpy	1.14.0
	Pandas	0.22.0

4.2   Evaluation Results

SVM is the most common binary classifier. It has good classification and prediction ability for unknown new samples, and has been widely used in Android malware detection [6, 7, 10, 12, 13]. So we compare our methods with the SVM-based method.

Precision (p) and recall rate (r) are two common metrics, and they can be merged into one metric called F-measure (F). It is worth noting that precision and recall rate affect each other. Under ideal circumstances, we hope to achieve both high precision and high recall rate. However, in general, the higher the precision, the lower the recall rate, and vice versa.

Comparison with the SVM-Based and KNN-Based Methods. We randomly select 42,999 samples to be a training set, and select 43,013 samples to be a test set. In order to evaluate the effectiveness of our two methods, we test the precision, recall rate,

F-meature as well as prediction time, and compare them with two common classifiers: SVM and KNN.

As stated before, we choose to use the K-mean clustering algorithm and the KNN classifier. There are two parameters in our methods. One is the k value in K-means, and the other is the k value in KNN. Table 2 gives the test results, where $k_m^{cluster}$ denotes the k value in K-means for malicious samples clustering and $k_b^{cluster}$ denotes the k value in K-means for benign samples clustering.

Table 2. Comparison of detection accuracy and prediction time

Method	Parameter	Accuracy			Prediction time
		p	r	F	(s)
SVM	/	0.996	0.679	0.797	315
KNN	$k = 1$	0.936	0.940	0.938	2427
	$k = 3$	0.945	0.930	0.937	3075
Mixed-clustering and classification	$k^{cluster} = 30$ $k^{knn} = 3$	0.940	0.924	0.932	549
Separate-clustering and classification	$k_m^{cluster} = 70$ $k_b^{cluster} = 70$ $k^{knn} = 3$	0.822	0.898	0.858	18

We can draw the following conclusions from Table 2:

- The SVM-based method can achieve very high precision, but the recall rate is not satisfactory.
- The KNN-based method has both high precision and high recall rate, but the prediction time is very long. The reason is that KNN needs to calculate the distance to each training sample for each test sample. So, for a large training set, pure KNN is not practical.
- The method based on mixed-clustering and classification has both high precision and high recall rate. Moreover, its prediction time is far shorter than the KNN-based method. It can be used for the offline detection of Android malware.
- The method based on separate-clustering and classification can achieve satisfactory precision and recall rate. Also, its F-measure is higher than the SVM-based method. More importantly, its prediction time is very short. So, it can be directly applied to mobile devices to detect malware online.

Detection Accuracy Comparison of Our Two Methods. Our tests show that the k value in KNN has little effect on the detection accuracy and prediction time. Therefore, we just choose different k value in K-means to test and compare the accuracy of our two methods. The k value in KNN is set to 3. Figures 5 and 6 give the test results.

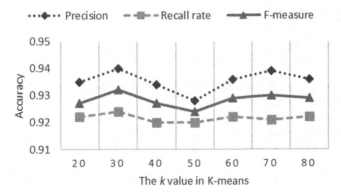

Fig. 5. The accuracy of the mixed-clustering and classification method

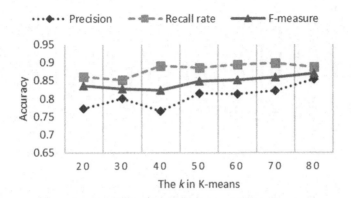

Fig. 6. The accuracy of the separate-clustering and classification method

From the above two figures we can see that:

- The detection accuracy of our two methods are not very sensitive to the k value in K-means. That is to say, the selection of the k value in K-means has little effect on the detection accuracy.
- Compared to the separate-clustering and classification method, the mixed-clustering and classification method has advantage on detection accuracy.

Detection Ability of Unknown Malware Families. Note that when testing the detection performance of a method, we should balance malware families in the training set. If the numbers of samples of certain malware families are much less than of other families, it will be hard to detect the malware of these families. In order to evaluate the detection ability of unknown malware families, in the below tests, we evaluate the detection ability for each of the 20 largest malware families [6] separately, and compare our methods with the SVM-based method.

In every test, the training set just contain 5 samples of a certain malware family, but the test set has a large number of samples of this family. The sizes of the training set and test set are both about 43,000. Figures 7 and 8 give the test results.

From the above two figures we can see that:

- In the aspect of recall rate, our two methods are both higher than that of the SVM-based method apparently.
- In the aspect of precision, there is no obvious difference between our methods and the SVM-based method.

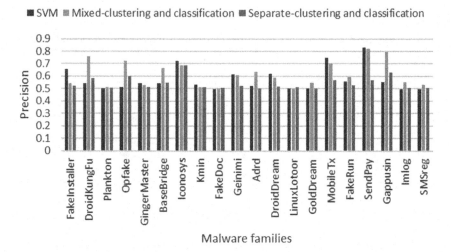

Fig. 7. The precision of detecting unknown malware families

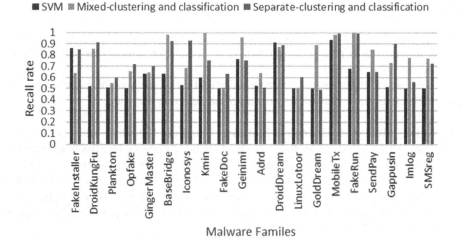

Fig. 8. The recall rate of detecting unknown malware families

Therefore, the detection ability of unknown malware families of our methods is better than that of the SVM-based method.

5 Conclusion

With the vigorous development of mobile Internet, Android platform has been widely used in various smartphones and tablet computers. Android malware poses a serious threat to our life, so Android malware detection is a challenging practical problem that needs to be resolved urgently. In this paper, we propose two static analysis methods for Android malware detection based on the combination of clustering and classification. The dataset utilized in this paper comes from Drebin. The main work of this paper includes two aspects. First, based on the analysis of the category and appearance frequency of each feature, we extract a part of key features for malware detection. As a result, the dimensionality of feature vector is reduced significantly, which contributes to shorten detection time and improve detection accuracy. Second, we propose two methods to distinguish malicious and benign applications. One is mixed-clustering combined with classification, which clusters the malicious and benign samples together; the other is separate-clustering combined with classification, which clusters the malicious and benign samples separately. Test results show the feasibility and effectiveness of the two methods. Especially, the method of mixed-clustering and classification is suitable for the offline detection of Android malware, while the method of separate-clustering and classification can be directly applied to mobile devices to detect malware online. Our future work is to assign different weights to different features according to their importance.

Acknowledgements. This work is supported by the Special Funds for Discipline and Specialty Construction of Guangdong Higher Education Institutions (2016KTSCX040).

References

1. Kantar Worldpanel. https://www.kantarworldpanel.com/cn/smartphone-os-market-share/. Accessed 30 Apr 2018
2. China Mobile Security Risk Report 2017. http://bbs.360.cn/thread-14972358-1-1.html. Accessed 30 Apr 2018
3. Chen, Z., et al.: Machine learning based mobile malware detection using highly imbalanced network traffic. Inf. Sci. **433–434**, 346–364 (2018)
4. Singh, L., Hofmann, M.: Dynamic behavior analysis of Android applications for malware detection. In: International Conference on Intelligent Communication and Computational Techniques, pp. 1-7. IEEE, Jaipur (2017)
5. Xiao, X., Xiao, X., Jiang, Y., Liu, X., Ye, R.: Identifying Android malware with system call co-occurrence matrices. Trans. Emerg. Telecommun. Technol. **27**(5), 675–684 (2016)
6. Arp, D., Spreitzenbarth, M., Huebner, M., Gascon, H., Rieck, K.: Drebin: Efficient and explainable detection of Android malware in your pocket. In: 21st Annual Network and Distributed System Security Symposium, pp. 1–15. Internet Society, San Diego (2014)

7. Fan, M., et al.: Android malware familial classification and representative sample selection via frequent subgraph analysis. IEEE Trans. Inf. Forensics Secur. **13**(8), 1890–1905 (2018)
8. Deypir, M., Horri, A.: Instance based security risk value estimation for Android applications. J. Inf. Secur. Appl. **40**, 20–30 (2018)
9. Morales-Ortega, S., Escamilla-Ambrosio, P.J., Rodriguez-Mota, A., Coronado-De-Alba, L. D.: Native malware detection in smartphones with Android OS using static analysis, feature selection and ensemble classifiers. In: 11th International Conference on Malicious and Unwanted Software, pp. 67–74. IEEE, Fajardo (2017)
10. Chen, T., Yang, Y., Chen, B.: Maldetect: An Android malware detection system based on abstraction of dalvik instructions. J. Comput. Res. Dev. **53**(10), 2299–2306 (2016)
11. Miao, X.C., Wang, R., Xu, L., Zhang, W.F., Xu, B.W.: Security analysis for Android applications using sensitive path identification. J. Softw. **28**(9), 2248–2263 (2017)
12. Kumar, A., Kuppusamy, K.S., Aghila, G.: FAMOUS: Forensic analysis of mobile devices using scoring of application permissions. Future Gener. Comput. Syst. **83**, 158–172 (2018)
13. Varsha, M.V., Vinod, P., Dhanya, K.A.: Identification of malicious Android app using manifest and opcode features. J. Comput. Virol. Hacking Tech. **13**(2), 125–138 (2017)
14. The Drebin Dataset. http://www.sec.cs.tu-bs.de/~danarp/drebin/index.html. Accessed 30 Apr 2018
15. Scikit-learn. http://scikit-learn.org/stable/. Accessed 30 Apr 2018

An OpenvSwitch Extension
for SDN Traceback

Danni Ren[1,3], Wenti Jiang[1], Huakang Li[1,2], and Guozi Sun[1,2(✉)]

[1] School of Computer Science, Nanjing University of Posts
and Telecommunications, Nanjing, China
danni_ren@qq.com,1121379147@qq.com,{huakanglee,sun}@njupt.edu.cn
[2] Institude of Computer Technology, Nanjing University of Posts
and Telecommunications, Nanjing, China
[3] Zhongxing Telecommunication Equipment Corporation, Nanjing, China

Abstract. While software-defined networking (SDN) opens a new
chapter for network administrators to manage and to maintain network,
the vital characteristic of logically centralized control draws attackers to
exploit different network technologies to hijack the controller. How to
develop a security mechanism to determine the root of an anomaly and
to identify the responsible entities is an urgent but challenging task now.
Therefore, in this paper we conduct a research on SDN traceback with an
OpenvSwitch extension, which is based on the technology of packet marking and logging. The traceback mainly consists of three functional mechanisms: mapping-table creation, packet marking and traceback, which is
used to reconstruct the forwarding path of the packet with given features without changing network behaviors. We describe the dependent
theoretical model and design concept of traceback, and demonstrate the
validity, feasibility and practicability of traceback with an experiment.
Similarly, the traceback we propose can play an important role in the
fields of debugger and network behavior analysis.

Keywords: Software-defined networking · OpenvSwitch · Traceback
Packet marking · Logging

1 Introduction

Software-defined networking (SDN), as a novel network architecture, is gradually coming into people's horizons [1]. It enables the decoupling of both data
and control planes, and abstracts the underlying network infrastructures from
the applications, which make network architecture more flexible and intelligent.
One of the main contributions of SDN is the southbound interface, a uniform
and vendor-agnostic interface that is responsible for the communications between
data and control planes. SDN controller can change the behaviors of network and
manage network by modifying and customizing the flow tables of switches. The
most common realization of this interface currently is the OpenFlow [2] protocol.

© Springer Nature Switzerland AG 2018
M. H. Au et al. (Eds.): NSS 2018, LNCS 11058, pp. 423–435, 2018.
https://doi.org/10.1007/978-3-030-02744-5_31

Another is the northbound interface, which provides an open interface of network resources for top business. Thus, researchers and developers can develop security services according to specific requirements, such as access control, traffic engineering and storage optimization [3].

Inevitably, with the development of SDN technology, along with the convenience SDN brings to us some huge safety hazards, including loops caused by flow table conflict, links changing caused by emergency situations, cyber-attacks (e.g., DDoS (Distributed Denial of Service) attack), and so on [4]. In view of above security threats, one solution is to locate the source of network failures and attacks, and even to trace back the path of packet forwarding [5,6], which can provide a theory basis for identifying the responsible entities and conduct forensics.

In this paper, we conduct a research of SDN traceback with an OpenvSwitch [7] extension, which is based on the technology of packet marking and logging. The framework of SDN traceback includes three functional mechanisms: mapping-table creation, packet marking and traceback. Mapping-table creation is used to generate the switch-mapping table in the process of constructing the network topology. Packet marking plans to mark packets that match with given features in the specific fields and store some packet information in the form of a file when the specific fields are full. Traceback can reconstruct the forwarding path of the packet with given features. Once the traceback is deployed successfully in SDN, it can help administrators adjust and configure policies to mitigate network attack and to improve network state when anomalies occur.

To summarize, the contributions of this paper are shown as follows:

- We introduce a theoretical model hypothesis (Sect. 2) which involves: (i) three main functional components (traffic detection, traceback and decision), (ii) the general trend of data flows.
- We present the main mechanisms of the traceback component (Sect. 2), including mapping-table creation, packet marking and traceback. Besides, we briefly describe the design concept of each mechanism and the relationship between them. In addition, we present detailed work procedure of packet marking mechanism and traceback mechanism with algorithms.
- We provide a simulation result to support our platform with an OpenvSwitch [7] extension (Sect. 3). Moreover, we explain the experimental results.
- We present a variety of outstanding related work on SDN traceback among different fields (Sect. 4), such as attack forensics and fusion system. Finally, we make a conclusion in Sect. 5.

2 Prevising

2.1 Theoretical Model Hypothesis

The study in the paper bases on a theoretical model hypothesis that is shown in Fig. 1. The theoretical model is mainly composed of three functional components: traffic detection, traceback and decision. Generally speaking, the traffic detection component is used to detect and to identify abnormal traffic and extract their various features if the traffic are suspicious. The traceback component can rebuild the forwarding path of packet with features as required. The decision component is responsible for adjusting and deploying policies after analyzing the results of traceback. Therefore, network administrators can manage and optimize the network more easily and efficiently with new and effective flow tables. In addition, the arrows indicate the general trend of different data flows according to the above illustration of three components. Remarkably, the traceback component is the focus of the paper. It must be executed after the traffic detection component in ordinary condition. That is to say, the various features extracted by traffic detection component are the input of the traceback component.

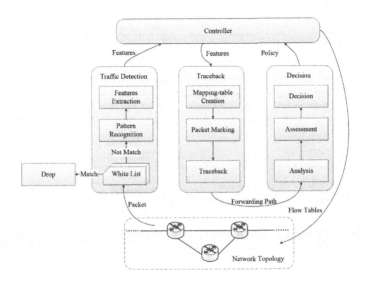

Fig. 1. Theoretical model

2.2   Design Concept of Traceback

This section describes how we envision the component of traceback to be designed. Obviously, the traceback component consists of three mechanisms: mapping-table creation, packet marking and traceback.

Mapping-Table Creation. Mapping-table creation is used to generate switch-mapping table, a one-to-one relationship between switches and identity information.

For example, assuming a network topology with three switches: S_1, S_2, and S_3. We can consider replacing switch names with various numbers to construct the switch-mapping table. Like number 0 represents the switch whose name is S_1 and so on. Meanwhile, the specific construction time needs to be recorded once a switch-mapping table is constructed. The operation of generating switch-mapping table must be completed in the process of constructing network topology.

Packet Marking. Packet marking is used to write the label of the current switch into the packet header, taking a labeling scheme of fixed-fields, and to store some packet information in the form of a file when the marking fields are full. Particularly, the mapping-table creation is the theoretical foundation of the packet marking. The information to be marked is gained by querying the switch-mapping table. We depict the relationship diagram between two mechanisms of mapping-table creation and packet marking in Fig. 2.

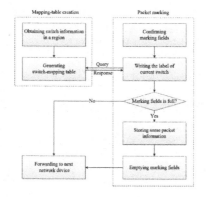

Fig. 2. The relationship diagram between two mechanisms of mapping-table creation and packet marking

On the basis of generating switch-mapping table, for packet marking mechanism, the first step is confirming marking fields. Next, the identity information of current switch that is obtained by querying the switch-mapping table should be written to packet header under the condition of marking fields are not full. If the space of marking fields is tight, it's necessary to store some valuable packet fields in the form of a file, to record storage order of the same packet and to save the current time. Subsequently, the marking fields also need to be emptied to provide space for the next writing. Finally, forwarding the packet to the next network device and executing repeatedly the steps above until the packet to destination.

Traceback. The traceback is designed to rebuild forwarding path for those packets that have been marked and stored combing with switch-mapping table. We give a simple topology to demonstrate basic process of rebuilding forwarding path, shown in Fig. 3. Assuming there is a need to rebuild forwarding path of a packet whose source host is H_2 and destination host is H_4, the key is extracting some features of the packet and amalgamating them into the $feature\_variable$. Then, the results can be obtained by using $feature\_variable$ as a query parameter from packets marking and storing files created by packet marking mechanism. Next, the identity information of switch can be converted into specific switch using switch-mapping table. Finally, the traceback result can be deduced by sorting the switches according to the retention time. Thus, the red arrows (Fig. 3) will be expected forwarding path (i.e., $H_2 \rightarrow S_2 \rightarrow S_3 \rightarrow S_4 \rightarrow H_4$) regarding the assumption, including three switches: S_2, S_3, S_4.

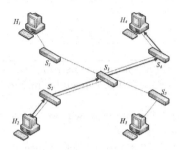

Fig. 3. A simple topology to demonstrate basic process of rebuilding forwarding path

2.3   Algorithm

Assuming that we have extracted the features that are used to justify the packet to be marked. The main process of the packet marking and traceback we implement is clarified as following using algorithms. A series of associated functions along with the required parameters in the algorithm are defined as following.

– $create\_map\_table()$: creating switch-mapping table with storing creation time when network topology is created.
– $match\_feature\_set(f, p)$: returning true if the features of the packet p match the features f in $feature\_set$, false otherwise.
– $init(t)$: initializing some special fields t that have only a small impact on the behaviors of forwarding packets.
– $mark(s)$: writing switch identity information s that is gained by querying switch-mapping table to special fields.
– $store(info)$: storing some information of packets $info$ in the form of files, including basic information of the packet, time, and storage order and so on.
– $IS\_sufficient(t)$: returning true if the remaining space of special fields t is sufficient, false otherwise.
– $IS\_arrive(ds)$: judging whether or not to arrive at the switch ds that is linked directly with destination host.
– $query\_feature(fv, pf)$: returning corresponding results when querying the $packet\_file$ pf created by the module of packet marking with taking feature variables fv as the query parameters.

- *integrate_result(pdata, time)*: classifying data stored in *packet_file* according to different time *time*.
- *query_map_table(time, mt)*: returning corresponding switch-mapping table when querying the *map_table mt* created by the module of packet marking with taking time *time* as the query parameters.
- *gain_switch(sf, cmt)*: returning corresponding switch name when querying a certain map table *cmt* with taking special fields *sf* determined before marking as the query parameters.
- *output(route)*: outputting and displaying the route information route with visualization technologies.

Algorithm 1. Packet marking: marking in special fields and storing some information of packets in the form of files, especially including time and sequences

---

Input:

    t : special fields to mark information of switches;

    s : the switch identity information;

    info : some information of the packet, including basic features of the packet, storing time, storage order of the same packet and so on;

    ds : the switch that is linked directly with destination host.

Output:

    map_table : the switch-mapping table;

    packet_file : the file to storing some information of packets.

1: *map_table ← create_map_table()*
2: **if** *match_feature_set(f, p)* **then**
3:    **while** *IS_arrive(ds) == false* **do**
4:      **if** *the packet p is reaching the first switch* **then**
5:        *init(t)*
6:        *mark(s)*
7:      **else if** *IS_sufficient(t) == true* **then**
8:        *mark(s)*
9:      **else**
10:       *packet_file ← store(info)*
11:       *init(t)*
12:     **end if**
13:    **end while**
14:    *packet_file ← store(info)*
15:    *init(t)*
16: **end if**
17: **return** *map_table, packet_file*

As for Algorithm 1, the packet marking mechanism bases on three premises: (i) a completed switch-mapping table, (ii) the features to be marked, (iii) the fields to be marked. When there is a new packet arriving at some switch, it needs to be marked if matching the given features, forwarded directly to next switch otherwise. Regarding marking, there are three aspects needing to be concerned:

Algorithm 2. Traceback: rebuilding the packet forwarding path

---

Input:

    $traceroute(x)$: keep the x packet path to the $traceroute(x)$;

    i,j : variables;

    fv : some feature variables being used for traceback.

 1: give some variables: i,j

 2: $packet\_result \leftarrow query\_feature(fv, packet\_file)$

 3: $result\_by\_time \leftarrow integrate\_result(packet\_result, time)$

 4: $i = 0$

 5: **for** each $pk \in result\_by\_time$ **do**

 6:    $pseq \leftarrow$ extract the field of storage order in each pk

 7:    **if** $pseq == 1$ **then**

 8:        $pkt \leftarrow$ extract the field of time in each pk

 9:        $cur\_map \leftarrow query\_map\_table(pkt, map\_table)$

10:        $i++$

11:    **end if**

12:    initialize $traceroute(i)$

13:    $special\_fields \leftarrow$ extract all data of marking fields in each pk

14:    **for** each $sf \in special\_fields$ **do**

15:        $traceroute(i) \leftarrow traceroute(i) \cup gain\_switch(sf, cur\_map)$

16:    **end for**

17:    $traceroute(i) \leftarrow traceroute(i) \cup pkt \cup cur\_map$

18: **end for**

19: **for** $j = 1$ to i **do**

20:    $output(traceroute(j))$

21: **end for**

(i) initializing the marking fields with zero before starting marking, (ii) if the space of marking fields is not sufficient, storing some valuable packet information to a file, including storage order of the same packet and the current time. Subsequently, setting the marking fields to zero again, (iii) if the packet arrives at the switch that is nearest to the destination, storing packet information to the same file same as (ii), which also means the end of the packet marking mechanism. In addition, two files of map_table and $packet\_file$ are the input of Algorithm 2.

As for Algorithm 2, the execution of the traceback mechanism primarily contains several steps as following: (i) obtaining relevant information $packet\_result$ from the file $packet\_file$ with feature parameters fv, (ii) classifying the result $packet\_result$ according to the storage time, (iii) obtaining the corresponding switch_mapping table cur_map for different time by querying file map_table, (iv) parsing marking fields to specific switch names based on switch-mapping table cur_map, (v) rebuilding the forwarding path, and compiling statistics and analysis to the traceback result. Particularly, the exception data also need to be recorded under the process of traceback.

3 Implementation

3.1 Experimental Environment

We build several different experimental topology environments using Mininet [8] to check the correctness and validity of traceback component. An example is shown in Fig. 4. The topology contains one controller, seven switches and eight hosts. The dotted line represents the link between the controller and switches while the solid line represents the link between switches and switches. The switches are software-based in Open vSwitch 2.3.0, and the controller is based on OpenDaylight [9] Helium supporting OpenFlow 1.3. Moreover, the packet marking, implemented in C, is an extension of Open vSwitch source code. We added several auxiliary files and modified some codes related to *ovs_dp_process_received_packet* function. The traceback, implemented in Python, is a relatively independent external program. We presented the traceback results with ECharts technology, which is based on the data that is stored in packet marking mechanism.

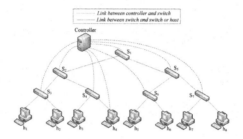

Fig. 4. An example of experimental topology

3.2 A Simple Experiment

Our experiment is working on the assumption that we should rebuild forwarding path of the packet fitting these features (shown in Table 1). In addition, we assume that the controller in our prototype is absolutely safe and unoccupied, and the packet loss rate and packet latency are very low that can be ignored.

Table 1. Some features needing to be matched when rebuilding

Feature variable	Source IP	Destination IP	Total length	Protocol	Source port	Destination port
Value	h_1	h_8	58	TCP	61000	1234

Packet Marking. We perform packet marking and storing by selecting host H_1 and H_8 to initiate TCP connection with the destination port is 1234. We consider the fields of TOS (8 bits), $Identification$ (16 bits) and RF (1 bit) to mark (the impact of packet forwarding is minimal), i.e., the special fields are for a grand total of 25 bits. In our experimental topology (Fig. 4), the node H_1 IP address is 10.0.0.1, and the node H_8 IP address is 10.0.0.8. The generated switch-mapping table is shown in Fig. 5, including the specific time of constructing network topology and the corresponding switch-mapping table. In the current experimental topology, there are 7 switches: S_1, S_2, S_3, S_4, S_5, S_6 and S_7. Moreover, number 0 represents the switch whose name is S_4, number 1 represents the switch whose name is S_5 and so on.

```
map table:
date         time         inteferface
2017-06-24,08:53:45,s4,s5,s3,s7,s2,s6,s1
```

Fig. 5. A screenshot showing of switch-mapping table file

Before marking, take a use case: suppose that there could be a maximum of 32 switches in our experimental topology combining with the concept of distributed computing. Thus, we conduct a simple marking design that assigns 5 bits for each switch. For the special fields possessing 25 bits, marking for 5 times is a cycle. The Fig. 6 illustrates the marking process. The marking process is performed based on marking field order from TOS to $Identification$ to RF.

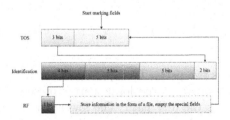

Fig. 6. The illustration of marking process

To strengthen the experimental contrast and broaden the range to mark packets, we extracted three feature variables from Table 1 as marking conditions in the experiment, which include source IP, destination IP and protocol. So the packet that node H_1 sends to node H_8 will be marked and then store some information about the packet in the forms of a file when special fields are not sufficient. Some contents of the storage file are shown in Fig. 7. We can see there are 13 feature variables stored in the file, such as date and time $date\_time$ and storage order of the same packet seq. The feature variable $match\_id$ represents number identity of switch that the packet reaches when this data is being stored.

```
packet route information:
date  time  seq src_ip  dest_ip  tot_len head_len pro src_port dest_port tos id RF match_id
2017-06-24,08:54:18,1,10.0.0.1,10.0.0.8,60,20 bytes,TCP,58906,1234,0x82,0x3098,0,3
2017-06-24,08:54:18,1,10.0.0.1,10.0.0.8,52,20 bytes,TCP,58906,1234,0x82,0x3098,0,3
2017-06-24,08:54:37,1,10.0.0.1,10.0.0.8,58,20 bytes,TCP,58906,1234,0x82,0x3098,0,3
2017-06-24,08:54:45,1,10.0.0.1,10.0.0.8,58,20 bytes,TCP,58906,1234,0x82,0x3098,0,3
2017-06-24,08:55:14,1,10.0.0.1,10.0.0.8,52,20 bytes,TCP,58906,1234,0x82,0x3098,0,3
2017-06-24,08:55:14,1,10.0.0.1,10.0.0.8,52,20 bytes,TCP,58906,1234,0x82,0x3098,0,3
2017-06-24,08:55:41,1,10.0.0.1,10.0.0.8,60,20 bytes,TCP,58909,1234,0x82,0x3098,0,3
2017-06-24,08:55:41,1,10.0.0.1,10.0.0.8,52,20 bytes,TCP,58909,1234,0x82,0x3098,0,3
2017-06-24,08:55:56,1,10.0.0.1,10.0.0.8,58,20 bytes,TCP,58909,1234,0x82,0x3098,0,3
2017-06-24,08:56:16,1,10.0.0.1,10.0.0.8,52,20 bytes,TCP,58909,1234,0x82,0x3098,0,3
2017-06-24,08:56:16,1,10.0.0.1,10.0.0.8,52,20 bytes,TCP,58909,1234,0x82,0x3098,0,3
```

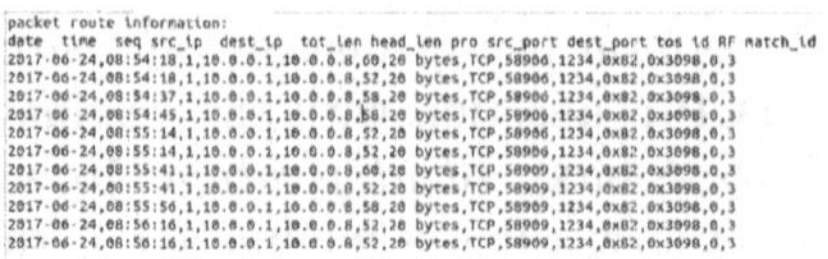

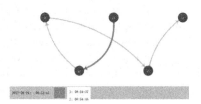

Fig. 7. Some contents of the storage file

Traceback. Deciding a testing topology shown in Fig. 4. Then realizing the whole process of traceback with Algorithm 2 by querying switch-mapping table and analyzing storage file. It is worth mentioning that data cleaning is necessary when rebuilding packet forwarding path. We should screen wrong data and save them to the corresponding file as an evidence when there is a need to analyze. Next, rebuilding forwarding path for the remaining data according to time, the restore process of special fields accords with the sequence of choosing marking fields in the packet marking mechanism. If a data is the last to be stored when a packet is forwarded, the rebuilding process of a packet will end with the condition that a value in special fields (TOS, $Identification$, RF) is equal to the value of $match_id$. The result of traceback is shown in Fig. 8.

Fig. 8. The result of traceback

The result contains two parts. The upper part shows the specific path information that a small square in the lower part represents when being clicked. The red row represents the first path. The lower part analyzes and integrates the distribution of various paths in various time, including the time to create switch-mapping table, the appearing numbers of a path and the storage time of a packet. In the case that there are some kinds of paths in a time, we regard the path with the maximal appearing number as the final forwarding path of a packet we expect. In addition, the path present in Fig. 8 is our current experimental result. In the testing topology shown in Fig. 4, the forwarding path of packets that match features shown in Table 1 is $S_3 \to S_2 \to S_1 \to S_5 \to S_7$. The result is the same as the actual path in our experimental topology.

4   Related Work

So far, more and more technical schemes are being proposed to solve the potential security threats of SDN, regardless of traditional technology improvements or new technology innovations.

Aiming at attack forensics, most research carry out surrounding the technology of backtracking attack path. NDB [10], a prototype network debugger inspired by gdb, provides direct evidence to rebuild the sequence of events and identify root cause leading to a network error by modifying forwarding state and logging packet digests with two primitives: *breakpoints* and *packet backtraces*. In [11], a new technique is proposed to focus on tracing back to the sources and finding all network paths of an anomaly leveraging a graph-based model and SDN without deploying any specific tool. Packet traceback [12] applies the "back policy" that is computed by a provably correct set of syntactic transformations on a given policy to packets of interest to determine all possible paths the packets leveraging Pyretic language without introducing any data-plane overhead. SDN traceroute [13] is an alternate tool for measuring paths of arbitrary packets by injecting the probes created by the production traffic at a certain point without changing actual forwarding rules. All of the works mentioned of attack forensics takes no consideration for the integration of different security mechanisms.

Aiming at fusion system, most research carry out surrounding the design of architecture. MalwareMonitor [14] introduces a security framework to detect and mitigate the malware infections with high speed using SDN, which elastically partitions network traffic and distributes detection load across a range of detectors. A SDN troubleshooting tool EPOXIDE [15], an Emacs based modular framework, aims to track down misconfigurations or bugs of a specific nature by effectively combining existing network and software troubleshooting tools in a single platform. Netography [16], a system that troubleshoots your network, locates and digs root causes of network issues with exporting packet behavior and flow rules obtained by actively sending probes related to normal packets. None of the works mentioned of attack forensics can compose the network path only through single packet under the condition of not increase workload of SDN controller.

Traceback approach we propose, however, can ensure security of network link and source data to some extend and provides direct evidence when needing to recover forwarding path of suspicious packets. Moreover, traceback need not change network behavior or increase SDN controllers burden. Particularly, traceback can act as extra specific tools, ranging from debugging to network behavior analysis.

5   Conclusion and Future Work

In this paper, we conduct a research of SDN traceback with an OpenvSwitch [7] extension, which is based on the technology of packet marking and logging. We introduce a theoretical model hypothesis and describe the detailed information of mapping-table creation, packet marking and traceback and their relationships. To verify the validity and feasibility of the traceback component, we make a simple experiment to illustrate the whole implementation process. In future, we plan to extend and improve our propose traceback component as the following aspects.

1. Multiple packet marking schemes. How to use the finite fields to store more information of path is an urgent issue to be solved. In view of the different application scenarios and network topologies, we need to design some various schemes to meet various requirements along with the higher utilization of marking fields. For example, we can design a method that is similar to that of frame boundary in traditional network. It is a choice to adopt and improve existing IP traceability algorithms, such as PPM (Probabilistic Packet Marking) and DPM (Deterministic Packet Marking).
2. Traceability design. How to rebuild the forwarding path is the one of the cores of the traceback component. We can consider some other designs to implement traceback with a better combination of SDN characteristics. For example, we still adopt the algorithms of packet marking and logging, but based on configuring flow table policies, taking advantages of the capacity of SDN controller that can control the global vision.
3. Actual practice about the theoretical model. The theoretical model we propose can strengthen and ensure SDN security from various perspectives. Once we can realize each component and intelligently merge them, then we will make a great contribution to the development and innovation of SDN.

Acknowledgment. The authors would like to thank the anonymous reviewers for their elaborate reviews and feedback. This paper is supported by the National Natural Science Foundation of China (No. 61502247), Open Project Program of the State Key Laboratory of Mathematical Engineering and Advanced Computing (No. 2017A10), and Key Lab of Information Network Security, Ministry of Public Security (No. C17611), Opening Project of Collaborative Innovation Center for Economics crime investigation and prevention technology (No. JXJZXTCX-015).

References

1. Feamster, N., Rexford, J., Zegura, E.: The road to SDN. Queue **11**(12), 20 (2013)
2. Mckeown, N., et al.: OpenFlow: enabling innovation in campus networks. ACM SIGCOMM Comput. Commun. Rev. **38**(2), 69–74 (2008)
3. Zinner, T., Jarschel, M., Hossfeld, T., Tran-Gia, P., Kellerer, W.: A compass through SDN networks. Informatik., Uni (2013)
4. Scott-Hayward, S., O'Callaghan, G., Sezer, S.: SDN security: a survey. In: Future Networks and Services, pp. 1–7 (2013)
5. Khan, S., et al.: Software-defined network forensics: motivation, potential locations, requirements, and challenges. IEEE Netw. **30**(6), 6–13 (2016)
6. Bates, A., Butler, K., Haeberlen, A., Sherr, M., Zhou, W.: Let SDN be your eyes: secure forensics in data center networks. In: The Workshop on Security of Emerging Networking Technologies (2014)

7. Pfaff, B., et al.: The design and implementation of Open vSwitch. In: NSDI, pp. 117–130 (2015)
8. Oliveira, R.L.S.D., Shinoda, A.A., Schweitzer, C.M., Prete, L.R.: Using mininet for emulation and prototyping software-defined networks. In: Communications and Computing, pp. 1–6 (2014)
9. Medved, J., Varga, R., Tkacik, A., Gray, K.: Opendaylight: towards a model-driven SDN controller architecture. In: World of Wireless, Mobile and Multimedia Networks, pp. 1–6 (2014)
10. Handigol, N., Heller, B., Jeyakumar, V., Mckeown, N.: Where is the debugger for my software-defined network? In: The Workshop on Hot Topics in Software Defined Networks, pp. 55–60 (2012)
11. Francois, J.: Anomaly traceback using software defined networking. In: International Workshop on Information Forensics & Security (2014)
12. Zhang, H., Reich, J., Rexford, J.: Packet traceback for software-defined networks, Department of Computer Science, Princeton University, Princeton. Technical report TR-978-15, vol. 201 (2015)
13. Agarwal, K., Dixon, C., Dixon, C., Carter, J.: SDN traceroute: tracing SDN forwarding without changing network behavior. In: The Workshop on Hot Topics in Software Defined Networking, pp. 145–150 (2014)
14. Abaid, Z., Rezvani, M., Jha, S.: Malware monitor: an SDN-based framework for securing large networks, pp. 40–42 (2014)
15. Lvai, T., Pelle, I., Nmeth, F., Gulys, A.: EPOXIDE: a modular prototype for SDN troubleshooting. ACM SIGCOMM Comput. Commun. Rev. 45(5), 359–360 (2015)
16. Zhao, Y., Zhang, P., Jin, Y.: Netography: troubleshoot your network with packet behavior in SDN. In: IEEE/IFIP Network Operations and Management Symposium, NOMS 2016, pp. 878–882 (2016)

Shoot at a Pigeon and Kill a Crow: On Strike Precision of Link Flooding Attacks

Jiahao Peng[1,2], Xiaobo Ma[1,2(✉)], Jianfeng Li[1,2], Lei Xue[3], and Wenjun Hu[4]

[1] Ministry of Education Key Laboratory of Intelligent Networks and Network Security, Xi'an Jiaotong University, Xi'an 710049, Shaanxi, China
xma.cs@xjtu.edu.cn
[2] School of Electronic and Information Engineering, Xi'an Jiaotong University, Xi'an 710049, Shaanxi, China
[3] Department of Computing, Hong Kong Polytechnic University, Hong Kong, China
[4] Palo Alto Networks, Santa Clara, CA, USA

Abstract. The emerging link flooding attacks (LFAs) increasingly attract significant attention in both academia and industry, due to their huge threat to the routing infrastructure. Compared with traditional distributed denial-of-service attacks (DDoS) that target servers, LFAs target critical links. Stemming from coordinated flows between bots and public servers or among bots, the attack traffic flows are aggregated at a critical link, thereby gradually making a network connected to the critical link disconnected as the aggregated attack traffic flows grow intensified. It is commonly believed that LFAs are far more sophisticated than traditional DDoS attacks. Nevertheless, whether such sophistication comes without a downside has never been investigated. In this paper, we advance the notion of *strike precision* of LFAs, and reveal that LFAs may exhibit *attack interference* which might restrict their applicability from the adversary's standpoint. Due to attack interference, strike precision of LFAs would be lowered. That is, while disconnecting a network, LFAs may unexpectedly interfere the connectivity of innocent networks nearby, undermining the stealthiness and persistence of LFAs. We tackle a series of questions surrounding strike precision, for fostering more research concerning the practical aspects of LFAs.

Keywords: Crossfire · Link flooding attack · Strike precision

1 Introduction

In contrast to traditional distributed denial-of-service (DDoS) attacks that target (end) computer servers [12,13,20,21], link flooding attacks (LFAs) target (intermediate) critical links that constitute the Internet backbone [14,25,26]. LFAs have recently come into practice after attracting the academia for years, posing severe threats to large-scale regional networks. For example, a few links of

© Springer Nature Switzerland AG 2018
M. H. Au et al. (Eds.): NSS 2018, LNCS 11058, pp. 436–451, 2018.
https://doi.org/10.1007/978-3-030-02744-5_32

major Internet exchange points in Europe and Asia were flooded to disconnect the anti-spam service Spamhaus, with up to 300 Gb/s traffic of LFAs [2].

LFAs are powerful, formidable and hard to defend against for three major reasons. First, stemming from coordinated flows between bots and public servers (e.g., web servers) or among bots, the attack traffic flows are aggregated at a critical link with a huge amount. As such, a network connected to the critical link will be gradually disconnected, as the aggregated attack traffic flows grow intensified. Second, the disconnected network, though having traditional DDoS countermeasures deployed at the network perimeter, might be blind to the attack, since the critical link is not within its administrative domain. Last, even for those ISPs who have the privilege to access the traffic flows crossing the critical link, it would be challenging for them to identify the attack traffic flows that are indistinguishable from legitimate ones.

Since the pioneering works of Studer and Perrig [19] and Kang et al. [9], considerable progress has been made to thwart LFAs, with a focus on detecting and mitigating the attack [3,4,7–10,19,22,26]. In all state-of-the-art studies, it is commonly believed that LFAs are far more sophisticated than traditional server-targeted DDoS attacks by design. Nevertheless, whether such sophistication comes without a downside has never been investigated.

In this paper, we take the first step to explore this problem. Particularly, we advance the notion of *strike precision* of LFAs, and reveal that LFAs may exhibit *attack interference* which might restrict their applicability from the adversary's standpoint. More precisely, when the adversary aims at disconnecting a specific network (e.g., $\mathcal{N}$) via attacking a critical link l, the connectivity of the networks surrounding $\mathcal{N}$ (e.g., $\bar{\mathcal{N}}$) might be interfered (i.e., attack interference), in whole or in part, depending on the importance of l for $\bar{\mathcal{N}}$ in respect of connectivity. Due to attack interference, strike precision of LFAs would be lowered in the sense that LFAs, while disconnecting a network, may unexpectedly interfere the connectivity of some innocent networks nearby.

At first glance, the adversary lacks interest in attack interference. For a terrorist adversary interested in mass destruction, it is true. However, for a rational adversary in consideration of attack stealthiness and persistence, it is not true. The reason is that attack interference tends to incentivize different victim networks to collaborate in defending against LFAs. Such collaboration is an effective countermeasure against LFAs, since it increases individual networks' visibility of coordinated attack traffic flows. The severer attack interference is, the stronger the incentive is. Therefore, for a rational adversary, attack interference and strike precision would be big concerns, especially in the long run.

Focusing on attack interference and strike precision, we attempt to answer the following research questions:

- **RQ1:** To what extent does attack interference exist, and how do they affect strike precision, in traditional LFAs that only seeks *strike efficiency*, i.e., interrupting more routes (destined to $\mathcal{N}$) by flooding fewer selected links?

- **RQ2**: What are the main factors affecting attack interference and strike precision? Can adversaries reduce attack interference (posed to $\bar{\mathcal{N}}$) and increase strike precision? What is their cost?

To answer RQ1, we first quantify strike precision, as well as strike efficiency. Then, we propose the Strike-Efficiency-Oriented (i.e., SEO) flooding strategy for traditional LFAs. The strategy interrupts more routes by flooding fewer selected links. Following the SEO flooding strategy, we perform traditional LFAs to gain insight into their strike precision. To tackle RQ2, taking into account the attack interference induced by attacking each link, we propose the Strike-Precision-Aware Hybrid (i.e., SPAH) flooding strategy, for impeding the attack toward links with more severe attack interferences while achieving larger strike efficiency. To approach these two questions, all experiments are conducted based on real-world traceroute data.

To our best knowledge, we are the *first* to advance the notion of strike precision for LFAs. Our contributions are summarized below.

- We quantify strike precision, as well as strike efficiency. Our quantification sheds light on a new angle of understanding LFAs, potentially fostering more research concerning the practical aspects of LFAs.
- Combining the greedy algorithm and the genetic algorithm, we propose the SEO flooding strategy for traditional LFAs, for interrupting more routes by flooding fewer selected links. Following the SEO flooding strategy, we perform traditional LFAs to gain insight into their strike precision. The experiments suggest that attack interference is pervasive and significantly lowers strike precision in traditional LFAs.
- Taking into account attack interference induced by attacking each link, we propose the SPAH flooding strategy, for impeding the attack toward links with more attack interference while achieving larger strike efficiency. The experiments show that our strategy can substantially increase strike precision.

Roadmap. In Sect. 2, we present background and motivation. Then, we describe the problem in Sect. 3, propose flooding strategies in Sect. 4, and conduct experiments in Sect. 5. We discuss and propose countermeasures in Sect. 6. Finally, we survey the literature in Sect. 7 and conclude in Sect. 8.

2   Background and Motivation

2.1   Background

As illustrated in Fig. 1, the goal of LFAs is to disconnect the intended victim network from the rest of the network, wherein the intended victim network could be a university, a city or even a country. To accomplish such a goal, the adversary analyzes the routing topology and finds a target link (or a set of target links) connecting the intended victim network and the rest of the network. By clogging the target link, the adversary can disconnect the intended victim network, rendering legitimate users unable to communicate with the intended victim network. A typical way that the adversary clogs the target link is to coordinate a huge number of traffic flows originating from bots and destined to decoy servers (or bots) inside or near the intended victim network. Decoy servers refer to public servers with open services such as HTTP, FTP. The coordinated traffic flows are required to be aggregated at the target link enormously. They are often indistinguishable from legitimate traffic flows for evading the detection.

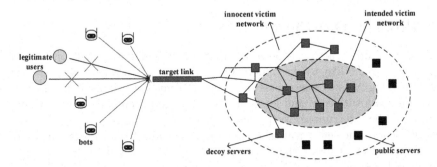

Fig. 1. A simplified example demonstrating LFAs, and that clogging the target link may disconnect the innocent victim network besides the intended one.

2.2   Motivation

By clogging the target link, the adversary can disconnect the intended victim network, while it is challenging for the intended victim network to defend against the attack using countermeasures deployed at its network perimeter. However, it can be argued that, though more sophisticated, powerful and hard to defend against, LFAs were born to have limitations in comparison to traditional DDoS attacks. As depicted in Fig. 1, clogging the target link will also result in the disconnection of the innocent victim network from the rest of the network, since the communication between legitimate users and hosts within the innocent victim network also crosses the target link.

We term the disconnection of the innocent victim network as attack interference. Due to attack interference, strike precision of LFAs would be lowered. Specifically, while disconnecting a network, LFAs may unexpectedly interfere the connectivity of innocent networks nearby. The root cause is that, when selecting the target links, the adversary does not consider the influence of clogging the selected target links to the networks surrounding the intended victim network. It is strike efficiency that the adversary only seeks in traditional LFAs, meaning that the adversary wants to interrupt more routes (destined to the intended victim network) by flooding fewer selected target links.

At first glance, the adversary lacks interest in attack interference. For a terrorist adversary interested in mass destruction, it is true. However, for a rational adversary in consideration of attack stealthiness and persistence, it is not true. The reason is that attack interference tends to incentivize different victim networks to collaborate with each other in defending against LFAs. Such collaboration is an effective countermeasure against LFAs, since it increases individual networks' visibility of coordinated attack traffic flows. The severer attack interference is, the stronger the incentive is. Moreover, the adversary's allies may exist in the innocent victim network, and disconnecting the innocent victim network cannot make the adversary better off whereas it renders the adversary face a more severe legal penalty. Therefore, for a rational adversary, attack interference and strike precision would be big concerns, especially in the long run.

3   Problem Description

Consider an adversary who performs LFAs. Let $\mathcal{N}$ denote a network that the adversary would like to disconnect from the rest of the network. Essentially disconnecting $\mathcal{N}$ is to select a set of target (intermediate) links along the routes between hosts within $\mathcal{N}$ and hosts outside of it, and then clog them so that the routes can be interrupted. Note that a route comprises a sequence of links.

We denote the set of routes between hosts within $\mathcal{N}$ and hosts outside of it by $\mathcal{R}_\mathcal{N}$, the set of links (that constitute $\mathcal{R}_\mathcal{N}$) by $\mathcal{L}_\mathcal{N}$, and the set of selected target links by $\mathcal{L}'_\mathcal{N} \subseteq \mathcal{L}_\mathcal{N}$. Normally, it is hard, if not impossible, to interrupt all routes in $\mathcal{R}_\mathcal{N}$ by clogging the links in $\mathcal{L}'_\mathcal{N}$. Suppose, by clogging the links in $\mathcal{L}'_\mathcal{N}$, the set of routes that the adversary interrupts is $\mathcal{R}'_\mathcal{N} \subseteq \mathcal{R}_\mathcal{N}$. Let $|\cdot|$ be the operator calculating the cardinality of a set. On a limited budget of $|\mathcal{L}'_\mathcal{N}|$, the adversary can strategically derive $\mathcal{L}'_\mathcal{N}$ for a larger value of $|\mathcal{R}'_\mathcal{N}|/|\mathcal{R}_\mathcal{N}|$, i.e., interrupting the routes in $\mathcal{R}_\mathcal{N}$ as many as possible.

To quantify the adversary's return on investment (ROI), we define *strike efficiency*, denoted by SE, to represent the number of routes that the adversary can interrupt by clogging one link on average.

Definition 3.1. Strike Efficiency.

$$SE = \frac{|\mathcal{R}'_\mathcal{N}|}{|\mathcal{L}'_\mathcal{N}|}. \tag{1}$$

When the adversary performs LFAs to disconnect $\mathcal{N}$, the connectivity of networks surrounding $\mathcal{N}$ may be interfered. Let $\bar{\mathcal{N}}$ denote the network(s) whose connectivity is interfered, $\mathcal{R}_{\bar{\mathcal{N}}}$ denote the set of routes between hosts within $\bar{\mathcal{N}}$ and hosts outside of it, and $\mathcal{R}'_{\bar{\mathcal{N}}} \subseteq \mathcal{R}_{\bar{\mathcal{N}}}$ denote the set of interrupted routes due to the adversary clogging the links in $\mathcal{L}'_\mathcal{N}$. We define *attack interference*, denoted by AI, posed to $\bar{\mathcal{N}}$ due to disconnecting $\mathcal{N}$, as $|\mathcal{R}'_{\bar{\mathcal{N}}}|/|\mathcal{R}_{\bar{\mathcal{N}}}|$. To minimize AI, $|\mathcal{R}'_{\bar{\mathcal{N}}}|$ should be minimized, since $|\mathcal{R}_{\bar{\mathcal{N}}}|$ is constant in a specific problem.

On a limited budget of $|\mathcal{L}'_\mathcal{N}|$ and a certain value of SE, $|\mathcal{R}'_\mathcal{N}|$ is determined. Therefore, minimizing AI is equivalent to maximizing $|\mathcal{R}'_\mathcal{N}|/(|\mathcal{R}'_{\bar{\mathcal{N}}}| + |\mathcal{R}'_\mathcal{N}|)$, which we define as *strike precision* and denote by SP.

Definition 3.2. Strike Precision.

$$SP = \frac{|\mathcal{R}'_\mathcal{N}|}{|\mathcal{R}'_{\bar{\mathcal{N}}}| + |\mathcal{R}'_\mathcal{N}|}. \tag{2}$$

It refers to the ratio of the number of interrupted routes associated with $\mathcal{N}$ to the total number of interrupted routes by clogging the links in $\mathcal{L}'_\mathcal{N}$.

We have three remarks on strike efficiency and strike precision. First, to evaluate LFAs comprehensively, both strike efficiency and strike precision should be measured, whereas existing studies neglect the latter. Second, for attack stealthiness and persistence, a rational adversary tends to seek larger strike efficiency while ensuring higher strike precision. Third, strategically deriving $\mathcal{L}'_\mathcal{N}$ is the core to achieve larger strike efficiency and higher strike precision.

Having strike efficiency and strike precision defined, we are interested in the research questions raised in Sect. 1 (i.e., **RQ1** and **RQ2**). To address these questions, we should explore different link flooding strategies, and then measure strike efficiency and strike precision under different strategies. Determining link flooding strategies are essentially to strategically derive $\mathcal{L}'_\mathcal{N}$ by setting different priorities for strike efficiency and strike precision.

4   Exploring Link Flooding Strategies

When deriving $\mathcal{L}'_\mathcal{N}$, traditional adversaries in LFAs seek high strike efficiency. We, accordingly, present two strike-efficiency-oriented (SEO) strategies, namely, the naive SEO strategy and the advanced SEO strategy that further improves strike efficiency of the naive one. Also, for rational adversaries concerning strike precision, we propose the strike-precision-aware hybrid strategy.

4.1   Naive Strike-Efficiency-Oriented (N-SEO) Strategy

Traditional adversaries heuristically derive $\mathcal{L}'_\mathcal{N}$ (i.e., the set of target links) in a greedy way [9]. They calculate $|\mathcal{R}'_\mathcal{N}|/|\mathcal{R}_\mathcal{N}|$ to quantify the degradation severity of the attack against $\mathcal{N}$. The N-SEO strategy is detailed in Algorithm 1.

In the N-SEO strategy, adversaries iteratively select a new link $l \in \mathcal{L}_\mathcal{N} \setminus \mathcal{L}'_\mathcal{N}$ maximizing the reward gain, $\delta_l(\mathcal{L}'_\mathcal{N}) = |\mathcal{R}'_\mathcal{N}(\mathcal{L}'_\mathcal{N} \cup \{l\})|/|\mathcal{R}_\mathcal{N}| - |\mathcal{R}'_\mathcal{N}(\mathcal{L}'_\mathcal{N})|/|\mathcal{R}_\mathcal{N}|$, and insert l into $\mathcal{L}'_\mathcal{N}$. Here, $\mathcal{R}'_\mathcal{N}(\cdot)$ is a function calculating the set of interrupted

---

Algorithm 1: Naive strike-efficiency-oriented strategy.

Input: $\mathcal{R}_\mathcal{N}$, $\mathcal{L}_\mathcal{N}$, ∇, Φ
Output: $\mathcal{L}'_\mathcal{N}$
1 $\mathcal{L}'_\mathcal{N} = \varnothing$, $\mathcal{R}'_\mathcal{N} = \varnothing$;
2 **for** $l \in \mathcal{L}_\mathcal{N}$ **do**
3 | calculate $\mathcal{R}'_\mathcal{N}(l)$;
4 **end**
5 **while** $|\mathcal{R}'_\mathcal{N}|/|\mathcal{R}_\mathcal{N}| < \nabla$ **do**
6 | $l = \arg\max_{l \in \mathcal{L}_\mathcal{N} \setminus \mathcal{L}'_\mathcal{N}} \delta_l(\mathcal{L}'_\mathcal{N})$;
7 | **if** $|\mathcal{L}'_\mathcal{N}| = \Phi$ **then**
8 | | break;
9 | **end**
10 | $\mathcal{L}'_\mathcal{N} = \mathcal{L}'_\mathcal{N} \cup \{l\}$;
11 | $\mathcal{R}'_\mathcal{N} = \mathcal{R}'_\mathcal{N} \cup \mathcal{R}'_\mathcal{N}(l)$;
12 | **for** $l \in \mathcal{L}_\mathcal{N}$ **do**
13 | | calculate $\mathcal{R}'_\mathcal{N}(l)$;
14 | **end**
15 **end**

routes to $\mathcal{N}$ due to clogging a set of links. Note that we recalculate $\mathcal{R}'_{\mathcal{N}}(l)$ for each l after removing the link with maximum reward gain at each iteration. This process repeats until $|\mathcal{R}'_{\mathcal{N}}|/|\mathcal{R}_{\mathcal{N}}|$ approaches a pre-specified goal ∇, or $|\mathcal{L}'_{\mathcal{N}}|$ reaches the budget of the number of selected links Φ.

4.2   Advanced Strike-Efficiency-Oriented (A-SEO) Strategy

To further improve strike efficiency achievable by the N-SEO strategy, we devise the A-SEO strategy to derive $\mathcal{L}'_{\mathcal{N}}$ using the genetic algorithm. Specifically, the A-SEO strategy initializes n different genes of the first generation. A gene is a binary vector indicating and corresponding to a set of selected target links. We denote the function that transforms the former to the latter by $gene2set()$, while the latter to the former by $set2gene()$. All genes are constructed based on $\mathcal{L}_{\mathcal{N}}$, differing from each other in the subset of selected target links (i.e., $\mathcal{L}'_{\mathcal{N}}$). Particularly, among all the initialized genes, one gene is obtained according to the $\mathcal{L}'_{\mathcal{N}}$ derived by the N-SEO strategy, while each of the remaining genes is generated according to randomly generated $\mathcal{L}'_{\mathcal{N}}$. Constituting the first generation, the set of initialized n different genes, denoted by $\mathcal{G}_1$, evolve from generation to generation, forming a sequence of generations $\mathcal{G}_1, \mathcal{G}_2, \mathcal{G}_3, \ldots$.

The evolution consists of selection, crossover, and mutation. Selection is for retaining better genes in each generation via roulette-wheel selection [11]. That is, probabilistically selecting a gene, say g, among n different genes in each generation, and a gene with a larger value of strike efficiency, say $SE(g)$, should be assigned a larger selection probability. In the early generations, $SE(g)$ varies to a wide extent. Hence, assigning g with a larger value of $SE(g)$ a larger selection probability is easy. However, as generations evolve, the value of $SE(g)$ tends to become closer to each other, resulting in similar selection probabilities between genes. To signify the discrepancy of selection probabilities between genes, we assign g in $\mathcal{G}_j$ a selection probability of Stoffa-$SE_j(g)$ ($SSE_j(g)$) using the Stoffa method [18]. $SSE_j(g)$ is calculated as follows:

$$SSE_j(g) = \frac{e^{SE(g)/T_j}}{\sum_{i=1}^{n} e^{SE(g)/T_j}}, \tag{3}$$

$$T_j = 0.99^{j-1}T_1, \tag{4}$$

where $j = 1, 2, 3, \ldots$ represents the sequence number of generations, and T_j is the temperature of the jth generation.

Crossover and mutation are leveraged to achieve cross-generation gene improvement. The self-adaptive genetic (SAG) algorithm is employed to adaptively adjust $P_c(g_k, g_q)$ (i.e., the probability of crossover between g_k and g_q acquired via roulette-wheel selection), $P_m(g)$ (i.e., the probability of mutation of g). Specifically, when the value of $SSE(g)^1$ becomes homogeneous, $P_c(g_k, g_q)$

---

[1] Unless otherwise stated, we remove the subscript j representing the number of generations, for the simplicity of representation.

and $P_m(g)$ defined below should be increased and otherwise decreased [6,16].

$$P_c(g_k, g_q) = \begin{cases} P_{c1} - \frac{(P_{c1}-P_{c2})(SSE'-SSE^{\mathrm{avg}})}{SSE^{\mathrm{max}}-SSE^{\mathrm{avg}}}, & SSE' \geq SSE^{\mathrm{avg}}, \\ P_{c1}, & SSE' < SSE^{\mathrm{avg}}, \end{cases} \quad (5)$$

$$P_m(g) = \begin{cases} P_{m1} - \frac{(P_{m1}-P_{m2})(SSE^{\mathrm{max}}-SSE(g))}{SSE^{\mathrm{max}}-SSE^{\mathrm{avg}}}, & SSE(g) \geq SSE^{\mathrm{avg}}, \\ P_{m1}, & SSE(g) < SSE^{\mathrm{avg}}, \end{cases} \quad (6)$$

where P_{c1}, P_{c2}, P_{m1}, P_{m2} are empirically specified constants, and the remaining notations are given in (7). Intuitively, the above equations render g with a value of $SSE(g)$ smaller (resp. larger) than the average have larger (resp. smaller) $P_c(g_k, g_q)$, $P_m(g)$. In this way, low-quality genes are likely to be improved.

$$\begin{aligned} SSE' &= \mathbf{max}\{SSE(g_k), SSE(g_q)\}, \\ SSE^{\mathrm{avg}} &= \tfrac{1}{n}\textstyle\sum_{g\in\mathcal{G}} SSE(g), \\ SSE^{\mathrm{max}} &= \mathbf{max}\{SSE(g)|g \in \mathcal{G}\}. \end{aligned} \quad (7)$$

To prevent a generation $\mathcal{G}_j$ from degrading to genes of lower quality, we introduce the evolution-with-restart mechanism. Specifically, when $SE_j^{\mathrm{max}} = \mathbf{max}\{SE(g)|g \in \mathcal{G}_j\}$ is smaller than $0.99SE_1^{\mathrm{max}}$, we assign all the elements in $\mathcal{G}_1$ to $\mathcal{G}_j$. The evolution runs until we reach the j^*th generation satisfying $SE_{j^*}^{\mathrm{max}}$ exceeds SE_1^{max}. We derive $\mathcal{L}'_{\mathcal{N}}$ from $\mathbf{arg\,max}_g\{SE(g) = SE_{j^*}^{\mathrm{max}}|g \in \mathcal{G}_{j^*}\}$.

We summarize the A-SEO strategy in Algorithm 2.

4.3 Strike-Precision-Aware Hybrid (SPAH) Strategy

To seek strike precision along with strike efficiency, we propose the SPAH strategy in Algorithm 3. Specifically, we maximize $|\mathcal{R}'_{\mathcal{N}}|/|\mathcal{R}_{\mathcal{N}}|$ and meanwhile minimize $|\mathcal{R}'_{\bar{\mathcal{N}}}|/|\mathcal{R}_{\bar{\mathcal{N}}}|$ (i.e., AI). Adversaries iteratively select a link $l \in \mathcal{L}_{\mathcal{N}} \setminus \mathcal{L}'_{\mathcal{N}}$ maximizing the reward gain, $\theta_l(\mathcal{L}'_{\mathcal{N}}) = (|\mathcal{R}'_{\mathcal{N}}(\mathcal{L}'_{\mathcal{N}} \cup \{l\})| - |\mathcal{R}'_{\bar{\mathcal{N}}}(\mathcal{L}'_{\mathcal{N}} \cup \{l\})|) - (|\mathcal{R}'_{\mathcal{N}}(\mathcal{L}'_{\mathcal{N}})| - |\mathcal{R}'_{\bar{\mathcal{N}}}(\mathcal{L}'_{\mathcal{N}})|)$. $\mathcal{R}'_{\bar{\mathcal{N}}}(\cdot)$ calculates the number of interrupted routes to $\bar{\mathcal{N}}$ due to clogging a set of links. This process repeats until $|\mathcal{R}'_{\mathcal{N}}|/|\mathcal{R}_{\mathcal{N}}|$ approaches a pre-specified goal ∇, or $|\mathcal{L}'_{\mathcal{N}}|$ reaches the budget of the number of selected links Φ.

5 Experiments

5.1 Dataset Preparation

We perform traceroute from source (Planetlab) servers distributed all over the world to target (public) servers in five regional networks. Figure 2 shows the locations of these servers. There are totally 81 source servers (40 in US, 7 in China, 5 in Canada, 4 in Australia, 4 in Brazil, 3 in Germany, and 18 in others), and 4,843 target servers (1048 in Taiwan, 962 in Switzerland, 957 in Singapore,

942 in Hong Kong, 934 in Japan). The entire dataset consists of more than 1.2×10^6 routes and 1.2×10^6 links.

We consider part of the networks in five different regions as intended victim networks, namely, Kowloon (KLN) in Hong Kong, Downtown (DT SG) in Singapore, Zurich (ZRH) in Switzerland, Tokyo (TYO) in Japan, Greater Taipei area (TPE) in Taiwan, and the complement part as innocent victim networks (e.g., the network in Hong Kong except KLN). In each attack, the adversary aims to disconnect one intended victim network by selecting target links to clog through the N-SEO strategy, the A-SEO strategy and the SPAH strategy. In the N-SEO strategy and the SPAH strategy, we assume $\Phi = |\mathcal{L}_\mathcal{N}|$. In the A-SEO strategy, we set $P_{c1} = 0.9$, $P_{c2} = 0.6$, $P_{m1} = 0.1$, $P_{m2} = 0.001$.

5.2   Measuring Strike Precision Under Different Strategies

Figure 3 shows attack interference (AI) when $|\mathcal{R}'_\mathcal{N}|/|\mathcal{R}_\mathcal{N}|$ (i.e., the percentage of interrupted routes) varies from 50% to 100%, with a step of 10%. Each line corresponds to a specific intended victim network.

We observe that, among the three strategies, the N-SEO strategies introduces the most attack interference, the SPAH strategy the least, while the A-SEO in the moderate, for a specific intended victim network. Apparently, the SPAH strategy substantially lowers attack interference by taking into account attack

---

Algorithm 2: Advanced strike-efficiency-oriented strategy.

Input: $\mathcal{R}_\mathcal{N}$, $\mathcal{L}_\mathcal{N}$, n, $\mathcal{L}'_\mathcal{N}$ from the N-SEO strategy
Output: $\mathcal{L}'_\mathcal{N}$

1 $\mathcal{G}_1 = \cup_{i=1,2,\ldots,n-1}\{set2gene(X_i)|X_i = \text{random target links}\} \cup \{set2gene(\mathcal{L}'_\mathcal{N})\}$;
2 $SE_1^{max} = \max\{SE(g)|g \in \mathcal{G}_1\}$;
3 $j = 1$;
4 **while** $SE_j^{max} \leq SE_1^{max}$ **do**
5 $\quad$ j++;
6 $\quad$ $\mathcal{G}_j = \varnothing$;
7 $\quad$ **while** $|\mathcal{G}_j| < n$ **do**
8 $\quad\quad$ select g_k and g_q over probability distribution $\{SSE_{j-1}(g)|g \in \mathcal{G}_{j-1}\}$;
9 $\quad\quad$ $\mathcal{G}_j = \mathcal{G}_j \cup \{g_k, g_q\}$;
10 $\quad\quad$ generate a random float r, $0 < r < 1$;
11 $\quad\quad$ **if** $r < P_c(g_k, g_q)$ **then**
12 $\quad\quad\quad$ $g_{k'}, g_{q'} = crossover(g_k, g_q)$;
13 $\quad\quad\quad$ $\mathcal{G}_j = \mathcal{G}_j \cup \{g_{k'}, g_{q'}\}$;
14 $\quad\quad$ **end**
15 $\quad$ **end**
16 $\quad$ **for** $g \in \mathcal{G}_j$ **do**
17 $\quad\quad$ **if** $r < P_m(g)$ **then**
18 $\quad\quad\quad$ $g_m = mutation(g)$;
19 $\quad\quad\quad$ $\mathcal{G}_j = (\mathcal{G}_j \setminus \{g\}) \cup \{g_m\}$;
20 $\quad\quad$ **end**
21 $\quad$ **end**
22 $\quad$ $SE_j^{max} = \max\{SE(g)|g \in \mathcal{G}_j\}$;
23 $\quad$ **if** $SE_j^{max} < 0.99 SE_1^{max}$ **then**
24 $\quad\quad$ $\mathcal{G}_j = \mathcal{G}_1$;
25 $\quad$ **end**
26 **end**
27 $\mathcal{L}'_\mathcal{N} = gene2set(\arg\max_g\{SE(g) = SE_j^{max}|g \in \mathcal{G}_j\})$;

Algorithm 3: Strike-precision-aware hybrid strategy.

$\quad$ **Input:** $\mathcal{R_N}$, $\mathcal{L_N}$, ∇, $\varPhi$
$\quad$ **Output:** $\mathcal{L'_N}$
1 $\mathcal{L'_N}=\varnothing, \mathcal{R'_N} = \varnothing$;
2 **for** $l \in \mathcal{L_N}$ **do**
3 $\quad$ | $\quad$ calculate $\mathcal{R'_N}(l)$;
4 **end**
5 **while** $|\mathcal{R'_N}|/|\mathcal{R_N}| < \nabla$ **do**
6 $\quad$ | $\quad l = \arg\max_{l \in \mathcal{L_N} \setminus \mathcal{L'_N}} \theta_l(\mathcal{L'_N})$;
7 $\quad$ | $\quad$ **if** $|\mathcal{L'_N}| = \varPhi$ **then**
8 $\quad$ | $\quad$ | $\quad$ break;
9 $\quad$ | $\quad$ **end**
10 $\quad$ | $\quad \mathcal{L'_N} = \mathcal{L'_N} \cup \{l\}$;
11 $\quad$ | $\quad \mathcal{R'_N} = \mathcal{R'_N} \cup \mathcal{R'_N}(l)$;
12 $\quad$ | $\quad$ **for** $l \in \mathcal{L_N}$ **do**
13 $\quad$ | $\quad$ | $\quad$ calculate $\mathcal{R'_N}(l)$;
14 $\quad$ | $\quad$ **end**
15 **end**

---

interference to innocent victim networks. In addition, for both the N-SEO strategy and the A-SEO strategy, AI grows roughly linearly as the percentage of interrupted routes increases. However, such a tendency is not significant for the SPAH strategy, indicating that no obvious attack interference would be introduced as more routes are interrupted.

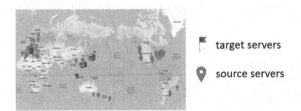

target servers

source servers

Fig. 2. The locations of source servers and target servers.

Under a specific strategy, attack interference to networks such as Tokyo in Japan is relatively lower, whereas that to networks like Kowloon in Hong Kong is relatively higher. The reason is that Tokyo is a small area for Japan, and Kowloon accounts for a large area for Hong Kong. In other words, the larger the ratio of the intended victim network size in the entire regional network is, the more interference to the entire regional network would be posed.

Figure 4 reports strike precision (SP) over $|\mathcal{R'_N}|/|\mathcal{R_N}|$ under different strategies, as further cross-validate the results about attack interference. Specifically, the SPAH strategy achieves the largest SP, the N-SEO strategy the least, while the A-SEO strategy in the moderate, for a specific intended victim network. Under the N-SEO strategy and the A-SEO strategy, the value of SP when Tokyo is disconnected is larger than those when the remaining intended victim networks are disconnected. This observation coincides with the lower attack

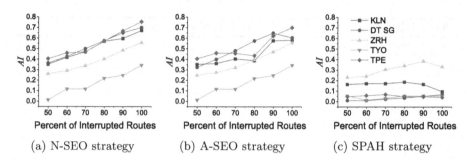

Fig. 3. Attack interference (AI) as the percentage of interrupted routes varies under different strategies.

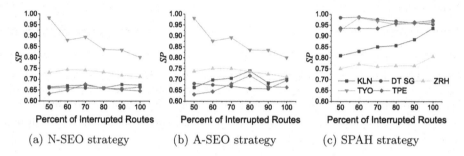

Fig. 4. Strike precision (SP) as the percentage of interrupted routes varies under different strategies.

interference when Tokyo is disconnected. To exemplify the selected links intuitively, we plot the geographical locations of selected target links via the N-SEO strategy and the SPAH strategy, when $\mathcal{N}$ ="KLN" (i.e., Kowloon in Hong Kong) and $|\mathcal{R}'_{\mathcal{N}}|/|\mathcal{R}_{\mathcal{N}}| = 0.8$ in Fig. 5. We label the links commonly selected by two strategies (20 links in red), and the links exclusively selected by each strategy (22 links by N-SEO, and 39 links by SPAH, both in black). This example demonstrates that the set of selected links by the SPAH strategy are different from and larger than those by the N-SEO strategy, suggesting that, when interrupting the same number of routes, the SPAH strategy comes at the cost of more selected links to clog.

5.3 Measuring Strike Efficiency Under Different Strategies

We also measure strike efficiency (SE) over $|\mathcal{R}'_{\mathcal{N}}|/|\mathcal{R}_{\mathcal{N}}|$ under different strategies. The result is shown in Fig. 6.

For all strategies, as the percentage of interrupted routes increases, SE drastically decreases. Compared with the N-SEO strategy, the A-SEO strategy has a higher value of SE. However, the strike efficiency of the SPAH strategy is just slightly lower than that of the SEO strategy. Since the SPAH strategy takes

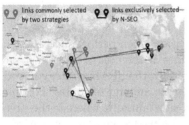
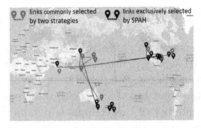

(a) N-SEO strategy (42 links)   (b) SPAH strategy (59 links)

Fig. 5. The locations of selected target links via different strategies, when $\mathcal{N}$ ="KLN" (i.e., Kowloon in Hong Kong) and $|\mathcal{R}'_{\mathcal{N}}|/|\mathcal{R}_{\mathcal{N}}| = 0.8$. (Color figure online)

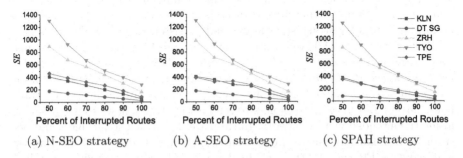

(a) N-SEO strategy   (b) A-SEO strategy   (c) SPAH strategy

Fig. 6. Strike efficiency (SE) as the percentage of interrupted routes varies under different strategies.

both strike precision and strike efficiency into account, it achieves high strike precision without significantly lowering strike efficiency.

Combining the results above, we answer **RQ1** and **RQ2** in Sect. 1 below.

The Answer to RQ1. According to Figs. 3 and 4, on average, when adversaries interrupt 80% of routes to the intended victim network by strategies that only consider strike efficiency, attack interference is severe and strike precision is low. More precisely, by the N-SEO strategy, we have $AI = 46.82\%, SP = 69.16\%$, and $AI = 40.36\%, SP = 72.18\%$ for the A-SEO strategy.

The Answer to RQ2. The main factors affecting attack interference and strike precision include the percentage of routes adversaries would like to interrupt (i.e., a larger percentage results in more attack interference and lower strike precision), the ratio of the size of the intended victim network to that of the innocent victim network (i.e., a larger ratio generally leads to less attack interference and higher strike precision). To lower attack interference and improve strike precision, the SPAH strategy can be used. On average, when adversaries interrupt 80% of routes to the intended victim network by the SPAH strategy, $AI = 13.34\%, SP = 91.79\%$, at the cost of slightly more selected links to clog but without significantly decreasing strike efficiency.

6   Discussion

Adversaries can effectively increase the precision when performing LFAs via the SPAH strategy. However, such precision comes at the cost of lowered strike efficiency. That is, compared with the SEO strategy, the SPAH strategy has to clog more target links in order to interrupt the same amount of routes. Fortunately, the number of target links is not increased substantially, whereas the precision is improved significantly. Furthermore, according to our data, the number of average (traceroute) hops from the target links selected by the SPAH strategy to the intended victim network equals 6.76, indicating that the attacked links are beyond the administrative domain of the intended victim network and thus defending these links against the attack remains difficult. We, therefore, envision that there is a tendency that adversaries take into account strike precision when performing LFAs for attack stealthiness and persistence.

Besides the cost of lowered strike efficiency, seeking strike precision may lead to the increase of the ratio of *the routes crossing the set of selected target links and destined to the intended victim network* to *all the routes crossing the set of selected target links*. Consequently, when coordinating attack traffic flows, adversaries have more choices to send attack traffic flows to decoy servers inside the intended victim network. In this case, for attack stealthiness and persistence, rational adversaries would construct attack traffic flows meeting two requirements. First, each attack traffic flow, when being inspected separately, is indistinguishable from legitimate traffic flows. Second, these attack traffic flows should exhibit diversity without similar behavioral patterns (e.g., visit different websites at different times) to evade correlation-based detection.

To defend against rational adversaries in consideration of strike precision, one solution is to monitor the performance (e.g., available bandwidth) of the set of links selected by the SPAH strategy in real time and trigger warnings upon anomaly occurs [25]. In addition, from the perspective of routing topology design, one can also increase the overlapping of the (intermediate) links of different networks, as well as the entropy of the distribution of link importance to different networks. Consider the extreme case where all links are equally important to different networks in terms of connectivity. It would be challenging for rational adversaries in consideration of strike precision to determine which network to disconnect, since clogging one link may interfere many other networks.

7   Related Work

The layered architecture of the Internet enables various types of connectivity structures [24]. CAIDA's Archipelago project [5] and DIMES [17] measured the router-level Internet topology via traceroute. Kang et al. analyzed the pervasiveness of routing bottlenecks in 15 countries and 15 cities around the world. Albert et al. [1] showed that if an adversary disables 4% of the highly connected routers, the entire Internet will be broken up into small isolated pieces. However, later work by Magoni [15] and Wang et al. [23] concluded that breaking the entire

Internet may not be infeasible because of the vast number of routers or links that need to be disconnected.

Recently, LFAs have gained attention in the literature. Kang et al. proposed LFAs that can effectively cut off the Internet connections of a target area *without* being detected [7,9]. The Coremelt attack could be considered a special case of LFAs [19]. Since LFAs result in abnormal link performance, traditional active link (and path) measurement techniques, such as packet pair and packet train, could naturally facilitate the detection of LFAs. To apply these techniques in detecting LFAs, LinkScope employs both end-to-end and hop-by-hop measurement to detect the links under such attacks [25,26].

To defend against LFAs, Gkounis *et al.* showed that both existing and novel traffic engineering modules can efficiently expose the attack. They implemented a defense prototype using simulation mechanisms and evaluated it extensively on multiple real topologies [3]. Attacks by cost-sensitive attackers try to fully utilize the bots' upstream bandwidth. Kang *et al.* tackled this root cause that it is sufficient to perform a rate change test, where they temporarily increased the effective bandwidth of the bottleneck core link and observed the response. Attackers will be detected since they are unable to demonstrably increase throughput after bandwidth expansion. Kang *et al.* designed a software-defined network (SDN) based system called SPIFFY that addresses key practical challenges in turning this high-level idea into a concrete defense mechanism, and provided a practical solution to force a tradeoff between cost and detectability for LFAs [8].

8   Conclusion

Despite making considerable research progresses regarding LFAs, existing studies do not consider attack interference and strike precision which might restrict the applicability of LFAs from the adversary's standpoint. We take the first step to take into account these issues, and advance the notion of strike precision. It is arguable that, for rational adversaries concerning attack stealthiness and persistence, attack interference and strike precision would be big concerns, especially in the long run. Using real-world traceroute data, we demonstrate that current link flooding strategies that only seek strike efficiency (i.e., interrupting more routes by flooding fewer links) may result in poor strike precision, severely interfering the connectivity of the networks surrounding the intended victim network. To increase strike precision of LFAs, we propose a strike-precision-aware hybrid link flooding strategy, which impedes the attack toward links with more attack interference while achieving larger strike efficiency. Our experiments show that the proposed hybrid strategy improves strike precision significantly at the cost of limited degradation of strike efficiency. We also discuss and propose countermeasures against rational adversaries who perform LFAs in consideration of attack interference and strike precision.

References

1. Albert, R., Jeong, H., Barabási, A.L.: Error and attack tolerance of complex networks. Nature **406**(6794), 378 (2000)
2. Bright, P.: Can a ddos break the internet? (2013). http://goo.gl/oM6XJt
3. Gkounis, D., Kotronis, V., Liaskos, C., Dimitropoulos, X.: On the interplay of link-flooding attacks and traffic engineering. ACM SIGCOMM Comput. Commun. Rev. **46**(2), 5–11 (2016)
4. Hirayama, T., Toyoda, K., Sasase, I.: Fast target link flooding attack detection scheme by analyzing traceroute packets flow. In: Proceedings of IEEE WIFS, pp. 1–6 (2015)
5. Hyun, Y.: Caida Monitors: The Archipelago Measurement Infrastructure (2009)
6. Jing, J., Li-dong, M., Shu-ling, L., Lin, J.: Simulation research based on a self-adaptive genetic algorithm. In: Proceedings of IEEE ICIS, pp. 267–269 (2010)
7. Kang, M.S., Gligor, V.D.: Routing bottlenecks in the internet: causes, exploits, and countermeasures. In: Proceedings of ACM SIGSAC, pp. 321–333 (2014)
8. Kang, M.S., Gligor, V.D., Sekar, V.: SPIFFY: Inducing cost-detectability tradeoffs for persistent link-flooding attacks. In: Proceedings of NDSS, pp. 1–15 (2016)
9. Kang, M.S., Lee, S.B., Gligor, V.D.: The crossfire attack. In: Proceedings of IEEE S&P, pp. 127–141 (2013)
10. Lee, S.B., Kang, M.S., Gligor, V.D.: CoDef: collaborative defense against large-scale link-flooding attacks. In: Proceedings of ACM CoNEXT, pp. 417–428 (2013)
11. Lipowski, A., Lipowska, D.: Roulette-wheel selection via stochastic acceptance, pp. 2193–2196. CoRR abs/1109.3627 (2012)
12. Luo, X., Chang, R.K.: On a new class of pulsing denial-of-service attacks and the defense. In: Proceedings of NDSS (2005)
13. Luo, X., Chang, R.K.: Optimizing the pulsing denial-of-service attacks. In: Proceedings of IEEE DSN, pp. 582–591 (2005)
14. Ma, X., Li, J., Tang, Y., An, B., Guan, X.: Protecting internet infrastructure against link flooding attacks: a techno-economic perspective. Inf. Sci. (2018, in press)
15. Magoni, D.: Tearing down the internet. IEEE J. Sel. Areas Commun. **21**(6), 949–960 (2003)
16. Qin, A.K., Suganthan, P.N.: Self-adaptive differential evolution algorithm for numerical optimization. In: Proceedings of IEEE TEVC, pp. 1785–1791 (2005)
17. Shavitt, Y., Shir, E.: DIMES: let the internet measure itself. ACM SIGCOMM Comput. Commun. Rev. **35**(5), 71–74 (2005)
18. Stoffa, P.L., Sen, M.K.: Nonlinear multiparameter optimization using genetic algorithms: inversion of plane-wave seismograms. Geophysics **56**(11), 1794–1810 (1991)
19. Studer, A., Perrig, A.: The coremelt attack. In: Backes, M., Ning, P. (eds.) ESORICS 2009. LNCS, vol. 5789, pp. 37–52. Springer, Heidelberg (2009). https://doi.org/10.1007/978-3-642-04444-1_3
20. Tang, Y., Luo, X., Hui, Q., Chang, R.K.: Modeling the vulnerability of feedback-control based internet services to low-rate DoS attacks. IEEE Trans. Inf. Forensics Secur. **9**(3), 339–353 (2014)
21. Wang, C., Miu, T.T., Luo, X., Wang, J.: SkyShield: a sketch-based defense system against application layer DDoS attacks. IEEE Trans. Inf. Forensics Secur. **13**(3), 559–573 (2018)
22. Wang, L., Li, Q., Jiang, Y., Wu, J.: Towards mitigating link flooding attack via incremental SDN deployment. In: Proceedings of IEEE ISCC, pp. 397–402 (2016)

23. Wang, Y., Xiao, S., Xiao, G., Fu, X., Cheng, T.H.: Robustness of complex communication networks under link attacks. In: Proceedings of ACM ICAIT, p. 61 (2008)
24. Willinger, W., Roughan, M.: Internet topology research redux. Recent Advances in Networking. ACM SIGCOMM eBook (2013)
25. Xue, L., Luo, X., Chan, E.W., Zhan, X.: Towards detecting target link flooding attack. In: Proceedings of USENIX LISA, pp. 81–96 (2014)
26. Xue, L., Ma, X., Luo, X., Chan, E.W., Miu, T.T., Gu, G.: Linkscope: Towards detecting target link flooding attacks. IEEE Trans. Inf. Forensics Secur. **13**, 2423–2438 (2018)

Creating and Managing Realism in the Next-Generation Cyber Range

Dragos-George Ionica[1], Florin Pop[1,2(✉)], and Aniello Castiglione[3]

[1] Computer Science Department, University Politehnica of Bucharest,
Bucharest, Romania
ionicadrgs@gmail.com, florin.pop@cs.pub.ro
[2] National Institute for Research and Development in Informatics (ICI),
Bucharest, Romania
[3] Department of Computer Science, University of Salerno, Fisciano, SA, Italy
castiglione@ieee.org

Abstract. There are numerous potential digital range arrangements and situations that a very much outlined range can achieve. We have experienced several use cases, and we acknowledged that every last mechanism requires distinctive human components, scale, and assault and safeguard standards. What you will likewise discover is that these things devour a lot of HR and set-up, readiness, and examination time, which compare to time and cash. These standards may make you oblige your activities to the point that they get to be distinctly lumbering and do not yield the outcomes that you need. You can without much of a stretch get overpowered with these essential variables to the disservice of your activities, consequently lessening your adequacy and precluding your benefits from having the capacity to prepare as they battle genuinely. This paper presents real-world attack-defence scenarios for cybersecurity training.

Keywords: Attack-defence · Cybersecurity training · Cyber range
Architecture · Technology development assessment

1 Introduction

Solidifying the versatility of key government, military, and business frameworks become essential for associations that are conveying digital extents, inconceivable proving grounds that permit war diversions and re-enactments went for fortifying digital security abilities and barriers. Conventional digital reaches require critical, expensive interests in equipment and faculty and, after its all said and done cannot scale adequately to address today's developing system activity volume and always complex assault vectors [1]. A digital range is genuinely just a sensible environment that is utilized for digital innovation advancement and digital lighting preparing. Digital innovation advancement applications may incorporate system execution assessment, application execution assessment, security improvement and confirmation as well as item evaluations and prepare to give some examples. Preparing applications then again integrate banner activities, digital rivalries and red, blue, white group preparing work out [3].

© Springer Nature Switzerland AG 2018
M. H. Au et al. (Eds.): NSS 2018, LNCS 11058, pp. 452–462, 2018.
https://doi.org/10.1007/978-3-030-02744-5_33

We need to demonstrate to you generally accepted methods to accomplish digital range testing and preparing without the requirement for the immediately old and inconceivable proving grounds of past digital extents. In this paper, we talk about models and situations connected with average digital range organizations and how you can accomplish the most advantage out of your digital range.

This paper presents the general features of digital cyber range in Sect. 2, the main aspects of architecture a cyber range in Sect. 3, then in Sect. 4 address the practical use of the cyber range. Section 5 presents the technology development assessment. We present a case study on SCADA in Sect. 6. The paper ends with a conclusion and future work presented in Sect. 7.

2 Digital Cyber Range

What the word goes in the term digital range is military wording for a run of the mill focusing on or dynamic range where you can send troops to sharpen their battling aptitudes with an assortment of reasonable all around arranged activities that may incorporate connections with weapons and ammo, tanks, warplanes, war boats, etc. In that way, the war contender can prepare as they would battle.

Essentially, a digital range gives your system and IT innovation workforce with a sensible stage for preparing identified with system assault and guard situations, emulating genuine cases in the lab so that they also can develop as they would battle. Digital range preparing concentrates on the best way to assess circumstances and apply the right arrangement/design for particular genuine assault circumstances [2].

Its likely genuinely clear why militaries need to prepare their digital resources [14]. They have to guarantee that their central goal basic war-battling framework performs satisfactorily in a period of war. It is insufficient to ensure that things work. They likewise must be secure against assault for an adversary who may never be going to budge on upsetting mission-basic foundation. Many organizations understand somewhat late in the diversion is this is not pertinent just to militaries and governments, but instead these situations are playing out every day around the globe, in regular day to day existence, and in private industry. Indeed, even in present-day "peace times", state-supported assaults are pervasive. Our associated world is under steady attack from criminal associations, activists, and rebel country states.

2.1 The Need of a Cyber Range

Each and every day, the news features shout out about new assaults on the money related industry, monetary extortion, charge card misrepresentation, wholesale fraud, information spillage of corporate privileged insights, safeguard contractual workers being besieged by entrance endeavors, open influence and water arrange interruptions, and politically or ideologically roused digital assaults. The basic actuality is that no industry is resistant to this new and predominant assault culture.

In the event that you have a huge online nearness, an assault that causes your administrations to go down notwithstanding for brief timeframes can bring about huge measures of lost income. Maybe venturing into the many thousands or even a huge number of dollars of loses for specific enterprises. In the event that you were on a shut system serving open frameworks.

In case your business relies on upon virtual private framework, a VPN advancement for your regular operations for a contrasting workforce over a nation or around the world, and a framework attack circumstance spoils or chops down segments of your VPN designing, you will wish you had arranged for the outcome in a computerized run condition before it hit [4].

In case you are a nuclear power plant whose basic databases are unfavorably changed or perhaps annihilated by a cyber-attack which is influencing your capacity to deliver your item or to penetrate, then you will completely wish that you had investigated that projection in a digital cyber testbed to have possessed the capacity to successfully relieve it early.

In case you are a security, expert and you can't deal with or moderate an botnet which runs over a large scale network went for your system by awkward country, or political substance, your clients and their business main concern are affected.

Who needs such a cyber testbed? All things considered, it's quite obvious that for all intents and purposes each association needs one. Nobody is safe to these issues and breaks. Each and every day it appears assaults are being disclosed in associations under steady assault.

We consistently know about the steady torrent of new security assaults and the commonness of security gaps. It just appears that there's not a single end to be seen. The way of the vast majority of the associated world makes securing our systems and information into a significant degree troublesome issue to handle [5]. On a par with the most significant programming and equipment advancement companies are, there is by all accounts no limit to the quantity of found security gaps, with security vulnerabilities being revealed every day over the globe for system frame-works IT and administrations. Organizations like Google, Mozilla, Apple, Oracle, Adobe, Microsoft, and numerous others are always applying security overhauls and fixes for a bunch of imperfections in their product.

There is by all accounts not a single end to be seen. These issues are not leaving. They reliably appear to deteriorate for the straightforward reason that system foundation and processing multifaceted nature is developing after some time. Where unpredictability exists, security issues will exist. We live with an incredibly complex registering and systems administration foundation surrounding us. Where multifaceted nature prospers, security issues will thrive, and the information demonstrates this out. As per the Secunia Vulnerability Review 2014, the pattern for security vulnerabilities for the first utilised programming programs has gone up altogether through the span of the most recent five years [6].

2.2 Tackling Security Issue

There's been an intriguing arrangement of dialogues continuing for a considerable length of time with contending perspectives in the matter of how to unravel these security issues in both the transient and the long haul. There are examinations about the advantages of open designs, advantages of shut structures, a shiny new as far as anyone knows "secure from the beginning" system and contending models, utilization of firewall, interruption and avoidance frameworks, zero-day assault acknowledgment, bound together risk administration frameworks (UMTS), and a plenty of other security designs and exchanges.

3   Architecture of a Cyber Range

Cyber Testbeds can be designed from multiple points of view however when all is said in done you can aggregate them into three classifications, physical, virtualized, and cross breed. We should investigate every range sort, and their focal points and weaknesses [7].

3.1   Physical Architecture

In a full physical range, you copy your whole physical system foundation, your switches, firewalls, servers, endpoints, and so on. You utilise that copied element for your preparation. This is incredible from a reasonable point of view since you can't get it any more practical than that since you're utilising fundamentally everything that you're using as a part of your range is genuine.

Be that as it may, this approach has some noteworthy drawbacks and these are genuinely imperative:

- One of the greatest disservices is the frequently extreme budgetary and staffing cost to recreate your run of the system environment that's running live.
- Another damage is the setup and teardown time to make new planning circumstances in that condition.
- Another is physical organization of the earth, constant operational cost examinations for things like cooling and power use of such an enormous complex physical range.
- The last one, and not be communicated delicately, is the inconvenience in cleaning an unadulterated physical range after a practice wraps up. This is crucial in light of the way that various circumstances running on your range will incorporate complex ambush vectors that can leave undesirable relics on your framework at some point later and that is terrible.

3.2   Virtual Architecture

In a virtual range, everything is preenacted. Virtual machines copy every segment. This approach offers some particular points of interest. The underlying capital cost and the progressing operational cost are altogether less costly than a full physical reconstructive range. The setup and teardown are commonly more straightforward too and are ordinarily known amounts regarding the time they take.

The range equipment gets to be distinctly more comfortable and that is on account of everything is virtualised to keep running on generally regular off the rack equipment and less master HR, or less master HR, are ordinarily required than for utterly physical documentation. The ancient assault rarities are likewise more effectively discarded. For instance, by returning to the known great depiction of your virtualised foundation [8].

Be that as it may, there are severe weaknesses to this approach too. Mostly, what you pick up in effortlessness and lower costs, you pay for in execution. Virtual frameworks will never perform to the same level from physical structures, paying little respect to what virtual merchants let you know and offer you. This can be an issue in preparing as you battle. Since in an environment, you will be unable to demonstrate specific assaults situations that you will discover in this present reality, directly on the premise of physical execution limitations of virtual models.

Two more cases of why unadulterated virtualisation can bring about issues are system throughput, which is dependably lower in a virtualised situation, and firewall IPS/IDS execution, which are significantly obliged regarding performance when those components are.

4   Effective Use of Cyber Range

We know we require a cross breed condition and we have a general considered what we have to virtualized and what we have to remain physical. Since the diverse sections can be virtual or physical depending upon the planning circumstance requirements, we won't cover the real utilization of an advanced range all around [9].

You may have an assortment of physical as well as virtual endpoint hardware on several sub-nets associated with a couple switches, with steering and firewall assets scattered as is basic on numerous topologies. Some of these exchanging and directing capacities possibly virtualized or they might be physical, contingent upon the practice prerequisites. A similar thing goes for the firewalls [10].

The steered correspondence connections could be anything also: ISP associations, coordinate pointto-point cabling, satellite interchanges, cell, or other. The truth is that whatever you're showing should be as sensible of course to meet the prerequisites of the practice and its goals. Potentially you have a couple of servers hanging off of a framework nonpartisan ground (DMZ).

The DMZ segment is an outer venture administration, for example, web facilitating and mail administrations. This may be your openly confronting e-mail or web servers for instance. They may likewise have full access through some special rules created in firewall to other assets and servers, making all this infrastructure most likely focused for assault by outside systems. Figure 1 shows an abnormal state topology of a Cyber Range which incorporates:

- Data-Center: Enterprise services from the Internal Network (Domain Controller, Exchange Server, SQL/Non-SQL Database Server, File Server, etc.).
- DMZ: Enterprise services from the External Network (web or e-mail hosting services etc.).
- Internal Clients:
  - Browsing the Internet;
  - Browsing the WWW from internal clients;
  - Accessing enterprise resources from the data center with internal clients

- External clients:
  - Clients from Internet that are willing to penetrate /harm the organization;
  - Internet Users accessing DMZ;
  - SYNC function from DNS and Mail;
  - Accessing from Internet via VPN with Internal Clients.

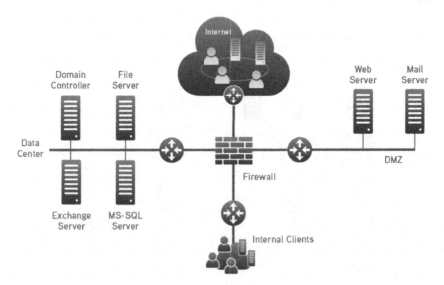

Fig. 1. Complex cyber range architecture.

5   Technology Development Assessment

How about we first discuss the innovation advancement evaluation case. At first look, this case has all the earmarks of being straightforward. You're utilising the range to survey execution in a specific gadget or administration under imperatives that you set. Utilizing the range furnishes you with a reliable lab environment, mapping to certain utilise cases that you can guarantee your gadget, benefit, arrangement, bug settle, and so forth will act not surprisingly once conveyed to creation.

The same thing would go, in case you're looking at various items in an item bakeoff. Perhaps an all the more fascinating example would be in case you're trying out a moment physical camcorder arrangement close by a current agreement. You have to perceive how it carries on and thinks about your existing foundation. Indeed, even in this environment, however, there is plenty of fundamental contemplations. For instance, how genuine is your range develop? Did you test the gadget's convention conduct and system data transfer capacity in segregation or amidst reason-able foundation organise the activity? These things have a large effect in the legitimacy of your examinations on your digital range. Note that authenticity is exceptionally essential in a digital range. If you don't have practical situations that include reasonable foundation activity and practical security assaults, then your scope is essentially pointless [10].

5.1   Technology Development Assessment

In preparing situations, it is anything but difficult to perceive how things can rapidly get a considerable amount more muddled. We utilise what we call red groups and blue groups to assault and shield the system, servers separately, and applications as a significant aspect of the digital range surrendered rules set by the white group. White groups are critical (Fig. 2).

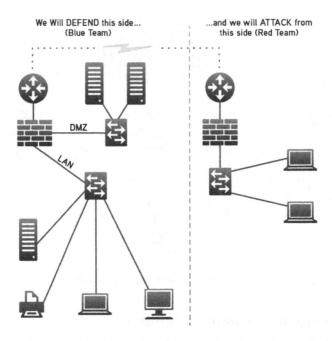

Fig. 2. Red vs blue team cyber range scenario. (Color figure online)

They set the objectives for the workout. These could be red group-based objectives, blue group-based objectives, or both. They deal with the preparation work out, have full permeability into the workout, and set the guidelines of engagement. The white group additionally guarantees the requirements under which the preparation practice will happen. They are kept mindful by the red groups and the blue groups of their advance amid the workout. For instance, a red group may guarantee that they have subverted a specific system asset. The white group once educated will have a way to confirm the reality of the claim. A blue group may assert a fruitful barrier against some known or obscure assault vector. The white group can confirm that also.

The white group can control different parts of practical foundation movement amid different phases of the practice to challenge the red group, the blue group, or both. Without a white group to all in all control the workout, you're preparing results will be severely restricted and you won't finish the objectives of the practice to develop as you battle.

Here you can see we have drawn a discretionary line directly down to the center got the system. Will safeguard one side and assaulting from the other. The white group would develop the range and relegate the assets to the different groups and capacities. At that point you start your preparation or essentially survey your current resistances from an innovation angle.

For instance, suppose the objective of one practice is to prepare your blue group strengths to guarantee that mission-basic camcorder frameworks can result in any case work under the nearness of two concurrent monstrous scale DDoS assaults against firewall and DMZ foundation in your defensive system. You could dole out your resistance from IT blue group assets and dole out the attack in red group strengths. The red group powers can be interior assets on the off chance that you have such ability on staff.

They could be outsider faculty that you employ on an impermanent premise to play out the assaults in your controlled range environment, working as indicated by the requirements set up by your white group. That line can be anyplace the white group needs it to be to accomplish the motivation behind the specific digital range situation that you may prepare for. For instance, you could choose a practice demonstrating an insider risk. Your white group has made a position where you have a security rupture inside your to-be ensured arrange (see taking after chart).

The objective is to check whether the blue group can identify pernicious exercises originating from the insider danger that could bring about necessary information going over your external correspondence connection to an adversary order and control server. This, for the most part, requires the guards having an inward firewall as well as system permeability arrangement set up to search for weird correspondences pathways that do not ordinarily exists on the system, and afterwards examination of profound parcel investigation (DPI) motors where exceptional mark location procedures isolate benevolent conduct from peculiar and vindictive behaviour.

Be that as it may, this can turn out to be exceedingly intricate. A decent range environment will permit you to perform only this sort of what we call behavioural displaying preparing if you find that you require it. Why is this so essential? Since the insider danger model is precisely the model that applies if you have been traded off by what is named Zero Day assaults. Most associations have been bargained with these sorts of attacks at some point.

5.2   Zero-Day Attacks

Zero Day assaults are a definitive assault vectors because by definition what they allude to are assaults that have not yet been found by security seller specialists. They are engendered by malevolent interests to pick up control of what you believed were well protected organise assets. On the off chance that these assaults are effective, and most by far of Zero Day assaults are, they frequently result in the establishment of an assortment of malignant programming (malware) to take control of your system and your information, permitting your essential information to be redirected to outside substances. They can likewise bring about an interruption or decimation of components of your order or your knowledge.

At times such malware can even lay in sit tight for an exact time when they are told to wreak facilitate destruction. You may never know whether or when that happens. They can likewise erase themselves, transform themselves, and do a wide range of other dreadful things in a situation. On the off chance that you have any mission-basic foundation in your surroundings and you are not preparing for these sorts of insider risk situations utilising demonstrating behavioural strategies, it won't be long until you procure the repercussions and they will be extreme.

5.3   Creating and Managing Realism in the Next-Gen Cyber Range

There are numerous potential digital range arrangements and situations that a very much out-lined range can achieve. We have experienced a few situations as of now. What you immediately acknowledged is that every last arrangement requires distinctive human components, scale, and assault and safeguard standards. What you'll likewise discover is that these things devour a lot of HR and set-up, readiness, and examination time, which compare to time and cash. This may make you oblige your activities to the point that they get to be distinctly lumbering and don't yield the outcomes that you need. You can without much of a stretch get overpowered with these basic variables to the disservice of your activities, consequently lessening your adequacy and precluding your benefits from having the capacity to genuinely prepare as they battle.

For instance, assume you have a thousand people who use your figuring resources in your affiliation. How are you going to indicate appropriate establishment development mixes that address their ordinary operations to scale without requiring each one of them to genuinely appreciate the range hone itself? How are you going to make suitably scaled, sensible ambush vectors when you don't have the battling resources of an overall botnet? By what means will you get the expertise that you need to effectively ambush your range works regardless to review your framework insurances when you won't not have that inclination.

6   Case Study – SCADA Scenario (SCCR Scenario)

If IT-class protections are inadequate, then how should we be protecting SCADA systems? To address this question, we must first understand cyber-attacks. Too many SCADA security practitioners do not study modern attack techniques, and they produce singularly vulnerable "secure" SCADA systems. Instead of attacks, too many of today's SCADA security and IT security practitioners spend far too much time thinking about vulnerabilities. Classic risk assessment calculations maintain that risk is a function of threats, vulnerabilities, exploits and consequences. Many practitioners, therefore, conclude that their job is to eliminate weaknesses. They reason that if we could only, somehow, eliminate all failings, then our systems would be invulnerable. This chain of reasoning quickly devolves into a preoccupation with known vulnerabilities and security update programs.

The first law of cybersecurity states that nothing is ever secure. For example, security updates repair only known product vulnerabilities, leaving countless unknowns waiting to be discovered and exploited. More generally, SCADA systems as a whole may have vulnerabilities that stem from how the systems are organised and configured, independent of any security defects in the product code.

These systems vulnerabilities are at the heart of many kinds of recent attacks (e.g., in Clouds to decrease the system performance [12] or to drain energy power in different ICT scenarios [13]). Frankly, our attackers are lazy - they prefer to use permissions we have configured into our SCADA networks rather than software vulnerabilities because exploiting agreements is less work. It takes considerable time and talent to analyse software applications to find undiscovered software vulnerabilities. It makes even more work to write the code needed to exploit those newly-discovered vulnerabilities (Fig. 3).

	Threat	Resources	Attack	Example
HIGH → **Potential Impact** → **LOW**	Nation States Military Grade	Nearly unlimited	Autonomous Targeted Malware	Stuxnet
	Intelligence Agencies	Professional	Remote Control Exploit New Vulnerabilities	Black Energy
	Hacktivists	Skilled Amateur	Remote Control Exploit Permissions	Ukraine
	SCADA Insiders	Amateur	Exploit Permissions	Maroochy
	Organized Crime	Professional	Indiscriminate Malware, Exploit Known Vulnerabilities	Zeus
	Corporate Insiders	Amateur	Exploit Permissions	Fraud

Fig. 3. Potential impact.

The standard permissions-based attack described in the section on intelligence agencies below easily defeats security updates, antivirus systems, intrusion detection systems, remote access jump hosts, firewalls and other IT-class protections routinely installed on SCADA systems. To anyone focused on vulnerabilities rather than attack techniques, this targeted, remote-control, permissions-based type of attack comes as a horrible surprise.

7   Conclusion

In outline, the continuous surge of creative applications and advancing security assaults immediately outpaced the exorbitant, static, work and hardware escalated customary digital scopes of the past. In the meantime, the emotional increment in digital dangers to undertakings must be tended to, driving the requirement for minimal digital extents that can fit inside a venture IT spending plan. A very much outlined digital range is the initial phase in empowering your association to perform complex innovation evaluations and in addition level today's playing field against muddled digital assault situations via preparing digital warriors.

A substantial digital range utilizes a half and half physical/virtual develop and incorporates application and security test apparatuses to help with reasonable blends of profoundly adaptable mission-basic foundation movement and assault activity while giving point by point investigation progressively and by means of complete reporting devices. With a digital range, you will enhance the abilities of your system barrier, consequently guaranteeing the flexibility of your systems and applications, and that your blue groups and red groups are set up for true digital situations by permitting them to prepare as they battle.

Acknowledgment. The research presented in this paper is supported by the projects: ROBIN (PNIII-P1-1.2-PCCDI-2017-0734), NETIO TEL-MONAER, ForestMon, SANTO (53/05.09.2016, SMIS2014 + 105976), and SPERO (PN-III-P2-2.1-SOL-2016-030046, 3Sol/2017. We would like to thank the reviewers for their time and expertise, constructive comments and valuable insight.

References

1. Branlat, M., Morison, A., Woods, D.: Challenges in Managing Uncertainty During Cyber Events: Lessons from the Staged-World Study Of A Large-Scale Adversarial Cyber Security Exercise. The Ohio State University (2011)
2. Brangetto, P., Caliskan, E., Roigas, H.: Cyber Red Teaming. NATO Cooperative Cyber Defence Centre of Excellence CCDCOE (2015)
3. ENISA - European Network and Information Security Agency. Good Practice Guide on National Exercises (2009)
4. Chen, J., Zhang, W., Urvoy-Keller, G.: Traffic profiling for modern enterprise networks: a case study. In: 2014 IEEE 20th International Workshop (2014)
5. Conklin, A., White, B.: E-government and cyber security: the role of cyber security exercises. In: 39th Hawaii International Conference on Systems Sciences (2006)
6. He, W., et al.: A game theoretical attack-defense model oriented to network security risk assessment. In: Computer Science and Software Engineering (2008)
7. Abrams, M., Weiss, J.: Malicious Control System Cyber Security Attack Case Study–Maroochy Water Services, Australia. The MITRE Corporation, McLean, VA (2008)
8. Andersson, G., et al.: Cyber-security of SCADA systems. In: Innovative Smart Grid Technologies (ISGT), 2012 IEEE PES. IEEE (2012)
9. Department of Homeland Security. (n.d.). Cyber Storm: securing cyber space. (DHS). http://www.dhs.gov/cyber-storm-securing-cyberspace. Accessed 6 June 2014
10. Eller, R.: Black Hat Japan 2004 - capture the flag games/ measuring skill with hacking contests, 15 October 2004. http://www.blackhat.com/presentations/bh-asia-04/bh-jp-04-pdfs/bh-jp-04-eller/bh-jp-04-eller.pdf
11. Ferrara, E.: Determine the business value of an effective security program - information security economics 101. Forrester Research (2002)
12. Catalin, N., Pop, F., Cristea, V., Bessis, N., Li, J.: Energy efficient cloud storage service: key issues and challenges. In: 2013 Fourth International Conference on Emerging Intelligent Data and Web Technologies (EIDWT), pp. 763–766. IEEE (2013)
13. Palmieri, F., Ricciardi, S., Fiore, U., Ficco, M., Castiglione, A.: Energy-oriented denial of service attacks: an emerging menace for large cloud infrastructures. J. Supercomput. 71(5), 1620–1641 (2015)
14. Castiglione, A., Raymond Choo, K.K., Nappi, M., Ricciardi, S.: Context aware ubiquitous biometrics in edge of military thing. IEEE Cloud Comput. 4(6), 16–20 (2017)

Understanding the Behaviors of
BGP-based DDoS Protection Services

Tony Miu Tung[1], Chenxu Wang[2,3(✉)], and Jinhe Wang[2]

[1] Nexusguard Ltd., Tsuen Wan, Hong Kong
[2] School of Software Engineering, Xi'an Jiaotong University, Xi'an, China
cxwang@mail.xjtu.edu.cn
[3] MoE Key Laboratory for INNS, Xi'an Jiaotong University, Xi'an 710049, China

Abstract. Distributed Denial of Service attacks has been one of the most challenges faced by the Internet for decades. Recently, DDoS protection services (DPS) have risen up to mitigate large-scale DDoS attacks by diverting the vast malicious traffic against the victims to affordable networks. One common approach is to reroute the traffic through the change of BGP policies, which may cause abnormal BGP routing dynamics. However, little is known about such behaviors and the consequences. To fill this gap, in this paper, we conduct the first study on the behaviors of BGP-based DPS through two steps. First, we propose a machine learning based approach to identify DDoS events because there usually lacks data for characterizing real DDoS events. Second, We design a new algorithm to analyze the behavior of DPS against typical DDoS attacks. In the case study of real DDoS attacks, we carefully analyze the policies used to mitigate the attacks and obtain several meaningful findings. This research sheds light on the design of effective DDoS attack mitigation schemes.

Keywords: DDoS attacks · BGP traffic · DPS behavior

1 Introduction

Distributed Denial of Service (DDoS) attacks has been threatening the infrastructure of the Internet for decades. In recent years, DDoS attacks are becoming even more popular with the emergence of the DDoS-as-a-service economy [10,15,17] and the over 1Tbps DDoS attack has been evidenced [2]. These attacks usually bring with victims great financial losses. As a result, the market of DDoS protection services (DPS), which provide the cleansing of traffic through traffic diversion, sees rapid growth in recent days [9].

Traffic diversion allows traffic to be routed through the DPS infrastructure, either in an always-on or on-demand manner. There are two main approaches to divert traffic, including the Domain Name System (DNS)-based method and Border Gateway Protocol (BGP)-based method, respectively. The DNS-based approach diverts network traffic through proper configurations of Domain Name

© Springer Nature Switzerland AG 2018
M. H. Au et al. (Eds.): NSS 2018, LNCS 11058, pp. 463–473, 2018.
https://doi.org/10.1007/978-3-030-02744-5_34

Severs or Anycast techniques. It is similar to what is done in the content delivery networks (CDN). The BGP-based scheme diverts traffic towards the DPS infrastructure for scrubbing by announcing an IP subnet of its customers. Although recent studies have measured the DNS-based approach [9], little is known about the behavior of BGP-based DPS.

To fill this gap, in this paper, we conduct the first study on the behaviors of BGP-based DPS by analyzing the dynamics of BGP messages. BGP is the de facto inter-domain protocol of the Internet and controls how packets are routed through autonomous systems (ASes). To provide a better understanding of BGP dynamics, several projects such as the Route Viewers Project and RIPE keep collecting the update information of edge routers through distributed vantage points. Our analysis consists of two steps. First, we design a machine learning based approach to identify DDoS events from BGP update messages because there usually lacks data for characterizing real DDoS events. It is non-trivial to identify DDoS events from BGP update messages because other disruptive events such as earthquakes, hurricanes, and blackouts may also disturb the BGP dynamics. To address this issue, we first detect BGP anomalies and then design a machine learning based method to determine whether or not a BGP anomaly is caused by DDoS attacks.

To train the classifier, we collect a sufficient number of DDoS attacks and disaster events which are reported to cause abnormal BGP dynamics. For each event, we collect the BGP update messages during the reported time period from the Route views project and then extract features from the BGP update messages within a fixed time interval. After classifying the events into two categories: DDoS attacks and disasters, we use the data to train a random forest classifier, which is utilized to determine the types of other detected abnormal events. More precisely, if a DDoS attack event is identified, we conduct an in-depth analysis of the BGP traffic to characterize how BGP-based DPS leverages BGP to mitigate the attack. To evaluate our approach, we perform retrospective studies on DDoS attacks and the DPS policies, and the experimental results demonstrate the effectiveness of our approach. In summary, we make the following contributions:

(1) We propose a new machine learning based approach to identify DDoS events by analyzing BGP update messages.
(2) We conduct the first analysis on the behavior of BGP-based DPS after DDoS attacks occur.
(3) We develop a new system based on our new algorithms and evaluate it through BGP data associated with real DDoS attacks.

The rest of this paper is organized as follows: In Sect. 2, we analyze the characteristics of extracted features. In Sect. 3, we describe the designed system. Section 4 describes the evaluation results of the system. In Sect. 4, we validate our system with extensive experiments. After reviewing relevant literature in Sect. 5, we conclude this work in Sect. 6.

2   Feature Analysis

We investigate 6 features from BGP update messages to character the fluctuation of the BGP traffic. Table 1 shows the description of the features. These features are borrowed from [12, 19]. Figure 1 demonstrates the distributions of features in different types of incidents.

Table 1. Description of features

Features	Definition
Ann	Number of announcements generalized by BGP speakers
WADiff	Number of new announced paths after an explicit withdrawal
AADupType1	Number of duplicate announcements to the same IP prefix
Unq_pfx_as	Number of unique prefixes originated by an AS
Max_AS_path_len	The maximum length of AS-PATHs
pfx_org_chg	Number of Prefix origin change

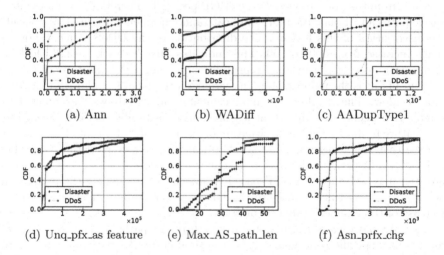

(a) Ann   (b) WADiff   (c) AADupType1

(d) Unq_pfx_as feature   (e) Max_AS_path_len   (f) Asn_prfx_chg

Fig. 1. CDF of the features

Ann is the number of paths announced by BGP speakers in a detection cycle. Figure 1(a) demonstrates that the Ann feature could help the distinction of DDoS events and disaster events. It is shown that DDoS events have about 80% of abnormal databins that have a value of the number of announcements less than 3000. However, no more than 50% of abnormal databins detected in disaster events that have a value less than 3000. This indicates that there will be fewer announcements to be sent in DDoS attacks than that in disaster events. The reason may be that disaster events usually last for a long time, and thus once a route is not available edge routers will announce a new path.

WADiff is the number of newly announced paths after an explicit withdrawal. When a previously announced path is withdrawn, other paths that depend on the withdrawn path may still be chosen and announced, only to be removed one by one [3], which results in the slow convergence of the Internet. We distinguish between explicit or implicit withdrawals based on whether a withdrawal message is sent or not. Explicit withdrawals are those associated with a withdrawal message; whereas an implicit withdrawal occurs when an existing route is replaced by the announcement of a new route to the destination prefix without an intervening withdrawal message. Figure 1(b) illustrates that there are more newly announced routes after an explicit withdrawal during the disaster events. This is because disaster events usually result in unreachability of some BGP routes and thus trigger peer routers to send explicit withdrawals.

AADupType1 is the number of duplicate announcements to the same prefix with all fields unchanged. Park et al. [16] studied the cause of duplicate announcements in BGP traffic and discovered that duplicates are caused by an unintended interaction between eBGP and iBGP. Routers receive updates via iBGP which differ in iBGP attribute values alone, and thus the router believes the updates to be unique. However, once the router processes the update, strips the iBGP attribute values, and sends the update to its eBGP peer, the two updates look identical from the point of view of the eBGP peer [16]. Therefore, the more alternative paths an AS has, the more duplicate announcements. Figure 1(c) presents the distribution of this feature. The distribution of the DDoS attacks shows a sharp increase from 500 to 600. This indicates DDoS attacks usually lead to similar responses of victims, e.g. repeatedly announcing the affected paths.

Unq_pfx_as is the number of unique prefixes originated from an AS in a given time window. The number of announcements and withdrawals exchanged by neighboring peers is an important feature during instability periods. We utilize this feature to model the stable situation of the normal state. From Fig. 1(d), we can see that this feature is more stable during disaster event period than that in DDoS event period. The reason is that when DDoS attacks occur, the DPS provider may well utilize a BGP-based approach by announcing the prefix that belongs to the victim to mitigate the DDoS attack traffic, which leads to the increase of the number of unique prefixes.

Max_AS_path_len is the maximum length of AS paths announced by BGP routers in a specific time window. In a normal state, AS paths announced by BGP routers usually have limited number of hops, since the BGP protocol prefers to short paths. However, when an AS is suffering from attacks, the operator might implicitly withdraw a pre-announced path by pre-pending a number of duplicated ASes in the AS-path field. This could significantly increase the lengths of AS paths. Figure 1(e) shows that the lengths of AS paths for DDoS attack events are concentrated in the range from 25 to 30, which results in the sharp increase of the distribution curve. However, the distribution of the maximum AS path lengths for disaster events is much evener than that for DDoS attacks. This is because that disaster events usually cause outages of the Internet, and thus there are more long paths during disaster events.

ASN (AS number) is a globally unique number that is used to identify an AS. It allows an AS to exchange exterior routing information between neighboring ASes. Asn_prfx_chg is the number of prefix changes of ASes in a time window. This feature is proposed based on the assumption that the Internet topology should not frequently change. It has been used as a single BGP feature to detect prefix hijacking attacks. However, it is also possible for an AS to alter the prefix in order to reroute the traffic of a subnet through the DPS AS. Figure 1(f) demonstrates that there are more prefix origin changes during DDoS attacks. The reason is that when DDoS attack events occur, the DPS provider will announce the prefix that belongs to the victim and scrub the traffic.

3 System Design

Figure 2 gives an overview of our investigation process. It consists of a training phase and a monitoring phase. In both phases, we extract a number of features from the BGP update data within a fixed time interval. We group the extracted features into a vector which is referred to as a databin in the rest of this paper. When a DDoS attack is identified, the BGP update traffic originated from the ASes of DPS will be further analyzed by the mitigation policy analysis module. We develop a prototype of the system, using Python running on a 64-bit Windows 10 system with an Intel(R) CUP Q9550 @2.83GH and 8.0GB RAM.

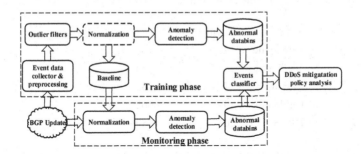

Fig. 2. The architecture of the system

3.1 Training Phase

We first collect many different kinds of events that will cause BGP changes, such as the hurricane, blackout, earthquake, cable cuts, and DDoS attacks. We manually searched the related news about these events to determine the occurrence times of these events. In the training phase, we collect the BGP update data in the time periods that cover the occurrence of these events. Since the BGP traffic is inherently dynamic and there are even some outliers during the normal state, we employ the k-means method to filter out the outlier databins in the normal period [12]. Specifically, the databins in the normal period are clustered into two groups based on their Euclidean distances. The group of the majority is expected to contain only normal databins and is used as the baseline of normality. To ensure that the occurrence periods contains a majority of normal databins, we then mix the normal databins with those in occurrence periods. Again, we employ the k-means method to cluster the mixed databins into two groups. The one of the majority is discriminated as normal and the other as abnormal. We further group the obtained abnormal databins according to the timestamps for obtaining consecutive abnormal databins. Such consecutive abnormal databins fulfill two requirements: (1) their intervals are less than 3 min and (2) they have at least 3 consecutive databins in the cluster. The obtained groups of consecutive abnormal databins are referred to as "incidents".

Second, we manually label the types of the incidents. In this paper, we only distinguish between disaster events and DDoS attacks. We collect 41 historical events and manually label the types of the incidents. The results are summarized in Table 2 and use these events to train the classification model of the random forest method. We only distinguish between disaster events and DDoS attack events. We use 5-fold cross validation method to evaluate the accuracy of the system. The detected abnormal databins in each category is divided into 5 folds and in each test, we use one of the 5 folds as test data and the other 4 folds as training data. The results are obtained by averaging the 5 results. Based on the collected data, we obtained an accuracy of 91.2%.

Table 2. A summary of the dataset

Type	Event number	Detected databins
Hurricane	4	30
Black out	4	14
Earthquake	4	152
Cable cut	9	602
DDoS	20	889

3.2   Monitoring Phase

In the monitoring phase, the newly collected BGP update messages are normalized using the baseline obtained in the training phase. More precisely, in this paper, we utilize a Z-score normalization method to normalize the databins. The Z-score value of a feature is calculated as $z = \frac{x - \mu}{\sigma}$, where μ is the mean of the obtained normal databins and σ is the standard deviation. The calculated mean and deviation are used to normalize the databins in the monitoring phase. The anomaly detection module will detect whether there is an anomaly in the BGP dynamics. If an anomaly is detected, the system utilizes the trained classifier to identify whether the abnormal event is caused by DDoS attacks.

It is worth noting that the system allows practitioners to utilize their experience knowledge to improve the performance of the system. When an alarm is raised, the practitioner could have a judgment on the result based on other external information source. If the prediction agrees with the judgment of the practitioner, the newly incoming databins will be added to the training databins. Otherwise, the prediction will be rejected.

3.3 Mitigation Policy Analysis

We provide a module to analyze the BGP-based mitigation policies utilized by DPS. After a DDoS event is confirmed, we use this module to examine the BGP policies adopted by DPS. It is worth noting that we allow practitioners to utilize their experiences and knowledge to improve the performance of the system. When an alarm is raised, the practitioner could have a judgment on the result based on other external information sources. If the prediction agrees with the judgment of the practitioner, the newly incoming databins will be added to the training databins. Otherwise, the prediction will be rejected.

We develop an algorithm to automatically extract the policies that adopted by DPS providers. When DPS providers find customers are under DDoS attacks, they can perform BGP prepending. Prepending means adding one or more AS numbers to the left side of the AS path. Normally this is done using one's own AS number, using someone else's AS number for this can have unintended side effects. Such protection process would start with a WADiff BGP update message and end with an AW BGP update message. We denote this process as B_0. In the prepending action, the ASN would appear in the BGP routing path, and the WADup BGP update message follows the AW BGP update message. We define the direct protection action as an action that DPS providers' ASN serves as the first hop of the BGP routing path, and the AADiff BGP update message follows the AADiff BGP update message. We denote the prepending action as B_1 and directed protection action as B_2. The algorithm works as follows. First, we label the BGP update records with AW, WWDup, AADupType1, AADupType2, AADiff, WADup, WADiff tags for each victim prefix. After we labeled the BGP update messages, we recognize the B_0, B_1 and B_2 sequences which reflects the policies adopted by DPS providers to protect the victims.

4 Experiments

4.1 Evaluation of DDoS Attack Detection

Our system succeeded to detect the DDoS attack against the Dyn in October, 2016 [8]. On October 21, 2016, the Dyn suffers from DNS queries from a large vast of clients, which consume the ability of the managed DNS network. This caused the unavailability of the DNS service of the Dyn. This further results in the difficulties in connecting numerous websites. During the attack, the traffic going to the other DNS providers increased dramatically and thus caused the wide-spread congestion of network traffic. This congestion eventually results in the abnormal dynamics of BGP traffic, which enables us to detect the Dyn DDoS attack event through the BGP dynamics.

Figure 3 illustrates the impact values versus the time. The impact value, which is the sum of the differences between the normalized features and the baseline, represents the distance of a databin from the normal ones. Three periods of abnormal dynamics are illustrated by three red blocks on October 21, 2016. Our anomaly detection module is able to identify these abnormal databins and correctly classified them as DDoS attacks. The detected abnormal periods are described as follows:

- The first period started at 04:30:22 (PDT), and fluctuations of BGP traffics began. Until around 06:16:00 (PDT), the fluctuations diminished. This coincides with the reported start and mitigation time of the incident [18]. During this period, the Dyn's DNS server platforms in the Asia Pacific and East Europe suffered from massive requests, and then the US-East region, resulting in the vast BGP route dynamics [8].
- According to our system detection results, the second period started at 08:41:44 (PDT) and ended at around 10:32:00 (PDT), which also agrees to the reported DDoS attack period [1].
- Our system also detected the third period of abnormal BGP dynamics which started at 13:19:28 and ended at around 14:08:0 (PDT). This is also consistent with the DDoS attack period reported in the news [8].

We also found some additional obvious fluctuations in the BGP traffic, which started at 01:22:23 (PDT) and 17:47:1 respectively, as shown in Fig. 3 with green blocks. However, these events are not reported by the Dyn.com or other news media. We speculate these events were caused by the initiation and aftershocks of the DDoS attacks (Table 3).

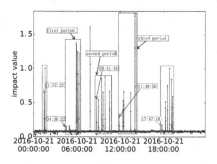

Fig. 3. Dyn DDoS attack overview

5   Related Work

Many studies have addressed the detection of instability or pathological behavior of the BGP dynamics. Labovitz et al. [11] investigated the BGP routing messages and found that the volume of routing update is more redundant than expected.

Table 3. DPS protection behaviors of update pattern sequences of three prefixs

Prefix	Update pattern sequence
58.64.128.119/32	WADiff→B1→B1→B1→B2→B1→AW
58.64.138.186/32	WADiff→B1→B1→B2→AW
58.64.135.102/32	B0→B0

Besides, they revealed several unexpected trends of both forwarding instability and routing policy fluctuations. Deshpande et al. [6] proposed an online instability detection architecture which applies statistical pattern recognition techniques to detect the instabilities of GBP dynamics. They found that features like AS path length and AS path edit distance are very effective in modeling the behaviors of the Internet topology. Chang et al. [4] proposed an algorithm to identify inter-domain path-change events from streams of BGP updates. Feldmann et al. [7] proposed a methodology to identify the origin of routing instability from BGP updates. Several studies utilize statistical pattern recognition techniques to detect the instabilities of BGP routing dynamics [6,11,13]. Compared to these studies, in this paper, we propose a machine learning based method to distinguish between DDoS attack events and disruptive disaster events, which are two main causes of abnormal BGP dynamics. This allows identifying whether there is a DDoS attack going on when a BGP traffic anomaly is detected.

Many retrospective studies have also been conducted by analyzing the impacts brought by historical events such as blackouts, cable cuts, worms, and prefix-hijacking attacks, etc. Cowie et al. [5] analyzed the global BGP routing instabilities caused by the Code Red II and Nimda worms occurred in July and September 2001, respectively. They found that the impact was more serious than publicly revealed in the blacked-out region. Li et al. [14] analyzed the BGP behavior during large-scale power outages from a perspective of both the global and prefix levels. They found there was an increase in the number of withdraws at the global level. Consequently, there was a sharp decrease in the number of edges and nodes at the prefix level. These studies mainly concern the impacts of disruptive events on the performance of BGP routing. In this paper, we focus on the disruptions caused by DDoS attack and impacts of different DPS policies.

6   Conclusion

In this paper, we investigate the behaviors of BGP-based DDoS protection services. To identify the abnormal BGP dynamics caused by DDoS attacks, rather than other disruptive events such as earthquake, blackout, cable cut, etc., we train a proper classifier based on a dataset of more than 40 manually collected events which have been demonstrated to cause abnormal behaviors of BGP dynamics. We also develop a system for detecting DDoS events through abnormal BGP update messages and design a new algorithm to analyze the behavior of DPS against typical DDoS attacks. By applying the system to real

DDoS attacks, we identify the policies used by DPS to mitigate the attacks and obtain several meaningful findings. This research sheds light on the design of effective DDoS attack mitigation schemes.

Acknowledgment. The research presented in this paper is supported in part by National Natural Science Foundation (No. 61602370, 61672026, 61772411, U1736205), Postdoctoral Foundation (No. 201659M2806, 2018T111066), Fundamental Research Funds for the Central Universities (No. 1191320006), Shaanxi Postdoctoral Foundation, Project JCYJ20170816100819428 supported by SZSTI, CCF-Tencent Open Fund WeBank Special Funding (No. CCF-Webank RAGR20180101), CCF-NSFOCUS Kun-Peng Research Fund (No. CCF-NSFOCUS 2018006).

References

1. How friday's massive ddos attack on the U.S. happened. https://en.wikipedia.org/wiki/2016_Dyn_cyberattackcite_note-wired-5/
2. OVH suffers from 1.1Tbps DDoS attack. https://www.scmagazineuk.com/ovh-suffers-11tbps-ddos-attack/article/532197/. Accessed 11 Mar 2017
3. Chandrashekar, J., Duan, Z., Zhang, Z.L., Krasky, J.: Limiting path exploration in BGP. In: 24th Annual Joint Conference of INFOCOM, vol. 4, pp. 2337–2348. IEEE (2005)
4. Chang, D.F., Govindan, R., Heidemann, J.: The temporal and topological characteristics of BGP path changes. In: ICNP, pp. 190–199. IEEE (2003)
5. Cowie, J., Ogielski, A.T., Premore, B., Yuan, Y.: Internet worms and global routing instabilities. In: ITCom 2002: The Convergence of Information Technologies and Communications, pp. 195–199 (2002)
6. Deshpande, S., Thottan, M., Ho, T.K., Sikdar, B.: An online mechanism for BGP instability detection and analysis. IEEE Trans. Comput. **58**(11), 1470–1484 (2009)
7. Feldmann, A., Maennel, O., Mao, Z.M., Berger, A., Maggs, B.: Locating internet routing instabilities. ACM SIGCOMM CCR **34**, 205–218 (2004)
8. Hilton, S.: Dyn analysis summary of friday october 21 attack. http://dyn.com/blog/dyn-analysis-summary-of-friday-october-21-attack/
9. Jonker, M., Sperotto, A., van Rijswijk-Deij, R., Sadre, R., Pras, A.: Measuring the adoption of DDoS protection services. In: Proceedings of the 2016 ACM on Internet Measurement Conference, pp. 279–285. ACM (2016)
10. Karami, M., McCoy, D.: Understanding the emerging threat of DDoS-as-a-service. In: LEET (2013)
11. Labovitz, C., Malan, G.R., Jahanian, F.: Internet routing instability. IEEE/ACM Trans. Netw. **6**(5), 515–528 (1998)
12. Li, J., Brooks, S.: I-seismograph: observing and measuring internet earthquakes. In: INFOCOM, 2011 Proceedings IEEE, pp. 2624–2632. IEEE (2011)
13. Li, J., Guidero, M., Wu, Z., Purpus, E., Ehrenkranz, T.: BGP routing dynamics revisited. ACM SIGCOMM CCR **37**(2), 5–16 (2007)
14. Li, J., Wu, Z., Purpus, E.: Cam04-5: Toward understanding the behavior of BGP during large-scale power outages. In: IEEE Globecom. IEEE (2006)
15. Noroozian, A., Korczyński, M., Gañan, C.H., Makita, D., Yoshioka, K., van Eeten, M.: Who gets the boot? analyzing victimization by DDoS-as-a-service. In: Monrose, F., Dacier, M., Blanc, G., Garcia-Alfaro, J. (eds.) RAID 2016. LNCS, vol. 9854, pp. 368–389. Springer, Cham (2016). https://doi.org/10.1007/978-3-319-45719-2_17

16. Park, J.H., Jen, D., Lad, M., Amante, S., McPherson, D., Zhang, L.: Investigating occurrence of duplicate updates in BGP announcements. In: Krishnamurthy, A., Plattner, B. (eds.) PAM 2010. LNCS, vol. 6032, pp. 11–20. Springer, Heidelberg (2010). https://doi.org/10.1007/978-3-642-12334-4_2
17. Santanna, J.J., et al.: Booters-an analysis of DDoS-as-a-service attacks. In: 2015 IFIP/IEEE International Symposium on Integrated Network Management (IM), pp. 243–251. IEEE (2015)
18. Smith, D.: How friday's massive ddos attack on the U.S. happened. https://blog. radware.com/security/2016/10/fridays-massive-ddos-attack-u-s-happened/
19. Zhang, M.: BGPInspector: A real-time extensible border gateway protocol monitoring framework. CAS (2014)

Position Paper on Blockchain Technology: Smart Contract and Applications

Weizhi Meng[1]([⊠]), Jianfeng Wang[2], Xianmin Wang[3], Joseph Liu[4],
Zuoxia Yu[5,6], Jin Li[3], Yongjun Zhao[7], and Sherman S. M. Chow[7]

[1] Department of Applied Mathematics and Computer Science,
Technical University of Denmark, Copenhagen, Denmark
weme@dtu.dk
[2] State Key Laboratory of Integrated Service Networks (ISN), Xidian University,
Xi'an, People's Republic of China
[3] School of Computer Science, Guangzhou University, Guangzhou, China
{xianmin,jinli71}@gzhu.edu.cn
[4] Faculty of Information Technology, Monash University, Melbourne, Australia
[5] Department of Computing, The Hong Kong Polytechnic University,
Hung Hom, Hong Kong SAR
[6] Department of Computing, The Hong Kong Polytechnic University Shenzhen
Research Institute, Shenzhen, China
[7] Department of Information Engineering, The Chinese University of Hong Kong,
Shatin, Hong Kong SAR

Abstract. Blockchain technology enables a transaction to be handled in a decentralized fashion. In this position paper, we aim to introduce the background of blockchain technology, discuss one of its important component — smart contract, and present its recent applications in many fields such as cryptocurrency, financial services, risk management, and Internet of Things.

Keywords: Blockchain technology · Smart contract
Practical applications · Financial services · Internet of Things
Risk management

1 Blockchain Background

Cryptocurrencies refer to digital currencies in which cryptographic techniques are used to regulate the generation of the currency units as well as securing their transaction. Research on cryptocurrency begins in the 1980's. The first electronic cash scheme was proposed by Chaum [9]. While extensive researches have been conducted (e.g., [3,14]), real-world deployment of cryptocurrency has seen little success.

The situation has changed dramatically with the invention of Bitcoin [32], which has become the most popular cryptocurrency to date. The main problem of previous cryptocurrencies is that they failed to be decentralized. Bitcoin

© Springer Nature Switzerland AG 2018
M. H. Au et al. (Eds.): NSS 2018, LNCS 11058, pp. 474–483, 2018.
https://doi.org/10.1007/978-3-030-02744-5_35

overcomes this problem by introducing a distributed ledger technology known as blockchain. Specifically, every Bitcoin transaction is recorded on blockchain with an underlying distributed consensus mechanism that can be compromised only if the attacker controls the majority of the whole world's computation power. Double-spending can be detected at the time of spending by referring to the blockchain. Bitcoin differs from some of the existing cryptocurrencies in the sense that it does not support offline transactions. However, since Bitcoin network is fully decentralized, peers can transact directly among each other within the network, without any centralized party such as the bank. According to CoinMarketCap[1], the total market cap of over 1700 cryptocurrencies exceeds 267 billion US dollar. The blockchain market size, according to a recent report published by Markets is expected to grow from 411 million USD in 2017 to 7683 million in the next five years.

Blockchain has attracted a lot of attention from both the industry and the academia. In a nutshell, blockchain offers a promising building block for applications which were otherwise only known to hold with the help of (offline) trusted third party (e.g., [15]). As a decentralized, append-only distributed ledger, blockchain technologies find applications beyond electronic currencies, money related applications such as trading, and other FinTech applications. Integrating with other techniques, it also allows recording, managing, and tracing of goods or spare parts, or in general, complicated procedures in the logistics process. Ethereum[2], the second largest cryptocurrency, introduces general computability into the blockchain platform. This makes blockchain-based applications more versatile.

1.1 Different Layers of Blockchain

Blockchain applications can be divided into several layers, namely, consensus, data structure, and ledger (or application). The consensus layer ensures different nodes in the network share the same view of the current blockchain and governs who is authorized to append a new block to the current blockchain. The data structure layer specifies how data are recorded and arranged while the application layer defines the format and meaning of the data recorded. Below we discuss how cryptography plays an important role in each of these layers in the Bitcoin blockchain.

Consensus. The consensus mechanism underlying Bitcoin is later known by the name of Nakamoto consensus, attributing to the original Bitcoin proposal of Nakamoto [32]. The longest chain rule specifies that the nodes to decide locally the current view of the blockchain by following the longest chain. This layer also defines the rules governing who is authorized to produce the next block to be appended to the current blockchain. In Bitcoin, this is enforced by proof-of-work. A node which wishes to publish a new block must find a

---

[1] https://coinmarketcap.com.

[2] https://www.ethereum.org.

nonce such that the hash value of this newly produced block is less than a certain threshold. Finding such a nonce requires a certain amount of work which explains the name proof-of-work. The actual amount of work is adjusted dynamically to ensures that new blocks are proposed at a constant rate on average. There are recent proposals [23,29] that aim to achieve higher block creation rate when more peers participate. Nevertheless, further research is needed to balance efficiency, security, and other requirements [16].

Data Structure. Data items in the Bitcoin blockchain are grouped into blocks. Each block is linked to the previous one through the use of a cryptographic hash function. Specifically, each block contains the hash of the previous block. As this structure forms a chain, hence the name of blockchain.

Application Layer. The original purpose of the Bitcoin blockchain is to support Bitcoin transaction. The original data format for the records in each block is rather simple. Each record is simply a Bitcoin transaction with an input and an output, except that the first transaction recorded on each blockchain does not require an output. This special transaction, sometimes known as the coinbase transaction, serves as an incentive mechanism for nodes to create new blocks, and also for Bitcoin unit creation. An output is merely (a hash of) a public key of a digital signature scheme and an amount, while the input is an unspent output of some previous transaction. The input-output has to be signed, using a secret key that matches the public key of the output to be spent. Transactions recorded in the same block are arranged into a Merkle tree. The block only stores the root of the Merkle tree to save storage space.

1.2 Privacy Aspects of Blockchain-Enabled Cryptocurrencies

Achieving security and privacy simultaneously has been the design goal for cryptocurrencies since its introduction [9]. Despite being regarded as highly anonymous by the general public, the privacy guarantee provided by Bitcoin is inferior to traditional cryptographic electronic cash. In particular, transactions in Bitcoin are linkable. For an example of analyses, it is possible to correlate Bitcoin address and IP address in Bitcoin blockchain [24].

To address the privacy issue, several new cryptocurrencies have been proposed. Created in 2014, Monero is an open-sourced decentralized cryptocurrency which employs linkable ring signatures [27] to hide the sender of the transaction. A ring signature scheme is a special kind of digital signatures which can convince a verifier that one out of several possible signers generated the signature, without revealing exactly whom. The linkability mandates that the signatures issued by the same signer for the same "context" can be publicly linkable[3]. This allows the actual sender to hide the fact that money is transferred from his account. Double-spending is prevented through the use of the one-time key in a way that signatures generated by the same key can be detected. Subsequently, Monero upgrades its protocol to ring confidential transaction, which also hides transaction amount and receiver [30].

---

[3] There are other variants of linkability. For example, escrowed linkability [17] only allows a designated party to link.

Zcash is another privacy-preserving cryptocurrency that makes heavy use of cryptographic techniques. It is based on Zerocash [5]. The core underlying cryptographic technique is zero-knowledge succinct non-interactive arguments of knowledge (ZK-SNARK), which allows a prover to produce a short proof to convince anyone that he knows some secret without revealing it. In Zcash, ZK-SNARK is employed to allow a spender to prove that he is spending a valid coin to a receiver without revealing any extra information. In general, ZK-SNARK is a powerful cryptographic technique which implies many other cryptographic primitives, such as multi-key homomorphic signatures unforgeable under insider corruption [25].

As more people consider applying blockchain for applications beyond cryptocurrency, the privacy issue attracts more and more attention. Improved cryptographic techniques are required to cope with these new use cases in an efficient manner.

2   Smart Contract

The concept of smart contracts was proposed by Szabo in 1994 [36]. With the great success of Bitcoin, Blockchain 2.0 introduces the support of smart contracts for executing diverse applications other than cryptocurrency [26]. In particular, Ethereum, the second largest blockchain, supports Turing-complete smart contracts. There are already more than 4 million smart contracts on Ethereum. Besides Ethereum, there are also some other blockchain systems supporting smart contracts [4], such as Counterparty, Stellar, Lisk, Monax, etc.[4]

A smart contract can be considered as an autonomous program that can be automatically executed according to the predefined program logic. Developers usually design and implement smart contracts using high-level languages, such as, Solidity, Serpent, LLL, etc. Then, the smart contract will be compiled into EVM (Ethereum virtual machine) bytecode and deployed to the Ethereum blockchain. Once the smart contract is invoked by a user or another smart contract, it will be executed in the EVM on every Ethereum node. EVM is a register-based virtual machine and its specification can be found in the Ethereum yellow paper [37]. For security consideration, EVM is sandboxed and the smart contract running in EVM cannot access the important resources (e.g., network, file system, etc.) of each Ethereum node. Different from traditional virtual machines, Ethereum introduces the *gas* mechanism such that the execution of each EVM operation costs a certain amount of money equal to the multiplication of the gas price and the gas cost of the operation. This indirectly guarantees that the execution of a smart contract will eventually stop.

The most severe threat to smart contracts is its software vulnerabilities. Nicola et al. carried out a systematic study on the attacks on Ethereum smart contract [2]. Loi et al. designed Oyente [28], a symbolic execution tool which identified four kinds of security vulnerabilities —

---

[4] `counterparty.io`, `stellar.org`, `lisk.io`, `monax.io`.

1. The reentrancy vulnerability results from the fact that when an Ethereum smart contract invokes another one, the current execution will wait until the invocation finishes. If the callee is malicious, it could exploit the intermediate state of the caller to launch attacks. Such vulnerability has led to 60 million USD worth of Ether theft [8].
2. The mishandled exceptions may happen when one smart contract calls another one. In particular, if the exception in the callee is not propagated to the caller or the caller does not take care of the return value from the callee, the execution logic of caller will be affected.
3. The transaction-ordering dependence refers to the potential attacks resulting from the unexpected order of transactions. Note that the miner that mines the block can determine the order of the transactions.
4. The timestamp dependence refers to the potential vulnerability in smart contracts that use the block timestamp to control the execution of some important operations. A malicious miner may change the block timestamp to affect the execution of those important operations.

Recently, Kalra et al. proposed a tool, named Zeus [22], which employs abstract interpretation, symbolic model checking, as well as constrained horn clauses to quickly discover security issues in smart contracts. Besides the above four security issues [28], they further investigated how to detect new vulnerabilities, such as unchecked send, failed send, integer overflow/underflow, etc. Further research is needed to improve the detection rate of vulnerabilities and decrease the false positive rate.

Attackers can also use smart contracts to conduct malicious activities and even attack the Ethereum platform. Juels et al. [21] showed that the criminal smart contracts can facilitate the leakage of confidential data, theft of private keys, and various "calling-card" crimes, such as murder, terrorism, etc. Malicious smart contracts have also been used to launch denial-of-service (DoS) attacks on the Ethereum platform [6,7]. Chen et al. designed a measurement approach to assess whether the gas price is properly set by Ethereum [11]. Unfortunately, their results show that although Ethereum has adjusted the gas prices of some operations to defend against known DoS attacks, there still exist underpriced operations that can be exploited by attackers to launch DoS attacks. To address this problem, they proposed an adaptive gas cost mechanism to defend against known and unknown DoS attacks. They further conducted the first systematic study on Ethereum and employed three types of graphs, including money flow graph, smart contract creation graph, and smart contract invocation graph to characterize the major activities on Ethereum. By conducting graph analyses, they revealed stealthy attacks on Ethereum [13]. Further research is desired to capture more stealthy attacks with low false positive rates.

Besides security issues, there are also various performance issues in Ethereum. Dinh et al. proposed the first evaluation framework to measure the performance of private blockchains in terms of throughput, latency, scalability, and fault-tolerance [19]. Zheng et al. designed a lightweight performance monitoring framework for blockchain systems, which can visualize detailed and real-time performance data [39]. Since the execution of smart contracts cost money, Chen et al. [10] found that gas-inefficient patterns are prevalent in existing smart contracts. In other words, a smart contract with gas-inefficient patterns costs more gas than necessary. They further designed GasReducer, a tool which automatically eliminates such gas-inefficient patterns in smart contracts [12]. Further research is needed to automatically identify and remove more gas-inefficient patterns.

3   Blockchain Applications Beyond Cryptocurrencies

The original application of blockchains is Bitcoin [32]. With the increasing number of adoptions, it has diverse application scenarios related to finance, Internet of Things, risk management, etc. Below we highlight some of these applications or the vision behind.

3.1   Financial Field

Blockchain technology is expected to optimize the global financial infrastructure and build an efficient economic system. Cocco et al. [18] noted that many banks are focusing on blockchain technology to promote economic growth and accelerate the development of green technologies —

> "Sustainability strategies try to minimize the impact on the environment, starting from making people more efficient, improved recording of environmental key performance indicators, efficient building technology, green travel to sustainable purchasing, and from the end-to-end management of resources and waste."

That is, they appreciate the effort of saving energy while using blockchains.

In addition, Hong Kong's de-facto central bank had planned to evaluate blockchain distributed ledger solutions by building an innovation hub [34]. The Hong Kong Monetary Authority (HKMA) is also working with the Hong Kong Applied Science and Technology Research Institute (ASTRI) to enhance such hub as a blockchain testbed. They believe that this innovation hub can be acted as a "neutral ground" for evaluating financial technology prior to its eventual release in near future.

3.2   Internet of Things (IoT)

The Internet of Things (IoT) represents a kind of network environment that consists of various Internet-enabled physical and embedded devices with electronics, software, and sensors, etc. Recently, blockchains have become a popular means to help address issues in an IoT environment. For example, Sharma et al. [35] proposed a blockchain-based distributed cloud architecture with a software-defined networking enabled controller at the network edge, providing low-cost, secure, and on-demand access to the most competitive computing infrastructures in an

IoT network. Novo [33] introduced an IoT architecture for arbitrating roles and permissions based on blockchain technology, which is a fully distributed access control system for IoT. Their method can operate in a single smart contract, simplifying the whole process in the blockchain network and reducing the communication overhead between the nodes.

IoT may involve many financial factors. Zhang and Wen [38] introduced an E-business architecture designed specifically for IoT through the Bitcoin protocol. They adopted distributed autonomous corporations as the transaction entity to handle the paid data and the smart property. In their e-commerce architecture, users can obtain IoT coins through P2M and DACs. How to combine blockchains and various IoT scenarios is one popular topic in both industry and academia.

3.3 Risk Management

Blockchain technology allows verification without a central authority or a trusted third party. It can be useful to enhance the existing risk management, including intrusion detection and trust computation.

Intrusion Detection. To examine system or network threats, intrusion detection system (IDS) is an important and commonly available tool for different organizations. Meng et al. [31] discussed how to combine distributed or collaborative IDSs (CIDS) with blockchain technology. They identified that blockchains can be used to solve data sharing and better establish mutual trust among collaborating parties by working as a permanent public ledger of contracts between data owners and other parties. Gu et al. [20] introduced a multi-feature detection method for detecting and classifying malware by establishing a fact-base of distributed Android malicious codes by blockchain technology. In particular, they proposed a framework, called "consortium blockchain for malware detection and evidence extraction, which is composed of two parts of mixed chains: detecting consortium chain by test members and public chain by users.

Trust Computation. It is an essential and critical task to evaluate the trustworthiness of nodes in a distributed IDS network environment. Traditionally, trust computation needs a certified third party or a central server, which may suffer from many attacks, especially insider attacks, where the intruders have authorized access to the network. With the advent of blockchains, it become feasible to perform a trust evaluation without any trusted third party. Alexopoulosetal et al. [1] described a blockchain-based CIDS framework, in which they considered the raw alerts generated by each IDS node as transactions in a blockchain.

4 Concluding Remarks

There is an increasing number of blockchain applications in various fields. This position paper briefly introduces what are blockchain and smart contract, and presents their recent applications in finance, IoT and risk management. More research is still needed to investigate how to design a robust, efficient, and privacy-preserving blockchain-based security mechanism.

Acknowledgement. Sherman S.M. Chow is supported by the General Research Fund (CUHK 14210217) of the Research Grants Council, University Grant Committee of Hong Kong.

References

1. Alexopoulos, N., Vasilomanolakis, E., Ivánkó, N.R., Mühlhäuser, M.: Towards blockchain-based collaborative intrusion detection systems. In: D'Agostino, G., Scala, A. (eds.) CRITIS 2017. LNCS, vol. 10707, pp. 1–12. Springer, Cham (2018)
2. Atzei, N., Bartoletti, M., Cimoli, T.: A survey of attacks on ethereum smart contracts (SoK). In: Maffei, M., Ryan, M. (eds.) POST 2017. LNCS, vol. 10204, pp. 164–186. Springer, Heidelberg (2017). https://doi.org/10.1007/978-3-662-54455-6_8
3. Au, M.H., Chow, S.S.M., Susilo, W.: Short E-cash. In: Maitra, S., Veni Madhavan, C.E., Venkatesan, R. (eds.) INDOCRYPT 2005. LNCS, vol. 3797, pp. 332–346. Springer, Heidelberg (2005). https://doi.org/10.1007/11596219_27
4. Bartoletti, M., Pompianu, L.: An empirical analysis of smart contracts: platforms, applications, and design patterns. In: Brenner, M., Rohloff, K., Bonneau, J., Miller, A., Ryan, P.Y.A., Teague, V., Bracciali, A., Sala, M., Pintore, F., Jakobsson, M. (eds.) FC 2017. LNCS, vol. 10323, pp. 494–509. Springer, Cham (2017). https://doi.org/10.1007/978-3-319-70278-0_31
5. Ben-Sasson, E., et al.: Decentralized anonymous payments from bitcoin. In: Proceedings of 2014 IEEE Symposium on Security and Privacy, SP 2014, 18–21 May 2014, pp. 459–474 (2014)
6. Buterin, V.: A state clearing FAQ (2016). https://goo.gl/x5QRrd. Accessed 30 July 2016
7. Buterin, V.: Transaction spam attack: next steps (2016). https://goo.gl/uKi9Ug. Accessed 30 July 2016
8. Castillo, M.: The DAO attacked: code issue leads to $60 million ether theft (2016). https://www.coindesk.com/dao-attacked-code-issue-leads-60-million-ether-theft
9. Chaum, D.: Blind signatures for untraceable payments. In: Chaum, D., Rivest, R.L., Sherman, A.T. (eds.) Advances in Cryptology: Proceedings of CRYPTO 1982, Santa Barbara, California, USA, August 23–25, pp. 199–203 (1982)
10. Chen, T., Li, X., Luo, X., Zhang, X.: Under-optimized smart contracts devour your money. In: Proceedings of SANER (2017)
11. Chen, T., et al.: An adaptive gas cost mechanism for ethereum to defend against under-priced DoS attacks. In: Liu, J.K., Samarati, P. (eds.) ISPEC 2017. LNCS, vol. 10701, pp. 3–24. Springer, Cham (2017). https://doi.org/10.1007/978-3-319-72359-4_1
12. Chen, T., et al.: Towards saving money in using smart contracts. In: Proceedings of ICSE (2018)
13. Chen, T., et al.: Understanding ethereum via graph analysis. In: Proceedings of INFOCOM (2018)
14. Chow, S.S.M.: Running on karma – P2P reputation and currency systems. In: Bao, F., Ling, S., Okamoto, T., Wang, H., Xing, C. (eds.) CANS 2007. LNCS, vol. 4856, pp. 146–158. Springer, Heidelberg (2007). https://doi.org/10.1007/978-3-540-76969-9_10
15. Chow, S.S.M., Hui, L.C.K., Yiu, S.-M., Chow, K.P.: Practical electronic lotteries with offline TTP. Comput. Commun. **29**(15), 2830–2840 (2006)

16. Chow, S.S.M., Lai, Z., Liu, C., Lo, E., Zhao, Y.,: Sharding blockchain (Invited Paper). In: The 2018 IEEE Internal Conference on Blockchain (2018)
17. Chow, S.S.M., Susilo, W., Yuen, T.H.: Escrowed linkability of ring signatures and its applications. In: Nguyen, P.Q. (ed.) VIETCRYPT 2006. LNCS, vol. 4341, pp. 175–192. Springer, Heidelberg (2006). https://doi.org/10.1007/11958239_12
18. Cocco, L., Pinna, A., Marchesi, M.: Banking on blockchain: costs savings thanks to the blockchain technology. Future Internet 9(3), 25 (2017)
19. Dinh, T.T.A., Wang, J., Chen, G., Liu, R., Ooi, B.C., Tan, K.: Blockbench: a framework for analyzing private blockchains. In: Proceedings of SIGMOD (2017)
20. Gu, J., Sun, B., Du, X., Wang, J., Zhuang, Y., Wang, Z.: Consortium blockchain-based malware detection in mobile devices. IEEE Access 6, 12118–12128 (2018)
21. Juels, A., Kosba, A., Shi, E.: The ring of Gyges: investigating the future of criminal smart contracts. In: Proceedings of CCS (2016)
22. Kalra, S., Goel, S., Dhawan, M., Sharma, S.: Zeus: analyzing safety of smart contracts. In: Proceedings of NDSS (2018)
23. Kokoris-Kogias, E., Jovanovic, P., Gasser, L., Gailly, N., Syta, E. Ford, B.: Omniledger: a secure, scale-out, decentralized ledger via sharding. In: IEEE Symposium on Security and Privacy, pp. 583–598 (2018)
24. Koshy, P., Koshy, D., McDaniel, P.: An analysis of anonymity in bitcoin using P2P network traffic. In: Christin, N., Safavi-Naini, R. (eds.) FC 2014. LNCS, vol. 8437, pp. 469–485. Springer, Heidelberg (2014). https://doi.org/10.1007/978-3-662-45472-5_30
25. Lai, R.W.F., Tai, R.K.H., Wong, H.W.H., Chow, S.S.M.: Multi-key homomorphic signatures unforgeable under insider corruption. In: ASIACRYPT (2018, to appear)
26. Li, P.J.X., Chen, T., Luo, X., Wen, Q.: A survey on the security of blockchain systems. Future Generation Computer Systems (2017)
27. Liu, J.K., Wei, V.K., Wong, D.S.: Linkable spontaneous anonymous group signature for Ad Hoc groups. In: Wang, H., Pieprzyk, J., Varadharajan, V. (eds.) ACISP 2004. LNCS, vol. 3108, pp. 325–335. Springer, Heidelberg (2004). https://doi.org/10.1007/978-3-540-27800-9_28
28. Luu, L., Chu, D.-H., Olickel, H., Saxena, P., Hobor, A.: Making smart contracts smarter. In: Proceedings of CCS (2016)
29. Luu, L., Narayanan, V., Zheng, C., Baweja, K., Gilbert, S., Saxena, P.: A secure sharding protocol for open blockchains. In: Proceedings of CCS (2016)
30. Maxwell, G.: Confidential transactions (2015). https://elementsproject.org/elements/confidential-transactions
31. Meng, W., Tischhauser, E., Wang, Q., Wang, Y., Han, J.: When intrusion detection meets blockchain technology: a review. IEEE Access 6, 10179–10188 (2018)
32. Nakamoto, S.: Bitcoin: a peer-to-peer electronic cash system (2008). https://bitcoin.org/bitcoin.pdf
33. Novo, O.: Blockchain meets IoT: an architecture for scalable access management in IoT. IEEE Internet Things J. 5(2), 1184–1195 (2018)
34. Rizzo, P.: Hong Kong's central bank to test blockchain (2018). http://www.coindesk.com/hong-kongs-central-bank-test-blockchain. Accessed 30 July 2018
35. Sharma, P.K., Chen, M.Y., Park, J.H.: A software defined fog node based distributed blockchain cloud architecture for IoT. IEEE Access 6, 115–124 (2018)
36. Szabo, N.: The Idea of Smart Contracts (1994). http://www.fon.hum.uva.nl/rob/Courses/InformationInSpeech/CDROM/Literature/LOTwinterschool2006/szabo.best.vwh.net/idea.html
37. Wood, G.: Ethereum: a secure decentralised generalised transaction ledger. https://ethereum.github.io/yellowpaper/paper.pdf

38. Zhang, Y., Wen, J.: The IoT electric business model: using blockchain technology for the internet of things. Peer-to-Peer Networking Appl. **10**(4), 983–994 (2017)
39. Zheng, P., Zheng, Z., Luo, X., Chen, X., Liu, X.: A detailed and real-time performance monitoring framework for blockchain systems. In: Proceedings of ICSE (2018)

Position Paper on Recent Cybersecurity Trends: Legal Issues, AI and IoT

Junbin Fang[1], Yun Ju Huang[2], Frankie Li[3], Jing Li[4(✉)], Xuan Wang[5], and Yang Xiang[6,7]

[1] Jinan University, Guangzhou, China
[2] Hong Kong Applied Science and Technology Research Institute (ASTRI), Shatin, Hong Kong SAR
[3] Dragon Advance Tech, China, Hong Kong SAR
[4] Guangzhou University, Guangzhou, China
lijingbeiyou@163.com
[5] Harbin Institute of Technology, Shenzhen, China
[6] State Key Laboratory of Integrated Service Networks (ISN), Xidian University, Xi'an, People's Republic of China
[7] Digital Research and Innovation Capability Platform, Swinburne University of Technology, Melbourne, Australia

Abstract. There is a large number of high-profile cyberattacks identified in the year of 2017, i.e., Ransomware attacks are one of the areas of cybercrime growing the fastest. These increasingly sophisticated cyberattacks are forcing various organisations to face security challenges and invest money building security and trust models. There will also be an increase in the use of recent development of security solutions that can help improve the detection performance and react to malicious events. In this position paper, we mainly introduce recent development trends in cybersecurity, including legal issues (e.g., GDPR), Artificial intelligence (AI), Mobile security and Internet of Things.

Keywords: Cybersecurity · Internet of Things
Artificial Intelligence · General Data Protection Regulation
Mobile security

1 Legal Regulation

With the development of data analytic techniques and the trend of ubiquitous computing, more companies are using the technologies to profile users and infer the whereabouts of the potential customers to provide more sophisticated marketing campaign and services. At the same time, there is a growing concern of user privacy. Besides, the collection and handling of user data poses an increasing risk of data leakage. In response to the growing concern on privacy, the legal system is also evolving to better regulate how user data should be handled.

The EU General Data Protection Regulation (GDPR), came into effect on 25 May 2018, is an prominent example of this phenomena. Replacing the previous

M. H. Au et al. (Eds.): NSS 2018, LNCS 11058, pp. 484–490, 2018.
https://doi.org/10.1007/978-3-030-02744-5_36

Data Protection Directive 95/46/EC, GDPR aims to protect data privacy of citizens of the EU countries. Under GDPR, organisations whose practices do not compliant with GDPR may face heavy fines.

The enforcement of these regulations may bring significant changes to the industry. Under GDPR, any information relating to an identifiable person, be it a direct or an indirect reference through the identifier, are regarded as personal data. It is required that personal data should be handled with care. It also include specific rules regarding child-tailored privacy protection [13]. Below we briefly discuss some of the requirement in GDPR and their potential impact to the companies.

- *Data protection by design and default.* It is required that any system handling personal data should be secure by design and by default.
- *Consent.* It is required that the company handling personal data must request for consent given in an explicit and unambitious way, with the purpose for data processing stated clearly.
- *Data portability.* It is required that users are entitled to the right to data portability. In other words, the user has the right to transmit those personal data into another system. Also, the user has the right to obtain from the data controller a copy of the provided personal data in a commonly used electronic format.
- *The right to be forgotten.* The user has the right to request removing any personal data stored in the system.

The steps in which the industry and system developers need to follow in order to achieve data protection compliant with GDPR has become an important topic that worth investigating. It is expected that more cybersecurity mechanism should be incorporated during the design of any system with the intention to handle user data. Some of the requirements could be addressed through the use of existing techniques while other may impose serious challenge. One frequently discussed example is the dilemma between the right to be forgotten and the use of blockchain technology, since immutability is an inherit feature of blockchain. One direction to address this contraction is to use blockchain that are retractable by authorised party as in [1].

Besides developing guidelines and technology to cope with these new regulations, another related topic is how can the general public be educated about their rights under these new regulations. In particular, from the viewpoint of security community, what should be the best way to educate the public about GDPR?

Besides data protection, there are other cybersecurity risks. In this broader scale, there are a number of cybersecurity standards, including ISO27001[1] and NIST Cybersecurity Framework (NIST CSF), which serve to help managing different types of cybersecurity risks. How we, cybersecurity professionals, could promote these standards is also an interesting topic worth discussing.

---

[1] More formally, ISO27001 is the most famous standard in the ISO/IEC 27000 family whiich provides the requirements for an Information security management systems.

Recently, China also issued its own standard on data protection, namely, the national standard on personal information protection entitled GB/T 35273-2017 Information Technology - Personal Information Security Specification. This standard come into effect on 1 May 2018. Promotion of this standard, and how these standard compare with others, are problems that worth looking into.

In 2018, it is encouraging to witness the development of these regulatory requirements with the goal of better protecting user privacy. It is expected that new cybersecurity mechanisms will be developed to cope with these new requirements. Education to the general public on this issue is another problem that the community as a whole should pay more attention to.

2   Artificial Intelligence

Generally, artificial intelligence (AI) enables software or systems in relation to security learning from the consequences of past events in order to help predict and identify malicious events. However, there is a concern on the AI development that hackers may use AI to launch even more sophisticated cyber-attacks.

2.1   Detection Improvement

Robots might be able to help defend against incoming cyber-attacks. In particular, AI and machine learning algorithms can be used to help improve the detection performance. One challenge is that security managers rarely get the chance to deal with them immediately. Loukas et al. [12] combined intrusion detection with deep learning in a small four-wheel robotic land vehicle. Their approach uses data captured in real-time that relate to both cyber and physical processes as input, and then feeds as time series data to a neural network architecture. Diro and Chilamkurti [2] identified that deep learning-based networks has been successful deployed in big data areas, and then proposed a distributed deep learning scheme of cyber-attack detection in fog-to-things computing.

Nguyen et al. [15] then applied deep learning for detecting malware, by introducing an enhanced form of Control flow graph (CFG), called lazy-binding CFG, aiming to reflect the behaviors of dynamically executed contents (DEC). Karbab et al. [10] designed MalDozer, an automatic Android malware detection and family attribution framework relying on sequences classification by means of deep learning techniques. MalDozer can automatically extract and learn the malicious and benign patterns from the actual samples to detect Android malware, in addition to app's API method calls. It can serve as a malware detection system that is deployed on both servers and IoT devices. Their results indicate that MalDozer can correctly detect malware and attribute them to their actual families with an F1-Score of 96%–99% and a false positive rate of 0.06%–2%, under all tested datasets and settings.

On the other hand, Jones and Kaufman [9] found that *"though AI can be used to predict a model of information norms and privacy violations, the normative conversations around risk, marginalization, power, and autonomy should supplement these rules. Normative conversations can and should be used to edit AI-formalized norms and expectations learned by looking at user behavior and preferences, providing an opportunity to address the challenges to privacy self-management mentioned above"*. That is, when we try to automate aspects of consent, we should ask ourselves whether we can enable or simulate consent, and the influence on partnership development among various parties.

2.2 AI-based Threat

AI will become an important tool to help automate detection and improve the accuracy of identifying threats, while AI can also be used to automate the collection of certain information from a particular organisation. Further, AI may be used to assist hackers when it comes to cracking passwords by reducing the password space. Additionally, AI may not always provide meaningful output that can reduce its effectiveness to security administrators or managers, the potential of deep learning was recently demonstrated when Google took the decision to turn off its machine learning toolset. Through deep learning, the machines were educating themselves to the extent that they had begun to create a new language which system developers cannot understand.

Currently, sophisticated attackers are willing to use polluting training data to maximally sabotage machine-learning classifiers. Chen et al. [6] investigated the feasibility of constructing crafted malware samples; examine how machine-learning classifiers can be misled under three different threat models; then conclude that injecting carefully crafted data into training data can significantly reduce detection accuracy. Chen et al. [3] explored the security of machine learning in Android malware detection on the basis of a learning-based classifier with the input of a set of features extracted from the Android applications (apps). They studied different features associated with their contributions to the classification problem as well as their manipulation costs, and presented a feature selection method (named SecCLS) to make the classifier harder to be evaded. They further developed a system called SecureDroid, which integrates their proposed methods (i.e., SecCLS and SecENS) to enhance machine learning-based Android malware detection.

3   Mobile Security and IoT Security

The great success of app economy poses lucrative and profitable targets for attackers. Mobile malware can causes severe impact on users and mobile networks, such as leaking users' sensitive information [23,24] and depleting network resources. The attackers usually insert malicious components into popular apps and then upload the repackaged apps to the third-party market. After luring the victims to install such malicious apps, the attackers often try to get the root privilege [19] and organize the compromised mobile devices into mobile botnets [5] for conducting various malicious activities.

Numerous research has been done to detect mobile malware [8,21]. The majority of them employ static code analysis [25] and/or dynamic behavior analysis to identify malicious behaviors [28]. Early works exploits permissions required by an app and other heuristics to detect malware. Recent detection solutions exploit many other features: (1) various features of code, such as API dependency graph, inter-component call graph, context information, etc.; (2) inconsistency between an app's textual data (e.g., description, privacy policy [23–25], and reviews [11]) and bytecode. Recently, some app hardening services (or packers) have been proposed to protect apps from being reserved, modified, and repackaged [28]. They usually hide the original executable file (i.e., dex file), impede the attempt of dumping the dex file, and prevent the apps from being debugged by others. Note that packed malware can evade signature-based detection and make it very difficult to conduct static analysis. Although a few unpacking tools have been proposed, further research is desired to deal with the advanced packing techniques.

Many existing dynamic malware detection systems require tracking information flows [27]. Several dynamic information flow tracking systems for Android (e.g., Malton [26], TaintDroid [7]) have been designed. Note that Android has replaced the Dalvik Virtual Machine (DVM) with a new runtime named ART, which compiles apps into native code during the installation and then runs them directly. Only Malton [26] supports ART whereas other analysis systems rely on DVM. For example, TaintDroid modifies the DVM. Although DroidScope [22] and NDroid [16] are built on top of QEMU, DroidScope exploits the features of DVM interpreter (i.e., mterp) to recover Dalvik instructions and NDroid propagates taints between Java context and native context by exploiting the implementation of Java native interface (JNI) between DVM and the underlying Linux system. Note that malware can evade emulator-based systems due to differences between emulator and smartphone. Therefore, further research is needed to conduct the in-depth analysis of mobile malware in real mobile device.

While around 8.4 billion connected Internet-of-things (IoT) devices will be in use worldwide next year, these devices have become the new targets for attackers because IoT devices usually lack of sufficient security protection and the compromised IoT devices will pose severe threats to cybersecurity. Vulnerable authentication mechanisms in various IoT devices have been widely reported [17]. Firmware modification attacks are also due to the vulnerability in the authentication mechanism. Recent research has demonstrated such attacks on many IoT devices, including printers [4], mouse [14], fitness trackers [18], etc. Unfortunately, most of these studies focus on specific IoT devices and heavily rely on manual analysis. To automate the discovery of issues in authentication mechanism, Shoshitaishvili et al. proposed Firmalice that conducts static analysis on firmware to detect three kinds of authentication vulnerabilities [20]. Since Firmalice only focuses on the firmware, it will miss other authentication vulnerabilities in the IoT devices. For further research, a systematic approach to discover the vulnerabilities in IoT systems is desired.

4   Concluding Remarks

Cybersecurity is developing at a rapid pace and is also making a great impact on the world. (1) If you want to operate a company in the European Union, then you should be ready for the General Data Protection Regulation (GDPR), and the infringements can provoke fines of at least 20 million euros. (2) Artificial intelligence has already made an impact on more organizations and it will be sure to play a bigger role in cybersecurity. To achieve good performance, these AI algorithms need to be trained and honed, but there is also a risk that AI may be exploited by cyber-criminals for more complex attacks. (3) People are rolling out more and more sensor-packed, internet-connected mobile devices, but IoT remains a major weak point for defenses, as they lack of basic security features, i.e., some of them rely upon default passwords that can give attackers easy access. As a result, there is a need to educate users and focus more on security when the system or software is designed.

References

1. Ateniese, G., Magri, B., Venturi, D., Andrade, E.R.: Redactable blockchain - or - rewriting history in bitcoin and friends. In: 2017 IEEE European Symposium on Security and Privacy, EuroS&P 2017, Paris, France, pp. 111–126 (2017)
2. Diro, A.A., Chilamkurti, N.: Deep learning: the frontier for distributed attack detection in Fog-to-Things computing. IEEE Commun. Mag. **56**(2), 169–175 (2018)
3. Chen, L., Hou, S., Ye, Y.: SecureDroid: enhancing security of machine learning-based detection against adversarial android malware attacks. In: Proceedings of ACSAC, pp. 362–372 (2017)
4. Cui, A., Costello, M., Stolfo, S.: When firmware modifications attack: a case study of embedded exploitation. In: Proceedings of NDSS (2013)
5. Chen, W., Luo, X., Yin, C., Xiao, B., Au, M.H., Tang, Y.: Cloudbot: advanced mobile botnets using ubiquitous cloud technologies. Pervasive Mob. Comput. **41**, 270–285 (2017)
6. Chen, S., et al.: Automated poisoning attacks and defenses in malware detection systems: an adversarial machine learning approach. Comput. Secur. **73**, 326–344 (2018)
7. Enck, W., et al.: TaintDroid: an information-flow tracking system for realtime privacy monitoring on smartphones. In: Proceedings of OSDI (2010)
8. Faruki, P., et al.: Android security: a survey of issues, malware penetration, and defenses. IEEE Commun. Surv. Tut. **17**(2), 998–1022 (2015)
9. Jones, M.L., Kaufman, E., Edenberg, E.: AI and the ethics of automating consent. IEEE Secur. Priv. **16**(3), 64–72 (2018)
10. Karbab, E.B., Debbabi, M., Derhab, A., Mouheb, D.: MalDozer: automatic framework for android malware detection using deep learning. Digit. Invest. **24**, S48–S59 (2018)
11. Kong, D., Cen, L., Jin, H.: AUTOREB: automatically understanding the review-to-behavior fidelity in android applications. In: Proceedings of CCS (2015)
12. Loukas, G., Vuong, T., Heartfield, R., Sakellari, G., Yoon, Y., Gan, D.: Cloud-based cyber-physical intrusion detection for vehicles using deep learning. IEEE Access **6**, 3491–3508 (2018)

13. Macenaite, M.: From universal towards child-specific protection of the right to privacy online: dilemmas in the EU general data protection regulation. New Media Soc. **19**(5), 765–779 (2017)
14. Maskiewicz, J., Ellis, B., Mouradian, J., Shacham, H.: Mouse trap: exploiting firmware updates in USB peripherals. In: Proceedings of WOOT (2014)
15. Nguyen, M.H., Nguyen, D.L., Nguyen, X.M., Quan, T.T.: Auto-detection of sophisticated malware using lazy-binding control flow graph and deep learning. Comput. Secur. **76**, 128–155 (2018)
16. Qian, C., Luo, X., Shao, Y., Chan, A.T.: On tracking information flows through JNI in android applications. In: Proceedings of DSN (2014)
17. Ronen, E., OFlynn, C., Shamir, A.: IoT goes nuclear: creating a ZigBee chain reaction. In: Proceedings of the IEEE Symposium on Security and Privacy (2017)
18. Rieck, J.: Attacks on fitness trackers revisited: a case-study of unfit firmware security. https://arxiv.org/abs/1604.03313. Accessed July 2018
19. Shao, Y., Luo, X., Qian, C.: Rootguard: protecting rooted android phones. IEEE Comput. **47**(6), 32–40 (2014)
20. Shoshitaishvili, Y., Wang, R., Hauser, C., Kruegel, C., Vigna, G.: Firmalice - automatic detection of authentication bypass vulnerabilities in binary firmware. In: Proceedings of NDSS (2015)
21. Sufatrio, Tan, D.J.J., Chua, T.W., Thing, V.L.: Securing android: a survey, taxonomy, and challenges. ACM Comput. Surv. **47**(4), 58 (2015)
22. Yan, L., Yin, H.: DroidScope: seamlessly reconstructing the OS and Dalvik semantic views for dynamic android malware analysis. In: Proceedings of USENIX Security (2012)
23. Yu, L., Luo, X., Qian, C., Wang, S., Leung, H.: Enhancing the description-to-behavior fidelity in android apps with privacy policy. IEEE Trans. Softw. Eng. **44**, 834–854 (2018)
24. Yu, L., Zhang, T., Luo, X., Xue, L., Chang, H.: Towards automatically generating privacy policy for android apps. IEEE Trans. Inform. Forensics Secur. **12**(4), 865–880 (2017)
25. Yu, L., Luo, X., Liu, X., Zhang, T.: Can we trust the privacy policies of android apps? In: Proceedings of IEEE/IFIP DSN (2016)
26. Xue, L., Zhou, Y., Chen, T., Luo, X., Gu, G.: Malton: towards on-device non-invasive mobile malware analysis for art. In: Proceedings of USENIX SEC (2017)
27. Xue, L., Qian, C., Luo, X.: AndroidPerf: a cross-layer profiling system for android applications. In: Proceedings of IWQoS (2015)
28. Zhang, Y., Luo, X., Yin, H.: DexHunter: toward extracting hidden code from packed android applications. In: Pernul, G., Ryan, P.Y.A., Weippl, E. (eds.) ESORICS 2015. LNCS, vol. 9327, pp. 293–311. Springer, Cham (2015). https://doi.org/10.1007/978-3-319-24177-7_15

Author Index

Printed in the United States
By Bookmasters